THIRD EDITION

iOS Programming Fundamentals with Swift

Swift, Xcode, and Cocoa Basics

Matt Neuburg

Beijing · Boston · Farnham · Sebastopol · Tokyo

iOS 10 Programming Fundamentals with Swift, Third Edition

by Matt Neuburg

Printed in the United States of America.

Published by O'Reilly Media, Inc., 1005 Gravenstein Highway North, Sebastopol, CA 95472.

O'Reilly books may be purchased for educational, business, or sales promotional use. Online editions are also available for most titles (*http://safaribooksonline.com*). For more information, contact our corporate/institutional sales department: 800-998-9938 or corporate@oreilly.com.

Editor: Rachel Roumeliotis
Production Editor: Kristen Brown
Proofreader: O'Reilly Production Services
Indexer: Matt Neuburg

Cover Designer: Karen Montgomery
Interior Designer: David Futato
Illustrator: Matt Neuburg

April 2015:   First Edition
October 2015:   Second Edition
October 2016:   Third Edition

Revision History for the Third Edition

2016-09-23:   First release

See *http://oreilly.com/catalog/errata.csp?isbn=9781491970072* for release details.

ISBN: 978-1-491-97007-2

[LSI]

Table of Contents

Preface.. xi

Part I. Language

1. The Architecture of Swift.. 3
Ground of Being   3
Everything Is an Object?   5
Three Flavors of Object Type   6
Variables   6
Functions   8
The Structure of a Swift File   9
Scope and Lifetime   11
Object Members   12
Namespaces   13
Modules   14
Instances   15
Why Instances?   17
self   19
Privacy   20
Design   22
   Object Types and APIs   23
   Instance Creation, Scope, and Lifetime   25
   Summary and Conclusion   26

2. Functions... 27
Function Parameters and Return Value   27
   Void Return Type and Parameters   31
   Function Signature   32

External Parameter Names   32
Overloading   34
Default Parameter Values   35
Variadic Parameters   36
Ignored Parameters   36
Modifiable Parameters   37
Function In Function   41
Recursion   43
Function As Value   43
Anonymous Functions   46
Define-and-Call   52
Closures   53
    How Closures Improve Code   54
    Function Returning Function   56
    Closure Setting a Captured Variable   58
    Closure Preserving Its Captured Environment   59
    Escaping Closures   60
Curried Functions   61
Function References and Selectors   62
    Function Reference Scope   65
    Selectors   66

3. Variables and Simple Types. 69
Variable Scope and Lifetime   69
Variable Declaration   71
Computed Initializer   74
Computed Variables   75
Setter Observers   78
Lazy Initialization   80
Built-In Simple Types   82
    Bool   82
    Numbers   84
    String   90
    Character   95
    Range   98
    Tuple   100
    Optional   103

4. Object Types. 117
Object Type Declarations and Features   117
    Initializers   119
    Properties   125

Methods	128
Subscripts	130
Nested Object Types	132
Instance References	133
Enums	135
Raw Values	137
Associated Values	138
Enum Initializers	139
Enum Properties	140
Enum Methods	141
Why Enums?	142
Structs	143
Struct Initializers, Properties, and Methods	144
Struct As Namespace	145
Classes	146
Value Types and Reference Types	146
Subclass and Superclass	151
Class Initializers	156
Class Deinitializer	164
Class Properties and Methods	164
Polymorphism	166
Casting	169
Type Reference	174
Protocols	179
Why Protocols?	181
Protocol Type Testing and Casting	183
Declaring a Protocol	183
Optional Protocol Members	185
Class Protocol	186
Implicitly Required Initializers	187
Literal Convertibles	189
Generics	190
Generic Declarations	192
Type Constraints	194
Explicit Specialization	196
Associated Type Chains	197
Additional Constraints	200
Extensions	203
Extending Object Types	203
Extending Protocols	206
Extending Generics	209
Umbrella Types	210

Any   211
AnyObject   212
AnyClass   215
Collection Types   216
  Array   216
  Dictionary   230
  Set   235

5. Flow Control and More. **241**
Flow Control   241
  Branching   242
  Loops   254
  Jumping   259
Operators   274
Privacy   277
  Private and Fileprivate   278
  Public and Open   280
  Privacy Rules   280
Introspection   281
Memory Management   282
  Weak References   284
  Unowned References   285
  Weak and Unowned References in Anonymous Functions   287
  Memory Management of Protocol-Typed References   290

Part II.   IDE

6. Anatomy of an Xcode Project. **293**
New Project   294
The Project Window   296
  The Navigator Pane   297
  The Utilities Pane   303
  The Editor   304
The Project File and Its Dependents   306
The Target   309
  Build Phases   310
  Build Settings   312
  Configurations   313
  Schemes and Destinations   314
From Project to Running App   316
  Build Settings   319

Property List Settings   319
Nib Files   320
Additional Resources   321
Code Files and the App Launch Process   324
Frameworks and SDKs   329
Renaming Parts of a Project   331

7. Nib Management. **333**
The Nib Editor Interface   335
   Document Outline   336
   Canvas   339
   Inspectors and Libraries   341
Nib Loading   342
   When Nibs Are Loaded   343
   Manual Nib Loading   344
Connections   346
   Outlets   346
   The Nib Owner   348
   Automatically Configured Nibs   351
   Misconfigured Outlets   352
   Deleting an Outlet   353
   More Ways to Create Outlets   354
   Outlet Collections   357
   Action Connections   357
   More Ways to Create Actions   360
   Misconfigured Actions   361
   Connections Between Nibs — Not!   361
Additional Configuration of Nib-Based Instances   362

8. Documentation. **367**
The Documentation Window   367
Class Documentation Pages   369
Quick Help   372
Symbols   374
Header Files   375
Sample Code   376
Internet Resources   376

9. Life Cycle of a Project. **379**
Device Architecture and Conditional Code   379
   Backward Compatibility   380
   Device Type   381

Version Control   383
Editing and Navigating Your Code   385
  Autocompletion   386
  Snippets   388
  Fix-it and Live Syntax Checking   389
  Navigation   390
  Finding   391
Running in the Simulator   393
Debugging   394
  Caveman Debugging   394
  The Xcode Debugger   396
Testing   403
Clean   409
Running on a Device   410
  Obtaining a Developer Program Membership   410
  Signing an App   411
  Automatic Development Signing   412
  Obtaining a Development Certificate Manually   415
  Obtaining a Development Provisioning Profile Manually   416
  Running the App   418
  Managing Certificates, Profiles, and Devices   418
Profiling   419
  Gauges   420
  Memory Debugging   421
  Instruments   422
Localization   425
  Localizing the Info.plist   426
  Localizing a Nib File   427
  Localizing Code Strings   429
  Localizing With XML Files   431
Distribution   433
  Making an Archive   433
  Obtaining a Distribution Certificate Manually   434
  Obtaining a Distribution Profile Manually   435
  Ad Hoc Distribution   436
Final App Preparations   437
  Icons in the App   437
  Other Icons   439
  Launch Images   439
  Screenshots and Video Previews   440
  Property List Settings   442

Submission to the App Store   443

Part III.   Cocoa

10. Cocoa Classes. **447**
   Subclassing   447
   Categories and Extensions   450
      How Swift Uses Extensions   451
      How You Use Extensions   451
      How Cocoa Uses Categories   452
   Protocols   453
      Informal Protocols   455
      Optional Methods   456
   Some Foundation Classes   458
      Useful Structs and Constants   459
      NSString and Friends   461
      NSDate and Friends   464
      NSNumber   465
      NSValue   467
      NSData   468
      NSMeasurement and Friends   469
      Equality and Comparison   469
      NSArray and NSMutableArray   471
      NSDictionary and NSMutableDictionary   473
      NSSet and Friends   473
      NSIndexSet   474
      NSNull   475
      Immutable and Mutable   475
      Property Lists   477
   Accessors, Properties, and Key–Value Coding   478
      Swift Accessors   479
      Key–Value Coding   481
      Uses of Key–Value Coding   482
      KVC and Outlets   483
      Key Paths   484
      Array Accessors   485
   The Secret Life of NSObject   486

11. Cocoa Events. **489**
   Reasons for Events   490
   Subclassing   490

Notifications   492
  Receiving a Notification   493
  Unregistering   495
  Posting a Notification   496
  Timer   497
Delegation   498
  Cocoa Delegation   499
  Implementing Delegation   500
Data Sources   502
Actions   503
The Responder Chain   506
  Deferring Responsibility   507
  Nil-Targeted Actions   508
Key–Value Observing   509
Swamped by Events   513
Delayed Performance   516

12. Memory Management. **519**
Principles of Cocoa Memory Management   519
Rules of Cocoa Memory Management   521
What ARC Is and What It Does   522
How Cocoa Objects Manage Memory   522
Autorelease Pool   523
Memory Management of Instance Properties   525
Retain Cycles and Weak References   526
Unusual Memory Management Situations   529
Nib Loading and Memory Management   532
Memory Management of CFTypeRefs   533
Property Memory Management Policies   535
Debugging Memory Management Mistakes   537

13. Communication Between Objects. **539**
Visibility by Instantiation   540
Visibility by Relationship   542
Global Visibility   543
Notifications and Key–Value Observing   544
Model–View–Controller   545

A. C, Objective-C, and Swift. **549**

Index. **579**

Preface

On June 2, 2014, Apple's WWDC keynote address ended with a shocking announcement: "We have a new programming language." This came as a huge surprise to the developer community, which was accustomed to Objective-C, warts and all, and doubted that Apple could ever possibly relieve them from the weight of its venerable legacy. The developer community, it appeared, had been wrong.

Having picked themselves up off the floor, developers immediately began to examine this new language — Swift — studying it, critiquing it, and deciding whether to use it. My own first move was to translate all my existing iOS apps into Swift; this was enough to convince me that, for all its faults, Swift deserved to be adopted by new students of iOS programming, and that my books, therefore, should henceforth assume that readers are using Swift.

The Swift language is designed from the ground up with these salient features:

Object-orientation
   Swift is a modern, object-oriented language. It is *purely* object-oriented: "Everything is an object."

Clarity
   Swift is easy to read and easy to write. Its syntax is clear, consistent, and explicit, with few hidden shortcuts and minimal syntactic trickery.

Safety
   Swift enforces strong typing to ensure that it knows, and that you know, what the type of every object reference is at every moment.

Economy
   Swift is a fairly small language, providing some basic types and functionalities and no more. The rest must be provided by your code, or by libraries of code that you use — such as Cocoa.

Memory management
> Swift manages memory automatically. You will rarely have to concern yourself with memory management.

Cocoa compatibility
> The Cocoa APIs are written in C and Objective-C. Swift is explicitly designed to interface with most of the Cocoa APIs.

These features make Swift an excellent language for learning to program iOS.

The alternative, Objective-C, still exists, and you can use it if you like. Indeed, it is easy to write an app that includes both Swift code and Objective-C code; and you may have reason to do so. Objective-C, however, lacks the very advantages that Swift offers. Objective-C agglomerates object-oriented features onto C. It is therefore only partially object-oriented; it has both objects and scalar data types, and its objects have to be slotted into one particular C data type (pointers). Its syntax can be difficult and tricky; reading and writing nested method calls can make one's eyes glaze over, and it invites hacky habits such as implicit nil-testing. Its type checking can be and frequently is turned off, resulting in programmer errors where a message is sent to the wrong type of object and the program crashes. It uses manual memory management; the recent introduction of ARC (automatic reference counting) has alleviated some of the programmer tedium and has greatly reduced the likelihood of programmer error, but errors are still possible, and memory management ultimately remains manual.

Recent revisions and additions to Objective-C — ARC, synthesis and autosynthesis, improved literal array and dictionary syntax, blocks — have made it easier and more convenient, but such patches have also made the language even larger and possibly even more confusing. Because Objective-C must encompass C, there are limits to how far it can be extended and revised. Swift, on the other hand, is a clean start. If you were to dream of *completely* revising Objective-C to create a *better* Objective-C, Swift might be what you would dream of. It puts a modern, rational front end between you and the Cocoa Objective-C APIs.

Therefore, Swift is the programming language used throughout this book. Nevertheless, the reader will also need some awareness of Objective-C (including C). The Foundation and Cocoa APIs, the built-in commands with which your code must interact in order to make anything happen on an iOS device, are still written in C and Objective-C. In order to interact with them, you have to know what those languages would expect. For example, in order to pass a Swift array where an NSArray is expected, you need to know what constitutes an object acceptable as an element of an Objective-C NSArray.

Therefore, in this edition, although I do not attempt to teach Objective-C, I do describe it in enough detail to allow you to read it when you encounter it in the documentation and on the Internet, and I occasionally show some Objective-C code.

Part III, on Cocoa, is really all about learning to think the way Objective-C thinks — because the structure and behavior of the Cocoa APIs are fundamentally based on Objective-C. And the book ends with an appendix that details how Swift and Objective-C communicate with one another, as well as explaining how your app can be written partly in Swift and partly in Objective-C.

The Scope of This Book

This book is actually one of a pair with my *Programming iOS 10*, which picks up exactly where this book leaves off. They complement and supplement one another. The two-book architecture should, I believe, render the size and scope of each book tractable for readers. Together, they provide a complete grounding in the knowledge needed to begin writing iOS apps; thus, when you *do* start writing iOS apps, you'll have a solid and rigorous understanding of what you are doing and where you are heading. If writing an iOS program is like building a house of bricks, this book teaches you what a brick is and how to handle it, while *Programming iOS 10* hands you some actual bricks and tells you how to assemble them.

When you have read this book, you'll know about Swift, Xcode, and the underpinnings of the Cocoa framework, and you will be ready to proceed directly to *Programming iOS 10*. Conversely, *Programming iOS 10* assumes a knowledge of this book; it begins, like Homer's *Iliad*, in the middle of the story, with the reader jumping with all four feet into views and view controllers, and with a knowledge of the language and the Xcode IDE already presupposed. If you started reading *Programming iOS 10* and wondered about such unexplained matters as Swift language basics, the UIApplicationMain function, the nib-loading mechanism, Cocoa patterns of delegation and notification, and retain cycles, wonder no longer — I didn't explain them there because I do explain them here.

The three parts of this book teach the underlying basis of all iOS programming:

- Part I introduces the Swift language, from the ground up — I do not assume that you know any other programming languages. My way of teaching Swift is different from other treatments, such as Apple's; it is systematic and Euclidean, with pedagogical building blocks piled on one another in what I regard as the most helpful order. At the same time, I have tried to confine myself to the essentials. Swift is not a big language, but it has some subtle and unusual corners. You don't need to dive deep into all of these, and my discussion will leave many of them unexplored. You will probably never encounter them, and if you do, you will have entered an advanced Swift world outside the scope of this discussion. To give an obvious example, readers may be surprised to find that I never mention Swift playgrounds or the REPL. My focus here is real-life iOS programming, and my explanation of Swift therefore concentrates on those common, practical aspects of the language that, in my experience, actually come into play in the course of programming iOS.

- Part II turns to Xcode, the world in which all iOS programming ultimately takes place. It explains what an Xcode project is and how it is transformed into an app, and how to work comfortably and nimbly with Xcode to consult the documentation and to write, navigate, and debug code, as well as how to bring your app through the subsequent stages of running on a device and submission to the App Store. There is also a very important chapter on nibs and the nib editor (Interface Builder), including outlets and actions as well as the mechanics of nib loading; however, such specialized topics as autolayout constraints in the nib are postponed to the other book.

- Part III introduces the Cocoa Touch framework. When you program for iOS, you take advantage of a suite of frameworks provided by Apple. These frameworks, taken together, constitute Cocoa; the brand of Cocoa that provides the API for programming iOS is Cocoa Touch. Your code will ultimately be almost entirely about communicating with Cocoa. The Cocoa Touch frameworks provide the underlying functionality that any iOS app needs to have. But to use a framework, you have to think the way the framework thinks, put your code where the framework expects it, and fulfill many obligations imposed on you by the framework. To make things even more interesting, Cocoa uses Objective-C, while you'll be using Swift: you need to know how your Swift code will interface with Cocoa's features and behaviors. Cocoa provides important foundational classes and adds linguistic and architectural devices such as categories, protocols, delegation, and notifications, as well as the pervasive responsibilities of memory management. Key–value coding and key–value observing are also discussed here.

The reader of this book will thus get a thorough grounding in the fundamental knowledge and techniques that any good iOS programmer needs. The book itself doesn't show how to write any particularly interesting iOS apps, but it does constantly use my own real apps and real programming situations to illustrate and motivate its explanations. And then you'll be ready for *Programming iOS 10*, of course!

Versions

This book is geared to Swift 3, iOS 10, and Xcode 8.

In general, only very minimal attention is given to earlier versions of iOS and Xcode. It is not my intention to embrace in this book any detailed knowledge about earlier versions of the software, which is, after all, readily and compendiously available in my earlier books. The book does contain, nevertheless, a few words of advice about backward compatibility (especially in Chapter 9).

The Swift language included with Xcode 8, Swift 3, has changed very significantly from its predecessor, Swift 2. A few important basic syntax changes were foreshadowed in Swift 2.2 and Swift 2.3, but Swift 3 adds many more, plus "renamification" has changed the names of many standard library and Cocoa methods, along with the new Foundation "overlay" that removes the "NS" prefix from certain type names. Fortunately, if you have existing Swift 2 code, Xcode 8 comes with a migrator that will update your Swift 2 code to Swift 3 in a remarkably intelligent fashion. This book, conversely, is totally incompatible with Swift 2 and doesn't discuss it; for the most part, I behave as if Swift 2 never existed. I do call out a few particularly noteworthy Swift 3 innovations, but by no means all of them.

In this edition, I have dropped my earlier convention of referring to Cocoa methods by their Objective-C name, because "renamification" has made it impossible to deduce the Swift 3 name of an Objective-C method. Instead, I give the name in Swift, as a function reference (as described in Chapter 2) — that is, the name plus the parameter labels followed by colon in parentheses. Now and then, if a method is already under discussion and there is no ambiguity, I'll use the bare name. (In a few places, such as Appendix A, where the Objective-C language is explicitly under discussion, I naturally do still use Objective-C method names.)

Please bear in mind that Apple continues to make adjustments to the Swift language. I have tried to keep my code up-to-date right up to the moment when the manuscript left my hands; but if, at some future time, a new version of Xcode is released along with a new version of Swift, some of the code in this book, and even some information about Swift itself, might be slightly incorrect. Please make allowances, and be prepared to compensate.

Screenshots of Xcode were taken using Xcode 8 under OS X 10.11 El Capitan. I have *not* upgraded my machine to macOS 10.12 Sierra, because at the time of this writing it was too new to be trusted with mission-critical work. If you are braver than I am and are running Sierra, your interface may naturally look very slightly different from the screenshots, but this difference will be minimal and shouldn't cause any confusion.

Acknowledgments

My thanks go first and foremost to the people at O'Reilly Media who have made writing a book so delightfully easy: Rachel Roumeliotis, Sarah Schneider, Kristen Brown, Dan Fauxsmith, Adam Witwer, and Sanders Kleinfeld come particularly to mind. And let's not forget my first and long-standing editor, Brian Jepson, whose influence is present throughout.

As in the past, I have been greatly aided by some fantastic software, whose excellences I have appreciated at every moment of the process of writing this book. I should like to mention, in particular:

- git (*http://git-scm.com*)
- SourceTree (*http://www.sourcetreeapp.com*)
- TextMate (*http://macromates.com*)
- AsciiDoc (*http://www.methods.co.nz/asciidoc*)
- Asciidoctor (*http://asciidoctor.org*)
- BBEdit (*http://barebones.com/products/bbedit/*)
- EasyFind (*http://www.devontechnologies.com/products/freeware.html*)
- Snapz Pro X (*http://www.ambrosiasw.com*)
- GraphicConverter (*http://www.lemkesoft.com*)
- OmniGraffle (*http://www.omnigroup.com*)

The book was typed and edited entirely on my faithful Unicomp Model M keyboard (*http://pckeyboard.com*), without which I could never have done so much writing over so long a period so painlessly. For more about my physical work environment, see *http://matt.neuburg.usesthis.com*.

From the Programming iOS 4 Preface

A programming framework has a kind of personality, an overall flavor that provides an insight into the goals and mindset of those who created it. When I first encountered Cocoa Touch, my assessment of its personality was: "Wow, the people who wrote this are really clever!" On the one hand, the number of built-in interface objects was severely and deliberately limited; on the other hand, the power and flexibility of some of those objects, especially such things as UITableView, was greatly enhanced over their OS X counterparts. Even more important, Apple created a particularly brilliant way (UIViewController) to help the programmer make entire blocks of interface come and go and supplant one another in a controlled, hierarchical manner, thus allowing that tiny iPhone display to unfold virtually into multiple interface worlds within a single app without the user becoming lost or confused.

The popularity of the iPhone, with its largely free or very inexpensive apps, and the subsequent popularity of the iPad, have brought and will continue to bring into the fold many new programmers who see programming for these devices as worthwhile and doable, even though they may not have felt the same way about OS X. Apple's own annual WWDC developer conventions have reflected this trend, with their emphasis shifted from OS X to iOS instruction.

The widespread eagerness to program iOS, however, though delightful on the one hand, has also fostered a certain tendency to try to run without first learning to walk. iOS gives the programmer mighty powers that can seem as limitless as imagination itself, but it also has fundamentals. I often see questions online from programmers who are evidently deep into the creation of some interesting app, but who are stymied in a way that reveals quite clearly that they are unfamiliar with the basics of the very world in which they are so happily cavorting.

It is this state of affairs that has motivated me to write this book, which is intended to ground the reader in the fundamentals of iOS. I love Cocoa and have long wished to write about it, but it is iOS and its popularity that has given me a proximate excuse to do so. Here I have attempted to marshal and expound, in what I hope is a pedagogically helpful and instructive yet ruthlessly Euclidean and logical order, the principles and elements on which sound iOS programming rests. My hope, as with my previous books, is that you will both read this book cover to cover (learning something new often enough to keep you turning the pages) and keep it by you as a handy reference.

This book is not intended to disparage Apple's own documentation and example projects. They are wonderful resources and have become more wonderful as time goes on. I have depended heavily on them in the preparation of this book. But I also find that they don't fulfill the same function as a reasoned, ordered presentation of the facts. The online documentation must make assumptions as to how much you already know; it can't guarantee that you'll approach it in a given order. And online documentation is more suitable to reference than to instruction. A fully written example, no matter how well commented, is difficult to follow; it demonstrates, but it does not teach.

A book, on the other hand, has numbered chapters and sequential pages; I can assume you know views before you know view controllers for the simple reason that Part I precedes Part II. And along with facts, I also bring to the table a degree of experience, which I try to communicate to you. Throughout this book you'll find me referring to "common beginner mistakes"; in most cases, these are mistakes that I have made myself, in addition to seeing others make them. I try to tell you what the pitfalls are because I assume that, in the course of things, you will otherwise fall into them just as naturally as I did as I was learning. You'll also see me construct many examples piece by piece or extract and explain just one tiny portion of a larger app. It is not a massive finished program that teaches programming, but an exposition of the thought process that developed that program. It is this thought process, more than anything else, that I hope you will gain from reading this book.

Conventions Used in This Book

The following typographical conventions are used in this book:

Italic
> Indicates new terms, URLs, email addresses, filenames, and file extensions.

`Constant width`
> Used for program listings, as well as within paragraphs to refer to program elements such as variable or function names, databases, data types, environment variables, statements, and keywords.

`Constant width bold`
> Shows commands or other text that should be typed literally by the user.

`Constant width italic`
> Shows text that should be replaced with user-supplied values or by values determined by context.

 This element signifies a tip or suggestion.

 This element signifies a general note.

 This element indicates a warning or caution.

Using Code Examples

Supplemental material (code examples, exercises, etc.) is available for download at *http://github.com/mattneub/Programming-iOS-Book-Examples*.

This book is here to help you get your job done. In general, if example code is offered with this book, you may use it in your programs and documentation. You do not need to contact us for permission unless you're reproducing a significant portion of the code. For example, writing a program that uses several chunks of code from this book does not require permission. Selling or distributing a CD-ROM of examples from O'Reilly books does require permission. Answering a question by citing this book and quoting example code does not require permission. Incorporating a significant amount of example code from this book into your product's documentation does require permission.

We appreciate, but do not require, attribution. An attribution usually includes the title, author, publisher, and ISBN. For example: "*iOS 10 Programming Fundamentals with Swift* by Matt Neuburg (O'Reilly). Copyright 2017 Matt Neuburg, 978-1-491-97007-2."

If you feel your use of code examples falls outside fair use or the permission given above, feel free to contact us at *permissions@oreilly.com*.

Safari® Books Online

 Safari Books Online is an on-demand digital library that delivers expert content in both book and video form from the world's leading authors in technology and business.

Technology professionals, software developers, web designers, and business and creative professionals use Safari Books Online as their primary resource for research, problem solving, learning, and certification training.

Safari Books Online offers a range of plans and pricing for enterprise, government, education, and individuals.

Members have access to thousands of books, training videos, and prepublication manuscripts in one fully searchable database from publishers like O'Reilly Media, Prentice Hall Professional, Addison-Wesley Professional, Microsoft Press, Sams, Que, Peachpit Press, Focal Press, Cisco Press, John Wiley & Sons, Syngress, Morgan Kaufmann, IBM Redbooks, Packt, Adobe Press, FT Press, Apress, Manning, New Riders, McGraw-Hill, Jones & Bartlett, Course Technology, and hundreds more. For more information about Safari Books Online, please visit us online.

How to Contact Us

Please address comments and questions concerning this book to the publisher:

O'Reilly Media, Inc.
1005 Gravenstein Highway North
Sebastopol, CA 95472
800-998-9938 (in the United States or Canada)
707-829-0515 (international or local)
707-829-0104 (fax)

We have a web page for this book, where we list errata, examples, and any additional information. You can access this page at *http://bit.ly/ios10-prog-fundamentals*.

To comment or ask technical questions about this book, send email to *bookquestions@oreilly.com*.

For more information about our books, courses, conferences, and news, see our website at *http://www.oreilly.com*.

Find us on Facebook: *http://facebook.com/oreilly*

Follow us on Twitter: *http://twitter.com/oreillymedia*

Watch us on YouTube: *http://www.youtube.com/oreillymedia*

PART I
Language

This part of the book teaches the Swift language, from the ground up. The description is rigorous and orderly. Here you'll become sufficiently conversant with Swift to be comfortable with it, so that you can proceed to the practical business of actual programming.

- Chapter 1 surveys the structure of a Swift program, both physically and conceptually. You'll learn how Swift code files are organized, and you'll be introduced to the most important underlying concepts of the object-oriented Swift language: variables and functions, scopes and namespaces, object types and their instances.

- Chapter 2 explores Swift functions. We start with the basics of how functions are declared and called; then we discuss parameters — external parameter names, default parameters, and variadic parameters. Then we dive deep into the power of Swift functions, with an explanation of functions inside functions, functions as first-class values, anonymous functions, functions as closures, curried functions, and function references and selectors.

- Chapter 3 starts with Swift variables — their scope and lifetime, and how they are declared and initialized, along with features such as computed variables and setter observers. Then some important built-in Swift types are introduced, including Booleans, numbers, strings, ranges, tuples, and Optionals.

- Chapter 4 is all about Swift object types — classes, structs, and enums. It explains how these three object types work, and how you declare, instantiate, and use them. Then it proceeds to polymorphism and casting, protocols, generics, and extensions. The chapter concludes with a discussion of Swift's umbrella types, such as Any and AnyObject, and collection types — Array, Dictionary, and Set (including option sets).

- Chapter 5 is a miscellany. We start with Swift's flow control structures for branching, looping, and jumping, including error handling. Then I'll explain how to create your own Swift operators. The chapter concludes by describing Swift access control (privacy), introspection (reflection), and memory management.

CHAPTER 1

The Architecture of Swift

It will be useful at the outset for you to have a general sense of how the Swift language is constructed and what a Swift-based iOS program looks like. This chapter will survey the overall architecture and nature of the Swift language. Subsequent chapters will fill in the details.

Ground of Being

A complete Swift command is a *statement*. A Swift text file consists of multiple *lines* of text. Line breaks are meaningful. The typical layout of a program is one statement, one line:

```
print("hello")
print("world")
```

(The print command provides instant feedback in the Xcode console.)

You can combine more than one statement on a line, but then you need to put a semicolon between them:

```
print("hello"); print("world")
```

You are free to put a semicolon at the end of a statement that is last or alone on its line, but no one ever does (except out of habit, because C and Objective-C *require* the semicolon):

```
print("hello");
print("world");
```

Conversely, a single statement can be broken into multiple lines, in order to prevent long statements from becoming long lines. But you should try to do this at sensible places so as not to confuse Swift. For example, after an opening parenthesis is a good place:

```
print(
    "world")
```

Comments are everything after two slashes in a line (so-called C++-style comments):

```
print("world") // this is a comment, so Swift ignores it
```

You can also enclose comments in /*...*/, as in C. Unlike C, C-style comments can be nested.

Many constructs in Swift use curly braces as delimiters:

```
class Dog {
    func bark() {
        print("woof")
    }
}
```

By convention, the contents of curly braces are preceded and followed by line breaks and are indented for clarity, as shown in the preceding code. Xcode will help impose this convention, but the truth is that Swift doesn't care, and layouts like this are legal (and are sometimes more convenient):

```
class Dog { func bark() { print("woof") }}
```

Swift is a *compiled* language. This means that your code must *build* — passing through the compiler and being turned from text into some lower-level form that a computer can understand — before it can *run* and actually do the things it says to do. The Swift compiler is very strict; in the course of writing a program, you will often try to build and run, only to discover that you can't even build in the first place, because the compiler will flag some *error*, which you will have to fix if you want the code to run. Less often, the compiler will let you off with a *warning*; the code can run, but in general you should take warnings seriously and fix whatever they are telling you about. The strictness of the compiler is one of Swift's greatest strengths, and provides your code with a large measure of audited correctness even before it ever starts running.

 The Swift compiler's error and warning messages range from the insightful to the obtuse to the downright misleading. You will often know that *something* is wrong with a line of code, but the Swift compiler will not be telling you clearly exactly *what* is wrong or even *where* in the line to focus your attention. My advice in these situations is to pull the line apart into several lines of simpler code until you reach a point where you can guess what the issue is. Try to love the compiler despite the occasional unhelpful nature of its messages. Remember, it knows more than you do, even if it is sometimes rather inarticulate about its knowledge.

Everything Is an Object?

In Swift, "everything is an object." That's a boast common to various modern object-oriented languages, but what does it mean? Well, that depends on what you mean by "object" — and what you mean by "everything."

Let's start by stipulating that an object, roughly speaking, is something you can send a message to. A message, roughly speaking, is an imperative instruction. For example, you can give commands to a dog: "Bark!" "Sit!" In this analogy, those phrases are messages, and the dog is the object to which you are sending those messages.

In Swift, the syntax of message-sending is *dot-notation*. We start with the object; then there's a dot (a period); then there's the message. (Some messages are also followed by parentheses, but ignore them for now; the full syntax of message-sending is one of those details we'll be filling in later.) This is valid Swift syntax:

```
fido.bark()
rover.sit()
```

The idea of *everything* being an object is a way of suggesting that even "primitive" linguistic entities can be sent messages. Take, for example, 1. It appears to be a literal digit and no more. It will not surprise you, if you've ever used any programming language, that you can say things like this in Swift:

```
let sum = 1 + 2
```

But it *is* surprising to find that 1 can be followed by a dot and a message. This is legal and meaningful in Swift (don't worry about what it actually means):

```
let s = 1.description
```

But we can go further. Return to that innocent-looking 1 + 2 from our earlier code. It turns out that this is actually a kind of syntactic trickery, a convenient way of expressing and hiding what's really going on. Just as 1 is actually an object, + is actually a message; but it's a message with special syntax (*operator* syntax). In Swift, every noun is an object, and every verb is a message.

Perhaps the ultimate acid test for whether something is an object in Swift is whether you can modify it. An object type can be *extended* in Swift, meaning that you can define your own messages on that type. For example, you can't normally send the say-Hello message to a number. But you can change a number type so that you can:

```
extension Int {
    func sayHello() {
        print("Hello, I'm \(self)")
    }
}
1.sayHello() // outputs: "Hello, I'm 1"
```

In Swift, then, 1 is an object. In some languages, such as Objective-C, it clearly is not; it is a "primitive" or *scalar* built-in data type. So the distinction being drawn here is between object types on the one hand and scalars on the other. In Swift, there are no scalars; *all* types are ultimately object types. That's what "everything is an object" really means.

Three Flavors of Object Type

If you know Objective-C or some other object-oriented language, you may be surprised by Swift's notion of what *kind* of object 1 is. In many languages, such as Objective-C, an object is a *class* or an instance of a class (I'll explain later what an instance is). Swift has classes, but 1 in Swift is not a class or an instance of a class: the type of 1, namely Int, is a *struct*, and 1 is an instance of a struct. And Swift has yet another kind of thing you can send messages to, called an *enum*.

So Swift has three kinds of object type: classes, structs, and enums. I like to refer to these as the three *flavors* of object type. Exactly how they differ from one another will emerge in due course. But they are all very definitely object types, and their similarities to one another are far stronger than their differences. For now, just bear in mind that these three flavors exist.

(The fact that a struct or enum is an object type in Swift will surprise you particularly if you know Objective-C. Objective-C has structs and enums, but they are not objects. Swift structs, in particular, are much more important and pervasive than Objective-C structs. This difference between how Swift views structs and enums and how Objective-C views them can matter when you are talking to Cocoa.)

Variables

A variable is a *name* for an object. Technically, it *refers* to an object; it is an object *reference*. Nontechnically, you can think of it as a shoebox into which an object is placed. The object may undergo changes, or it may be replaced inside the shoebox by another object, but the name has an integrity all its own. The object to which the variable refers is the variable's *value*.

In Swift, no variable comes implicitly into existence; all variables must be *declared*. If you need a name for something, you must say "I'm creating a name." You do this with one of two keywords: let or var. In Swift, declaration is usually accompanied by *initialization* — you use an equal sign to give the variable a value immediately, as part of the declaration. These are both variable declarations (and initializations):

```
let one = 1
var two = 2
```

Once the name exists, you are free to use it. For example, we can change the value of two to be the same as the value of one:

```
let one = 1
var two = 2
two = one
```

The last line of that code uses both the name one and the name two declared in the first two lines: the name one, on the right side of the equal sign, is used merely to *refer* to the value inside the shoebox one (namely 1); but the name two, on the left side of the equal sign, is used to *replace* the value inside the shoebox two. A statement like that, with a variable name on the left side of an equal sign, is called an *assignment*, and the equal sign is the *assignment operator*. The equal sign is not an assertion of equality, as it might be in an algebraic formula; it is a command. It means: "Get the value of what's on the right side of me, and use it to replace the value of what's on the left side of me."

The two kinds of variable declaration differ in that a name declared with let *cannot have its value replaced*. A variable declared with let is a *constant*; its value is assigned once and stays. This won't even compile:

```
let one = 1
var two = 2
one = two // compile error
```

It is always possible to declare a name with var to give yourself the most flexibility, but if you know you're never going to replace the initial value of a variable, it's better to use let, as this permits Swift to behave more efficiently — so much more efficiently, in fact, that the Swift compiler will actually call your attention to any case of your using var where you could have used let, offering to change it for you.

Variables also have a *type*. This type is established when the variable is declared and *can never change*. For example, this won't compile:

```
var two = 2
two = "hello" // compile error
```

Once two is declared and initialized as 2, it is a number (properly speaking, an Int) and it must always be so. You can replace its value with 1 because that's also an Int, but you can't replace its value with "hello" because that's a string (properly speaking, a String) — and a String is not an Int.

Variables literally have a life of their own — more accurately, a *lifetime* of their own. As long as a variable exists, it keeps its value alive. Thus, a variable can be not only a way of conveniently *naming* something, but also a way of *preserving* it. I'll have more to say about that later.

By convention, type names such as String or Int (or Dog or Cat) start with a capital letter; variable names start with a small letter. *Do not violate this convention.* If you do, your code might still compile and run just fine, but I will personally send agents to your house to remove your kneecaps in the dead of night.

Functions

Executable code, like `fido.bark()` or `one = two`, cannot go just anywhere in your program. In general, it must live inside the body of a *function*. A function is a batch of code that can be told, as a batch, to run. Typically, a function has a name, and it gets that name through a function declaration. Function declaration syntax is another of those details that will be filled in later, but here's an example:

```
func go() {
    let one = 1
    var two = 2
    two = one
}
```

That describes a sequence of things to do — declare `one`, declare `two`, change the value of `two` to match the value of `one` — and it gives that sequence a *name*, `go`; but it doesn't *perform* the sequence. The sequence is performed when someone *calls* the function. Thus, we might say, elsewhere:

```
go()
```

That is a command to the `go` function that it should actually run. But again, that command is itself executable code, so it cannot live on its own either. It might live in the body of a different function:

```
func doGo() {
    go()
}
```

But wait! This is getting a little nutty. That, too, is just a function declaration; to run it, someone must call `doGo` by saying `doGo()` — and that's executable code too. This seems like some kind of infinite regression; it looks like none of our code will *ever* run. If all executable code has to live in a function, who will tell *any* function to run? The initial impetus must come from somewhere.

In real life, fortunately, this regression problem doesn't arise. Remember that your goal is ultimately to write an iOS app. Thus, your app will be run on an iOS device (or the Simulator) by a runtime that already wants to call certain functions. So you start by writing special functions that you know the runtime itself will call. That gives your app a way to get started and gives you places to put functions that will be called by the runtime at key moments — such as when the app launches, or when the user taps a button in your app's interface.

Swift also has a special rule that a file called *main.swift*, exceptionally, *can* have executable code at its top level, outside any function body, and this is the code that actually runs when the program runs. You can construct your app with a *main.swift* file, but in general you won't need to.

The Structure of a Swift File

A Swift program can consist of one file or many files. In Swift, a file is a meaningful unit, and there are definite rules about the structure of the Swift code that can go inside it. (I'm assuming that we are *not* in a *main.swift* file.) Only certain things can go at the top level of a Swift file — chiefly the following:

Module `import` *statements*
> A module is an even higher-level unit than a file. A module can consist of multiple files, and these can all see each other automatically; but a module can't see another module without an `import` statement. For example, that is how you are able to talk to Cocoa in an iOS program: the first line of your file says `import UIKit`.

Variable declarations
> A variable declared at the top level of a file is a *global* variable: all code will be able to see and access it, without explicitly sending a message to any object, and it lives as long as the program runs.

Function declarations
> A function declared at the top level of a file is a *global* function: all code will be able to see and call it, without explicitly sending a message to any object.

Object type declarations
> The declaration for a class, a struct, or an enum.

For example, this is a legal Swift file containing (just to demonstrate that it can be done) an `import` statement, a variable declaration, a function declaration, a class declaration, a struct declaration, and an enum declaration:

```
import UIKit
var one = 1
func changeOne() {
}
class Manny {
}
struct Moe {
}
enum Jack {
}
```

That's a very silly and mostly empty example, but remember, our goal is to survey the parts of the language and the structure of a file, and the example shows them.

Furthermore, the curly braces for each of the things in that example can all have variable declarations, function declarations, and object type declarations within them! Indeed, *any* structural curly braces can contain such declarations.

You'll notice that I did *not* say that executable code can go at the top level of a file. That's because it can't! *Only a function body can contain executable code.* A statement like one = two or print(name) is executable code, and can't go at the top level of a file. But in our previous example, func changeOne() is a function declaration, so executable code *can* go inside its curly braces, because they constitute a function body:

```
var one = 1
func changeOne() {
    let two = 2
    one = two
}
```

Executable code also can't go directly inside the curly braces that accompany the class Manny declaration; that's the top level of a class declaration, not a function body. But a class declaration *can* contain a function declaration, and that function declaration *can* contain executable code:

```
class Manny {
    let name = "manny"
    func sayName() {
        print(name)
    }
}
```

To sum up, Example 1-1 is a legal Swift file, schematically illustrating the structural possibilities. (Ignore the hanky-panky with the name variable declaration inside the enum declaration for Jack; enum top-level variables have some special rules that I'll explain later.)

Example 1-1. Schematic structure of a legal Swift file

```
import UIKit
var one = 1
func changeOne() {
    let two = 2
    func sayTwo() {
        print(two)
    }
    class Klass {}
    struct Struct {}
    enum Enum {}
    one = two
}
class Manny {
    let name = "manny"
    func sayName() {
```

```
            print(name)
        }
        class Klass {}
        struct Struct {}
        enum Enum {}
    }
}
struct Moe {
    let name = "moe"
    func sayName() {
        print(name)
    }
    class Klass {}
    struct Struct {}
    enum Enum {}
}
enum Jack {
    var name : String {
        return "jack"
    }
    func sayName() {
        print(name)
    }
    class Klass {}
    struct Struct {}
    enum Enum {}
}
```

Obviously, we can recurse down as far we like: we could have a class declaration containing a class declaration containing a class declaration, and so on. But there's no point illustrating *that*.

Scope and Lifetime

In a Swift program, things have a *scope*. This refers to their ability to be seen by other things. Things are nested inside of other things, making a nested hierarchy of things. The rule is that things can see things *at their own level and at a higher level containing them*. The levels are:

- A module is a scope.
- A file is a scope.
- Curly braces are a scope.

When something is declared, it is declared at some level within that hierarchy. Its place in the hierarchy — its scope — determines whether it can be seen by other things.

Look again at Example 1-1. Inside the declaration of Manny is a name variable declaration and a sayName function declaration; the code *inside* sayName's curly braces can see things *outside* those curly braces *at a higher containing level*, and can therefore see the name variable. Similarly, the code inside the body of the changeOne function can see the one variable declared at the top level of the file; indeed, *everything* throughout this file can see the one variable declared at the top level of the file.

Scope is thus a very important way of *sharing information*. Two different functions declared inside Manny would *both* be able to see the name declared at Manny's top level. Code inside Jack and code inside Moe can *both* see the one declared at the file's top level.

Things also have a *lifetime*, which is effectively equivalent to their scope. A thing lives as long as its surrounding scope lives. Thus, in Example 1-1, the variable one lives as long as the file lives — namely, as long the program runs. It is global *and persistent*. But the variable name declared at the top level of Manny exists only so long as a Manny instance exists (I'll talk in a moment about what that means).

Things declared at a deeper level live even shorter lifetimes. Consider this code:

```
func silly() {
    if true {
        class Cat {}
        var one = 1
        one = one + 1
    }
}
```

That code is silly, but it's legal: remember, I said that variable declarations, function declarations, and object type declarations can appear in *any* structural curly braces. In that code, the class Cat and the variable one will not even come into existence until someone calls the silly function, and even then they will exist only during the brief instant that the path of code execution passes through the if construct. So, suppose the function silly is called; the path of execution then enters the if construct. Here, Cat is declared and comes into existence; then one is declared and comes into existence; then the executable line one = one + 1 is executed; and then the scope ends and both Cat and one vanish in a puff of smoke. And throughout their brief lives, Cat and one were completely invisible to the rest of the program. (Do you see why?)

Object Members

Inside the three object types (class, struct, and enum), things declared at the top level have special names, mostly for historical reasons. Let's use the Manny class as an example:

```
class Manny {
    let name = "manny"
    func sayName() {
        print(name)
    }
}
```

In that code:

- `name` is a variable declared at the top level of an object declaration, so it is called a *property* of that object.
- `sayName` is a function declared at the top level of an object declaration, so it is called a *method* of that object.

Things declared at the top level of an object declaration — properties, methods, and any objects declared at that level — are collectively the *members* of that object. Members have a special significance, because they define the *messages* you are allowed to send to that object!

Namespaces

A *namespace* is a named region of a program. A namespace has the property that the names of things inside it cannot be reached by things outside it without somehow first passing through the barrier of saying that region's name. This is a good thing because it allows the same name to be used in different places without a conflict. Clearly, namespaces and scopes are closely related notions.

Namespaces help to explain the significance of declaring an object at the top level of an object, like this:

```
class Manny {
    class Klass {}
}
```

This way of declaring Klass makes Klass a *nested type*. It effectively "hides" Klass inside Manny. Manny is a namespace! Code *inside* Manny can see (and say) Klass directly. But code outside Manny can't do that. It has to specify the namespace *explicitly* in order to pass through the barrier that the namespace represents. To do so, it must say Manny's name first, followed by a dot, followed by the term Klass. In short, it has to say `Manny.Klass`.

The namespace does not, of itself, provide secrecy or privacy; it's a convenience. Thus, in Example 1-1, I gave Manny a Klass class, and I also gave Moe a Klass class. But they don't conflict, because they are in different namespaces, and I can differentiate them, if necessary, as `Manny.Klass` and `Moe.Klass`.

It will not have escaped your attention that the syntax for diving explicitly into a namespace is the message-sending dot-notation syntax. They are, in fact, the same thing.

In effect, message-sending allows you to see into scopes you can't see into otherwise. Code inside Moe can't *automatically* see the Klass declared inside Manny, but it *can* see it by taking one easy extra step, namely by speaking of `Manny.Klass`. It can do *that* because it *can* see Manny (because Manny is declared at a level that code inside Moe can see).

Modules

The top-level namespaces are *modules*. By default, your app is a module and hence a namespace; that namespace's name is, roughly speaking, the name of the app. For example, if my app is called `MyApp`, then if I declare a class Manny at the top level of a file, that class's *real* name is `MyApp.Manny`. But I don't usually need to use that real name, because my code is already inside the same namespace, and can see the name Manny directly.

Frameworks are also modules, and hence they are also namespaces. When you import a module, all the top-level declarations of that module become visible to your code, without your having to use the module's namespace explicitly to refer to them.

For example, Cocoa's Foundation framework, where NSString lives, is a module. When you program iOS, you will say `import Foundation` (or, more likely, you'll say `import UIKit`, which itself imports Foundation), thus allowing you to speak of NSString without saying `Foundation.NSString`. But you *could* say `Foundation.NSString`, and if you were so silly as to declare a different NSString in your own module, you would *have* to say `Foundation.NSString`, in order to differentiate them. You can also create your own frameworks, and these, too, will be modules.

Swift itself is defined in a module — the Swift module. Your code *always implicitly imports the Swift module*. You could make this explicit by starting a file with the line `import Swift`; there is no need to do this, but it does no harm either.

That fact is important, because it solves a major mystery: where do things like `print` come from, and why is it possible to use them outside of any message to any object? `print` is in fact a function declared at the top level of the Swift module, and your code can see the Swift module's top-level declarations because it imports Swift. The `print` function thus becomes, as far as your code is concerned, an ordinary top-level function like any other; it is global to your code, and your code can speak of it without specifying its namespace. You *can* specify its namespace — it is perfectly legal to say things like `Swift.print("hello")` — but you probably never will, because there's no name conflict to resolve.

You can actually *see* the Swift top-level declarations and read and study them, and this can be a useful thing to do. To do so, Command-click the term `print` in your code. Alternatively, explicitly `import Swift` and Command-click the term `Swift`. Behold, there's the Swift top-level declarations! You won't see any executable Swift *code* here, but you will see the declarations for all the available Swift terms, including top-level functions like `print`, operators like +, and built-in types such as Int and String (look for `struct Int`, `struct String`, and so on).

Instances

Object types — class, struct, and enum — have an important feature in common: they can be *instantiated*. In effect, when you declare an object type, you are only defining a *type*. To instantiate a type is to make a thing — an *instance* — of that type.

So, for example, I can declare a Dog class, and I can give my class a method:

```
class Dog {
    func bark() {
        print("woof")
    }
}
```

But I don't actually have any Dog objects in my program yet. I have merely described the *type* of thing a Dog *would* be if I had one. To get an actual Dog, I have to *make* one. The process of making an actual Dog object whose type is the Dog class is the process of instantiating Dog. The result is a new object — a Dog *instance*.

In Swift, instances can be created by using the object type's name as a function name and calling the function. This involves using parentheses. When you append parentheses to the name of an object type, you are sending a very special kind of message to that object type: Instantiate yourself!

So now I'm going to make a Dog instance:

```
let fido = Dog()
```

There's a lot going on in that code! I did two things. I instantiated Dog, thus causing me to end up with a Dog instance. I also put that Dog instance into a shoebox called `fido` — I declared a variable and initialized the variable by assigning my new Dog instance to it. Now `fido` *is a Dog instance*. (Moreover, because I used `let`, `fido` will always be this same Dog instance. I could have used `var` instead, but even then, initializing `fido` as a Dog instance would have meant `fido` could only be some Dog instance after that.)

Now that I have a Dog instance, I can send *instance messages* to it. And what do you suppose they are? They are Dog's properties and methods! For example:

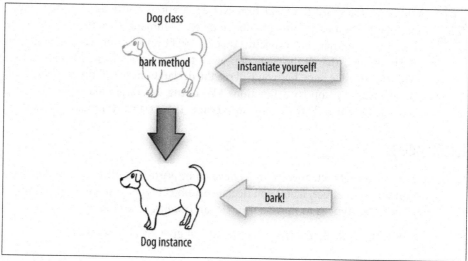

Figure 1-1. Making an instance and calling an instance method

```
let fido = Dog()
fido.bark()
```

That code is legal. Not only that, it is effective: it actually does cause "woof" to appear in the console. I made a Dog and I made it bark! (See Figure 1-1.)

There's an important lesson here, so let me pause to emphasize it. By default, properties and methods are *instance* properties and methods. You can't use them as messages to the object type itself; you have to have an *instance* to send those messages to. As things stand, this is illegal and won't compile:

```
Dog.bark() // compile error
```

It is possible to declare a function bark in such a way that saying Dog.bark() *is* legal, but that would be a different kind of function — a *class* function or a *static* function — and you would need to say so when you declare it.

The same thing is true of properties. To illustrate, let's give Dog a name property. The only respect in which any Dog has had a name up to now has been the name of the variable to which it is assigned. But that name is not intrinsic to the Dog object *itself*. The name property will be:

```
class Dog {
    var name = ""
}
```

That allows me to set a Dog's name, but it needs to be an *instance* of Dog:

```
let fido = Dog()
fido.name = "Fido"
```

It is possible to declare a property `name` in such a way that saying `Dog.name` is legal, but that would be a different kind of property — a *class* property or a *static* property — and you would need to say so when you declare it.

Why Instances?

Even if there were no such thing as an instance, an object type is itself an object. We know this because it is possible to send a message to an object type: it is possible to treat an object type as a namespace and to dive explicitly into that namespace (the phrase `Manny.Klass` is a case in point). Moreover, since class and static members exist, it is possible to call a method directly on a class, a struct, or an enum type, and to refer to a property of a class, a struct, or an enum type. Why, then, do instances exist at all?

The answer has mostly to do with the nature of instance properties. The value of an instance property is defined with respect to *a particular instance*. This is where instances get their real usefulness and power.

Consider again our Dog class. I'll give it a `name` property and a `bark` method; remember, these are an instance property and an instance method:

```
class Dog {
    var name = ""
    func bark() {
        print("woof")
    }
}
```

A Dog instance comes into existence with a blank `name` (an empty string). But its `name` property is a `var`, so once we have any Dog instance, we can assign to its `name` a new String value:

```
let dog1 = Dog()
dog1.name = "Fido"
```

We can also ask for a Dog instance's `name`:

```
let dog1 = Dog()
dog1.name = "Fido"
print(dog1.name) // "Fido"
```

The important thing is that we can make more than one Dog instance, and that two different Dog instances can have two different `name` property values (Figure 1-2):

```
let dog1 = Dog()
dog1.name = "Fido"
let dog2 = Dog()
dog2.name = "Rover"
print(dog1.name) // "Fido"
print(dog2.name) // "Rover"
```

Figure 1-2. Two dogs with different property values

Note that a Dog instance's name property has nothing to do with the name of the variable to which a Dog instance is assigned. The variable is just a shoebox. You can pass an instance from one shoebox to another. But the instance itself maintains its own internal integrity:

```
let dog1 = Dog()
dog1.name = "Fido"
var dog2 = Dog()
dog2.name = "Rover"
print(dog1.name) // "Fido"
print(dog2.name) // "Rover"
dog2 = dog1
print(dog2.name) // "Fido"
```

That code didn't change Rover's name; it changed which dog was inside the dog2 shoebox, replacing Rover with Fido.

The full power of object-based programming has now emerged. There is a Dog object type which defines *what it is to be a Dog*. Our declaration of Dog says that a Dog instance — *any* Dog instance, *every* Dog instance — has a name property and a bark method. But *each* Dog instance can have its own name property *value*. They are *different* instances and maintain their own internal *state*. So multiple instances of the same object type *behave* alike — both Fido and Rover can bark, and will do so when they are sent the bark message — but they are different instances and can have different property values: Fido's name is "Fido" while Rover's name is "Rover".

So an instance is a reflection of the instance methods of its type, but that isn't *all* it is; it's also a collection of instance properties. The object type is responsible for *what* properties the instance has, but not necessarily for the *values* of those properties. The values can change as the program runs, and apply only to a particular instance. An instance is a cluster of particular property values.

An instance is responsible not only for the values but also for the *lifetimes* of its properties. Suppose we bring a Dog instance into existence and assign to its name property the value "Fido". Then this Dog instance is keeping the string "Fido" alive just so long as we do not replace the value of its name with some other value *and just so long as this instance lives.*

In short, an instance is both code and data. The code it gets from its type and in a sense is shared with all other instances of that type, but the data belong to it alone. The data can persist as long as the instance persists. The instance has, at every moment, a state — the complete collection of its own personal property values. An instance is a device for maintaining state. It's a box for storage of data.

self

An instance is an object, and an object is the recipient of messages. Thus, an instance needs a way of sending a message to itself. This is made possible by the magic word self. This word can be used wherever an instance of the appropriate type is expected.

For example, let's say I want to keep the thing that a Dog says when it barks — namely "woof" — in a property. Then in my implementation of bark I need to refer to that property. I can do it like this:

```
class Dog {
    var name = ""
    var whatADogSays = "woof"
    func bark() {
        print(self.whatADogSays)
    }
}
```

Similarly, let's say I want to write an instance method speak which is merely a synonym for bark. My speak implementation can consist of simply calling my own bark method. I can do it like this:

```
class Dog {
    var name = ""
    var whatADogSays = "woof"
    func bark() {
        print(self.whatADogSays)
    }
```

```
    func speak() {
        self.bark()
    }
}
```

Observe that the term `self` in that example appears only in instance methods. When an instance's code says `self`, it is referring to *this* instance. If the expression `self.name` appears in a Dog instance method's code, it means the `name` of *this* Dog instance, the one whose code is running at that moment.

It turns out that every use of the word `self` I've just illustrated is completely optional. You can omit it and all the same things will happen:

```
class Dog {
    var name = ""
    var whatADogSays = "woof"
    func bark() {
        print(whatADogSays)
    }
    func speak() {
        bark()
    }
}
```

The reason is that if you omit the message recipient and the message you're sending can be sent to `self`, the compiler supplies `self` as the message's recipient under the hood. However, I *never* do that (except by mistake). As a matter of style, I like to be *explicit* in my use of `self`. I find code that omits `self` harder to read and understand. And there are situations where you *must* say `self`, so I prefer to use it whenever I'm allowed to.

Privacy

Earlier, I said that a namespace is not, of itself, an insuperable barrier to accessing the names inside it. But such a barrier is sometimes desirable. For example, not all data stored by an instance is intended for alteration by, or even visibility to, another instance. And not every instance method is intended to be called by other instances. Any decent object-based programming language needs a way to endow its object members with *privacy* — a way of making it harder for other objects to see those members if they are not supposed to be seen.

Consider, for example:

```
class Dog {
    var name = ""
    var whatADogSays = "woof"
    func bark() {
        print(self.whatADogSays)
    }
```

```
    func speak() {
        print(self.whatADogSays)
    }
}
```

Here, other objects can come along and change my property `whatADogSays`. Since that property is used by both `bark` and `speak`, we could easily end up with a Dog that, when told to `bark`, says `"meow"`. This seems somehow undesirable:

```
let dog1 = Dog()
dog1.whatADogSays = "meow"
dog1.bark() // meow
```

You might reply: Well, silly, why did you declare `whatADogSays` with `var`? Declare it with `let` instead. Make it a constant! Now no one can change it:

```
class Dog {
    var name = ""
    let whatADogSays = "woof"
    func bark() {
        print(self.whatADogSays)
    }
    func speak() {
        print(self.whatADogSays)
    }
}
```

That is a good answer, but it is not quite good enough. There are two problems. Suppose I want a Dog instance itself to be able to change `self.whatADogSays`. Then `whatADogSays` *has* to be a `var`; otherwise, even the instance itself can't change it. Also, suppose I don't want any other object to *know* what this Dog says, except by calling `bark` or `speak`. Even when declared with `let`, other objects can still *read* the value of `whatADogSays`. Maybe I don't like that.

To solve this problem, Swift provides the `private` keyword. I'll talk later about all the ramifications of this keyword, but for now it's enough to know that it solves the problem:

```
class Dog {
    var name = ""
    private var whatADogSays = "woof"
    func bark() {
        print(self.whatADogSays)
    }
    func speak() {
        print(self.whatADogSays)
    }
}
```

Reserved Words

Certain terms, like `class` and `func` and `var` and `let` and `if` and `private` and `import`, are *reserved* in Swift; they are part of the language. That means you can't use them as *identifiers* — as the name of a class, a function, or a variable, for example. If you try to do so, you'll get a compile error with the word "identifier" in it.

To force a reserved word to be an identifier, surround it by backticks (`` ` ``). Thus, this (extraordinarily confusing) code is legal:

```
class `func` {
    func `if`() {
        let `class` = 1
    }
}
```

Now `name` is a public property, but `whatADogSays` is a private property: it can't be seen by other types of object. A Dog instance can speak of `self.whatADogSays`, but a Cat instance with a reference to a Dog instance as `fido` cannot say `fido.whatADogSays`.

The important lesson here is that object members are public by default, and if you want privacy, you have to ask for it. The class declaration defines a namespace; this namespace requires that other objects use an extra level of dot-notation to refer to what's inside the namespace, but other objects *can* still refer to what's inside the namespace; the namespace does not, in and of itself, close any doors of visibility. The `private` keyword lets you close those doors.

Design

What object types will your program need, what methods and properties should they have, when and how will they be instantiated, and what should you do with those instances when you have them? Those aren't easy decisions, and there are no clear-cut answers. Object-based programming is an art.

In real life, when you're programming iOS, many object types you'll be working with will not be yours but Apple's. Swift itself comes with a few useful object types, such as String and Int; you'll also `import UIKit`, which includes a *huge* number of object types, all of which spring to life in your program. You didn't create any of those object types, so their design is not your problem; instead, you must learn to use them. Apple's object types are aimed at enabling the *general* functionality that any app might need. At the same time, your app will probably have *specific* functionality, unique to its purpose, and you will have to design object types to serve that purpose.

Object-based program design must be founded upon a secure understanding of the nature of objects. You want to design object types that encapsulate the right sort of functionality (methods) accompanied by the right set of data (properties). Then, when you instantiate those object types, you want to make sure that your instances have the right lifetimes, sufficient exposure to one another, and an appropriate ability to communicate with one another.

Object Types and APIs

Your program files will have very few, if any, top-level functions and variables. Methods and properties of object types — in particular, instance methods and instance properties — will be where most of the action is. Object types give each actual instance its specialized abilities. They also help to organize your program's code meaningfully and maintainably.

We may summarize the nature of objects in two phrases: encapsulation of functionality, and maintenance of state. (I first used this summary many years ago in my book *REALbasic: The Definitive Guide*.)

Encapsulation of functionality
Each object does its own job, and presents to the rest of the world — to other objects, and indeed in a sense to the programmer — an opaque wall whose only entrances are the methods to which it promises to respond and the actions it promises to perform when the corresponding messages are sent to it. The details of how, behind the scenes, it actually implements those actions are secreted within itself; no other object needs to know them.

Maintenance of state
Each individual instance is a bundle of data that it maintains. Often that data is private, so it's encapsulated as well; no other object knows what that data is or in what form it is kept. The only way to discover from outside what private data an object is maintaining is if there's a public method or property that reveals it.

As an example, imagine an object whose job is to implement a stack — it might be an instance of a Stack class. A *stack* is a data structure that maintains a set of data in LIFO order (last in, first out). It responds to just two messages: push and pop. Push means to add a given piece of data to the set. Pop means to remove from the set the piece of data that was most recently pushed and hand it out. It's like a stack of plates: plates are placed onto the top of the stack or removed from the top of the stack one by one, so the first plate to go onto the stack can't be retrieved until all other subsequently added plates have been removed (Figure 1-3).

The stack object illustrates encapsulation of functionality because the outside world knows nothing of how the stack is actually implemented. It might be an array, it might be a linked list, it might be any of a number of other implementations. But a client object — an object that actually sends a push or pop message to the stack object — knows nothing of this and cares less, provided the stack object adheres to its con-

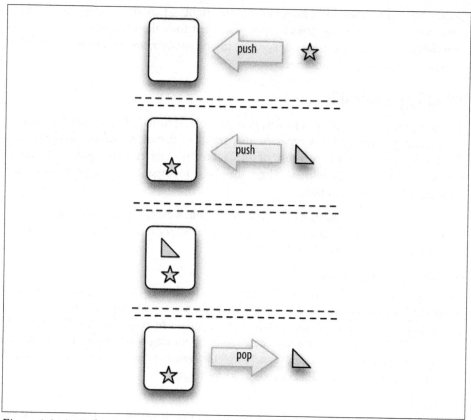

Figure 1-3. A stack

tract of behaving like a stack. This is also good for the programmer, who can, as the program develops, safely substitute one implementation for another without harming the vast machinery of the program as a whole.

The stack object illustrates maintenance of state because it isn't just the gateway to the stack data — it *is* the stack data. Other objects can get access to that data, but only by virtue of having access to the stack object itself, and only in the manner that the stack object permits. The stack data is effectively inside the stack object; no one else can see it. All that another object can do is push or pop.

The sum total of messages that each object type is eligible to be sent by other objects — its *API* (application programming interface) — is like a list or menu of things you can ask this type of object to do. Your object types divide up your code; their APIs form the basis of communication between those divisions. The same is true of objects that you didn't design. Apple's Cocoa documentation consists largely of lists of object APIs. For example, to know what messages you can send to an NSString instance, you'd start by studying the NSString class documentation. That page is really just a big list of properties and methods, so it tells you what an NSString object can do — and thus constitutes the bulk of what you need to know in order to use NSStrings in your program.

Instance Creation, Scope, and Lifetime

The important moment-to-moment entities in a Swift program are mostly instances. Object types define what *kinds* of instances there can be and how each kind of instance behaves. But the actual instances of those types are the state-carrying individual "things" that the program is all about, and instance methods and properties are messages that can be sent to instances. So there need to *be* instances in order for the program to *do* anything.

By default, however, there are *no* instances! Looking back at Example 1-1, we defined some object types, but we made no instances of them. If we were to run this program, our object types would exist from the get-go, but that's all that would exist. We've created a world of pure potentiality — some types of object that *might* exist. In that world, nothing would actually *happen*.

Instances do not come into being by magic. You have to instantiate a type in order to obtain an instance. Much of the action of your program, therefore, will consist of instantiating types. And of course you will want those instances to persist, so you will also assign each newly created instance to a variable as a shoebox to hold it, name it, and give it a lifetime. The instance will *persist* according to the lifetime of the variable that refers to it. And the instance will be *visible* to other instances according to the scope of the variable that refers to it.

Much of the art of object-based programming involves giving instances a sufficient lifetime and making them visible to one another. You will often put an instance into a particular shoebox — assigning it to a particular variable, declared at a certain scope — exactly so that, thanks to the rules of variable lifetime and scope, this instance will *persist* long enough to keep being useful to your program while it will still be needed, and so that other code can *get a reference* to this instance and talk to it later.

Planning how you're going to create instances, and working out the lifetimes and communication between those instances, may sound daunting. Fortunately, in real life, when you're programming iOS, the Cocoa framework itself will provide an initial scaffolding for you. Before you write a single line of code, the framework ensures that your app, as it launches, is given some instances that will persist for the lifetime of the app, providing the basis of your app's visible interface and giving you an initial place to put your own instances and give them sufficiently long lifetimes.

Summary and Conclusion

As we imagine constructing an object-based program for performing a particular task, we bear in mind the nature of objects. There are types and instances. A type is a set of methods describing what all instances of that type can do (encapsulation of functionality). Instances of the same type differ only in the value of their properties (maintenance of state). We plan accordingly. Objects are an organizational tool, a set of boxes for encapsulating the code that accomplishes a particular task. They are also a conceptual tool. The programmer, being forced to think in terms of discrete objects, must divide the goals and behaviors of the program into discrete tasks, each task being assigned to an appropriate object.

At the same time, no object is an island. Objects can cooperate with one another, namely by communicating with one another — that is, by sending messages to one another. The ways in which appropriate lines of communication can be arranged are innumerable. Coming up with an appropriate arrangement — an *architecture* — for the cooperative and orderly relationship between objects is one of the most challenging aspects of object-based programming. In iOS programming, you get a boost from the Cocoa framework, which provides an initial set of object types and a practical basic architectural scaffolding.

Using object-based programming effectively to make a program do what you want it to do while keeping it clear and maintainable is itself an art; your abilities will improve with experience. Eventually, you may want to do some further reading on effective planning and construction of the architecture of an object-based program. I recommend in particular two classic, favorite books. *Refactoring*, by Martin Fowler (Addison-Wesley, 1999), describes why you might need to rearrange what methods belong to what classes (and how to conquer your fear of doing so). *Design Patterns*, by Erich Gamma, Richard Helm, Ralph Johnson, and John Vlissides (also known as "the Gang of Four"), is the bible on architecting object-based programs, listing all the ways you can arrange objects with the right powers and the right knowledge of one another (Addison-Wesley, 1994).

CHAPTER 2

Functions

Nothing is so characteristic of Swift syntax as the way you declare and call functions. Probably nothing is so important, either! As I said in Chapter 1, all your code is going to be in functions; they are where the action is.

Function Parameters and Return Value

A function is like one of those pseudoscientific machines for processing miscellaneous stuff that you probably drew in your math textbook in elementary school. You know the ones I mean: with a funnel-like "hopper" at the top, and then a bunch of gears and cranks, and then a tube at the bottom where something is produced. A function is a machine like that: you feed some stuff in, the stuff is processed in accordance with what this particular machine does, and something is produced.

The stuff that goes in is the input; what comes out is the output. More technically, a function that expects input has *parameters*; a function that produces output has a *result*. For example, here's a very silly but perfectly valid function that expects two Int values, adds them together, and produces that sum:

```
func sum (_ x:Int, _ y:Int) -> Int {
    let result = x + y
    return result
}
```

The syntax here is very strict and well-defined, and you can't use Swift unless you understand it perfectly. Let's pause to appreciate it in full detail; I'll break the first line into pieces so that I can call them out individually:

```
func sum                          ❶
    (_ x:Int, _ y:Int)            ❷❸
    -> Int {                      ❹❺
        let result = x + y        ❻
        return result             ❼
}
```

❶ The declaration starts with the keyword func, followed by the *name* of this function; here, it's sum. This is the name that must be used in order to *call* the function — that is, in order to run the code that the function contains.

❷ The name of the function is followed by its *parameter list*. It consists, minimally, of parentheses. If this function takes parameters (input), they are listed inside the parentheses, separated by comma. Each parameter has a strict format: the *name* of the parameter, a colon, and the *type* of the parameter.

❸ This particular function declaration also has an underscore (_) and a space before each parameter name in the parameter list. *I'm not going to explain that underscore yet.* I need it for the example, so just trust me for now.

❹ After the parentheses is an arrow operator ->, followed by the type of value that this function will return.

❺ Then we have curly braces enclosing the *body* of the function — its actual code.

❻ Within the curly braces, in the function body, the variables defined as the parameter names have sprung to life, with the types specified in the parameter list.

❼ If the function is to return a value, it must do so with the keyword return followed by that value. And, not surprisingly, the type of that value must match the type declared earlier for the return value (after the arrow operator).

Here are some further points to note about the parameters and return type of our function:

Parameters

Our sum function expects two parameters — an Int, to which it gives the name x, and another Int, to which it gives the name y. The function body code won't run unless code elsewhere calls this function and actually passes values of the specified types for its parameters. (In fact, if I were to try to call this function *without* providing a value for each of these two parameters, or if either of the values I provide were *not* an Int, the compiler would stop me with an error.) In the body of the function, therefore, we can confidently use those values, referring to them by those names, secure in the knowledge that such values will exist and that they will be Int values, as specified by our parameter list. This provides certainty for not only the programmer, but also the compiler.

Observe that these names, x and y, are arbitrary and purely local (*internal*) to this function. They are different from any other x and y that may be used in other functions or at a higher level of scope. These names are defined so that the parameter values will have names by which they can be referred to in the code within the function body. The parameter declaration is, indeed, a kind of variable declaration: we are declaring variables x and y for use inside this function.

Return type

The last statement of our sum function's body returns the value of a variable called result; this variable was created by adding two Int values together, so it is an Int, which is what this function is supposed to produce. If I tried to return a String (return "howdy"), or if I were to omit the return statement altogether, the compiler would stop me with an error.

Note that the keyword return actually does *two* things. It returns the accompanying value, and it also halts execution of the function. It is permitted for more lines of code to follow a return statement, but the compiler will warn if this means that those lines of code can never be executed.

The function declaration before the curly braces is, in short, a *contract* about what kinds of values will be used as input and about what kind of output will be produced. According to this contract, the function *expects* a certain number of parameters, each of a certain type, and *yields* a certain type of result. Everything must correspond to this contract. The function body, inside the curly braces, can use the parameters as local variables. The returned value must match the declared return type.

The same contract applies to code elsewhere that *calls* this function. Here's some code that calls our sum function:

```
let z = sum(4,5)
```

Focus your attention on the right side of the equal sign — sum(4,5). That's the function call. How is it constructed? It uses the *name* of the function; that name is followed by *parentheses*; and inside those parentheses, separated by a comma, are the *values* to be passed to each of the function's parameters. Technically, these values are called *arguments*. Here, I'm using literal Int values, but I'm perfectly free to use Int variables instead; the only requirement is that I use things that have the correct type:

```
let x = 4
let y = 5
let z = sum(y,x)
```

In that code, I purposely used the names x and y for the variables whose values are passed as arguments, and I purposely reversed them in the call, to emphasize that these names have *nothing to do* with the names x and y inside the function parameter list and the function body. These names do not magically make their way to the function. Their *values* are all that matter; their values are the arguments.

What about the value returned by the function? That value is magically *substituted* for the function call, at the point where the function call is made. It happens that in the preceding code, the result is 9. So the last line is exactly as if I had said:

```
let z = 9
```

The programmer and the compiler both know what type of thing this function returns, so they also know where it is and isn't legal to call this function. It's fine to call this function as the initialization part of the declaration of the variable z, just as it would be to use 9 as the initialization part of that declaration: in both cases, we have an Int, and so z ends up being declared as an Int. But it would not be legal to write this:

```
let z = sum(4,5) + "howdy" // compile error
```

Because sum returns an Int, that's the same as trying to add an Int to a String — and by default, you can't do that in Swift.

Observe that it is legal to ignore the value returned from a function call:

```
sum(4,5)
```

That code is sort of silly in this particular situation, because we have made our sum function go to all the trouble of adding 4 and 5 for us and we have then thrown away the answer without capturing or using it. The compiler knows this, and will warn that we are failing to use the result of our function call. Nevertheless, a warning is not an error; that code is legal. There are, in fact, lots of situations where it is perfectly reasonable to ignore the value returned from a function call; in particular, the function may do other things (technically called *side effects*) in addition to returning a value, and the purpose of your call to that function may be those other things.

 If you're ignoring a function call result deliberately, you can silence the compiler warning by assigning the function call to _ (a variable without a name) — for example, _ = sum(4,5). Alternatively, if the function being called is your own, you can prevent the warning by marking the function declaration with @discardableResult.

If you can call sum wherever you can use an Int, and if the parameters of sum have to be Int values, doesn't that mean you can call sum inside a call to sum? Of course it does! This is perfectly legal (and reasonable):

```
let z = sum(4,sum(5,6))
```

The only argument against writing code like that is that you might confuse yourself and that it might make things harder to debug later. But, technically, it's legal, and quite normal.

Void Return Type and Parameters

Let's return to our function declaration. With regard to a function's parameters and return type, there are two degenerate cases that allow us to express a function declaration more briefly:

A function without a return type
No law says that a function *must* return a value. A function may be declared to return *no* value. In that case, there are three ways to write the declaration: you can write it as returning Void; you can write it as returning (), an empty pair of parentheses; or you can omit the arrow operator and the return type entirely. These are all legal:

```
func say1(_ s:String) -> Void { print(s) }
func say2(_ s:String) -> () { print(s) }
func say3(_ s:String) { print(s) }
```

If a function returns no value, then its body need not contain a `return` statement. If it does contain a `return` statement, its purpose will be purely to end execution of the function at that point.

A call to a function that returns no value is made purely for the function's side effects; it has no useful return value that can be made part of a larger expression, so the statement will usually consist of the function call and nothing else.

A function without any parameters
No law says that a function *must* take any parameters. If it doesn't, the parameter list in the function declaration can be completely empty. But you can't omit the parameter list parentheses themselves! They will be present in the function declaration, after the function's name:

```
func greet1() -> String { return "howdy" }
```

Obviously a function can lack both a return value and parameters; these are all ways of expressing the same thing:

```
func greet1() -> Void { print("howdy") }
func greet2() -> () { print("howdy") }
func greet3() { print("howdy") }
```

Just as you cannot omit the parentheses (the parameter list) from a function declaration, you cannot omit the parentheses from a function call. Those parentheses will be empty if the function takes no parameters, but they must be present. For example:

```
greet1()
```

Notice the parentheses!

Even a function that returns no value technically *does* in fact return a value — namely, a value of type Void, which may be expressed as the literal (). (I'll explain in Chapter 3 what the literal () really represents.) Thus, it is legal for such a function to say return (); whether it says that or not, () is what it returns, and it is legal (though nearly always pointless) to capture that value.

Function Signature

If we ignore for a moment the parameter names in the function declaration, we can completely characterize a function by the types of its inputs and its output, using an expression like this:

```
(Int, Int) -> Int
```

That in fact is a legal expression in Swift. It is the *signature* of a function. In this case, it's the signature of our sum function. Of course, there can be other functions that take two Int parameters and return an Int — and that's just the point. This signature characterizes *all* functions that have this number of parameters, of these types, and that return a result of this type. A function's signature is, in effect, *its* type — the type *of the function*. The fact that functions have types will be of great importance later on.

The signature of a function must include both the parameter list (without parameter names) and the return type, even if one or both of those is empty; so, the signature of a function that takes no parameters and returns no value may be written in any of four equivalent ways, including (Void) -> Void and () -> ().

External Parameter Names

A function can *externalize* the names of its parameters. The external names must then appear in a call to the function as *labels* to the arguments. There are several reasons why this is a good thing:

- It clarifies the purpose of each argument; each argument label can give a clue as to how that argument contributes to the behavior of the function.
- It distinguishes one function from another; two functions with the same name (before the parentheses) and the same signature but different externalized parameter names are two distinct functions.
- It helps Swift to interface with Objective-C and Cocoa, where method parameters nearly always have externalized names.

Externalized parameter names are so standard in Swift that there's a rule: by default, *all* parameter names are externalized *automatically*, using the internal name as the externalized name. Thus, if you want a parameter name to be externalized, and if you want the externalized name to be the same as the internal name, *do nothing* — that will happen all by itself.

If you want to depart from the default behavior, you can do either of the following in your function declaration:

Change the name of an external parameter
> If you want to change the external name of a parameter to be different from its internal name, precede the internal name with the external name and a space.

Suppress the externalization of a parameter
> To suppress a parameter's external name, precede the internal name with an underscore and a space.

> (That explains my declaration func sum (_ x:Int, _ y:Int) -> Int at the start of this chapter: I was suppressing the externalization of the parameter names, so as not to have to explain argument labels at the outset.)

Here's the declaration for a function that concatenates a string with itself a given number of times:

```
func echoString(_ s:String, times:Int) -> String {
    var result = ""
    for _ in 1...times { result += s }
    return result
}
```

That function's first parameter has an internal name only, but its second parameter has an external name, which will be the same as its internal name, namely times. And here's how to call it:

```
let s = echoString("hi", times:3)
```

In the call, as you can see, the external name precedes the argument as a label, separated by a colon.

Now let's say that in our echoString function we prefer to use times purely as an external name for the second parameter, with a different name — say, n — as the internal name. And let's strip the string off the function's name (before the parentheses) and make it the external name of the first parameter. Then the declaration would look like this:

```
func echo(string s:String, times n:Int) -> String {
    var result = ""
    for _ in 1...n { result += s}
    return result
}
```

In the body of that function, there is now no `times` variable available; `times` is purely an external name, for use in the call. The internal name is `n`, and that's the name the code refers to. And here's how to call it:

```
let s = echo(string:"hi", times:3)
```

 The existence of external names doesn't mean that the call can use a different parameter order from the declaration. For example, our echo(string:times:) expects a String parameter and an Int parameter, *in that order*. The order can't be different in the call, even though the label might appear to disambiguate which argument goes with which parameter.

Overloading

In Swift, function overloading is legal (and common). This means that two functions with exactly the same name, *including* their external parameter names, can coexist as long as they have different signatures.

Thus, for example, these two functions can coexist:

```
func say (_ what:String) {
}
func say (_ what:Int) {
}
```

The reason overloading works is that Swift has strict typing. A String is not an Int. Swift can tell them apart in the declaration, and Swift can tell them apart in a function call. Thus, Swift knows unambiguously that `say("what")` is different from `say(1)`.

Overloading works for the return type as well. Two functions with the same name and parameter types can have different return types. But the context of the call must disambiguate; that is, it must be clear what return type the caller is expecting.

For example, these two functions can coexist:

```
func say() -> String {
    return "one"
}
func say() -> Int {
    return 1
}
```

But now you can't call `say` like this:

```
let result = say() // compile error
```

The call is ambiguous, and the compiler tells you so. The call must be used in a context where the expected return type is clear. For example, suppose we have another function that is not overloaded, and that expects a String parameter:

```
func giveMeAString(_ s:String) {
    print("thanks!")
}
```

Then `giveMeAString(say())` is legal, because only a String can go in this spot, so we must be calling the `say` that returns a String. Similarly:

```
let result = say() + "two"
```

Only a String can be "added" to a String, so this must be the `say()` that returns a String.

The legality of overloading in Swift is particularly striking if you're coming from Objective-C, where overloading is *not* legal. If you tried to declare two overloaded versions of the same method in Objective-C, you'd get a "Duplicate declaration" compile error. And indeed, if you try to declare two overloaded methods in Swift, but in a place where Objective-C can see them (see Appendix A for what that means), you'll get a Swift compile error, because such overloading is incompatible with Objective-C.

 Two functions with the same signature but different external parameter names do *not* constitute a case of overloading; the functions have different external parameter names, so they are simply two different functions with two different names.

Default Parameter Values

A parameter can have a default value. This means that the caller can omit the parameter entirely, supplying no argument for it; the value will then be the default.

To specify a default value in a function declaration, append = and the default value after the parameter type:

```
class Dog {
    func say(_ s:String, times:Int = 1) {
        for _ in 1...times {
            print(s)
        }
    }
}
```

In effect, there are now *two* functions — `say(_:)` and `say(_:times:)`. If you just want to say something once, you can call `say(_:)` with a single unlabeled argument, and a `times:` parameter value of 1 will be supplied for you:

```
let d = Dog()
d.say("woof") // same as saying d.say("woof", times:1)
```

If you want repetition, call `say(_:times:)`:

```
let d = Dog()
d.say("woof", times:3)
```

Variadic Parameters

A parameter can be *variadic*. This means that the caller can supply as many values of this parameter's type as desired, separated by comma; the function body will receive these values as an array.

To indicate in a function declaration that a parameter is variadic, follow it by three dots, like this:

```
func sayStrings(_ arrayOfStrings:String ...) {
    for s in arrayOfStrings { print(s) }
}
```

And here's how to call it:

```
sayStrings("hey", "ho", "nonny nonny no")
```

The global print function takes a variadic first parameter, so you can output multiple values with a single command:

```
print("Manny", 3, true) // Manny 3 true
```

The print function's default parameters dictate further details of the output. The default separator: (for when you provide multiple values) is a space, and the default terminator: is a newline; you can change either or both:

```
print("Manny", "Moe", separator:", ", terminator:", ")
print("Jack")
// output is "Manny, Moe, Jack" on one line
```

A function can declare a maximum of one variadic parameter (because otherwise it might be impossible to determine where the list of values ends).

 Unfortunately, there's a hole in the Swift language: there's no way to convert an array into a comma-separated list of arguments (comparable to splatting in Ruby). If what you're starting with is an array of some type, you can't use it where a variadic of that type is expected.

Ignored Parameters

A parameter whose local name is an underscore is ignored. The caller must supply an argument, but it has no name within the function body and cannot be referred to there. For example:

```
func say(_ s:String, times:Int, loudly _:Bool) {
```

No loudly parameter makes its way into the function body, but the caller must still provide the third parameter:

```
say("hi", times:3, loudly:true)
```

The declaration needn't have an externalized name for the ignored parameter:

```
func say(_ s:String, times:Int, _:Bool) {
```

But the caller must still supply it:

```
say("hi", times:3, true)
```

What's the purpose of this feature? It isn't to satisfy the compiler, because the compiler doesn't complain if a parameter is never referred to in the function body. I use it primarily as a kind of note to myself, a way of saying, "Yes, I know there is a parameter here, and I am deliberately not using it for anything."

Modifiable Parameters

In the body of a function, a parameter is essentially a local variable. By default, it's a variable implicitly declared with let. You can't assign to it:

```
func say(_ s:String, times:Int, loudly:Bool) {
    loudly = true // compile error
}
```

If your code needs to assign to a parameter name within the body of a function, declare a var local variable inside the function body and assign the parameter value to it; your local variable can even have the same name as the parameter:

```
func say(_ s:String, times:Int, loudly:Bool) {
    var loudly = loudly
    loudly = true // no problem
}
```

In that code, loudly is a local variable; assigning to it doesn't change the value of any variable outside the function body. However, it is also possible to configure a parameter in such a way that assigning to it *does* modify the value of a variable outside the function body! One typical use case is that you want your function to return more than one result. For example, here I'll write a rather advanced function that removes all occurrences of a given character from a given string and returns the number of occurrences that were removed:

```
func removeCharacter(_ c:Character, from s:String) -> Int {
    var s = s
    var howMany = 0
    while let ix = s.characters.index(of:c) {
        s.remove(at:ix)
```

```
        howMany += 1
    }
    return howMany
}
```

And you call it like this:

```
let s = "hello"
let result = removeCharacter("l", from:s) // 2
```

That's nice, but we forgot one little thing: the original string, s, is still "hello"! In the function body, we removed all occurrences of the character from the *local* copy of the String parameter, but this change didn't affect the *original* string.

If we want our function to alter the *original* value of an argument passed to it, we must do the following:

- The type of the parameter we intend to modify must be declared inout.

- When we call the function, the variable holding the value we intend to tell it to modify must be declared with var, not let.

- Instead of passing the variable as an argument, we must pass its *address*. This is done by preceding its name with an ampersand (&).

Our removeCharacter(_:from:) now looks like this:

```
func removeCharacter(_ c:Character, from s: inout String) -> Int {
    var howMany = 0
    while let ix = s.characters.index(of:c) {
        s.remove(at:ix)
        howMany += 1
    }
    return howMany
}
```

And our call to removeCharacter(_:from:) now looks like this:

```
var s = "hello"
let result = removeCharacter("l", from:&s)
```

After the call, result is 2 *and* s is "heo". Notice the ampersand before name of s as the first argument in our function call! I like this requirement, because it forces us to acknowledge explicitly to the compiler, and to ourselves, that we're about to do something potentially dangerous: we're letting this function, as a side effect, modify a value outside of itself.

 When a function with an inout parameter is called, the variable whose address was passed as argument to that parameter is *always* set, even if the function makes no changes to that parameter.

You may encounter variations on this pattern when you're using Cocoa. The Cocoa APIs are written in C and Objective-C, so you probably won't see the Swift term inout. You'll probably see some mysterious type such as UnsafeMutablePointer. From your point of view as the caller, however, it's the same thing. You'll prepare a var variable and pass its address.

For instance, consider the problem of learning a UIColor's RGBA components. There are four such components: the color's red, green, blue, and alpha values. A function that, given a UIColor, returned the components of that color, would need to return four values at once — and that is something that Objective-C cannot do. So a different strategy is used. The UIColor method getRed(_:green:blue:alpha:) returns only a Bool reporting whether the component extraction succeeded. Instead of returning the actual components, it says: "You hand me four CGFloats *as arguments*, and I will *modify* them for you so that they are the results of this operation." Here's how the declaration for getRed(_:green:blue:alpha:) appears in Swift:

```
func getRed(_ red: UnsafeMutablePointer<CGFloat>,
    green: UnsafeMutablePointer<CGFloat>,
    blue: UnsafeMutablePointer<CGFloat>,
    alpha: UnsafeMutablePointer<CGFloat>) -> Bool
```

How would you call this function? The parameters are each an UnsafeMutablePointer to a CGFloat. You'll create four var CGFloat variables beforehand, giving them each some value even though that value will be replaced when you call get-Red(_:green:blue:alpha:). You'll pass the addresses of those variables as arguments. Those variables are where the component values will be after the call; and you'll probably be so sure that the component extraction will succeed, that you won't even bother to capture the call's actual result! So, for example:

```
let c = UIColor.purple
var r : CGFloat = 0
var g : CGFloat = 0
var b : CGFloat = 0
var a : CGFloat = 0
c.getRed(&r, green: &g, blue: &b, alpha: &a)
// now r, g, b, a are 0.5, 0.0, 0.5, 1.0
```

Sometimes, Cocoa will call *your* function with an UnsafeMutablePointer parameter, and *you* will want to change its value. To do this, you cannot assign directly to it, as we did with the inout variable s in our implementation of remove(from:character:). You're talking to Objective-C, not to Swift, and this is an UnsafeMutablePointer, not an inout parameter. The technique here is to assign to the UnsafeMutablePointer's pointee property. Here (without further explanation) is an example from my own code:

```
func popoverPresentationController(
    _ popoverPresentationController: UIPopoverPresentationController,
    willRepositionPopoverTo rect: UnsafeMutablePointer<CGRect>,
    in view: AutoreleasingUnsafeMutablePointer<UIView>) {
        view.pointee = self.button2
        rect.pointee = self.button2.bounds
}
```

There is one very common situation where your function can modify a parameter *without* declaring it as `inout` — namely, when the parameter is an *instance of a class*. This is a special feature of classes, as opposed to the other two object type flavors, enum and struct. String isn't a class; it's a struct. That's why we had to use `inout` in order to modify a String parameter. So I'll illustrate by declaring a Dog class with a `name` property:

```
class Dog {
    var name = ""
}
```

Here's a function that takes a Dog instance parameter and a String, and sets that Dog instance's `name` to that String. Notice that no `inout` is involved:

```
func changeName(of d:Dog, to newName:String) {
    d.name = newName
}
```

Here's how to call it. There's no `inout`, so we pass a Dog instance *directly*:

```
let d = Dog()
d.name = "Fido"
print(d.name) // "Fido"
changeName(of:d, to:"Rover")
print(d.name) // "Rover"
```

Observe that we were able to change a property of our Dog instance d, even though it wasn't passed as an `inout` parameter, and even though it was declared originally with `let`, not `var`. This appears to be an exception to the rules about modifying parameters — but it isn't. It's a feature of class instances, namely that they are themselves mutable. In `changeName(of:to:)`, we didn't actually attempt to modify the *parameter itself*. To do that, we would have had to *substitute a different Dog instance*. That is *not* what we tried to do, and if we did want to do it, the Dog parameter *would* need to be declared `inout` (and d would have to be declared with `var` and we would have to pass its address as argument).

Technically, we say that classes are *reference types*, whereas the other object type flavors are *value types*. When you pass an instance of a struct as an argument to a function, you effectively wind up with a *separate copy* of the struct instance. But when you pass an instance of a class as an argument to a function, you pass a reference to the class instance *itself*. I'll discuss this topic in more detail in Chapter 4.

Function In Function

A function can be declared anywhere, including inside the body of a function. A function declared in the body of a function (also called a *local function*) is available to be called by later code within the same scope, but is completely invisible elsewhere.

This feature is an elegant architecture for functions whose sole purpose is to assist another function. If only function A ever needs to call function B, function B might as well be packaged inside function A.

Here's a typical example from one of my apps (I've omitted everything except the structure):

```
func checkPair(_ p1:Piece, and p2:Piece) -> Path? {
    // ...
    func addPathIfValid(_ midpt1:Point, _ midpt2:Point) {
        // ...
    }
    for y in -1..._yct {
        addPathIfValid((pt1.x,y),(pt2.x,y))
    }
    for x in -1..._xct {
        addPathIfValid((x,pt1.y),(x,pt2.y))
    }
    // ...
}
```

What I'm doing in the first for loop (for y) and what I'm doing in the second for loop (for x) are the same — but with a different set of starting values. We could write out the functionality in full inside each for loop, but that would be an unnecessary and confusing repetition. (Such a repetition would violate the principle often referred to as *DRY*, for "Don't Repeat Yourself.") To prevent that repetition, we could refactor the repeated code into an instance method to be called by both for loops, but that exposes this functionality more broadly than we need, as it is called *only* by these two for loops inside checkPair. A local function is the perfect compromise.

Sometimes, it's worth using a local function even when that function will be called in only *one* place. Here's another example from my code (it's actually another part of the same function):

```
func checkPair(_ p1:Piece, and p2:Piece) -> Path? {
    // ...
    if arr.count > 0 {
        func distance(_ pt1:Point, _ pt2:Point) -> Double { ❶
            // utility to learn physical distance between two points
            let deltax = pt1.0 - pt2.0
            let deltay = pt1.1 - pt2.1
            return sqrt(Double(deltax * deltax + deltay * deltay))
        }
        for thisPath in arr {
            var thisLength = 0.0
            for ix in thisPath.indices.dropLast() {
                thisLength += distance(thisPath[ix],thisPath[ix+1]) ❷
            }
            // ...
        }
    }
    // ...
}
```

Again, the structure is clear (even though the code uses some Swift features I haven't discussed yet). Deep inside the function checkPair, a moment comes when I have an array (arr) of paths, and I need to know the length of every path. Each path is itself an array of points, so to learn its length, I need to sum the distances between each pair of points. To get the distance between a pair of points, I use the Pythagorean theorem. I could apply the Pythagorean theorem and express the calculation right there inside the for loop (for ix). Instead:

❶ I've expressed the Pythagorean theorem as a local function, distance, and then...

❷ Inside the for loop I call that function.

There is no savings whatever in the number of lines of code; in fact, declaring distance makes my code longer! Nor, strictly speaking, am I in danger of repeating myself; the application of the Pythagorean theorem is repeated many times, but it occurs at only one spot in my code, namely inside this one for loop. Nevertheless, abstracting the code into a more general distance-calculation utility makes my code much clearer: in effect, I announce in general form what I'm about to do ("Look! I'm going to calculate distances between points now!"), and then I do it. The function name, distance, gives my code *meaning*; it is more understandable and maintainable than if I had directly written out the steps of the distance calculation inline.

 Local functions are really local variables with function values (a notion that I'll explain later in this chapter). Therefore, a local function can't have the same name as a local variable in the same scope, and two local functions can't have the same name as one another in the same scope.

Recursion

A function can call itself. This is called *recursion*. Recursion seems a little scary, rather like jumping off a cliff, because of the danger of creating an infinite loop; but if you write the function correctly, you will always have a "stopper" condition that handles the degenerate case and prevents the loop from being infinite:

```
func countDownFrom(_ ix:Int) {
    print(ix)
    if ix > 0 { // stopper
        countDownFrom(ix-1) // recurse!
    }
}
```

Function As Value

If you've never used a programming language where functions are first-class citizens, perhaps you'd better sit down now, because what I'm about to tell you might make you feel a little faint: In Swift, a function *is* a first-class citizen. This means that a function can be used wherever a value can be used. For example, a function can be assigned to a variable; a function can be passed as an argument in a function call; a function can be returned as the result of a function.

Swift has strict typing. You can only assign a value to a variable or pass a value into or out of a function if it is the right *type* of value. In order for a function to be used as a value, it needs to *have* a type. And indeed it does! Have you guessed what it is? A function's *signature* is its type.

The chief purpose of using a function as a value is so that this function can later be called without a definite knowledge of *what* function it is. Here's the world's simplest (and silliest) example, just to show the syntax and structure:

```
func doThis(_ f:()->()) {
    f()
}
```

That is a function doThis that takes one parameter (and returns no value). The parameter, f, is itself a function; we know this because the type of the parameter is given as a function signature, ()->(), meaning (as you know) a function that takes no parameters and returns no value. The function doThis then *calls* the function f that it received as its parameter, by saying f().

Having declared the function doThis, how would you call it? To do so, you'd need to pass it a function as argument. Here's one way to do that:

```
func doThis(_ f:()->()) {
    f()
}
func whatToDo() {
    print("I did it")
}
doThis(whatToDo)
```

First, we declare a function (`whatToDo`) *of the proper type* — a function that takes no parameters and returns no value. Then, we call `doThis`, passing as argument a *function reference* — in effect, the bare name of the function. Notice that we are not *calling* `whatToDo` here; we are *passing* it. Sure enough, this works: we pass `whatToDo` as argument to `doThis`; `doThis` calls the function that it receives as its parameter; and the string `"I did it"` appears in the console.

But what's the point of being able to do *that*? If our goal is to call `whatToDo`, why don't we just call it? What's useful about being able to tell some *other* function to call it? In the example I just gave, there is *nothing* useful about it; I was just showing you the syntax and structure. But in real life, this is a very valuable thing to do. Encapsulating function-calling in a function can reduce repetition and opportunity for error. Moreover, the other function may call the parameter function in some special way; for example, it might call it after doing other things, or at some later time.

Here's a case from my own code. A common thing to do in Cocoa is to draw an image, directly, in code. This involves four steps:

```
let size = CGSize(width:45, height:20)
UIGraphicsBeginImageContextWithOptions(size, false, 0) ❶
let p = UIBezierPath(
    roundedRect: CGRect(x:0, y:0, width:45, height:20), cornerRadius: 8)
p.stroke() ❷
let result = UIGraphicsGetImageFromCurrentImageContext()! ❸
UIGraphicsEndImageContext() ❹
```

❶ Open an image context.

❷ Draw into the context.

❸ Extract the image.

❹ Close the image context.

That's terribly ugly. The sole purpose of all that code is to obtain `result`, the image; but that purpose is buried in all the other code. At the same time, the entire structure is boilerplate; every time I do this in any app, step 1, step 3, and step 4 are exactly the same. Moreover, I live in mortal fear of forgetting a step; for example, if I were to omit step 4 by mistake, the universe would explode.

The only thing that's different every time I draw is step 2. Thus, step 2 is the only part I should have to write out! The entire problem is solved by writing a utility function expressing the boilerplate:

```
func imageOfSize(_ size:CGSize, _ whatToDraw:() -> ()) -> UIImage {
    UIGraphicsBeginImageContextWithOptions(size, false, 0)
    whatToDraw()
    let result = UIGraphicsGetImageFromCurrentImageContext()!
    UIGraphicsEndImageContext()
    return result
}
```

My imageOfSize utility is so useful that I declare it at the top level of a file, where all my files can see it. To make an image, I perform step 2 (the actual drawing) in a function and pass that function as argument to the imageOfSize utility:

```
func drawing() {
    let p = UIBezierPath(
        roundedRect: CGRect(x:0, y:0, width:45, height:20),
        cornerRadius: 8)
    p.stroke()
}
let image = imageOfSize(CGSize(width:45, height:20), drawing)
```

Now *that* is a beautifully expressive and clear way to turn drawing instructions into an image.

 Evidently Apple agrees with my criticism of UIGraphicsBeginImageContext..., because iOS 10 introduces a new class, UIGraphicsImageRenderer, that expresses itself using syntax similar to my imageOfSize. Nevertheless, I'll continue using imageOfSize in this chapter, because it illustrates important aspects of Swift functions.

The Cocoa API is full of situations where you'll pass a function to be called by the runtime in some special way or at some later time. Some common Cocoa situations even involve passing *two* functions. For instance, when you perform view animation, you'll often pass one function prescribing the action to be animated and another function saying what to do afterward:

```
func whatToAnimate() { // self.myButton is a button in the interface
    self.myButton.frame.origin.y += 20
}
func whatToDoLater(finished:Bool) {
    print("finished: \(finished)")
}
UIView.animate(withDuration:
    0.4, animations: whatToAnimate, completion: whatToDoLater)
```

That means: Change the frame origin (that is, the position) of this button in the interface, but do it over time (four-tenths of a second); and then, when that's finished, print a log message in the console saying whether the animation was performed or not.

The Cocoa documentation will often describe a function to be passed in this way as a *handler*, and will refer it as a *block*, because that's the Objective-C syntactic construct needed here; in Swift, it's a function, so just think of it as a function and pass a function.

Anonymous Functions

Consider once again this earlier example:

```
func whatToAnimate() { // self.myButton is a button in the interface
    self.myButton.frame.origin.y += 20
}
func whatToDoLater(finished:Bool) {
    print("finished: \(finished)")
}
UIView.animate(withDuration:
    0.4, animations: whatToAnimate, completion: whatToDoLater)
```

There's a slight bit of ugliness in that code. I'm declaring functions `whatToAnimate` and `whatToDoLater`, just because I want to pass those functions in the last line. I don't really need the *names* `whatToAnimate` and `whatToDoLater` for anything, except to refer to them in the last line; neither the names nor the functions will ever be used again. Therefore, it would be nice to be able to pass just the *body* of those functions *without* a declared name.

That's called an *anonymous* function, and it's legal and common in Swift. To form an anonymous function, you do two things:

1. Create the function body itself, including the surrounding curly braces, but with no function declaration.

2. If necessary, express the function's parameter list and return type as the first line *inside* the curly braces, followed by the keyword in.

Let's practice by transforming our named function declarations into anonymous functions. Here's the named function declaration for whatToAnimate:

```
func whatToAnimate() {
    self.myButton.frame.origin.y += 20
}
```

Here's an anonymous function that does the same thing. Notice how I've moved the parameter list and return type inside the curly braces:

```
{
    () -> () in
    self.myButton.frame.origin.y += 20
}
```

Here's the named function declaration for whatToDoLater:

```
func whatToDoLater(finished:Bool) {
    print("finished: \(finished)")
}
```

Here's an anonymous function that does the same thing:

```
{
    (finished:Bool) -> () in
    print("finished: \(finished)")
}
```

Now that we know how to make anonymous functions, let's use them. The point where we need the functions is the point where we're passing arguments to animate(withDuration:animations:completion:). We can create and pass anonymous functions *right at that point*, like this:

```
UIView.animate(withDuration:0.4,
    animations: {
        () -> () in
        self.myButton.frame.origin.y += 20
    },
    completion: {
        (finished:Bool) -> () in
        print("finished: \(finished)")
    }
)
```

We can make the same improvement in the way we call the `imageOfSize` function from the preceding section. Earlier, we called that function like this:

```
func drawing() {
    let p = UIBezierPath(
        roundedRect: CGRect(x:0, y:0, width:45, height:20),
        cornerRadius: 8)
    p.stroke()
}
let image = imageOfSize(CGSize(width:45, height:20), drawing)
```

We now know, however, that we don't need to declare the `drawing` function separately. We can call `imageOfSize` with an anonymous function:

```
let image = imageOfSize(CGSize(width:45, height:20), {
    () -> () in
    let p = UIBezierPath(
        roundedRect: CGRect(x:0, y:0, width:45, height:20),
        cornerRadius: 8)
    p.stroke()
})
```

Anonymous functions are very commonly used in Swift, so make sure you can read and write that code! Anonymous functions, in fact, are *so* common and *so* important, that some shortcuts for writing them are provided:

Omission of the return type

If the anonymous function's return type is already known to the compiler, you can omit the arrow operator and the specification of the return type:

```
UIView.animate(withDuration:0.4, animations: {
    () in
    self.myButton.frame.origin.y += 20
    }, completion: {
        (finished:Bool) in
        print("finished: \(finished)")
})
```

Omission of the in *line when there are no parameters*

If the anonymous function takes no parameters, and if the return type can be omitted, the `in` line itself can be omitted entirely:

```
UIView.animate(withDuration:0.4, animations: {
    self.myButton.frame.origin.y += 20
    }, completion: {
        (finished:Bool) in
        print("finished: \(finished)")
})
```

Omission of the parameter types

If the anonymous function takes parameters and their types are already known to the compiler, the types can be omitted:

```
UIView.animate(withDuration:0.4, animations: {
    self.myButton.frame.origin.y += 20
    }, completion: {
        (finished) in
        print("finished: \(finished)")
})
```

Omission of the parentheses

If the parameter types are omitted, the parentheses around the parameter list can be omitted:

```
UIView.animate(withDuration:0.4, animations: {
    self.myButton.frame.origin.y += 20
    }, completion: {
        finished in
        print("finished: \(finished)")
})
```

Omission of the in *line even when there are parameters*

If the return type can be omitted, and if the parameter types are already known to the compiler, you can omit the in line and refer to the parameters directly within the body of the anonymous function by using the magic names $0, $1, and so on, in order:

```
UIView.animate(withDuration:0.4, animations: {
    self.myButton.frame.origin.y += 20
    }, completion: {
        print("finished: \($0)")
})
```

Omission of the parameter names

If the anonymous function body doesn't need to refer to a parameter, you can substitute an underscore for its name in the parameter list in the in line; in fact, if the anonymous function body doesn't need to refer to *any* of the parameters, you can substitute *one* underscore for *the entire parameter list*:

```
UIView.animate(withDuration:0.4, animations: {
    self.myButton.frame.origin.y += 20
    }, completion: {
        _ in
        print("finished!")
})
```

But note that if the anonymous function takes parameters, you *must* acknowledge them somehow. You can omit the in line and use the parameters by the magic names $0 and so on, or you can keep the in line and ignore the parameters with an underscore, but you can't omit the in line altogether *and* not use the parameters by their magic names! If you do, your code won't compile.

Omission of the function argument label

If, as will just about always be the case, your anonymous function is the *last* argument being passed in this function call, you can close the function call with a right parenthesis *before* this last argument, and then put just the anonymous function body *without a label* (this is called a *trailing function*):

```
UIView.animate(withDuration:0.4, animations: {
    self.myButton.frame.origin.y += 20
}) {
    _ in
    print("finished!")
}
```

Omission of the calling function parentheses

If you use the trailing function syntax, and if the function you are calling takes no parameters other than the function you are passing to it, you can omit the empty parentheses from the call. This is the *only* situation in which you can omit the parentheses from a function call! To illustrate, I'll declare and call a different function:

```
func doThis(_ f:()->()) {
    f()
}
doThis { // no parentheses!
    print("Howdy")
}
```

Omission of the keyword return

If the anonymous function body consists of *exactly one statement* and that statement consists of returning a value with the keyword return, the keyword return can be omitted. To put it another way, in a context that expects a function that returns a value, if an anonymous function body consists of exactly one statement, Swift *assumes* that this statement is an expression whose value is to be returned from the anonymous function:

```
func greeting() -> String {
    return "Howdy"
}
func performAndPrint(_ f:()->String) {
    let s = f()
    print(s)
```

```
    }
performAndPrint {
    greeting() // meaning: return greeting()
}
```

When writing anonymous functions, you will frequently find yourself taking advantage of all the omissions you are permitted. In addition, you'll often shorten the *layout* of the code (though not the code itself) by putting the whole anonymous function together with the function call *on one line*. Thus, Swift code involving anonymous functions can be extremely compact.

Here's a typical example. We start with an array of Int values and generate a new array consisting of all those values multiplied by 2, by calling the map(_:) instance method. The map(_:) method of an array takes a function that takes one parameter of the same type as the array's elements, and returns a new value; here, our array is made of Int values, and we are passing to the map(_:) method a function that takes one Int parameter and returns an Int. We could write out the whole function, like this:

```
let arr = [2, 4, 6, 8]
func doubleMe(i:Int) -> Int {
    return i*2
}
let arr2 = arr.map(doubleMe) // [4, 8, 12, 16]
```

That, however, is not very Swifty. We don't need the name doubleMe for anything else, so this may as well be an anonymous function:

```
let arr = [2, 4, 6, 8]
let arr2 = arr.map ({
    (i:Int) -> Int in
    return i*2
})
```

Fine, but now let's start shortening our anonymous function. Its parameter type is known in advance, so we don't need to specify that. Its return type is known by inspection of the function body, so we don't need to specify that. There's just one parameter and we are going to use it, so we don't need the in line as long we refer to the parameter as $0. Our function body consists of just one statement, and it is a return statement, so we can omit return. And map(_:) doesn't take any other parameters, so we can omit the parentheses and follow the name directly with a trailing function:

```
let arr = [2, 4, 6, 8]
let arr2 = arr.map {$0*2}
```

It doesn't get any Swiftier than that!

Define-and-Call

A pattern that's surprisingly common in Swift is to define an anonymous function and call it, all in one move:

```
{
    // ... code goes here
}()
```

Notice the parentheses after the curly braces. The curly braces define an anonymous function body; the parentheses call that anonymous function.

Why would anyone do such a thing? If you want to run some code, you can just run it; why would you embed it in a deeper level as a function body, only to turn around and run that function body immediately?

For one thing, an anonymous function can be a good way to make your code less imperative and more, well, functional: an action can be taken at the point where it is needed, rather than in a series of preparatory steps. Here's a common Cocoa example: we create and configure an NSMutableParagraphStyle and then use it as an argument in a call to the NSMutableAttributedString method addAttribute(_:value:range:), like this:

```
let para = NSMutableParagraphStyle()
para.headIndent = 10
para.firstLineHeadIndent = 10
// ... more configuration of para ...
content.addAttribute( // content is an NSMutableAttributedString
    NSParagraphStyleAttributeName,
    value:para,
    range:NSRange(location:0, length:1))
```

I find that code ugly. We don't need para except to pass it as the value: argument within the call to addAttribute(_:value:range:), so it would be much nicer to create and configure it right there within the call, as the value: argument. That sounds like an anonymous function — except that the value: parameter is not a function, but an NSMutableParagraphStyle object. We can solve the problem by providing, as the value: argument, an anonymous function that *produces* an NSMutableParagraphStyle object *and calling it* so that it *does* produce an NSMutableParagraphStyle object:

```
content.addAttribute(
    NSParagraphStyleAttributeName,
    value: {
        let para = NSMutableParagraphStyle()
        para.headIndent = 10
        para.firstLineHeadIndent = 10
```

```
    // ... more configuration of para ...
       return para
}(),
range:NSRange(location:0, length:1))
```

I'll demonstrate some further uses of define-and-call in Chapter 3.

Closures

Swift functions are *closures*. This means they can *capture* references to external variables in scope within the body of the function. What do I mean by that? Well, recall from Chapter 1 that code in curly braces constitutes a scope, and this code can "see" variables and functions declared in a surrounding scope:

```
class Dog {
    var whatThisDogSays = "woof"
    func bark() {
        print(self.whatThisDogSays)
    }
}
```

In that code, the body of the function bark refers to a variable whatThisDogSays. That variable is *external* to the body of the function, because it is declared outside the body of the function. It is *in scope* for the body of the function, because the code inside the body of the function can see it. And the code inside the body of the function *refers* to it — it says, explicitly, whatThisDogSays.

So far, so good; but we now know that the function bark can be passed as a value. In effect, it can travel from one environment to another! When it does, what happens to that reference to whatThisDogSays? Let's find out:

```
func doThis(_ f : (Void) -> Void) {
    f()
}
let d = Dog()
d.whatThisDogSays = "arf"
let barkFunction = d.bark
doThis(barkFunction) // arf
```

We run that code, and "arf" appears in the console.

Perhaps that result doesn't seem very surprising to you. But think about it. We do not directly *call* d.bark(). We make a Dog instance and *pass* its bark function as a value into the function doThis. There, it is called. Now, whatThisDogSays is an instance property of a particular Dog. Inside the function doThis there is no whatThisDog-Says. Indeed, inside the function doThis there is no Dog instance! Nevertheless the call f() still works. The function d.bark, as it is passed around, can *still* see that variable whatThisDogSays, declared *outside* itself, even though it is *called* in an environment where there is no longer any Dog instance and no longer any instance property whatThisDogSays.

But there's more. I'll move the line where we set d.whatThisDogSays to *after* we assign d.bark into our variable barkFunction:

```
func doThis(_ f : (Void) -> Void) {
    f()
}
let d = Dog()
let barkFunction = d.bark
d.whatThisDogSays = "arf" // *
doThis(barkFunction) // arf
```

Do you see what this proves? At the time we assigned d.bark to barkFunction, d.whatThisDogSays was "woof". We then changed d.whatThisDogSays to "arf", and passed barkFunction into doThis, where it was called — and we got "arf". This proves that barkFunction is maintaining its reference to this actual Dog, the one that we call d. The bark function, as it is passed around, is carrying its environment with it — including the instance of which it is an instance method (because it refers, in its body, to self). That environment is still there later when the bark function is called in some other environment. So, by "capture" I mean that when a function is passed around as a value, it carries along its internal references to external variables. That is what makes a function a closure.

How Closures Improve Code

Once you understand that functions are closures, you can take advantage of this fact to improve your code's syntax. Closures can help make your code more general, and hence more useful. Here, once again, is my earlier example of a function that accepts drawing instructions and performs them to generate an image:

```
func imageOfSize(_ size:CGSize, _ whatToDraw:() -> ()) -> UIImage {
    UIGraphicsBeginImageContextWithOptions(size, false, 0)
    whatToDraw()
    let result = UIGraphicsGetImageFromCurrentImageContext()!
    UIGraphicsEndImageContext()
    return result
}
```

We can call imageOfSize with a trailing anonymous function:

```
let image = imageOfSize(CGSize(width:45, height:20)) {
    let p = UIBezierPath(
        roundedRect: CGRect(x:0, y:0, width:45, height:20),
        cornerRadius: 8)
    p.stroke()
}
```

That code, however, contains an annoying repetition. This is a call to create an image of a given size consisting of a rounded rectangle of that size. We are repeating the size; the pair of numbers 45,20 appears twice. That's silly. Let's prevent the repetition by putting the size into a variable at the outset:

```
let sz = CGSize(width:45, height:20)
let image = imageOfSize(sz) {
    let p = UIBezierPath(
        roundedRect: CGRect(origin:CGPoint.zero, size:sz),
        cornerRadius: 8)
    p.stroke()
}
```

The variable sz, declared outside our anonymous function at a higher level, is visible inside it. Thus we can refer to it inside the anonymous function — and we do so. In the fourth line, we are not calling CGRect(origin:size:) and passing the value of sz to it *now*. Everything inside the curly braces is just a function body. It won't be *executed* until imageOfSize calls it. Nevertheless, the value of sz persists. The anonymous function is a function. Therefore it is a closure. Therefore the anonymous function captures the reference to sz, and carries it on into the call to imageOfSize.

Now let's go further. So far, we've been hard-coding the size of the desired rounded rectangle. Imagine, though, that creating images of rounded rectangles of various sizes is something we do often. It would make sense to package this code up as a function, where sz is not a fixed value but a parameter; the function will then return the image:

```
func makeRoundedRectangle(_ sz:CGSize) -> UIImage {
    let image = imageOfSize(sz) {
        let p = UIBezierPath(
            roundedRect: CGRect(origin:CGPoint.zero, size:sz),
            cornerRadius: 8)
        p.stroke()
    }
    return image
}
```

In the expression CGRect(origin:CGPoint.zero, size:sz), we refer to sz. This expression is part of an anonymous function to be passed to imageOfSize. The term sz refers to the sz parameter that arrives into the surrounding function makeRounded-Rectangle. A parameter of the surrounding function is a variable external to and in scope within the anonymous function, and the anonymous function is a closure, so it captures the reference to that parameter as it is passed to imageOfSize.

Our code is becoming beautifully compact. To call makeRoundedRectangle, supply a size; an image is returned. Thus, I can perform the call, obtain the image, and put that image into my interface, all in one move, like this:

```
self.myImageView.image = makeRoundedRectangle(CGSize(width:45, height:20))
```

Function Returning Function

But now let's go even further! Instead of returning an image, our function can return *a function* that makes rounded rectangles *of the specified size*. If you've never seen a function returned as a value from a function, you may now be gasping for breath. But a function, after all, can be used as a value. We have already passed a function *into* a function as an argument in the function call; now we are going to receive a function *from* a function call as its result:

```
func makeRoundedRectangleMaker(_ sz:CGSize) -> () -> UIImage { ❶
    func f () -> UIImage { ❷
        let im = imageOfSize(sz) {
            let p = UIBezierPath(
                roundedRect: CGRect(origin:CGPoint.zero, size:sz),
                cornerRadius: 8)
            p.stroke()
        }
        return im
    }
    return f ❸
}
```

Let's analyze that code slowly:

❶ The declaration is the hardest part. What on earth is the type (signature) of this function makeRoundedRectangleMaker? It is (CGSize) -> () -> UIImage. That expression has *two* arrow operators. To understand it, keep in mind that every-thing after each arrow operator is the type of a returned value. So makeRounded-RectangleMaker is a function that takes a CGSize parameter and returns a () -> UIImage. Okay, and what's a () -> UIImage? We already know that: it's a func-tion that takes no parameters and returns a UIImage. So makeRoundedRectangle-Maker is a function that takes a CGSize parameter and returns *a function* — a function that itself, when called with *no* parameters, will return a UIImage.

❷ Now here we are in the body of the function makeRoundedRectangleMaker, and our first step is to declare a function (a function-in-function, or local function) of precisely the type we intend to return, namely, one that takes no parameters and returns a UIImage. Here, we're naming this function f. The way this function works is simple and familiar: it calls imageOfSize, passing it an anonymous func-tion that makes an image of a rounded rectangle (im) — and then it returns the image.

❸ Finally, we *return* the function we just made (f). We have thus fulfilled our con-tract: we said we would return a function that takes no parameters and returns a UIImage, and we do so.

But perhaps you are still gazing open-mouthed at makeRoundedRectangleMaker, wondering how you would ever call it and what you would get if you did. Let's try it:

```
let maker = makeRoundedRectangleMaker(CGSize(width:45, height:20))
```

What is the variable maker after that code runs? It's a *function* — a function that takes no parameters and that, when called, produces the image of a rounded rectangle of size 45,20. You don't believe me? I'll prove it — by *calling* the function that is now the value of maker:

```
let maker = makeRoundedRectangleMaker(CGSize(width:45, height:20))
self.myImageView.image = maker()
```

Now that you've gotten over your stunned surprise at the notion of a function that produces a function as its result, turn your attention once again to the implementation of makeRoundedRectangleMaker and let's analyze it again, a different way. Remember, I didn't write that function to show you that a function can produce a function. I wrote it to illustrate closures! Let's think about how the environment gets captured:

```
func makeRoundedRectangleMaker(_ sz:CGSize) -> () -> UIImage {
    func f () -> UIImage {
        let im = imageOfSize(sz) { // *
            let p = UIBezierPath(
                roundedRect: CGRect(origin:CGPoint.zero, size:sz), // *
                cornerRadius: 8)
            p.stroke()
        }
        return im
    }
    return f
}
```

The function f takes no parameters. Yet, twice within the function body of f (I've marked the places with asterisk comments), there are references to a size value sz. The body of the function f can see sz, the incoming parameter to the surrounding function makeRoundedRectangleMaker, because it is in a surrounding scope. The function f *captures* the reference to sz at the time makeRoundedRectangleMaker is called, and *keeps* that reference when f is returned and assigned to maker:

```
let maker = makeRoundedRectangleMaker(CGSize(width:45, height:20))
```

That is why maker is now a function that, when it is called, creates and returns an image of the particular size 45,20 even though it itself will be called *with no parameters*. We have *baked* the knowledge of what size of image to produce into maker.

Looking at it another way, makeRoundedRectangleMaker is a *factory* for creating a whole family of functions similar to maker, each of which produces an image of one particular size. That's a dramatic illustration of the power of closures.

Before I leave `makeRoundedRectangleMaker`, I'd like to rewrite it in a Swiftier fashion. Within `f`, there is no need to create `im` and then return it; we can return the result of calling `imageOfSize` directly:

```
func makeRoundedRectangleMaker(_ sz:CGSize) -> () -> UIImage {
    func f () -> UIImage {
        return imageOfSize(sz) {
            let p = UIBezierPath(
                roundedRect: CGRect(origin:CGPoint.zero, size:sz),
                cornerRadius: 8)
            p.stroke()
        }
    }
    return f
}
```

But there is no need to declare `f` and then return it either; it can be an anonymous function and we can return it directly:

```
func makeRoundedRectangleMaker(_ sz:CGSize) -> () -> UIImage {
    return {
        return imageOfSize(sz) {
            let p = UIBezierPath(
                roundedRect: CGRect(origin:CGPoint.zero, size:sz),
                cornerRadius: 8)
            p.stroke()
        }
    }
}
```

But our anonymous function consists of just one statement, returning the result of the call to `imageOfSize`. (The anonymous function parameter to `imageOfSize` is consists of multiple statements, but the `imageOfSize` call itself is still just one Swift statement.) Thus there is no need to say `return`:

```
func makeRoundedRectangleMaker(_ sz:CGSize) -> () -> UIImage {
    return {
        imageOfSize(sz) {
            let p = UIBezierPath(
                roundedRect: CGRect(origin:CGPoint.zero, size:sz),
                cornerRadius: 8)
            p.stroke()
        }
    }
}
```

Closure Setting a Captured Variable

The power that a closure gets through its ability to capture its environment is even greater than I've shown so far. If a closure captures a reference to a variable outside itself, and if that variable is settable, *the closure can set the variable*.

For example, let's say I've declared this simple function. All it does is to accept a function that takes an Int parameter, and to call that function with an argument of 100:

```
func pass100 (_ f:(Int)->()) {
    f(100)
}
```

Now, look closely at this code and try to guess what will happen when we run it:

```
var x = 0
print(x)
func setX(newX:Int) {
    x = newX
}
pass100(setX)
print(x)
```

The first `print(x)` call obviously produces 0. The second `print(x)` call produces 100! The `pass100` function has reached into my code and changed the value of my variable x! That's because the function `setX` that I passed to `pass100` contains a reference to x; not only does it contain it, but it captures it; not only does it capture it, but it sets its value. That x *is my* x. Thus, `pass100` was able to set my x just as readily as I would have set it by calling `setX` directly.

Closure Preserving Its Captured Environment

When a closure captures its environment, it *preserves* that environment *even if nothing else does*. Here's an example calculated to blow your mind — a function that modifies a function:

```
func countAdder(_ f: @escaping ()->()) -> () -> () {
    var ct = 0
    return {
        ct = ct + 1
        print("count is \(ct)")
        f()
    }
}
```

The function `countAdder` accepts a function as its parameter and returns a function as its result. (I'll explain the `@escaping` attribute in the next section.) The function that it returns calls the function that it accepts, with a little bit added: it increments a variable and reports the result. So now try to guess what will happen when we run this code:

```
func greet () {
    print("howdy")
}
let countedGreet = countAdder(greet)
countedGreet()
countedGreet()
countedGreet()
```

What we've done here is to take a function greet, which prints "howdy", and pass it through countAdder. What comes out the other side of countAdder is a new function, which we've named countedGreet. We then call countedGreet three times. Here's what appears in the console:

```
count is 1
howdy
count is 2
howdy
count is 3
howdy
```

Clearly, countAdder has added to the functionality of the function that was passed into it *the ability to report how many times it is called*. Now ask yourself: Where on earth is the variable that maintains this count? Inside countAdder, it was a local variable ct. But it isn't declared inside the anonymous function that countAdder returns. That's deliberate! If it *were* declared inside the anonymous function, we would be setting ct to 0 every time countedGreet is called — we wouldn't be counting. Instead, ct is initialized to 0 once *and then captured* by the anonymous function. Thus, this variable is preserved as part of the *environment* of countedGreet — it is *outside* countedGreet in some mysterious environment-preserving world, so that it can be incremented every time countedGreet is called.

Escaping Closures

If a function passed as parameter to a function will be preserved for later execution, rather than being called directly, its type must be marked @escaping, to signal that this is a closure that captures and preserves its environment. The compiler will detect violations of this rule, so if you find the rule confusing, don't worry about it; just let the compiler enforce it for you.

So, for example, this function is legal because it receives a function and calls it directly:

```
func funcCaller(f:()->()) {
    f()
}
```

And this function is legal, even though it returns a function to be executed later, because it also *creates* that function internally:

```
func funcMaker() -> () -> () {
    return { print("hello world") }
}
```

But this function is illegal. It returns a function to be executed later, and it *acquires* that function as a parameter:

```
func funcPasser(f:()->()) -> () -> () { // compile error
    return f
}
```

The solution is to mark the type of the incoming parameter f as @escaping, and the compiler will prompt you to do so:

```
func funcPasser(f:@escaping ()->()) -> () -> () {
    return f
}
```

A secondary consequence of this distinction is that if an anonymous function passed as an @escaping parameter refers to a property or method of self, the compiler will insist that you say self explicitly. That's because such a reference *captures* self, and the compiler wants you to acknowledge this fact by *saying* self.

Curried Functions

Return once more to makeRoundedRectangleMaker:

```
func makeRoundedRectangleMaker(_ sz:CGSize) -> () -> UIImage {
    return {
        imageOfSize(sz) {
            let p = UIBezierPath(
                roundedRect: CGRect(origin:CGPoint.zero, size:sz),
                cornerRadius: 8)
            p.stroke()
        }
    }
}
```

There's something I don't like about this method: the size of the rounded rectangle that it creates is a parameter (sz), but the cornerRadius of the rounded rectangle is hard-coded as 8. I'd like the ability to specify a value for the corner radius as well. I can think of two ways to do it. One is to give makeRoundedRectangleMaker itself another parameter:

```
func makeRoundedRectangleMaker(_ sz:CGSize, _ r:CGFloat) -> () -> UIImage {
    return {
        imageOfSize(sz) {
            let p = UIBezierPath(
                roundedRect: CGRect(origin:CGPoint.zero, size:sz),
                cornerRadius: r)
```

```
            p.stroke()
        }
    }
}
```

And we would then call it like this:

```
let maker = makeRoundedRectangleMaker(CGSize(width:45, height:20), 8)
```

But there's another way. The function that we are returning from `makeRounded-RectangleMaker` takes no parameters. Instead, *it* could take the extra parameter:

```
func makeRoundedRectangleMaker(_ sz:CGSize) -> (CGFloat) -> UIImage {
    return {
        r in
        imageOfSize(sz) {
            let p = UIBezierPath(
                roundedRect: CGRect(origin:CGPoint.zero, size:sz),
                cornerRadius: r)
            p.stroke()
        }
    }
}
```

Now `makeRoundedRectangleMaker` returns a function that, itself, takes one parameter, so we must remember to supply that when we call it:

```
let maker = makeRoundedRectangleMaker(CGSize(width:45, height:20))
self.myImageView.image = maker(8)
```

If we don't need to conserve `maker` for anything, we can of course do all that in one line — a function call that yields a function which we immediately call to obtain our image:

```
self.myImageView.image = makeRoundedRectangleMaker(CGSize(width:45, height:20))(8)
```

 When a function returns a function that takes a parameter in this way, it is called a *curried* function (after the computer scientist Haskell Curry).

Function References and Selectors

Throughout this chapter, wherever I wanted to refer to a function by name — for example, in order to pass it as argument to another function — I've been using its bare name, like this:

```
func whatToAnimate() { // self.myButton is a button in the interface
    self.myButton.frame.origin.y += 20
}
func whatToDoLater(finished:Bool) {
```

```
        print("finished: \(finished)")
    }
    UIView.animate(withDuration:
        0.4, animations: whatToAnimate, completion: whatToDoLater) // *
```

A bare name like whatToAnimate or whatToDoLater is a *function reference*. Use of the bare name as a function reference is legal because it's unambiguous in this particular context: thus, there's only one function called whatToDoLater in scope, and I'm using its name as argument in a function call where the parameter type is known (namely, (Bool) -> Void).

But now consider the following situation. Just as I can pass a function as an argument, I can assign a function as a value to a variable. And suppose I have *two* functions with the same name, one that takes a parameter, and one that doesn't:

```
class Dog {
    func bark() {
        print("woof")
    }
    func bark(_ loudly:Bool) {
        if loudly {
            print("WOOF")
        } else {
            self.bark()
        }
    }
    func test() {
        let barkFunction = bark // compile error
        // ...
    }
}
```

That code won't compile, because the bare name bark is ambiguous in this context: which bark method does it refer to? To solve this problem, Swift 2.2 introduced a more elaborate notation allowing you to refer to a function more precisely. This notation has two parts:

Full name
    The full name of a Swift function is the name that precedes the parentheses, plus parentheses containing the external names of its parameters, each followed by colon. If the external name of a parameter is suppressed, we can represent its external name as an underscore.

    For example, a function declared func say(_ s:String, times:Int) has the full name say(_:times:).

Signature
    The signature of a Swift function may be specified explicitly by appending it to its bare name or full name with the keyword as.

For example, a function declared func say(_ s:String, times:Int) may be referred to as say as (String,Int) -> Void.

In our bark example, use of the full name solves the problem if the function to which we want a reference is the one that takes a parameter:

```
class Dog {
    func bark() {
        // ... as before ...
    }
    func bark(loudly:Bool) {
        // ... as before ...
    }
    func test() {
        let barkFunction = bark(_:) // fine
    }
}
```

But use of the full name *doesn't* solve the problem if the function to which we want a reference is the one that takes *no* parameters, because in that case the full name is the bare name, which is exactly what's ambiguous in this context. Use of the signature solves the problem:

```
class Dog {
    func bark() {
        // ... as before ...
    }
    func bark(loudly:Bool) {
        // ... as before ...
    }
    func test() {
        let barkFunction = bark as (Void) -> Void // fine
    }
}
```

Obviously, an explicit signature is needed also when a function is *overloaded.* For example:

```
class Dog{
    func bark() {
    }
    func bark(_ loudly:Bool) {
    }
    func bark(_ times:Int) {
    }
    func test() {
        let barkFunction = bark(_:) // compile error
    }
}
```

Here, we have said that we want the `bark` that takes one parameter, but there are *two* such `bark` functions, one whose parameter is a Bool, the other whose parameter is an Int. The signature disambiguates (and we can use the bare name):

```
let barkFunction = bark as (Int) -> Void // "times", not "loudly"
```

Function Reference Scope

In the foregoing examples of function references, there was no need to tell the compiler *where* the function is defined. That's because the function is already in scope at the point where the function reference appears. If you would be able to *call* the function without supplying further information, you can form the function *reference* without supplying further information.

However, a function reference *can* supply further information about where a function is defined; and sometimes it *must* do so. Therefore, you can prefix an instance or class to the function reference, using dot-notation. For example, there are situations where the compiler would force you to use `self` to call a function; in those situations, you will have to use `self` to refer to the function as well:

```
class Dog {
    func bark() {
    }
    func bark(_ loudly:Bool) {
    }
    func test() {
        let f = {
            return self.bark(_:) // self required here
        }
    }
}
```

To form a function reference to an instance method of another type, you have two choices. If you have on hand an instance of that type, you can use dot-notation with a reference to that instance:

```
class Cat {
    func purr() {
    }
}
class Dog {
    let cat = Cat()
    func test() {
        let purrFunction = cat.purr
    }
}
```

The other possibility is to use *the type* with dot-notation (this works even if the function is an instance method):

```
class Cat {
    func purr() {
    }
}
class Dog {
    func bark() {
    }
    func test() {
        let barkFunction = Dog.bark // legal but not necessary
        let purrFunction = Cat.purr
    }
}
```

Selectors

In Objective-C, a selector is a kind of method reference. In iOS programming, you'll often have to supply a Cocoa method with a selector as one of its parameters; very typically, this parameter will be named either `selector:` or `action:`. To call such a method requires you to pass a selector to Cocoa, along with a *target* (an object reference); later, the runtime can call the method by turning the selector into a message and sending that message to that target.

This architecture is the most prolific source of runtime errors (also known as crashes) in iOS programming. The reason is that it is all too easy to get the selector wrong. To form the selector, it is necessary to construct a *literal string* representing a method's Objective-C name. If you construct that name incorrectly, then when the time comes to send the message to the target, the runtime will find that the target can't handle that message, because it has no such method, and the app comes to a violent and premature halt, dumping the dreaded phrase "unrecognized selector" into the console.

For example, here's a typical recipe for failure:

```
class ViewController : UIViewController {
    @IBOutlet var b : UIButton!
    func viewDidLoad() {
        super.viewDidLoad()
        self.b.addTarget( // prepare to crash!
            self, action: "buttonPressed", for: .touchUpInside)
    }
    func buttonPressed(_ sender: Any) {
        // ...
    }
}
```

In that code, `self.b` is a button in the interface, and we are configuring it by calling `addTarget(action:for:)`, so that when the button is tapped, our `buttonPressed` method will be called. But we are configuring it incorrectly! Unfortunately, `"button-Pressed"` is *not* the Objective-C name of our `buttonPressed` method; the correct name would have been `"buttonPressed:"`, with a colon. (I'll explain why in Appendix A.) Therefore, our app will crash when the user taps that button. If you don't know the rules for forming a selector string — or even if you do, but you make a typing mistake — an "unrecognized selector" crash is likely to be in your future.

Thankfully, there is a solution to the problem: `#selector` syntax. To form an Objective-C selector, you use `#selector(...)` with a function reference inside the parentheses. Thus, we would rewrite our button action example like this:

```
class ViewController : UIViewController {
    @IBOutlet var button : UIButton!
    func viewDidLoad() {
        super.viewDidLoad()
        self.b.addTarget(
            self, action: #selector(buttonPressed), for: .touchUpInside)
    }
    func buttonPressed(_ sender: Any) {
        // ...
    }
}
```

When you use that notation, two wonderful things happen:

The compiler validates the function reference
   If your function reference isn't valid, your code won't even compile. The compiler also checks that this function is exposed to Objective-C; there's no point forming a selector for a method that Objective-C can't see, as your app would crash if Objective-C were to try to call such a method. (For a method to be exposed to Objective-C, either the class must be an NSObject subclass or the method must be marked with the `@objc` attribute.)

The compiler forms the Objective-C selector for you
   If your code compiles, the actual selector that will be passed into this parameter is guaranteed to be correct. *You* might form the selector incorrectly, but the compiler won't! Thus, it is impossible that the resulting selector should fail to match the method, and there is no chance of an "unrecognized selector" crash.

Very rarely, you still might need to create a selector manually. You can use a literal string, or you can instantiate Selector with the literal method name as argument — for example, `Selector("woohoo:")`.

 You can still crash, even with `#selector` syntax, by sending an action message to the wrong target. In the preceding example, if you changed `self`, the first argument of the `addTarget` call, to `self.b`, you'd crash at runtime with "unrecognized selector." The compiler won't help you with this kind of mistake.

CHAPTER 3

Variables and Simple Types

A variable is a named "shoebox" whose contained value must be of a single well-defined type. Every variable must be explicitly and formally declared. To put an object into the shoebox, thus causing the variable name to *refer* to that object, you *assign* the object to the variable. (As we know from Chapter 2, a function, too, has a type, and can be assigned to a variable.)

This chapter goes into detail about declaration and initialization of variables. It then discusses all the primary built-in Swift simple types. (I mean "simple" as opposed to collections; the primary built-in collection types are discussed at the end of Chapter 4.)

Variable Scope and Lifetime

Aside from the convenience of giving a reference a name, a variable, by virtue of *where it is declared*, endows its referent with a particular *scope* (visibility) and *lifetime*; assigning something to a variable is a way of ensuring that it can be *seen* by code that needs to see it and that it *persists* long enough to serve its purpose.

In the structure of a Swift file (see Example 1-1), a variable can be declared just about anywhere. It will be useful to distinguish several levels of variable scope and lifetime:

Global variables
> A global variable, or simply a *global*, is a variable declared at the top level of a Swift file. A global variable lives as long as the file lives, which is as long as the program runs. A global variable is visible everywhere (that's what "global" means). It is visible to all code within the *same* file, because it is at top level, so any other code in the same file must be at the same level or at a lower contained level of scope. Moreover, it is visible (by default) to all code within any *other* file

in the same module, because Swift files in the same module can automatically see one another, and hence can see one another's top levels. For example:

```
// File1:
let globalVariable = "global"
class Dog {
    func printGlobal() {
        print(globalVariable) // *
    }
}
// File2:
class Cat {
    func printGlobal() {
        print(globalVariable) // *
    }
}
```

Properties

A *property* is a variable declared at the top level of an object type declaration (an enum, struct, or class). There are two kinds of properties: instance properties and static/class properties.

Instance properties

By default, a property is an *instance* property. Its value can differ for each instance of this object type. Its lifetime is the same as the lifetime of the instance. Recall from Chapter 1 that an instance comes into existence through deliberate instantiation of an object type; the subsequent lifetime of the instance, and hence of its instance properties, depends on the lifetime of the variable to which the instance itself is assigned.

Static/class properties

A property is a static/class property if its declaration is preceded by the keyword static or class. (I'll go into detail about those terms in Chapter 4.) Its lifetime is the same as the lifetime of the object type. If the object type is declared at the top level of a file, the property lives as long as the program runs.

A property is visible to code *inside* the object declaration. For example, an object's methods can see that object's properties. Such code can refer to the property using dot-notation with self, and I always do this as a matter of style, but self can usually be omitted except for purposes of disambiguation. An instance property is also visible (by default) to other code, provided the other code has a reference to this instance; in that case, the property can be referred to through dot-notation with the instance reference. A static/class property is visible (by default) to other code that can see the name of this object type; in that case, it can be referred to through dot-notation with the object type. For example:

```
// File1:
class Dog {
    static let staticProperty = "staticProperty"
    let instanceProperty = "instanceProperty"
    func printInstanceProperty() {
        print(self.instanceProperty) // *
    }
}
// File2:
class Cat {
    func printDogStaticProperty() {
        print(Dog.staticProperty) // *
    }
    func printDogInstanceProperty() {
        let d = Dog()
        print(d.instanceProperty) // *
    }
}
```

Local variables

A local variable is a variable declared inside a function body. A local variable lives only as long as its surrounding curly-braces scope lives: it comes into existence when the path of execution passes into the scope and reaches the variable declaration, and it goes out of existence when the path of execution exits the scope. Local variables are sometimes called *automatic,* to signify that they come into and go out of existence automatically. A local variable can be seen only by *subsequent* code within the same scope (including a subsequent deeper scope within the same scope). For example:

```
class Dog {
    func printLocalVariable() {
        let localVariable = "local"
        print(localVariable) // *
    }
}
```

Variable Declaration

A variable is declared with let or var:

- With let, the variable becomes a *constant* — its value can never be changed after the first assignment of a value (*initialization*).

- With var, the variable is a true variable, and its value can be changed by subsequent assignment.

A variable's *type,* however, can *never* be changed. A variable declared with var can be given a different value, but that value must conform to the variable's type. Thus, when a variable is declared, it must be *given* a type, which it will have forever after. You can give a variable a type explicitly or implicitly:

Explicit variable type declaration
After the variable's name in the declaration, add a colon and the name of the type:

```
var x : Int
```

Implicit variable type by initialization
If you initialize the variable as part of the declaration, and if you provide no explicit type, Swift will *infer* its type, based on the value with which it is initialized:

```
var x = 1 // and now x is an Int
```

It is perfectly possible to declare a variable's type explicitly *and* assign it an initial value, all in one move:

```
var x : Int = 1
```

In that example, the explicit type declaration is superfluous, because the type (Int) would have been inferred from the initial value. Sometimes, however, providing an explicit type, even while also assigning an initial value, is *not* superfluous. Here are the main situations where that's the case:

Swift's inference would be wrong
A very common case in my own code is when I want to provide the initial value as a numeric literal. Swift will infer either Int or Double, depending on whether the literal contains a decimal point. But there are a lot of other numeric types! When I mean one of those, I will provide the type explicitly, like this:

```
let separator : CGFloat = 2.0
```

Swift can't infer the type
Sometimes, the type of the initial value is completely unknown to the compiler unless you tell it. A very common case involves option sets (discussed in Chapter 4). This won't compile:

```
var opts = [.autoreverse, .repeat] // compile error
```

The problem is that the name .autoreverse is a shortcut for UIViewAnimation-Options.autoreverse (and so too for .repeat), but Swift doesn't know that unless we tell it. Explicitly typing the variable is an elegant way of doing that:

```
let opts : UIViewAnimationOptions = [.autoreverse, .repeat]
```

The programmer can't infer the type
I frequently include a superfluous explicit type declaration as a kind of note to myself. Here's an example from my own code:

```
let duration : CMTime = track.timeRange.duration
```

In that code, `track` is an AVAssetTrack. Swift knows perfectly well that the `duration` property of an AVAssetTrack's `timeRange` property is a CMTime. But I don't! In order to remind myself of that fact, I've shown the type explicitly.

Because explicit variable typing is possible, a variable doesn't have to be initialized when it is declared. It is legal to write this:

```
let x : Int
```

Now x is an empty shoebox — an Int variable without an initial value. I strongly urge you, however, not to do that with a local variable if you can possibly avoid it. It isn't a disaster — the Swift compiler will stop you from trying to use a variable that has never been assigned a value — but it's not a good habit.

The exception that proves the rule is what we might call *conditional initialization*. Sometimes, we don't *know* a variable's initial value until we've performed some sort of conditional test. The variable itself, however, can be declared only once; so it must be declared in advance and conditionally initialized afterward. This sort of thing is not unreasonable (though there are other, possibly better ways to write it, to which I'll come in due course):

```
let timed : Bool
if val == 1 {
    timed = true
} else {
    timed = false
}
```

When a variable's *address* is to be passed as argument to a function, the variable must be declared *and initialized* beforehand, even if the initial value is fake. Recall this example from Chapter 2:

```
var r : CGFloat = 0
var g : CGFloat = 0
var b : CGFloat = 0
var a : CGFloat = 0
c.getRed(&r, green: &g, blue: &b, alpha: &a)
```

After that code runs, our four CGFloat 0 values will have been replaced; they were just momentary placeholders, to satisfy the compiler.

On rare occasions, you'll want to call a Cocoa method that returns a value immediately and later uses that value in a function passed to that same method. For example, Cocoa has a UIApplication instance method declared like this:

```
func beginBackgroundTask(
    expirationHandler handler: (() -> Void)? = nil)
        -> UIBackgroundTaskIdentifier
```

`beginBackgroundTask(expirationHandler:)` returns a number (a UIBackground-TaskIdentifier is just an Int), and will later call the `expirationHandler:` function passed to it — a function in which you will want to *use* the number that was returned at the outset. Swift's safety rules won't let you declare the variable that holds this number and use it in an anonymous function all in the same statement:

```
let bti = UIApplication.shared.beginBackgroundTask {
    UIApplication.shared.endBackgroundTask(bti)
} // error: variable used within its own initial value
```

Therefore, you need to declare the variable beforehand; but then Swift has another complaint:

```
var bti : UIBackgroundTaskIdentifier
bti = UIApplication.shared.beginBackgroundTask {
    UIApplication.shared.endBackgroundTask(bti)
} // error: variable captured by a closure before being initialized
```

The solution is to declare the variable beforehand and give it a fake initial value as a placeholder:

```
var bti : UIBackgroundTaskIdentifier = 0
bti = UIApplication.shared.beginBackgroundTask {
    UIApplication.shared.endBackgroundTask(bti)
}
```

 Instance properties of an object (at the top level of an enum, struct, or class declaration) can be initialized in the object's initializer function rather than by assignment in their declaration. It is legal and common for both constant (`let`) and variable (`var`) instance properties to have an explicit type and no directly assigned initial value. I'll have more to say about that in Chapter 4.

Computed Initializer

Sometimes, you'd like to run several lines of code in order to compute a variable's initial value. A simple and compact way to express this is with an anonymous function that you call immediately (see "Define-and-Call" on page 52). I'll illustrate by rewriting an earlier example:

```
let timed : Bool = {
    if val == 1 {
        return true
    } else {
        return false
    }
}()
```

You can do the same thing when you're initializing an instance property. In this class, there's an image (a UIImage) that I'm going to need many times later on. It makes sense to create this image in advance as a constant instance property of the class. To create it means to draw it. That takes several lines of code. So I declare and initialize the property by defining and calling an anonymous function, like this (for my image-OfSize utility, see Chapter 2):

```
class RootViewController : UITableViewController {
    let cellBackgroundImage : UIImage = {
        return imageOfSize(CGSize(width:320, height:44)) {
            // ... drawing goes here ...
        }
    }()
    // ... rest of class goes here ...
}
```

Indeed, a define-and-call anonymous function is often the *only* legal way to compute an instance property's initial value with multiple lines of code. The reason is that, when you're initializing an instance property, you can't call an instance method, because there is no instance yet — the instance, after all, is what you are in the process of creating.

Computed Variables

The variables I've been describing so far in this chapter have all been *stored* variables. The shoebox analogy applies. The variable is a name, like a shoebox; a value can be put into the shoebox by assigning it to the variable, and it then sits there and can be retrieved later by referring to the variable, for as long the variable lives.

Alternatively, a variable can be *computed*. This means that the variable, instead of having a value, has *functions*. One function, the *setter*, is called when the variable is assigned to. The other function, the *getter*, is called when the variable is referred to. Here's some code illustrating schematically the syntax for declaring a computed variable:

```
var now : String { ❶
    get { ❷
        return Date().description ❸
    }
    set { ❹
        print(newValue) ❺
    }
}
```

❶ The variable must be declared with var (not let). Its type must be declared explicitly. The type is followed *immediately* by curly braces.

❷ The getter function is called get. There is no formal function declaration; the word get is simply followed immediately by a function body in curly braces.

❸ The getter function *must* return a value of the same type as the variable.

❹ The setter function is called set. There is no formal function declaration; the word set is simply followed immediately by a function body in curly braces.

❺ The setter behaves like a function taking one parameter. By default, this parameter arrives into the setter function body with the local name newValue.

Here's some code that illustrates the use of our computed variable. You don't treat it any differently than any other variable! To assign to the variable, assign to it; to use the variable, use it. Behind the scenes, though, the setter and getter functions are called:

```
now = "Howdy" // Howdy ❶
print(now) // 2016-06-26 17:03:30 +0000 ❷
```

❶ Assigning to now calls its setter. The argument passed into this call is the assigned value; here, that's "Howdy". That value arrives in the set function as newValue. Our set function prints newValue to the console.

❷ Fetching now calls its getter. Our get function obtains the current date-time and translates it into a string, and returns the string. Our code then prints that string to the console.

Observe that when we set now to "Howdy" in the first line, the string "Howdy" wasn't stored anywhere. It had no effect, for example, on the value of now in the second line. A set function *can* store a value, but it can't store it in this computed variable; a computed variable isn't storage! It's a shorthand for calling its getter and setter functions.

There are a couple of variants on the basic syntax I've just illustrated:

- The name of the set function parameter doesn't have to be newValue. To specify a different name, put it in parentheses after the word set, like this:

  ```
  set (val) { // now you can use "val" inside the setter function body
  ```

- There doesn't have to be a setter. If the setter is omitted, this becomes a *read-only* variable. Attempting to assign to it is a compile error. A computed variable with no setter is the *primary* way to create a read-only variable in Swift.

- There must always be a getter! However, if there is no setter, the word get and the curly braces that follow it can be omitted. Thus, this is a legal declaration of a read-only variable:

  ```
  var now : String {
      return Date().description
  }
  ```

A computed variable can be useful in many ways. Here are the ones that occur most frequently in my real programming life:

Read-only variable

A computed variable is the simplest way to make a read-only variable. Just omit the setter from the declaration. Typically, the variable will be a global variable or a property; there probably wouldn't be much point in a local read-only variable.

Façade for a function

When a value can be readily calculated by a function each time it is needed, it often makes for simpler syntax to express it as a read-only calculated variable. Here's an example from my own code:

```
var mp : MPMusicPlayerController {
    return MPMusicPlayerController.systemMusicPlayer()
}
```

It's no bother to call `MPMusicPlayerController.systemMusicPlayer()` every time I want to refer to this object, but it's more compact to refer to it by a simple name, `mp`. And since `mp` represents a thing, rather than the performance of an action, it's nicer for `mp` to appear as a variable, so that to all appearances it *is* the thing, rather than as a function, which *returns* the thing.

Façade for other variables

A computed variable can sit in front of one or more stored variables, acting as a gatekeeper on how those stored variables are set and fetched. This is comparable to an accessor method in Objective-C. In the extreme case, a public computed variable is backed by a private stored variable:

```
private var _p : String = ""
var p : String {
    get {
        return self._p
    }
    set {
        self._p = newValue
    }
}
```

That's a silly example, because we're not *doing* anything interesting with our accessors: we are just setting and getting the private stored variable directly, so there's no effective difference between p and _p. But based on that template, you could now add functionality so that something useful happens during setting and getting.

 As the preceding example demonstrates, a computed instance property function can refer to other instance properties; it can also call instance methods. This is important, because in general the initializer for a stored property can do neither of those things. The reason this is legal for a computed property is that its functions won't be called until the instance actually exists.

Here's a practical example of a computed variable used as a façade for storage. My class has an instance property myBigData, holding a very large stored piece of data, which can alternatively be nil (it's an Optional, as I'll explain later). When my app goes into the background, I want to reduce memory usage (because iOS kills back-grounded apps that use too much memory). So I plan to save the data of myBigData as a file to disk, and then set the variable itself to nil, thus releasing its data from memory. Now consider what should happen when my app comes back to the front and my code tries to fetch myBigData. If it isn't nil, we just fetch its value. But if it *is* nil, this might be because we saved its value to disk. So now I want to restore its value by reading it from disk, and *then* fetch its value. This is a perfect use of a computed variable façade:

```
private var _myBigData : Data! = nil
var myBigData : Data! {
    set (newdata) {
        self._myBigData = newdata
    }
    get {
        if _myBigData == nil {
            // ... get a reference to file on disk, f ...
            if let d = try? Data(contentsOf:f) {
                self._myBigData = d
                // ... erase the file ...
            }
        }
        return self._myBigData
    }
}
```

Setter Observers

Computed variables are not needed as a stored variable façade as often as you might suppose. That's because Swift has another feature, which lets you inject functionality into the setter of a stored variable — setter observers. These are functions that are called just before and just after other code *sets* a stored variable.

The syntax for declaring a variable with a setter observer is very similar to the syntax for declaring a computed variable; you can write a willSet function, a didSet function, or both:

```
var s = "whatever" { ❶
    willSet { ❷
        print(newValue) ❸
    }
    didSet { ❹
```

```
        print(oldValue) ❺
        // self.s = "something else"
    }
}
```

❶ The variable must be declared with var (not let). It can be assigned an initial value. It is then followed *immediately* by curly braces.

❷ The willSet function, if there is one, is the word willSet followed immediately by a function body in curly braces. It is called when other code sets this variable, just *before* the variable actually receives its new value.

❸ By default, the willSet function receives the incoming new value as newValue. You can change this name by writing a different name in parentheses after the word willSet. The old value is still sitting in the stored variable, and the willSet function can access it there.

❹ The didSet function, if there is one, is the word didSet followed immediately by a function body in curly braces. It is called when other code sets this variable, just *after* the variable actually receives its new value.

❺ By default, the didSet function receives the old value, which has already been replaced as the value of the variable, as oldValue. You can change this name by writing a different name in parentheses after the word didSet. The new value is already sitting in the stored variable, and the didSet function can access it there. Moreover, it is legal for the didSet function to *set the stored variable to a different value.*

 Setter observer functions are *not* called when the stored variable is initialized or when the didSet function changes the stored variable's value. That would be circular!

In practice, I find myself using setter observers, rather than a computed variable, in the vast majority of situations where I would have used a setter override in Objective-C. Here's an example. This is an instance property of a view class. Every time this property changes, we need to change the interface to reflect it. Not only do we change the interface, but also we "clamp" the incoming value within a fixed limit:

```
var angle : CGFloat = 0 {
    didSet {
        // angle must not be smaller than 0 or larger than 5
        if self.angle < 0 {
            self.angle = 0
        }
        if self.angle > 5 {
            self.angle = 5
        }
```

```
    // modify interface to match
    self.transform = CGAffineTransform(rotationAngle: self.angle)
  }
}
```

 A computed variable can't have setter observers. But it doesn't need them! There's a setter function, so anything additional that needs to happen during setting can be programmed directly into that setter function.

Lazy Initialization

The term *lazy* is not a pejorative ethical judgment; it's a formal description of an important behavior. If a stored variable is assigned an initial value as part of its declaration, and if it uses lazy initialization, then the initial value is not actually evaluated and assigned until running code accesses the variable's value.

There are three types of variable that can be initialized lazily in Swift:

Global variables
> Global variables are *automatically lazy*. This makes sense if you ask yourself when they should be initialized. As the app launches, files and their top-level code are encountered. It would make no sense to initialize globals now, because the app isn't even running yet. Thus global initialization must be postponed to some moment that *does* make sense. Therefore, a global variable's initialization doesn't happen until other code first refers to that global. Under the hood, this behavior is protected with the equivalent of dispatch_once; this makes initialization both singular (it can happen only once) and thread-safe.

Static properties
> Static properties are *automatically lazy*. They behave exactly like global variables, and for basically the same reason. (There are no stored class properties in Swift, so class properties can't be initialized and thus can't have lazy initialization.)

Instance properties
> An instance property is not lazy by default, but it may be made lazy by marking its declaration with the keyword lazy. This property must be declared with var, not let. The initializer for such a property might *never* be evaluated, namely if code assigns the property a value before any code fetches the property's value.

 In Swift 3, dispatch_once itself is unavailable; use a global or static variable to obtain the same behavior.

Lazy initialization is often used to implement *singleton*. Singleton is a pattern where all code is able to get access to a single shared instance of a certain class:

```
class MyClass {
    static let sharedSingleton = MyClass()
}
```

Now other code can obtain a reference to MyClass's singleton by saying
`MyClass.sharedSingleton`. The singleton instance is not created until the first time
other code says this; subsequently, no matter how many times other code may say
this, the instance returned is always that same instance. (Observe that that is *not* what
would happen if this were a computed read-only property whose getter calls
`MyClass()` and returns that instance; do you see why?)

Now let's talk about lazy initialization of instance properties. Why might you want
this? One reason is obvious: the initial value might be expensive to generate, so you'd
like to avoid generating it unless it is actually needed. But there's another reason that
turns out to be even more important: a lazy initializer can do things that a normal
initializer can't. In particular, it can *refer to the instance*. A normal initializer can't do
that, because the instance doesn't yet exist at the time that a normal initializer would
need to run (*ex hypothesi*, we're in the middle of creating the instance, so it isn't ready
yet). A lazy initializer, by contrast, won't run until some time after the instance has
fully come into existence, so referring to the instance is fine. For example, this code
would be illegal if the `arrow` property weren't declared `lazy`:

```
class MyView : UIView {
    lazy var arrow : UIImage = self.arrowImage()
    func arrowImage () -> UIImage {
        // ... big image-generating code goes here ...
    }
}
```

A very common idiom is to initialize a lazy instance property with a define-and-call
anonymous function:

```
lazy var prog : UIProgressView = {
    let p = UIProgressView(progressViewStyle: .default)
    p.alpha = 0.7
    p.trackTintColor = UIColor.clear
    p.progressTintColor = UIColor.black
    p.frame = CGRect(x:0, y:0, width:self.view.bounds.size.width, height:20)
    p.progress = 1.0
    return p
}()
```

 There are some holes in the language. Lazy instance properties can't have setter
observers; and there's no `lazy let`, so you can't readily make a lazy instance
property read-only. Moreover, lazy instance properties aren't atomic, so there's a
danger of multiple initialization under certain circumstances. (Global and static
variables don't have these issues: they are thread-safe and atomic.)

Built-In Simple Types

Every variable, and every value, must have a type. But what types are there? Up to this point, I've assumed the existence of some types, such as Int and String, without formally telling you about them. Here's a survey of the primary simple types provided by Swift, along with some instance methods, global functions, and operators that apply to them. (Collection types will be discussed at the end of Chapter 4.)

Bool

The Bool object type (a struct) has only two values, commonly regarded as true and false (or yes and no). You can represent these values using the literal keywords `true` and `false`, and it is natural to think of a Bool value as *being* either `true` or `false`:

```
var selected : Bool = false
```

In that code, `selected` is a Bool variable initialized to `false`; it can subsequently be set to `false` or `true`, and to no other values. Because of its simple yes-or-no state, a Bool variable of this kind is often referred to as a *flag*.

Cocoa methods very often expect a Bool parameter or return a Bool value. For example, when your app launches, Cocoa calls a method in your code declared like this:

```
func application(_ application: UIApplication,
    didFinishLaunchingWithOptions
    launchOptions: [UIApplicationLaunchOptionsKey : Any]?)
    -> Bool {
```

You can do anything you like in that method; often, you will do nothing. But you must return a Bool! And in real life, that Bool will probably be `true`. A minimal implementation thus looks like this:

```
func application(_ application: UIApplication,
    didFinishLaunchingWithOptions
    launchOptions: [UIApplicationLaunchOptionsKey : Any]?)
    -> Bool {
        return true
}
```

A Bool is useful in conditions; as I'll explain in Chapter 5, when you say `if` *something*, the *something* is the condition, and is a Bool — or an expression that evaluates to a Bool. For example, when you compare two values with the equality comparison operator ==, the result is a Bool — `true` if they are equal to each other, `false` if they are not:

```
if meaningOfLife == 42 { // ...
```

(I'll talk more about equality comparison in a moment, when we come to discuss types that can be compared, such as Int and String.)

When preparing a condition, you will sometimes find that it enhances clarity to store the Bool value in a variable beforehand:

```
let comp = self.traitCollection.horizontalSizeClass == .compact
if comp { // ...
```

Observe that, when employing that idiom, we use the Bool variable *directly* as the condition. There is no need to test explicitly whether a Bool equals `true` or `false`; the conditional expression itself is already testing that. It is silly — and arguably wrong — to say `if comp == true`, because `if comp` already *means* "if comp is `true`."

Since a Bool can be used as a condition, a call to a function that returns a Bool can be used as a condition. Here's an example from my own code. I've declared a function that returns a Bool to say whether the cards the user has selected constitute a correct answer to the puzzle:

```
func evaluate(_ cells:[CardCell]) -> Bool { // ...
```

Thus, elsewhere I can say this:

```
if self.evaluate(cellsToTest) { // ...
```

Unlike many computer languages, nothing else in Swift is implicitly coerced to or treated as a Bool. In C, for example, a boolean is actually a number, and 0 is false. But in Swift, nothing is false but `false`, and nothing is true but `true`.

The type name, Bool, comes from the English mathematician George Boole; Boolean algebra provides operations on logical values. Bool values are subject to these same operations:

`!`

Not. The `!` unary operator reverses the truth value of the Bool to which it is applied as a prefix. If ok is `true`, `!ok` is `false` — and *vice versa*.

`&&`

Logical-and. Returns `true` only if both operands are `true`; otherwise, returns `false`. If the first operand is `false`, the second operand is not even evaluated (thus avoiding possible side effects).

`||`

Logical-or. Returns `true` if either operand is `true`; otherwise, returns `false`. If the first operand is `true`, the second operand is not even evaluated (thus avoiding possible side effects).

If a logical operation is complicated or elaborate, parentheses around subexpressions can help clarify both the logic and the order of operations.

Numbers

The main numeric types are Int and Double, meaning that, left to your own devices, these are the types you'll use. Other numeric types exist mostly for compatibility with the C and Objective-C APIs that Swift needs to be able to talk to when you're programming iOS.

Int

The Int object type (a struct) represents an integer between Int.max and Int.min inclusive. The actual values of those limits might depend on the platform and architecture under which the app runs, so don't count on them to be absolute; in my testing at this moment, they are 2^{63}-1 and -2^{63} respectively (64-bit words).

The easiest way to represent an Int value is as a numeric literal. A simple numeric literal without a decimal point is taken as an Int by default. Internal underscores are legal; this is useful for making long numbers readable. Leading zeroes are legal; this is useful for padding and aligning values in your code.

You can write an Int literal using binary, octal, or hexadecimal digits. To do so, start the literal with 0b, 0o, or 0x respectively. Thus, for example, 0x10 is decimal 16.

Double

The Double object type (a struct) represents a floating-point number to a precision of about 15 decimal places (64-bit storage).

The easiest way to represent a Double value is as a numeric literal. Any numeric literal containing a decimal point is taken as a Double by default. Internal underscores and leading zeroes are legal.

A Double literal may *not* begin with a decimal point (unlike C and Objective-C). If the value to be represented is between 0 and 1, start the literal with a leading 0.

You can write a Double literal using scientific notation. Everything after the letter e is the exponent of 10. You can omit the decimal point if the fractional digits would be zero. For example, 3e2 is 3 times 10^2 (300).

You can write a Double literal using hexadecimal digits. To do so, start the literal with 0x. You can use exponentiation here too (and again, you can omit the decimal point); everything after the letter p is the exponent of 2. For example, 0x10p2 is decimal 64, because you are multiplying 16 by 2^2.

There's a static property Double.infinity and an instance property isZero, among others.

Numeric coercion

Coercion is the conversion of a value from one type to another, and numeric coercion is the conversion of a value from one numeric type to another. Swift doesn't really have explicit coercion, but it has something that serves the same purpose — instantiation. To convert an Int explicitly into a Double, instantiate Double with an Int in the parentheses. To convert a Double explicitly into an Int, instantiate Int with a Double in the parentheses; this will truncate the original value (everything after the decimal point will be thrown away):

```
let i = 10
let x = Double(i)
print(x) // 10.0, a Double
let y = 3.8
let j = Int(y)
print(j) // 3, an Int
```

When numeric values are assigned to variables or passed as arguments to a function, Swift will perform implicit coercion *of literals only*. This code is legal:

```
let d : Double = 10
```

But this code is not legal, because what you're assigning is a *variable* (not a literal) of a different type; the compiler will stop you:

```
let i = 10
let d : Double = i // compile error
```

The solution is to *coerce explicitly* as you assign or pass the variable:

```
let i = 10
let d : Double = Double(i)
```

The same rule holds when numeric values are combined by an arithmetic operation. Swift will perform implicit coercion *of literals only*. The usual situation is an Int combined with a Double; the Int is treated as a Double:

```
let x = 10/3.0
print(x) // 3.33333333333333
```

But *variables* of different numeric types *must be coerced explicitly* so that they are the *same* type if you want to combine them in an arithmetic operation. Thus, for example:

```
let i = 10
let n = 3.0
let x = i / n // compile error; you need to say Double(i)
```

These rules are evidently a consequence of Swift's strict typing; but (as far as I am aware) they constitute very unusual treatment of numeric values for a modern computer language, and will probably drive you mad in short order. The examples I've given so far were easily solved, but things can become more complicated if an arithmetic expression is longer, and the problem is compounded by the existence of other numeric types that are needed for compatibility with Cocoa, as I shall now proceed to explain.

Other numeric types

If you weren't programming iOS — if you were using Swift in some isolated, abstract world — you could probably do all necessary arithmetic with Int and Double alone. Unfortunately, to program iOS you need Cocoa, which is full of other numeric types; and Swift has types that match every one of them. Thus, in addition to Int, there are signed integers of various sizes — Int8, Int16, Int32, Int64 — plus the unsigned integer UInt along with UInt8, UInt16, UInt32, and UInt64. In addition to Double, there is the lower-precision Float (32-bit storage, about 6 or 7 decimal places of precision) and the extended-precision Float80; plus, in the Core Graphics framework, CGFloat (whose size can be that of Float or Double, depending on the bitness of the architecture).

You may also encounter a C numeric type when trying to interface with a C API. These types, as far as Swift is concerned, are just type aliases, meaning that they are alternate names for another type; for example, a CDouble (corresponding to C's double) is just a Double by another name, a CLong (C's long) is an Int, and so on. Many other numeric type aliases will arise in various Cocoa frameworks; for example, TimeInterval (Objective-C NSTimeInterval) is merely a type alias for Double.

Here's the problem. I have just finished telling you that you can't assign, pass, or combine values of different numeric types using variables; you have to coerce those values explicitly to the correct type. But now it turns out that you're being flooded by Cocoa with numeric values of many types! Cocoa will often hand you a numeric value that is neither an Int nor a Double — and you won't necessarily realize this, until the compiler stops you dead in your tracks for some sort of type mismatch. You must then figure out what you've done wrong and coerce everything to the same type.

Here's a typical example from one of my apps. A slider, in the interface, is a UISlider, whose minimumValue and maximumValue are Floats. In this code, s is a UISlider, g is a UIGestureRecognizer, and we're trying to use the gesture recognizer to move the slider's "thumb" to wherever the user tapped within the slider:

```
let pt = g.location(in:s) ❶
let percentage = pt.x / s.bounds.size.width ❷
let delta = percentage * (s.maximumValue - s.minimumValue) // compile error ❸
```

That won't compile. Here's why:

❶ pt is a CGPoint, and therefore pt.x is a CGFloat.

```
let percentage = pt.x / s.bounds.size.width
```

Figure 3-1. Quick Help displays a variable's type

❷ Luckily, `s.bounds.size.width` is also a CGFloat, so the second line compiles; `percentage` is now inferred to be a CGFloat.

❸ We now try to combine `percentage` with `s.maximumValue` and `s.minimumValue` — and they are Floats, not CGFloats. That's a compile error.

This sort of thing is not an issue in C or Objective-C, where there is implicit coercion; but in Swift, a CGFloat can't be combined with Floats. We must coerce explicitly:

```
let delta = Float(percentage) * (s.maximumValue - s.minimumValue)
```

The good news here is that if you can get enough of your code to compile, Xcode's Quick Help feature will tell you what type Swift has inferred for a variable (Figure 3-1). This can assist you in tracking down your issues with numeric types.

> In the rare circumstance where you need to assign or pass an integer type where another integer type is expected and you don't actually know what that other integer type is, you can get Swift to coerce dynamically by calling the global `numericCast(_:)` function. For example, if `i` and `j` are previously declared variables of different integer types, `i = numericCast(j)` coerces `j` to the integer type of `i`.

Arithmetic operations

Swift's arithmetic operators are as you would expect; they are familiar from other computer languages as well as from real arithmetic:

+

Addition operator. Add the second operand to the first and return the result.

-

Subtraction operator. Subtract the second operand from the first and return the result. A different operator (unary minus), used as a prefix, looks the same; it returns the additive inverse of its single operand. (There is, in fact, also a unary plus operator, which returns its operand unchanged.)

*

Multiplication operator. Multiply the first operand by the second and return the result.

/

Division operator. Divide the first operand by the second and return the result.

 As in C, division of one Int by another Int yields an Int; any remaining fraction is stripped away. 10/3 is 3, not 3-and-one-third.

%

Remainder operator. Divide the first operand by the second and return the remainder. The result can be negative, if the first operand is negative; if the second operand is negative, it is treated as positive. Floating-point operands are legal.

Integer types can be treated as binary bitfields and subjected to binary bitwise operations:

&

Bitwise-and. A bit in the result is 1 if and only if that bit is 1 in both operands.

|

Bitwise-or. A bit in the result is 0 if and only if that bit is 0 in both operands.

^

Bitwise-or, exclusive. A bit in the result is 1 if and only if that bit is not identical in both operands.

~

Bitwise-not. Precedes its single operand; inverts the value of each bit and returns the result.

<<

Shift left. Shift the bits of the first operand leftward the number of times indicated by the second operand.

>>

Shift right. Shift the bits of the first operand rightward the number of times indicated by the second operand.

 Technically, the shift operators perform a logical shift if the integer is unsigned, and an arithmetic shift if the integer is signed.

Integer overflow or underflow — for example, adding two Int values so as to exceed Int.max — is a runtime error (your app will crash). In simple cases the compiler will stop you, but you can get away with it easily enough:

```
let i = Int.max - 2
let j = i + 12/2 // crash
```

Under certain circumstances you might want to force such an operation to succeed, so special overflow/underflow methods are supplied. These methods return a tuple; I'll show you an example even though I haven't discussed tuples yet:

```
let i = Int.max - 2
let (j, over) = Int.addWithOverflow(i,12/2)
```

Now j is Int.min + 3 (because the value has wrapped around from Int.max to Int.min) and over is true (to report the overflow).

If you don't care to hear about whether or not there was an overflow/underflow, special arithmetic operators let you suppress the error: &+, &-, &*.

You will frequently want to combine the value of an existing variable arithmetically with another value and store the result in the same variable. Remember that to do so, you will need to have declared the variable as a var:

```
var i = 1
i = i + 7
```

As a shorthand, operators are provided that perform the arithmetic operation and the assignment all in one move:

```
var i = 1
i += 7
```

The shorthand (*compound*) assignment arithmetic operators are +=, -=, *=, /=, %=, &=, |=, ^=, <<=, >>=.

Operation precedence is largely intuitive: for example, * has a higher precedence than +, so x+y*z multiplies y by z first, and then adds the result to x. Use parentheses to disambiguate when in doubt; for example, (x+y)*z performs the addition first.

Global functions include abs (absolute value), max, and min:

```
let i = -7
let j = 6
print(abs(i)) // 7
print(max(i,j)) // 6
```

New in Swift 3, many mathematical functions, such as square roots and rounding, are implemented natively as methods; thus you can say 2.squareRoot() or 5.5.rounded().

Global mathematical functions, such as trigonometry and random numbers, come from the C standard libraries that are visible because you've imported UIKit. You still have to be careful about numeric types. For example, arc4random_uniform takes and returns a UInt32. So if n is an Int and you want to get a random Int between between 0 and n-1, you can't say arc4random_uniform(n); you have to coerce the argument and the result, saying Int(arc4random_uniform(UInt32(n))).

Comparison

Numbers are compared using the comparison operators, which return a Bool. For example, the expression `i==j` tests whether `i` and `j` are equal; when `i` and `j` are numbers, "equal" means numerically equal. So `i==j` is `true` only if `i` and `j` are "the same number," in exactly the sense you would expect.

The comparison operators are:

`==`

Equality operator. Returns `true` if its operands are equal.

`!=`

Inequality operator. Returns `false` if its operands are equal.

`<`

Less-than operator. Returns `true` if the first operand is less than the second operand.

`<=`

Less-than-or-equal operator. Returns `true` if the first operand is less than or equal to the second operand.

`>`

Greater-than operator. Returns `true` if the first operand is greater than the second operand.

`>=`

Greater-than-or-equal operator. Returns `true` if the first operand is greater than or equal to the second operand.

Keep in mind that, because of the way computers store numbers, equality comparison of Double values may not succeed where you would expect. To test whether two Doubles are effectively equal, it can be more reliable to compare the difference between them to a very small value (usually called an *epsilon*):

```
let isEqual = abs(x - y) < 0.000001
```

String

The String object type (a struct) represents text. The easiest way to represent a String value is with a literal, which is delimited by double quotes:

```
let greeting = "hello"
```

A Swift string is thoroughly modern; under the hood, it's Unicode, and you can include any character directly in a string literal. If you don't want to bother typing a

Unicode character whose codepoint you know, use the notation \u{...}, where what's between the curly braces is up to eight hex digits:

```
let leftTripleArrow = "\u{21DA}"
```

The backslash in that string representation is the *escape* character; it means, "I'm not really a backslash; I indicate that the next character gets special treatment." Various nonprintable and ambiguous characters are entered as escaped characters; the most important are:

\n

A Unix newline character

\t

A tab character

\"

A quotation mark (escaped to show that this is not the end of the string literal)

\\

A backslash (escaped because a lone backslash is the escape character)

One of Swift's coolest features is *string interpolation*. This permits you to embed any value that can be output with print inside a literal string *as a string*, even if it is not itself a string. The notation is escaped parentheses: \(...). For example:

```
let n = 5
let s = "You have \(n) widgets."
```

Now s is the string "You have 5 widgets." The example is not very compelling, because we know what n is and could have typed 5 directly into our string; but imagine that we *don't* know what n is! Moreover, the stuff in escaped parentheses doesn't have to be the name of a variable; it can be almost any expression that evaluates as legal Swift. If you don't know how to add, this example is more compelling:

```
let m = 4
let n = 5
let s = "You have \(m + n) widgets."
```

To combine (concatenate) two strings, the simplest approach is to use the + operator:

```
let s = "hello"
let s2 = " world"
let greeting = s + s2
```

This convenient notation is possible because the + operator is *overloaded*: it does one thing when the operands are numbers (numeric addition) and another when the operands are strings (concatenation). As I'll explain in Chapter 5, *all* operators can be overloaded, and you can overload them to operate in some appropriate way on your own types.

The + operator comes with a += assignment shortcut; naturally, the variable on the left side must have been declared with var:

```
var s = "hello"
let s2 = " world"
s += s2
```

As an alternative to +=, you can call the append(_:) instance method:

```
var s = "hello"
let s2 = " world"
s.append(s2)
```

Another way of concatenating strings is with the joined(separator:) method. You start with an array (yes, I know we haven't gotten to arrays yet) of strings to be concatenated, and hand it the string that is to be inserted between all of them:

```
let s = "hello"
let s2 = "world"
let space = " "
let greeting = [s,s2].joined(separator:space)
```

The comparison operators are also overloaded so that they all work with String operands. Two String values are equal (==) if they are, in the natural sense of the words, "the same text." A String is less than another if it is alphabetically prior.

A few additional convenient instance methods and properties are provided. isEmpty returns a Bool reporting whether this string is the empty string (""). hasPrefix(_:) and hasSuffix(_:) report whether this string starts or ends with another string; for example, "hello".hasPrefix("he") is true. The uppercased and lowercased methods provide uppercase and lowercase versions of the original string.

Coercion between a String and an Int is possible. To make a string that represents an Int, it is sufficient to use string interpolation; alternatively, use the Int as a String initializer, just as if you were coercing between numeric types:

```
let i = 7
let s = String(i) // "7"
```

Your string can also represent an Int in some other base; supply a radix: argument expressing the base:

```
let i = 31
let s = String(i, radix:16) // "1f"
```

A String that might represent a number can be coerced to a numeric type; an integer type will accept a radix: argument expressing the base. The coercion might fail, though, because the String might *not* represent a number of the specified type; so the result is not a number but an Optional wrapping a number (I haven't talked about Optionals yet, so you'll have to trust me for now; failable initializers are discussed in Chapter 4):

```
let s = "31"
let i = Int(s) // Optional(31)
let s2 = "1f"
let i2 = Int(s2, radix:16) // Optional(31)
```

 Coercion to String is in fact the basis of string interpolation, and of representation in the console with `print`. You can make *any* object coercible to String, by making it conform to any of three protocols: Streamable, CustomStringConvertible, and CustomDebugStringConvertible. I'll give an example when I explain what a protocol is, in Chapter 4.

The length of a String, in characters, is given by the `count` property of its `characters` property:

```
let s = "hello"
let length = s.characters.count // 5
```

Why isn't there simply a `length` property of a String? It's because a String doesn't really have a simple length. The String is stored as a sequence of Unicode codepoints, but multiple Unicode codepoints can combine to form a character; so, in order to know how many characters are represented by such a sequence, we actually have to walk through the sequence and resolve it into the characters that it represents.

You, too, can walk through a String's characters. The simplest way is with the `for...in` construct (see Chapter 5). What you get when you do this are Character objects; I'll talk more about Character objects later:

```
let s = "hello"
for c in s.characters {
    print(c) // print each Character on its own line
}
```

At an even deeper level, you can decompose a String into its UTF-8 codepoints or its UTF-16 codepoints, using the `utf8` and `utf16` properties:

```
let s = "\u{BF}Qui\u{E9}n?"
for i in s.utf8 {
    print(i) // 194, 191, 81, 117, 105, 195, 169, 110, 63
}
for i in s.utf16 {
    print(i) // 191, 81, 117, 105, 233, 110, 63
}
```

There is also a `unicodeScalars` property representing a collection (a `String.Unicode-ScalarView`) of the String's UTF-32 codepoints expressed as UnicodeScalar structs. To illustrate, here's a utility function that turns a two-letter country abbreviation into an emoji representation of its flag:

```
func flag(country:String) -> String {
    let base : UInt32 = 127397
    var s = ""
    for v in country.unicodeScalars {
        s.unicodeScalars.append(UnicodeScalar(base + v.value)!)
    }
    return String(s)
}
// and here's how to use it:
let s = flag(country:"DE")
```

The curious thing is that there aren't more methods for standard string manipulation. How, for example, do you capitalize a string, or find out whether a string contains a given substring? Most modern programming languages have a compact, convenient way of doing things like that; Swift doesn't. The reason appears to be that missing features are provided by the Foundation framework, to which you'll always be linked in real life (importing UIKit imports Foundation). A Swift String is bridged to a Foundation NSString. This means that, to a large extent, Foundation NSString properties and methods magically spring to life whenever you are using a Swift String. For example:

```
let s = "hello world"
let s2 = s.capitalized // "Hello World"
```

The `capitalized` property comes from the Foundation framework; it's provided by Cocoa, not by Swift. It's an NSString property; it appears tacked on to String "for free." Similarly, here's how to locate a substring of a string:

```
let s = "hello"
let range = s.range(of:"ell") // Optional(Range(1..<4))
```

I haven't explained yet what an Optional is or what a Range is (I'll talk about them later in this chapter), but that innocent-looking code has made a remarkable round-trip from Swift to Cocoa and back again: the Swift String s becomes an NSString, an NSString method is called, a Foundation NSRange struct is returned, and the NSRange is converted to a Swift Range and wrapped up in an Optional.

It will often happen, however, that you don't want this round-trip conversion. For various reasons, you might want to stay in the Foundation world and receive the answer as a Foundation NSRange. To accomplish that, you have to cast your string explicitly to an NSString, using the as operator (I'll discuss casting formally in Chapter 4):

```
let s = "hello"
let range = (s as NSString).range(of:"ell") // (1,3), an NSRange
```

Here's another example, also involving NSRange. Suppose you want to derive the string "ell" from "hello" by its range — the second, third, and fourth characters. Foundation's NSString method substring(with:) requires that you supply a range

— meaning an NSRange. You can readily form the NSRange, but when you do, your code doesn't compile:

```
let s = "hello"
let ss = s.substring(with:NSRange(location:1, length:3)) // compile error
```

The reason for the compile error is that Swift has absorbed NSString's substring(with:), and expects you to supply a Swift Range here. I'll explain in a moment how to do that, but you may find it simpler to tell Swift to stay in the Foundation world, by casting:

```
let s = "hello"
let ss = (s as NSString).substring(with:NSRange(location: 1, length:3))
```

Character

The Character object type (a struct) represents a single Unicode grapheme cluster — what you would naturally think of as one character of a string. A String object can be decomposed into a sequence of Character objects by taking its characters property. Formally, this is a String.CharacterView struct; but I'll call it simply a *character sequence*. As I mentioned earlier, you can walk through a character sequence with for...in to obtain the String's Characters, one by one:

```
let s = "hello"
for c in s.characters {
    print(c) // print each Character on its own line
}
```

It isn't common to encounter Character objects outside of some character sequence of which they are a part. There isn't even a way to write a literal Character. To make a Character from scratch, initialize it from a single-character String:

```
let c = Character("h")
```

By the same token, you can initialize a String from a Character:

```
let c = Character("h")
let s = (String(c)).uppercased()
```

Characters can be compared for equality; "less than" means what you would expect it to mean.

A character sequence has many properties and methods that can come in handy. By virtue of being a Collection, it has a first and last property; these are Optionals, because the string might be empty:

```
let s = "hello"
let c1 = s.characters.first // Optional("h")
let c2 = s.characters.last // Optional("o")
```

The index(of:) method locates the first occurrence of a given character within the sequence and returns its index. Again, this is an Optional, because the character might be absent:

```
let s = "hello"
let firstL = s.characters.index(of:"l") // Optional(2)
```

All Swift indexes are numbered starting with 0, so 2 means the third character. The index value here, however, is not an Int; I'll explain in a moment what it is and what it's good for.

By virtue of being a Sequence, a character sequence has a contains(_:) method that returns a Bool, reporting whether a certain character is present:

```
let s = "hello"
let ok = s.characters.contains("o") // true
```

Alternatively, contains(_:) can take a function that takes a Character and returns a Bool. (The index(of:) method has an alternative form, index(where:), that can do this too.) This code reports whether the target string contains a vowel:

```
let s = "hello"
let ok = s.characters.contains {"aeiou".characters.contains($0)} // true
```

The filter(_:) method takes a function that takes a Character and returns a Bool, effectively eliminating those characters for which false is returned. The result is a character sequence, but you can coerce that to a String. Thus, here's how to delete all nonvowels from a String:

```
let s = "hello"
let s2 = String(s.characters.filter {"aeiou".characters.contains($0)}) // "eo"
```

The dropFirst and dropLast methods return (in effect) a new character sequence without the first or last character, respectively:

```
let s = "hello"
let s2 = String(s.characters.dropFirst()) // "ello"
```

prefix(_:) and suffix(_:) extract the character sequence of a given length from the start or end of the original character sequence:

```
let s = "hello"
let s2 = String(s.characters.prefix(4)) // "hell"
```

split(_:) breaks a character sequence up into an array, according to a function that takes a Character and returns a Bool. In this example, I obtain the words of a String, where a "word" is simplemindedly defined as a run of Characters other than a space:

```
let s = "hello world"
let arr = s.characters.split{$0 == " "}
```

The result, once again, is an array of character sequences; to get String objects, we can apply the map(_:) function and coerce them all to Strings. I'll talk about map(_:) in Chapter 4, so you'll have to trust me for now:

```
let s = "hello world"
let arr = s.characters.split{$0 == " "}.map{String($0)} // ["hello", "world"]
```

A String — in reality, its underlying character sequence — can also be manipulated similarly to an array. For example, you can use subscripting to obtain the character at a certain position. Unfortunately, this isn't as easy as it might be. For example, what's the second character of "hello"? This doesn't compile:

```
let s = "hello"
let c = s[1] // compile error
```

The reason is that the indexes on a String (which are actually indexes on its character sequence) are a special nested type, a String.Index (which is actually a type alias for String.CharacterView.Index). To make an object of this type is rather tricky. Start with a String's (or a character sequence's) startIndex or endIndex, or with the return value from the index(of:) method; you can then call the index(_:offsetBy:) method to derive the index you want:

```
let s = "hello"
let ix = s.startIndex
let ix2 = s.index(ix, offsetBy:1)
let c = s[ix2] // "e"
```

The reason for this clumsy circumlocution is that Swift doesn't know where the characters of a character sequence actually are until it walks the sequence; calling `index(_:offsetBy:)` is how you make Swift do that.

To offset an index by a single position, you can obtain the next or preceding index value with the `index(after:)` and `index(before:)` methods. Thus, I could have written the preceding example like this:

```
let s = "hello"
let ix = s.startIndex
let c = s[s.index(after:ix)] // "e"
```

Once you've obtained a desired character index value, you can use it to modify the String. For example, the `insert(contentsOf:at:)` method inserts a character sequence — not a String! — into a String:

```
var s = "hello"
let ix = s.index(s.startIndex, offsetBy:1)
s.insertContentsOf("ey, h".characters, at: ix) // s is now "hey, hello"
```

Similarly, `remove(at:)` deletes a single character, and also returns that character. (Manipulations involving longer character stretches require use of a Range, which is the subject of the next section.)

Note that a character sequence can be coerced directly to an Array of Character objects — for example, `Array("hello".characters)`. It could be worth your while to do that, because array indexes *are* Ints, and are thus easy to work with. Once you've manipulated the array of Characters, you can coerce it directly to a String. I'll give an example in the next section (and I'll discuss arrays, and say more about collections and sequences, in Chapter 4).

Range

The Range object type (a struct) represents a pair of endpoints. There are two operators for forming a Range literal; you supply a start value and an end value, with one of the Range operators between them:

...

Closed range operator. The notation a...b means "everything from a up to b, *including* b."

..<

Half-open range operator. The notation a..<b means "everything from a up to but *not* including b."

Spaces around a Range operator are legal.

The types of a Range's endpoints will typically be some kind of number — most often, Ints:

```
let r = 1...3
```

If the end value is a negative literal, it has to be enclosed in parentheses or preceded by whitespace:

```
let r = -1000 ... -1
```

A very common use of a Range is to loop through numbers with for...in:

```
for ix in 1...3 {
    print(ix) // 1, then 2, then 3
}
```

There are no reverse Ranges: the start value of a Range can't be greater than the end value (the compiler won't stop you, but you'll crash at runtime). In practice, you can use Range's reversed() method to iterate from a higher value to a lower one:

```
for ix in (1...3).reversed() {
    print(ix) // 3, then 2, then 1
}
```

In Chapter 5 I'll show how to create a custom operator that effectively generates a reverse Range.

You can also use a Range's contains(_:) instance method to test whether a value falls within given limits:

```
let ix = // ... an Int ...
if (1...3).contains(ix) { // ...
```

For purposes of testing containment, a Range's endpoints can be Doubles:

```
let d = // ... a Double ...
if (0.1...0.9).contains(d) { // ...
```

There are also methods for learning whether two ranges overlap, and for clamping one range to another.

Another common use of a Range is to index into a sequence. For example, here's one way to get the second, third, and fourth characters of a String. As I suggested at the end of the preceding section, we coerce the String's characters to an Array; we can then use an Int Range as an index into that array, and coerce back to a String:

```
let s = "hello"
let arr = Array(s.characters)
let result = arr[1...3]
let s2 = String(result) // "ell"
```

Alternatively, you can use a Range to index directly into a String (or its underlying character sequence), but then it has to be a Range of String.Index, which, as I've already pointed out, is rather clumsy to obtain. One way to get one is to let Swift convert the NSRange that you get back from a Cocoa method call into a Swift Range for you:

```
let s = "hello"
let r = s.range(of:"ell") // a Swift Range (wrapped in an Optional)
```

You can also generate your Range endpoints as index values. Once you have a Range of the proper type, you can extract a substring by subscripting:

```
let s = "hello"
let ix1 = s.index(s.startIndex, offsetBy:1)
let ix2 = s.index(ix1, offsetBy:2)
let s2 = s[ix1...ix2] // "ell"
```

The `replaceSubrange(_:with:)` method splices into a range, thus modifying the string:

```
var s = "hello"
let ix = s.startIndex
let r = s.index(ix, offsetBy:1)...s.index(ix, offsetBy:3)
s.replaceSubrange(r, with: "ipp") // s is now "hippo"
```

Similarly, you can delete a stretch of characters with the `removeSubrange(_:)` method:

```
var s = "hello"
let ix = s.startIndex
let r = s.index(ix, offsetBy:1)...s.index(ix, offsetBy:3)
s.removeSubrange(r) // s is now "ho"
```

A Swift Range and a Cocoa NSRange are constructed very differently from one another. A Swift Range is defined by two endpoints. A Cocoa NSRange is defined by a starting point and a length. But you can coerce a Swift Range whose endpoints are Ints to an NSRange, and you can convert from an NSRange to a Swift Range with the toRange method (which returns an Optional wrapping a Range).

Sometimes, Swift goes even further. For example, when we say "hello".range(of:"ell"), Swift bridges between Range and NSRange for us, correctly taking account of the fact that Swift and Cocoa interpret characters and string length differently, as well as the fact that an NSRange's values are Ints, while the endpoints of a Range describing a Swift substring are String.Index.

Tuple

A *tuple* is a lightweight custom ordered collection of multiple values. As a type, it is expressed by surrounding the types of the contained values with parentheses and separating them by commas. For example, here's a declaration for a variable whose type is a tuple of an Int and a String:

```
var pair : (Int, String)
```

The literal value of a tuple is expressed in the same way — the contained values, surrounded with parentheses and separated by commas:

```
var pair : (Int, String) = (1, "Two")
```

Those types can be inferred, so there's no need for the explicit type in the declaration:

```
var pair = (1, "Two")
```

Tuples are a pure Swift language feature; they are not compatible with Cocoa and Objective-C, so you'll use them only for values that Cocoa never sees. Within Swift, however, they have many uses. For example, a tuple is an obvious solution to the problem that a function can return only one value; a tuple *is* one value, but it *contains* multiple values, so using a tuple as the return type of a function permits that function to return multiple values.

Tuples come with numerous linguistic conveniences. You can assign to a tuple of variable names as a way of assigning to multiple variables simultaneously:

```
var ix: Int
var s: String
(ix, s) = (1, "Two")
```

That's such a convenient thing to do that Swift lets you do it in one line, declaring and initializing multiple variables simultaneously:

```
var (ix, s) = (1, "Two") // can use let or var here
```

To ignore one of the assigned values, use an underscore to represent it in the receiving tuple:

```
let pair = (1, "Two")
let (_, s) = pair // now s is "Two"
```

Assigning variable values to one another through a tuple swaps them safely:

```
var s1 = "hello"
var s2 = "world"
(s1, s2) = (s2, s1) // now s1 is "world" and s2 is "hello"
```

 There's also a global function swap that swaps values in a more general way.

The enumerated method lets you walk a sequence with for...in and receive, on each iteration, each successive element's index number along with the element itself; this double result comes to you as — you guessed it — a tuple:

```
let s = "hello"
for (ix,c) in s.characters.enumerated() {
    print("character \(ix) is \(c)")
}
```

I also pointed out earlier that numeric instance methods such as addWithOverflow return a tuple.

You can refer to the individual elements of a tuple directly, in two ways. The first way is by index number, using a *literal number* (not a variable value) as the name of a message sent to the tuple with dot-notation:

```
let pair = (1, "Two")
let ix = pair.0 // now ix is 1
```

If you have a var reference to a tuple, you can assign into it by the same means:

```
var pair = (1, "Two")
pair.0 = 2 // now pair is (2, "Two")
```

The second way to access tuple elements is to give them labels. The notation is like that of function parameters, and must appear as part of the explicit or implicit type declaration. Thus, here's one way to establish tuple element labels:

```
let pair : (first:Int, second:String) = (1, "Two")
```

And here's another way:

```
let pair = (first:1, second:"Two")
```

The labels are now part of the type of this value, and travel with it through subsequent assignments. You can then use them as literal messages, just like (and together with) the numeric literals:

```
var pair = (first:1, second:"Two")
let x = pair.first // 1
pair.first = 2
let y = pair.0 // 2
```

You can assign from a tuple without labels into a corresponding tuple with labels (and *vice versa*):

```
let pair = (1, "Two")
let pairWithNames : (first:Int, second:String) = pair
let ix = pairWithNames.first // 1
```

You can also pass, or return from a function, a tuple without labels where a corresponding tuple with labels is expected:

```
func tupleMaker() -> (first:Int, second:String) {
    return (1, "Two") // no labels here
}
let ix = tupleMaker().first // 1
```

If you're going to be using a certain type of tuple consistently throughout your program, it might be useful to give it a type name. To do so, use Swift's typealias keyword. For example, in my LinkSame app I have a Board class describing and manipulating the game layout. The board is a grid of Piece objects. I needed a way to describe positions of the grid. That's a pair of integers, so I define my own type as a tuple:

```
class Board {
    typealias Point = (x:Int, y:Int)
    // ...
}
```

The advantage of that notation is that it now becomes easy to use Points throughout my code. For example, given a Point, I can fetch the corresponding Piece:

```
func piece(at p:Point) -> Piece? {
    let (i,j) = p
    // ... error-checking goes here ...
    return self.grid[i][j]
}
```

 Void, the type of value returned by a function that doesn't return a value, is actually a type alias for an empty tuple. That's why it is also notated as ().

Optional

The Optional object type (an enum) wraps another object of any type. What makes an Optional optional is this: it *might* wrap another object, but then again it might not. Think of an Optional as being itself a kind of shoebox — a shoebox which can quite legally be empty.

Let's start by creating an Optional that does wrap an object. Suppose we want an Optional wrapping the String "howdy". One way to create it is with the Optional initializer:

```
var stringMaybe = Optional("howdy")
```

If we log stringMaybe to the console with print, we'll see an expression identical to the corresponding initializer: Optional("howdy").

After that declaration and initialization, stringMaybe is typed, not as a String, nor as an Optional plain and simple, but as an Optional wrapping a String. This means that any other Optional wrapping a String can be assigned to it — but not an Optional wrapping some other type. This code is legal:

```
var stringMaybe = Optional("howdy")
stringMaybe = Optional("farewell")
```

This code, however, is not legal:

```
var stringMaybe = Optional("howdy")
stringMaybe = Optional(123) // compile error
```

Optional(123) is an Optional wrapping an Int, and you can't assign an Optional wrapping an Int where an Optional wrapping a String is expected.

Optionals are so important to Swift that special syntax for working with them is baked into the language. The usual way to make an Optional is not to use the Optional initializer (though you can certainly do that), but to assign or pass a value of some type to a reference that is already typed as an Optional wrapping that type. This seems as if it should not be legal — but it is. For example, once `stringMaybe` is typed as an Optional wrapping a String, it is legal to assign a String directly to it. The outcome is that the assigned String is wrapped in an Optional for us, automatically:

```
var stringMaybe = Optional("howdy")
stringMaybe = "farewell" // now stringMaybe is Optional("farewell")
```

We also need a way of typing something *explicitly* as an Optional wrapping a String. Otherwise, we cannot declare a variable or parameter with an Optional type. Formally, an Optional is a generic, so an Optional wrapping a String is an `Optional<String>` (I'll explain that syntax in Chapter 4). However, you don't have to write that. The Swift language supports syntactic sugar for expressing an Optional type: use the name of the wrapped type followed by a question mark. For example:

```
var stringMaybe : String?
```

Thus I don't need to use the Optional initializer at all. I can type the variable as an Optional wrapping a String and assign a String into it for wrapping, all in one move:

```
var stringMaybe : String? = "howdy"
```

That, in fact, is the normal way to make an Optional in Swift.

Once you've got an Optional wrapping a particular type, you can use it wherever an Optional wrapping that type is expected — just like any other value. If a function expects an Optional wrapping a String as its parameter, you can pass `stringMaybe` as argument to that parameter:

```
func optionalExpecter(_ s:String?) {}
let stringMaybe : String? = "howdy"
optionalExpecter(stringMaybe)
```

Moreover, where an Optional wrapping a certain type of value is expected, you can pass a value of that wrapped type instead. That's because parameter passing is just like assignment: an unwrapped value will be wrapped implicitly for you. For example, if a function expects an Optional wrapping a String, you can pass a String argument, which will be wrapped into an Optional in the received parameter:

```
func optionalExpecter(_ s:String?) {
    // ... here, s will be an Optional wrapping a String ...
    print(s)
}
optionalExpecter("howdy") // console prints: Optional("howdy")
```

But you cannot do the opposite — you cannot use an Optional wrapping a type where the wrapped type is expected. This won't compile:

```
func realStringExpecter(_ s:String) {}
let stringMaybe : String? = "howdy"
realStringExpecter(stringMaybe) // compile error
```

The error message reads: "Value of optional type String? not unwrapped; did you mean to use ! or ??" You're going to be seeing that sort of message a lot in Swift, so get used to it! As that message suggests, if you want to use an Optional where the type of thing it wraps is expected, you must *unwrap* the Optional — that is, you must reach inside it and *retrieve* the actual thing that it wraps. Now I'm going to talk about how to do that.

Unwrapping an Optional

We have seen more than one way to wrap an object in an Optional. But what about the opposite procedure? How do we unwrap an Optional to get at the object wrapped inside it? One way is to use the *unwrap operator* (or *forced unwrap operator*), which is a postfixed exclamation mark. For example:

```
func realStringExpecter(_ s:String) {}
let stringMaybe : String? = "howdy"
realStringExpecter(stringMaybe!)
```

In that code, the stringMaybe! syntax expresses the operation of reaching inside the Optional stringMaybe, grabbing the wrapped value, and substituting it at that point. Since stringMaybe is an Optional wrapping a String, the thing inside it is a String. That is exactly what the realStringExpecter function wants as its parameter! string-Maybe is an Optional *wrapping* the String "howdy", but stringMaybe! *is* the String "howdy".

If an Optional wraps a certain type, you cannot send it a message expected by that type. You must unwrap it first. For example, let's try to get an uppercase version of stringMaybe:

```
let stringMaybe : String? = "howdy"
let upper = stringMaybe.uppercased() // compile error
```

The solution is to unwrap stringMaybe to get at the String inside it. We can do this directly, in place, using the unwrap operator:

```
let stringMaybe : String? = "howdy"
let upper = stringMaybe!.uppercased()
```

If an Optional is to be used several times where the unwrapped type is expected, and if you're going to be unwrapping it with the unwrap operator each time, your code can quickly start to look like the dialog from a 1960s Batman comic. For example, in iOS programming, an app's window is an Optional UIWindow property of the app delegate (self.window):

```
// self.window is an Optional wrapping a UIWindow
self.window!.rootViewController = RootViewController()
self.window!.backgroundColor = UIColor.white
self.window!.makeKeyAndVisible()
```

That sort of thing soon gets old (or silly). One obvious alternative is to assign the unwrapped value *once* to a variable of the wrapped type and then use that variable:

```
// self.window is an Optional wrapping a UIWindow
let window = self.window!
// now window (not self.window) is a UIWindow, not an Optional
window.rootViewController = RootViewController()
window.backgroundColor = UIColor.white
window.makeKeyAndVisible()
```

However, there's another way, as I shall now explain.

Implicitly unwrapped Optional

Swift provides another way of using an Optional where the wrapped type is expected: you can declare the Optional *type* as being *implicitly unwrapped*. An implicitly unwrapped Optional is an Optional, but the compiler permits some special magic associated with it: its value can be used *directly* where the wrapped type is expected. You *can* unwrap an implicitly unwrapped Optional explicitly, but you don't have to, because it will be unwrapped for you, automatically, if you try to use it where the wrapped type is expected. As with Optional, Swift provides syntactic sugar for expressing an implicitly unwrapped Optional type. Just as an Optional wrapping a String can be expressed as String?, an implicitly unwrapped Optional wrapping a String can be expressed as String!. For example:

```
func realStringExpecter(_ s:String) {}
var stringMaybe : String! = "howdy"
realStringExpecter(stringMaybe) // no problem
```

Bear in mind that *an implicitly unwrapped Optional is still an Optional*. It's just a convenience. By declaring something as an implicitly unwrapped Optional, you are asking the compiler, if you happen to use this value where the wrapped type is expected, to forgive you and to unwrap the value for you.

As far as their *values* are concerned, a normal Optional wrapping a certain type (such as a String?) and an implicitly unwrapped Optional wrapping that same type (such as a String!) are considered interchangeable: you can pass either one where either one is expected.

In Swift 3, however, an implicitly unwrapped Optional type is not really a distinct type; it is merely an Optional marked in a special way that allows it to be used where the unwrapped type is expected. As a result, certain behaviors that were previously legal are no longer permitted. For example, implicit unwrapping does not propagate by assignment. Here's a case in point. If `self` is a UIViewController, then `self.view` is typed as UIView!. As a result, this expression is legal:

```
self.view.addSubview(v)
```

But this is not legal:

```
let mainview = self.view
mainview.addSubview(v) // compile error
```

The problem is that, although `self.view` is an implicitly unwrapped Optional wrapping a UIView, `mainview` is a *normal* Optional wrapping a UIView, and so it would have to be unwrapped explicitly before you could send it the `addSubview` message. Alternatively, you could unwrap the implicitly unwrapped Optional explicitly at the outset:

```
let mainview = self.view!
mainview.addSubview(v)
```

The magic word nil

I have talked so far about Optionals that contain a wrapped value. But what about an Optional that *doesn't* contain any wrapped value? Such an Optional is, as I've already said, a perfectly legal entity; that, indeed, is the whole point of Optionals.

You are going to need a way to *ask* whether an Optional contains a wrapped value, and a way to *specify* an Optional *without* a wrapped value. Swift makes both of those things easy, through the use of a special keyword, `nil`:

To learn whether an Optional contains a wrapped value
> Test the Optional for equality against `nil`. If the test succeeds, the Optional is empty. An empty Optional is also reported in the console as `nil`.

To specify an Optional with no wrapped value
> Assign or pass `nil` where the Optional type is expected. The result is an Optional of the expected type, containing no wrapped value.

For example:

```
var stringMaybe : String? = "Howdy"
print(stringMaybe) // Optional("Howdy")
if stringMaybe == nil {
    print("it is empty") // does not print
}
stringMaybe = nil
```

```
print(stringMaybe) // nil
if stringMaybe == nil {
    print("it is empty") // prints
}
```

The magic word `nil` lets you express the concept, "an Optional wrapping the appropriate type, but not actually containing any object of that type." Clearly, that's very convenient magic; you'll want to take advantage of it. It is very important to understand, however, that it *is* magic: `nil` in Swift is *not* a thing and is *not* a value. *It is a shorthand.* It is natural to think and speak as if this shorthand were real. For example, I will say that something "is `nil`." But in reality, nothing "is `nil`"; `nil` isn't a thing. What I really mean is that this thing is equatable with `nil`, because it is an Optional not wrapping anything. (I'll explain in Chapter 4 how `nil`, and Optionals in general, really work.)

Because a variable typed as an Optional can be `nil`, Swift follows a special initialization rule: a variable (`var`) typed as an Optional *is* `nil`, automatically. This is legal:

```
func optionalExpecter(_ s:String?) {}
var stringMaybe : String?
optionalExpecter(stringMaybe)
```

That code is interesting because it looks as if it should be illegal. We declared a variable `stringMaybe`, but we never assigned it a value. Nevertheless we are now passing it around as if it were an actual thing. That's because it *is* an actual thing. This variable has been *implicitly initialized* — to `nil`. A variable (`var`) typed as an Optional is the *only* sort of variable that gets implicit initialization in Swift.

We come now to perhaps the most important rule in all of Swift: You *cannot unwrap an Optional containing nothing* (an Optional equatable with `nil`). Such an Optional contains nothing; there's nothing to unwrap. Like Oakland, there's no there there. In fact, explicitly unwrapping an Optional containing nothing will *crash your program* at runtime:

```
var stringMaybe : String?
let s = stringMaybe! // crash
```

The crash message reads: "Fatal error: unexpectedly found `nil` while unwrapping an Optional value." Get used to it, because you're going to be seeing it a lot. This is an easy mistake to make. Unwrapping an Optional that contains no value is, in fact, probably the most common way to crash a Swift program. You should look upon this kind of crash as a blessing. Very often, in fact, you will *want* to crash if your Optional contains no value, because it *should* contain a value, and the fact that it doesn't indicates that you've made a mistake elsewhere.

In the long run, however, crashing is bad. To eliminate this kind of crash, you need to ensure that your Optional contains a value, and *don't* unwrap it if it doesn't! Ensuring that an Optional contains a value before attempting to unwrap it is clearly a very important thing to do. Accordingly, Swift provides several convenient ways of doing it. I'll describe some of them now, and I'll discuss others in Chapter 5.

One obvious approach is to test your Optional against `nil` explicitly before you unwrap it:

```
var stringMaybe : String?
// ... stringMaybe might be assigned a real value here ...
if stringMaybe != nil {
    let s = stringMaybe!
    // ...
}
```

But there's a more elegant way, as I shall now explain.

Optional chains

A common situation is that you want to send a message to the value wrapped inside an Optional. To do so, you can unwrap the Optional in place. I gave an example earlier:

```
let stringMaybe : String? = "howdy"
let upper = stringMaybe!.uppercased()
```

That form of code is called an *Optional chain*. In the middle of a chain of dot-notation, you have unwrapped an Optional.

You *cannot* send a message to an Optional *without* unwrapping it. Optionals themselves don't respond to any messages. (Well, they do respond to some messages, but very few, and you are unlikely to use them — and in any case they are not the messages to which the thing inside them responds.) If you try to send to an Optional a message intended for the thing inside it, you will get an error message from the compiler:

```
let stringMaybe : String? = "howdy"
let upper = stringMaybe.uppercased() // compile error
```

We have already seen, however, that if you unwrap an Optional that contains no wrapped object, you'll crash. So what if you're *not sure* whether this Optional contains a wrapped object? How can you send a message to an Optional in that situation? Swift provides a special shorthand for exactly this purpose. To send a message *safely* to an Optional that might be empty, you can *unwrap the Optional optionally*. To do so, unwrap the Optional with the question mark postfix operator instead of the exclamation mark:

```
var stringMaybe : String?
// ... stringMaybe might be assigned a real value here ...
let upper = stringMaybe?.uppercased()
```

That's an Optional chain in which you used a question mark to unwrap the Optional. By using that notation, you have unwrapped the Optional optionally — meaning conditionally. The condition in question is one of safety; a test for nil is performed for us. Our code means: "If stringMaybe contains a String, unwrap it and send it the uppercased message. If it doesn't (that is, if it equates to nil), *do not* unwrap it and *do not* send it any messages!"

Such code is a double-edged sword. On the one hand, if stringMaybe is nil, you won't crash at runtime. On the other hand, if stringMaybe is nil, that line of code won't do anything useful — you won't get any uppercase string.

But now there's a new question. In that code, we initialized a variable upper to an expression that involves sending the uppercased message. Now it turns out that the uppercased message might not even be sent. So what, exactly, is upper initialized *to*?

To handle this situation, Swift has a special rule. If an Optional chain contains an optionally unwrapped Optional, and if this Optional chain produces a value, that value is itself *wrapped in an Optional*. Thus, upper is typed as an Optional wrapping a String. This works brilliantly, because it covers both possible cases. Let's say, first, that stringMaybe contains a String:

```
var stringMaybe : String?
stringMaybe = "howdy"
let upper = stringMaybe?.uppercased() // upper is a String?
```

After that code, upper is *not* a String; it is *not* "HOWDY". It is an Optional wrapping "HOWDY"! On the other hand, if the attempt to unwrap the Optional fails, the Optional chain can return nil instead:

```
var stringMaybe : String?
let upper = stringMaybe?.uppercased() // upper is a nil String?
```

Unwrapping an Optional optionally in this way is elegant and safe; even if string-Maybe is nil, we won't crash at runtime. On the other hand, we've ended up with yet another Optional on our hands! upper is typed as an Optional wrapping a String, and in order to use that String, we're going to have to unwrap upper. And we don't know whether upper is nil, so we have exactly the same problem we had before — we need to make sure that we unwrap upper safely, and that we don't accidentally unwrap an empty Optional.

Longer Optional chains are legal. No matter how many Optionals are unwrapped in the course of the chain, if any of them is unwrapped optionally, the entire expression produces an Optional wrapping the type it would have produced if the Optionals were unwrapped normally, and is free to fail safely at any point along the way. For example:

```
// self is a UIViewController
let f = self.view.window?.rootViewController?.view.frame
```

The `frame` property of a view is a CGRect. But after that code, `f` is *not* a CGRect. It's an Optional wrapping a CGRect. If *any* of the optional unwrapping along the chain fails (because the Optional we propose to unwrap is `nil`), `f` will be `nil` to indicate failure.

(Observe that the preceding code does *not* end up nesting Optionals; it doesn't produce a CGRect wrapped in an Optional wrapped in an Optional, merely because there are two Optionals being optionally unwrapped in the chain! However, it is possible, for other reasons, to end up with an Optional wrapped in an Optional. I'll give an example in Chapter 4.)

If a function call returns an Optional, you can unwrap the result and use it. You don't necessarily have to capture the result in order to do that; you can unwrap it in place, by putting an exclamation mark or a question mark after the function call (that is, after the closing parenthesis). That's really no different from what we've been doing all along, except that instead of an Optional property or variable, this is a function call that returns an Optional. For example:

```
class Dog {
    var noise : String?
    func speak() -> String? {
        return self.noise
    }
}
let d = Dog()
let bigname = d.speak()?.uppercased()
```

After that, don't forget, `bigname` is not a String — it's an Optional wrapping a String.

You can also assign safely into an Optional chain. If any of the optionally unwrapped Optionals in the chain turns out to be `nil`, nothing happens:

```
// self is a UIViewController
self.navigationController?.hidesBarsOnTap = true
```

A view controller might or might not have a navigation controller, so its `navigationController` property is an Optional. In that code, we are setting our navigation controller's `hidesBarsOnTap` property safely; if we happen to have no navigation controller, no harm is done — because nothing happens.

When assigning into an Optional chain, if you also want to know whether the assignment succeeded, you can capture the result of the assignment as an Optional wrapping a Void and test it for `nil`. For example:

```
let ok : Void? = self.navigationController?.hidesBarsOnTap = true
```

Now, if `ok` is not `nil`, `self.navigationController` was safely unwrapped and the assignment succeeded.

The ! and ? postfix operators, which respectively unconditionally and condition-ally unwrap an Optional, have basically *nothing* to do with the ! and ? used with type names as syntactic sugar for expressing Optional types (such as String? to mean an Optional wrapping a String, and String! to mean an implicitly unwrapped Optional wrapping a String). The outward similarity has confused many a beginner.

Comparison with Optional

In an equality comparison with something other than nil, an Optional gets special treatment: the wrapped value, not the Optional itself, is compared. So, for example, this works:

```
let s : String? = "Howdy"
if s == "Howdy" { // ... they _are_ equal!
```

That shouldn't work — how can an Optional be the same as a String? — but it does. Instead of comparing the Optional itself with "Howdy", Swift automagically (and safely) compares its wrapped value (if there is one) with "Howdy", and the comparison succeeds. If the wrapped value is not "Howdy", the comparison fails. If there is *no* wrapped value (s is nil), the comparison fails too — safely! Thus, you can compare s to nil or to a String, and the comparison works correctly in all cases.

The same, however, is *not* true for an inequality comparison, using the greater-than and less-than operators:

```
let i : Int? = 2
if i < 3 { // compile error
```

Such code was legal in Swift 2 and before, but in Swift 3 it isn't, partly because the implementation was buggy, and partly because such an expression might represent a programming mistake that the compiler couldn't catch. The loss is not a serious one, as you can always unwrap safely and perform the comparison directly on the unwrap-ped value:

```
if i != nil && i! < 3 { // ... it _is_ less
```

Do not compare an implicitly unwrapped Optional with anything; you can crash at runtime (and, as of this writing, you can even crash the compiler).

Why Optionals?

Now that you know *how* to use an Optional, you are probably wondering *why* to use an Optional. Why does Swift have Optionals at all? What are they good for?

One very important purpose of Optionals is to provide *interchange of object values with Objective-C*. In Objective-C, *any* object reference can be nil. You thus need a way to send `nil` to Objective-C and to receive `nil` from Objective-C. Swift Optionals provide your only way to do that.

Swift will typically assist you by a judicious use of appropriate types in the Cocoa APIs. For example, consider a UIView's `backgroundColor` property. It's a UIColor, but it can be `nil`, and you are allowed to set it to `nil`. Thus, it is typed as a `UIColor?`. You don't need to work directly with Optionals in order to *set* such a value! Remember, assigning the wrapped type to an Optional is legal, as the assigned value will be wrapped for you. Thus, you can set `myView.backgroundColor` to a UIColor — or to `nil`. But if you *get* a UIView's `backgroundColor`, you now have an Optional wrapping a UIColor, *and you must be conscious of this fact*, for all the reasons I've already discussed: if you're not, surprising things can happen:

```
let v = UIView()
let c = v.backgroundColor
let c2 = c.withAlphaComponent(0.5) // compile error
```

You're trying to send the `withAlphaComponent` message to c, as if it were a UIColor. It *isn't* a UIColor. It's an Optional wrapping a UIColor. Xcode will try to help you in this situation; if you use code completion (Chapter 9) to enter the name of the `withAlpha-Component` method, Xcode will insert a question mark after c, thus (optionally) unwrapping the Optional and giving you legal code:

```
let v = UIView()
let c = v.backgroundColor
let c2 = c?.withAlphaComponent(0.5)
```

In the vast majority of situations, however, a Cocoa object type will *not* be marked as an Optional. That's because, although in *theory* it *could* be `nil` (because any Objective-C object reference can be `nil`), in practice it won't be. Swift thus saves you a step by treating the value as the object type itself. This magic is performed by hand-tweaking the Cocoa APIs (also called *auditing*). In the very first public version of Swift (in June of 2014), *all* object values received from Cocoa were in fact typed as Optionals (usually implicitly unwrapped Optionals). But then Apple embarked on the massive project of hand-tweaking the APIs to eliminate Optionals that didn't need to be Optionals, and in Swift 3 and Xcode 8, that project is essentially complete.

Another important use of Optionals is to *defer initialization* of an instance property. If a variable (declared with `var`) is typed as an Optional, it has a value even if you don't initialize it — namely `nil`. That comes in very handy in situations where you know something *will* have a value, but not right away. A typical example in real-life iOS programming is an outlet, which is a reference to something in your interface such as a button:

```
class ViewController: UIViewController {
    @IBOutlet var myButton: UIButton!
    // ...
}
```

Ignore, for now, the @IBOutlet designation, which is an internal hint to Xcode (as I'll explain in Chapter 7). The important thing is that this property, myButton, won't have a value when our ViewController instance first comes into existence, but shortly thereafter the view controller's view will be loaded and myButton will be set so that it points to an actual UIButton object in the interface. Therefore, the variable is typed as an implicitly unwrapped Optional. It's an Optional because we need a placeholder value (namely nil) for myButton when the ViewController instance first comes into existence. It's implicitly unwrapped so that in our code, once self.myButton has been assigned a UIButton value, we can treat it as a reference to an actual UIButton, passing through the Optional without noticing that it *is* an Optional.

A closely related situation is when a variable, again typically an instance property, represents data that will take time to acquire. For example, in my Albumen app, as we launch, I create an instance of my root view controller. I also want to gather a bunch of data about the user's music library and store that data in instance properties of the root view controller instance. But gathering that data will take time. Therefore I must instantiate the root view controller *first* and gather the data *later*, because if we pause to gather the data *before* instantiating the root view controller, the app will take too long to launch — the delay will be perceptible, and we might even crash (because iOS forbids long launch times). Therefore the data properties are all typed as Optionals; they are nil until the data are gathered, at which time they are assigned their "real" values:

```
class RootViewController : UITableViewController {
    var albums : [MPMediaItemCollection]! // initialized to nil
    // ...
```

Finally, one of the most important uses of Optionals is to permit a value to be *marked as empty or erroneous*. The preceding code is a good illustration. When my Albumen app launches, it displays a table listing all the user's music albums. At launch time, however, that data has not yet been gathered. My table-display code tests albums to see whether it's nil and, if it is, displays an empty table. After gathering the data, I tell my table to display its data *again*. This time, the table-display code finds that albums is *not* nil, but rather consists of actual data — and it now displays that data. The use of an Optional allows one and the same value, albums, to store the data or to state that there is no data.

Many built-in Swift functions use an Optional in a similar way. For example:

```
let arr = [1,2,3]
let ix = arr.index(of:4)
if ix == nil { // ...
```

Swift's index(of:) method returns an Optional because the object sought might not be present, in which case it has no index at all. The type returned cannot be an Int, because there is no Int value that can be taken to mean, "I didn't find this object at all." Returning an Optional solves the problem neatly: nil means "I didn't find the object," and otherwise the actual Int result is sitting there wrapped up in the Optional.

Swift is cleverer than Objective-C in this regard. If a reference is an object, Objective-C can return nil to report failure; but not everything in Objective-C is an object. Thus, many important Cocoa methods do return a special value to indicate failure, and you have to know this and remember to test for it.

For example, if you call NSArray's index(of:) (as opposed to Swift Array's index(of:)), the result *is* an Int, not an Optional wrapping an Int. To indicate that the object wasn't found at all, Cocoa must fall back on returning an Int with a special meaning — namely, NSNotFound, which is actually just a very large negative number. And you have to remember to test for this:

```
let arr = [1,2,3]
let ix = (arr as NSArray).indexOfObject(4)
if ix == NSNotFound { // ...
```

In some cases, Swift will help you by bridging intelligently from Objective-C. For example, NSString's range(of:) might not find the given substring in the target string; in that case, it returns an NSRange whose length is zero and whose location is (you guessed it) NSNotFound. Fortunately, a knowledge of this fact is built into the Swift bridge to the Cocoa API: Swift types the returned value as an Optional wrapping a Range, and if range(of:) does return an NSRange whose location is NSNotFound, Swift neatly expresses it as nil.

CHAPTER 4

Object Types

In the preceding chapter, I discussed some built-in object types. But I have not yet explained object types themselves. As I mentioned in Chapter 1, Swift object types come in three flavors: enum, struct, and class. What are the differences between them? And how would you create your own object type? That's what this chapter is about.

I'll describe object types in general, and then each of the three flavors. Then I'll explain three Swift ways of giving an object type greater flexibility: protocols, generics, and extensions. Finally, the survey of Swift's built-in types will conclude with three umbrella types and three collection types.

Object Type Declarations and Features

Object types are declared with the flavor of the object type (enum, struct, or class), the name of the object type (which should start with a capital letter), and curly braces:

```
class Manny {
}
struct Moe {
}
enum Jack {
}
```

The visibility (*scope*), and hence the usability, of an object type by other code depends upon where its declaration appears:

- Object types declared at the *top level of a file* will, by default, be visible to all files in the same module. This is the usual place for object type declarations.

- Sometimes it's useful to declare a type *inside the declaration of another type*, thus giving it a namespace. This is called a *nested type*.

- An object type declared *within the body of a function* will exist only inside the scope of the curly braces that surround it; such declarations are legal but rare.

Declarations for any object type may contain within their curly braces the following things:

Initializers

An object type is merely the *type* of an object. The purpose of declaring an object type will usually (though not always) be so that you can make an actual object — an *instance* — that *has* this type. An initializer is a function, declared and called in a special way, allowing you to do that.

Properties

A variable declared at the top level of an object type declaration is a *property*. By default, it is an *instance property*. An instance property is scoped to an instance: it is accessed through a particular instance of this type, and its value can be different for every instance of this type.

Alternatively, a property can be a *static/class property*. For an enum or struct, it is declared with the keyword `static`; for a class, it may instead be declared with the keyword `class`. Such a property belongs to the object type itself: it is accessed through the type, and it has just one value, associated with the type.

Methods

A function declared at the top level of an object type declaration is a *method*. By default, it is an *instance method*: it is called by sending a message to a particular instance of this type. Inside an instance method, `self` is the instance.

Alternatively, a method can be a *static/class method*. For an enum or struct, it is declared with the keyword `static`; for a class, it may be declared instead with the keyword `class`. It is called by sending a message to the type. Inside a static/class method, `self` is the type.

Subscripts

A subscript is a special kind of instance method. It is called by appending square brackets to an instance reference.

Object type declarations

An object type declaration can contain an object type declaration — a nested type. From inside the containing object type, the nested type is in scope; from outside the containing object type, the nested type must be referred to through the containing object type. Thus, the containing object type is a namespace for the nested type.

Initializers

An *initializer* is a function called in order to bring an instance of an object type into existence. Strictly speaking, it is a static/class method, because it is called by talking to the object type. It is usually called using special syntax: the name of the type is followed directly by parentheses, as if the type itself were a function. When an initializer is called, a new instance is created and returned as a result. You will usually do something with the returned instance, such as assigning it to a variable, in order to preserve it and work with it in subsequent code.

For example, suppose we have a Dog class:

```
class Dog {
}
```

Then we can make a Dog instance like this:

```
Dog()
```

That code, however, though legal, is silly — so silly that it warrants a warning from the compiler. We have created a Dog instance, but there is no reference to that instance. Without such a reference, the Dog instance comes into existence and then immediately vanishes in a puff of smoke. The usual sort of thing is more like this:

```
let fido = Dog()
```

Now our Dog instance will persist as long as the variable fido persists (see Chapter 3) — and the variable fido gives us a reference to our Dog instance, so that we can use it.

Observe that Dog() calls an initializer even though our Dog class doesn't declare any initializers! The reason is that object types may have *implicit initializers*. These are a convenience that save you the trouble of writing your own initializers. But you *can* write your own initializers, and you will often do so.

An initializer is a kind of function, and its declaration syntax is rather like that of a function. To declare an initializer, you use the keyword init followed by a parameter list, followed by curly braces containing the code. An object type can have multiple initializers, distinguished by their parameters. A frequent use of the parameters is to set the values of instance properties.

For example, here's a Dog class with two instance properties, name (a String) and license (an Int). We give these instance properties default values that are effectively placeholders — an empty string and the number zero. Then we declare three initializers, so that the caller can create a Dog instance in three different ways: by supplying a name, by supplying a license number, or by supplying both. In each initializer, the parameters supplied are used to set the values of the corresponding properties:

```
class Dog {
    var name = ""
    var license = 0
    init(name:String) {
        self.name = name
    }
    init(license:Int) {
        self.license = license
    }
    init(name:String, license:Int) {
        self.name = name
        self.license = license
    }
}
```

Observe that in that code, in each initializer, I've given each parameter the same name as the property to which it corresponds. There's no reason to do that apart from stylistic clarity. In the code for each initializer, I can distinguish the parameter from the property by using self to access the property.

The result of that declaration is that I can create a Dog in three different ways:

```
let fido = Dog(name:"Fido")
let rover = Dog(license:1234)
let spot = Dog(name:"Spot", license:1357)
```

What I *can't* do is to create a Dog with *no* initializer parameters. I wrote initializers, so my implicit initializer went away. This code is no longer legal:

```
let puff = Dog() // compile error
```

Of course, I could *make* that code legal by explicitly declaring an initializer with no parameters:

```
class Dog {
    var name = ""
    var license = 0
    init() {
    }
    init(name:String) {
        self.name = name
    }
    init(license:Int) {
        self.license = license
    }
    init(name:String, license:Int) {
        self.name = name
        self.license = license
    }
}
```

Now, the truth is that we don't need those four initializers, because an initializer is a function, and a function's parameters can have default values. Thus, I can condense all that code into a single initializer, like this:

```
class Dog {
    var name = ""
    var license = 0
    init(name:String = "", license:Int = 0) {
        self.name = name
        self.license = license
    }
}
```

I can still make an actual Dog instance in four different ways:

```
let fido = Dog(name:"Fido")
let rover = Dog(license:1234)
let spot = Dog(name:"Spot", license:1357)
let puff = Dog()
```

Now comes the really interesting part. In my property declarations, I can *eliminate* the assignment of default initial values (as long as I declare explicitly the *type* of each property):

```
class Dog {
    var name : String // no default value!
    var license : Int // no default value!
    init(name:String = "", license:Int = 0) {
        self.name = name
        self.license = license
    }
}
```

That code is legal (and common) — because an initializer initializes! In other words, I don't have to give my properties initial values in their declarations, *provided I give them initial values in all initializers*. That way, I am guaranteed that all my instance properties have values when the instance comes into existence, which is what matters. Conversely, an instance property without an initial value when the instance comes into existence *is illegal*. A property *must* be initialized either as part of its declaration or by every initializer, and the compiler will stop you otherwise.

The Swift compiler's insistence that all instance properties be properly initialized is a valuable feature of Swift. (Contrast Objective-C, where instance properties can go uninitialized — and often do, leading to mysterious errors later.) Don't fight the compiler; work with it. The compiler will help you by giving you an error message ("Return from initializer without initializing all stored properties") until *all* your initializers initialize *all* your instance properties:

```
class Dog {
    var name : String
    var license : Int
    init(name:String = "") {
        self.name = name // compile error
    }
}
```

Because setting an instance property in an initializer counts as initialization, it is legal even if the instance property is a constant declared with let:

```
class Dog {
    let name : String
    let license : Int
    init(name:String = "", license:Int = 0) {
        self.name = name
        self.license = license
    }
}
```

In our artificial examples, we have been very generous with our initializer: we are letting the caller instantiate a Dog without supplying a name: argument or a license: argument. Usually, however, the purpose of an initializer is just the opposite: we want to *force* the caller to supply *all* needed information at instantiation time. Thus, in real life, it is much more likely that our Dog class would look like this:

```
class Dog {
    let name : String
    let license : Int
    init(name:String, license:Int) {
        self.name = name
        self.license = license
    }
}
```

In that code, our Dog has a name property and a license property, and values for these *must* be supplied at instantiation time (there are no default values), and those values can never be changed thereafter (these properties are constants). In this way, we enforce a rule that every Dog must have a meaningful name and license. There is now only *one* way to make a Dog:

```
let spot = Dog(name:"Spot", license:1357)
```

Optional properties

Sometimes, there is no meaningful default value that can be assigned to an instance property during initialization. For example, perhaps the initial value of this property will not be obtained until some time has elapsed *after* this instance has come into existence. This situation conflicts with the requirement that all instance properties be initialized either in their declaration or through an initializer. You could, of course, just circumvent the problem by assigning a default initial value anyway; but this fails to communicate to your own code the fact that this isn't a "real" value.

A sensible and common solution, as I explained in Chapter 3, is to declare your instance property as a var having an Optional type. An Optional has a value, namely nil, signifying that no "real" value has been supplied; and an Optional var is initialized to nil automatically. Thus, your code can test this instance property against nil and, if it is nil, it won't use the property. Later, the property will be given its "real" value. Of course, that value is now wrapped in an Optional; but if you declare this property as an implicitly unwrapped Optional, you can use the wrapped value directly, without explicitly unwrapping it — as if this weren't an Optional at all — once you're sure it is safe to do so:

```
// this property will be set automatically when the nib loads
@IBOutlet var myButton: UIButton!
// this property will be set after time-consuming gathering of data
var albums : [MPMediaItemCollection]!
```

Referring to self

Except in order to set an instance property, an initializer may not refer to self, explicitly or implicitly, until all instance properties have been initialized. This rule guarantees that the instance is fully formed before it is used. This code, for example, is illegal:

```
struct Cat {
    var name : String
    var license : Int
    init(name:String, license:Int) {
        self.name = name
        meow() // too soon - compile error
        self.license = license
    }
    func meow() {
        print("meow")
    }
}
```

The call to the instance method meow is implicitly a reference to self — it means self.meow(). The initializer can say that, but not until it has fulfilled its primary contract of initializing all uninitialized properties. The call to the instance method meow simply needs to be moved down one line, so that it comes *after* both name and license have been initialized.

Delegating initializers

Initializers within an object type can call one another by using the syntax self.init(...). An initializer that calls another initializer is called a *delegating ini-*

tializer. When an initializer delegates, the other initializer — the one that it delegates to — must completely initialize the instance first, and then the delegating initializer can work with the fully initialized instance, possibly setting again a `var` property that was already set by the initializer that it delegated to.

A delegating initializer appears to be an exception to the rule against saying `self` too early. But it isn't, because it is saying `self` in order to delegate — and delegating will cause all instance properties to be initialized. In fact, the rules about a delegating initializer saying `self` are even more stringent: a delegating initializer cannot refer to `self`, *not even* to set a property, until after the call to the other initializer. For example:

```
struct Digit {
    var number : Int
    var meaningOfLife : Bool
    init(number:Int) {
        self.number = number
        self.meaningOfLife = false
    }
    init() { // this is a delegating initializer
        self.init(number:42)
        self.meaningOfLife = true
    }
}
```

Moreover, a delegating initializer cannot set an immutable property (a `let` variable) at all. That is because it cannot refer to the property until after it has called the other initializer, and at that point the instance is fully formed — initialization proper is over, and the door for initialization of immutable properties has closed. Thus, the preceding code would be illegal if `meaningOfLife` were declared with `let`, because the second initializer is a delegating initializer and cannot set an immutable property.

Be careful not to delegate recursively! If you tell an initializer to delegate to itself, or if you create a vicious circle of delegating initializers, the compiler won't stop you (I regard that as a bug), but your running app will hang. For example, don't say this:

```
struct Digit { // do not do this!
    var number : Int = 100
    init(value:Int) {
        self.init(number:value)
    }
    init(number:Int) {
        self.init(value:number)
    }
}
```

Failable initializers

An initializer can return an Optional wrapping the new instance. In this way, nil can be returned to signal failure. An initializer that behaves this way is a *failable initializer*. To mark an initializer as failable when declaring it, put a question mark after the keyword init. If your failable initializer needs to return nil, explicitly write return nil. It is up to the caller to test the resulting Optional for equivalence with nil, unwrap it, and so forth, as with any Optional.

Here's a version of Dog with an initializer that returns an Optional, returning nil if the name: or license: arguments are invalid:

```
class Dog {
    let name : String
    let license : Int
    init?(name:String, license:Int) {
        if name.isEmpty {
            return nil
        }
        if license <= 0 {
            return nil
        }
        self.name = name
        self.license = license
    }
}
```

The resulting value is typed as an Optional wrapping a Dog, and the caller will need to unwrap that Optional (if isn't nil) before sending any messages to it.

Cocoa and Objective-C conventionally return nil from initializers to signal failure; the API for such initializers has been hand-tweaked as a Swift failable initializer if initialization really might fail. For example, the UIImage initializer init?(named:) is a failable initializer, because there might be no image with the given name. It is not implicitly unwrapped, so the resulting value is a UIImage?, and will typically have to be unwrapped before using it. (Most Objective-C initializers, however, are *not* bridged as failable initializers, even though in theory *any* Objective-C initializer might return nil.)

Properties

A *property* is a variable — one that happens to be declared at the top level of an object type declaration. This means that everything said about variables in Chapter 3 applies. A property has a fixed type; it can be declared with var or let; it can be stored or computed; it can have setter observers. An instance property can also be declared lazy.

A stored instance property must be given an initial value. But, as I explained a moment ago, this doesn't have to be through assignment in the declaration; it can be through an initializer instead. Setter observers are not called during initialization of properties.

Code that initializes a property cannot fetch an instance property or call an instance method. Such behavior would require a reference, explicit or implicit, to self; and during initialization, there is no self yet — self is exactly what we are in the process of initializing. Making this mistake can result in some of Swift's most perplexing compile error messages. For example, this is illegal (and removing the explicit references to self doesn't make it legal):

```
class Moi {
    let first = "Matt"
    let last = "Neuburg"
    let whole = self.first + " " + self.last // compile error
}
```

One solution in that situation would be to make whole a computed property:

```
class Moi {
    let first = "Matt"
    let last = "Neuburg"
    var whole : String {
        return self.first + " " + self.last
    }
}
```

That's legal because the computation won't actually be performed until after self exists. Another solution is to declare whole as lazy:

```
class Moi {
    let first = "Matt"
    let last = "Neuburg"
    lazy var whole : String = self.first + " " + self.last
}
```

Again, that's legal because the reference to self won't be performed until after self exists. Similarly, a property initializer can't call an instance method, but a computed property can, and so can a lazy property.

As I demonstrated in Chapter 3, a variable's initializer can consist of multiple lines of code if you write it as a define-and-call anonymous function. If this variable is an instance property, and if that code is to refer to other instance properties or instance methods, the variable must be declared lazy:

```
class Moi {
    let first = "Matt"
    let last = "Neuburg"
    lazy var whole : String = {
        var s = self.first
```

```
            s.append(" ")
            s.append(self.last)
            return s
        }()
    }
```

If a property is an instance property (the default), it can be accessed only through an instance, and its value is separate for each instance. For example, let's start once again with a Dog class:

```
class Dog {
    let name : String
    let license : Int
    init(name:String, license:Int) {
        self.name = name
        self.license = license
    }
}
```

Our Dog class has a name instance property. Then we can make two different Dog instances with two different name values, and we can access each Dog instance's name through the instance:

```
let fido = Dog(name:"Fido", license:1234)
let spot = Dog(name:"Spot", license:1357)
let aName = fido.name // "Fido"
let anotherName = spot.name // "Spot"
```

A static/class property, on the other hand, is accessed through the type, and is scoped to the type, which usually means that it is global and unique. I'll use a struct as an example:

```
struct Greeting {
    static let friendly = "hello there"
    static let hostile = "go away"
}
```

Now code elsewhere can fetch the values of Greeting.friendly and Greeting.hostile. That example is neither artificial nor trivial; immutable static properties are a convenient and effective way to supply your code with nicely name-spaced constants.

Unlike instance properties, static properties can be initialized with reference to one another; the reason is that static property initializers are lazy (see Chapter 3):

```
struct Greeting {
    static let friendly = "hello there"
    static let hostile = "go away"
    static let ambivalent = friendly + " but " + hostile
}
```

Notice the lack of `self` in that code. In static/class code, `self` means the type itself. I like to use `self` explicitly wherever it would be implicit, but here I can't use it without arousing the ire of the compiler (I regard this as a bug). To clarify the status of the terms `friendly` and `hostile`, I can use the name of the type, just as any other code would do:

```
struct Greeting {
    static let friendly = "hello there"
    static let hostile = "go away"
    static let ambivalent = Greeting.friendly + " but " + Greeting.hostile
}
```

On the other hand, if I write `ambivalent` as a computed property, I *can* use `self`:

```
struct Greeting {
    static let friendly = "hello there"
    static let hostile = "go away"
    static var ambivalent : String {
        return self.friendly + " but " + self.hostile
    }
}
```

On the other other hand, I'm not allowed to use `self` when the initial value is set by a define-and-call anonymous function (again, I regard this as a bug):

```
struct Greeting {
    static let friendly = "hello there"
    static let hostile = "go away"
    static var ambivalent : String = {
        return self.friendly + " but " + self.hostile // compile error
    }()
}
```

Methods

A *method* is a function — one that happens to be declared at the top level of an object type declaration. This means that everything said about functions in Chapter 2 applies.

By default, a method is an instance method. This means that it can be accessed only through an instance. Within the body of an instance method, `self` is the instance. To illustrate, let's continue to develop our Dog class:

```
class Dog {
    let name : String
    let license : Int
    let whatDogsSay = "Woof"
    init(name:String, license:Int) {
        self.name = name
        self.license = license
    }
```

```
    func bark() {
        print(self.whatDogsSay)
    }
    func speak() {
        self.bark()
        print("I'm \(self.name)")
    }
}
```

Now I can make a Dog instance and tell it to speak:

```
let fido = Dog(name:"Fido", license:1234)
fido.speak() // Woof I'm Fido
```

In my Dog class, the speak method calls the instance method bark by way of self, and obtains the value of the instance property name by way of self; and the bark instance method obtains the value of the instance property whatDogsSay by way of self. This is because instance code can use self to refer to this instance. Such code can omit self if the reference is unambiguous; thus, for example, I could have written this:

```
func speak() {
    bark()
    print("I'm \(name)")
}
```

But I *never* write code like that (except by accident). Omitting self, in my view, makes the code harder to read and maintain; the loose terms bark and name seem mysterious and confusing. Moreover, sometimes self cannot be omitted. For example, in my implementation of init(name:license:), I *must* use self to disambiguate between the parameter name and the property self.name.

A static/class method is accessed through the type, and self means the type. I'll use our Greeting struct as an example:

```
struct Greeting {
    static let friendly = "hello there"
    static let hostile = "go away"
    static var ambivalent : String {
        return self.friendly + " but " + self.hostile
    }
    static func beFriendly() {
        print(self.friendly)
    }
}
```

And here's how to call the static beFriendly method:

```
Greeting.beFriendly() // hello there
```

There is a kind of conceptual wall between static/class members, on the one hand, and instance members on the other; even though they may be declared within the same object type declaration, they inhabit different worlds. A static/class method can't refer to "the instance" because there is no instance; thus, a static/class method cannot directly refer to any instance properties or call any instance methods. An instance method, on the other hand, can refer to the type by name, and can thus access static/class properties and can call static/class methods.

For example, let's return to our Dog class and grapple with the question of what dogs say. Presume that all dogs say the same thing. We'd prefer, therefore, to express what-DogsSay not at instance level but at class level. This would be a good use of a static property. Here's a simplified Dog class that illustrates:

```
class Dog {
    static var whatDogsSay = "Woof"
    func bark() {
        print(Dog.whatDogsSay)
    }
}
```

Now we can make a Dog instance and tell it to bark:

```
let fido = Dog()
fido.bark() // Woof
```

(I'll talk later in this chapter about another way in which an instance method can refer to the type.)

Subscripts

A *subscript* is an instance method that is called in a special way — by appending square brackets to an instance reference. The square brackets can contain arguments to be passed to the subscript method. You can use this feature for whatever you like, but it is suitable particularly for situations where this is an object type with *elements* that can be appropriately accessed by key or by index number. I have already described (in Chapter 3) the use of this syntax with strings, and it is familiar also from dictionaries and arrays; you can use square brackets with strings and dictionaries and arrays exactly because Swift's String and Dictionary and Array types declare subscript methods.

The syntax for declaring a subscript method is somewhat like a function declaration and somewhat like a computed property declaration. That's no coincidence! A subscript is like a function in that it can take parameters: arguments can appear in the square brackets when a subscript method is called. A subscript is like a computed property in that the call is used like a reference to a property: you can fetch its value or you can assign into it.

To illustrate, I'll write a struct that treats an integer as if it were a digit sequence, returning a digit that can be specified by an index number in square brackets; for simplicity, I'm deliberately omitting any sort of error-checking:

The Secret Life of Instance Methods

Here's a secret: instance methods are actually static/class methods. For example, this is legal (but strange):

```
class MyClass {
    var s = ""
    func store(_ s:String) {
        self.s = s
    }
}
let m = MyClass()
let f = MyClass.store(m) // what just happened!?
```

Even though `store` is an instance method, we are able to call it as a class method — with a parameter that is an instance of this class! The reason is that an instance method is actually a curried static/class method composed of two functions — one function that takes an instance, and another function that takes the parameters of the instance method. Thus, after that code, `f` is the *second* of those functions, and can be called as a way of passing a parameter to the `store` method *of the instance m:*

```
f("howdy")
print(m.s) // howdy
```

```
struct Digit {
    var number : Int
    init(_ n:Int) {
        self.number = n
    }
    subscript(ix:Int) -> Int { ❶ ❷
        get { ❸
            let s = String(self.number)
            return Int(String(s[s.index(s.startIndex, offsetBy:ix)]))!
        }
    }
}
```

❶ After the keyword `subscript` we have a parameter list stating what parameters are to appear inside the square brackets; by default, *their names are not externalized* (I regard this a bug in the language).

❷ Then, after the arrow operator, we have the type of value that is passed out (when the getter is called) or in (when the setter is called); this is parallel to the type declared for a computed property, even though the syntax with the arrow operator is like the syntax for the returned value in a function declaration.

❸ Finally, we have curly braces whose contents are exactly like those of a computed property. You can have `get` and curly braces for the getter, and `set` and curly braces for the setter. If there's a getter and no setter, the word get and its curly braces can be omitted. The setter receives the new value as newValue, but you can change that name by supplying a different name in parentheses after the word set.

Here's an example of calling the getter; the instance with appended square brackets containing the arguments is used just as if you were getting a property value:

```
var d = Digit(1234)
let aDigit = d[1] // 2
```

Now I'll expand my Digit struct so that its subscript method includes a setter (and again I'll omit error-checking):

```
struct Digit {
    var number : Int
    init(_ n:Int) {
        self.number = n
    }
    subscript(ix:Int) -> Int {
        get {
            let s = String(self.number)
            return Int(String(s[s.index(s.startIndex, offsetBy:ix)]))!
        }
        set {
            var s = String(self.number)
            let i = s.index(s.startIndex, offsetBy:ix)
            s.replaceSubrange(i...i, with: String(newValue))
            self.number = Int(s)!
        }
    }
}
```

And here's an example of calling the setter; the instance with appended square brackets containing the arguments is used just as if you were setting a property value:

```
var d = Digit(1234)
d[0] = 2 // now d.number is 2234
```

An object type can declare multiple subscript methods, distinguished by their parameters.

Nested Object Types

An object type may be declared inside an object type declaration, forming a nested type:

```
class Dog {
    struct Noise {
        static var noise = "Woof"
    }
```

```
    func bark() {
        print(Dog.Noise.noise)
    }
}
```

A nested object type is no different from any other object type, but the rules for referring to it from the outside are changed; the surrounding object type acts as a namespace, and must be referred to explicitly in order to access the nested object type:

```
Dog.Noise.noise = "Arf"
```

Here, the Noise struct is namespaced inside the Dog class. This namespacing provides clarity: the name Noise does not float free, but is explicitly associated with the Dog class to which it belongs. Namespacing also allows more than one Noise struct to exist, without any clash of names. Swift built-in object types often take advantage of namespacing; for example, the String struct is one of several structs that contain an Index struct, with no clash of names.

Instance References

On the whole, the names of object types will be global, and you will be able to refer to them simply by using their names. Instances, however, are another story. Instances must be deliberately created, one by one. That is what instantiation is for. Once you have created an instance, you can cause that instance to persist, by storing the instance in a variable with sufficient lifetime; using that variable as a reference, you can send instance messages to that instance, accessing instance properties and calling instance methods.

Instantiation may involve you calling an initializer, or some other object may create or provide the instance for you. A simple example is what happens when you manipulate a String, like this:

```
let s = "Hello, world"
let s2 = s.uppercased()
```

In that code, we end up with two String instances. The first one, s, we created using a string literal. The second one, s2, was created for us when we called the first string's uppercased method. Thus we have two instances, and they will persist independently as long as our references to them persist; but we didn't get either of them by calling an initializer.

In other cases, the instance you are interested in will *already* exist in some persistent fashion; the problem will then be to find a way of *getting a reference* to that instance.

Let's say, for example, that this is a real-life iOS app. You will certainly have a root view controller, which will be an instance of some type of UIViewController. Let's say it's an instance of the ViewController class. Once your app is up and running, this instance already exists. It would then be utterly counterproductive to attempt to speak to the root view controller by *instantiating* the ViewController class:

```
let theVC = ViewController() // legal but stupid
```

All that code does is to make a *second, different* instance of the ViewController class, and your messages to that instance will be wasted, as it is not *the particular already existing instance* that you wanted to talk to. That is a very common beginner mistake; don't make it.

Getting a reference to an already existing instance can be, of itself, an interesting problem. The process always starts with something you already have a reference to. Often, this will be a class. In iOS programming, the app itself is an instance, and there is a class that holds a reference to that instance and will hand it to you whenever you ask for it. That class is the UIApplication class, and the way to get a reference to the app instance is through its `shared` class property:

```
let app = UIApplication.shared
```

Now we have a reference to the application instance. The application instance has a `keyWindow` property:

```
let window = app.keyWindow
```

Now we have a reference to our app's key window. That window owns the root view controller, and will hand us a reference to it, as its own `rootViewController` property; the app's `keyWindow` is an Optional, so to get at its `rootViewController` we must unwrap the Optional:

```
let vc = window?.rootViewController
```

And voilà, we have a reference to our app's root view controller. To obtain the reference to this persistent instance, we created, in effect, a chain of method calls and properties leading from the known to the unknown, from a globally available class to the particular desired instance:

```
let app = UIApplication.shared
let window = app.keyWindow
let vc = window?.rootViewController
```

Clearly, we can write that chain as an actual chain, using repeated dot-notation:

```
let vc = UIApplication.shared.keyWindow?.rootViewController
```

You don't *have* to chain your instance messages into a single line — chaining through multiple `let` assignments is completely efficient, possibly more legible, and certainly easier to debug — but it's a handy formulaic convenience and is particularly characteristic of dot-notated object-oriented languages like Swift.

The general problem of getting a reference to a particular already existing instance is so interesting and pervasive that I will devote much of Chapter 13 to it.

Enums

An *enum* is an object type whose instances represent *distinct predefined alternative values*. Think of it as a list of known possibilities. An enum is the Swift way to express a set of constants that are alternatives to one another. An enum declaration includes case statements. Each case is the name of one of the alternatives. An instance of an enum will represent exactly one alternative — one case.

For example, in my Albumen app, different instances of the same view controller can list any of four different sorts of music library contents: albums, playlists, podcasts, or audiobooks. The view controller's behavior is slightly different in each case. So I need a sort of four-way switch that I can set once when the view controller is instantiated, saying which sort of contents this view controller is to display. That sounds like an enum!

Here's the basic declaration for that enum; I call it Filter, because each case represents a different way of filtering the contents of the music library:

```
enum Filter {
    case albums
    case playlists
    case podcasts
    case books
}
```

That enum doesn't have an initializer. You *can* write an initializer for an enum, as I'll demonstrate in a moment; but there is a default mode of initialization that you'll probably use most of the time — the name of the enum followed by dot-notation and one of the cases. For example, here's how to make an instance of Filter representing the albums case:

```
let type = Filter.albums
```

As a shortcut, if the type is known in advance, you can omit the name of the enum; the bare case must still be preceded by a dot. For example:

```
let type : Filter = .albums
```

You can't say .albums just anywhere out of the blue, because Swift doesn't know what enum it belongs to. But in that code, the variable is explicitly declared as a Filter, so Swift knows what .albums means. A similar thing happens when passing an enum instance as an argument in a function call:

```
func filterExpecter(_ type:Filter) {}
filterExpecter(.albums)
```

In the second line, I create an instance of Filter and pass it, all in one move, without having to include the name of the enum. That's because Swift knows from the function declaration that a Filter is expected here.

Inference of Type Name with Static/Class Members

Just as you can use the bare name of an enum case, preceded by a dot, where an instance of that enum is expected, you can do the same thing when referring to a type's static/class member whose value is an instance of that type. For example, UIColor has many class properties that produce a UIColor instance, so you can omit UIColor where a UIColor is expected:

```
p.trackTintColor = .red // instead of UIColor.red
```

Similarly, suppose we have a struct Thing with static constants whose values are Thing instances (I'll explain later what RawRepresentable means):

```
struct Thing : RawRepresentable {
    let rawValue : Int
    static let one : Thing = Thing(rawValue:1)
    static let two : Thing = Thing(rawValue:2)
}
```

Then we can refer to Thing.one as .one where a Thing instance is expected:

```
let thing : Thing = .one
```

Many Objective-C enums are bridged to Swift as this kind of struct, and I'll talk about them later in this chapter.

In real life, the space savings when omitting the enum name can be considerable — especially because, when talking to Cocoa, the enum type names are often long. For example:

```
let v = UIView()
v.contentMode = .center
```

A UIView's contentMode property is typed as a UIViewContentMode enum. Our code is neater and simpler because we don't have to include the name UIViewContentMode explicitly here; .center is nicer than UIViewContentMode.center. But either is legal.

Instances of an enum with the same case are regarded as equal. Thus, you can compare an enum instance for equality against a case. Again, the type of enum is known from the first term in the comparison, so the second term can omit the enum name:

```
func filterExpecter(_ type:Filter) {
    if type == .albums {
        print("it's albums")
    }
}
filterExpecter(.albums) // "it's albums"
```

Raw Values

Optionally, when you declare an enum, you can add a type declaration. The cases then all carry with them a fixed (constant) value of that type. If the type is an integer numeric type, the values can be implicitly assigned, and will start at zero by default. For example:

```
enum PepBoy : Int {
    case manny
    case moe
    case jack
}
```

In that code, `.manny` carries a value of 0, `.moe` carries of a value of 1, and so on.

If the type is String, the implicitly assigned values are the string equivalents of the case names. For example:

```
enum Filter : String {
    case albums
    case playlists
    case podcasts
    case books
}
```

In that code, `.albums` carries a value of `"albums"`, and so on.

Regardless of the type, you can assign values explicitly as part of the case declarations, like this:

```
enum Filter : String {
    case albums = "Albums"
    case playlists = "Playlists"
    case podcasts = "Podcasts"
    case books = "Audiobooks"
}
```

The types attached to an enum in this way are limited to numbers and strings, and the values assigned must be literals. The values carried by the cases are called their *raw values*. An instance of this enum has just one case, so it has just one fixed raw value, which can be retrieved with its `rawValue` property:

```
let type = Filter.albums
print(type.rawValue) // Albums
```

Having each case carry a fixed raw value can be quite useful. In my Albumen app, the Filter cases really do have those String values, and `type` is a view controller property; and so when the view controller wants to know what title string to put at the top of the screen, it simply retrieves `self.type.rawValue`.

The raw value associated with each case must be unique within this enum; the compiler will enforce this rule. Therefore, the mapping works the other way: given a raw value, you can derive the case. For example, you can instantiate an enum that has raw values by using its `init(rawValue:)` initializer:

```
let type = Filter(rawValue:"Albums")
```

However, the attempt to instantiate the enum in this way might fail, because you might supply a raw value corresponding to no case; therefore, this is a failable initializer, and the value returned is an Optional. In that code, `type` is not a Filter; it's an Optional wrapping a Filter. This might not be terribly important, however, because the thing you are most likely to want to do with an enum is to compare it for equality with a case of the enum; you can do that with an Optional without unwrapping it. This code is legal and works correctly:

```
let type = Filter(rawValue:"Albums")
if type == .albums { // ...
```

Associated Values

The raw values discussed in the preceding section are fixed in advance: a given case carries with it a certain raw value, and that's that. Alternatively, you can construct a case whose constant value can be set *when the instance is created*. To do so, do not declare any type for the enum as a whole; instead, append a tuple type to the name of the case. There will usually be just one type in this tuple, so what you'll write will look like a type name in parentheses. Any type may be declared. Here's an example:

```
enum Error {
    case number(Int)
    case message(String)
    case fatal
}
```

That code means that, at instantiation time, an Error instance with the `.number` case must be assigned an Int value, an Error instance with the `.message` case must be assigned a String value, and an Error instance with the `.fatal` case can't be assigned any value. Instantiation with assignment of a value is really a way of calling an initialization function, so to supply the value, you pass it as an argument in parentheses:

```
let err : Error = .number(4)
```

The attached value here is called an *associated value*. What you are supplying as you specify the associated value is actually a tuple, so it can contain literal values or value references; this is legal:

```
let num = 4
let err : Error = .number(num)
```

The tuple can contain more than one value, with or without labels; if the values have labels, they must be used at initialization time:

```
enum Error {
    case number(Int)
    case message(String)
    case fatal(n:Int, s:String)
}
let err : Error = .fatal(n:-12, s:"Oh the horror")
```

An enum case that declares an associated value is actually an initialization function, so you can capture a reference to that function and call the function later:

```
let fatalMaker = Error.fatal
let err = fatalMaker(n:-1000, s:"Unbelievably bad error")
```

I'll explain how to *extract* the associated value from an actual instance of such an enum in Chapter 5.

At the risk of sounding like a magician explaining his best trick, I will now reveal how an Optional works. An Optional is simply an enum with two cases: .none and .some. If it is .none, it carries no associated value, and it equates to nil. If it is .some, it carries the wrapped value *as its associated value*.

Enum Initializers

An explicit enum initializer must do what default initialization does: it must return a particular case of this enum. To do so, set self to the case. In this example, I'll expand my Filter enum so that it can be initialized with a numeric argument:

```
enum Filter : String {
    case albums = "Albums"
    case playlists = "Playlists"
    case podcasts = "Podcasts"
    case books = "Audiobooks"
    static var cases : [Filter] = [.albums, .playlists, .podcasts, .books]
    init(_ ix:Int) {
        self = Filter.cases[ix]
    }
}
```

Now there are three ways to make a Filter instance:

```
let type1 = Filter.albums
let type2 = Filter(rawValue:"Playlists")!
let type3 = Filter(2) // .podcasts
```

In that example, we'll crash in the third line if the caller passes a number that's out of range (less than 0 or greater than 3). If we want to avoid that, we can make this a failable initializer and return nil if the number is out of range:

```
enum Filter : String {
    case albums = "Albums"
    case playlists = "Playlists"
    case podcasts = "Podcasts"
```

```
        case books = "Audiobooks"
        static var cases : [Filter] = [.albums, .playlists, .podcasts, .books]
        init?(_ ix:Int) {
            if !(0...3).contains(ix) {
                return nil
            }
            self = Filter.cases[ix]
        }
    }
```

An enum can have multiple initializers. Enum initializers can delegate to one another by saying self.init(...). The only requirement is that, at some point in the calling chain, self must be set to a case; if that doesn't happen, your enum won't compile.

In this example, I improve my Filter enum so that it can be initialized with a String raw value without having to say rawValue: in the call. To do so, I declare a failable initializer with a string parameter that delegates to the built-in failable rawValue: initializer:

```
enum Filter : String {
    case albums = "Albums"
    case playlists = "Playlists"
    case podcasts = "Podcasts"
    case books = "Audiobooks"
    static var cases : [Filter] = [.albums, .playlists, .podcasts, .books]
    init?(_ ix:Int) {
        if !(0...3).contains(ix) {
            return nil
        }
        self = Filter.cases[ix]
    }
    init?(_ rawValue:String) {
        self.init(rawValue:rawValue)
    }
}
```

Now there are four ways to make a Filter instance:

```
let type1 = Filter.albums
let type2 = Filter(rawValue:"Playlists")
let type3 = Filter(2) // .Podcasts, wrapped in an Optional
let type4 = Filter("Playlists")
```

Enum Properties

An enum can have instance properties and static properties, but there's a limitation: an enum instance property can't be a stored property. This makes sense, because if two instances of the same case could have different stored instance property values, they would no longer be equal to one another — which would undermine the nature and purpose of enums.

Computed instance properties are fine, however, and the value of the property can vary by rule in accordance with the case of self. In this example from my real code, I've associated an MPMediaQuery (obtained by calling an MPMediaQuery factory class method) with each case of my Filter enum, suitable for fetching the songs of that type from the music library:

```
enum Filter : String {
    case albums = "Albums"
    case playlists = "Playlists"
    case podcasts = "Podcasts"
    case books = "Audiobooks"
    var query : MPMediaQuery {
        switch self {
        case .albums:
            return .albums()
        case .playlists:
            return .playlists()
        case .podcasts:
            return .podcasts()
        case .books:
            return .audiobooks()
        }
    }
}
```

If an enum instance property is a computed variable with a setter, other code can assign to this property. However, that code's reference to the enum instance must be a variable (var), not a constant (let). If you try to assign to an enum instance property through a let reference, you'll get a compile error.

Enum Methods

An enum can have instance methods (including subscripts) and static methods. Writing an enum method is straightforward. Here's an example from my own code. In a card game, the cards draw themselves as rectangles, ellipses, or diamonds. I've abstracted the drawing code into an enum that draws itself as a rectangle, an ellipse, or a diamond, depending on its case:

```
enum Shape {
    case rectangle
    case ellipse
    case diamond
    func addShape (to p: CGMutablePath, in r : CGRect) -> () {
        switch self {
        case .rectangle:
            p.addRect(r)
        case .ellipse:
            p.addEllipse(in:r)
        case .diamond:
            p.move(to: CGPoint(x:r.minX, y:r.midY))
```

```
            p.addLine(to: CGPoint(x: r.midX, y: r.minY))
            p.addLine(to: CGPoint(x: r.maxX, y: r.midY))
                p.addLine(to: CGPoint(x: r.midX, y: r.maxY))
            p.closeSubpath()
        }
    }
}
```

An enum instance method that modifies the enum itself must be marked as mutating. For example, an enum instance method might assign to an instance property of self; even though this is a computed property, such assignment is illegal unless the method is marked as mutating. An enum instance method can even change the case of self, by assigning to self; but again, the method must be marked as mutating. The caller of a mutating instance method must have a variable reference to the instance (var), not a constant reference (let).

In this example, I add an advance method to my Filter enum. The idea is that the cases constitute a sequence, and the sequence can cycle. By calling advance, I transform a Filter instance into an instance of the next case in the sequence:

```
enum Filter : String {
    case albums = "Albums"
    case playlists = "Playlists"
    case podcasts = "Podcasts"
    case books = "Audiobooks"
    static var cases : [Filter] = [.albums, .playlists, .podcasts, .books]
    mutating func advance() {
        var ix = Filter.cases.index(of:self)!
        ix = (ix + 1) % 4
        self = Filter.cases[ix]
    }
}
```

And here's how to call it:

```
var type = Filter.books
type.advance() // type is now Filter.albums
```

(A subscript setter is always considered mutating and does not have to be specially marked.)

Why Enums?

An enum is a switch whose states have names. There are many situations where that's a desirable thing. You could implement a multistate value yourself; for example, if there are five possible states, you could use an Int whose values can be 0 through 4. But then you would have to provide a lot of additional overhead — making sure that no other values are used, and interpreting those numeric values correctly. A list of five named cases is much better! Even when there are only *two* states, an enum is often better than, say, a mere Bool, because the enum's states have names. With a Bool, you have to know what `true` and `false` signify in a particular usage; with an enum, the name of the enum and the names of its cases *tell* you its significance. Moreover, you can store extra information in an enum's associated value or raw value; you can't do that with a mere Bool.

For example, in my LinkSame app, the user can play a real game with a timer or a practice game without a timer. At various places in the code, I need to know which type of game this is. The game types are the cases of an enum:

```
enum InterfaceMode : Int {
    case timed = 0
    case practice = 1
}
```

The current game type is stored in an instance property `interfaceMode`, whose value is an InterfaceMode. Thus, it's easy to set the game type by case name:

```
// ... initialize new game ...
self.interfaceMode = .timed
```

And it's easy to examine the game type by case name:

```
// notify of high score only if user is not just practicing
if self.interfaceMode == .timed { // ...
```

So what are the raw value integers for? That's the really clever part. They correspond to the segment indexes of a UISegmentedControl in the interface! Whenever I change the `interfaceMode` property, a setter observer also selects the corresponding segment of the UISegmentedControl (`self.timedPractice`), simply by fetching the `rawValue` of the current enum case:

```
var interfaceMode : InterfaceMode = .timed {
    willSet (mode) {
        self.timedPractice?.selectedSegmentIndex = mode.rawValue
    }
}
```

Structs

A *struct* is the Swift object type *par excellence*. An enum, with its fixed set of cases, is a reduced, specialized kind of object. A class, at the other extreme, will often turn out to be overkill; it has some features that a struct lacks, but if you don't need those features, a struct may be preferable.

Of the numerous object types declared in the Swift header, only three are classes (and you are unlikely to encounter any of them consciously). On the contrary, nearly all the built-in object types provided by Swift itself are structs. A String is a struct. An Int is a struct. A Range is a struct. An Array is a struct. And so on. That shows how powerful a struct can be.

Struct Initializers, Properties, and Methods

A struct that doesn't have an explicit initializer and that doesn't *need* an explicit initializer — because it has no stored properties, or because all its stored properties are assigned default values as part of their declaration — automatically gets an implicit initializer with no parameters, init(). For example:

```
struct Digit {
    var number = 42
}
```

That struct can be initialized by saying Digit(). But if you add any explicit initializers of your own, you lose that implicit initializer:

```
struct Digit {
    var number = 42
    init(number:Int) {
        self.number = number
    }
}
```

Now you can say Digit(number:42), but you can't say Digit() any longer. Of course, you can add an explicit initializer that does the same thing:

```
struct Digit {
    var number = 42
    init() {}
    init(number:Int) {
        self.number = number
    }
}
```

Now you can say Digit() once again, as well as Digit(number:42).

A struct that has stored properties and that doesn't have an explicit initializer automatically gets an implicit initializer derived from its instance properties. This is called the *memberwise initializer*. For example:

```
struct Digit {
    var number : Int // could use "let" here instead
}
```

That struct is legal — indeed, it is legal even if the number property is declared with let instead of var — even though it seems we have not fulfilled the contract requiring us to initialize all stored properties in their declaration or in an initializer. The reason is that this struct automatically has a memberwise initializer which *does* initialize all its properties. In this case, the memberwise initializer is init(number:), and you can say Digit(number:42).

The memberwise initializer exists even for `var` stored properties that are assigned a default value in their declaration; thus, this struct has a memberwise initializer `init(number:)`, in addition to its implicit `init()` initializer:

```
struct Digit {
    var number = 42
}
```

But if you add any explicit initializers of your own, you lose the memberwise initializer (though of course you can write an explicit initializer that does the same thing).

If a struct has any explicit initializers, then they must fulfill the contract that all stored properties must be initialized either by direct initialization in the declaration or by all initializers. If a struct has multiple explicit initializers, they can delegate to one another by saying `self.init(...)`.

A struct can have instance properties and static properties, and they can be stored or computed variables. If other code wants to set a property of a struct instance, its reference to that instance must be a variable (`var`), not a constant (`let`).

A struct can have instance methods (including subscripts) and static methods. If an instance method sets a property, it must be marked as `mutating`, and the caller's reference to the struct instance must be a variable (`var`), not a constant (`let`). A `mutating` instance method can even replace this instance with another instance, by setting `self` to a different instance of the same struct. (A subscript setter is always considered `mutating` and does not have to be specially marked.)

Struct As Namespace

I very often use a degenerate struct as a handy namespace for constants. I call such a struct "degenerate" because it consists entirely of static members; I don't intend to use this object type to make any instances.

For example, let's say I'm going to be storing user preference information in Cocoa's UserDefaults. UserDefaults is a kind of dictionary: each item is accessed through a key. The keys are typically strings. A common programmer mistake is to write out these string keys literally every time a key is used; if you then misspell a key name, there's no penalty at compile time, but your code will mysteriously fail to work correctly. The proper approach is to embody these keys as constant strings and use the names of the strings; that way, if you make a mistake typing the name of a string, the compiler can catch you. A struct with static members is a great way to define those constant strings and clump their names into a namespace:

```
struct Default {
    static let rows = "CardMatrixRows"
    static let columns = "CardMatrixColumns"
    static let hazyStripy = "HazyStripy"
}
```

That code means that I can now refer to a UserDefaults key with a name, such as
`Default.hazyStripy`.

Classes

A *class* is similar to a struct, with the following key differences:

Reference type
> Classes are reference types. This means, among other things, that a class instance
> has two remarkable features that are not true of struct instances or enum instan-
> ces:

Mutability
> A class instance is mutable in place. Even if your reference to an instance of a
> class is a constant (`let`), you can change the value of an instance property
> through that reference. An instance method of a class never has to be
> marked `mutating` (and cannot be).

Multiple references
> When a given instance of a class is assigned to multiple variables or passed as
> argument to a function, you get multiple references to *one and the same
> object*.

Inheritance
> A class can have a superclass. A class that has a superclass is a *subclass* of that
> superclass. Class types can thus form a hierarchical tree.

In Objective-C, classes are the only object type. Some built-in Swift struct types are
magically bridged to Objective-C class types, but your custom struct types don't have
that magic. Thus, when programming iOS with Swift, a primary reason for declaring
a class, rather than a struct, is as a form of interchange with Objective-C and Cocoa.

Value Types and Reference Types

A major difference between enums and structs, on the one hand, and classes, on the
other, is that enums and structs are *value types*, whereas classes are *reference types*.

A value type is *not mutable in place*, even though it seems to be. For example, consider a struct. A struct is a value type:

```
struct Digit {
    var number : Int
    init(_ n:Int) {
        self.number = n
    }
}
```

Now, Swift's syntax of assignment would lead us to believe that changing a Digit's number is possible:

```
var d = Digit(123)
d.number = 42
```

But in reality, when you apparently mutate an instance of a value type, you are actually *replacing* that instance with a *different* instance. To see that this is true, add a setter observer:

```
var d : Digit = Digit(123) {
    didSet {
        print("d was set")
    }
}
d.number = 42 // "d was set"
```

That explains why it is impossible to mutate a value type instance if the reference to that instance is declared with let:

```
struct Digit {
    var number : Int
    init(_ n:Int) {
        self.number = n
    }
}
let d = Digit(123)
d.number = 42 // compile error
```

Under the hood, this change would require us to *replace* the Digit instance pointed to by d with another Digit instance — and we can't do that, because it would mean assigning into d, which is exactly what the let declaration forbids.

That, in turn, is why an instance method of a struct or enum that sets a property of the instance must be marked explicitly with the mutating keyword. For example:

```
struct Digit {
    var number : Int
    init(_ n:Int) {
        self.number = n
    }
    mutating func changeNumberTo(_ n:Int) {
        self.number = n
    }
}
```

Without the `mutating` keyword, that code won't compile. The `mutating` keyword assures the compiler that you understand what's really happening here. If that method is called, it replaces the instance; therefore, it can be called only on a reference declared with `var`, not `let`:

```
let d = Digit(123)
d.changeNumberTo(42) // compile error
```

None of what I've just said, however, applies to class instances! Class instances are reference types, not value types. An instance property of a class, to be settable, must be declared with `var`, obviously; but the reference to a class instance does *not* have to be declared with `var` in order to set that property through that reference:

```
class Dog {
    var name : String = "Fido"
}
let rover = Dog()
rover.name = "Rover" // fine
```

In the last line of that code, the class instance pointed to by `rover` is being *mutated in place*. No implicit assignment to `rover` is involved, and so the `let` declaration is powerless to prevent the mutation. A setter observer on a Dog variable is *not* called when a property is set:

```
var rover : Dog = Dog() {
    didSet {
        print("did set rover")
    }
}
rover.name = "Rover" // nothing in console
```

The setter observer would be called if we were to set `rover` explicitly (to another Dog instance), but it is not called merely because we change a property of the Dog instance already pointed to by `rover`.

Those examples involve a declared variable reference. Exactly the same difference between a value type and a reference type may be seen with a parameter of a function call. When we receive an instance of a value type as a parameter into a function body, the compiler will stop us in our tracks if we try to assign to its instance property. This doesn't compile:

```
func digitChanger(_ d:Digit) {
    d.number = 42 // compile error
}
```

But this does compile:

```
func dogChanger(_ d:Dog) {
    d.name = "Rover"
}
```

With a reference type, there is in effect a concealed level of indirection between your reference to the instance and the instance itself; the reference actually refers to a *pointer* to the instance. This, in turn, has another important implication: it means that when a class instance is assigned to a variable or passed as an argument to a function or as the result of a function, you can wind up with *multiple references to the same object*. That is not true of structs and enums. When an enum instance or a struct instance is assigned or passed, what is assigned or passed is essentially a *new copy* of that instance. But when a class instance is assigned or passed, what is assigned or passed is a reference to the *same* instance.

To prove it, I'll assign one reference to another, and then mutate the second reference — and then I'll examine what happened to the first reference. Let's start with the struct:

```
var d = Digit(123)
print(d.number) // 123
var d2 = d // assignment!
d2.number = 42
print(d.number) // 123
```

In that code, we changed the number property of d2, a struct instance; but nothing happened to the number property of d. Now let's try the class:

```
var fido = Dog()
print(fido.name) // Fido
var rover = fido // assignment!
rover.name = "Rover"
print(fido.name) // Rover
```

In that code, we changed the name property of rover, a class instance — and the name property of fido was changed as well! That's because, after the assignment in the third line, fido and rover refer to *one and the same instance*.

The same thing is true of parameter passing. With a class instance, what is passed is a reference to the *same* instance:

```
func dogChanger(_ d:Dog) {
    d.name = "Rover"
}
var fido = Dog()
print(fido.name) // "Fido"
dogChanger(fido)
print(fido.name) // "Rover"
```

The change made to d inside the function dogChanger affected *our* Dog instance fido! You can't do that with an enum or struct instance parameter, because the instance is effectively *copied* as it is passed. But handing a class instance to a function does *not* copy that instance; it is more like *lending* that instance to the function.

The ability to generate multiple references to the same instance is significant particularly in a world of object-based programming, where objects persist and can have properties that persist along with them. If object A and object B are both long-lived objects, and if they both have a Dog property (where Dog is a class), and if they have each been handed a reference to one and the same Dog instance, then either object A or object B can mutate its Dog, and this mutation will affect the other's Dog. You can thus be holding on to an object, only to discover that it has been mutated by someone else behind your back. If that happens unexpectedly, it can put your program into an invalid state.

Class instances are also more complicated behind the scenes. Swift has to manage their memory (as I'll explain in detail in Chapter 12), precisely because there can be multiple references to the same object; this management can involve quite a bit of overhead. At an even lower level, the mere storage of class instances in memory entails some necessary overhead.

On the whole, therefore, you should prefer a value type (such as a struct) to a reference type (a class) wherever possible. Struct instances are not shared between references, and so you are relieved from any worry about such an instance being mutated behind your back; moreover, under the hood, storage and memory management are far simpler as well. New in Swift 3, the language itself will help you by imposing value types in front of many Cocoa Foundation reference types. For example, Objective-C NSDate and NSData are classes, but Swift 3 will steer you toward using struct types Date and Data instead. (I'll talk about these types in detail in Chapter 10.)

But don't get the wrong idea. Classes are not bad; they're good! For one thing, a class instance is very efficient to pass around, because all you're passing is a pointer. No matter how big and complicated a class instance may be, no matter how many properties it may have containing vast amounts of data, passing the instance is incredibly fast and efficient, because no new data is generated.

Even more important, there are many situations where the independent identity of a class instance, no matter how many times it is referred to, is exactly what you want. The extended lifetime of a class instance, as it is passed around, can be crucial to its functionality and integrity. In particular, only a class instance can successfully represent an *independent reality*. For example, a UIView needs to be a class, not a struct, because an individual UIView instance, no matter how it gets passed around, must continue to represent the same single real and persistent view in your running app's interface.

Still another reason for preferring a class over a struct or enum is when you need recursive references. A value type cannot be structurally recursive: a stored instance property of a value type cannot be an instance of the same type. This code won't compile:

```
struct Dog { // compile error
    var puppy : Dog?
}
```

More complex circular chains, such as a Dog with a Puppy property and a Puppy
with a Dog property, are similarly illegal. But if Dog is a class instead of a struct,
there's no error. This is a consequence of the nature of memory management of value
types as opposed to reference types. The moral is clear: if you need a property of a
Dog to be a Dog, Dog has to be a class.

 An enum case's associated value *can* be an instance of that enum, provided the
case (or the entire enum) is marked indirect:

```
enum Node {
    case None(Int)
    indirect case left(Int, Node)
    indirect case right(Int, Node)
    indirect case both(Int, Node, Node)
}
```

Subclass and Superclass

Two classes can be *subclass* and *superclass* of one another. For example, we might have
a class Quadruped and a class Dog and make Quadruped the superclass of Dog. A
class may have many subclasses, but a class can have only one immediate superclass. I
say "immediate" because that superclass might itself have a superclass, and so on in a
rising chain, until we get to the ultimate superclass, called the *base class*, or *root class*.

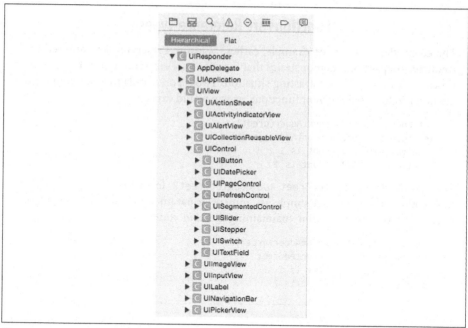

Figure 4-1. Part of the Cocoa class hierarchy as shown in Xcode

Because a class can have many subclasses but only one superclass, there is a hierarchical tree of subclasses, each branching from its superclass, and so on, with a single class, the base class, at the top.

As far as the Swift language itself is concerned, there is no requirement that a class should have any superclass, or, if it does have a superclass, that it should ultimately be descended from any particular base class. Thus, a Swift program can have many classes that have no superclass, and it can have many independent hierarchical subclass trees, each descended from a different base class.

Cocoa, however, doesn't work that way. In Cocoa, there is effectively just one base class — NSObject, which embodies all the functionality necessary for a class to *be* a class in the first place — and all other classes are subclasses, at some level, of that one base class. Cocoa thus consists of one huge tree of hierarchically arranged classes, even before you write a single line of code or create any classes of your own.

We can imagine diagramming this tree as an outline. And in fact Xcode will *show* you this outline (Figure 4-1): in an iOS project window, choose View → Navigators → Show Symbol Navigator and click Hierarchical, with the first and third icons in the filter bar selected (blue). The Cocoa classes are the part of the tree descending from NSObject.

The reason for having a superclass–subclass relationship in the first place is to allow related classes to *share functionality*. Suppose, for example, we have a Dog class and a Cat class, and we are considering declaring a walk method for both of them. We might reason that both a dog and a cat walk in pretty much the same way, by virtue of both being quadrupeds. So it might make sense to declare walk as a method of the Quadruped class, and make both Dog and Cat subclasses of Quadruped. The result is that both Dog and Cat can be sent the walk message, even if neither of them has a walk method, because each of them has a superclass that *does* have a walk method. We say that a subclass *inherits* the methods of its superclass.

To declare that a certain class is a subclass of a certain superclass, add a colon and the superclass name after the class's name in its declaration. So, for example:

```
class Quadruped {
    func walk () {
        print("walk walk walk")
    }
}
class Dog : Quadruped {}
class Cat : Quadruped {}
```

Now let's prove that Dog has indeed inherited walk from Quadruped:

```
let fido = Dog()
fido.walk() // walk walk walk
```

Observe that, in that code, the walk message can be sent to a Dog instance just as if the walk instance method were declared in the Dog class, even though the walk instance method is in fact declared in a superclass of Dog. That's inheritance at work.

The purpose of subclassing is not *merely* so that a class can inherit another class's methods; it's so that it can also declare methods *of its own*. Typically, a subclass consists of the methods inherited from its superclass *and then some*. If Dog has no methods of its own, after all, it's hard to see why it should exist separately from Quadruped. But if a Dog knows how to do something that not every Quadruped knows how to do — let's say, bark — then it makes sense as a separate class. If we declare bark in the Dog class, and walk in the Quadruped class, and make Dog a subclass of Quadruped, then Dog inherits the ability to walk from the Quadruped class *and also* knows how to bark:

```
class Quadruped {
    func walk () {
        print("walk walk walk")
    }
}
class Dog : Quadruped {
```

```
    func bark () {
        print("woof")
    }
}
```

Again, let's prove that it works:

```
let fido = Dog()
fido.walk() // walk walk walk
fido.bark() // woof
```

Within a class, it is a matter of indifference whether that class has an instance method because that method is declared in that class or because the method is declared in a superclass and inherited. A message to self works equally well either way. In this code, we have declared a barkAndWalk instance method that sends two messages to self, without regard to where the corresponding methods are declared (one is native to the subclass, one is inherited from the superclass):

```
class Quadruped {
    func walk () {
        print("walk walk walk")
    }
}
class Dog : Quadruped {
    func bark () {
        print("woof")
    }
    func barkAndWalk() {
        self.bark()
        self.walk()
    }
}
```

And here's proof that it works:

```
let fido = Dog()
fido.barkAndWalk() // woof walk walk walk
```

It is also permitted for a subclass to *redefine* a method inherited from its superclass. For example, perhaps some dogs bark differently from other dogs. We might have a class NoisyDog, for instance, that is a subclass of Dog. Dog declares bark, but Noisy-Dog also declares bark, and defines it differently from how Dog defines it. This is called *overriding*. The very natural rule is that if a subclass overrides a method inherited from its superclass, then when the corresponding message is sent to an instance of that subclass, it is the subclass's version of that method that is called.

In Swift, when you override something inherited from a superclass, you must explicitly acknowledge this fact by preceding its declaration with the keyword override. So, for example:

```
class Quadruped {
    func walk () {
        print("walk walk walk")
    }
}
class Dog : Quadruped {
    func bark () {
        print("woof")
    }
}
class NoisyDog : Dog {
    override func bark () {
        print("woof woof woof")
    }
}
```

And let's try it:

```
let fido = Dog()
fido.bark() // woof
let rover = NoisyDog()
rover.bark() // woof woof woof
```

Observe that a subclass method by the same *name* as a superclass's method is not necessarily, of itself, an override. Recall that Swift can distinguish two functions with the
same name, provided they have different *signatures*. Those are different functions,
and so an implementation of one in a subclass is not an override of the other in a
superclass. An override situation exists only when the subclass redefines the *same*
method that it inherits from a superclass — using the same name, including the
external parameter names, and the same signature.

It often happens that we want to override something in a subclass and yet access the
thing overridden in the superclass. This is done by sending a message to the keyword
super. Our bark implementation in NoisyDog is a case in point. What NoisyDog
really does when it barks is the same thing Dog does when *it* barks, but more times.
We'd like to express that relationship in our implementation of NoisyDog's bark. To
do so, we have NoisyDog's bark implementation send the bark message, not to self
(which would be circular), but to super; this causes the search for a bark instance
method implementation to start in the superclass rather than in our own class:

```
class Dog : Quadruped {
    func bark () {
        print("woof")
    }
}
class NoisyDog : Dog {
    override func bark () {
        for _ in 1...3 {
```

```
                    super.bark()
            }
        }
    }
```

And it works:

```
let fido = Dog()
fido.bark() // woof
let rover = NoisyDog()
rover.bark() // woof woof woof
```

A subscript function is a method. If a superclass declares a subscript, the subclass can declare a subscript with the same signature, provided it designates it with the `override` keyword. To call the superclass subscript implementation, the subclass can use square brackets after the keyword `super` (e.g. `super[3]`).

Along with methods, a subclass also inherits its superclass's properties. Naturally, the subclass may also declare additional properties of its own. It is possible to override an inherited property (with some restrictions that I'll talk about later).

A class declaration can prevent the class from being subclassed by preceding the class declaration with the `final` keyword. A class declaration can prevent a class member from being overridden by a subclass by preceding the member's declaration with the `final` keyword.

Class Initializers

Initialization of a class instance is considerably more complicated than initialization of a struct or enum instance, because of the existence of class inheritance. The chief task of an initializer is to ensure that all properties have an initial value, thus making the instance well-formed as it comes into existence; and an initializer may have other tasks to perform that are essential to the initial state and integrity of this instance. A class, however, may have a superclass, which may have properties and initializers of its own. Thus we must somehow ensure that when a subclass is initialized, its superclass's properties are initialized and the tasks of its initializers are performed in good order, in addition to initializing the properties and performing the initializer tasks of the subclass itself.

Swift solves this problem coherently and reliably — and ingeniously — by enforcing some clear and well-defined rules about what a class initializer must do.

Kinds of class initializer

The rules begin with a distinction between the kinds of initializer that a class can have:

Designated initializer

A class initializer, by default, is a *designated* initializer. A class with any stored properties that are *not* initialized as part of their declaration *must* have at least one designated initializer, and when the class is instantiated, exactly one of its designated initializers must be called, and must see to it that all stored properties are initialized. A designated initializer may *not* delegate to another initializer in the same class; it is *illegal* for a designated initializer to use the phrase `self.init(...)`.

Convenience initializer

A *convenience* initializer is marked with the keyword `convenience`. It is a delegating initializer; it *must* contain the phrase `self.init(...)`. Moreover, a convenience initializer must delegate to a designated initializer: when it says `self.init(...)`, it must call a designated initializer in the same class — or else it must call another convenience initializer in the same class, thus forming a chain of convenience initializers which ends by calling a designated initializer in the same class.

Implicit initializer

A class with no stored properties, or with stored properties all of which are initialized as part of their declaration, and that has *no explicit designated initializers*, has an *implicit* designated initializer `init()`.

Here are some examples. This class has no stored properties, so it has an implicit `init()` designated initializer:

```
class Dog {
}
let d = Dog()
```

This class's stored properties have default values, so it has an implicit `init()` designated initializer too:

```
class Dog {
    var name = "Fido"
}
let d = Dog()
```

This class's stored properties have default values, but it has no implicit `init()` initializer because it has an explicit designated initializer:

```
class Dog {
    var name = "Fido"
    init(name:String) {self.name = name}
}
let d = Dog(name:"Rover") // ok
let d2 = Dog() // compile error
```

This class's stored properties have default values, and it has an explicit initializer, but it also has an implicit `init()` initializer because its explicit initializer is a convenience initializer. Moreover, the implicit `init()` initializer is a designated initializer, so the convenience initializer can delegate to it:

```
class Dog {
    var name = "Fido"
    convenience init(name:String) {
        self.init()
        self.name = name
    }
}
let d = Dog(name:"Rover")
let d2 = Dog()
```

This class has stored properties without default values; it has an explicit designated initializer, and all of those properties are initialized in that designated initializer:

```
class Dog {
    var name : String
    var license : Int
    init(name:String, license:Int) {
        self.name = name
        self.license = license
    }
}
let d = Dog(name:"Rover", license:42)
```

This class is similar to the previous example, but it also has convenience initializers forming a chain that ends with a designated initializer:

```
class Dog {
    var name : String
    var license : Int
    init(name:String, license:Int) {
        self.name = name
        self.license = license
    }
    convenience init(license:Int) {
        self.init(name:"Fido", license:license)
    }
    convenience init() {
        self.init(license:1)
    }
}
let d = Dog()
```

Note that the rules about what else an initializer can say and when it can say it, as I described them earlier in this chapter, are still in force:

- A designated initializer cannot, except in order to initialize a property, say `self` until *all* of this class's properties have been initialized.

- A convenience initializer is a delegating initializer, so it cannot say `self` until after it has called, directly or indirectly, a designated initializer (and cannot set an immutable property at all).

Subclass initializers

Having defined and distinguished between designated initializers and convenience initializers, we are ready for the rules about what happens with regard to initializers when a class is itself a subclass of some other class:

No declared initializers
> If a subclass doesn't have to have any initializers of its own, and if it declares no initializers of its own, then its initializers consist of the initializers inherited from its superclass. (A subclass has no implicit `init()` initializer unless it inherits it from its superclass.)

Convenience initializers only
> If a subclass doesn't have to have any initializers of its own, it is eligible to declare convenience initializers, and these work exactly as convenience initializers always do, because inheritance supplies `self` with the designated initializers that the convenience initializers must call.

Designated initializers
> If a subclass declares any designated initializers of its own, the entire game changes drastically. Now, no initializers are inherited! The existence of an explicit designated initializer *blocks initializer inheritance*. The only initializers the subclass now has are the initializers that you explicitly write. (However, there's an exception, which I'll come to in a moment.)

> Every designated initializer in the subclass now has an extra requirement: it must call one of the *superclass's designated initializers*, by saying `super.init(...)`. Moreover, the rules about saying `self` continue to apply. A subclass designated initializer must do things in this order:

> 1. It must ensure that all properties of *this* class (the subclass) are initialized.

> 2. It must call `super.init(...)`, and the initializer that it calls must be a designated initializer.

> 3. Only then may this initializer say `self` for any other reason — to call an instance method, say, or to access an inherited property.

If a designated initializer doesn't call super.init(...), then super.init() is called implicitly if possible. (I don't like this feature of Swift: in my view, Swift should not indulge in secret behavior, even if that behavior might be considered "helpful.")

Designated and convenience initializers

If a subclass declares both designated and convenience initializers, the convenience initializers in the subclass are still subject to the rules I've already outlined. They must call self.init(...), calling a designated initializer directly or (through a chain of convenience initializers) indirectly. There are no inherited initializers, so the designated initializer that a convenience initializer calls must be declared in the subclass.

Override initializers

Superclass initializers can be overridden in the subclass, in accordance with these restrictions:

- An initializer whose parameters match a *convenience* initializer of the superclass can be a designated initializer or a convenience initializer, and is *not* marked override.

- An initializer whose parameters match a *designated* initializer of the superclass can be a designated initializer or a convenience initializer, and *must* be marked override. The superclass designated initializer that an override designated initializer calls with super.init(...) can be the one that it overrides.

Generally, if a subclass has *any* designated initializers, *no* initializers are inherited. But if a subclass overrides *all* of its superclass's *designated* initializers, then the subclass *does* inherit the superclass's *convenience* initializers.

Failable initializers

If an initializer called by a failable initializer is failable, the calling syntax does not change, and no additional test is needed — if a called failable initializer fails, the whole initialization process will fail (and will be aborted) immediately.

There are some additional restrictions on failable initializers:

- init can override init?, but not *vice versa*.

- init? can call init.

- init can call init? by saying init and unwrapping the result with an exclamation mark (and if the init? fails, you'll crash).

At no time can a subclass initializer set a constant (let) property of a superclass. This is because, by the time the subclass is allowed to do anything other than initialize its own properties and call another initializer, the superclass has finished its own initialization and the door for initializing its constants has closed.

Here are some basic examples. We start with a class whose subclass has no explicit initializers of its own:

```
class Dog {
    var name : String
    var license : Int
    init(name:String, license:Int) {
        self.name = name
        self.license = license
    }
    convenience init(license:Int) {
        self.init(name:"Fido", license:license)
    }
}
class NoisyDog : Dog {
}
```

Given that code, you can make a NoisyDog like this:

```
let nd1 = NoisyDog(name:"Fido", license:1)
let nd2 = NoisyDog(license:2)
```

That code is legal, because NoisyDog inherits its superclass's initializers. However, you can't make a NoisyDog like this:

```
let nd3 = NoisyDog() // compile error
```

That code is illegal. Even though a NoisyDog has no properties of its own, it has no implicit init() initializer; its initializers are its inherited initializers, and its superclass, Dog, has no implicit init() initializer to inherit.

Now here is a class whose subclass's only explicit initializer is a convenience initializer:

```
class Dog {
    var name : String
    var license : Int
    init(name:String, license:Int) {
        self.name = name
        self.license = license
    }
    convenience init(license:Int) {
        self.init(name:"Fido", license:license)
    }
}
class NoisyDog : Dog {
```

```
        convenience init(name:String) {
            self.init(name:name, license:1)
        }
    }
```

Observe how NoisyDog's convenience initializer fulfills its contract by calling self.init(...) to call a designated initializer — which it happens to have inherited. Given that code, there are three ways to make a NoisyDog, just as you would expect:

```
let nd1 = NoisyDog(name:"Fido", license:1)
let nd2 = NoisyDog(license:2)
let nd3 = NoisyDog(name:"Rover")
```

Next, here is a class whose subclass declares a designated initializer:

```
class Dog {
    var name : String
    var license : Int
    init(name:String, license:Int) {
        self.name = name
        self.license = license
    }
    convenience init(license:Int) {
        self.init(name:"Fido", license:license)
    }
}
class NoisyDog : Dog {
    init(name:String) {
        super.init(name:name, license:1)
    }
}
```

NoisyDog's explicit initializer is now a designated initializer. It fulfills its contract by calling a designated initializer in super. NoisyDog has now *cut off inheritance* of all initializers; the *only* way to make a NoisyDog is like this:

```
let nd1 = NoisyDog(name:"Rover")
```

Finally, here is a class whose subclass overrides its designated initializers:

```
class Dog {
    var name : String
    var license : Int
    init(name:String, license:Int) {
        self.name = name
        self.license = license
    }
    convenience init(license:Int) {
        self.init(name:"Fido", license:license)
    }
}
class NoisyDog : Dog {
```

```
    override init(name:String, license:Int) {
        super.init(name:name, license:license)
    }
}
```

NoisyDog has overridden *all* of its superclass's designated initializers, so it inherits its superclass's convenience initializers. There are thus two ways to make a NoisyDog:

```
let nd1 = NoisyDog(name:"Rover", license:1)
let nd2 = NoisyDog(license:2)
```

Those examples illustrate the main rules that you should keep in your head. You probably don't need to memorize the remaining rules, because the compiler will enforce them, and will keep slapping you down until you get them right.

Required initializers

There's one more thing to know about class initializers: a class initializer may be preceded by the keyword `required`. This means that a subclass may not lack it. This, in turn, means that if a subclass implements designated initializers, thus blocking inheritance, it *must* override this initializer. Here's a (rather pointless) example:

```
class Dog {
    var name : String
    required init(name:String) {
        self.name = name
    }
}
class NoisyDog : Dog {
    var obedient = false
    init(obedient:Bool) {
        self.obedient = obedient
        super.init(name:"Fido")
    }
} // compile error
```

That code won't compile. `init(name:)` is marked `required`; thus, our code won't compile unless we inherit or override `init(name:)` in NoisyDog. But we cannot inherit it, because, by implementing the NoisyDog designated initializer `init(obedient:)`, we have blocked inheritance. Therefore we must override it:

```
class Dog {
    var name : String
    required init(name:String) {
        self.name = name
    }
}
class NoisyDog : Dog {
    var obedient = false
    init(obedient:Bool) {
        self.obedient = obedient
        super.init(name:"Fido")
```

```
    }
    required init(name:String) {
        super.init(name:name)
    }
}
```

Observe that our overridden required initializer is not marked with `override`, but *is* marked with `required`, thus guaranteeing that the requirement continues drilling down to any further subclasses.

I have explained what declaring an initializer as `required` does, but I have not explained *why* you'd need to do it. I'll give examples later in this chapter.

Class Deinitializer

A class, and only a class (not the other flavors of object type), can have a deinitializer. This is a function declared with the keyword `deinit` followed by curly braces containing the function body. You never call this function yourself; it is called by the runtime when an instance of this class goes out of existence. If a class has a superclass, the subclass's deinitializer (if any) is called before the superclass's deinitializer (if any).

The idea of a deinitializer is that you might want to perform some cleanup, or just log to the console to prove to yourself that your instance is going out of existence in good order. I'll take advantage of deinitializers when I discuss memory management issues in Chapter 5.

Class Properties and Methods

A subclass can override its inherited properties. The override must have the same name and type as the inherited property, and must be marked with `override`. (A property cannot have the same name as an inherited property but a different type, as there is no way to distinguish them.)

The chief restriction here is that an `override` property *cannot be a stored property*. More specifically:

- If the superclass property is writable (a stored property or a computed property with a setter), the subclass's override may consist of adding setter observers to this property.

- Alternatively, the subclass's override may be a computed property. In that case:

  - If the superclass property is stored, the subclass's computed property override must have both a getter and a setter.

  - If the superclass property is computed, the subclass's computed property override must reimplement all the accessors that the superclass implements. If the superclass property is read-only (it has just a getter), the override can add a setter.

The overriding property's functions may refer to — and may read from and write to — the inherited property, through the super keyword.

A class can have static members, marked static, just like a struct or an enum. It can also have class members, marked class. Both static and class members are inherited by subclasses.

The chief difference between static and class methods from the programmer's point of view is that a static method cannot be overridden; it is as if static were a synonym for class final.

Here, for example, I'll use a static method to express what dogs say:

```
class Dog {
    static func whatDogsSay() -> String {
        return "woof"
    }
    func bark() {
        print(Dog.whatDogsSay())
    }
}
```

A subclass now inherits whatDogsSay, but can't override it. No subclass of Dog may contain any implementation of a class method or a static method whatDogsSay with this same signature.

Now I'll use a class method to express what dogs say:

```
class Dog {
    class func whatDogsSay() -> String {
        return "woof"
    }
    func bark() {
        print(Dog.whatDogsSay())
    }
}
```

A subclass inherits whatDogsSay, and *can* override it, either as a class method or as a static method:

```
class NoisyDog : Dog {
    override class func whatDogsSay() -> String {
        return "WOOF"
    }
}
```

The difference between static properties and class properties is similar, but with an additional, rather dramatic qualification: static properties can be stored, but class properties can only be computed.

Here, I'll use a static class property to express what dogs say:

```
class Dog {
    static var whatDogsSay = "woof"
    func bark() {
        print(Dog.whatDogsSay)
    }
}
```

A subclass inherits whatDogsSay, but can't override it; no subclass of Dog can declare a class or static property whatDogsSay.

Now I'll use a class property to express what dogs say. It cannot be a stored property, so I'll have to use a computed property instead:

```
class Dog {
    class var whatDogsSay : String {
        return "woof"
    }
    func bark() {
        print(Dog.whatDogsSay)
    }
}
```

A subclass inherits whatDogsSay and can override it either as a class property or as a static property. But even as a static property the subclass's override cannot be a stored property, in keeping with the rules of property overriding that I outlined earlier:

```
class NoisyDog : Dog {
    override static var whatDogsSay : String {
        return "WOOF"
    }
}
```

Polymorphism

When a computer language has a hierarchy of types and subtypes, it must resolve the question of what such a hierarchy means for the relationship between the type of an *object* and the declared type of a *reference* to that object. Swift obeys the principles of *polymorphism*. In my view, it is polymorphism that turns an object-based language into a full-fledged object-oriented language. We may summarize Swift's polymorphism principles as follows:

Substitution
    Wherever a certain type is expected, a subtype of that type may be used instead.

Internal identity

An object's type is a matter of its internal nature, regardless of how the object is referred to.

To see what these principles mean in practice, imagine we have a Dog class, along with its subclass, NoisyDog:

```
class Dog {
}
class NoisyDog : Dog {
}
let d : Dog = NoisyDog()
```

The substitution rule says that the last line is legal: we can assign a NoisyDog instance to a reference, d, that is typed as a Dog. The internal identity rule says that, under the hood, d now *is* a NoisyDog.

You may be asking: How is the internal identity rule manifested? If a reference to a NoisyDog is typed as a Dog, in what sense is this "really" a NoisyDog? To illustrate, let's examine what happens when a subclass overrides an inherited method. Let me redefine Dog and NoisyDog to demonstrate:

```
class Dog {
    func bark() {
        print("woof")
    }
}
class NoisyDog : Dog {
    override func bark() {
        super.bark(); super.bark()
    }
}
```

Now try to guess what happens when this code runs:

```
func tellToBark(_ d:Dog) {
    d.bark()
}
var nd = NoisyDog()
tellToBark(nd)
```

That code is legal, because, by the substitution principle, we can pass nd, typed as a NoisyDog, where a Dog is expected. Now, inside the tellToBark function, d is typed as a Dog. How will it react to being told to bark? On the one hand, d is *typed* as a Dog, and a Dog barks by saying "woof" once. On the other hand, in our code, when tellToBark is called, what is *really* passed is a NoisyDog instance, and a NoisyDog barks by saying "woof" twice. What will happen? Let's find out:

```
func tellToBark(_ d:Dog) {
    d.bark()
}
var nd = NoisyDog()
tellToBark(nd) // woof woof
```

The result is "woof woof". The internal identity rule says that what matters when a message is sent is not how the recipient of that message is *typed* through this or that *reference*, but what that recipient actually *is*. What arrives inside tellToBark is a NoisyDog, regardless of the type of variable that holds it; thus, the bark message causes this object to say "woof" twice.

Here's another important consequence of polymorphism — the meaning of the keyword self. It means the actual instance, and thus its meaning depends upon the type of the actual instance — even if the word self *appears* in a superclass's code. For example:

```
class Dog {
    func bark() {
        print("woof")
    }
    func speak() {
        self.bark()
    }
}
class NoisyDog : Dog {
    override func bark() {
        super.bark(); super.bark()
    }
}
```

What happens when we tell a NoisyDog to speak? Let's try it:

```
let nd = NoisyDog()
nd.speak() // woof woof
```

The speak method is declared in Dog, the superclass — not in NoisyDog. The speak method calls the bark method. It does this by way of the keyword self. (I could have omitted the explicit reference to self here, but self would still be involved implicitly, so I'm not cheating by making self explicit.) There's a bark method in Dog, and an override of the bark method in NoisyDog. Which bark method will be called?

The word self is encountered within the Dog class's implementation of speak. But what matters is not *where* the word self *appears* but what it *means*. It means *this instance*. And the internal identity principle tells us that this instance is a NoisyDog! Thus, it is NoisyDog's override of bark that is called.

Polymorphism applies to Optional types in the same way that it applies to the type of thing wrapped by the Optional. Suppose we have a reference typed as an Optional wrapping a Dog. You already know that you can assign a Dog to it. Well, you can also assign a NoisyDog, or an Optional wrapping a NoisyDog, and the underlying wrapped object will maintain its integrity:

```
var d : Dog?
d = Dog()
d = NoisyDog()
d = Optional(NoisyDog())
```

(The applicability of polymorphism to Optionals derives from a special dispensation of the Swift language: Optionals are *covariant*. I'll talk more about that later in this chapter.)

Thanks to polymorphism, you can take advantage of subclasses to add power and customization to existing classes. This is important particularly in the world of iOS programming, where most of the classes are defined by Cocoa and don't belong to you. The UIViewController class, for example, is defined by Cocoa; it has lots of built-in methods that Cocoa will call, and these methods perform various important tasks — but in a generic way. In real life, you'll make a UIViewController *subclass* and *override* those methods to do the tasks appropriate to your particular app. This won't bother Cocoa in the slightest, because (substitution principle) wherever Cocoa expects to receive or to be talking to a UIViewController, it will accept without question an instance of your UIViewController subclass. And this substitution will also work as expected, because (internal identity principle) whenever Cocoa calls one of those UIViewController methods on your subclass, it is your subclass's override that will be called. I'll talk more about subclassing Cocoa classes in Chapter 10.

 Polymorphism is cool, but it is also slow. It requires *dynamic dispatch*, meaning that the compiler can't perform certain optimizations, and that the runtime has to think about what a message to a class instance means. You can reduce the need for dynamic dispatch by declaring a class or a class member final or private, or by turning on Whole Module Optimization (see Chapter 6). Or use a struct, if appropriate; structs don't need dynamic dispatch.

Casting

The Swift compiler, with its strict typing, imposes severe restrictions on what messages can be sent to an object reference. The messages that the compiler will permit to be sent to an object reference depend upon the reference's *declared* type. But the internal identity principle of polymorphism says that, under the hood, an object may have a *real* type that is different from its reference's declared type. Such an object may be capable of receiving messages that the compiler won't permit us to send.

To illustrate, let's give NoisyDog a method that Dog doesn't have:

```
class Dog {
    func bark() {
        print("woof")
    }
}
class NoisyDog : Dog {
    override func bark() {
        super.bark(); super.bark()
    }
    func beQuiet() {
        self.bark()
    }
}
```

In that code, we configure a NoisyDog so that we can tell it to beQuiet. Now look at what happens when we try to tell an object typed as a Dog to be quiet:

```
func tellToHush(_ d:Dog) {
    d.beQuiet() // compile error
}
let nd = NoisyDog()
tellToHush(nd)
```

Our code doesn't compile. We can't send the beQuiet message to the reference d inside the function body, because it is typed as a Dog — and a Dog has no beQuiet method. But there is a certain irony here: for once, we happen to know more than the compiler does — namely, that this object is *in fact* a NoisyDog and *does* have a beQuiet method! Our code would run correctly — because d really is a NoisyDog — if only we could get our code to compile in the first place. We need a way to say to the compiler, "Look, compiler, just trust me: this thing is going to turn out to be a Noisy-Dog when the program actually runs, so let me send it this message."

There is in fact a way to do this — *casting*. To cast, you use a form of the keyword as followed by the name of the type you claim something really is. Swift will not let you cast just any old type to any old other type — for example, you can't cast a String to an Int — but it will let you cast a superclass to a subclass. This is called *casting down*. When you cast down, the form of the keyword as that you must use is as! with an exclamation mark. The exclamation mark reminds you that you are *forcing* the compiler to do something it would rather not do:

```
func tellToHush(_ d:Dog) {
    (d as! NoisyDog).beQuiet()
}
let nd = NoisyDog()
tellToHush(nd)
```

That code compiles, and works. A useful way to rewrite the example is like this:

```
func tellToHush(_ d:Dog) {
    let d2 = d as! NoisyDog
    d2.beQuiet()
    // ... other NoisyDog messages to d2 can go here ...
}
let nd = NoisyDog()
tellToHush(nd)
```

The reason that way of rewriting the code is useful is in case we have *other* NoisyDog messages to send to this object. Instead of casting *every time* we want to send a message to it, we cast the object *once* to its internal identity type, and assign it to a variable. Now that variable's type — inferred, in this case, from the cast — *is* the internal identity type, and we can send multiple messages to the variable.

A moment ago, I said that the `as!` operator's exclamation mark reminds you that you are forcing the compiler's hand. It also serves as a warning: your code can now crash! The reason is that you might be lying to the compiler. Casting down is a way of telling the compiler to relax its strict type checking and to let you call the shots. If you use casting to make a false claim, the compiler may permit it, but you will crash when the app runs:

```
func tellToHush(_ d:Dog) {
    (d as! NoisyDog).beQuiet() // compiles, but prepare to crash...!
}
let d = Dog()
tellToHush(d)
```

In that code, we told the compiler that this object would turn out to be a NoisyDog, and the compiler obediently took its hands off and allowed us to send the beQuiet message to it. But in fact, this object was a Dog when our code ran, and so we ultimately crashed when the cast failed because this object was *not* a NoisyDog.

To prevent yourself from lying accidentally, you can *test* the type of an instance at runtime. One way to do this is with the keyword `is`. You can use `is` in a condition; if the condition passes, *then* cast, in the knowledge that your cast is safe:

```
func tellToHush(_ d:Dog) {
    if d is NoisyDog {
        let d2 = d as! NoisyDog
        d2.beQuiet()
    }
}
```

The result is that we won't cast d to a NoisyDog unless it really *is* a NoisyDog.

An alternative way to solve the same problem is to use Swift's `as?` operator. This casts down, but with the option of failure; therefore what it casts to is (you guessed it) an Optional — and now we are on familiar ground, because we know how to deal safely with an Optional:

```
func tellToHush(_ d:Dog) {
    let noisyMaybe = d as? NoisyDog // an Optional wrapping a NoisyDog
    if noisyMaybe != nil {
        noisyMaybe!.beQuiet()
    }
}
```

That doesn't look much cleaner or shorter than our previous approach. But remember that we can safely send a message to an Optional by optionally unwrapping the Optional! Thus we can skip the assignment and condense to a single line:

```
func tellToHush(_ d:Dog) {
    (d as? NoisyDog)?.beQuiet()
}
```

First we use the `as?` operator to obtain an Optional wrapping a NoisyDog (or nil). Then we optionally unwrap that Optional and send a message to it. If d isn't a Noisy-Dog, the Optional will be nil and the message won't be sent. If d *is* a NoisyDog, the Optional will be unwrapped and the message will be sent. Thus, that code is safe.

Recall from Chapter 3 that comparison operators applied to an Optional are automatically applied to the object wrapped by the Optional. The `is`, `as!`, and `as?` operators work the same way.

Let's start with `is`. Consider an Optional d ostensibly wrapping a Dog (that is, d is a Dog? object). It might, in actual fact, be wrapping either a Dog or a NoisyDog. To find out which it is, you might be tempted to use `is`. But can you? After all, an Optional is neither a Dog nor a NoisyDog — it's an Optional! Nevertheless, Swift knows what you mean; when the thing on the left side of `is` is an Optional, Swift pretends that it's the value wrapped in the Optional. Thus, this works just as you would hope:

```
let d : Dog? = NoisyDog()
if d is NoisyDog { // it is!
```

When using `is` with an Optional, the test fails in good order if the Optional is nil. Thus our `is` test really does *two* things: it checks whether the Optional is nil, and if it is not, it then checks whether the wrapped value is the type we specify.

What about casting? You can't really cast an Optional to anything. Nevertheless, Swift knows what you mean; you can use the `as!` operator with an Optional. When the thing on the left side of `as!` is an Optional, Swift treats it as the wrapped type. Moreover, the consequence of applying the `as!` operator is that two things happen: Swift unwraps first, and then casts. This code works, because d is unwrapped to give us d2, which is a NoisyDog:

```
let d : Dog? = NoisyDog()
let d2 = d as! NoisyDog
d2.beQuiet()
```

That code, however, is not safe. You shouldn't cast like that, without testing first, unless you are very sure of your ground. If d were `nil`, you'd crash in the second line because you're trying to unwrap a `nil` Optional. And if d were a Dog, not a Noisy-Dog, you'd *still* crash in the second line when the cast fails. That's why there's also an `as?` operator, which *is* safe — but yields an Optional:

```
let d : Dog? = NoisyDog()
let d2 = d as? NoisyDog
d2?.beQuiet()
```

Another way you'll use casting is during a value interchange between Swift and Objective-C when two types are *equivalent*. For example, you can cast a Swift String to a Cocoa NSString, and *vice versa*. That's not because one is a subclass of the other, but because they are *bridged* to one another; in a very real sense, they are the same type. When you cast from String to NSString, you're not casting down, and what you're doing is not dangerous, so you use the `as` operator, with no exclamation mark. I gave an example, in Chapter 3, of a situation where you might need to do that:

```
let s = "hello"
let range = (s as NSString).range(of:"ell") // (1,3), an NSRange
```

The cast from String to NSString tells Swift to stay in the Cocoa world as it calls `range(of:)`, and thus causes the result to be the Cocoa result, an NSRange, rather than a Swift Range.

In Swift 3, in general, to cross the bridge from a Swift type to a bridged Objective-C type, you will need to cast explicitly (except in the case of a string literal):

```
let s : NSString = "howdy"         // literal string to NSString
let s2 = "howdy"
let s3 : NSString = s2 as NSString // String to NSString
let i : NSNumber = 1 as NSNumber   // Int to NSNumber
```

That sort of code, however, is rather artificial. In real life, you won't be casting all that often, because the Cocoa API will present itself to you in terms of Swift types. For example, this is legal with no cast:

```
let name = "MyNib" // Swift String
let vc = ViewController(nibName:name, bundle:nil)
```

That's legal, not because the Swift String name magically crosses the bridge to NSString as it is assigned to `nibName:`, but because `nibName:` is typed as a Swift String (actually, an Optional wrapping a String). The bridge, in effect, is crossed *later*. Similarly, no cast is required here:

```
let ud = UserDefaults.standard
let s = "howdy"
ud.set(s, forKey:"Test")
```

The Swift String s doesn't magically cross the bridge when you use it as the first argument to set(_:forKey:); rather, the first argument of set(_:forKey:) is typed as a Swift type, namely Any (actually, an Optional wrapping Any) — and any Swift type can be used, without casting, where an Any is expected. I'll talk more about Any later in this chapter.

Coming back the other way, it is possible that you'll receive from Objective-C a value about whose real underlying type Swift has no information. In that case, you'll probably want to cast explicitly to the underlying type — and now you are casting down, with all that that implies. For example, here's what happens when we go to retrieve the "howdy" that we put into UserDefaults in the previous example:

```
let ud = UserDefaults.standard
let test = ud.object(forKey:"Test") as! String
```

When we call ud.object(forKey:), Swift has no type information; the result is an Any (actually, an Optional wrapping Any). But we know that this particular call should yield a string — because that's what we put in to begin with. So we can force-cast this value down to a String — and it works. However, if ud.object(forKey:"Test") were *not* a string (or if it were nil), we'd crash. If you're not sure of your ground, use is or as? to be safe. I'll discuss this kind of downcasting in more detail later on.

Type Reference

It can be useful for an instance to refer to its own type — for example, to send a message to that type. In an earlier example, a Dog instance method fetched a Dog class property by sending a message to the Dog type explicitly — by using the word Dog:

```
class Dog {
    class var whatDogsSay : String {
        return "Woof"
    }
    func bark() {
        print(Dog.whatDogsSay)
    }
}
```

The expression Dog.whatDogsSay seems clumsy and inflexible. Why should we have to hard-code into Dog a knowledge of what class it is? It *has* a class; it should just *know* what it is.

In Swift, you can access the type of an object reference's underlying object through the type(of:) function. Thus, if you don't like the notion of a Dog instance calling a Dog class method by saying Dog explicitly, there's another way:

```
class Dog {
    class var whatDogsSay : String {
        return "Woof"
    }
    func bark() {
        print(type(of:self).whatDogsSay)
    }
}
```

An important thing about using `type(of:)` instead of hard-coding a class name is
that it obeys polymorphism:

```
class Dog {
    class var whatDogsSay : String {
        return "Woof"
    }
    func bark() {
        print(type(of:self).whatDogsSay)
    }
}
class NoisyDog : Dog {
    override class var whatDogsSay : String {
        return "Woof woof woof"
    }
}
```

Now watch what happens:

```
let nd = NoisyDog()
nd.bark() // Woof woof woof
```

If we tell a NoisyDog instance to `bark`, it says `"Woof woof woof"`. The reason is that
`type(of:)` means, "The type that this object actually is, right now." We send the `bark`
message to a NoisyDog instance. The `bark` implementation refers to `type(of:self)`;
`self` means this instance, which is a NoisyDog, and so `type(of:self)` is the Noisy-
Dog class, and it is NoisyDog's version of `whatDogsSay` that is fetched.

 You can also use `type(of:)` for learning the name of an object's type, as a string
— typically for debugging purposes. When you say `print(type(of:myObject))`,
you'll see the type name in the console.

In some situations, you may want to pass an object type as a value. That is legal; an
object type is itself an object. Here's what you need to know:

- To *declare* that an object type is acceptable — for example, as the type of a variable or parameter — use dot-notation with the name of the type and the keyword
  `Type`.

```
```

- To *use* an object type as a value — for example, to assign a type to a variable or pass it to a function — use the type's name followed by the keyword `self` using dot-notation, or hand an object to `type(of:)`.

For example, here's a function `dogTypeExpecter` that accepts a Dog type as its parameter:

```
func dogTypeExpecter(_ whattype:Dog.Type) {
}
```

And here's an example of calling that function:

```
dogTypeExpecter(Dog.self)
```

Or you could call it like this:

```
let d = Dog()
dogTypeExpecter(type(of:d))
```

The substitution principle applies, so you could call `dogTypeExpecter` starting with a NoisyDog instead:

```
dogTypeExpecter(NoisyDog.self)
let nd = NoisyDog()
dogTypeExpecter(type(of:nd))
```

Why might you want to do something like that? A typical situation is that your function is a factory for instances: given a type, it creates an instance of that type, possibly prepares it in some way, and returns it. You can use a variable reference to a type — what Swift calls a *metatype* — to make an instance of that type, by explicitly sending it an `init(...)` message.

For example, here's a Dog class with an `init(name:)` initializer, and its NoisyDog subclass:

```
class Dog {
    var name : String
    init(name:String) {
        self.name = name
    }
}
class NoisyDog : Dog {
}
```

And here's a factory method that creates a Dog or a NoisyDog, as specified by its parameter, gives it a name, and returns it:

```
func dogMakerAndNamer(_ whattype:Dog.Type) -> Dog {
    let d = whattype.init(name:"Fido") // compile error
    return d
}
```

However, there's a problem. The code doesn't compile. The reason is that the compiler is in doubt as to whether the init(name:) initializer is implemented by every possible subtype of Dog. To reassure it, we must declare that initializer with the required keyword:

```
class Dog {
    var name : String
    required init(name:String) {
        self.name = name
    }
}
class NoisyDog : Dog {
}
```

I promised I'd tell you why you might need to declare an initializer as required; now I'm fulfilling that promise! The required designation reassures the compiler; every subclass of Dog must inherit or reimplement init(name:), so it's legal to send the init(name:) message to a type reference that might refer to Dog or some subclass of Dog. Now our code compiles, and we can call our function:

```
let d = dogMakerAndNamer(Dog.self) // d is a Dog named Fido
let d2 = dogMakerAndNamer(NoisyDog.self) // d2 is a NoisyDog named Fido
```

In a class method, self stands for the class — polymorphically. This means that, in a class method, you can send a message to self to call an initializer polymorphically. Here's an example. Let's say we want to move our instance factory method into Dog itself, as a class method. Let's call this class method makeAndName. We want this class method to create and return a named Dog of whatever class we send the makeAndName message to. If we say Dog.makeAndName(), we should get a Dog. If we say NoisyDog.makeAndName(), we should get a NoisyDog. So our makeAndName class method initializes polymorphic self:

```
class Dog {
    var name : String
    required init(name:String) {
        self.name = name
    }
    class func makeAndName() -> Dog {
        let d = self.init(name:"Fido")
        return d
    }
}
class NoisyDog : Dog {
}
```

It works as expected:

```
let d = Dog.makeAndName() // d is a Dog named Fido
let d2 = NoisyDog.makeAndName() // d2 is a NoisyDog named Fido
```

But there's a problem. Although d2 is in fact a NoisyDog, it is *typed* as a Dog. This is because our makeAndName class method is declared as returning a Dog. That isn't what we meant to declare. What we want to declare is that this method returns an instance of the same type as the class to which the makeAndName message was originally sent. In other words, we need a polymorphic type declaration! That type is Self (notice the capitalization). It is used as a return type in a method declaration to mean "an instance of whatever type this is at runtime." Thus:

```
class Dog {
    var name : String
    required init(name:String) {
        self.name = name
    }
    class func makeAndName() -> Self {
        let d = self.init(name:"Fido")
        return d
    }
}
class NoisyDog : Dog {
}
```

Now when we call NoisyDog.makeAndName() we get a NoisyDog typed as a Noisy-Dog.

Self also works for instance method declarations. Therefore, we can write an instance method version of our factory method. Here, we start with a Dog or a Noisy-Dog and tell it to have a puppy of the same type as itself:

```
class Dog {
    var name : String
    required init(name:String) {
        self.name = name
    }
    func havePuppy(name:String) -> Self {
        return type(of:self).init(name:name)
    }
}
class NoisyDog : Dog {
}
```

And here's some code to test it:

```
let d = Dog(name:"Fido")
let d2 = d.havePuppy(name:"Fido Junior")
let nd = NoisyDog(name:"Rover")
let nd2 = nd.havePuppy(name:"Rover Junior")
```

As expected, d2 is a Dog, but nd2 is a NoisyDog typed as a NoisyDog.

All this terminology can get a bit confusing, so here's a quick summary:

```
type(of:)
```
Applied to an object: the polymorphic (internal) type of the object, regardless of how a reference is typed. Static/class members are accessible by passing an object to `type(of:)`.

```
.Type
```
Sent to a type in a type declaration: the polymorphic type. For example, in a function parameter declaration, `Dog` means a Dog instance is expected (or an instance of one its subclasses), but `Dog.Type` means that the Dog type itself is expected (or the type of one of its subclasses).

```
.self
```
Sent to a type: the type. For example, to pass the Dog type where `Dog.Type` is expected, you can pass `Dog.self`.

```
self
```
In instance code, this instance, polymorphically. In static/class code, this type, polymorphically; `self.init(...)` instantiates the type.

```
Self
```
In a method declaration, when specifying the return type, this class or this instance's class, polymorphically.

Protocols

A *protocol* is a way of expressing commonalities between otherwise unrelated types. For example, a Bee object and a Bird object might need to have certain features in common by virtue of the fact that both a bee and a bird can fly. Thus, it might be useful to define a Flier type. The question is: In what sense can both Bee and Bird be Fliers?

One possibility, of course, is class inheritance. If Bee and Bird are both classes, there's a class hierarchy of superclasses and subclasses. So Flier could be the superclass of both Bee and Bird. The problem is that there may be other reasons why Flier *can't* be the superclass of both Bee and Bird. A Bee is an Insect; a Bird isn't. Yet they both have the power of flight — independently. We need a type that cuts across the class hierarchy somehow, tying remote classes together.

Moreover, what if Bee and Bird are *not* both classes? In Swift, that's a very real possibility. Important and powerful objects can be structs instead of classes. But there is no struct hierarchy of superstructs and substructs! That, after all, is one of the major differences between structs and classes. Yet structs need the ability to possess and express formal commonalities every bit as much as classes do. How can a Bee struct and a Bird struct both be Fliers?

Swift solves this problem through the use of protocols. Protocols are tremendously important in Swift; the Swift header defines over 70 of them! Moreover, Objective-C has protocols as well; Swift protocols correspond roughly to these, and can interchange with them. Cocoa makes heavy use of protocols.

A protocol is an object *type*, but there are no protocol *objects* — you can't instantiate a protocol. A protocol is much more lightweight than that. A protocol declaration is just a list of properties and methods. The properties have no values, and the methods have no code! The idea is that a "real" object type can formally declare that it belongs to a protocol type; this is called *adopting* or *conforming to* the protocol. An object type that adopts a protocol is signing a contract stating that it actually implements the properties and methods listed by the protocol.

For example, let's say that being a Flier consists of no more than implementing a `fly` method. Then a Flier protocol could specify that there must be a `fly` method; to do so, it lists the `fly` method *with no function body*, like this:

```
protocol Flier {
    func fly()
}
```

Any type — an enum, a struct, a class, or even another protocol — can then adopt this protocol. To do so, it lists the protocol after a colon after its name in its declaration. (If the adopter is a class with a superclass, the protocol comes after a comma after the superclass specification.)

Let's say Bird is a struct. Then it can adopt Flier like this:

```
struct Bird : Flier {
} // compile error
```

So far, so good. But that code won't compile. The Bird struct has made a promise to implement the features listed in the Flier protocol. Now it must keep that promise! The `fly` method is the only requirement of the Flier protocol. To satisfy that requirement, I'll just give Bird an empty `fly` method:

```
protocol Flier {
    func fly()
}
struct Bird : Flier {
    func fly() {
    }
}
```

That's all there is to it! We've defined a protocol, and we've made a struct adopt that protocol. Of course, in real life you'll probably want to make the adopter's implementation of the protocol's methods *do* something; but the protocol says nothing about that.

A protocol can also declare a method *and provide its implementation*, thanks to protocol extensions, which I'll discuss later in this chapter.

Why Protocols?

Perhaps at this point you're scratching your head over *why* this is a useful thing to do. We made a Bird a Flier, but so what? If we wanted a Bird to know how to fly, why didn't we just give Bird a `fly` method *without* adopting any protocol? The answer has to do with types. Don't forget, a protocol is a type. Our protocol, Flier, is a type. Therefore, I can use Flier wherever I would use a type — to declare the type of a variable, for example, or the type of a function parameter:

```
func tellToFly(_ f:Flier) {
    f.fly()
}
```

Think about that code for a moment, because it embodies the entire point of protocols. A protocol is a type — so *polymorphism applies*. Protocols give us another way of expressing the notion of type and subtype. This means that, by the substitution principle, a Flier here could be an instance of any object type — an enum, a struct, or a class. It doesn't matter *what* object type it is, *as long as it adopts the Flier protocol*. If it adopts the Flier protocol, it can be passed where a Flier is expected. Moreover, if it adopts the Flier protocol, then it must have a `fly` method, because that's exactly what it *means* to adopt the Flier protocol! Therefore the compiler is willing to let us send the `fly` message to this object.

The converse, however, is not true: an object with a `fly` method is *not* automatically a Flier. It isn't enough to *obey* the requirements of a protocol; the object type must *adopt* the protocol. This code won't compile:

```
struct Bee {
    func fly() {
    }
}
let b = Bee()
tellToFly(b) // compile error
```

A Bee *can* be sent the `fly` message, *qua* Bee. But `tellToFly` doesn't take a Bee parameter; it takes a Flier parameter. Formally, a Bee is *not* a Flier. To make a Bee a Flier, simply declare formally that Bee adopts the Flier protocol. This code does compile:

```
struct Bee : Flier {
    func fly() {
    }
}
let b = Bee()
tellToFly(b)
```

Enough of birds and bees; we're ready for a real-life example! As I've already said, Swift is chock full of protocols already. Let's make one of our own object types adopt one. One of the most useful Swift protocols is CustomStringConvertible. The CustomStringConvertible protocol requires that we implement a `description` String property. If we do that, a wonderful thing happens: when an instance of this type is used in string interpolation or `print` (or the `po` command in the console), the `description` property value is used automatically to represent it.

Recall, for example, the Filter enum, from earlier in this chapter. I'll add a `description` property to it:

```
enum Filter : String {
    case albums = "Albums"
    case playlists = "Playlists"
    case podcasts = "Podcasts"
    case books = "Audiobooks"
    var description : String { return self.rawValue }
}
```

But that isn't enough, in and of itself, to give Filter the power of the CustomStringConvertible protocol; to do that, we also need to *adopt* the CustomStringConvertible protocol formally. There is already a colon and a type in the Filter declaration, so an adopted protocol comes after a comma:

```
enum Filter : String, CustomStringConvertible {
    case albums = "Albums"
    case playlists = "Playlists"
    case podcasts = "Podcasts"
    case books = "Audiobooks"
    var description : String { return self.rawValue }
}
```

We have now made Filter formally adopt the CustomStringConvertible protocol. The CustomStringConvertible protocol requires that we implement a `description` String property; we *do* implement a `description` String property, so our code compiles. Now we can hand a Filter to `print`, or interpolate it into a string, and its `description` will appear automatically:

```
let type = Filter.albums
print(type) // Albums
print("It is \(type)") // It is Albums
```

Behold the power of protocols. You can give *any* object type the power of string conversion in exactly the same way.

Note that a type can adopt more than one protocol! For example, the built-in Double type adopts CustomStringConvertible, Hashable, Comparable, and other built-in protocols. To declare adoption of multiple protocols, list each one after the first protocol in the declaration, separated by comma. For example:

```
struct MyType : CustomStringConvertible, Hashable, Comparable {
    // ...
}
```

(Of course, that code won't compile unless I also declare the required methods in MyType, so that MyType really *does* adopt those protocols.)

Protocol Type Testing and Casting

A protocol is a type, and an adopter of a protocol is its subtype. Polymorphism applies. Therefore, the operators for mediating between an object's declared type and its real type work when the object is declared as a protocol type. For example, given a protocol Flier that is adopted by both Bird and Bee, we can use the `is` operator to test whether a particular Flier is in fact a Bird:

```
func isBird(_ f:Flier) -> Bool {
    return f is Bird
}
```

Similarly, `as!` and `as?` can be used to cast an object declared as a protocol type down to its actual type. This is important to be able to do, because the adopting object will typically be able to receive messages that the protocol can't receive. For example, let's say that a Bird can get a worm:

```
struct Bird : Flier {
    func fly() {
    }
    func getWorm() {
    }
}
```

A Bird can `fly` *qua* Flier, but it can `getWorm` only *qua* Bird. Thus, you can't tell just any old Flier to get a worm:

```
func tellGetWorm(_ f:Flier) {
    f.getWorm() // compile error
}
```

But if this Flier is a Bird, clearly it *can* get a worm. That is exactly what casting is all about:

```
func tellGetWorm(f:Flier) {
    (f as? Bird)?.getWorm()
}
```

Declaring a Protocol

Protocol declaration can take place only at the top level of a file. To declare a protocol, use the keyword `protocol` followed by the name of the protocol, which, being an object type, should start with a capital letter. Then come curly braces which may contain the following:

Properties

A property declaration in a protocol consists of `var` (not `let`), the property name, a colon, its type, and curly braces containing the word `get` or the words `get set`. In the former case, the adopter's implementation of this property *can* be writable, while in the latter case, it *must* be: the adopter may not implement a `get set` property as a read-only computed property or as a constant (`let`) stored property.

To declare a static/class property, precede it with the keyword `static`. A class adopter is free to implement this as a `class` property.

Methods

A method declaration in a protocol is a function declaration without a function body — that is, it has no curly braces and thus it has no code. Any object function type is legal, including `init` and `subscript`. (The syntax for declaring a subscript in a protocol is the same as the syntax for declaring a subscript in an object type, except that there will be no function bodies, so the curly braces, like those of a property declaration in a protocol, will contain `get` or `get set`.)

To declare a static/class method, precede it with the keyword `static`. A class adopter is free to implement this as a `class` method.

If a method, as implemented by an enum or struct, might need to be declared `mutating`, the protocol must specify the `mutating` designation; the adopter cannot add `mutating` if the protocol lacks it. However, the adopter may omit `mutating` if the protocol has it.

A protocol can itself adopt one or more protocols; the syntax is just as you would expect — a colon after the protocol's name in the declaration, followed by a comma-separated list of the protocols it adopts. In effect, this gives you a way to create an entire secondary hierarchy of types! The Swift headers make heavy use of this.

A protocol that adopts another protocol may repeat the contents of the adopted protocol's curly braces, for clarity; but it doesn't have to, as this repetition is implicit. An object type that adopts such a protocol must satisfy the requirements of this protocol and all protocols that the protocol adopts.

 If the only purpose of a protocol would be to combine other protocols by adopting all of them, without adding any new requirements, and if this combination is used in just one place in your code, you can avoid formally declaring the protocol in the first place by creating the combining protocol on the fly. To do so, join the protocol names with &. This is called *protocol composition*.

Optional Protocol Members

In Objective-C, a protocol member can be declared optional, meaning that this member doesn't have to be implemented by the adopter, but it may be. For compatibility with Objective-C, Swift allows optional protocol members, but only in a protocol explicitly bridged to Objective-C by preceding its declaration with the @objc attribute. In such a protocol, an optional member is declared by preceding its declaration with the keywords @objc optional:

```
@objc protocol Flier {
    @objc optional var song : String {get}
    @objc optional func sing()
}
```

Only a class can adopt such a protocol, and this feature will work only if the class is an NSObject subclass, or if the optional member is marked with the @objc attribute:

```
class Bird : Flier {
    @objc func sing() {
        print("tweet")
    }
}
```

(All these @objc markings are needed because optional protocol members are not really a Swift feature; they are an Objective-C feature! Therefore, everything about an optional protocol member must be explicitly exposed to Objective-C, so that Objective-C can implement it. I'll explain in Chapter 10 *how* Objective-C implements optional protocol members.)

An optional member is not guaranteed to be implemented by the adopter, so Swift doesn't know whether it's safe to send a Flier either the song message or the sing message.

In the case of an optional property like song, Swift solves the problem by wrapping its value in an Optional. If the Flier adopter doesn't implement the property, the result is nil and no harm done:

```
let f : Flier = Bird()
let s = f.song // s is an Optional wrapping a String
```

This is one of those rare situations where you can wind up with a double-wrapped Optional. For example, if the value of the optional property song were itself a String?, then fetching its value from a Flier would yield a String??:

```
@objc protocol Flier {
    @objc optional var song : String? {get}
    @objc optional func sing()
}
let f : Flier = Bird()
let s = f.song // s is an Optional wrapping an Optional wrapping a String
```

An optional property can be declared {get set} by its protocol, but there is no legal syntax for setting such a property in an object of that protocol type. For example, if f is a Flier and song is declared {get set}, you can't set f.song. I regard this as a bug in the language.

In the case of an optional method like sing, things are more elaborate. If the method is not implemented, we must not be permitted to call it in the first place. To handle this situation, the method *itself* is automatically typed as an Optional version of its declared type. To send the sing message to a Flier, therefore, you must unwrap it. The safe approach is to unwrap it optionally, with a question mark:

```
let f : Flier = Bird()
f.sing?()
```

That code compiles — and it also runs safely. The effect is to send the sing message to f *only if this Flier adopter implements* sing. If this Flier adopter *doesn't* implement sing, nothing happens. You could have force-unwrapped the call — f.sing!() — but then your app would crash if the adopter doesn't implement sing.

If an optional method returns a value, that value is wrapped in an Optional as well. For example:

```
@objc protocol Flier {
    @objc optional var song : String {get}
    @objc optional func sing() -> String
}
```

If we now call sing?() on a Flier, the result is an Optional wrapping a String:

```
let f : Flier = Bird()
let s = f.sing?() // s is an Optional wrapping a String
```

If we force-unwrap the call — sing!() — the result is either a String (if the adopter implements sing) or a crash (if it doesn't).

Many Cocoa protocols have optional members. For example, your iOS app will have an app delegate class that adopts the UIApplicationDelegate protocol; this protocol has many methods, all of them optional. That fact, however, will have no effect on how you implement those methods; you don't need to mark them in any special way. Your app delegate class is already a subclass of NSObject, so this feature just works. Either you implement a method or you don't. (I'll talk more about Cocoa protocols in Chapter 10, and about delegate protocols in Chapter 11.)

Class Protocol

A protocol declared with the keyword class after the colon after its name is a *class protocol*, meaning that it can be adopted only by class object types:

```
protocol SecondViewControllerDelegate : class {
    func accept(data:Any!)
}
```

(There is no need to say `class` if this protocol is already marked `@objc`; the `@objc` attribute implies that this is also a class protocol.)

A typical reason for declaring a class protocol is to take advantage of special memory management features that apply only to classes. I haven't discussed memory management yet, but I'll continue the example anyway (and I'll repeat it when I do talk about memory management, in Chapter 5):

```
class SecondViewController : UIViewController {
    weak var delegate : SecondViewControllerDelegate?
    // ...
}
```

The keyword `weak` marks the `delegate` property as having special memory management. Only a class instance can participate in this kind of special memory management. The `delegate` property is typed as a protocol, and a protocol might be adopted by a struct or an enum type. So to satisfy the compiler that this object *will* in fact be a class instance, and *not* a struct or enum instance, the protocol is declared as a class protocol.

Implicitly Required Initializers

Suppose that a protocol declares an initializer. And suppose that a class adopts this protocol. By the terms of this protocol, this class and any subclass it may ever have must implement this initializer. Therefore, the class must not only implement the initializer, but it must also mark it as `required`. An initializer declared in a protocol is thus *implicitly required*, and the class is forced to make that requirement explicit.

Consider this simple example, which won't compile:

```
protocol Flier {
    init()
}
class Bird : Flier {
    init() {} // compile error
}
```

That code generates an elaborate but perfectly informative compile error message: "Initializer requirement `init()` can only be satisfied by a `required` initializer in non-final class Bird." To compile our code, we must designate our initializer as `required`:

```
protocol Flier {
    init()
}
class Bird : Flier {
    required init() {}
}
```

The alternative, as the compile error message informs us, would be to mark the Bird class as final. This would mean that it *cannot have any subclasses* — thus guaranteeing that the problem will never arise in the first place. If Bird were marked final, there would be no need to mark its init as required.

In the above code, Bird is *not* marked as final, and its init *is* marked as required. This, as I've already explained, means in turn that any subclass of Bird that implements any designated initializers — and thus loses initializer inheritance — must implement the required initializer and mark it required as well.

That fact is responsible for a strange and annoying feature of real-life iOS programming with Swift. Let's say you subclass the built-in Cocoa class UIViewController — something that you are extremely likely to do. And let's say you give your subclass an initializer — something that you are also extremely likely to do:

```
class ViewController: UIViewController {
    init() {
        super.init(nibName: "ViewController", bundle: nil)
    }
}
```

That code won't compile. The compile error says: "required initializer init(coder:) must be provided by subclass of UIViewController."

What's going on here? It turns out that UIViewController adopts a protocol, NSCoding. And this protocol requires an initializer init(coder:). None of that is your doing; UIViewController and NSCoding are declared by Cocoa, not by you. But that doesn't matter! This is the same situation I was just describing. Your UIViewController subclass must either inherit init(coder:) or must explicitly implement it and mark it required. Well, your subclass has implemented a designated initializer of its own — thus cutting off initializer inheritance. Therefore it must implement init(coder:) and mark it required.

But that makes no sense if you are not expecting init(coder:) ever to be *called* on your UIViewController subclass. You are being forced to write an initializer for which you can provide no meaningful functionality! Fortunately, Xcode's Fix-it feature will offer to write the initializer for you, like this:

```
required init?(coder aDecoder: NSCoder) {
    fatalError("init(coder:) has not been implemented")
}
```

That code satisfies the compiler. (I'll explain in Chapter 5 why it's a legal initializer even though it doesn't fulfill an initializer's contract.) It also deliberately crashes if it is ever called.

If you *do* have functionality for this initializer, you will delete the `fatalError` line and insert your own functionality in its place. A minimum meaningful implementation would be `super.init(coder:aDecoder)`, but of course if your class has properties that need initialization, you will need to initialize them first.

Not only UIViewController but *lots* of built-in Cocoa classes adopt NSCoding. You will encounter this problem if you subclass *any* of those classes and implement your own initializer. It's just something you'll have to get used to.

Literal Convertibles

One of the wonderful things about Swift is that so many of its features, rather than being built-in and accomplished by magic, are implemented *in* Swift and are exposed to view in the Swift header. Literals are a case in point. The reason you can say 5 to make an Int whose value is 5, instead of formally initializing Int by saying `Int(5)`, is not because of magic (or at least, not entirely because of magic). It's because Int adopts a protocol, ExpressibleByIntegerLiteral. Not only Int literals, but *all* literals work this way. The following protocols are declared in the Swift header:

- ExpressibleByNilLiteral
- ExpressibleByBooleanLiteral
- ExpressibleByIntegerLiteral
- ExpressibleByFloatLiteral
- ExpressibleByStringLiteral
- ExpressibleByStringInterpolation
- ExpressibleByExtendedGraphemeClusterLiteral
- ExpressibleByUnicodeScalarLiteral
- ExpressibleByArrayLiteral
- ExpressibleByDictionaryLiteral

Your own object type can adopt a literal convertible protocol as well. This means that a literal can appear where an instance of your object type is expected! For example, here we declare a Nest type that contains some number of eggs (its `eggCount`):

```
struct Nest : ExpressibleByIntegerLiteral {
    var eggCount : Int = 0
    init() {}
    init(integerLiteral val: Int) {
        self.eggCount = val
    }
}
```

Because Nest adopts ExpressibleByIntegerLiteral, we can pass an Int where a Nest is expected, and our init(integerLiteral:) will be called automatically, causing a new Nest object with the specified eggCount to come into existence at that moment:

```
func reportEggs(_ nest:Nest) {
    print("this nest contains \(nest.eggCount) eggs")
}
reportEggs(4) // this nest contains 4 eggs
```

Generics

A *generic* is a sort of placeholder for a type, into which an actual type will be slotted later. This is useful because of Swift's strict typing. Without sacrificing that strict typing, there are situations where you can't or don't want to specify too precisely in a certain region of your code what the exact type of something is going to be.

An Optional is a good example. Any type of value can be wrapped up in an Optional. Yet there is no doubt as to what type is wrapped up in a *particular* Optional. How can this be? It's because Optional is a generic type. Here's how an Optional works.

I have already said that an Optional is an enum, with two cases: .none and .some. If an Optional's case is .some, it has an associated value — the value that is wrapped by this Optional. But what is the type of that associated value? On the one hand, one wants to say that it can be any type; that, after all, is why anything can be wrapped up in an Optional. On the other hand, any given Optional that wraps a value wraps a value of some specific type. When you unwrap an Optional, that unwrapped value needs to be typed as what it is, so that it can be sent messages appropriate for that type.

The solution to this sort of problem is a Swift generic. The declaration for the Optional enum in the Swift header starts like this:

```
enum Optional<Wrapped> {
    // ...
}
```

That syntax means: "In the course of this declaration, I'm going to be using a made-up type — a type *placeholder* — that I call Wrapped. It's a real and individual type, but I'm not going to say more about it right now. All you need to know is that whenever I say Wrapped, I mean this one particular type. When an actual Optional is created, it will be perfectly clear what type Wrapped stands for, and then, wherever I say Wrapped, you should substitute the type that it stands for."

Let's look at more of the Optional declaration:

```
enum Optional<Wrapped> {
    case none
    case some(Wrapped)
    init(_ some: Wrapped)
    // ...
}
```

Having declared that Wrapped is a placeholder, we proceed to use it. There's a case .none. There's also a case .some, which has an associated value — of type Wrapped. We also have an initializer, which takes a parameter — of type Wrapped. Thus, the type with which we are initialized — whatever type that may be — *is* type Wrapped, and thus is the type of value that is associated with the .some case.

Now, in the declaration of the Optional enum, Wrapped is a placeholder. But in real life, when an actual Optional is created, it will be initialized with an actual value of some definite type. Usually, we'll use the question-mark syntactic sugar (type String?) and the initializer will be called for us behind the scenes, but let's call the initializer explicitly for the sake of clarity:

```
let s = Optional("howdy")
```

Obviously, "howdy" here is a String. But we're calling init(_ some: Wrapped), so "howdy" is being supplied here as a Wrapped instance. As a result, the compiler knows that Wrapped is String *throughout* this particular Optional<Wrapped>. This is called *resolving* (or *specializing*) the generic. Under the hood, wherever Wrapped appears in the declaration of the Optional enum, the compiler now substitutes String. Thus, the declaration for the *particular* Optional referred to by the variable s looks, in the compiler's mind, like this:

```
enum Optional<String> {
    case None
    case Some(String)
    init(_ some: String)
    // ...
}
```

That is the pseudocode declaration of an Optional whose Wrapped placeholder has been replaced everywhere with the String type. We can summarize this by saying that s is an Optional<String>. In fact, that is legal syntax! We can create the same Optional like this:

```
let s : Optional<String> = "howdy"
```

As that example demonstrates, generics do not in any way relax Swift's strict typing. In particular, they do not postpone resolution of a type until runtime. When you use a generic, your code will still specify its real type; that real type is known with complete specificity at compile time! The particular region of your code where the type is *expected* uses a generic so that *it* doesn't have to specify the type fully, but at the point where that code is *used* by other code, the type *is* specified. The placeholder is generic, but it is *resolved* to an actual specific type whenever the generic is used.

Generic Declarations

Here's a list of the places where generics, in one form or another, can be declared in Swift:

Generic protocol with Self

In a protocol, use of the keyword Self (note the capitalization) turns the protocol into a generic. Self is a placeholder meaning the *type of the adopter*. For example, here's a Flier protocol that declares a method that takes a Self parameter:

```
protocol Flier {
    func flockTogetherWith(_ f:Self)
}
```

That means that if the Bird object type were to adopt the Flier protocol, its implementation of flockTogetherWith would need to declare its parameter as a Bird.

Generic protocol with associated type

A protocol can declare an *associated type* using an associatedtype statement. This turns the protocol into a generic; the associated type name is a placeholder. For example:

```
protocol Flier {
    associatedtype Other
    func flockTogetherWith(_ f:Other)
    func mateWith(_ f:Other)
}
```

An adopter will declare some particular type where the generic uses the associated type name, thus resolving the placeholder. If the Bird struct adopts the Flier protocol and declares the parameter of flockTogetherWith as a Bird, that declaration resolves Other to Bird for this particular adopter — and now Bird must declare the parameter for mateWith as a Bird as well:

```
struct Bird : Flier {
    func flockTogetherWith(_ f:Bird) {}
    func mateWith(_ f:Bird) {}
}
```

Generic functions

A function declaration can use a generic placeholder type for any of its parameters, for its return type, and within its body. Declare the placeholder name in angle brackets after the function name:

```
func takeAndReturnSameThing<T> (_ t:T) -> T {
    return t
}
```

The caller will use some particular type where the placeholder appears in the function declaration, thus resolving the placeholder:

```
let thing = takeAndReturnSameThing("howdy")
```

Here, the type of the argument "howdy" used in the call resolves T to String; therefore this call to takeAndReturnSameThing will also return a String, and the variable capturing the result, thing, is inferred to String as well.

Generic object types

An object type declaration can use a generic placeholder type anywhere within its curly braces. Declare the placeholder name in angle brackets after the object type name:

```
struct HolderOfTwoSameThings<T> {
    var firstThing : T
    var secondThing : T
    init(thingOne:T, thingTwo:T) {
        self.firstThing = thingOne
        self.secondThing = thingTwo
    }
}
```

A user of this object type will use some particular type where the placeholder appears in the object type declaration, thus resolving the placeholder:

```
let holder = HolderOfTwoSameThings(thingOne:"howdy", thingTwo:"getLost")
```

Here, the type of the thingOne argument, "howdy", used in the initializer call, resolves T to String; therefore thingTwo must also be a String, and the properties firstThing and secondThing are Strings as well.

For generic functions and object types, which use the angle bracket syntax, the angle brackets may contain multiple placeholder names, separated by comma. For example:

```
func flockTwoTogether<T, U>(_ f1:T, _ f2:U) {}
```

The two parameters of flockTwoTogether can now be resolved to two different types (though they do not *have* to be different).

Type Constraints

All our examples so far have permitted any type to be substituted for the placeholder. Alternatively, you can limit the types that are eligible to be used for resolving a particular placeholder. This is called a *type constraint*. The simplest form of type constraint is to put a colon and a type name after the placeholder's name when it first appears. The type name after the colon can be a class name or a protocol name.

For example, let's return to our Flier and its `flockTogetherWith` function. Suppose we want to say that the parameter of `flockTogetherWith` should be declared by the adopter as a type that adopts Flier. You would *not* do that by declaring the type of that parameter as Flier in the protocol:

```
protocol Flier {
    func flockTogetherWith(_ f:Flier)
}
```

That code says: You can't adopt this protocol unless you declare a function `flock-TogetherWith` whose parameter is declared as Flier:

```
struct Bird : Flier {
    func flockTogetherWith(_ f:Flier) {}
}
```

That isn't what we want to say! We want to say that Bird should be able to adopt Flier while declaring its parameter as being of *some Flier adopter type*, such as Bird. The way to say that is to use a placeholder constrained as a Flier. For example, we could do it like this:

```
protocol Flier {
    associatedtype Other : Flier
    func flockTogetherWith(_ f:Other)
}
```

Unfortunately, that's illegal: a protocol can't use itself as a type constraint. The workaround is to declare an extra protocol that Flier itself will adopt, and constrain Other to that protocol:

```
protocol Superflier {}
protocol Flier : Superflier {
    associatedtype Other : Superflier
    func flockTogetherWith(_ f:Other)
}
```

Now Bird can be a legal adopter like this:

```
struct Bird : Flier {
    func flockTogetherWith(_ f:Bird) {}
}
```

In a generic function or a generic object type, the type constraint appears in the angle brackets. For example:

```
func flockTwoTogether<T:Flier>(_ f1:T, _ f2:T) {}
```

If Bird and Insect both adopt Flier, this flockTwoTogether function can be called with two Bird arguments or with two Insect arguments — but not with a Bird and an Insect, because T is just one placeholder, signifying one Flier adopter type. And you can't call flockTwoTogether with two String parameters, because a String is not a Flier.

A type constraint on a placeholder is often useful as a way of assuring the compiler that some message can be sent to an instance of the placeholder type. For example, let's say we want to implement a function myMin that returns the smallest from a list of the same type. Here's a promising implementation as a generic function, but there's one problem — it doesn't compile:

```
func myMin<T>(_ things:T...) -> T {
    var minimum = things[0]
    for ix in 1..<things.count {
        if things[ix] < minimum { // compile error
            minimum = things[ix]
        }
    }
    return minimum
}
```

The problem is the comparison things[ix] < minimum. How does the compiler know that the type T, the type of things[ix] and minimum, will be resolved to a type that can in fact be compared using the less-than operator in this way? It doesn't, and that's exactly why it rejects that code. The solution is to promise the compiler that the resolved type of T *will* in fact work with the less-than operator. The way to do that, it turns out, is to constrain T to Swift's built-in Comparable protocol; adoption of the Comparable protocol exactly guarantees that the adopter *does* work with the less-than operator:

```
func myMin<T:Comparable>(_ things:T...) -> T {
```

Now myMin compiles, because it cannot be called except by resolving T to an object type that adopts Comparable and hence can be compared with the less-than operator. Naturally, built-in object types that you think should be comparable, such as Int, Double, String, and Character, do in fact adopt the Comparable protocol! If you look in the Swift headers, you'll find that the built-in min global function is declared in just this way, and for just this reason.

 A generic protocol (a protocol whose declaration mentions Self or has an associated type) can be used as a type *only* in a generic, as a type constraint. If you try to use it in any other way, you'll get a compile error: "Protocol can only be used as a generic constraint." There's a way around this restriction, called *type erasure*; for an excellent discussion of type erasure, see *http://robnapier.net/erasure*.

Explicit Specialization

In the examples so far, the user of a generic resolves the placeholder's type through inference. But there's another way to perform resolution: the user can resolve the type manually. This is called *explicit specialization*. In some situations, explicit specialization is mandatory — namely, if the placeholder type cannot be resolved through inference. There are two forms of explicit specialization:

Generic protocol with associated type

  The adopter of a protocol can resolve the protocol's associated type manually through a typealias declaration using the protocol's associated type name with an explicit type assignment. For example:

```
protocol Flier {
    associatedtype Other
}
struct Bird : Flier {
    typealias Other = String
}
```

Generic object type

  The user of a generic object type can resolve the object's placeholder type(s) manually using the same angle bracket syntax used to declare the generic in the first place, with actual type names in the angle brackets. For example:

```
class Dog<T> {
    var name : T?
}
let d = Dog<String>()
```

  (That explains the Optional<String> type used earlier in this chapter and in Chapter 3.)

You cannot explicitly specialize a generic function. You can, however, declare a generic type with a nongeneric function that uses the generic type's placeholder; explicit specialization of the generic type resolves the placeholder, and thus resolves the function:

```
protocol Flier {
    init()
}
struct Bird : Flier {
    init() {}
}
struct FlierMaker<T:Flier> {
    static func makeFlier() -> T {
        return T()
    }
}
let f = FlierMaker<Bird>.makeFlier() // returns a Bird
```

Generics are Not Covariant

A generic type specialized to a subtype is not polymorphic with respect to the same generic type specialized to a supertype. For example, suppose we have a simple generic struct along with a class and its subclass:

```
struct Wrapper<T> {
}
class Cat {
}
class CalicoCat : Cat {
}
```

Then you can't assign a Wrapper specialized to CalicoCat where a Wrapper specialized to Cat is expected:

```
let w : Wrapper<Cat> = Wrapper<CalicoCat>() // compile error
```

It appears that polymorphism is failing here — but it isn't. The two generic types, Wrapper<Cat> and Wrapper<CalicoCat>, are not superclass and subclass. Rather, if this assignment were possible, we would say that the types are *covariant*, meaning that the polymorphic relationship between the specializations of the placeholders is applied to the generic types themselves. Certain Swift built-in generic types *are* covariant; Optional is a clear example! But it's not a *general* language feature, and there's no way for you to specify that *your* generic types should be covariant.

When a class is generic, you can subclass it, provided you resolve the generic. You can do this either through a matching generic subclass or by resolving the superclass generic explicitly. For example, here's a generic Dog:

```
class Dog<T> {
    var name : T?
}
```

You can subclass it as a generic whose placeholder matches that of the superclass:

```
class NoisyDog<T> : Dog<T> {}
```

That's legal because the resolution of the NoisyDog placeholder T will resolve the Dog placeholder T. The alternative is to subclass an explicitly specialized Dog:

```
class NoisyDog : Dog<String> {}
```

Associated Type Chains

When a generic placeholder is constrained to a generic protocol with an associated type, you can refer to that type using a dot-notation chain: the placeholder name, a dot, and the associated type name.

Here's an example. Imagine that in a game program, soldiers and archers are enemies of one another. I'll express this by subsuming a Soldier struct and an Archer struct under a Fighter protocol that has an Enemy associated type, which is itself constrained to be a Fighter (again, I'll need an extra protocol that Fighter adopts):

```
protocol Superfighter {}
protocol Fighter : Superfighter {
    associatedtype Enemy : Superfighter
}
```

I'll resolve that associated type manually for both structs:

```
struct Soldier : Fighter {
    typealias Enemy = Archer
}
struct Archer : Fighter {
    typealias Enemy = Soldier
}
```

Now I'll create a generic struct to express the opposing camps of these fighters:

```
struct Camp<T:Fighter> {
}
```

Now suppose that a camp may contain a spy from the opposing camp. What is the type of that spy? Well, if this is a Soldier camp, it's an Archer; and if it's an Archer camp, it's a Soldier. More generally, since T is a Fighter, it's the type of the Enemy of this adopter of Fighter. I can express that neatly by a chain consisting of the placeholder name T, a dot, and the associated type name Enemy:

```
struct Camp<T:Fighter> {
    var spy : T.Enemy?
}
```

The result is that if, for a particular Camp, T is resolved to Soldier, T.Enemy means Archer — and *vice versa*. We have created a correct and inviolable rule for the type that a Camp's spy must be. This won't compile:

```
var c = Camp<Soldier>()
c.spy = Soldier() // compile error
```

We've tried to assign an object of the wrong type to this Camp's spy property. But this does compile:

```
var c = Camp<Soldier>()
c.spy = Archer()
```

Longer chains of associated type names are possible — in particular, when a generic protocol has an associated type which is itself constrained to a generic protocol with an associated type.

For example, let's give each type of Fighter a characteristic weapon: a soldier has a sword, while an archer has a bow. I'll make a Sword struct and a Bow struct, and I'll unite them under a Wieldable protocol:

```
protocol Wieldable {
}
struct Sword : Wieldable {
}
struct Bow : Wieldable {
}
```

I'll add a Weapon associated type to Fighter, which is constrained to be a Wieldable, and once again I'll resolve it manually for each type of Fighter:

```
protocol Superfighter {
    associatedtype Weapon : Wieldable
}
protocol Fighter : Superfighter {
    associatedtype Enemy : Superfighter
}
struct Soldier : Fighter {
    typealias Weapon = Sword
    typealias Enemy = Archer
}
struct Archer : Fighter {
    typealias Weapon = Bow
    typealias Enemy = Soldier
}
```

Now let's say that every Fighter has the ability to steal his enemy's weapon. I'll give the Fighter generic protocol a steal(weapon:from:) method. How can the Fighter generic protocol express the parameter types in a way that causes its adopter to declare this method with the proper types?

The from: parameter type is this Fighter's Enemy. We already know how to express that: it's the placeholder plus dot-notation with the associated type name. Here, the placeholder is the adopter of this protocol — namely, Self. So the from: parameter type is Self.Enemy. And what about the weapon: parameter type? That's the Weapon of that Enemy! So the weapon: parameter type is Self.Enemy.Weapon:

```
protocol Fighter : Superfighter {
    associatedtype Enemy : Superfighter
    func steal(weapon:Self.Enemy.Weapon, from:Self.Enemy)
}
```

(We could omit Self from that code, and it would still compile and would mean the same thing. But Self would still be the implicit start of the chain, and I think it makes the meaning of the code clearer.)

The result is that the following declarations for Soldier and Archer correctly adopt the Fighter protocol, and the compiler approves:

```
struct Soldier : Fighter {
    typealias Weapon = Sword
    typealias Enemy = Archer
    func steal(weapon:Bow, from:Archer) {
    }
}
struct Archer : Fighter {
    typealias Weapon = Bow
    typealias Enemy = Soldier
    func steal (weapon:Sword, from:Soldier) {
    }
}
```

The example is artificial, but the concept is not. The Swift headers make heavy use of associated type chains; the associated type chain `Iterator.Element` is particularly common, because it expresses the type of the element of a sequence. (The Sequence generic protocol has an associated type Iterator, which is constrained to be an adopter of the generic IteratorProtocol, which in turn has an associated type Element.) Even longer associated type chains are not uncommon; for example, the LazyCollection-Protocol `filter` method refers to a type `Self.Elements.Iterator.Element`.

Additional Constraints

A simple type constraint limits the types eligible for resolving a placeholder to a single type. Sometimes, you want to limit the eligible resolving types still further: you want additional constraints.

In a generic protocol, the colon in an associated type constraint is effectively the same as the colon that appears in a type declaration. Thus, it can be followed by multiple protocols, or by a superclass and multiple protocols:

```
class Dog {
}
class FlyingDog : Dog, Flier {
}
protocol Flier {
}
protocol Walker {
}
protocol Generic {
    associatedtype T : Flier, Walker
    associatedtype U : Dog, Flier
}
```

In the Generic protocol, the associated type T can be resolved only as a type that adopts the Flier protocol *and* the Walker protocol, and the associated type U can be resolved only as a type that is a Dog (or a subclass of Dog) *and* that adopts the Flier protocol.

In the angle brackets of a generic function or object type, that syntax is illegal. In the simple case where a type is to adopt more than one protocol, you can use protocol composition:

```
func flyAndWalk<T: Flier & Walker> (_ f:T) {}
```

More generally, you can append a where clause, consisting of one or more comma-separated additional constraints on a declared placeholder:

```
func flyAndWalk<T> (_ f:T) where T:Flier, T:Walker {} // or T: Flier & Walker
func flyAndWalk2<T> (_ f:T) where T:Flier, T:Dog {}
```

A where clause can also impose additional constraints on the associated type of a generic protocol that already constrains a placeholder, using an associated type chain (described in the preceding section). This pseudocode shows what I mean; I've omitted the content of the where clause, to focus on what the where clause will be constraining:

```
protocol Flier {
    associatedtype Other
}
func flockTogether<T:Flier> (_ f:T) where T.Other /*???*/ {}
```

As you can see, the placeholder T is already constrained to be a Flier. Flier is itself a generic protocol, with an associated type Other. Thus, whatever type resolves T will resolve Other. The where clause is going to constrain T.Other; thus, it will constrain further the types eligible to resolve T, by restricting the types eligible to resolve Other.

So what sort of restriction are we allowed to impose on our associated type chain? One possibility is the same sort of restriction as in the preceding example — a colon followed by a protocol that it must adopt, or by a class that it must descend from. Here's an example with a protocol:

```
protocol Flier {
    associatedtype Other
}
struct Bird : Flier {
    typealias Other = String
}
struct Insect : Flier {
    typealias Other = Bird
}
func flockTogether<T:Flier> (_ f:T) where T.Other:Equatable {}
```

Both Bird and Insect adopt Flier, but they are not both eligible as the argument in a call to the flockTogether function. The flockTogether function can be called with a Bird argument, because a Bird's Other associated type is resolved to String, which adopts the built-in Equatable protocol. But flockTogether can't be called with an Insect argument, because an Insect's Other associated type is resolved to Bird, which doesn't adopt the Equatable protocol:

```
flockTogether(Bird()) // okay
flockTogether(Insect()) // compile error
```

Instead of a colon, we can use an equality operator == followed by a type. The type at the end of the associated type chain must then *be* this exact type — not merely an adopter or subclass. For example:

```
protocol Flier {
    associatedtype Other
}
protocol Walker {
}
struct Kiwi : Walker {
}
struct Bird : Flier {
    typealias Other = Kiwi
}
struct Insect : Flier {
    typealias Other = Walker
}
func flockTogether<T:Flier> (_ f:T) where T.Other == Walker {}
```

The flockTogether function can be called with an Insect argument, because Insect adopts Flier and resolves Other to Walker. But it can't be called with a Bird argument. Bird adopts Flier, and it resolves Other to *an adopter of* Walker, namely Kiwi — but that isn't good enough to satisfy the == restriction.

The type on the right side of the == operator can itself be an associated type chain. The resolved types at the ends of the two chains must then be identical. For example:

```
protocol Flier {
    associatedtype Other
}
struct Bird : Flier {
    typealias Other = String
}
struct Insect : Flier {
    typealias Other = Int
}
func flockTwoTogether<T:Flier, U:Flier> (_ f1:T, _ f2:U)
    where T.Other == U.Other {}
```

The flockTwoTogether function can be called with a Bird and a Bird, and it can be called with an Insect and an Insect, but it can't be called with an Insect and a Bird, because they don't resolve the Other associated type to the same type.

The Swift header makes extensive use of where clauses with an == operator, especially as a way of restricting a sequence type. Take, for example, the String append(contentsOf:) method, declared like this:

```
mutating func append<S : Sequence>(contentsOf newElements: S)
    where S.Iterator.Element == Character
```

A String must consist of only Characters. The constraint means that a character sequence — but *not* a sequence of something else, such as Int — can be concatenated to a String:

```
var s = "hello"
s.append(contentsOf: " world".characters) // "hello world"
```

The Array `append(contentsOf:)` method is declared a little differently:

```
mutating func append<S : Sequence>(contentsOf newElements: S)
    where S.Iterator.Element == Element
```

An Array can consist of any type — but only *one* type. Array is a generic struct whose Element placeholder is the type of its elements. The constraint here enforces a rule that you can append to an Array the elements of any sort of Sequence, but only if they are the same kind of element as the elements of this array. If the array consists of String elements, you can add more String elements to it, but not Int elements.

Extensions

An *extension* is a way of injecting your own code into an object type that has already been declared elsewhere; you are *extending* an existing object type. You can extend your own object types; you can also extend one of Swift's object types or one of Cocoa's object types, in which case you are *adding functionality* to a type that doesn't belong to you!

Extension declaration can take place only at the top level of a file. To declare an extension, put the keyword `extension` followed by the name of an existing object type, then optionally a colon plus the names of any protocols you want to add to the list of those adopted by this type, and finally curly braces containing the usual things that go inside an object type declaration — with the following restrictions:

- An extension can't override an existing member (but it can overload an existing method).
- An extension can't declare a stored property (but it can declare a computed property).
- An extension of a class can't declare a designated initializer or a deinitializer (but it can declare a convenience initializer).

Extending Object Types

In my real programming life, I sometimes extend a built-in Swift or Cocoa type just to encapsulate some missing functionality by expressing it as a property or method. Here are some examples from actual apps.

In a card game, I need to shuffle the deck, which is stored in an array. I extend Swift's built-in Array type to give it a `shuffle` method:

```
extension Array {
    mutating func shuffle () {
        for i in (0..<self.count).reversed() {
            let ix1 = i
            let ix2 = Int(arc4random_uniform(UInt32(i+1)))
            (self[ix1], self[ix2]) = (self[ix2], self[ix1])
        }
    }
}
```

Cocoa's Core Graphics framework has many useful functions associated with the CGRect struct, and Swift already extends CGRect to add some helpful properties and methods; but there's no shortcut for getting the center point (a CGPoint) of a CGRect, something that in practice one very often needs. I extend CGRect to give it a `center` property:

```
extension CGRect {
    var center : CGPoint {
        return CGPoint(x:self.midX, y:self.midY)
    }
}
```

An extension can declare a static or class member; since an object type is usually globally available, this can be a good way to slot a global function into an appropriate namespace. For example, in one of my apps, I find myself frequently using a certain color (a UIColor). Instead of creating that color repeatedly, it makes sense to encapsulate the instructions for generating it in a global function. But instead of making that function *completely* global, I make it — appropriately enough — a read-only class variable of UIColor:

```
extension UIColor {
    class var myGolden : UIColor {
        return self.init(
            red:1.000, green:0.894, blue:0.541, alpha:0.900
        )
    }
}
```

Now I can use that color throughout my code as `UIColor.myGolden`, completely parallel to built-in class properties such as `UIColor.red`.

Another good use of an extension is to make built-in Cocoa classes work with your private data types. For example, in my Zotz app, I've defined an enum whose raw values are the key strings to be used when archiving or unarchiving a property of a Card:

```
enum Archive : String {
    case color = "itsColor"
    case number = "itsNumber"
    case shape = "itsShape"
    case fill = "itsFill"
}
```

The only problem is that in order to use this enum when archiving, I have to take its rawValue each time:

```
coder.encode(self.color, forKey:Archive.color.rawValue)
coder.encode(self.number, forKey:Archive.number.rawValue)
coder.encode(self.shape, forKey:Archive.shape.rawValue)
coder.encode(self.fill, forKey:Archive.fill.rawValue)
```

That's just ugly. An elegant fix (suggested in a WWDC 2015 video) is to teach NSCoder, the class of coder, what to do when the forKey: argument is an Archive instead of a String. In an extension, I overload the encode(_:forKey:) method:

```
extension NSCoder {
    func encode(_ objv: Any?, forKey key: Archive) {
        self.encode(objv, forKey:key.rawValue)
    }
}
```

In effect, I've moved the rawValue call out of my code and into NSCoder's code. Now I can archive a Card without saying rawValue:

```
coder.encode(self.color, forKey:Archive.color)
coder.encode(self.number, forKey:Archive.number)
coder.encode(self.shape, forKey:Archive.shape)
coder.encode(self.fill, forKey:Archive.fill)
```

Extensions on one's own object types can help to organize one's code. A frequently used convention is to add an extension for each protocol one's object type needs to adopt, like this:

```
class ViewController: UIViewController {
    // ... UIViewController method overrides go here ...
}
extension ViewController : UIPopoverPresentationControllerDelegate {
    // ... UIPopoverPresentationControllerDelegate methods go here ...
}
extension ViewController : UIToolbarDelegate {
    // ... UIToolbarDelegate methods go here ...
}
```

An extension on your own object type is also a way to spread your definition of that object type over multiple files, if you feel that several shorter files are better than one long file.

When you extend a Swift struct, a curious thing happens with initializers: it becomes possible to declare an initializer and keep the implicit initializers:

```
struct Digit {
    var number : Int
}
extension Digit {
    init() {
        self.init(number:42)
    }
}
```

In that code, the explicit declaration of an initializer through an extension did not cause us to lose the implicit memberwise initializer, as would have happened if we had declared the same initializer inside the original struct declaration. Now we can instantiate a Digit by calling the explicitly declared initializer — `Digit()` — or by calling the implicit memberwise initializer — `Digit(number:7)`.

Extending Protocols

When you extend a protocol, you can add methods and properties to the protocol, just as for any object type. Unlike a protocol declaration, these methods and properties are not mere requirements, to be fulfilled by the adopter of the protocol; they are actual methods and properties, to be *inherited* by the adopter of the protocol! For example:

```
protocol Flier {
}
extension Flier {
    func fly() {
        print("flap flap flap")
    }
}
struct Bird : Flier {
}
```

Observe that Bird can now adopt Flier without implementing the `fly` method. That's because the Flier protocol extension *supplies* the `fly` method! Bird thus *inherits* an implementation of `fly`:

```
let b = Bird()
b.fly() // flap flap flap
```

An adopter can provide its own alternative implementation of a method inherited from a protocol extension:

```
protocol Flier {
}
extension Flier {
    func fly() {
        print("flap flap flap")
    }
}
struct Insect : Flier {
```

```
    func fly() {
        print("whirr")
    }
}
let i = Insect()
i.fly() // whirr
```

But be warned: this kind of inheritance is *not polymorphic*. The adopter's implementation is not an override; it is merely another implementation. The internal identity rule does *not* apply; it matters how a reference is typed:

```
let f : Flier = Insect()
f.fly() // flap flap flap
```

Even though f is internally an Insect (as we can discover with the is operator), the fly message is being sent to an object reference typed as a Flier, so it is Flier's implementation of the fly method that is called, not Insect's implementation.

To get something that looks like polymorphic inheritance, we must declare fly as a requirement *in the original protocol*:

```
protocol Flier {
    func fly() // *
}
extension Flier {
    func fly() {
        print("flap flap flap")
    }
}
struct Insect : Flier {
    func fly() {
        print("whirr")
    }
}
```

Now an Insect maintains its internal integrity:

```
let f : Flier = Insect()
f.fly() // whirr
```

The chief benefit of protocol extensions is that they allow code to be moved to an appropriate scope. Here's an example from my Zotz app. I have four enums, each representing an attribute of a Card: Fill, Color, Shape, and Number. They all have an Int raw value. I was tired of having to say rawValue: every time I initialized one of these enums from its raw value, so I gave each enum a delegating initializer with no externalized parameter name, that calls the built-in init(rawValue:) initializer:

```
enum Fill : Int {
    case empty = 1
    case solid
    case hazy
    init?(_ what:Int) {
```

```
            self.init(rawValue:what)
        }
    }
    enum Color : Int {
        case color1 = 1
        case color2
        case color3
        init?(_ what:Int) {
            self.init(rawValue:what)
        }
    }
    // ... and so on ...
```

However, I didn't like the repetition of my initializer declaration. This initializer is shared by all four enums, so I'd like to write it once, as part of some type from which all four enums can inherit it. That sounds like a protocol extension! An enum with a raw value automatically adopts the built-in generic RawRepresentable protocol, where the raw value type is an associated type called RawValue. So I can shoehorn my initializer into the RawRepresentable protocol:

```
    extension RawRepresentable {
        init?(_ what:RawValue) {
            self.init(rawValue:what)
        }
    }
    enum Fill : Int {
        case empty = 1
        case solid
        case hazy
    }
    enum Color : Int {
        case color1 = 1
        case color2
        case color3
    }
    // ... and so on ...
```

The Swift standard library makes heavy use of protocol extensions. Again, this is because protocol extensions allow code to be moved to an appropriate scope. The Swift standard library declares a lot of important protocols; protocol extensions allow those protocols to be given *methods*, like this:

```
    extension Sequence {
        func enumerated() -> EnumeratedSequence<Self>
    }
```

Without protocol extensions, the only way to apply enumeration to a Sequence, and *only* to a Sequence, would be to declare a *global generic function* with a constraint restricting the parameter to Sequence adopters. (And before Swift 2.0, when protocol extensions were introduced, that's exactly what *was* declared.)

Extending Generics

When you extend a generic type, the placeholder type names are visible to your extension declaration. That's good, because you might need to use them; but it can make your code a little mystifying, because you seem to be using an undefined type name out of the blue. It might be a good idea to add a comment, to remind yourself what you're up to:

```
class Dog<T> {
    var name : T?
}
extension Dog {
    func sayYourName() -> T? { // T is the type of self.name
        return self.name
    }
}
```

A generic type extension declaration can include a where clause. This has the same effect as any generic constraint: it limits which resolvers of the generic can call the code injected by this extension, and assures the compiler that your code is legal for those resolvers.

As with protocol extensions, this means that a global function can be turned into a method. Recall this example from earlier in this chapter:

```
func myMin<T:Comparable>(_ things:T...) -> T {
    var minimum = things[0]
    for ix in 1..<things.count {
        if things[ix] < minimum {
            minimum = things[ix]
        }
    }
    return minimum
}
```

That's a global function. I'd prefer to inject it into Array as a method. Array is a generic struct whose placeholder type is called Element. To make this work, I need somehow to bring along the Comparable type constraint that makes this code legal; without it, as you remember, my use of < won't compile. I can do that with a where clause:

```
extension Array where Element:Comparable {
    func myMin() -> Element {
        var minimum = self[0]
        for ix in 1..<self.count {
            if self[ix] < minimum {
                minimum = self[ix]
            }
        }
```

```
        }
            return minimum
        }
    }
```

The where clause is a constraint guaranteeing that this array's elements adopt Comparable, so the compiler permits the use of the < operator — and it doesn't permit the myMin method to be called on an array whose elements *don't* adopt Comparable.

The Swift standard library makes heavy use of generic extensions. For example, in real life, there is already a min method; myMin isn't needed. The min method is a Sequence method — and it is declared just like myMin, namely through an extension on the generic Sequence protocol with a constraint guaranteeing that the sequence's elements are comparable:

```
extension Sequence where Iterator.Element : Comparable {
    func min() -> Self.Iterator.Element?
}
```

An interesting problem arises when you want your generic extension where clause to specify type equality (==) instead of protocol adoption or class inheritance (:). The problem is that you can't do that with a generic struct. Suppose, for example, that I want to give Array a sum method when the elements are Ints. I can't do it:

```
extension Array where Element == Int { // compile error
    func sum() -> Int {
        return self.reduce(0, +)
    }
}
```

But you *can* do it with a generic protocol, so the trick is to extend a generic protocol adopted by your struct. In this case, there is already a generic protocol adopted by Array, namely Sequence; so the solution is extend that instead:

```
extension Sequence where Iterator.Element == Int {
    func sum() -> Int {
        return self.reduce(0, +)
    }
}
```

(I'll discuss reduce later in this chapter.)

Umbrella Types

Swift provides a few built-in types as general umbrella types, capable of embracing multiple real types under a single heading.

Any

The Any type is the universal Swift umbrella type. Where an Any object is expected, absolutely any object or function can be passed, without casting:

```
func anyExpecter(_ a:Any) {}
anyExpecter("howdy")      // a struct instance
anyExpecter(String.self) // a struct type
anyExpecter(Dog())        // a class instance
anyExpecter(Dog.self)     // a class type
anyExpecter(anyExpecter) // a function
```

Going the other way, of course, if you want to type an Any object as a more specific type, you will generally have to cast down. Such a cast is legal for any specific object type or function type. A forced cast isn't safe, but you can easily make it safe, because you can also test an Any object against any specific object type or function type. Here, anything is typed as Any:

```
if anything is String {
    let s = anything as! String
    // ...
}
```

In Swift 3, the Any umbrella type is of great importance because it is the general medium of interchange between Swift and the Cocoa Objective-C APIs. When an Objective-C object type is nonspecific (Objective-C id), it will appear to Swift as Any. Commonly encountered examples are UserDefaults, NSCoding, and key–value coding (Chapter 10); all of these allow you to *pass* an object of indeterminate class along with a string key name, and they allow you to *retrieve* an object of indeterminate class by a string key name. That object is typed, in Swift, as Any (or as an Optional wrapping Any, so that it can be nil).

For example:

```
let ud = UserDefaults.standard
let s = "howdy"
ud.set(s, forKey:"Test")
```

The first parameter of UserDefaults set(_:forKey:) is typed as Any. Thus, Any functions as a general conduit for crossing the bridge between the Swift world and Cocoa's Objective-C world.

However, merely casting or assigning to Any does not in fact cross the bridge there and then. Rather, the bridge will be crossed later, when Objective-C actually receives this value and has to do something with it. At that time, it will be transformed into an object type that Objective-C can deal with. Objective-C objects must be class types. Certain common Swift types are structs, which would be meaningless to Objective-C; therefore they are automatically bridged to Objective-C class types. For example, a String becomes an NSString, and an Int becomes an NSNumber. Nonclass types that are not automatically bridged are boxed up in a way that allows them to survive the journey into Objective-C's world, even though Objective-C can't do anything directly with such types.

Coming back the other way, if Objective-C hands you an Any object, you will need to cast it down to its underlying type in order to do anything useful with it:

```
let ud = UserDefaults.standard
let test = ud.object(forKey:"Test") as! String
```

The result returned from UserDefaults object(forKey:) is typed as Any — actually, as an Optional wrapping an Any, because UserDefaults might need to return nil to indicate that no object exists for that key. But you know that it's supposed to be a string, so you cast it down to String. Of course, you'd better be telling the truth when you cast down with as!, or you will crash when the code runs and the cast turns out to be impossible. You can use the as? and is operators, if you're in doubt, to make sure your cast is safe:

```
let ud = UserDefaults.standard
let test = ud.object(forKey:"Test") as? String
if test != nil {
    // ...
}
```

AnyObject

AnyObject is an empty protocol (requiring no properties or methods) with the special feature that *all class types* conform to it automatically. Although Objective-C APIs present Objective-C id *as* Any in Swift, Swift AnyObject *is* Objective-C id. In Swift 3, AnyObject is useful primarily when you want to take advantage of the *behavior* of Objective-C id, as I'll demonstrate in a moment.

A class type can be assigned directly where an AnyObject is expected; to retrieve it as its original type, you'll need to cast down:

```
class Dog {
}
let d = Dog()
let anyo : AnyObject = d
let d2 = anyo as! Dog
```

Assigning to an AnyObject requires crossing the bridge to Objective-C then and there. If you're not starting with a class type, you must cast (with as). If this type is automatically bridged to an Objective-C class type, it becomes that type; other types are boxed up in a way that allows them to survive the journey into Objective-C's world, even though Objective-C can't deal with them directly:

```
let s = "howdy" as AnyObject   // String to NSString to AnyObject
let i = 1 as AnyObject          // Int to NSNumber to AnyObject
let r = CGRect() as AnyObject  // CGRect to boxed type to AnyObject
```

Thus we may imagine that when you hand a Swift object off to Objective-C as an Any value, as in the previous section, it later crosses the bridge by being cast, behind the scenes, to AnyObject.

Suppressing type checking

Because AnyObject is Objective-C id, it can be used, like Objective-C id, to suspend the compiler's judgment as to whether a certain message can be sent to an object. Thus, you can send a message to an AnyObject without bothering to cast down to its real type.

You can't send just any old message to an AnyObject; the message must correspond to a class member that meets one of the following criteria:

- It is a member of an Objective-C class.

- It is a member of your own Swift subclass of an Objective-C class.

- It is a member of your own Swift extension of an Objective-C class.

- It is a member of a Swift class or protocol marked @objc.

This feature is fundamentally parallel to optional protocol members, which I discussed earlier in this chapter. Let's start with two classes:

```
class Dog {
    @objc var noise : String = "woof"
    @objc func bark() -> String {
        return "woof"
    }
}
class Cat {}
```

The Dog property noise and the Dog method bark are marked @objc, so they are visible as potential messages to be sent to an AnyObject. To prove it, I'll type a Cat as an AnyObject and send it one of these messages. Let's start with the noise property:

```
let c : AnyObject = Cat()
let s = c.noise
```

That code, amazingly, compiles. Moreover, it doesn't crash when the code runs! The noise property has been typed as an Optional wrapping its original type. Here, that's an Optional wrapping a String. If the object typed as AnyObject doesn't implement noise, the result is nil and no harm done.

Now let's try it with a method call:

```
let c : AnyObject = Cat()
let s = c.bark?()
```

Again, that code compiles and is safe. If the Object typed as AnyObject doesn't implement bark, no bark() call is performed; the method result type has been wrapped in
an Optional, so s is typed as String? and has been set to nil. If the AnyObject turns
out to have a bark method (for example, if it had been a Dog), the result is an
Optional wrapping the returned String. If you call bark!() on the AnyObject instead,
the result will be a String, but you'll crash if the AnyObject doesn't implement bark.
Unlike an optional protocol member, you can even send the message *with no unwrapping*. This is legal:

```
let c : AnyObject = Cat()
let s = c.bark()
```

That's just like force-unwrapping the call: the result is a String, but it's possible to
crash.

Object identity

Sometimes, what you want to know is not what *type* an object is, but whether an
object itself is the *particular object* you think it is. This problem can't arise with a
value type, but it can arise with a reference type, where there can be more than one
distinct reference to one and the same object. A class is a reference type, so the problem can arise with class instances.

Swift's solution is the identity operator (===). It is defined for operands whose type is
AnyObject?, and compares one object reference with another. It is not a comparison
of values for equality, like the equality operator (==); you're asking whether two object
references refer to one and the same object. There is also a negative version of the
identity operator (!==).

A typical use case is that a class instance arrives from Cocoa, and you need to know
whether it is in fact a particular object to which you already have a reference. For
example, a Notification has an object property that helps identify the notification
(usually, it is the original sender of the notification). We can use === to test whether
this object is the same as some object to which we already have a reference. However, object is typed as Any in Swift 3 (actually, as an Optional wrapping Any), so we
must cast to AnyObject? in order to take advantage of the identity operator:

```
func changed(_ n:Notification) {
    let player = MPMusicPlayerController.applicationMusicPlayer()
    if n.object as AnyObject? === player {
        // ...
    }
}
```

AnyClass

AnyClass is the type of AnyObject. It corresponds to the Objective-C Class type. It arises typically in declarations where a Cocoa API wants to say that a class is expected.

For example, the UIView `layerClass` class property is declared, in its Swift translation, like this:

```
class var layerClass : AnyClass {get}
```

That means: if you override this class property, implement your getter to return a class. This will presumably be a CALayer subclass. To return an actual class in your implementation, send the `self` message to the name of the class:

```
override class var layerClass : AnyClass {
    return CATiledLayer.self
}
```

A reference to an AnyClass object behaves much like a reference to an AnyObject object. You can send it any Objective-C message that Swift knows about — any Objective-C *class* message. To illustrate, once again I'll start with two classes:

```
class Dog {
    @objc static var whatADogSays : String = "woof"
}
class Cat {}
```

Objective-C can see `whatADogSays`, and it sees it as a class property. Therefore you can send `whatADogSays` to an AnyClass reference:

```
let c : AnyClass = Cat.self
let s = c.whatADogSays
```

A reference to a class, such as you can obtain by applying `type(of:)` to an object, or by sending `self` to the type name, is of a type that adopts AnyClass, and you can compare references to such types with the `===` operator. In effect, this is a way of finding out whether two references to classes refer to the same class. This construct is valuable because you can't use the `is` operator when the thing on the right side is a type *reference* rather than a literal type name. For example:

```
func typeTester(_ d:Dog, _ whattype:Dog.Type) {
    if type(of:d) === whattype {
        // ...
    }
}
```

The condition is `true` only if d is identically of type `whattype`. For example, if Dog has a subclass NoisyDog, then the condition is `true` if the parameters are `Dog()` and `Dog.self`, or if they are `NoisyDog()` and `NoisyDog.self`, but not if they are `NoisyDog()` and `Dog.self`.

Collection Types

Swift, in common with most modern computer languages, has built-in collection types Array and Dictionary, along with a third type, Set. Array and Dictionary are sufficiently important that the language accommodates them with some special syntax. At the same time, like most Swift types, they are quite thinly provided with related functions; some missing functionality is provided by Cocoa's NSArray and NSDictionary, to which they are respectively bridged. The Set collection type is bridged to Cocoa's NSSet.

Array

An array (Array, a struct) is an ordered collection of object instances (the *elements* of the array) accessible by index number, where an index number is an Int numbered from 0. Thus, if an array contains four elements, the first has index 0 and the last has index 3. A Swift array cannot be sparse: if there is an element with index 3, there is also an element with index 2 and so on.

The salient feature of Swift arrays is their strict typing. Unlike some other computer languages, a Swift array's elements must be *uniform* — that is, the array must consist solely of elements of the same definite type. Even an empty array must have a definite element type, despite lacking elements at this moment. An array is itself typed in accordance with its element type. Arrays whose elements are of different types are considered, themselves, to be of two different types: an array of Int elements is of a different type from an array of String elements.

If all this reminds you of Optionals, it should. Like an Optional, a Swift array is a generic. It is declared as `Array<Element>`, where the placeholder Element is the type of a particular array's elements. And, like an Optional, Array types are covariant, meaning that they behave polymorphically in accordance with their element types: if NoisyDog is a subclass of Dog, then an array of NoisyDog can be used where an array of Dog is expected.

To declare or state the type of a given array's elements, you could explicitly resolve the generic placeholder; an array of Int elements would thus be an `Array<Int>`. However, Swift offers syntactic sugar for stating an array's element type, using square brackets around the name of the element type, like this: `[Int]`. That's the syntax you'll use most of the time.

A literal array is represented as square brackets containing a list of its elements separated by comma (and optional spaces): for example, `[1,2,3]`. The literal for an empty array is empty square brackets: `[]`.

An array's default initializer init(), called by appending empty parentheses to the array's type, yields an empty array of that type. Thus, you can create an empty array of Int like this:

```
var arr = [Int]()
```

Alternatively, if a reference's type is known in advance, the empty array [] can be inferred to that type. Thus, you can also create an empty array of Int like this:

```
var arr : [Int] = []
```

If you're starting with a literal array containing elements, you won't usually need to declare the array's type, because Swift will infer it by looking at the elements. For example, Swift will infer that [1,2,3] is an array of Int. If the array element types consist of a class and its subclasses, like Dog and NoisyDog, Swift will infer the common superclass as the array's type. However, in some cases you will need to declare an array reference's type explicitly even while assigning a literal to that array:

```
let arr : [Any] = [1, "howdy"]           // mixed bag
let arr2 : [Flier] = [Insect(), Bird()] // protocol adopters
```

An array also has an initializer whose parameter is a sequence. This means that if a type is a sequence, you can split an instance of it into the elements of an array. For example:

- Array(1...3) generates the array of Int [1,2,3].
- Array("hey".characters) generates the array of Character ["h","e","y"].
- Array(d), where d is a Dictionary, generates an array of tuples of the key–value pairs of d.

Another array initializer, init(repeating:count:), lets you populate an array with the same value. In this example, I create an array of 100 Optional strings initialized to nil:

```
let strings : [String?] = Array(repeating:nil, count:100)
```

That's the closest you can get in Swift to a sparse array; we have 100 slots, each of which might or might not contain a string (and to start with, none of them do).

Array casting and type testing

When you assign, pass, or cast an array of a certain type to another array type, you are really operating on the individual elements of the array. Thus, for example:

```
let arr : [Int?] = [1,2,3]
```

That code is actually syntactic sugar: assigning an array of Int where an array of Optionals wrapping Int is expected constitutes a request that each individual Int in the original array should be wrapped in an Optional. And that is exactly what happens:

```
let arr : [Int?] = [1,2,3]
print(arr) // [Optional(1), Optional(2), Optional(3)]
```

Similarly, suppose we have a Dog class and its NoisyDog subclass; then this code is legal:

```
let dog1 : Dog = NoisyDog()
let dog2 : Dog = NoisyDog()
let arr = [dog1, dog2]
let arr2 = arr as! [NoisyDog]
```

In third line, we have an array of Dog. In the fourth line, we apparently cast this array down to an array of NoisyDog — which really means that we cast each individual Dog in the first array to a NoisyDog (and we won't crash when we do that, provided each element of the first array really *is* a NoisyDog).

Similarly, the as? operator will cast an array to an Optional wrapping an array, which will be nil if the requested cast cannot be performed for each element individually:

```
let dog1 : Dog = NoisyDog()
let dog2 : Dog = NoisyDog()
let dog3 : Dog = Dog()
let arr = [dog1, dog2]
let arr2 = arr as? [NoisyDog] // Optional wrapping an array of NoisyDog
let arr3 = [dog2, dog3]
let arr4 = arr3 as? [NoisyDog] // nil
```

Finally, you can test each element of an array with the is operator by testing the array itself. For example, given the array of Dog from the previous code, you can say:

```
if arr is [NoisyDog] { // ...
```

That will be true if each element of the array is in fact a NoisyDog.

Array comparison

Array equality works just as you would expect: two arrays are equal if they contain the same number of elements and all the elements are pairwise equal in order:

```
let i1 = 1
let i2 = 2
let i3 = 3
let arr : [Int] = [1,2,3]
if arr == [i1,i2,i3] { // they are equal!
```

Two arrays don't have to be of the same type to be compared against one another for equality, but the test won't succeed unless they do in fact contain objects that are equal to one another. Here, I compare a Dog array against a NoisyDog array; this is legal if equatability is defined for two Dogs. (For example, Dog might be an NSObject subclass; or you might make Dog adopt Equatable, as I'll explain in Chapter 5.) The two arrays are in fact equal, because the dogs they contain are the same dogs in the same order:

```
let nd1 = NoisyDog()
let d1 = nd1 as Dog
let nd2 = NoisyDog()
let d2 = nd2 as Dog
if [d1,d2] == [nd1,nd2] { // they are equal!
```

Arrays are value types

Because an array is a struct, it is a value type, not a reference type. This means that every time an array is assigned to a variable or passed as argument to a function, it is effectively copied. I do not mean to imply, however, that merely assigning or passing an array is expensive, or that a lot of actual copying takes place every time. If the reference to an array is a constant, clearly no copying is necessary; and even operations that yield a new array derived from another array, or that mutate an array, may be quite efficient. You just have to trust that the designers of Swift have thought about these problems and have implemented arrays efficiently behind the scenes.

Although an array itself is a value type, its elements are treated however those elements would normally be treated. In particular, an array of class instances, assigned to multiple variables, results in multiple references to the same instances.

Array subscripting

The Array struct implements subscript methods to allow access to elements using square brackets after a reference to an array. You can use an Int inside the square brackets. For example, in an array consisting of three elements, if the array is referred to by a variable arr, then arr[1] accesses the second element.

You can also use a Range of Int inside the square brackets. For example, if arr is an array with three elements, then arr[1...2] signifies the second and third elements. Technically, an expression like arr[1...2] yields something called an ArraySlice. However, an ArraySlice is very similar to an array; for example, you can subscript an ArraySlice in just the same ways you would subscript an array, and an ArraySlice can be passed where an array is expected.

In general, therefore, you will probably pretend that an ArraySlice *is* an array. However, they are not the same thing. An ArraySlice is not a new object; it's a way of pointing into a section of the original array. For this reason, its index numbers are those of the original array. For example:

```
let arr = ["manny", "moe", "jack"]
let slice = arr[1...2]
print(slice[1]) // moe
```

The ArraySlice `slice` consists of `"moe"` and `"jack"` — and these are not merely `"moe"` and `"jack"` taken *from* the original array, but the `"moe"` and `"jack"` *in* the original array. For this reason, their index numbers are 1 and 2, just as in the original array. If you want to extract a new array based on this slice, coerce the slice to an Array:

```
let arr2 = Array(slice)
print(arr2[1]) // jack
```

If the reference to an array is mutable (`var`, not `let`), then a subscript expression can be assigned to. This alters what's in that slot. Of course, what is assigned must accord with the type of the array's elements:

```
var arr = [1,2,3]
arr[1] = 4 // arr is now [1,4,3]
```

If the subscript is a range, what is assigned must be a slice. You can assign a literal array, because it will be cast for you to an ArraySlice; but if what you're starting with is an array reference, you'll have to cast it to a slice yourself. Such assignment can change the length of the array being assigned to:

```
var arr = [1,2,3]
arr[1..<2] = [7,8] // arr is now [1,7,8,3]
arr[1..<2] = [] // arr is now [1,8,3]
arr[1..<1] = [10] // arr is now [1,10,8,3] (no element was removed!)
let arr2 = [20,21]
// arr[1..<1] = arr2 // compile error! You have to say this:
arr[1..<1] = ArraySlice(arr2) // arr is now [1,20,21,10,8,3]
```

It is a runtime error to access an element by a number larger than the largest element number or smaller than the smallest element number. If `arr` has three elements, speaking of `arr[-1]` or `arr[3]` is not illegal linguistically, but your program will crash.

Nested arrays

It is legal for the elements of an array to be arrays. For example:

```
let arr = [[1,2,3], [4,5,6], [7,8,9]]
```

That's an array of arrays of Int. Its type declaration, therefore, is `[[Int]]`. (No law says that the contained arrays have to be the same length; that's just something I did for clarity.)

To access an individual Int inside those nested arrays, you can chain subscript operations:

```
let arr = [[1,2,3], [4,5,6], [7,8,9]]
let i = arr[1][1] // 5
```

If the outer array reference is mutable, you can also write into a nested array:

```
var arr = [[1,2,3], [4,5,6], [7,8,9]]
arr[1][1] = 100
```

You can modify the inner arrays in other ways as well; for example, you can insert additional elements into them.

Basic array properties and methods

An array is a Collection, which is itself a Sequence. If those terms have a familiar ring, they should: the same is true of a String's characters, which I called a character sequence in Chapter 3. For this reason, an array and a character sequence bear some striking similarities to one another.

As a collection, an array's count read-only property reports the number of elements it contains. If an array's count is 0, its isEmpty property is true.

An array's first and last read-only properties return its first and last elements, but they are wrapped in an Optional because the array might be empty and so these properties would need to be nil. This is one of those rare situations in Swift where you can wind up with an Optional wrapping an Optional. For example, consider an array of Optionals wrapping Ints, and what happens when you get the last property of such an array.

An array's largest accessible index is one less than its count. You may find yourself calculating index values with reference to the count; for example, to refer to the last two elements of arr, you can say:

```
let arr = [1,2,3]
let slice = arr[arr.count-2...arr.count-1] // [2,3]
```

Swift doesn't adopt the modern convention of letting you use negative numbers as a shorthand for that calculation. On the other hand, for the common case where you want the last n elements of an array, you can use the suffix(_:) method:

```
let arr = [1,2,3]
let slice = arr.suffix(2) // [2,3]
```

Both suffix(_:) and its companion prefix(_:) yield ArraySlices, and have the remarkable feature that there is no penalty for going out of range:

```
let arr = [1,2,3]
let slice = arr.suffix(10) // [1,2,3] (and no crash)
```

Instead of describing the size of the suffix or prefix by its count, you can express the limit of the suffix or prefix by its index:

```
let arr = [1,2,3]
let slice = arr.suffix(from:1)    // [2,3]
let slice2 = arr.prefix(upTo:1)    // [1]
let slice3 = arr.prefix(through:1) // [1,2]
```

An array's `startIndex` property is 0, and its `endIndex` property is its `count`. An array's `indices` property is a half-open range whose endpoints are the array's `startIndex` and `endIndex` — that is, a range accessing the entire array. Moreover, these values are Ints, so you can use ordinary arithmetic operations on them:

```
let arr = [1,2,3]
let slice = arr[arr.endIndex-2..<arr.endIndex] // [2,3]
```

But the `startIndex`, `endIndex`, and `indices` of an ArraySlice are measured against the original array; for example, after the previous code, `slice.startIndex` is 1.

The `index(of:)` method reports the index of the first occurrence of an element in an array, but it is wrapped in an Optional so that `nil` can be returned if the element doesn't appear in the array. If the array consists of Equatables, the comparison uses `==` behind the scenes to identify the element being sought:

```
let arr = [1,2,3]
let ix = arr.index(of:2) // Optional wrapping 1
```

Alternatively, you can call `index(where:)`, supplying your own function that takes an element type and returns a Bool, and you'll get back the index of the first element for which that Bool is `true`. In this example, my Bird struct has a `name` String property:

```
let aviary = [Bird(name:"Tweety"), Bird(name:"Flappy"), Bird(name:"Lady")]
let ix = aviary.index {$0.name.characters.count < 5} // Optional(2)
```

If what you want is not the index but the object itself, the `first(where:)` method returns it — wrapped, naturally, in an Optional.

As a sequence, an array's `contains(_:)` method reports whether it contains an element. Again, you can rely on the `==` operator if the elements are Equatables, or you can supply your own function that takes an element type and returns a Bool:

```
let arr = [1,2,3]
let ok = arr.contains(2) // true
let ok2 = arr.contains {$0 > 3} // false
```

The `starts(with:)` method reports whether an array's starting elements match the elements of a given sequence of the same type. Once more, you can rely on the `==` operator for Equatables, or you can supply a function that takes two values of the element type and returns a Bool stating whether they match:

```
let arr = [1,2,3]
let ok = arr.starts(with:[1,2]) // true
let ok2 = arr.starts(with:[1,-2]) {abs($0) == abs($1)} // true
```

The `elementsEqual(_:)` method is the sequence generalization of array comparison: the two sequences must be of the same length, and either their elements must be Equatables or you can supply a matching function.

The min and max methods return the smallest or largest element in an array, wrapped in an Optional in case the array is empty. If the array consists of Comparables, you can let the < operator do its work; alternatively, you can call min(by:) or max(by:), supplying a function that returns a Bool stating whether the smaller of two given elements is the first:

```
let arr = [3,1,-2]
let min = arr.min() // Optional(-2)
let min2 = arr.min {abs($0)<abs($1)} // Optional(1)
```

If the reference to an array is mutable, the append(_:) and append(contentsOf:) instance methods add elements to the end of it. The difference between them is that append(_:) takes a single value of the element type, while append(contentsOf:) takes a sequence of the element type. For example:

```
var arr = [1,2,3]
arr.append(4)
arr.append(contentsOf:[5,6])
arr.append(contentsOf:7...8) // arr is now [1,2,3,4,5,6,7,8]
```

The + operator is overloaded to behave like append(contentsOf:) (not append(_:)!) when the left-hand operand is an array, except that it generates a new array, so it works even if the reference to the array is a constant (let). If the reference to the array is mutable (var), you can append to it in place with the += operator. Thus:

```
let arr = [1,2,3]
let arr2 = arr + [4] // arr2 is now [1,2,3,4]
var arr3 = [1,2,3]
arr3 += [4] // arr3 is now [1,2,3,4]
```

If the reference to an array is mutable, the instance method insert(at:) inserts a single element at the given index. To insert multiple elements at once, call the insert(contentsOf:at:) method. Assignment into a range-subscripted array, which I described earlier, is even more flexible.

If the reference to an array is mutable, the instance method remove(at:) removes the element at that index; the instance method removeLast removes the last element. These methods also *return* the value that was removed from the array; you can ignore the returned value if you don't need it. These methods do not wrap the returned value in an Optional, and accessing an out-of-range index will crash your program. On the other hand, popLast does wrap the returned value in an Optional, and is thus safe even if the array is empty.

Similar to removeLast and popLast are removeFirst and popFirst. Alternate forms removeFirst(_:) and removeLast(_:) allow you to specify how many elements to remove, but return no value; they, too, can crash if there aren't that many elements. popFirst, remarkably, operates on a slice, not an array. This is presumably for the sake of efficiency: all it has to do is increase the slice's `startIndex` (whereas with an array, the whole array must be renumbered).

Alternatively, or if the reference is *not* mutable, you can use the `dropFirst` and `drop-Last` methods to return a slice with the end element removed. Again, you can supply a parameter stating how many elements to drop. And again, there is no penalty for dropping too many elements; you simply end up with an empty slice.

The `joined(separator:)` instance method starts with an array of arrays. It extracts their individual elements, and interposes between each sequence of extracted elements the elements of the `separator:`. The result is an intermediate sequence called a JoinSequence, and might have to be coerced further to an Array if that's what you were after. For example:

```
let arr = [[1,2], [3,4], [5,6]]
let joined = Array(arr.joined(separator:[10,11]))
// [1, 2, 10, 11, 3, 4, 10, 11, 5, 6]
```

Calling `joined()` with no `separator:` is a way to flatten an array of arrays. Again, it returns an intermediate sequence (or collection), so you might want to coerce to an Array:

```
let arr = [[1,2], [3,4], [5,6]]
let arr2 = Array(arr.flatten())
// [1, 2, 3, 4, 5, 6]
```

The `reversed` instance method yields a new array whose elements are in the opposite order from the original.

The `sort` and `sorted` instance methods respectively sort the original array (if the reference to it is mutable) and yield a new sorted array based on the original. Once again, you get two choices: if this is an array of Comparables, you can let the < operator dictate the new order; alternatively, you can call `sort(by:)` or `sorted(by:)`, supplying a function that takes two parameters of the element type and returns a Bool stating whether the first parameter should be ordered before the second (just like `min` and `max`). For example:

```
var arr = [4,3,5,2,6,1]
arr.sort() // [1, 2, 3, 4, 5, 6]
arr.sort {$0 > $1} // [6, 5, 4, 3, 2, 1]
```

In that last line, I provided an anonymous function. Alternatively, of course, you can pass as argument the name of a declared function. In Swift, comparison operators *are* the names of functions! Therefore, I can do the same thing like this:

```
var arr = [4,3,5,2,6,1]
arr.sort(by: >) // [6, 5, 4, 3, 2, 1]
```

The `split` instance method breaks an array into an array of slices at elements matching the parameter, if you call `split(separator:)`, or at elements that pass a specified test, if you call `split(isSeparator:)`; in the latter, the parameter is a function that takes a value of the element type and returns a Bool. The separator elements themselves are eliminated:

```
let arr = [1,2,3,4,5,6]
let arr2 = arr.split {$0 % 2 == 0} // split at evens: [[1], [3], [5]]
```

Array enumeration and transformation

An array is a sequence, and so you can enumerate it, inspecting or operating with each element in turn. The simplest way is by means of a for...in loop; I'll have more to say about this construct in Chapter 5:

```
let pepboys = ["Manny", "Moe", "Jack"]
for pepboy in pepboys {
    print(pepboy) // prints Manny, then Moe, then Jack
}
```

Alternatively, you can use the `forEach(_:)` instance method. Its parameter is a function that takes an element of the array (or other sequence) and returns no value. Think of it as the functional equivalent of the imperative for...in loop:

```
let pepboys = ["Manny", "Moe", "Jack"]
pepboys.forEach {print($0)} // prints Manny, then Moe, then Jack
```

If you need the index numbers as well as the elements, call the `enumerated` instance method and loop on the result; what you get on each iteration is a tuple:

```
let pepboys = ["Manny", "Moe", "Jack"]
for (ix,pepboy) in pepboys.enumerated() {
    print("Pep boy \(ix) is \(pepboy)") // Pep boy 0 is Manny, etc.
}
// or:
pepboys.enumerated().forEach {print("Pep boy \($0.0) is \($0.1)")}
```

Swift also provides some powerful array transformation instance methods. Like `forEach(_:)`, these methods all enumerate the array for you, so that the loop is buried implicitly inside the method call, making your code tighter and cleaner.

Let's start with the `filter(_:)` instance method. It yields a new array, each element of which is an element of the old array, in the same order; but some of the elements of the old array may be omitted — they were filtered out. What filters them out is a function that you supply; it accepts a parameter of the element type and returns a Bool stating whether this element should go into the new array. For example:

```
let pepboys = ["Manny", "Moe", "Jack"]
let pepboys2 = pepboys.filter {$0.hasPrefix("M")} // [Manny, Moe]
```

The map(_:) instance method yields a new array, each element of which is the result of passing the corresponding element of the old array through a function that you supply. This function accepts a parameter of the element type and returns a result which may be of some other type; Swift can usually infer the type of the resulting array elements by looking at the type returned by the function.

For example, here's how to multiply every element of an array by 2:

```
let arr = [1,2,3]
let arr2 = arr.map {$0 * 2} // [2,4,6]
```

Here's another example, to illustrate the fact that map(_:) can yield an array with a different element type:

```
let arr = [1,2,3]
let arr2 = arr.map {Double($0)} // [1.0, 2.0, 3.0]
```

Here's a real-life example showing how neat and compact your code can be when you use map(_:). In order to remove all the table cells in a section of a UITableView, I have to specify the cells as an array of IndexPath objects. If sec is the section number, I can form those IndexPath objects individually like this:

```
let path0 = IndexPath(row:0, section:sec)
let path1 = IndexPath(row:1, section:sec)
// ...
```

Hmmm, I think I see a pattern here! I could generate my array of IndexPath objects by looping through the row values using for...in. But with map(_:), there's a much tighter way to express the same loop (ct is the number of rows in the section):

```
let paths = Array(0..<ct).map {IndexPath(row:$0, section:sec)}
```

Actually, map(_:) is a Collection instance method — and a Range is itself a Collection. Therefore, I don't need the Array coercion:

```
let paths = (0..<ct).map {IndexPath(row:$0, section:sec)}
```

The map(_:) method has a specialized companion, flatMap(_:). Applied to an array, flatMap(_:) first calls map(_:), and then does one of two oddly unrelated things to the resulting array, depending on its type:

An array of arrays

If the map function produces an array of arrays, flatMap(_:) flattens the inner arrays. For instance, [[1],[2]].flatMap{$0} is [1,2]. Here's a more interesting example:

```
let arr = [[1, 2], [3, 4]]
let arr2 = arr.flatMap{$0.map{String($0)}} // ["1", "2", "3", "4"]
```

First we coerce the individual elements of each inner array to a string, thus yield-
ing an array of arrays of String. That's an array of arrays, so flatMap(_:) flattens
it, and we end up with a simple array of String.

An array of Optionals

If the map function produces an array of Optionals, flatMap(_:) safely unwraps
them, eliminating any nil elements. For example:

```
let arr : [Any] = [1, "hey", 2, "ho"]
let arr2 = arr.flatMap{$0 as? String} // ["hey", "ho"]
```

First we map the original array to an array of Optionals wrapping String: [nil,
Optional("hey"), nil, Optional("ho")]. Then flatMap(_:) unwraps each
element safely, resulting in an array of String; the nil elements are filtered out.
This neatly solves a class of problem that arises surprisingly often.

Finally, we come to the reduce instance method. If you've learned LISP or Scheme,
you're probably accustomed to reduce; otherwise, it can be a bit mystifying at first.
It's a way of *combining* all the elements of an array (actually, a sequence) into a single
value. This value's type — the result type — doesn't have to be the same as the array's
element type. You supply, as the second parameter, a function that takes two parameters; the first is of the result type, the second is of the element type, and the result is
the combination of those two parameters, as the result type. The result of each iteration becomes the function's first parameter in the *next* iteration, along with the next
element of the array as the second parameter. Thus, the output of combining pairs
accumulates, and the final accumulated value is the final output of the function.
However, that doesn't explain where the first parameter for the *first* iteration comes
from. The answer is that you have to supply it as the first argument of the reduce call.

That will all be easier to understand with a simple example. Let's assume we've got an
array of Int. Then we can use reduce to sum all the elements of the array. Here's some
pseudocode where I've left out the first argument of the call, so that you can think
about what it needs to be:

```
let sum = arr.reduce(/*???*/) {$0 + $1}
```

Each pair of parameters will be added together to get the first parameter on the next
iteration. The second parameter on every iteration is an element of the array. So the
question is, what should the first element of the array be added to? We want the
actual sum of all the elements, no more and no less; so clearly the first element of the
array should be added to 0! So here's actual working code:

```
let arr = [1, 4, 9, 13, 112]
let sum = arr.reduce(0) {$0 + $1} // 139
```

The + operator is the name of a function of the required type, so here's another way to
write the same thing:

```
let sum = arr.reduce(0, +)
```

In my real iOS programming life, I depend heavily on these methods, often using two or even all three of them together, nested or chained or both. Here's an example. I have a table view that displays data divided into sections. Under the hood, the data is an array of arrays of String — a `[[String]]` — where each subarray represents the rows of a section. Now I want to filter that data to eliminate all strings that don't contain a certain substring. I want to keep the sections intact, but if removing strings removes *all* of a section's strings, I want to eliminate that section array entirely.

The heart of the action is the test for whether a string contains a substring. I'm going to use a Cocoa method for that, in part because it lets me do a case-insensitive search. If s is a string from my array, and `target` is the substring we're looking for, then the code for looking to see whether s contains `target` case-insensitively is as follows:

```
let found = s.range(of:target, options:.caseInsensitive)
```

Recall the discussion of `range(of:)` in Chapter 3. If `found` is not `nil`, the substring was found. Here, then, is the actual code, preceded by some sample data for exercising it:

```
let arr = [["Manny", "Moe", "Jack"], ["Harpo", "Chico", "Groucho"]]
let target = "m"
let arr2 = arr.map {
    $0.filter {
        let found = $0.range(of:target, options:.caseInsensitive)
        return (found != nil)
    }
}.filter {$0.count > 0}
```

After the first two lines, setting up the sample data, what remains is a *single statement* — a map call, whose function consists of a filter call, with a filter call chained to it. If that code doesn't prove to you that Swift is cool, nothing will.

Swift Array and Objective-C NSArray

When you're programming iOS, you import the Foundation framework (or UIKit, which imports Foundation) and thus the Objective-C NSArray type. Swift's Array is bridged to Objective-C's NSArray. The most general medium of array interchange is [Any]; if an Objective-C API specifies an NSArray, with no further type information, Swift will see this as an array of Any. This reflects the fact that Objective-C's rules for what can be an element of an NSArray are looser than Swift's: the elements of an NSArray do not all have to be of the same type. On the other hand, the elements of an Objective-C NSArray must be Objective-C *objects* — that is, they must be class types.

Passing a Swift array to Objective-C is thus usually easy. Typically, you'll just pass the array, either by assignment or as an argument in a function call:

```
let arr = [UIBarButtonItem(), UIBarButtonItem()]
self.navigationItem.leftBarButtonItems = arr
```

The objects that you pass as elements of the array will cross the bridge to Objective-C in the usual way. For example:

```
let lay = CAGradientLayer()
lay.locations = [0.25, 0.5, 0.75]
```

CAGradientLayer's locations property is typed as an array of NSNumber. But we can pass Double values directly, because Double is bridged to NSNumber.

On the other hand, if a Swift type can't be seen usefully by Objective-C, automatic crossing of the bridge isn't going to do you any good. For example, in this code, anim is a CAKeyframeAnimation, and points is a Swift array of CGPoint:

```
let points = [oldP,p1,p2,newP] // [CGPoint]
anim.values = points
```

That's *legal*, but it isn't going to *work*. A CGPoint is a struct, which isn't an object in Objective-C, so this array is effectively opaque to Objective-C; Objective-C knows that this is an NSArray containing four objects, but it can't extract points from those objects and do anything with them. It is up to *you* to wrap these CGPoints as objects. In particular, you must do with them exactly what you would do if you were writing this code *in* Objective-C — you must put them inside NSValue wrappers:

```
let points = [oldP,p1,p2,newP]
anim.values = points.map {NSValue(cgPoint:$0)}
```

To call an NSArray method on a Swift array, you may have to cast to NSArray:

```
let arr = ["Manny", "Moe", "Jack"]
let s = (arr as NSArray).componentsJoined(by:", ")
// s is "Manny, Moe, Jack"
```

A Swift Array seen through a var reference is mutable, but an NSArray isn't mutable no matter how you see it. For mutability in Objective-C, you need an NSMutable-Array, a subclass of NSArray. You can't cast, assign, or pass a Swift array as an NSMutableArray; you have to coerce. The best way is to call the NSMutableArray initializer init(array:), to which you can pass a Swift array directly. To convert back from an NSMutableArray to a Swift array, you can cast:

```
var arr = ["Manny", "Moe", "Jack"]
let arr2 = NSMutableArray(array:arr)
arr2.remove("Moe")
arr = arr2 as NSArray as! [String]
```

Now let's talk about what happens when an NSArray arrives from Objective-C into Swift. There won't be any problem crossing the bridge: the NSArray will arrive safely as a Swift Array. But a Swift Array *of what?*

Of itself, an NSArray carries no information about what type of element it contains. Starting in Xcode 7, however, the Objective-C language was modified so that the declaration of an NSArray, NSDictionary, or NSSet — the three collection types that are bridged to Swift — can include element type information. (Objective-C calls this a *lightweight generic.*) Thus, for the most part, the arrays you receive from Cocoa will be correctly typed.

For example, this elegant code was previously impossible:

```
let arr = UIFont.familyNames.map {
    UIFont.fontNamesForFamilyName($0)
}
```

The result is an array of arrays of String, listing all available fonts grouped by family. That code is possible because both of those UIFont class methods are now seen by Swift as returning an array of String. Previously, those arrays were untyped, and casting down to an array of String was up to *you*.

On the other hand, lightweight generics are not always present. You might read an array from a *.plist* file stored on disk with NSArray's initializer init(contentsOf:); you might retrieve an array from UserDefaults; you might even be dealing with an Objective-C API that hasn't been updated to use lightweight generics. In such a situation, you're going to end up with a plain vanilla NSArray or a Swift array of Any. If that happens, then usually you will want to cast down or otherwise transform this array into an array of some specific Swift type. Here's an Objective-C class containing a method whose return type of NSArray hasn't been marked up with an element type:

```
@implementation Pep
- (NSArray*) boys {
    return @[@"Manny", @"Moe", @"Jack"];
}
@end
```

To call that method and do anything useful with the result, it will be necessary to cast that result down to an array of String. If I'm sure of my ground, I can force the cast:

```
let p = Pep()
let boys = p.boys() as! [String]
```

As with any cast, though, be sure you don't lie! An Objective-C array can contain more than one type of object. Don't force such an array to be cast down to a type to which not all the elements can be cast, or you'll crash when the cast fails; you'll need a more deliberate strategy for eliminating or otherwise transforming the problematic elements.

Dictionary

A dictionary (Dictionary, a struct) is an unordered collection of object pairs. In each pair, the first object is the *key*; the second object is the *value*. The idea is that you use a key to access a value. Keys are usually strings, but they don't have to be; the formal requirement is that they be types that are Equatable and also Hashable, meaning that they implement an Int hashValue property such that equal keys have equal hash values. Thus, the hash values can be used behind the scenes for rapid key access. Swift numeric types, strings, and enums are Hashables.

As with arrays, a given dictionary's types must be uniform. The key type and the value type don't have to be the same as one another, and they often will not be. But within any dictionary, all keys must be of the same type, and all values must be of the same type. Formally, a dictionary is a generic, and its placeholder types are ordered key type, then value type: Dictionary<Key,Value>. As with arrays, however, Swift provides syntactic sugar for expressing a dictionary's type, which is what you'll usually use: [Key: Value]. That's square brackets containing a colon (and optional spaces) separating the key type from the value type. This code creates an empty dictionary whose keys (when they exist) will be Strings and whose values (when they exist) will be Strings:

```
var d = [String:String]()
```

The colon is used also between each key and value in the literal syntax for expressing a dictionary. The key–value pairs appear between square brackets, separated by comma, just like an array. This code creates a dictionary by describing it literally (and the dictionary's type of [String:String] is inferred):

```
var d = ["CA": "California", "NY": "New York"]
```

The literal for an empty dictionary is square brackets containing just a colon: [:]. This notation can be used provided the dictionary's type is known in some other way. Thus, this is another way to create an empty [String:String] dictionary:

```
var d : [String:String] = [:]
```

If you try to fetch a value through a nonexistent key, there is no error, but Swift needs a way to report failure; therefore, it returns nil. This, in turn, implies that the value returned when you successfully access a value through a key must be an Optional wrapping the real value!

Access to a dictionary's contents is usually by subscripting. To fetch a value by key, subscript the key to the dictionary reference:

```
let d = ["CA": "California", "NY": "New York"]
let state = d["CA"]
```

Bear in mind, however, that after that code, state is not a String — it's an Optional wrapping a String! Forgetting this is a common beginner mistake.

If the reference to a dictionary is mutable, you can also assign into a key subscript expression. If the key already exists, its value is replaced. If the key doesn't already exist, it is created and the value is attached to it:

```
var d = ["CA": "California", "NY": "New York"]
d["CA"] = "Casablanca"
d["MD"] = "Maryland"
// d is now ["MD": "Maryland", "NY": "New York", "CA": "Casablanca"]
```

Alternatively, call updateValue(forKey:); it has the advantage that it returns the old value wrapped in an Optional, or nil if the key wasn't already present.

By a kind of shorthand, assigning nil into a key subscript expression removes that key–value pair if it exists:

```
var d = ["CA": "California", "NY": "New York"]
d["NY"] = nil // d is now ["CA": "California"]
```

Alternatively, call removeValue(forKey:); it has the advantage that it returns the removed value before it removes the key–value pair. The removed value is returned wrapped in an Optional, so a nil result tells you that this key was never in the dictionary to begin with.

As with arrays, a dictionary type is legal for casting down, meaning that the individual elements will be cast down. Typically, only the value types will differ:

```
let dog1 : Dog = NoisyDog()
let dog2 : Dog = NoisyDog()
let d = ["fido": dog1, "rover": dog2]
let d2 = d as! [String : NoisyDog]
```

As with arrays, is can be used to test the actual types in the dictionary, and as? can be used to test and cast safely. Dictionary equality, like array equality, works as you would expect.

Basic dictionary properties and enumeration

A dictionary has a count property reporting the number of key–value pairs it contains, and an isEmpty property reporting whether that number is 0.

A dictionary has a keys property reporting all its keys, and a values property reporting all its values. They are effectively opaque structs (a LazyMapCollection, if you must know), but when you enumerate them with for...in, you get the expected type:

```
var d = ["CA": "California", "NY": "New York"]
for s in d.keys {
    print(s) // s is a String
}
```

 A dictionary is unordered! You can enumerate it (or its keys, or its values), but do not expect the elements to arrive in any particular order.

You can extract all a dictionary's keys or values at once, by coercing the keys or values property to an array:

```
var d = ["CA": "California", "NY": "New York"]
var keys = Array(d.keys)
```

You can also enumerate a dictionary itself. As you might expect from what I've already said, each iteration provides a key–value tuple:

```
var d = ["CA": "California", "NY": "New York"]
for (abbrev, state) in d {
    print("\(abbrev) stands for \(state)")
}
```

You can extract a dictionary's entire contents at once as an array (of key–value tuples) by coercing the dictionary to an array:

```
var d = ["CA": "California", "NY": "New York"]
let arr = Array(d) // [("NY", "New York"), ("CA", "California")]
```

Like an array, a dictionary and its keys property and its values property are Collections and Sequences. Therefore, everything I said about arrays as Collections and Sequences in the previous section is applicable! For example, if a dictionary d has Int values, you can sum them with the reduce instance method:

```
let sum = d.values.reduce(0, +)
```

You can obtain its smallest value (wrapped in an Optional):

```
let min = d.values.min()
```

You can list the values that match some criterion:

```
let arr = Array(d.values.filter{$0 < 2})
```

(The coercion to Array is needed because the sequence that results from calling filter is lazy: there isn't really anything in it until we enumerate it or collect it into an array.) You can sort the keys:

```
let keysSorted = d.keys.sorted()
```

Swift Dictionary and Objective-C NSDictionary

The Foundation framework dictionary type is NSDictionary, and Swift's Dictionary type is bridged to it. The untyped API characterization of an NSDictionary will be [AnyHashable:Any] (AnyHashable is a *type eraser*, meaning that we can cope with the possibility that the keys will be of different hashable types).

Like NSArray, NSDictionary key and value types can now be marked in Objective-C. The most common key type in a real-life Cocoa NSDictionary is NSString, so you might well receive an NSDictionary as a [String:Any]. Specific typing of an NSDictionary's *values*, however, is much rarer; dictionaries that you pass to and receive from Cocoa will very often have values of *multiple* types. It is not at all surprising to have a dictionary whose keys are strings but whose values include a string, a number, a color, and an array. For this reason, you will usually *not* cast down the entire dictionary's type; instead, you'll work with the dictionary as having Any values, and cast when fetching an *individual value* from the dictionary. Since the value returned from subscripting a key is itself an Optional, you will typically unwrap and cast the value as a standard single move.

Here's an example. A Cocoa Notification object comes with a userInfo property. It is an NSDictionary that might itself be nil, so the Swift API characterizes it as [Any-Hashable:Any]?. Let's say I'm expecting this dictionary to be present and to contain a "progress" key whose value is an NSNumber containing a Double. My goal is to extract that NSNumber and assign the Double that it contains to a property, self.progress. Here's one way to do that safely, using optional unwrapping and optional casting (n is the Notification object):

```
let prog = (n.userInfo?["progress"] as? NSNumber)?.doubleValue
if prog != nil {
    self.progress = prog!
}
```

That's an Optional chain that ends by fetching an NSNumber's doubleValue property, so prog is implicitly typed as an Optional wrapping a Double. The code is safe, because if there is no userInfo dictionary, or if it doesn't contain a "progress" key, or if that key's value isn't an NSNumber, nothing happens, and prog will be nil. I then test prog to see whether it *is* nil; if it isn't, I know that it's safe to force-unwrap it, and that the unwrapped value is the Double I'm after.

(In Chapter 5 I'll describe another syntax for accomplishing the same goal, using conditional binding.)

Conversely, here's a typical example of creating a dictionary and handing it off to Cocoa. This dictionary is a mixed bag: its values are a UIFont, a UIColor, and an NSShadow. Its keys are all strings, which I obtain as constants from Cocoa. I form the dictionary as a literal and pass it, all in one move, with no need to cast anything (titleTextAttributes is typed as an Optional wrapping a [String:Any]):

```
UINavigationBar.appearance().titleTextAttributes = [
    NSFontAttributeName : UIFont(name: "ChalkboardSE-Bold", size: 20)!,
    NSForegroundColorAttributeName : UIColor.darkText,
    NSShadowAttributeName : {
        let shad = NSShadow()
        shad.shadowOffset = CGSize(width:1.5,height:1.5)
        return shad
    }()
]
```

As with NSArray and NSMutableArray, if you want Cocoa to mutate a dictionary, you must coerce to NSDictionary's subclass NSMutableDictionary. In this example, I want to do a join between two dictionaries, so I harness the power of NSMutable-Dictionary, which has an addEntries(from:) method:

```
var d1 = ["NY":"New York", "CA":"California"]
let d2 = ["MD":"Maryland"]
let mutd1 = NSMutableDictionary(dictionary:d1)
mutd1.addEntries(from:d2)
d1 = mutd1 as NSDictionary as! [String:String]
// d1 is now ["MD": "Maryland", "NY": "New York", "CA": "California"]
```

That sort of thing is needed quite often, because there's no native Swift method for adding the elements of one dictionary to another dictionary. Indeed, native utility methods involving dictionaries in Swift are disappointingly thin on the ground: there really aren't any. Still, Cocoa and the Foundation framework are right there, so perhaps Apple feels there's no point duplicating in the Swift standard library the functionality that already exists in Foundation. If having to drop into Cocoa bothers you, you can write your own library; for example, addEntries(from:) is easily reimplemented as a Swift Dictionary instance method through an extension:

```
extension Dictionary {
    mutating func addEntries(from d:[Key:Value]) {
        for (k,v) in d {
            self[k] = v
        }
    }
}
```

Set

A set (Set, a struct) is an unordered collection of unique objects. Its elements must be all of one type; it has a count and an isEmpty property; it can be initialized from any sequence; you can cycle through its elements with for...in. But the order of elements is not guaranteed, and you should make no assumptions about it.

The uniqueness of set elements is implemented by constraining their type to be Equatable and Hashable, just like the keys of a Dictionary. Thus, the hash values can be used behind the scenes for rapid access. Checking whether a set contains a given element, which you can do with the contains(_:) instance method, is *very* efficient — far more efficient than doing the same thing with an array. Therefore, if element uniqueness is acceptable (or desirable) and you don't need indexing or a guaranteed order, a set can be a much better choice of collection than an array.

The fact that a set's elements are Hashables means that they must also be Equatables. This makes sense, because the notion of uniqueness depends upon being able to answer the question of whether a given object is already in the set.

There are no set literals in Swift, but you won't need them because you can pass an array literal where a set is expected. There is no syntactic sugar for expressing a set type, but the Set struct is a generic, so you can express the type by explicitly specializing the generic:

```
let set : Set<Int> = [1, 2, 3, 4, 5]
```

In that particular example, however, there was no need to specialize the generic, as the Int type can be inferred from the array.

It sometimes happens (more often than you might suppose) that you want to examine one element of a set as a kind of sample. Order is meaningless, so it's sufficient to obtain *any* element, such as the first element. For this purpose, use the first instance property; it returns an Optional, just in case the set is empty.

The distinctive feature of a set is the uniqueness of its objects. If an object is added to a set and that object is already present, it isn't added a second time. Conversion from an array to a set and back to an array is thus a quick and reliable way of *uniquing* the array — though of course order is not preserved:

```
let arr = [1,2,1,3,2,4,3,5]
let set = Set(arr)
let arr2 = Array(set) // [5, 2, 3, 1, 4], perhaps
```

A set is a Collection and a Sequence, so it is analogous to an array or a dictionary, and what I have already said about those types generally applies to a set as well. For example, Set has a map(_:) instance method; it returns an array, but of course you can turn that right back into a set if you need to:

```
let set : Set = [1,2,3,4,5]
let set2 = Set(set.map {$0+1}) // {6, 5, 2, 3, 4}, perhaps
```

If the reference to a set is mutable, a number of instance methods spring to life. You can add an object with insert(_:); there is no penalty for trying to add an object that's already in the set. (To learn what happened, capture and examine the result of the insert call.) You can remove an object and return it by specifying the object itself, or something equatable to it, with the remove(_:) method; it returns the object wrapped in an Optional, or nil if the object was not present. You can remove and return the first object, whatever "first" may mean, with removeFirst; it crashes if the set is empty, so take precautions — or use popFirst, which is safe.

Equality comparison (==) is defined for sets as you would expect; two sets are equal if every element of each is also an element of the other.

If the notion of a set brings to your mind visions of Venn diagrams from elementary school, that's good, because sets have instance methods giving you all those set operations you remember so fondly. The parameter can be a set, or it can be any sequence, which will be converted to a set; for example, it might be an array, a range, or even a character sequence:

intersection(_:), formIntersection(_:)
> Yields the elements of this set that also appear in the parameter. The first forms a new Set; the second is mutating.

union(_:), formUnion(_:)
> Yields the elements of this set along with the (unique) elements of the parameter. The first forms a new Set; the second is mutating.

symmetricDifference(_:), formSymmetricDifference(_:)
> Yields the elements of this set that don't appear in the parameter, plus the (unique) elements of the parameter that don't appear in this set. The first forms a new Set; the second is mutating.

subtracting(_:), subtract(_:)
> Yields the elements of this set except for those that appear in the parameter. The first forms a new Set; the second is mutating.

isSubset(of:), isStrictSubset(of:)

isSuperset(of:), isStrictSuperset(of:)
> Returns a Bool reporting whether the elements of this set are respectively embraced by or embrace the elements of the parameter. The "strict" variant yields false if the two sets consist of the same elements.

isDisjoint(with:)
> Returns a Bool reporting whether this set and the parameter have no elements in common.

Here's a real-life example of elegant Set usage from one of my apps. I have a lot of numbered pictures, of which we are to choose one randomly. But I don't want to choose a picture that has recently been chosen. Therefore, I keep a list of the numbers of all recently chosen pictures. When it's time to choose a new picture, I convert the list of all possible numbers to a Set, convert the list of recently chosen picture numbers to a Set, and subtract(_:) to get a list of unused picture numbers! Now I choose a picture number at random and add it to the list of recently chosen picture numbers:

```
let ud = UserDefaults.standard
var recents = ud.object(forKey:Defaults.recents) as? [Int]
if recents == nil {
    recents = []
}
var forbiddenNumbers = Set(recents!)
let legalNumbers = Set(1...PIXCOUNT).subtracting(forbiddenNumbers)
let newNumber = Array(legalNumbers)[
```

```
        Int(arc4random_uniform(UInt32(legalNumbers.count)))
    ]
    forbiddenNumbers.insert(newNumber)
    ud.set(Array(forbiddenNumbers), forKey:Defaults.recents)
```

Option sets

An *option set* (OptionSet struct) is Swift's way of treating as a struct a certain type of Cocoa enumeration. It is not, strictly speaking, a Set; but it is deliberately set-like, sharing common features with Set through the SetAlgebra protocol. Thus, an option set has contains(_:), insert(_:), and remove(_:) methods, along with all the various set operation methods.

The purpose of option sets is to help you grapple with Objective-C *bitmasks*. A bitmask is an integer whose bits are used as switches when multiple options are to be specified simultaneously. Such bitmasks are very common in Cocoa. In Objective-C, bitmasks are manipulated through the arithmetic bitwise-or and bitwise-and operators. Such manipulation can be mysterious and error-prone. Thanks to option sets, bitmasks can be manipulated through set operations instead.

For example, when specifying how a UIView is to be animated, you are allowed to pass an options: argument whose value comes from the UIViewAnimationOptions enumeration, whose definition (in Objective-C) begins as follows:

```
typedef NS_OPTIONS(NSUInteger, UIViewAnimationOptions) {
    UIViewAnimationOptionLayoutSubviews        = 1 << 0,
    UIViewAnimationOptionAllowUserInteraction  = 1 << 1,
    UIViewAnimationOptionBeginFromCurrentState = 1 << 2,
    UIViewAnimationOptionRepeat                = 1 << 3,
    UIViewAnimationOptionAutoreverse           = 1 << 4,
    // ...
};
```

Pretend that an NSUInteger is 8 bits (it isn't, but let's keep things simple and short). Then this enumeration means that (in Swift) the following name–value pairs are defined:

```
UIViewAnimationOptions.layoutSubviews        0b00000001
UIViewAnimationOptions.allowUserInteraction  0b00000010
UIViewAnimationOptions.beginFromCurrentState 0b00000100
UIViewAnimationOptions.repeat                0b00001000
UIViewAnimationOptions.autoreverse           0b00010000
```

These values can be combined into a single value — a *bitmask* — that you pass as the options: argument for your animation. All Cocoa has to do to understand your intentions is to look to see which bits in the value that you pass are set to 1. So, for example, 0b00011000 would mean that UIViewAnimationOptions.repeat and UIViewAnimationOptions.autoreverse are both true (and that the others are all false).

The question is how to *form* the value `0b00011000` in order to pass it. You could form it directly as a literal and set the `options:` argument to `UIViewAnimation-Options(rawValue:0b00011000)`; but that's not a very good idea, because it's error-prone and makes your code incomprehensible. In Objective-C, you'd use the arithmetic bitwise-or operator, analogous to this Swift code:

```
let val =
    UIViewAnimationOptions.autoreverse.rawValue |
    UIViewAnimationOptions.repeat.rawValue
let opts = UIViewAnimationOptions(rawValue: val)
```

The UIViewAnimationOptions type, however, is an option set struct (because it is marked as `NS_OPTIONS` in Objective-C), and therefore can be treated much like a Set. For example, given a UIViewAnimationOptions value, you can add an option to it using `insert(_:)`:

```
var opts = UIViewAnimationOptions.autoreverse
opts.insert(.repeat)
```

Alternatively, you can start with an array literal, just as if you were initializing a Set:

```
let opts : UIViewAnimationOptions = [.autoreverse, .repeat]
```

 To indicate that no options are to be set, pass an empty option set (`[]`) or, where permitted, omit the `options:` parameter altogether.

The inverse situation is that Cocoa hands *you* a bitmask, and you want to know whether a certain bit is set. In this example from a UITableViewCell subclass, the cell's `state` comes to us as a bitmask; we want to know about the bit indicating that the cell is showing its edit control. You could do this by extracting the raw values and using the bitwise-and operator:

```
override func didTransition(to state: UITableViewCellStateMask) {
    let editing = UITableViewCellStateMask.showingEditControlMask.rawValue
    if state.rawValue & editing != 0 {
        // ... the ShowingEditControlMask bit is set ...
    }
}
```

That's a tricky formula, all too easy to get wrong. But this is an option set, so the `contains(_:)` method tells you the answer:

```
override func didTransition(to state: UITableViewCellStateMask) {
    if state.contains(.showingEditControlMask) {
        // ... the ShowingEditControlMask bit is set ...
    }
}
```

Swift Set and Objective-C NSSet

Swift's Set type is bridged to Objective-C NSSet. The untyped medium of interchange is Set<AnyHashable>. Coming back from Objective-C, if Objective-C doesn't know what this is a set of, you would probably cast down as needed. As with NSArray, however, NSSet can be marked up to indicate its element type, in which case no casting will be necessary:

```
override func touchesBegan(_ touches: Set<UITouch>, with event: UIEvent?) {
    let t = touches.first // an Optional wrapping a UITouch
    // ...
}
```

CHAPTER 5

Flow Control and More

This chapter is a miscellany, presenting various remaining aspects of the Swift language. I'll start by describing the syntax of Swift's flow control constructs for branching, looping, and jumping. Then I'll talk about how to override operators and how to create your own operators. The chapter ends with a survey of Swift's privacy and introspection features, and some specialized modes of reference type memory management.

Flow Control

A computer program has a *path of execution* through its code statements. Normally, this path follows a simple rule: execute each statement in succession. But there is another possibility. Flow control can be used to make the path of execution skip some code statements, or repeat some code statements. Flow control is what makes a computer program "intelligent," and not merely a simple fixed sequence of steps. By testing the truth value of a *condition* — an expression that evaluates to a Bool and is thus true or false — the program decides *at that moment* how to proceed. Flow control based on testing a condition may be divided into two general types:

Branching
> The code is divided into alternative chunks, like roads that diverge in a wood, and the program is presented with a choice of possible ways to go: the truth of a condition is used to determine which chunk will actually be executed.

Looping
> A chunk of code is marked off for possible repetition: the truth of a condition is used to determine whether the chunk should be executed, and then whether it should be executed again. Each repetition is called an *iteration*. Typically, some feature of the environment (such as the value of a variable) is changed on each

iteration, so that the repetitions are not identical, but are successive stages in progressing through an overall task.

The chunks of code in flow control, which I refer to as *blocks*, are demarcated by curly braces. These curly braces constitute a scope. New local variables can be declared here, and go out of existence automatically when the path of execution exits the curly braces (Chapter 3). For a loop, this means that local variables come into existence and go out of existence on each iteration. As with any scope, code inside the curly braces can see the surrounding higher scope (Chapter 1).

Swift flow control is fairly simple, and by and large is similar to flow control in C and related languages. There are two fundamental syntactic differences between Swift and C, both of which make Swift simpler and clearer: in Swift, a condition *does not have to be wrapped in parentheses*, and the curly braces *can never be omitted*. Moreover, Swift adds some specialized flow control features to help you grapple more conveniently with Optionals, and boasts a particularly powerful form of switch statement.

Branching

Swift has two forms of branching: the if construct, and the switch statement. I'll also discuss conditional evaluation, a compact form of if construct.

If construct

The Swift branching construct with `if` is similar to C. Many examples of if constructs have appeared already in this book. The construct may be formally summarized as shown in Example 5-1.

Example 5-1. The Swift if construct

```
if condition {
    statements
}

if condition {
    statements
} else {
    statements
}

if condition {
    statements
} else if condition {
    statements
} else {
    statements
}
```

The third form, containing else if, can have as many else if blocks as needed, and the final else block may be omitted.

Here's a real-life if construct that lies at the heart of one of my apps:

```
// okay, we've tapped a tile; there are three cases
if self.selectedTile == nil { // no selected tile: select and play this tile
    self.select(tile:tile)
    self.play(tile:tile)
} else if self.selectedTile == tile { // selected tile tapped: deselect it
    self.deselectAll()
    self.player?.pause()
} else { // there was a selected tile, another tile was tapped: swap them
    self.swap(self.selectedTile, with:tile, check:true, fence:true)
}
```

Conditional binding

In Swift, if can be followed immediately by a variable declaration and assignment — that is, by let or var and a new local variable name, possibly followed by a colon and a type declaration, then an equal sign and a value. This syntax, called a *conditional binding*, is actually a shorthand for conditionally unwrapping an Optional. The assigned value is expected to be an Optional — the compiler will stop you if it isn't — and this is what happens:

- If the Optional is nil, the condition fails and the block is not executed.
- If the Optional is *not* nil, then:

1. The Optional is unwrapped.
2. The unwrapped value is assigned to the declared local variable.
3. The block is executed with the local variable in scope.

Thus, a conditional binding is a convenient shorthand for safely passing an unwrapped Optional into a block. The Optional is unwrapped, and the block is executed, only if the Optional *can* be unwrapped.

It is perfectly reasonable for the local variable in a conditional binding to have the same name as an existing variable in the surrounding scope. It can even have the same name as the Optional being unwrapped! There is then no need to make up a new name, and inside the block the unwrapped value of the Optional overshadows the original Optional, which thus cannot be accessed accidentally.

Here's an example of a conditional binding. Recall this code from Chapter 4, where I optionally unwrap a Notification's userInfo dictionary, attempt to fetch a value from the dictionary using the "progress" key, and proceed only if that value turns out to be an NSNumber:

```
let prog = (n.userInfo?["progress"] as? NSNumber)?.doubleValue
if prog != nil {
    self.progress = prog!
}
```

We can rewrite that code as a conditional binding:

```
if let prog = (n.userInfo?["progress"] as? NSNumber)?.doubleValue {
    self.progress = prog
}
```

It is also possible to nest conditional bindings. To illustrate, I'll rewrite the previous example to use a separate conditional binding for every Optional in the chain:

```
if let ui = n.userInfo {
    if let prog = ui["progress"] as? NSNumber {
        self.progress = prog.doubleValue
    }
}
```

The result, if the chain involves many optional unwrappings, can be somewhat verbose and the nest can become deeply indented — Swift programmers like to call this the "pyramid of doom" — but in my view it is also considerably more legible, because the structure reflects perfectly the successive stages of testing. To help avoid the indentation, successive conditional bindings can be combined into a *condition list*, with each condition separated by comma:

```
if let ui = n.userInfo, let prog = ui["progress"] as? NSNumber {
    self.progress = prog.doubleValue
}
```

In that code, the assignment to prog won't even be attempted if the assignment to ui fails (because n.userInfo is nil).

Condition lists do not have to consist solely of conditional bindings. They can include ordinary conditions. The important thing is the left-to-right order of evaluation, which allows each condition to depend upon the previous one. Here's a real-life example from my own code (which I'll explain further in Chapter 11). The "pyramid of doom" consists of four nested conditions:

```
override func observeValue(forKeyPath keyPath: String?,
    of object: Any?, change: [NSKeyValueChangeKey : Any]?,
    context: UnsafeMutableRawPointer?) {
    if keyPath == readyForDisplay {
        if let obj = object as? AVPlayerViewController {
            if let ok = change?[.newKey] as? Bool {
                if ok {
                    // ...
                }
```

```
        }
      }
    }
  }
```

Alternatively, those four conditions can be combined into a single list:

```
override func observeValue(forKeyPath keyPath: String?,
    of object: Any?, change: [NSKeyValueChangeKey : Any]?,
    context: UnsafeMutableRawPointer?) {
        if keyPath == readyForDisplay,
        let obj = object as? AVPlayerViewController,
        let ok = change?[.newKey] as? Bool,
        ok {
            // ...
        }
}
```

But whether the second version is more legible is an open question.

Alternatively, you can express the chain of conditions as a series of guard statements (see "Guard" on page 272); I think I like this idiom best:

```
override func observeValue(forKeyPath keyPath: String?,
    of object: Any?, change: [NSKeyValueChangeKey : Any]?,
    context: UnsafeMutableRawPointer?) {
        guard keyPath == readyForDisplay else {return}
        guard let obj = object as? AVPlayerViewController else {return}
        guard let ok = change?[.newKey] as? Bool else {return}
        guard ok else {return}
        // ...
}
```

Switch statement

A switch statement is a neater way of writing an extended if...else if...else construct. In C (and Objective-C), a switch statement contains hidden traps; Swift eliminates those traps, and adds power and flexibility. As a result, switch statements are commonly used in Swift (whereas they are relatively rare in my Objective-C code).

In a switch statement, the condition involves the comparison of different possible values, called *cases*, against a single value, called the *tag*. The case comparisons are performed *successively in order*. As soon as a case comparison succeeds, that case's code is executed and the entire switch statement is exited. The schema is shown in Example 5-2; there can be as many cases as needed, and the default case can be omitted (subject to restrictions that I'll explain in a moment).

Example 5-2. The Swift switch statement

```
switch tag {
case pattern1:
    statements
case pattern2:
    statements
default:
    statements
}
```

Here's an actual example:

```
switch i {
case 1:
    print("You have 1 thingy!")
case 2:
    print("You have 2 thingies!")
default:
    print("You have \(i) thingies!")
}
```

In that code, a variable i functions as the tag. The value of i is first compared to the value 1. If it *is* 1, that case's code is executed and that's all. If it is *not* 1, it is compared to the value 2. If it *is* 2, *that* case's code is executed and that's all. If the value of i matches neither of those, the default case's code is executed.

In Swift, a switch statement must be *exhaustive*. This means that *every* possible value of the tag must be covered by a case. The compiler will stop you if you try to violate this rule. The rule makes intuitive sense when a value's type allows only a limited number of possibilities; the usual example is an enum, which itself has a small, fixed set of cases as its possible values. But when, as in the preceding example, the tag is an Int, there is an infinite number of possible individual cases. Thus, a "mop-up" case *must* appear, to mop up all the cases that you didn't write explicitly. A common way to write a "mop-up" case is to use a default case.

Each case's code can consist of multiple lines; it doesn't have to be a single line, as the cases in the preceding example happen to be. However, it must consist of *at least* a single line; it is illegal for a Swift switch case to be completely empty. It is legal for the first (or only) line of a case's code to appear on the same line as the case, after the colon; thus, I could have written the preceding example like this:

```
switch i {
case 1: print("You have 1 thingy!")
case 2: print("You have 2 thingies!")
default: print("You have \(i) thingies!")
}
```

The minimum single line of case code is the keyword break; used in this way, break acts as a placeholder meaning, "Do nothing." It is very common for a switch statement to include a `default` (or other "mop-up" case) consisting of nothing but the keyword `break`; in this way, you exhaust all possible values of the tag, but if the value is one that no case explicitly covers, you do nothing.

Now let's focus on the comparison between the tag value and the case value. In the preceding example, it works like an equality comparison (`==`); but that isn't the only possibility. In Swift, a case value is actually a special expression called a *pattern*, and the pattern is compared to the tag value using a "secret" pattern-matching operator, `~=`. The more you know about the syntax for constructing a pattern, the more powerful your case values and your switch statements will be.

A pattern can include an underscore (`_`) to absorb all values without using them. An underscore case is thus an alternative form of "mop-up" case:

```swift
switch i {
case 1:
    print("You have 1 thingy!")
case _:
    print("You have many thingies!")
}
```

A pattern can include a declaration of a local variable name (an unconditional binding) to absorb all values and use the actual value. This is another alternative form of "mop-up" case:

```swift
switch i {
case 1:
    print("You have 1 thingy!")
case let n:
    print("You have \(n) thingies!")
}
```

When the tag is a Comparable, a case can include a Range; the test involves sending the Range the `contains` message:

```swift
switch i {
case 1:
    print("You have 1 thingy!")
case 2...10:
    print("You have \(i) thingies!")
default:
    print("You have more thingies than I can count!")
}
```

When the tag is an Optional, a case can test it against `nil`. Thus, a possible way to unwrap an Optional safely is to test against `nil` *first* and then unwrap in a subsequent case, since we'll never reach the unwrapping if the `nil` test succeeds. In this example, `i` is an Optional wrapping an Int:

```
switch i {
case nil: break
default:
    switch i! {
    case 1:
        print("You have 1 thingy!")
    case let n:
        print("You have \(n) thingies!")
    }
}
```

That seems a bit clumsy, however, so there's a special syntax: appending ? to a case pattern safely unwraps an Optional tag. Thus, we can rewrite that example like this:

```
switch i {
case 1?:
    print("You have 1 thingy!")
case let n?:
    print("You have \(n) thingies!")
case nil: break
}
```

When the tag is a Bool, a case can test it against a condition. Thus, by a clever perversion, you can use the cases to test *any* conditions you like — by using true as the tag! A switch statement thus becomes a genuine substitute for an extended if...else if construct. In this example from my own code, I could have used if...else if, but each case is just one line, so a switch statement seems clearer:

```
func position(for bar: UIBarPositioning) -> UIBarPosition {
    switch true {
    case bar === self.navbar:  return .topAttached
    case bar === self.toolbar: return .bottom
    default:                   return .any
    }
}
```

A pattern can include a where clause adding a condition to limit the truth value of the case. This is often, though not necessarily, used in combination with a binding; the condition can refer to the variable declared in the binding:

```
switch i {
case let j where j < 0:
    print("i is negative")
case let j where j > 0:
    print("i is positive")
case 0:
    print("i is 0")
default:break
}
```

A pattern can include the is operator to test the tag's type. In this example, assume that we have a Dog class and its NoisyDog subclass, and that d is typed as Dog:

```
switch d {
case is NoisyDog:
    print("You have a noisy dog!")
case _:
    print("You have a dog.")
}
```

A pattern can include a cast with the as (not as?) operator. Typically, you'll combine this with a binding that declares a local variable; despite the use of unconditional as, the value is conditionally cast and, if the cast succeeds, the local variable carries the cast value into the case code. Again, d is typed as Dog; assume that Dog implements bark and that NoisyDog implements beQuiet:

```
switch d {
case let nd as NoisyDog:
    nd.beQuiet()
case let d:
    d.bark()
}
```

You can also use as (not as?) to cast down the tag (and possibly unwrap it) conditionally as part of a test against a specific match; in this example, i might be an Any or an Optional wrapping an Any:

```
switch i {
case 0 as Int:
    print("It is 0")
default:break
}
```

You can perform multiple tests at once by expressing the tag as a tuple and wrapping the corresponding tests in a tuple. The case passes only if every test in the test tuple succeeds against the corresponding member of the tag tuple. In this example, we start with a dictionary d typed as [String:Any]. Using a tuple, we can safely attempt to extract and cast two values at once:

```
switch (d["size"], d["desc"]) {
case let (size as Int, desc as String):
    print("You have size \(size) and it is \(desc)")
default:break
}
```

When a tag is an enum, the cases can be cases of the enum. A switch statement is thus an excellent way to handle an enum. Here's the Filter enum:

```
enum Filter {
    case albums
    case playlists
    case podcasts
    case books
}
```

And here's a switch statement, where the tag, type, is a Filter; no mop-up is needed, because I've exhausted the cases:

```
switch type {
case .albums:
    print("Albums")
case .playlists:
    print("Playlists")
case .podcasts:
    print("Podcasts")
case .books:
    print("Books")
}
```

A switch statement provides a way to extract an associated value from an enum case. Recall this enum from Chapter 4:

```
enum Error {
    case number(Int)
    case message(String)
    case fatal
}
```

To extract the error number from an Error whose case is .number, or the message string from an Error whose case is .message, I can use a switch statement. Recall that the associated value is actually a tuple. A tuple of patterns after the matched case name is applied to the associated value. If a pattern is a binding variable, it captures the associated value. The let (or var) can appear inside the parentheses or after the case keyword; this code illustrates both alternatives:

```
switch err {
case .number(let theNumber):
    print("It is a number: \(theNumber)")
case let .message(theMessage):
    print("It is a message: \(theMessage)")
case .fatal:
    print("It is fatal")
}
```

If the let (or var) appears after the case keyword, I can add a where clause:

```
switch err {
case let .number(n) where n > 0:
    print("It's a positive error number \(n)")
case let .number(n) where n < 0:
    print("It's a negative error number \(n)")
case .number(0):
    print("It's a zero error number")
default:break
}
```

If I don't want to extract the error number but just want to match against it, I can use some other pattern inside the parentheses:

```
switch err {
case .number(1...Int.max):
    print("It's a positive error number")
case .number(Int.min...(-1)):
    print("It's a negative error number")
case .number(0):
    print("It's a zero error number")
default:break
}
```

This same pattern also gives us yet another way to deal with an Optional tag. An Optional, as I explained in Chapter 4, is in fact an enum. It has two cases, .none and .some, where the wrapped value is the .some case's associated value. But now we know how to extract the associated value! Thus we can rewrite yet again the earlier example where i is an Optional wrapping an Int:

```
switch i {
case .none: break
case .some(1):
    print("You have 1 thingy!")
case .some(let n):
    print("You have \(n) thingies!")
}
```

When all you want to do is extract an associated value from an enum, a full switch statement may seem a bit heavy-handed. The lightweight if case construct lets you use in a condition the same sort of pattern syntax you'd use in a case of a switch statement. Where a switch case pattern is compared against a previously stated tag, an if case pattern is followed by an equal sign and the tag. Thus, for example, this is another way to extract an associated value from an enum; err is our Error enum once again:

```
if case let .number(n) = err {
    print("The error number is \(n)")
}
```

The condition starting with case is a condition like any other, and can be part of a longer comma-separated condition list:

```
if case let .number(n) = err, n < 0 {
    print("The negative error number is \(n)")
}
```

To combine switch case tests (with an implicit logical-or), separate them with a comma:

```
switch i {
case 1,3,5,7,9:
    print("You have a small odd number of thingies.")
case 2,4,6,8,10:
    print("You have a small even number of thingies.")
default:
    print("You have too many thingies for me to count.")
}
```

In this example, i is declared as an Any:

```
switch i {
case is Int, is Double:
    print("It's some kind of number.")
default:
    print("I don't know what it is.")
}
```

New in Swift 3, a comma can even combine patterns that declare binding variables, provided they declare the same variable of the same type:

```
switch err {
case let .number(n) where n > 0, let .number(n) where n < 0:
    print("It's a nonzero error number \(n)")
case .number(0):
    print("It's a zero error number")
default:break
}
```

Another way of combining cases is to jump from one case to the next by using a fallthrough statement. When a fallthrough statement is encountered, the current case code is *aborted* immediately and the next case code runs *unconditionally*. The test of the next case is not performed, so the next case can't declare any binding variables, because they would never be set. It is not uncommon for a case to consist entirely of a fallthrough statement:

```
switch pep {
case "Manny": fallthrough
case "Moe": fallthrough
case "Jack":
    print("\(pep) is a Pep boy")
default:
    print("I don't know who \(pep) is")
}
```

Conditional evaluation

An interesting problem arises when you'd like to decide what value to use — for example, what value to assign to a variable. This seems like a good use of a branching construct. You can, of course, declare the variable first without initializing it, and then set it from within a subsequent branching construct. It would be nice, however, to use a branching construct *as* the variable's value. Here, for example, I try (and fail) to write a variable assignment where the equal sign is followed directly by a branching construct:

```
let title = switch type { // compile error
case .albums:
    "Albums"
case .playlists:
    "Playlists"
case .podcasts:
    "Podcasts"
case .books:
    "Books"
}
```

There are languages that let you talk that way, but Swift is not one of them. However, an easy workaround does exist — use a define-and-call anonymous function, as I suggested in Chapter 2:

```
let title : String = {
    switch type {
    case .albums:
        return "Albums"
    case .playlists:
        return "Playlists"
    case .podcasts:
        return "Podcasts"
    case .books:
        return "Books"
    }
}()
```

In the special case where a value can be decided by a two-pronged condition, Swift provides the C ternary operator (`:?`). Its scheme is as follows:

```
condition ? exp1 : exp2
```

If the condition is `true`, the expression *exp1* is evaluated and the result is used; otherwise, the expression *exp2* is evaluated and the result is used. Thus, you can use the ternary operator while performing an assignment, using this schema:

```
let myVariable = condition ? exp1 : exp2
```

What `myVariable` gets initialized to depends on the truth value of the condition. I use the ternary operator heavily in my own code. Here's an example:

```
cell.accessoryType =
    ix.row == self.currow ? .checkmark : .disclosureIndicator
```

The context needn't be an assignment; here, we're deciding what value to pass as a function argument:

```
context.setFillColor(self.hilite ? purple.cgColor : beige.cgColor)
```

The ternary operator can also be used to determine the receiver of a message. In this example, one of two UIViews will have its background color set:

```
(self.firstRed ? v1 : v2).backgroundColor = .red
```

In Objective-C, there's a collapsed form of the ternary operator that allows you to test a value against nil. If it is nil, you get to supply a substitute value. If it *isn't* nil, the tested value itself is used. In Swift, the analogous operation would involve testing an Optional: if the tested Optional is nil, use the substitute value; if it *isn't* nil, *unwrap* the Optional and use the unwrapped value. Swift has such an operator — the ?? operator (called the *nil-coalescing* operator).

In this example, arr is a Swift array of Optional strings, and I'm converting it to a form that can be processed by a method written in Objective-C. An Objective-C NSArray can't contain nil, so Cocoa provides a special class, NSNull, whose singleton instance, NSNull(), can stand in for nil where an object is needed. So I propose to unwrap those Optional strings that aren't nil and substitute NSNull() for those that are. Here's a perfectly effective implementation:

```
let arr2:[Any] = arr.map {if $0 != nil {return $0!} else {return NSNull()}}
```

But we can write the same thing much more neatly using the ternary operator:

```
let arr2 = arr.map {$0 != nil ? $0! : NSNull() as Any}
```

And the nil-coalescing operator is even neater:

```
let arr2 = arr.map {$0 ?? NSNull() as Any}
```

Expressions using ?? can be chained:

```
let someNumber = i1 as? Int ?? i2 as? Int ?? 0
```

That code tries to cast i1 to an Int and use that Int. If that fails, it tries to cast i2 to an Int and use *that* Int. If *that* fails, it gives up and uses 0.

Loops

The usual purpose of a loop is to repeat a block of code with some simple difference on each iteration. This difference will typically serve also as a signal for when to stop the loop. Swift provides two basic loop structures: while loops and for loops.

While loops

A while loop comes in two forms, schematized in Example 5-3.

Example 5-3. The Swift while loop

```
while condition {
    statements
}

repeat {
    statements
} while condition
```

The chief difference between the two forms is the timing of the test. In the second form, the condition is tested after the block has executed — meaning that the block will be executed at least once.

Usually, the code inside the block will change something that alters both the environment and the condition, thus eventually bringing the loop to an end. Here's a typical example from my own code (`movenda` is an array):

```
while self.movenda.count > 0 {
    let p = self.movenda.removeLast()
    // ...
}
```

Each iteration removes an element from `movenda`, so eventually its `count` falls to `0` and the loop is no longer executed; execution then proceeds to the next line after the closing curly braces.

The first form of while loop can involve a conditional binding of an Optional. This provides a compact way of safely unwrapping an Optional and looping until the Optional is `nil`; the local variable containing the unwrapped Optional is in scope inside the curly braces. Thus, my code can be rewritten more compactly:

```
while let p = self.movenda.popLast() {
    // ...
}
```

There is no Swift `repeat...until` construct; instead, negate the `while` condition. In my own code, for example, I commonly need to walk my way up or down a hierarchy. Here, `textField` is a subview, at some depth, of some table view cell, and I want to know *which* table view cell it is a subview of. So I keep walking up the view hierarchy, investigating each superview in turn, until either I reach a table view cell or I hit the top of the view hierarchy:

```
var v : UIView? = textField
repeat {v = v?.superview} while !(v is UITableViewCell || v == nil)
if let c = v as? UITableViewCell {
    // ... if we get here, c is the cell
}
```

Similar to the `if case` construct, `while case` lets you use a switch case pattern. In this rather artificial example, we have an array of various Error enums:

```
let arr : [Error] = [
    .message("ouch"), .message("yipes"), .number(10), .number(-1), .fatal
]
```

We can extract the `.message` associated string values from the start of the array, like this:

```
var i = 0
while case let .message(message) = arr[i]  {
    print(message) // "ouch", then "yipes"; then the loop stops
    i += 1
}
```

For loops

The Swift for loop is schematized in Example 5-4.

Example 5-4. The Swift for loop

```
for variable in sequence {
    statements
}
```

The `for...in` construct that forms the basis of Swift's for loop is similar to Objective-C's `for...in` construct. In Objective-C, this syntax is available whenever a class conforms to the NSFastEnumeration protocol. In Swift, it is available whenever a type adopts the Sequence protocol.

In the `for...in` construct, the variable is implicitly declared with `let` on each iteration; it is thus immutable by default. (If you need to assign to the variable within the block, write `for var`.) The variable is also local to the block. On each iteration, a successive element of the sequence is used to initialize the variable, which is then in scope inside the block.

A common use of for loops is to iterate through successive numbers. This is easy in Swift, because you can readily create a sequence of numbers on the fly — a Range:

```
for i in 1...5 {
    print(i)
}
```

Under the hood, a Sequence has a `makeIterator` method which yields an iterator object adopting IteratorProtocol. According to this protocol, the iterator has a mutating next method that returns the next object in the sequence wrapped in an Optional, or `nil` if there is no next object. Thus, `for...in` is actually a kind of while loop:

```
var g = (1...5).makeIterator()
while let i = g.next() {
    print(i)
}
```

Sometimes you may find that writing out the while loop explicitly in that way makes the loop easier to control and to customize.

The sequence will often be an existing value. It might be a character sequence, in which case the variable values are the successive Characters. It might be an array, in which case the variable values are the successive elements of the array. It might be a dictionary, in which case the variable values are key–value tuples, and you will probably express the variable as a tuple of two names in order to capture them. Many examples have already appeared in earlier chapters.

As I explained in Chapter 4, you may encounter an array coming from Objective-C whose elements will need to be cast down from Any. It is quite typical to do this as part of the sequence specification:

```
let p = Pep()
for boy in p.boys() as! [String] {
    // ...
}
```

The sequence enumerated method yields a succession of tuples preceding each element of the original sequence with its index number:

```
for (i,v) in self.tiles.enumerated() {
    v.center = self.centers[i]
}
```

If you need to skip some values of the sequence, you can append a where clause:

```
for i in 0...10 where i % 2 == 0 {
    print(i) // 0, 2, 4, 6, 8, 10
}
```

Like if case and while case, there's also for case, letting us use a switch case pattern in a for loop. The tag is each successive value of the sequence, so no assignment operator is used. Return to our example of an array of Error enums:

```
let arr : [Error] = [
    .message("ouch"), .message("yipes"), .number(10), .number(-1), .fatal
]
```

Here we cycle through the whole array, extracting just the .number associated values:

```
for case let .number(i) in arr {
    print(i) // 10, -1
}
```

Similarly, here's how to work safely with an array each of whose elements might or might not be castable to a certain type:

```
let arr : [Any] = ["hey", 1, "ho"]
for case let s as String in arr {
    print(s) // hey, ho
}
```

A sequence also has instance methods, such as `map(_:)`, `filter(_:)`, and `reversed`; you can apply these to hone the sequence through which we will cycle. In this example, I count backward by even numbers:

```
let range = (0...10).reversed().filter{$0 % 2 == 0}
for i in range {
    print(i) // 10, 8, 6, 4, 2, 0
}
```

Yet another approach is to generate the sequence by calling `stride(from:through:by)` or `stride(from:to:by:)`. These are global functions whose first parameter must adopt the Strideable protocol, which is adopted by numeric types and anything else that can be incremented and decremented. Which form you use depends on whether or not you want the sequence to include the final value. The by: argument can be negative:

```
for i in stride(from: 10, through: 0, by: -2) {
    print(i) // 10, 8, 6, 4, 2, 0
}
```

For maximum flexibility, you can use the global `sequence` function (new in Swift 3) to generate your sequence by rule. It takes two parameters — an initial value, and a generation function that returns the next value based on what has gone before. In theory, the sequence generated by the `sequence` function can be infinite in length — though this is not a problem, because the resulting sequence is "lazy," meaning that an element isn't generated until you ask for it. In reality, you'll use one of two techniques to limit the result. The generation function can limit the sequence by returning `nil` to signal that the end has been reached:

```
let seq = sequence(first:1) {$0 >= 10 ? nil : $0 + 1}
for i in seq {
    print(i) // 1,2,3,4,5,6,7,8,9,10
}
```

Alternatively you can request just a piece of the infinite sequence — for example, by cycling through the sequence for a while and then stopping, or by taking a finite `prefix`:

```
let seq = sequence(first:1) {$0 + 1}
for i in seq.prefix(5) {
    print(i) // 1,2,3,4,5
}
```

The `sequence` function comes in two forms. The first form, `sequence(first:next:)`, initially hands `first` into the next: function and subsequently hands the previous result of the next: function into the next: function, as illustrated in the preceding examples. The second form, sequence(state:next:), is more general: it repeatedly hands state into the next: function as an inout parameter; the next: function is expected to set that parameter, using it as a scratchpad, in addition to returning the next value in the sequence. An obvious illustration is the Fibonacci sequence:

```
let fib = sequence(state:(0,1)) {
    (pair: inout (Int,Int)) -> Int in
    let n = pair.0 + pair.1
    pair = (pair.1,n)
    return n
}
for i in fib.prefix(10) {
    print(i) // 1, 2, 3, 5, 8, 13, 21, 34, 55, 89
}
```

You can cycle through two sequences simultaneously using the global zip function, which takes two sequences and yields a Zip2Sequence struct, which is itself a sequence. The value on each iteration through a Zip2Sequence is a tuple of the corresponding elements from both original sequences; if one of the original sequences is longer than the other, the extra elements are ignored:

```
let arr1 = ["CA", "MD", "NY", "AZ"]
let arr2 = ["California", "Maryland", "New York"]
var d = [String:String]()
for (s1,s2) in zip(arr1,arr2) {
    d[s1] = s2
} // now d is ["MD": "Maryland", "NY": "New York", "CA": "California"]
```

Jumping

Although branching and looping constitute the bulk of the decision-making flow of code execution, sometimes even they are insufficient to express the logic of what needs to happen next. On certain occasions, it is useful to be able to interrupt your code's progress completely and *jump* to a different place within it.

The most general way to jump from anywhere to anywhere is the goto command, common in early programming languages, but now notoriously "considered harmful." Swift doesn't have a goto command, but it does provide a repertory of controlled ways of jumping, which will, in practice, cover any real-life situation. Swift's modes of jumping are all forms of *early exit* from the current flow of code.

Shortcircuiting and labels

One of the most important constructs in Swift is the function call (Chapter 2). One function calls another, which may call another, and so on, forming a call stack. When a return statement is encountered, accompanied by a return value if needed, execution of the function code is aborted immediately and the path of execution comes back to the point at which the call is made. In effect, we have jumped one level up the call stack.

Swift also has several ways of shortcircuiting the flow of branch and loop constructs:

`fallthrough`
> A `fallthrough` statement in a switch case aborts execution of the current case code and immediately begins executing the code of the next case. There must *be* a next case or the compiler will stop you.

`continue`
> A `continue` statement in a loop construct aborts execution of the current iteration and proceeds to the next iteration:
>
> - In a while loop, `continue` means to perform immediately the conditional test.
>
> - In a for loop, `continue` means to proceed immediately to the next iteration if there is one.

`break`
> A `break` statement aborts the current construct:
>
> - In a loop, `break` aborts the loop completely.
>
> - In the code of a switch case, `break` aborts the entire switch construct.

When constructs are nested, you may need to specify which construct you want to continue or break. Therefore, Swift permits you to put a *label* before the start of a do block, an if construct, a switch statement, a while loop, or a for loop. The label is an arbitrary name followed by a colon. You can then use that label name as a second term in a continue or break statement within the labeled construct at any depth, to specify that this is the construct you are referring to.

Here's an artificial example to illustrate the syntax. First, I'll nest two for loops with no label:

```
for i in 1...5 {
    for j in 1...5 {
        print("\(i), \(j);")
        break
    }
}
// 1, 1; 2, 1; 3, 1; 4, 1; 5, 1;
```

As you can see from the output, that code keeps aborting the inner loop after one iteration, while the outer loop proceeds normally through all five iterations. But what if you wanted to abort the entire nested construct? The solution is a label:

```
outer: for i in 1...5 {
    for j in 1...5 {
        print("\(i), \(j);")
        break outer
    }
}
// 1, 1;
```

Throwing and catching errors

Sometimes a situation arises where further coherent progress is impossible: the entire operation in which we are engaged has failed. It can then be desirable to abort the current scope, and possibly the current function, and possibly even the function that called it, and so on, exiting to a point where we can acknowledge this failure and proceed in good order in some other way.

For this purpose, Swift provides a mechanism for *throwing and catching errors*. In keeping with its usual insistence on safety and clarity, Swift imposes certain strict conditions on the use of this mechanism, and the compiler will ensure that you adhere to them.

An *error*, in this sense, is a kind of message, presumably indicating what went wrong. This message is passed up the nest of scopes and function calls as part of the error-handling process, and the code that recovers from the failure can, if desired, read the message and determine how to proceed.

In Swift, an error must be an object of a type that adopts the Error protocol, which has just two requirements: a String _domain property and an Int _code property. The purpose of those properties is to help errors cross the bridge between Swift and Objective-C; in real life, you will be unaware of them (and in fact you won't even see them listed in the Swift header). What you will see and use will be one of the following:

A Swift type that adopts Error
> As soon as a Swift type formally declares adoption of the Error protocol, it is ready to be used as an error object; the protocol requirements are magically fulfilled for you, behind the scenes. Typically, this type will be an enum, which will communicate its message by means of its cases: different cases will distinguish different kinds of possible failure, perhaps with raw values or associated types to carry further information.

NSError
> NSError is Cocoa's class for communicating the nature of a problem; Swift extends NSError to adopt Error and bridges them to one another. If your call to a Cocoa method generates a failure, Cocoa will send you an NSError instance typed as an Error; you can examine its properties, such as its domain, code, localizedDescription, and so forth, to learn what went wrong and to present a

coherent alert to the user. You can also create your own NSError instance by calling its designated initializer, `init(domain:code:userInfo:)`.

There are two stages of the error mechanism to consider: throwing an error, and catching an error. Throwing an error aborts the current path of execution and hands an error object to the error mechanism. Catching an error receives that error object from the error mechanism and responds in good order, with the path of execution resuming after the point of catching. In effect, we have *jumped* from the throwing point to the catching point.

To *throw an error*, use the keyword `throw` followed by an error object. That's all it takes! The current block of code is immediately aborted, and the error mechanism takes over. However, to ensure that the `throw` command is used coherently, Swift imposes a rule that you can say `throw` *only in a context where the error can be caught*. What is such a context?

The primary context for throwing and catching an error is the `do...catch` construct. This consists of a do block and one or more catch blocks. It is legal to throw in the do block; an accompanying catch block can then be fed any errors thrown from within the do block. The `do...catch` construct's schema looks like Example 5-5.

Example 5-5. The Swift do...catch construct

```
do {
    statements // a throw can happen here
} catch errortype {
    statements
} catch {
    statements
}
```

A single do block can be accompanied by multiple catch blocks. Catch blocks are like the cases of a switch statement, and will usually have the same logic: first, you might have specialized catch blocks, each of which is designed to handle some limited set of possible errors; finally, you might have a general catch block that acts as the default, mopping up any errors that were not caught by any of the specialized catch blocks.

In fact, the *syntax* used by a catch block to specify what sorts of error it catches *is* the pattern syntax used by a case in a switch statement! Imagine that this *is* a switch statement, and that the tag is the error object. Then the matching of that error object to a particular catch block is performed just as if you had written `case` instead of `catch`. Typically, when the Error is an enum, a specialized catch block will state at least the enum that it catches, and possibly also the case of that enum; it can have a binding, to capture the enum or its associated type; and it can have a `where` clause to limit the possibilities still further.

To illustrate, I'll start by defining a couple of errors:

```
enum MyFirstError : Error {
    case firstMinorMistake
    case firstMajorMistake
    case firstFatalMistake
}
enum MySecondError : Error {
    case secondMinorMistake(i:Int)
    case secondMajorMistake(s:String)
    case secondFatalMistake
}
```

Now here's a do...catch construct designed to demonstrate some of the different
ways we can catch different errors in different catch blocks:

```
do {
    // throw can happen here
} catch MyFirstError.firstMinorMistake {
    // catches MyFirstError.firstMinorMistake
} catch let err as MyFirstError {
    // catches all other cases of MyFirstError
} catch MySecondError.secondMinorMistake(let i) where i < 0 {
    // catches e.g. MySecondError.secondMinorMistake(i:-3)
} catch {
    // catches everything else
}
```

In a catch block with an accompanying pattern, it is up to you to capture in the pattern any desired information about the error. For example, if you want the error itself
to travel as a variable into the catch block, you'll need a binding in the pattern. A
catch block whose pattern is *only* a binding catches *any* error under that name; for
example, catch let mistake is a "mop-up" catch block that catches any error and
calls the error object mistake. In a "mop-up" catch block with *no* accompanying pattern, the error object arrives into the block *automatically* as a variable called error.

Thus, let's look again at the previous example, but this time we'll note whether and
how the error object arrives into each catch block:

```
do {
    // throw can happen here
} catch MyFirstError.firstMinorMistake {
    // no error object, but we know it's MyFirstError.firstMinorMistake
} catch let err as MyFirstError {
    // MyFirstError arrives as err
} catch MySecondError.secondMinorMistake(let i) where i < 0 {
    // only i arrives, but we know it's MySecondError.secondMinorMistake
} catch {
    // error object arrives as error
}
```

However, as I said earlier, there's something else that can happen to a thrown error; instead of being caught directly, it can percolate up the calling chain, leaving the current function and arriving at the point where this function was called. In this situation, the error won't be caught here, at the point of throwing; it needs to be caught further up the calling chain. Moreover, suppose a do...catch construct lacks a "mop-up" catch block. Then a throw inside the do block might *not* be caught here, and again, the error will percolate up the calling chain, and needs to be caught further up the calling chain.

We therefore need a way to say to the compiler: "Look, I understand that it looks like this throw is not happening in a context where it can be caught, but that's only because you're not looking far enough up the calling chain. If you do look far enough, you'll see that a throw at this point *is* eventually caught." That way is the throws keyword.

If you mark a function with the throws keyword, then its *entire body* becomes a legal place for throwing. The syntax for declaring a throws function is that the keyword throws appears immediately after the parameter list (and before the arrow operator, if there is one) in the function's declaration. For example:

```
enum NotLongEnough : Error {
    case iSaidLongIMeantLong
}
func giveMeALongString(_ s:String) throws {
    if s.characters.count < 5 {
        throw NotLongEnough.iSaidLongIMeantLong
    }
    print("thanks for the string")
}
```

The addition of throws to a function declaration creates a distinct function type. The type of giveMeALongString is not (String) -> (), but rather (String) throws -> (). If a function receives as parameter a function that can throw, that parameter's type needs to be specified accordingly:

```
func receiveThrower(_ f:(String) throws -> ()) {
    // ...
}
```

That function can now be called with giveMeALongString as argument:

```
func callReceiveThrower() {
    receiveThrower(giveMeALongString)
}
```

An anonymous function, if necessary, can include the keyword throws in its in line, in the same place where it would appear in a normal function declaration. But this is not necessary if, as is usually the case, the anonymous function's type is known by inference:

```
func receiveThrower(_ f:(String) throws -> ()) {
    // ...
}
func callReceiveThrower() {
    receiveThrower {
        s in // can say "s throws in", but not required
        if s.characters.count < 5 {
            throw NotLongEnough.iSaidLongIMeantLong
        }
        print("thanks for the string")
    }
}
```

Swift also imposes a requirement on the *caller* of a throws function: the caller must precede the call with the keyword try. This keyword acknowledges, to the programmer and to the compiler, that this function can throw. But since this function can throw, there is a further requirement: this call must take place where throwing is legal! A function called with try can throw, so saying try is just like saying throw: you must say it either in the do block of a do...catch construct or in the body of a throws function.

So, for example:

```
func stringTest() {
    do {
        try giveMeALongString("is this long enough for you?")
    } catch {
        print("I guess it wasn't long enough: \(error)")
    }
}
```

But Swift also provides a clever shorthand. If you are very sure that a throws function will in fact *not* throw, then you can call it with the keyword try! instead of try. This relieves you of all further responsibility: you can say try! *anywhere*, without catching the possible throw. But be warned: if you're wrong, and this function *does* throw when your program runs, your program can crash at that moment, because you have allowed an error to percolate, uncaught, all the way up to the top of the calling chain.

Thus, this is legal but dangerous; we are calling a throws function *not* in a do...catch block and *not* in another throws function, and telling the compiler to trust us and let us do it:

```
func stringTest() {
    try! giveMeALongString("okay")
}
```

In between try and try! is try?. This has the advantage that, like try!, you can use it anywhere; but, like a do...catch construct, it catches the throw if there is one, without crashing. If there's a throw, you don't receive any error information, as you would with a catch block; but try? tells you if there *was* a throw, by returning nil.

Thus, `try?` is useful particularly in situations where its expression returns a value. If there's a throw, it returns `nil`. If there's no throw, it wraps the returned value in an Optional. Commonly, you'll unwrap that Optional safely in the same line with a conditional binding. I'll give an example in a moment.

Even if your own code never uses the keyword `throw` explicitly, you're still very likely, in real life, to call Cocoa methods that are marked with `throws`. Therefore, you need to know how Swift's error mechanism relates to Cocoa and Objective-C. Recall that an Objective-C method can return only one value (there are no tuples). So if a Cocoa method that returns a value has a failure and wants to hand back an NSError, how can it do it? The answer is that such a method will return `nil` to indicate failure, and will also take an `NSError**` parameter as a way of communicating an error to the caller in addition to the method result; the `NSError**` parameter is similar to a Swift `inout` parameter.

For example, NSString has an initializer declared in Objective-C like this:

```
- (instancetype)initWithContentsOfFile:(NSString *)path
                              encoding:(NSStringEncoding)enc
                                 error:(NSError **)error;
```

Objective-C code that calls that initializer must test to see whether the resulting NSString is in fact `nil`, and can examine the resulting error if it is:

```
NSError* err;
NSString* s =
    [[NSString alloc] initWithContentsOfFile:f
                                    encoding:NSUTF8StringEncoding
                                       error:&err];
if (s == nil) {
    NSLog(@"%@", err);
}
```

As you can see, the whole procedure is a lot like using a Swift `inout` parameter. An NSError variable must be prepared beforehand, and its address must be passed as the `error:` argument. Then we have to test the result for `nil` explicitly, to see whether the initialization succeeded. This is an annoyingly elaborate but necessary dance in Objective-C, and in Swift, prior to Swift 2.0, the dance was effectively the same.

In modern Swift, however, there's a *different* dance — a much simpler, more pleasant one. Such an Objective-C method is *automatically recast* to take advantage of the error mechanism. The `error:` parameter is removed from the Swift translation of the declaration, and is replaced by a `throws` marker:

```
init(contentsOfFile path: String, encoding enc: String.Encoding) throws
```

Thus there is no need to declare an NSError variable beforehand, and no need to receive the NSError by indirection. Instead, you just call the method, within the controlled conditions dictated by Swift. And what are those conditions? One way is to say try, in a place where throwing is legal. The result in that case can never be nil; it's a String, plain and simple, because if the initialization fails, the call will throw and no result will arrive at all. Here's an example (the encoding: parameter is optional, and defaults to .utf8):

```
do {
    let f = // path to some file, maybe
    let s = try String(contentsOfFile: f)
    // ... if successful, do something with s ...
} catch {
    print(error.localizedDescription)
}
```

Alternatively, you're very sure the initialization won't fail, you can skip the do...catch construct and use try! instead; again, the result can never be nil, so it's just a String:

```
let f = // path to some file, maybe
let s = try! String(contentsOfFile: f)
```

Finally, you can skip the do...catch construct and still proceed safely by using try?, in which case the value returned is an Optional wrapping a String, which you can test for nil to learn whether the initialization succeeded. You'll probably unwrap the Optional safely at the same point where you make the call, like this:

```
let f = // path to some file, maybe
if let s = try? String(contentsOfFile: f) {
    // ...
}
```

Objective-C NSError and Swift Error are bridged to one another. Thus, in a catch block a moment ago, I examined the error variable using an NSError property. Moreover, you can catch the specific NSError by its name. The name you'll use is the NSError domain, and optionally (with dot-notation) the Cocoa name of its code.

For example, let's say we call init(contentsOfFile:) and we want specifically to catch the error thrown when there is no such file. This NSError's domain, according to Cocoa, is "NSCocoaErrorDomain"; Swift sees that as CocoaError. Its code is 260, for which Cocoa provides the name NSFileReadNoSuchFileError (I found that out by looking in the *FoundationErrors.h* header file in Objective-C); Swift sees that as .fileReadNoSuchFile. Thus we can catch this specific error under the name CocoaError.fileReadNoSuchFile, like this:

```
do {
    let f = // path to some file, maybe
    let s = try String(contentsOfFile: f)
    // ... if successful, do something with s ...
} catch CocoaError.fileReadNoSuchFile {
```

```
        print("no such file")
    } catch {
        print(error)
    }
```

Objective-C sees a Swift error coherently as well. It receives a Swift error as an NSError whose domain is the name of the Swift object type. If the Swift object type is an enum, the NSError's code is the index number of its case; otherwise, the code is 1.

Nested scopes

Sometimes, when you know that a local variable needs to exist only for a few lines of code, you might like to define an artificial scope — a custom nested scope, at the start of which you can introduce your local variable, and at the end of which that variable will be permitted to go out of scope, destroying its value automatically.

Swift, however, does not permit you to use bare curly braces to do this. Instead, use a bare do construct without a catch:

```
do {
    var myVar = "howdy"
    // ... use myVar here ...
}
// now myVar is out of scope and its value is destroyed
```

Defer

The purpose of the defer statement is to *ensure* that a certain block of code will be executed at the time the path of execution flows out of the current scope, no matter how.

A defer statement applies to the scope in which it appears, such as a function body, a while block, an if construct, a do block, and so on. Wherever you say defer, curly braces surround it somehow; the defer block will be executed *when the path of execution leaves those curly braces*. Leaving the curly braces can involve reaching the last line of code within the curly braces, or any of the forms of early exit described earlier in this section.

To see why this is useful, consider the following pair of commands:

UIApplication.shared.beginIgnoringInteractionEvents()
   Stops all user touches from reaching any view of the application.

UIApplication.shared.endIgnoringInteractionEvents()
   Restores the ability of user touches to reach views of the application.

It can be valuable to turn off user interactions at the start of some slightly time-consuming operation and then turn them back on after that operation, especially when, *during* the operation, the interface or the app's logic will be in some state where the user's tapping a button, say, could cause things to go awry. Thus, it is not uncommon for a method to be constructed like this:

```
func doSomethingTimeConsuming() {
    UIApplication.shared.beginIgnoringInteractionEvents()
    // ... do stuff ...
    UIApplication.shared.endIgnoringInteractionEvents()
}
```

All well and good — *if* we can guarantee that the only path of execution out of this function will be by way of that last line. But what if we need to return early from this function? Our code now looks like this:

```
func doSomethingTimeConsuming() {
    UIApplication.shared.beginIgnoringInteractionEvents()
    // ... do stuff ...
    if somethingHappened {
        return
    }
    // ... do more stuff ...
    UIApplication.shared.endIgnoringInteractionEvents()
}
```

Oops! We've just made a terrible mistake. By providing an additional path out of our doSomethingTimeConsuming function, we've created the possibility that our code might never encounter the call to endIgnoringInteractionEvents. We might leave our function by way of the return statement — and the user will then be left unable to interact with the interface. Obviously, we need to add another endIgnoring... call inside the if construct, just before the return statement. But as we continue to develop our code, we must remember, if we add *further* ways out of this function, to add *yet another* endIgnoring... call for *each* of them. This is madness!

The defer statement solves the problem. It lets us specify *once* what should happen when we leave this scope, *no matter how*. Our code now looks like this:

```
func doSomethingTimeConsuming() {
    defer {
        UIApplication.shared.endIgnoringInteractionEvents()
    }
    UIApplication.shared.beginIgnoringInteractionEvents()
    // ... do stuff ...
    if somethingHappened {
        return
    }
    // ... do more stuff ...
}
```

The endIgnoring... call in the defer block will be executed, not where it appears, but before the return statement, or before the last line of the method — whichever path of execution ends up leaving the function. The defer statement says: "Eventually, and as late as possible, be sure to execute this code." We have thus ensured the necessary balance between turning off user interactions and turning them back on again. Most uses of the defer statement will probably come under this same rubric: you'll use it to balance a command or restore a disturbed state.

Observe that in the preceding code, I placed the defer block very early in its surrounding scope, even though this caused the endIgnoring... call to precede visually the beginIgnoring... call that it balances. This placement is important because a defer block is itself, as a whole, executable code. If a defer block is not actually *encountered* by the path of execution before we exit from the surrounding scope, *it won't be executed.* For this reason, always place your defer block as close to the start of its surrounding block as you can, to ensure that it will in fact be encountered.

 If the current scope has multiple defer blocks pending, they will be called in the reverse of the order in which they were originally encountered. In effect, there is a defer *stack*; each successive defer statement, as it is encountered, pushes its code onto the top of the stack, and exiting the scope in which a defer statement appeared pops that code and executes it.

Aborting the whole program

Aborting the whole program is an extreme form of flow control; the program stops dead in its tracks. In effect, you have deliberately crashed your own program. This is an unusual thing to do, but it can be useful as a way of raising a very red flag: you don't really *want* to abort, so if you *do* abort, things must be so bad that you've no choice.

One way to abort is by calling the global function `fatalError`. It takes a String parameter permitting you to provide a message to appear in the console. I've already given this example:

```
required init?(coder aDecoder: NSCoder) {
    fatalError("init(coder:) has not been implemented")
}
```

That code says, in effect, that execution should *never* reach this point. We have declared `init(coder:)` just because it is `required`, and we need to satisfy the compiler; but we have no real implementation of `init(coder:)`, and we do not expect to be initialized this way. If we *are* initialized this way, something has gone very wrong, and we *want* to crash, because our program has a serious bug.

An initializer containing a `fatalError` call does not have to initialize any properties. This is because `fatalError` is declared as returning Never, which causes the compiler to abandon any contextual requirements. Similarly, a function that returns a value does not have to return any value if a `fatalError` call is encountered.

You can also abort conditionally by calling the `assert` function. Its first parameter is a condition — something that evaluates as a Bool. If the condition is `false`, we will abort; the second parameter is a String message to appear in the console if we *do* abort. The idea here is that you are making a bet (an *assertion*) that the condition is `true` — a bet that you feel so strongly about that if the condition is `false`, there's a serious bug in your program and you want to crash so you can learn of this bug and fix it.

By default, `assert` works only when you're developing your program. When your program is to be finalized and made public, you throw a different build switch, telling the compiler that `assert` should be ignored. In effect, the conditions in your `assert` calls are then disregarded; they are all seen as `true`. This means that you can safely leave `assert` calls in your code. By the time your program ships, of course, none of your assertions should be failing; any bugs that caused them to fail should already have been ironed out.

The disabling of assertions in shipping code is performed in an interesting way. The condition parameter is given an extra layer of indirection by declaring it as an `@autoclosure` function. This means that, even though the parameter is *not* in fact a function, the compiler will wrap it in a function; thus, the runtime needn't call that function unless it has to. In shipping code, the runtime will *not* call that function. This mechanism averts expensive and unnecessary evaluation: an `assert` condition test may involve side effects, but the test won't even be performed when assertions are turned off in your shipping program.

In addition, Swift provides the `assertionFailure` function. It's like an `assert` that always fails — and, like an `assert`, it *doesn't* fail in your shipping program where assertions are turned off. It's a convenient synonym for `assert(false)`, as a way of assuring yourself that your code never goes where it's never supposed to go. By contrast, `precondition` and `preconditionFailure` are similar to `assert` and `assertion-Failure`, except that they *do* fail even in a shipping program.

Guard

If the need for jumping might arise, you will probably want to test a condition that decides whether to jump. Swift provides a special syntax for this situation — the guard statement. In effect, a guard statement is an if statement where you *must* exit early in response to failure of the condition. Its form is shown in Example 5-6.

Example 5-6. The Swift guard statement

```
guard condition else {
    statements
    exit
}
```

A guard statement, as you can see, consists solely of a condition and an `else` block. The `else` block *must* jump out of the current scope, by any of the means that Swift provides, such as `return`, `break`, `continue`, `throw`, or `fatalError` — anything that guarantees to the compiler that, in case of failure of the condition, execution absolutely will not proceed within the block that contains the guard statement.

An elegant consequence of this architecture is that, because the guard statement guarantees an exit on failure of the condition, the compiler knows that the condition has succeeded after the guard statement if we do *not* exit. Thus, a conditional binding in the condition *is in scope after the guard statement*, without introducing a further nested scope. For example:

```
guard let s = optionalString else {return}
// s is now a String (not an Optional)
```

A series of guard statements, as I demonstrated earlier, can be a nice alternative to the "pyramid of doom":

```
override func observeValue(forKeyPath keyPath: String?,
    of object: Any?, change: [NSKeyValueChangeKey : Any]?,
    context: UnsafeMutableRawPointer?) {
        guard keyPath == readyForDisplay else {return}
        guard let obj = object as? AVPlayerViewController else {return}
```

```
        guard let ok = change?[.newKey] as? Bool else {return}
        guard ok else {return}
        // ...
}
```

A guard statement will also come in handy in conjunction with try?. Let's presume
we can't proceed unless String(contentsOfFile:) succeeds. Then we can rewrite
our earlier example like this:

```
let f = // path to some file, maybe
guard let s = try? String(contentsOfFile: f)
    else {return}
// s is now a String (not an Optional)
```

There is also a guard case construct, forming the logical inverse of if case. To illustrate, we'll use our Error enum once again:

```
guard case let .number(n) = err else {return}
// n is now the extracted number
```

guard case helps to solve an interesting problem. Suppose we have a function whose
returned value we want to check in a guard statement:

```
guard howMany() > 10 else {return}
```

All well and good; but suppose also that in the *next* line we want to *use* the value
returned from that function. We don't want to call the function *again*; it might be
time-consuming and it might have side effects. We want to *capture* the result of calling the function and pass that captured result on into the subsequent code. But we
can't do that with guard let, because that requires an Optional, and our function
doesn't return an Optional.

What should we do? Well, we could wrap the returned value from our function in an
Optional just so we can unwrap it again:

```
guard let output = Optional(howMany()), output > 10 else {return}
// now output is in scope (not an Optional)
```

That happens to work, but it's horrible. guard case to the rescue:

```
guard case let output = howMany(), output > 10 else {return}
// now output is in scope
```

Note that a guard statement's conditional binding can't use on the left side of the
equal sign a name already declared in the same scope. This is illegal:

```
let s = // ... some Optional
guard let s = s else {return} // compile error
```

The reason is that guard let, unlike if let and while let, doesn't declare the
bound variable for a nested scope; it declares it for *this* scope. Thus, we can't declare s
here because s has already been declared in the same scope.

Operators

Swift operators such as + and > are not magically baked into the language. They are, in fact, functions; they are explicitly declared and implemented just like any other function. That is why, as I pointed out in Chapter 4, the term + can be passed as the second parameter in a reduce call; reduce expects a function taking two parameters and returning a value whose type matches that of the first parameter, and + is in fact the name of such a function. It also explains how Swift operators can be overloaded for different value types. You can use + with numbers, strings, or arrays — with a different meaning in each case — because two functions with the same name but different parameter types (different signatures) are two *different* functions; from the parameter types, Swift is able to determine *which* + function you are calling.

These facts are not merely an intriguing behind-the-scenes implementation detail. They have practical implications for you and your code. You are free to overload existing operators to apply to *your* object types. You can even invent *new* operators! In this section, we'll do both.

First, we must talk about how operators are declared. Clearly there is some sort of syntactical hanky-panky (a technical computer science term), because you don't *call* an operator function in the same way as a normal function. You don't say +(1,2); you say 1+2. Even so, 1 and 2 in that second expression *are* the parameters to a + function call. How does Swift know that the + function uses this special syntax?

To see the answer, look in the Swift header:

```
infix operator + : AdditionPrecedence
```

That is an operator declaration. An operator declaration announces that this symbol *is* an operator, and tells how many parameters it has and what the usage syntax will be in relation to those parameters. The really important part is the stuff before the colon: the keyword operator, preceded by an operator *type* — here, infix — and followed by the name of the operator. The types are:

infix
> This operator takes two parameters and appears between them.

prefix
> This operator takes one parameter and appears before it.

postfix
> This operator takes one parameter and appears after it.

The term after the colon in an operator declaration is the name of a precedence group. I'm not going to go into the details of how precedence groups are defined. The Swift header declares about a dozen of them, and you can easily see how those declarations work. You will probably have no need to declare a new precedence group; instead, you'll just look for an operator similar to yours and copy its precedence group (or omit the colon and the precedence group from your declaration).

An operator is also a function, so you also need a function declaration stating the type of the parameters and the result type of the function. Again, the Swift header shows us an example:

```
func +(lhs: Int, rhs: Int) -> Int
```

That is one of many declarations for the + function in the Swift header. In particular, it is the declaration for when the parameters are both Int. In that situation, the result is itself an Int. (The local parameter names lhs and rhs, which don't affect the special calling syntax, presumably stand for "left-hand side" and "right-hand side.")

An operator declaration must appear at the top level of a file. The corresponding function declaration may appear either at the top level of a file or at the top level of a type declaration; in the latter case, it must be marked static. If the operator is a prefix or postfix operator, the function declaration must start with the word prefix or postfix; the default is infix and can be omitted.

We now know enough to override an operator to work with an object type of our own! As a simple example, imagine a Vial full of bacteria:

```
struct Vial {
    var numberOfBacteria : Int
    init(_ n:Int) {
        self.numberOfBacteria = n
    }
}
```

When two Vials are combined, you get a Vial with all the bacteria from both of them. So the way to add two Vials is to add their bacteria:

```
extension Vial {
    static func +(lhs:Vial, rhs:Vial) -> Vial {
        let total = lhs.numberOfBacteria + rhs.numberOfBacteria
        return Vial(total)
    }
}
```

And here's code to test our new + operator override:

```
let v1 = Vial(500_000)
let v2 = Vial(400_000)
let v3 = v1 + v2
print(v3.numberOfBacteria) // 900000
```

In the case of a compound assignment operator, the first parameter is the thing being assigned to. Therefore, to implement such an operator, the first parameter must be declared inout. Let's do that for our Vial class:

```
extension Vial {
    static func +=(lhs:inout Vial, rhs:Vial) {
        let total = lhs.numberOfBacteria + rhs.numberOfBacteria
        lhs.numberOfBacteria = total
    }
}
```

Here's code to test our += override:

```
var v1 = Vial(500_000)
let v2 = Vial(400_000)
v1 += v2
print(v1.numberOfBacteria) // 900000
```

It might be useful also to override the equality comparison operator == for our Vial class. This satisfies the requirement for Vial to adopt the Equatable protocol, but of course it won't actually adopt it unless we tell it to:

```
extension Vial : Equatable {
    static func ==(lhs:Vial, rhs:Vial) -> Bool {
        return lhs.numberOfBacteria == rhs.numberOfBacteria
    }
}
```

Now that Vial is an Equatable, it becomes a candidate for use with methods such as index(of:):

```
let v1 = Vial(500_000)
let v2 = Vial(400_000)
let arr = [v1,v2]
let ix = arr.index(of:v1) // Optional wrapping 0
```

What's more, the complementary inequality operator != has sprung to life for Vials automatically! That's because it's already defined for *any* Equatable in terms of the == operator. By the same token, if we now override < for Vial and tell it to adopt Comparable, the other three comparison operators spring to life automatically.

Next, let's invent a completely new operator. As an example, I'll inject an operator into Int that raises one number to the power of another. As my operator symbol, I'll use ^^ (I'd like to use ^ but it's already in use for something else). For simplicity, I'll omit error-checking for edge cases (such as exponents less than 1):

```
infix operator ^^
extension Int {
    static func ^^(lhs:Int, rhs:Int) -> Int {
        var result = lhs
        for _ in 1..<rhs {result *= lhs}
        return result
    }
}
```

That's all it takes! Here's some code to test it:

```
print(2^^2) // 4
print(2^^3) // 8
print(3^^3) // 27
```

Here's another example. I've already illustrated the use of Range's reversed method to allow iteration from a higher value to a lower one. That works, but I find the notation unpleasant. There's an asymmetry with how you iterate up; the endpoints are in the wrong order, and you have to remember to surround a literal range with parentheses:

```
let r1 = 1..<10
let r2 = (1..<10).reversed()
```

Let's define a custom operator that calls reversed() for us:

```
infix operator >>> : RangeFormationPrecedence
func >>><Bound>(maximum: Bound, minimum: Bound)
    -> ReversedRandomAccessCollection<CountableRange<Bound>>
    where Bound : Comparable & Strideable, Bound.Stride : Integer {
        return (minimum..<maximum).reversed()
}
```

Now our expressions can be more symmetrical and compact:

```
let r1 = 1..<10
let r2 = 10>>>1
```

The Swift manual lists the special characters that can be used as part of a custom operator name:

```
/ = - + ! * % < > & | ^ ? ~
```

An operator name can also contain many other symbol characters (that is, characters that can't be mistaken for some sort of alphanumeric) that are harder to type; see the manual for a formal list.

Privacy

Privacy (also known as *access control*) refers to the explicit modification of the normal scope rules. I gave an example in Chapter 1:

```
class Dog {
    var name = ""
    private var whatADogSays = "woof"
    func bark() {
        print(self.whatADogSays)
    }
}
```

The intention here is to limit how other objects can see the Dog property whatADog-Says. It is a private property, intended primarily for the Dog class's own internal use: a Dog can speak of self.whatADogSays, but other objects should not be aware that it even exists.

Swift 3 has five levels of privacy:

`internal`

> The default rule is that declarations are *internal,* meaning that they are globally visible to *all code in all files within the containing module.* That is why Swift files within the same module can see one another's top-level contents *automatically,* with no effort on your part. (That's different from C and Objective-C, where files can't see each other at all unless you explicitly show them to one another through `include` or `import` statements.)

`fileprivate` *(narrower than* `internal`*)*

> A thing declared `fileprivate` is visible *only within its containing file.* For example, two object types declared in the same file can see one another's members declared `fileprivate`, but code in other files cannot see those members.

`private` *(even narrower than* `fileprivate`*)*

> A thing declared `private` is visible *only within its containing curly braces.* In effect, the visibility of an object type's member declared `private` is limited to code within this class declaration. (A `private` declaration at the top level of a file is equivalent to `fileprivate`.)

`public` *(wider than* `internal`*)*

> A thing declared `public` is visible *even outside its containing module.* Another module must first import this module before it can see anything at all. But once another module *has* imported this module, it still won't be able to see anything in this module that hasn't been explicitly declared public. If you don't write any modules, you might never need to declare anything public. If you do write a module, you *must* declare *something* public, or your module is useless.

`open` *(even wider than* `public`*)*

> If a class is declared `open`, code in another module can subclass it; it can't do that if the class is declared merely `public`. If an open class member is declared `open`, code in another module that subclasses this class can override this member; it can't do that without the open declaration.

 `fileprivate` and `open` are new in Swift 3. Before Swift 3, `private` meant `fileprivate`, and `public` implied `open`.

Private and Fileprivate

Declaring something private restricts its visibility. In this way, you specify by inversion what the public API of this object is. Here's an example from my own code:

```
class CancelableTimer: NSObject {
    private var q = DispatchQueue(label: "timer")
    private var timer : DispatchSourceTimer!
    private var firsttime = true
    private var once : Bool
    private var handler : () -> ()
    init(once:Bool, handler:@escaping ()->()) {
        // ...
    }
    func start(withInterval interval:Double) {
        // ...
    }
    func cancel() {
        // ...
    }
}
```

The initializer `init(once:handler:)` and the `start(withInterval:)` and `cancel` methods, which are *not* marked `private`, are this class's public API. They say, "Please feel free to call me!" The properties, however, are all private; no other code can see them, either to get them or to set them. They are purely for the internal use of the methods of this class. They maintain state, but it is not a state that any other code needs to know about.

Why would you declare something `fileprivate` rather than `private`? One common reason has to do with extensions. The rules about `private` are very strict; the surrounding curly braces are an absolute barrier. Well, an extension to a class is outside the curly braces that define that class. Therefore, code in an extension to a class can't see members of that class declared `private`! That is unlikely to be what you want, so you'll have to declare those members `fileprivate` instead.

By the same token, privacy is not magically violated by the existence of a special object relationship. For example, even a subclass cannot see its superclass's private members. (This comes as a surprise to those coming from a language with a `protected` privacy level.) You can work around this by declaring the class and its subclass in the same file and declaring those members `fileprivate` instead of `private`.

It may be that on some occasions you will want to draw a distinction between the privacy of a variable regarding setting and its privacy regarding getting. To draw this distinction, place the word `set` in parentheses after its own privacy declaration. Thus, `private(set) var myVar` or `fileprivate(set) var myVar` means that the *setting* of this variable is restricted, but says nothing about the *getting* of this variable, which is left at the default. Similarly, you can say `public private(set) var myVar` to make getting this variable public, while setting this variable is kept private. (You can use this same syntax with a `subscript` function.)

Public and Open

If you write a module, you'll need to specify at least some object type declaration as public, or code that imports your module won't be able to see that type. Other declarations that are not declared public are internal, meaning that they are private to the module. Thus, judicious use of `public` declarations configures the public API of your module.

For example, in my Zotz app, which is a card game, the object types for creating and portraying cards and for combining them into a deck are bundled into a framework called ZotzDeck. Many of these types, such as Card and Deck, are declared public. Many utility object types, however, are not; the classes within the ZotzDeck module can see and use them, but code outside the module doesn't need to be aware of them at all.

The members of a public object type are not, themselves, automatically public. If you want a method to be public, you have to declare it public. This is an excellent default behavior, because it means that these members are not shared outside the module unless you want them to be. (As Apple puts it, you must "opt in to publishing" object members.)

For example, in my ZotzDeck module, the Card class is declared public but its initializer is not. Why not? Because it doesn't need to be. The way you (meaning the importer of the ZotzDeck module) get cards is by initializing a Deck; the initializer for Deck *is* declared public, so you can do that. There is never any reason to make a card independently of a Deck, and thanks to the privacy rules, you can't.

 If the only initializer for a `public` type is implicit, code in another module can't see it and thus cannot create an instance of this type. If you want other code to be able to create an instance of this type, you must declare the initializer explicitly and declare it `public`.

New in Swift 3, a further access level open draws a further distinction. It is applicable only to classes and to members of open classes. A `public` class can't be subclassed in another module that can see this class; an open class can. A `public` member of an open class that has been subclassed in another module can't be overridden in that subclass; an open member can. (Prior to Swift 3, `public` also meant open; Swift 3 thus draws a distinction that provides a form of protection that was previously impossible.)

Privacy Rules

It took time for Apple to add access control to Swift in the early months of the language's release, mostly because the compiler had to be taught an extensive set of rules for ensuring that the privacy level of related things is coherent. For example:

- A variable can't be public if its type is private, because other code wouldn't be able to use such a variable.
- A subclass can't be public unless the superclass is public.
- A subclass can change an overridden member's access level, but it cannot even *see* its superclass's private members unless they are declared in the same file together.

And so on. I could proceed to list all the rules, but I won't. There is no need for me to enunciate them formally. They are spelled out in great detail in the Swift manual, which you can consult if you need to. In general, you probably won't need to; the privacy rules make intuitive sense, and you can rely on the compiler to help you with useful error messages if you violate one.

Introspection

Swift provides limited ability to *introspect* an object, letting an object display the names and values of its properties. This feature is intended for debugging, not for use in your program's logic. For example, you can use it to modify the way your object is displayed in the Xcode Debug pane.

To introspect an object, use it as the `reflecting:` parameter when you instantiate a Mirror. The Mirror's `children` will then be name–value tuples describing the original object's properties. Here, for example, is a Dog class with a `description` property that takes advantage of introspection. Instead of hard-coding a list of the class's instance properties, we introspect the instance to obtain the names and values of the properties. This means that we can later add more properties without having to modify our `description` implementation:

```
struct Dog : CustomStringConvertible {
    var name = "Fido"
    var license = 1
    var description : String {
        var desc = "Dog ("
        let mirror = Mirror(reflecting:self)
        for (k,v) in mirror.children {
            desc.append("\(k!): \(v), ")
        }
        let c = desc.characters.count
        return String(desc.characters.prefix(c-2)) + ")"
    }
}
```

If we now instantiate Dog and pass that instance to `print`, this is what we see in the console:

```
Dog (name: Fido, license: 1)
```

If your object type adopts both the CustomStringConvertible protocol (description property) and the CustomDebugStringConvertible protocol (debugDescription property), the description will be preferred, but you can output the debugDescription with the debugPrint function.

By adopting the CustomReflectable protocol, we can take charge of what a Mirror's children are. To do so, we supply the customMirror property to return our own custom Mirror object whose children property we have configured as a collection of name–value tuples.

In this (silly) example, we implement customMirror to supply altered names for our properties:

```
struct Dog : CustomReflectable {
    var name = "Fido"
    var license = 1
    var customMirror: Mirror {
        let children : [Mirror.Child] = [
            ("ineffable name", self.name),
            ("license to kill", self.license)
        ]
        let m = Mirror(self, children:children)
        return m
    }
}
```

The outcome is that when we po a Dog instance in the Xcode Debug pane console, our custom property names are displayed:

```
- ineffable name : "Fido"
- license to kill : 1
```

Memory Management

Swift memory management is handled automatically, and you will usually be unaware of it. Objects come into existence when they are instantiated and go out of existence as soon as they are no longer needed. Memory management of reference type objects, however, is quite tricky under the hood; I'll devote Chapter 12 to a discussion of the underlying mechanism. Even for the Swift user, things can occasionally go wrong in this regard. (Value types do not require the sort of complex memory management that reference types do, so no memory management issues can arise for them.)

Trouble typically arises when two class instances have references to one another. When that's the case, you can have a *retain cycle* which will result in a *memory leak*, meaning that the two instances *never* go out of existence. Some computer languages solve this sort of problem with a periodic "garbage collection" phase that detects retain cycles and cleans them up, but Swift doesn't do that; you have to fend off retain cycles manually.

One way to test for and observe a memory leak is to implement a class's deinit. This method is called when the instance goes out of existence. If the instance never goes out of existence, deinit is never called. That's a bad sign, if you were expecting that the instance *should* go out of existence.

Here's an example. First, I'll make two class instances and watch them go out of existence:

```swift
func testRetainCycle() {
    class Dog {
        deinit {
            print("farewell from Dog")
        }
    }
    class Cat {
        deinit {
            print("farewell from Cat")
        }
    }
    let d = Dog()
    let c = Cat()
}
testRetainCycle() // farewell from Cat, farewell from Dog
```

When we run that code, both "farewell" messages appear in the console. We created a Dog instance and a Cat instance, but the only references to them are automatic (local) variables inside the testRetainCycle function. When execution of that function's body comes to an end, all automatic variables are destroyed; that is what it means to be an automatic variable. There are no other references to our Dog and Cat instances that might make them persist, and so they are destroyed in good order.

Now I'll change that code by giving the Dog and Cat objects references to each other:

```swift
func testRetainCycle() {
    class Dog {
        var cat : Cat?
        deinit {
            print("farewell from Dog")
        }
    }
    class Cat {
        var dog : Dog?
        deinit {
            print("farewell from Cat")
        }
    }
    let d = Dog()
    let c = Cat()
}
```

```
        d.cat = c // create a...
        c.dog = d // ...retain cycle
    }
    testRetainCycle() // nothing in console
```

When we run that code, *neither* "farewell" message appears in the console. The Dog and Cat objects have references to one another. Those are *persisting* references (also called *strong* references). A persisting reference sees to it that, for example, as long as our Dog has a reference to a particular Cat, that Cat will not be destroyed. That's a good thing, and is a fundamental principle of sensible memory management. The bad thing is that the Dog and the Cat have persisting references *to one another*. That's a retain cycle! Neither the Dog instance nor the Cat instance can be destroyed, because neither of them can "go first" — it's like Alphonse and Gaston who can never get through the door because each requires the other to precede him. The Dog can't be destroyed first because the Cat has a persisting reference to him, and the Cat can't be destroyed first because the Dog has a persisting reference to him.

These objects are therefore now *leaking*. Our code is over; both d and c are gone. There are *no* further references to either of these objects; neither object can ever be referred to again. No code can mention them; no code can reach them. But they live on, floating, useless, and taking up memory.

Weak References

One solution to a retain cycle is to mark the problematic reference as weak. This means that the reference is *not* a persisting reference. It is a *weak reference*. The object referred to can now go out of existence even while the referrer continues to exist. Of course, this presents a terrible danger, because now the object referred to may be destroyed behind the referrer's back. But Swift has a solution for that, too: only an Optional reference can be marked as weak. That way, if the object referred to *is* destroyed behind the referrer's back, the referrer will see something coherent, namely nil. Also, the reference must be a var reference, precisely because it can change spontaneously to nil.

Thus, this code breaks the retain cycle and prevents the memory leak:

```
func testRetainCycle() {
    class Dog {
        weak var cat : Cat?
        deinit {
            print("farewell from Dog")
        }
    }
    class Cat {
        weak var dog : Dog?
        deinit {
            print("farewell from Cat")
        }
```

```
    }
    let d = Dog()
    let c = Cat()
    d.cat = c
    c.dog = d
}
testRetainCycle() // farewell from Cat, farewell from Dog
```

I've gone overboard in that code. To break the retain cycle, there's no need to make *both* Dog's cat and Cat's dog weak references; making just *one* of the two a weak reference is sufficient to break the cycle. That, in fact, is the usual solution when a retain cycle threatens. One of the pair will be more of an "owner" than the other; the one that is *not* the "owner" will have a weak reference to its "owner."

Although, as I mentioned earlier, value types are not subject to the same memory management issues as reference types, a value type can still be *involved* in a retain cycle with a class instance. In my retain cycle example, if Dog is a class and Cat is a struct, we still get a retain cycle. The solution is the same: make Cat's dog a weak reference. (You can't make Dog's cat a weak reference if Cat is a struct; only a reference to a class type can be declared weak.)

Do *not* use weak references unless you have to! Memory management is not to be toyed with lightly. Nevertheless, there are real-life situations in which weak references are the right thing to do, even when no retain cycle appears to threaten. For example, a view controller's references to *subviews of its own view* are usually weak, because the view itself already has persisting references to those subviews, and we would not typically want those subviews to persist in the absence of the view itself:

```
class HelpViewController: UIViewController {
    weak var wv : UIWebView?
    override func viewWillAppear(_ animated: Bool) {
        super.viewWillAppear(animated)
        let wv = UIWebView(frame:self.view.bounds)
        // ... further configuration of wv here ...
        self.view.addSubview(wv)
        self.wv = wv
    }
    // ...
}
```

In that code, `self.view.addSubview(wv)` causes the UIWebView wv to persist; our own reference to it, `self.wv`, can thus be weak.

Unowned References

There's another Swift solution for retain cycles. Instead of marking a reference as weak, you can mark it as unowned. This approach is useful in special cases where one object absolutely cannot exist without a reference to another, but where this reference need not be a persisting reference.

For example, let's pretend that a Boy may or may not have a Dog, but every Dog must have a Boy — and so I'll give Dog an init(boy:) initializer. The Dog needs a reference to its Boy, and the Boy needs a reference to his Dog if he has one; that's potentially a retain cycle:

```
func testUnowned() {
    class Boy {
        var dog : Dog?
        deinit {
            print("farewell from Boy")
        }
    }
    class Dog {
        let boy : Boy
        init(boy:Boy) { self.boy = boy }
        deinit {
            print("farewell from Dog")
        }
    }
    let b = Boy()
    let d = Dog(boy: b)
    b.dog = d
}
testUnowned() // nothing in console
```

We can solve this by declaring Dog's boy property unowned:

```
func testUnowned() {
    class Boy {
        var dog : Dog?
        deinit {
            print("farewell from Boy")
        }
    }
    class Dog {
        unowned let boy : Boy // *
        init(boy:Boy) { self.boy = boy }
        deinit {
            print("farewell from Dog")
        }
    }
    let b = Boy()
    let d = Dog(boy: b)
    b.dog = d
}
testUnowned() // farewell from Boy, farewell from Dog
```

An advantage of an unowned reference is that it doesn't have to be an Optional — in fact, it *cannot* be an Optional — and it can be a constant (let). But an unowned reference is also dangerous, because the object referred to can go out of existence behind the referrer's back, and an attempt to use that reference will cause a crash, as I can demonstrate by this rather forced code:

```
var b = Optional(Boy())
let d = Dog(boy: b!)
b = nil // destroy the Boy behind the Dog's back
print(d.boy) // crash
```

Thus, you should use unowned only if you are absolutely certain that the object referred to will outlive the referrer.

Weak and Unowned References in Anonymous Functions

A subtle variant of a retain cycle arises when an instance property's value is a function referring to the instance:

```
class FunctionHolder {
    var function : ((Void) -> Void)?
    deinit {
        print("farewell from FunctionHolder")
    }
}
func testFunctionHolder() {
    let fh = FunctionHolder()
    fh.function = {
        print(fh)
    }
}
testFunctionHolder() // nothing in console
```

Oops! I've created a retain cycle, by referring, inside the anonymous function, to the object that is holding a reference to it. Because functions are closures, the Function-Holder instance fh, declared outside the anonymous function, is captured by the anonymous function as a persisting reference. But the function property of this FunctionHolder contains this anonymous function, and that's a persisting reference too. So that's a retain cycle: the FunctionHolder persistently refers to the function, which persistently refers to the FunctionHolder.

In this situation, I *cannot* break the retain cycle by declaring the function property as weak or unowned. Only a reference to a class type can be declared weak or unowned, and a function is not a class. Thus, I must declare the captured value fh *inside the anonymous function* as weak or unowned instead.

Swift provides an ingenious syntax for doing that. At the very start of the anonymous function body, where the in line would go (and before the in line if there is one), you put square brackets containing a comma-separated list of any problematic references that will be captured from the surrounding environment, each reference preceded by weak or unowned. This list is called a *capture list*. If you have a capture list, you must follow it by the keyword in if you are not already including the keyword in for other reasons:

```
class FunctionHolder {
    var function : ((Void) -> Void)?
    deinit {
        print("farewell from FunctionHolder")
    }
}
func testFunctionHolder() {
    let fh = FunctionHolder()
    fh.function = {
        [weak fh] in // *
        print(fh)
    }
}
testFunctionHolder() // farewell from FunctionHolder
```

This syntax solves the problem. But marking a reference as weak in a capture list has a mild side effect that you will need to be aware of: such a reference passes into the anonymous function as an Optional. This is good, because it means that if the object referred to goes out of existence behind our back, the value of the Optional is nil. But of course you must also adjust your code accordingly, unwrapping the Optional as needed in order to use it. The usual technique is to perform the *weak–strong dance*: you unwrap the Optional once, right at the start of the function, in a conditional binding:

```
class FunctionHolder {
    var function : ((Void) -> Void)?
    deinit {
        print("farewell from FunctionHolder")
    }
}
func testFunctionHolder() {
    let fh = FunctionHolder()
    fh.function = {    // here comes the weak-strong dance...
        [weak fh] in  // weak
        guard let fh = fh else { return }
        print(fh)      // strong
    }
}
testFunctionHolder() // farewell from FunctionHolder
```

The conditional binding let fh = fh accomplishes two goals. First, it unwraps the Optional version of fh that arrived into the anonymous function. Second, it declares another fh that is a normal (strong) reference. So if the unwrapping succeeds, this new fh will persist for the rest of this scope.

In that particular example, there is no way on earth that this FunctionHolder instance, fh, can go out of existence while the anonymous function lives on. There are no other references to the anonymous function; it persists only as a property of fh. Therefore I can avoid some behind-the-scenes bookkeeping overhead, as well as the weak–strong dance, by declaring fh as unowned in my capture list instead.

In real life, my own most frequent use of unowned is precisely in this context. Very often, the reference marked as unowned in the capture list will be self. Here's an example from my own code:

```
class MyDropBounceAndRollBehavior : UIDynamicBehavior {
    let v : UIView
    init(view v:UIView) {
        self.v = v
        super.init()
    }
    override func willMove(to anim: UIDynamicAnimator?) {
        guard let anim = anim else { return }
        let sup = self.v.superview!
        let grav = UIGravityBehavior()
        grav.action = {
            [unowned self] in
            let items = anim.items(in:sup.bounds) as! [UIView]
            if items.index(of:self.v) == nil {
                anim.removeBehavior(self)
                self.v.removeFromSuperview()
            }
        }
        self.addChildBehavior(grav)
        grav.addItem(self.v)
        // ...
    }
    // ...
}
```

There's a potential (and rather elaborate) retain cycle here: self.addChild-Behavior(grav) causes a persistent reference to grav, grav has a persistent reference to grav.action, and the anonymous function assigned to grav.action refers to self. To break the retain cycle, I declare the reference to self as unowned in the anonymous function's capture list.

 Don't panic! Beginners have a tendency to backstop *all* their anonymous functions with [weak self]. That's unnecessary and wrong. Only a retained function can raise even the possibility of a retain cycle. Merely passing a function does *not* introduce such a possibility, especially if the function being passed will be called immediately. Always confirm that you actually *have* a retain cycle before concerning yourself with how to prevent a retain cycle.

Memory Management of Protocol-Typed References

Only a reference to an instance of a class type can be declared weak or unowned. A reference to an instance of a struct or enum type cannot be so declared, because its memory management doesn't work the same way (and is not subject to retain cycles).

A reference that is declared as a protocol type, therefore, has a problem. A protocol might be adopted by a struct or an enum. Therefore you cannot wantonly declare such a reference weak or unowned. You can only declare a protocol-typed reference weak or unowned if it is a class protocol — that is, if it is marked with @objc or class.

In this code, SecondViewControllerDelegate is a protocol that I've declared. This code won't compile unless SecondViewControllerDelegate is declared as a class protocol:

```
class SecondViewController : UIViewController {
    weak var delegate : SecondViewControllerDelegate?
    // ...
}
```

Here's the actual declaration of SecondViewControllerDelegate; it *is* declared as a class protocol, and that's why the preceding code is legal:

```
protocol SecondViewControllerDelegate : class {
    func accept(data:Any!)
}
```

A protocol declared in Objective-C is implicitly marked as @objc and is a class protocol. Thus, this declaration from my real-life code is legal:

```
weak var delegate : WKScriptMessageHandler?
```

WKScriptMessageHandler is a protocol declared by Cocoa (in particular, by the Web Kit framework). Thus, it is implicitly marked @objc; only a class can adopt WKScriptMessageHandler, and so the compiler is satisfied that the delegate variable will be an instance of a class, and thus the reference can be treated as weak.

PART II

IDE

By now, you're doubtless anxious to jump in and start writing an app. To do that, you need a solid grounding in the tools you'll be using. The heart and soul of those tools can be summed up in one word: Xcode. In this part of the book we explore Xcode, the *IDE* (integrated development environment) in which you'll be programming iOS. Xcode is a big program, and writing an app involves coordinating a lot of pieces; this part of the book will help you become comfortable with Xcode. Along the way, we'll generate a simple working app through some hands-on tutorials.

- Chapter 6 tours Xcode and explains the architecture of the *project*, the collection of files from which an app is generated.
- Chapter 7 is about nibs. A *nib* is a file containing a drawing of your interface. Understanding nibs — knowing how they work and how they relate to your code — is crucial to your use of Xcode and to proper development of just about any app.
- Chapter 8 pauses to discuss the Xcode documentation and other sources of information on the API.
- Chapter 9 explains editing your code, testing and debugging your code, and the various steps you'll take on the way to submitting your app to the App Store. You'll probably want to skim this chapter quickly at first, returning to it as a detailed reference later while developing and submitting an actual app.

CHAPTER 6

Anatomy of an Xcode Project

Xcode is the application used to develop an iOS app. An Xcode *project* is the source for an app; it's the entire collection of files and settings used to construct the app. To create, develop, and maintain an app, you must know how to manipulate and navigate an Xcode project. So you must know something about Xcode, and you must know something about the nature and structure of Xcode projects and how Xcode shows them to you. That's the subject of this chapter.

 The term "Xcode" is used in two ways. It's the name of the application in which you edit and build your app, and it's the name of an entire suite of utilities that accompanies it — in the latter sense, Instruments and the Simulator are part of Xcode. This ambiguity should generally present little difficulty.

Xcode is a powerful, complex, and extremely large program. My approach in introducing Xcode is to suggest that you adopt a kind of deliberate tunnel vision: if you don't understand something, don't worry about it — don't even look at it, and don't touch it, because you might change something important. Our survey of Xcode will chart a safe, restricted, and essential path, focusing on aspects of Xcode that you most need to understand immediately, and resolutely ignoring everything else.

For full information, study Apple's own documentation (choose Help → Xcode Help); it may seem overwhelming at first, but what you need to know is probably in there somewhere. There are also entire books devoted to describing and explaining Xcode.

 New in Xcode 8, Xcode Help and individual help topics that can be summoned through the contextual menu within Xcode will appear in Apple's Help View, not the documentation window discussed in Chapter 8.

New Project

Even before you've written any code, an Xcode project is quite elaborate. To see this, let's make a new, essentially "empty" project; you'll find that it isn't empty at all.

1. Start up Xcode and choose File → New → Project.

2. The "Choose a template" dialog appears. The *template* is your project's initial set of files and settings. When you pick a template, you're really picking an existing folder full of files; this folder is hidden deep inside the Xcode bundle, at *Xcode.app/Contents/Developer/Platforms/iPhoneOS.platform/Developer/Library/ Xcode/Templates/Project Templates/iOS/Application*. This template folder will essentially be copied, and a few values will be filled in, in order to create your project.

   So, in this case, select iOS; under Application, select the Single View app template. Click Next.

3. You are now asked to provide a name for your project (Product Name). Let's call our new project *Empty Window*.

   In a real project, you should give some thought to the project's name, as you're going to be living in close quarters with it. As Xcode copies the template folder, it's going to use the project's name to "fill in the blank" in several places, including the name of the app. Thus, whatever you type at this moment is something you'll be seeing throughout your project. You are not locked into the name of your project forever, though, and there's a separate setting allowing you to change at any time the name of the app that it produces. I'll talk later about name changes ("Renaming Parts of a Project" on page 331).

   It's fine to use spaces in a project name. Spaces are legal in the project name, the app name, and the various names of files and folders that Xcode will generate automatically; and in the few places where spaces are problematic (such as the bundle identifier, which I'll discuss in a moment), the name you type as the Product Name will have its spaces converted to hyphens. But do *not* use any other punctuation in your project name! Such punctuation can cause Xcode features to break in subtle ways.

4. New in Xcode 8 is the Team pop-up menu. Ignore this for now; I'll discuss its significance in Chapter 9. Ignore the Organization Name as well; it is used only in some automatically generated code comments.

5. Note the Organization Identifier field. The first time you create a project, this field will be blank, and you should fill it in. The goal here is to create a unique string identifying you or your organization. The convention is to start the organization identifier with com. and to follow it with a string (possibly with multiple dot-components) that no one else is likely to use. For example, I use

`com.neuburg.matt`. Every app on a device or submitted to the App Store needs a unique bundle identifier. Your app's bundle identifier, which is shown in gray below the organization identifier, will consist of the organization identifier plus a version of the project's name; if you give every project a unique name within your personal world, the bundle identifier will uniquely identify this project and the app that it produces (or you can change the bundle identifier manually later if necessary).

6. The Language pop-up menu lets you choose between Swift and Objective-C. This choice is not positively binding; it dictates the initial structure and code of the project template, but you are free to add Swift files to an Objective-C project, or Objective-C files to a Swift project. You can even start with an Objective-C project and decide later to convert it completely to Swift. (See "Bilingual Targets" on page 575.) For now, choose Swift.

7. Make sure the Devices pop-up menu is set to iPhone. Again, this choice is not positively binding; but for now, let's assume that our app is to run on iPhone only.

8. Make sure Use Core Data, Include Unit Tests, and Include UI Tests are *not* checked. Click Next.

9. You've now told Xcode how to construct your project. Basically, it's going to copy the *Single View Application.xctemplate* folder from within the *Project Templates* folder I mentioned earlier. But you need to tell it where to copy this template folder *to*. That's why Xcode is now presenting a Save dialog with a Create button. You are to specify the location of a folder that is about to be created — the *project folder* for this project. The project folder can go just about anywhere, and you can move it after creating it. I usually create new projects on the Desktop.

10. Xcode also offers, through a checkbox, to create a git repository for your project. (You might need to click Options to see the checkbox.) In real life, this can be a great convenience (see Chapter 9), but for now, uncheck that checkbox. Click Create.

11. The *Empty Window* project folder is created on disk (on the Desktop, if that's the location you just specified), and the project window for the Empty Window project opens in Xcode.

The project we've just created is a working project; it really does build an iOS app called Empty Window. To see this, make sure that the scheme and destination in the project window's toolbar are listed as Empty Window → iPhone 6. (The scheme and destination are actually pop-up menus, so you can click on them to change their values if needed.) Choose Product → Run. After some delay, the iOS Simulator application eventually opens and displays your app running — an empty white screen.

To *build* a project is to compile its code and assemble the compiled code, together with various resources, into the actual app. Typically, if you want to know whether your code compiles and your project is consistently and correctly constructed, you'll build the project (Product → Build). Alternatively, you can compile an individual file (choose Product → Perform Action → Compile [File-name]). To *run* a project is to launch the built app, in the Simulator or on a connected device; if you want to know whether your code works as expected, you'll run the project (Product → Run), which automatically builds first if necessary.

The Project Window

An Xcode project embodies a lot of information about what files constitute the project and how they are to be used when building the app, such as:

- The source files (your code) that are to be compiled
- Any *.storyboard* or *.xib* files, graphically expressing interface objects to be instantiated as your app runs
- Any resources, such as icons, images, or sound files, that are to be part of the app
- All settings (instructions to the compiler, to the linker, and so on) that are to be obeyed as the app is built
- Any frameworks that the code will need when it runs

A single Xcode project window presents all of this information, as well as letting you access, edit, and navigate your code, plus reporting the progress and results of such procedures as building or debugging an app and more. This window displays a lot of information and embodies a lot of functionality! A project window is powerful and elaborate; learning to navigate and understand it takes time. Let's pause to explore this window and see how it is constructed.

A project window has four main parts (Figure 6-1):

1. On the left is the Navigator pane. Show and hide it with View → Navigators → Show/Hide Navigator (Command-0) or with the first View button at the right end of the toolbar.

2. In the middle is the Editor pane (or simply "editor"). This is the main area of a project window. A project window nearly always displays an Editor pane, and can display multiple Editor panes simultaneously.

3. On the right is the Utilities pane. Show and hide it with View → Utilities → Show/Hide Utilities (Command-Option-0) or with the third View button at the right end of the toolbar.

Figure 6-1. The project window

4. At the bottom is the Debug pane. Show and hide it with View → Debug Area → Show/Hide Debug Area (Command-Shift-Y) or with the second View button at the right end of the toolbar.

> All Xcode keyboard shortcuts can be customized; see the Key Bindings pane of the Preferences window. Keyboard shortcuts that I cite are the defaults.

The Navigator Pane

The Navigator pane is the column of information at the left of the project window. Among other things, it's your primary mechanism for controlling what you see in the main area of the project window (the editor). An important use pattern for Xcode is: you select something in the Navigator pane, and that thing is displayed in the editor.

It is possible to toggle the visibility of the Navigator pane (View → Navigators → Hide/Show Navigator, or Command-0); for example, once you've used the Navigator pane to reach the item you want to see or work on in the editor, you might hide the Navigator pane temporarily to maximize your screen real estate (especially on a smaller monitor). You can change the Navigator pane's width by dragging the vertical line at its right edge.

The Navigator pane itself can display eight different sets of information; thus, there are actually eight navigators. These are represented by the eight icons across its top; to switch among them, use these icons or their keyboard shortcuts (Command-1, Command-2, and so on). If the Navigator pane is hidden, pressing a navigator's keyboard shortcut both shows the Navigator pane and switches to that navigator.

Figure 6-2. The Project navigator

Depending on your settings in the Behaviors pane of Xcode's preferences, a navigator might show itself automatically when you perform a certain action. For example, by default, when you build your project, if warning messages or error messages are generated, the Issue navigator will appear. This automatic behavior will not prove troublesome, because it is generally precisely the behavior you want, and if it isn't, you can change it; plus you can easily switch to a different navigator at any time.

Let's begin experimenting immediately with the various navigators:

Project navigator (Command-1)
> Click here for basic navigation through the files that constitute your project (Figure 6-2). For example, in the Empty Window folder (these folder-like things in the Project navigator are actually called *groups*), click *AppDelegate.swift* to view its code in the editor.
>
> At the top level of the Project navigator, with a blue Xcode icon, is the Empty Window project itself; click it to view the settings associated with your project and its targets. Don't change anything here without knowing what you're doing! I'll talk later in this chapter about what these settings are for.
>
> The filter bar at the bottom of the Project navigator lets you limit what files are shown; when there are many files, this is great for quickly reaching a file with a known name. For example, try typing "delegate" in the filter bar search field. Don't forget to remove your filter when you're done experimenting.

 Once you've filtered a navigator, it stays filtered until you remove the filter — even if you close the project! A common mistake is to filter a navigator, forget that you've done so, fail to notice the filter (because you're looking at the navigator itself, not down at the bottom where the filter bar is), and wonder, "Hey, where did all my files go?"

Symbol navigator (Command-2)
> A *symbol* is a name, typically the name of a class or method. Among other things, this can be useful for navigating your code. For example, highlight the first two

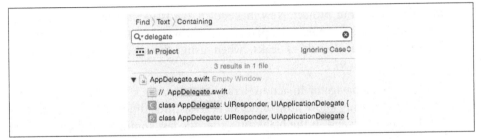

Figure 6-3. The Find navigator

icons in the filter bar (the first two are blue, the third is dark), and see how quickly you can reach the definition of AppDelegate's `applicationDidBecome-Active(_:)` method.

Try highlighting the filter bar icons in various ways to see how the contents of the Symbol navigator change. Type in the search field in the filter bar to limit what appears in the Symbol navigator; for example, try typing "active" in the search field, and see what happens.

 When the second filter icon is not highlighted, you are shown all symbols, including those defined by Swift and those defined by Cocoa (Figure 4-1). This is a great way to learn what object types exist, and to reach the headers where those types are declared (an important form of documentation: see Chapter 8).

Find navigator (Command-3)
This is a powerful search facility for finding text globally in your project. You can also summon the Find navigator with Find → Find in Project (Command-Shift-F). The words above the search field show what options are currently in force; they are pop-up menus, so click one to change the options. Try searching for "delegate" (Figure 6-3). Click a search result to jump to it in your code.

Below the search field, at the left, is the current *search scope*. This limits what files will be searched. Click it to see the Search Scopes panel. You can limit the search to a group (folder) within your project. You can also define a new scope: click New Scope to summon the scope configuration popover, where you can examine your options. Scopes are defined per user, not per project; scopes that you create here will appear in other projects.

You can type in the other search field, the one in the filter bar at the bottom, to limit further which search results are displayed. (I'm going to stop calling your attention to the filter bar now, but every navigator has it in some form.)

Issue navigator (Command-4)
You'll need this navigator primarily when your code has issues. This doesn't refer to emotional instability; it's Xcode's term for warning and error messages emitted

when you build your project. New in Xcode 8, the Issue navigator, in addition to displaying buildtime issues (compile errors and warnings), can also display certain runtime issues (such as leaks, when using the memory sanitizer, as I'll explain in Chapter 9).

To see the Issue navigator in action, let's give your code a buildtime issue. Navigate (as you already know how to do, in at least three different ways) to the file *AppDelegate.swift*, and in the blank line after the last comment at the top of the file's contents, above the import line, type howdy. Build the project (Command-B). The Issue navigator, in its Buildtime pane, will display some error messages, showing that the compiler is unable to cope with this illegal word appearing in an illegal place. Click an issue to see it within its file. In your code, issue "balloons" may appear to the right of lines containing issues; if you're distracted or hampered by these, toggle their visibility with Editor → Issues → Hide/Show All Issues (Command-Control-M).

Now that you've made Xcode miserable, select "howdy" and delete it; save and build again, and your issues will be gone. If only real life were this easy!

Test navigator (Command-5)

This navigator lists test files and individual test methods and permits you to run your tests and see whether they succeeded or failed. A test is code that isn't part of your app; rather, it calls a bit of your app's code to see whether it behaves as expected. I'll talk more about tests in Chapter 9.

Debug navigator (Command-6)

By default, this navigator will appear when your code is paused while you're debugging it. There is not a strong distinction in Xcode between running and debugging; the milieu is the same. The difference is mostly a matter of whether breakpoints are obeyed (more about that, and about debugging in general, in Chapter 9).

To see the Debug navigator in action, you'll need to give your code a breakpoint. Navigate once more to the file *AppDelegate.swift*, select in the line that says return true, and choose Debug → Breakpoints → Add Breakpoint at Current Line to make a blue breakpoint arrow appear on that line. Run the project. By default, as the breakpoint is encountered, the Navigator pane switches to the Debug navigator, and the Debug pane appears at the bottom of the window. This overall layout (Figure 6-4) will rapidly become familiar as you debug your projects.

The Debug navigator starts with several numeric and graphical displays of profiling information (at a minimum, you'll see CPU, Memory, Disk, and Network); click one to see extensive graphical information in the editor. This information allows you to track possible misbehavior of your app as you run it, without the

Figure 6-4. The Debug layout

added complexity of running the Instruments utility (discussed in Chapter 9). To toggle the visibility of the profiling information at the top of the Debug navigator, click the "gauge" icon (to the right of the process's name).

The Debug navigator also displays the call stack, with the names of the nested methods in which a pause occurs; as you would expect, you can click on a method name to navigate to it. You can shorten or lengthen the list with the first button in the filter bar at the bottom of the navigator. The second icon to the right of the process's name summons a pop-up menu that lets you toggle between display by thread (View Process by Thread) and display by queue (View Process by Queue). I'll discuss in Chapter 9 what the other two entries in that pop-up menu do.

The Debug pane, which can be shown or hidden at will (View → Debug Area → Hide/Show Debug Area, or Command-Shift-Y), consists of two subpanes:

The variables list (on the left)
It is populated with the variables in scope for the selected method in the call stack at the point where we are paused.

The console (on the right)
Here the debugger displays text messages; that's how you learn of exceptions thrown by your running app, plus you can have your code deliberately send you log messages describing your app's progress and behavior. Such messages are important, so keep an eye on the console as your app runs. You can also use the console to enter commands to the debugger. This can often be a better way to explore values during a pause than the variables list.

Either the variables list or the console can be hidden using the two buttons at the bottom right of the pane. The console can also be summoned by choosing View → Debug Area → Activate Console.

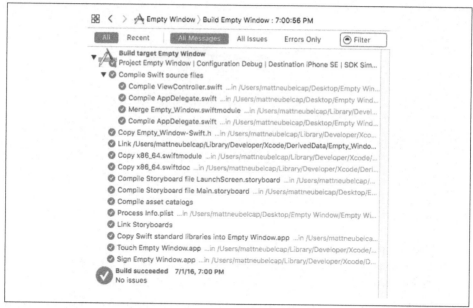

Figure 6-5. Viewing a report

Breakpoint navigator (Command-7)

This navigator lists all your breakpoints. At the moment you have only one, but when you're actively debugging a large project with many breakpoints, you'll be glad of this navigator. Also, this is where you create special breakpoints (such as symbolic breakpoints), and in general it's your center for managing existing breakpoints. We'll return to this topic in Chapter 9.

Report navigator (Command-8)

This navigator lists your recent major actions, such as building or running (debugging) your project. Click a listing to see (in the editor) the report generated when you performed that action. The report might contain information that isn't displayed in any other way, and also it lets you dredge up console messages from the recent past ("What was that exception I got while debugging a moment ago?").

For example, by clicking on the listing for a successful build, and by choosing to display All and All Messages using the filter switches at the top of the report, we can see the steps by which a build takes place (Figure 6-5). To reveal the full text of a step, click on that step and then click the Expand Transcript button that appears at the far right (and see also the menu items in the Editor menu).

When navigating by clicking in the Navigator pane, modifications to your click can determine where navigation takes place. By default, Option-click navigates in an assistant pane (discussed later in this chapter), double-click navigates by opening a new window, and Option-Shift-click summons a little heads-up pane where you can specify where to navigate (a new window, a new tab, or a new assistant pane). For the settings that govern these click modifications, see the Navigation pane of Xcode's preferences.

The Utilities Pane

The Utilities pane is the column at the right of the project window. It contains inspectors that provide information about the current selection or its settings; if those settings can be changed, this is where you change them. It also contains libraries that function as a source of objects you may need while editing your project. The Utilities pane's importance emerges mostly when you're editing a *.storyboard* or *.xib* file (Chapter 7). But it can be useful also while editing code, because Quick Help, a form of documentation (Chapter 8), is displayed here as well, plus the Utilities pane is the source of code snippets (Chapter 9). To toggle the visibility of the Utilities pane, choose View → Utilities → Hide/Show Utilities (Command-Option-0). You can change the Utilities pane's width by dragging the vertical line at its left edge.

The Utilities pane consists of numerous palettes, which are clumped into multiple sets, which are themselves divided into two major groups: the top half of the pane and the bottom half of the pane. You can change the relative heights of these two halves by dragging the horizontal line that separates them.

The top half
> What appears in the top half of the Utilities pane depends on what's selected in the current editor. For example:

A code file is being edited
> The top half of the Utilities pane shows either the File inspector or Quick Help. Toggle between them with the icons at the top of this half of the Utilities pane, or with their keyboard shortcuts (Command-Option-1, Command-Option-2). The File inspector is rarely needed, but Quick Help can be useful because it displays documentation (Chapter 8). The File inspector consists of multiple sections, each of which can be expanded or collapsed by clicking its header.

A .storyboard or .xib file is being edited
> The top half of the Utilities pane shows, in addition to the File inspector and Quick Help, the Identity inspector (Command-Option-3), the Attributes inspector (Command-Option-4), the Size inspector (Command-Option-5), and the Connections inspector (Command-Option-6). These can consist of multiple sections, each of which can be expanded or collapsed by clicking its header.

> Other forms of editing may cause other inspector combinations to appear here.

The bottom half

The bottom half of the Utilities pane shows one of four libraries. Toggle between them with the icons at the top of this half of the Utilities pane, or with their keyboard shortcuts. They are the File Template library (Command-Option-Control-1), the Code Snippet library (Command-Option-Control-2), the Object library (Command-Option-Control-3), and the Media library (Command-Option-Control-4). The Object library is the most important; you'll use it heavily when editing a *.storyboard* or *.xib* file.

To see a help pop-up describing the currently selected item in a library, press Spacebar.

The Editor

In the middle of the project window is the *editor*. This is where you get actual work done, reading and writing your code (Chapter 9), or designing your interface in a *.storyboard* or *.xib* file (Chapter 7). The editor is the core of the project window. You can hide the Navigator pane, the Utilities pane, and the Debug pane, but there is no such thing as a project window without an editor (though you can cover the editor completely with the Debug pane).

The editor provides its own form of navigation, the *jump bar* across the top. Not only does the jump bar show you hierarchically what file is currently being edited, but also it allows you to switch to a different file. In particular, each path component in the jump bar is also a pop-up menu. These pop-up menus can be summoned by clicking on a path component, or by using keyboard shortcuts (shown in the second section of the View → Standard Editor submenu). For example, Control-4 summons a hierarchical pop-up menu, which can be navigated entirely with the keyboard, allowing you to choose a different file in your project to edit. Moreover, each pop-up menu in the jump bar also has a filter field; to see it, summon a pop-up menu from the jump bar and start typing. Thus you can navigate your project even if the Project navigator isn't showing.

The symbol at the left end of the jump bar (Control-1) summons a hierarchical menu (the Related Items menu) allowing navigation to files related to the current one. What appears here depends not only on what file is currently being edited but on the current selection within that file. This is an extremely powerful and convenient menu, and you should take time to explore it. You can navigate to related class files (Superclasses, Subclasses, and Siblings; siblings are classes with the same superclass); you can view methods called by the currently selected method, and that call the currently selected method. Choose Generated Interface to view the public API of a Swift file or Objective-C header file as seen by Swift, or Original Source to switch from a Swift generated interface to the Objective-C original.

The editor remembers the history of things it has displayed, and you can return to previously viewed content with the Back button in the jump bar, which is also a pop-up menu from which you can choose. Alternatively, choose Navigate → Go Back (Command-Control-Left).

It is likely, as you develop a project, that you'll want to edit more than one file simultaneously, or obtain multiple views of a single file so that you can edit two areas of it simultaneously. This can be achieved in three ways: assistants, tabs, and secondary windows.

Assistants

You can split the editor into multiple editors by summoning an *assistant* pane. To do so, click the second Editor button in the toolbar ("Show the Assistant editor"), or choose View → Assistant Editor → Show Assistant Editor (Command-Option-Return). Also, by default, adding the Option key to navigation opens an assistant pane; for example, Option-click in the Navigator pane, or Option-choose in the jump bar, to navigate by opening an assistant pane (or to navigate in an existing assistant pane if there is one). To remove the assistant pane, click the first Editor button in the toolbar, or choose View → Standard Editor → Show Standard Editor (Command-Return), or click the X button at the assistant pane's top right.

You can determine how assistant panes are to be arranged. To do so, choose from the View → Assistant Editor submenu. I usually prefer All Editors Stacked Vertically, but it's purely a matter of taste. Once you've summoned an assistant pane, you can split it further into additional assistant panes. To do so, click the Plus button at the top right of an assistant pane. To dismiss an assistant pane, click the X button at its top right.

What makes an assistant pane an assistant, and not just a form of split-pane editing, is that it can bear a special relationship to the primary editor pane. The primary editor pane is the one whose contents, by default, are determined by what you click on in the Navigator pane; an assistant pane, meanwhile, can respond to what file is being edited in the primary editor pane by changing intelligently what file it (the assistant pane) is editing. This is called *tracking*. To configure the tracking behavior of an assistant pane, use the first component in its jump bar (Control-4). This is the Tracking menu; it's like the Related Items menu that I discussed a moment ago, but selecting a category determines automatic tracking behavior. If a category has multiple files, a pair of arrow buttons appears at the right end of the assistant's jump bar, with which you can navigate between them (or use the second jump bar component, Control-5). You can turn off tracking by setting the assistant's first jump bar component to Manual.

Tabs

You can embody the entire project window interface as a tab. To do so, choose File → New → Tab (Command-T), revealing the tab bar (just below the toolbar) if it wasn't showing already. Use of a tabbed interface will likely be familiar from applications such as Safari. You can switch between tabs by clicking on a tab, or with Command-Shift-}. At first, your new tab will look largely identical to the original window from which it was spawned. But then you can make changes in a tab — change what panes are showing or what file is being edited, for example — without affecting any other tabs. Thus you can get multiple views of your project. You can assign a descriptive name to a tab: double-click on a tab name to make it editable.

Secondary windows

A secondary project window is similar to a tab, but it appears as a separate window instead of a tab in the same window. To create one, choose File → New → Window (Command-Shift-T). Alternatively, you can promote a tab to be a window by dragging it right out of its current window.

There isn't a strong difference between a tab and a secondary window; which you use, and for what, will be a matter of taste and convenience. I find that the advantage of a secondary window is that you can see it at the same time as the main window, and that it can be small. Thus, when I have a file I frequently want to refer to, I might spawn off a secondary window displaying that file, sized fairly small and without any panes other than the editor.

Tabs and windows come in handy in connection with custom behaviors. For example, as I mentioned before, it's important to be able to view the console while debugging; I like to see it at the full size of the project window, but I also want to be able to switch back to viewing my code. So I've created a custom behavior (click the Plus button at the bottom of the Behaviors pane of the Preferences window) that performs two actions: Show tab named Console in active window, and Show debugger with Console View. Moreover, I've given that behavior a keyboard shortcut. Thus at any time I can press my keyboard shortcut, and we switch to the Console tab (creating it if it doesn't exist), displaying nothing but the console. This is just a tab, so I can easily switch between it and my code in the other tab.

The Project File and Its Dependents

The first item in the Project navigator (Command-1) represents the project itself. (In the Empty Window project that we created earlier in this chapter, it is called Empty Window.) Hierarchically dependent upon it are items that contribute to the building of the project. Many of these items, as well as the project itself, correspond to items on disk in the project folder.

Figure 6-6. The Project navigator and the project folder

To survey this correspondence, let's examine the project folder in the Finder simultaneously with the Xcode project window. Select the project listing in the Project navigator and choose File → Show in Finder. The Finder displays the contents of your project folder (Figure 6-6).

 Never, never, *never* touch anything in a project folder by way of the Finder, except for double-clicking the project file to open the project. Don't put anything directly into a project folder. Don't remove anything from a project folder. Don't rename anything in a project folder. Don't touch anything in a project folder! Do all your interaction with the project through the project window in Xcode. (When you're an Xcode power user, you'll know when you can disobey this rule. Until then, just obey it blindly.)

The reason is that the project expects things in the project folder to be a certain way. If you make any alterations to the project folder directly in the Finder, behind the project's back, you can upset those expectations and break the project. When you work in the project window, it is Xcode itself that makes any necessary changes in the project folder, and all will be well.

The most important thing in the project folder is *Empty Window.xcodeproj*. This is the *project file*, corresponding to the project listed in the Project navigator. All Xcode's knowledge about your project — what files it consists of and how to build the project — is stored in this file. To open a project from the Finder, double-click the project file. Alternatively, you can drag the project folder onto Xcode's icon (in the Finder, in the Dock, or in the application switcher) and Xcode will locate the project file and open it for you; thus, you might never need to open the project folder at all!

Let's consider how the groups and files displayed hierarchically down from the project in the Project navigator correspond to reality on disk as portrayed in the Finder (Figure 6-6). Recall that *group* is the technical term for the folder-like objects shown in the Project navigator:

- The Empty Window group corresponds directly to the *Empty Window* folder on disk. Groups in the Project navigator don't necessarily correspond to folders on disk in the Finder, and folders on disk in the Finder don't necessarily correspond to groups in the Project navigator. But in this case, there is such a correspondence!

- Files within the Empty Window group, such as *AppDelegate.swift*, correspond to real files on disk that are inside the *Empty Window* folder. If you were to create additional code files (which, in real life, you would almost certainly do in the course of developing your project), you would likely put them in the Empty Window group in the Project navigator, and they, too, would then be in the *Empty Window* folder on disk. (That, however, is not a requirement; your files can live anywhere and your project will still work fine.)

- Two files in the Empty Window group, *Main.storyboard* and *LaunchScreen.storyboard*, appear in the Finder inside a folder that doesn't visibly correspond to anything in the Project navigator, called *Base.lproj*. This arrangement has to do with *localization*, which I'll discuss in Chapter 9.

- The item *Assets.xcassets* in the Project navigator corresponds to a specially structured folder *Assets.xcassets* on disk. This is an *asset catalog*; you add resources to the asset catalog in Xcode, which maintains that folder on disk for you. I'll talk more about the asset catalog later in this chapter, and in Chapter 9.

You may be tempted to find all this confusing. Don't! Remember what I said about not involving yourself with the project folder on disk in the Finder. You've seen it; you know that it has contents; you know that they bear some relation to the Project navigator; now forget about them. Keep your attention on the Project navigator, make your modifications to the project there, and all will be well.

Feel free, as you develop your project and add files to it, to add further groups to the Project navigator. The purpose of groups is to make the Project navigator work well for you! They don't affect how the app is built, and by default they don't correspond to any folder on disk; they are just an organizational convenience within the Project navigator. To make a new group, choose File → New → Group. To rename a group, select it in the Project navigator and press Return to make the name editable. For example, if some of your code files have to do with a login screen that your app sometimes presents, you might clump them together in a Login group. If your app is to contain some sound files, you might put them into a Sounds group. And so on.

The Products group and its contents don't correspond to anything in the project folder. Xcode generates a reference to the executable bundle generated by building each target in your project, and by convention these references appear in the Products group.

Another conventional group is the Frameworks group, listing frameworks on which your code depends. Your code does depend on some frameworks, but by default they are not listed in the Project navigator, and the Project navigator has no Frameworks group, because these frameworks are not explicitly linked into your build; instead, your code uses *modules*, which means that the import statements at the top of your files are sufficient to cause linkage to take place implicitly. However, if you were to link *explicitly* to a framework, it would be listed in the Project navigator, and you might then create a Frameworks group, just to give that listing a nice place to live. I'll discuss frameworks later in this chapter.

The Target

A *target* is a collection of parts along with rules and settings for how to build a product from them. Whenever you build, what you're really building is a target (possibly more than one target).

Select the Empty Window project at the top of the Project navigator, and you'll see two things on the left side of the editor (Figure 6-7): the project itself, and a list of your targets. Our Empty Window project comes with one target — the *app target*, called Empty Window (just like the project itself). The app target is the target that you use to build and run your app. Its settings are the settings that tell Xcode how your app is to be built; its product is the app itself.

Under certain circumstances, you might add further targets to a project:

- You might want to perform unit tests or interface tests; to do so, you'd add a target. (I'll talk more about testing in Chapter 9.)
- You might write a framework as part of your iOS app; with a custom framework, you can factor common code into a single locus, and you can configure its privacy details as a namespace. A custom framework needs to be built, so it, too, is a target. (I'll talk more about frameworks later in this chapter.)
- You might write an application extension, such as a today extension (content to appear in the notification center) or a photo editing extension (custom photo editing interface to appear in the Photos app). Those, too, are targets.

The project name and the list of targets can appear in two ways (Figure 6-7): either as a column on the left side of the editor, or, if that column is collapsed to save space, as a pop-up menu at the top left of the editor. If, in the column or pop-up menu, you select the *project*, you *edit the project*; if you select a *target*, you *edit the target*. I'll use those expressions a lot in later instructions.

Figure 6-7. Two ways of showing the project and targets

Figure 6-8. The app target's build phases

Build Phases

Edit the app target and click Build Phases at the top of the editor (Figure 6-8). These are the stages by which your app is built. The *build phases* are both a report to you on how the target will be built and a set of instructions to Xcode on how to build the target; if you change the build phases, you change the build process. Click each build phase to see a list of the files in your target to which that build phase will apply.

Two of the build phases have contents. The meanings of these build phases are pretty straightforward:

Compile Sources

Certain files (your code) are compiled, and the resulting compiled code is copied into the app.

This build phase typically applies to all of the target's *.swift* files; those are the code files that constitute the target. Sure enough, it currently contains *View-Controller.swift* and *AppDelegate.swift*. If you add a new Swift file to your project (typically in order to declare another class), you'll specify that it should be part of the app target, and it will automatically be added to the Compile Sources build phase.

Copy Bundle Resources
Certain files are copied into the app, so that your code or the system can find them there when the app runs.

This build phase currently applies to the asset catalog; any resources you add to the asset catalog will be copied into your app as part of the catalog. It also currently lists your launch storyboard file, *LaunchScreen.storyboard*, and your app's interface storyboard file, *Main.storyboard*.

Copying doesn't necessarily mean making an identical copy. Certain types of file are automatically treated in special ways as they are copied into the app bundle. For example, copying the asset catalog means that icons in the catalog are written out to the top level of the app bundle, and the asset catalog itself is transformed into a *.car* file; copying a *.storyboard* file means that it is transformed into a *.storyboardc* file, which is itself a bundle containing nib files.

You can alter these lists manually, and sometimes you may need to do so. For instance, if something in your project, such as a sound file, was not in Copy Bundle Resources and you wanted it copied into the app during the build process, you would drag it from the Project navigator into the Copy Bundle Resources list, or (easier) click the Plus button beneath the Copy Bundle Resources list to get a helpful dialog listing everything in your project. Conversely, if something in your project was in Copy Bundle Resources and you *didn't* want it copied into the app, you would delete it from the list; this would not delete it from your project, from the Project navigator, or from the Finder, but only from the list of things to be copied into your app.

It is possible that you might need to alter the Link Binary With Libraries build phase. Certain libraries, usually frameworks, are linked to the compiled code (now referred to, following compilation, as the *binary*), thus telling your code to expect those libraries to be present on the device when the app runs. Our Empty Window project does link to some frameworks, but it doesn't use this build phase to do it; instead, it imports the frameworks as modules and the frameworks are linked automatically. However, in some cases you would need to link the binary with additional frameworks explicitly; I'll talk about that later in this chapter.

A useful trick is to add a Run Script build phase, which runs a custom shell script late in the build process. To do so, choose Editor → Add Build Phase → Add Run Script Build Phase. Open the newly added Run Script build phase to edit the custom shell script. A minimal shell script might read:

```
echo "Running the Run Script build phase"
```

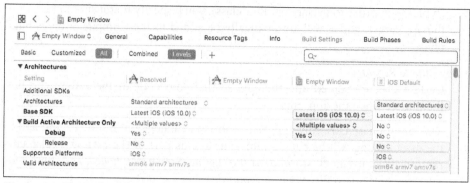

Figure 6-9. Target build settings

The "Show environment variables in build log" checkbox causes the build process's environment variables and their values to be listed in the build report during the Run Script build phase. This alone can be a reason to add a Run Script build phase; you can learn a lot about how the build process works by examining the environment variables.

Build Settings

Build phases are only one aspect of how a target knows how to build the app. The other aspect is *build settings*. To see them, edit the target and click Build Settings at the top of the editor (Figure 6-9). Here you'll find a long list of settings, most of which you'll never touch. Xcode examines this list in order to know what to do at various stages of the build process. Build settings are the reason your project compiles and builds the way it does.

You can determine what build settings are displayed by clicking Basic or All. The settings are combined into categories, and you can close or open each category heading to save room. If you know something about a setting you want to see, such as its name, you can use the search field at the top right to filter what settings are shown.

You can determine how build settings are displayed by clicking Combined or Levels; in Figure 6-9, I've clicked Levels, in order to discuss what levels are. It turns out that not only does a *target* contain values for the build settings, but the *project* also contains values for the same build settings; furthermore, Xcode has certain built-in default build setting values. The Levels display shows all of these levels at once, so you can understand the derivation of the actual values used for every build setting.

To understand the chart, read from right to left. For example, the iOS default for the Build Active Architecture Only setting's Debug configuration (far right) is No. But then the project comes along (second column from the right) and sets it to Yes. The target (third column from the right) doesn't change that setting, so the result (fourth column from the right) is that the setting resolves to Yes.

Figure 6-10. Configurations

You will rarely have occasion to manipulate build settings directly, as the defaults are usually acceptable. Nevertheless, you *can* change build setting values, and this is where you would do so. You can change a value at the project level or at the target level. You can select a build setting and show Quick Help in the Utilities pane to learn more about it.

Configurations

There are actually multiple lists of build setting values — though only one such list applies when a particular build is performed. Each such list is called a *configuration*. Multiple configurations are needed because you build in different ways at different times for different purposes, and thus you'll want certain build settings to take on different values under different circumstances.

By default, there are two configurations:

Debug
This configuration is used throughout the development process, as you write and run your app.

Release
This configuration is used for late-stage testing, when you want to check performance on a device, and for archiving the app to be submitted to the App Store.

Configurations exist at all because the project says so. To see where the project says so, edit the project and click Info at the top of the editor (Figure 6-10). Note that these configurations are just names. You can make additional configurations, and when you do, you're just adding to the list of names. The importance of configurations emerges only when those names are coupled with build setting values. Configurations can affect build setting values both at the project level and at the target level.

For example, return to the target build settings (Figure 6-9) and type "Optim" into the search field. Now you can look at the Optimization Level build setting (Figure 6-11).

Figure 6-11. How configurations affect build settings

The Debug configuration value for Optimization Level is None: while you're developing your app, you build with the Debug configuration, so your code is just compiled line by line in a straightforward way. The Release configuration value for Optimization Level is Fast, Whole Module Optimization. When your app is ready to ship, you build it with the Release configuration, so the resulting binary is optimized for speed, which is great for your users running the app on a device, but would be no good while you're developing the app because breakpoints and stepping in the debugger wouldn't work properly. In addition, Whole Module Optimization allows the Swift compiler to survey all your code files at once. Compilation may take considerably longer, but the resulting optimization can be better; for example, the compiler may be able to deduce that certain class members don't need dynamic dispatch, thus making your code even faster. And you won't mind the delay, because you won't do a Release build very often.

Schemes and Destinations

So far, I have not said how Xcode knows *which* configuration to use during a particular build. This is determined by a scheme.

A *scheme* unites a target (or multiple targets) with a build configuration, with respect to the purpose for which you're building. A new project comes by default with a single scheme, named after the project. Thus the Empty Window project's single scheme is currently called Empty Window. To see it, choose Product → Scheme → Edit Scheme. The scheme editor dialog opens (Figure 6-12).

On the left side of the scheme editor are listed various actions you might perform from the Product menu. Click an action to see its corresponding settings in this scheme.

The first action, the Build action, is different from the other actions, because it is common to all of them — the other actions all implicitly involve building. The Build action merely determines what target(s) will be built when each of the other actions is performed. For our project this means that the app target is always to be built, regardless of the action you perform.

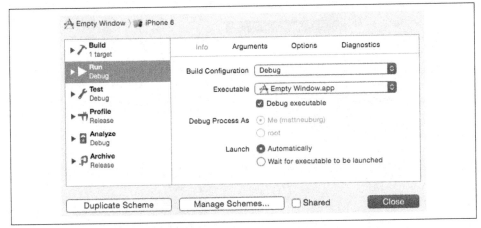

Figure 6-12. The scheme editor

The second action, the Run action, determines the settings that will be used when you build and run. The Build Configuration pop-up menu (in the Info pane) is set to Debug. That explains where the current build configuration comes from: at the moment, whenever you build and run (Product → Run, or click the Run button in the toolbar), you're using the Debug build configuration and the build setting values that correspond to it, because you're using this scheme, and that's what this scheme says to do when you build and run.

You can edit an existing scheme, and this can be useful especially as a temporary measure for doing certain kinds of specialized debugging. For example, the Run action's Diagnostics tab contains checkboxes that let you switch on the Address Sanitizer or the Thread Sanitizer, each of which can be useful for tracking down certain types of obscure runtime error. You'd check the checkbox, build and run, work on the error, and then uncheck the checkbox again.

Handy access to schemes and their management is through the Scheme pop-up menu in the project window toolbar (Figure 6-13).

The Scheme pop-up menu is something you're going to be using a lot. Your schemes are all listed here, and thus you can easily switch between them before you build and run. Hierarchically appended to each scheme are the destinations. A *destination* is effectively a machine that can run your app. On any given occasion, you might want to run the app on a physical device or in the Simulator — and, if in the Simulator, you might want to specify that a particular type of device should be simulated. To make that choice, pick a destination in the Scheme pop-up menu.

Destinations and schemes have nothing to do with one another. The presence of destinations in the Scheme pop-up menu is intended as a convenience, allowing you to use this one pop-up menu to choose either a scheme or a destination, or both, in a

Figure 6-13. The Scheme pop-up menu

single move. To switch easily among destinations without changing schemes, click the destination name in the Scheme pop-up menu. To switch among schemes, possibly also determining the destination (as shown in Figure 6-13), click the scheme name in the Scheme pop-up menu.

Each simulated device has a system version that is installed on that device. At the moment, all our simulated devices are running iOS 10.0; thus, there is no distinction to be drawn, and the system version is not shown. However, you can download additional SDKs (systems) in Xcode's Components preference pane. If you do, and if your app can run under more than one system version, you might also see a system version listed in the Scheme pop-up menu as part of a Simulator destination name. For example, if you've installed the iOS 9.3 SDK, and if your project's deployment target (see Chapter 9) is 9.0, the Scheme pop-up menu in the project window toolbar might say "iOS 10.0" or "iOS 9.3" after the destination name.

To manage destinations, choose Window → Device to summon the Devices window. This is where you manage what simulated devices exist. Here you can create, delete, and rename simulated devices, and specify whether a simulated device actually appears as a destination in the Scheme pop-up menu.

From Project to Running App

An app file is really a special kind of folder called a *package* (and a special kind of package called a *bundle*). The Finder normally disguises a package as a file and does

Figure 6-14. The built app, in the Finder

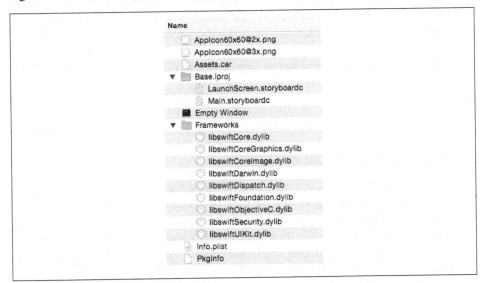

Figure 6-15. Contents of the app package

not dive into it to reveal its contents to the user, but you can bypass this protection and investigate an app bundle with the Show Package Contents command. By doing so, you can study the internal structure of your built app bundle.

We'll use the Empty Window app that we built earlier as a sample minimal app to investigate. You'll have to locate it in the Finder; by default, it should be somewhere in your user *Library/Developer/Xcode/DerivedData* folder, as shown in Figure 6-14.

In the Finder, Control-click the Empty Window app, and choose Show Package Contents from the contextual menu. Here you can see the results of the build process (Figure 6-15).

Think of the app bundle as a transformation of the project folder:

Empty Window

Our app's compiled code. The build process has compiled *ViewController.swift* and *AppDelegate.swift* into this single file, our app's binary. This is the heart of the app, its actual executable material. When the app is launched, the binary is linked to the various frameworks, and the code begins to run. (Later in this chapter, I'll explain in detail what "begins to run" involves.)

Main.storyboardc

Our app's interface storyboard file. The project's *Main.storyboard* is where our app's interface comes from — in this case, an empty white view occupying the entire window. The build process has compiled *Main.storyboard* (using the ibtool command-line tool) into a tighter format, resulting in a *.storyboardc* file, which is actually a bundle of nib files to be loaded as required while the app runs. One of these nib files, loaded as our app launches, will be the source of the white view displayed in the interface. *Main.storyboardc* occupies the same subfolder location (inside *Base.lproj*) as *Main.storyboard* does in the project folder; as I said earlier, this folder structure has to do with localization (to be discussed in Chapter 9).

LaunchScreen.storyboardc

Our app's launch screen file. This file, the compiled version of *LaunchScreen.storyboard*, contains the interface that will be displayed briefly during the time it takes for our app to launch.

Assets.car, AppIcon60x60@2x.png, AppIcon60x60@3x.png

An asset catalog and a pair of icon files. In preparation for this build, I added some icon images and some other image resources to the original asset catalog, *Assets.xcassets*. This file has been processed (using the actool command-line tool), resulting in a compiled asset catalog file (*.car*) containing any resources that have been added to the catalog. At the same time, the icon files have been written out to the top level of the app bundle, where the system can find them.

Info.plist

A configuration file in a strict text format (a *property list* file). It is derived from, but is not identical to, the project's *Info.plist*. It contains instructions to the system about how to treat and launch the app. For example, the project's *Info.plist* has a calculated bundle name derived from the product name, $(PRODUCT_NAME); in the built app's *Info.plist*, this calculation has been performed, and the value reads Empty Window. Also, in conjunction with the asset catalog writing out our icon files to the app bundle's top level, a setting has been added to the built app's *Info.plist* telling the system the name of those icon files.

Frameworks

A number of frameworks have been added to the built app. Our app uses Swift; these frameworks contain the entirety of the Swift language! Other frameworks used by our app are built into the system, but not Swift. This packaging of the Swift frameworks into the app bundle permits Apple to evolve the Swift language rapidly and independently of any system version, and allows Swift to be backward compatible to older systems. The downside is that these frameworks increase the size of our app; but this is a small price to pay for the power and flexibility of Swift. (Perhaps in the future, when the Swift language has settled down, it will be built into the system instead of the individual app, and Swift-based apps will become smaller.)

PkgInfo

A tiny text file reading APPL????, signifying the type and creator codes for this app. The *PkgInfo* file is something of a dinosaur; it isn't really necessary for the functioning of an iOS app and is generated automatically. You'll never need to touch it.

In real life, an app bundle may contain more files, but the difference will be mostly one of degree, not kind. For example, our project might have additional *.storyboard* or *.xib* files, additional frameworks, or additional resources such as sound files. All of these would make their way into the app bundle. In addition, an app bundle built to run on a device will contain some security-related files.

You are now in a position to appreciate, in a general sense, how the components of a project are treated and assembled into an app, and what responsibilities accrue to you, the programmer, in order to ensure that the app is built correctly. The rest of this section outlines what goes into the building of an app from a project, as well as how the constituents of that app are used at launch time to get the app up and running.

Build Settings

We have already talked about how build settings are determined. Xcode itself, the project, and the target all contribute to the resolved build setting values, some of which may differ depending on the build configuration. Before building, you, the programmer, will have specified a scheme; the scheme determines the build configuration, meaning the specific set of build setting values that will apply as this build proceeds.

Property List Settings

Your project contains a property list file that will be used to generate the built app's *Info.plist* file. The file in the project does not have to be named *Info.plist*! The app target knows what file it is because it is specified in the Info.plist File build setting. For example, in our project, the value of the app target's Info.plist File build setting has been set to *Empty Window/Info.plist*. (Take a look at the build settings and see!)

The property list file is a collection of key–value pairs. You can edit it, and you may need to do so. There are three main ways to edit your project's *Info.plist*:

- Select the *Info.plist* file in the Project navigator and edit in the editor. By default, the key names (and some of the values) are displayed descriptively, in terms of their functionality; for example, it says "Bundle name" instead of the actual key, which is CFBundleName. But you can view the actual keys: click in the editor and then choose Editor → Show Raw Keys & Values, or use the contextual menu.

  In addition, you can see and edit the *Info.plist* file in its true XML form: Control-click the *Info.plist* file in the Project navigator and choose Open As → Source Code from the contextual menu. (But editing an *Info.plist* as raw XML is risky, because if you make a mistake you can invalidate the XML, causing things to break with no warning.)

- Edit the target, and switch to the Info pane. The Custom iOS Target Properties section shows effectively the same information as editing the *Info.plist* in the editor.

- Edit the target, and switch to the General pane. Some of the settings here are effectively ways of editing the *Info.plist*. For example, when you click a Device Orientation checkbox here, you are changing the value of the "Supported interface orientations" key in the *Info.plist*. (Other settings here are effectively ways of editing build settings. For example, when you change the Deployment Target here (in the Deployment Info section), you are changing the value of the iOS Deployment Target build setting.)

Some values in the project's *Info.plist* are processed to transform them into their final values in the built app's *Info.plist*. This step is performed late in the build process. For example, the "Executable file" key's value in the project's *Info.plist* is $(EXECUTABLE_NAME); for this will be substituted the value of the EXECUTABLE_NAME build environment variable (which, as I mentioned earlier, you can discover by means of a Run Script build phase). Also, some additional key–value pairs are injected into the *Info.plist* during processing.

For a complete list of the possible keys and their meanings, consult Apple's document *Information Property List Key Reference*. I'll talk more in Chapter 9 about some *Info.plist* settings that you're particularly likely to edit.

Nib Files

A nib file is a description of a piece of user interface in a compiled format contained in a file with the extension *.nib*. Every app that you write is likely to contain at least one nib file. You prepare these nib files by editing a *.storyboard* or *.xib* file graphically in Xcode; in effect, you are designing some objects that you want instantiated when the app runs and the nib file loads.

A nib file is generated during the build process by compilation (using the `ibtool` command-line tool) either from a *.xib* file, which results in a single nib file, or from a *.storyboard* file, which results in a *.storyboardc* bundle containing multiple nib files. This compilation takes place by virtue of the *.storyboard* or *.xib* file being listed in the app target's Copy Bundle Resources build phase.

Our Empty Window project generated from the Single View app template contains an interface *.storyboard* file called *Main.storyboard*. This one file is subject to special treatment as the app's main storyboard, not because of its name, but because it is pointed to in the *Info.plist* file by the key "Main storyboard file base name" (`UIMain-StoryboardFile`), using its name ("Main") without the *.storyboard* extension — edit the *Info.plist* file and see! The result is that as the app launches, the first nib generated from this *.storyboard* file is loaded automatically to help create the app's initial interface.

I'll talk more about the app launch process and the main storyboard later in this chapter. See Chapter 7 for more about editing *.storyboard* and *.xib* files and how they create instances when your code runs.

Additional Resources

Resources are ancillary files embedded in your app bundle, to be fetched as needed when the app runs, such as images you want to display or sounds you want to play. A real-life app is likely to involve many such additional resources. Making such resources available when your app runs will usually be up to your code (or to the code implied by the loading of a nib file): basically, the runtime simply reaches into your app bundle and pulls out the desired resource. In effect, your app bundle is being treated as a folder full of extra stuff.

There are two places to add resources to your project, corresponding to two different places where they will end up in your app bundle:

The Project navigator
> If you add a resource to the Project navigator, also ensuring that it appears in the Copy Bundle Resources build phase, it is copied by the build process to the top level of your app bundle. (In Figure 6-15, that's the same level as the icon image files, such as *AppIcon60x60@2x.png*.)

An asset catalog
> If you add a resource to an asset catalog, then when the asset catalog is copied and compiled by the build process to the top level of your app bundle (like *Assets.car* in Figure 6-15), the resource will be inside it.

Figure 6-16. Options when adding a resource to a project

I'll describe both ways of adding resources to your project.

Resources in the Project navigator

To add a resource to your project through the Project navigator, choose File → Add Files to [Project], or drag the resource from the Finder into the Project navigator. A dialog appears in which you make the following settings (Figure 6-16; you might have to click Options to see them):

Destination

You should almost certainly check this checkbox ("Copy items if needed"). Doing so causes the resource to be copied into the project folder. If you leave this checkbox unchecked, your project will be relying on a file that's outside the project folder, where you might delete or change it unintentionally. Keeping everything your project needs inside the project folder is far safer.

Added folders

This choice matters only if what you're adding to the project is a folder; the difference is in how the project references the folder contents:

Create groups

The folder name becomes the name of an ordinary group within the Project navigator; the folder contents appear in this group, but they are listed individually in the Copy Bundle Resources build phase, so by default they will all be copied individually into the top level of the app bundle.

Create folder references

The folder is shown in blue in the Project navigator (a *folder reference*); moreover, it is listed as a folder in the Copy Bundle Resources build phase, meaning that the build process will copy *the entire folder and its contents* into the app bundle. This means that the resources inside the folder won't be at the top level of the app bundle, but in a subfolder within it. Such an arrangement can be valuable if you have many resources and you want to separate them into categories (rather than clumping them all at the top level of the app bundle) or if the folder hierarchy among resources is meaningful to your app. The downside of this arrangement is that the code you write for accessing a resource will have to be specific about what subfolder of the app bundle contains that resource.

Add to targets

Checking the checkbox for a target causes the resource to be added to that target's Copy Bundle Resources build phase. Thus you will almost certainly want to check it for the app target; why else would you be adding this resource to the project? If this checkbox accidentally goes unchecked and you realize later that a resource listed in the Project navigator needs to be added to the Copy Bundle Resources build phase for a particular target, you can add it manually, as I described earlier.

Resources in an asset catalog

Prior to Xcode 7, asset catalogs were intended only for image files. Other resources, such as sound files, could be added only in the Project navigator. Now, however, asset catalogs can accommodate any kind of data file. Keeping your resources in an asset catalog provides many advantages over keeping them at the top level of the app bundle by way of the project navigator.

For example, in the case of image files, asset catalogs allow you to draw easily a distinction that otherwise would depend upon special conventions involving the *name* of the image file. Because iOS 10 can run on single-resolution, double-resolution, and triple-resolution devices, you need up to three sizes of every image. In order to work properly with the framework's image-loading methods, such related image files must obey a special naming convention — for example, *listen.png*, *listen@2x.png*, and *listen@3x.png*. The resulting proliferation of image files in the Project navigator can be overwhelming and error-prone.

Asset catalogs alleviate the problem by providing the special names, behind the scenes, automatically. I edit the asset catalog, click the Plus button at the bottom of the first column, and choose New Image Set. The result is an image set called *Image* with slots for three images at three different sizes. I drag the images from the Finder into their proper slots. The names of the original image files don't matter! The images are automatically copied into the project folder (inside the asset catalog folder), and there is no need for me to specify the target membership of these image files, because they are part of an asset catalog which already has correct target membership. I can rename the image set to something more descriptive than *Image* — let's call it *listen*. The result is that my code can now load the correct image for the current screen resolution by referring to it as "listen", without regard to the original name (or extension) of the images.

 The image entries in an asset catalog can be inspected by selecting an image and using the Attributes inspector (Command-Option-4). This shows the original name and (more important) the pixel size of the image.

A parallel procedure applies to resources of other kinds. Let's say I want to add to my app bundle a sound file called *theme.mp3*. I edit the asset catalog, click the Plus button, and choose New Data Set. A data set called Data appears, with a single Universal slot into which I can now drag my sound file. I rename the data set — let's call it *theme* — and now my code can access this resource by the name "theme" (by means of the NSDataAsset class).

Asset catalogs also allow you to specify different versions of a resource to be supplied for different hardware configurations — the device's screen resolution, for example (in the case of an image), or iPhone vs. iPad (for any type of resource).

Moreover, folders in the asset catalog can be used to provide namespaces: for example, if my *theme* data set is inside an asset catalog folder called *music*, and if I've checked Provides Namespace in the Attributes inspector for that folder, then the data set can be accessed by the name "music/theme". Thus, the sheer organizational convenience of asset catalogs is, all by itself, an incentive to use them, rather than cluttering the Project navigator and the app bundle's top level with resource files.

 Resources in your app can be stored on Apple's servers instead of being included in the app bundle that the user downloads initially from the App Store. Your code subsequently downloads, in the background, any stored resources that the user is likely to need, and can purge them when they are no longer needed. For more information, see Apple's *On-Demand Resources Guide*.

Code Files and the App Launch Process

The build process knows what code files to compile to form the app's binary because they are listed in the app target's Compile Sources build phase. In the case of our Empty Window project, these are *ViewController.swift* and *AppDelegate.swift*. As development of your app proceeds, you will probably add further code files to the project, and you will ensure that they are part of the target and thus that they, too, are listed in its Compile Sources build phase. What typically happens is that you want to add a new object type declaration to your code; you will often do so by adding a new file to the project, because this makes your object type declaration easier to find, and because Swift privacy depends upon code being isolated in individual files (Chapter 5).

When you choose File → New → File to create a new file, you can specify either the Cocoa Touch Class template or the Swift File template. The Swift File template is little more than a blank file: it imports the Foundation framework and that's all. If your goal is to subclass a Cocoa class, the Cocoa Touch Class template will usually be more suitable; it imports the UIKit framework, plus Xcode will write the initial class declaration for you, and in the case of some commonly subclassed superclasses, such as UIViewController and UITableViewController, it even provides stub declarations of some of that class's methods.

When the app launches, the system knows where to find the binary inside the app's bundle because the app bundle's *Info.plist* file has an "Executable file" key (CFBundle-Executable) whose value is the name of the binary; by default, the binary's name comes from the EXECUTABLE_NAME environment variable (such as "Empty Window").

The entry point

The trickiest part of the app launch process is getting started. Having located and loaded the binary, the system must call into it. But where? If this app were an Objective-C program, the answer would be clear. Objective-C is C, so the entry point is the main function. Our project would typically have a *main.m* file containing the main function, like this:

```
int main(int argc, char *argv[]) {
    @autoreleasepool {
        return UIApplicationMain(argc, argv, nil,
            NSStringFromClass([AppDelegate class]));
    }
}
```

The main function does just two things:

- It sets up a memory management environment — the @autoreleasepool and the curly braces that follow it.

- It calls the UIApplicationMain function, which does the heavy lifting of helping your app pull itself up by its bootstraps and get running.

Our app, however, is a Swift program. It has no main function! Instead, Swift has a special attribute: @UIApplicationMain. If you look in the *AppDelegate.swift* file, you can see it, attached to the declaration of the AppDelegate class:

```
@UIApplicationMain
class AppDelegate: UIResponder, UIApplicationDelegate {
```

This attribute essentially does everything that the Objective-C *main.m* file was doing: it creates an entry point that calls UIApplicationMain to get the app started.

Under certain circumstances, you might like to remove the @UIApplicationMain attribute and substitute a *main* file. You are free to do this. Your file can be an Objective-C file or a Swift file. Let's say it's to be a Swift file. You would create a *main.swift* file and make sure it is added to the app target. The name is crucial, because a file called *main.swift* gets a special dispensation: it is allowed to put executable code at the top level of the file (Chapter 1). The file should contain essentially the Swift equivalent of the Objective-C call to UIApplicationMain, like this:

```
import UIKit
UIApplicationMain(
    CommandLine.argc,
    UnsafeMutableRawPointer(CommandLine.unsafeArgv)
        .bindMemory(
            to: UnsafeMutablePointer<Int8>.self,
            capacity: Int(CommandLine.argc)),
    nil,
    NSStringFromClass(AppDelegate.self)
)
```

Why might you do that sort of thing? Presumably, it would be because you want to do other things in the *main.swift* file, or because you want to customize the call to `UIApplicationMain`.

UIApplicationMain

Regardless of whether you write your own *main.swift* file or you rely on the Swift `@UIApplicationMain` attribute, you are calling `UIApplicationMain`. This one function call is the primary thing your app does. Your entire app is really nothing but a single gigantic call to `UIApplicationMain`! Moreover, `UIApplicationMain` is responsible for solving some tricky problems as your app gets going. Where will your app get its initial instances? What instance methods will initially be called on those instances? Where will your app's initial interface come from? Let's pause to understand what `UIApplicationMain` does:

1. `UIApplicationMain` creates your app's *first instance* — the shared application instance, which subsequently is to be accessible in code as `UIApplication.shared`. The third argument in the call to `UIApplicationMain` specifies, as a string, what class the shared application instance should be an instance of. If this argument is `nil`, as will usually be the case, the default class is UIApplication. If, however, you needed to subclass UIApplication, you would specify that subclass here, by substituting an explicit value, such as `NSStringFromClass(MyAppSubclass.self)` (depending on what the subclass is called) as the third argument in the call to `UIApplicationMain`.

2. `UIApplicationMain` also creates your app's *second instance* — the application instance's *delegate*. Delegation is an important and pervasive Cocoa pattern, described in detail in Chapter 11. It is crucial that every app you write have an app delegate instance. The fourth argument in the call to `UIApplicationMain` specifies, as a string, what class the app delegate instance should be. In our manual version of *main.swift*, that specification is `NSStringFromClass(AppDelegate.self)`. If we use the `@UIApplicationMain` attribute, that attribute is attached, by default, to the AppDelegate class declaration in *AppDelegate.swift*; the attribute means: "*This* is the application delegate class!"

3. If the *Info.plist* file specifies a main storyboard file, `UIApplicationMain` loads it and looks inside it to find the view controller that is designated as this story-board's *initial view controller* (or *storyboard entry point*); it instantiates this view controller, thus creating your app's *third instance*. In the case of our Empty Window project, as constructed for us from the Single View app template, that view controller will be an instance of the class called ViewController; the code file defining this class, *ViewController.swift*, was also created by the template.

4. If there was a main storyboard file, `UIApplicationMain` now creates your app's *window* — this is your app's *fourth instance*, an instance of UIWindow (or your app delegate can substitute an instance of a UIWindow subclass). It assigns this window instance as the app delegate's `window` property; it also assigns the initial view controller instance as the window instance's `rootViewController` property. This view is now the app's *root view controller*.

5. `UIApplicationMain` now turns to the app delegate instance and starts calling some of its code, such as `application(_:didFinishLaunchingWithOptions:)`. This is an opportunity for your own code to run! `application(_:didFinish-LaunchingWithOptions:)` is a good place to put your code that initializes values and performs startup tasks; but you don't want anything time-consuming to happen here, because your app's interface still hasn't appeared.

6. If there was a main storyboard, `UIApplicationMain` now causes your app's inter-face to appear. It does this by calling the UIWindow instance method `makeKeyAnd-Visible`.

7. The window is now about to appear. This, in turn, causes the window to turn to the root view controller and tell it to obtain its main view, which will occupy and appear in the window. If this view controller gets its view from a *.storyboard* or *.xib* file, that view nib file is now loaded; its objects are instantiated and initial-ized, and they become the objects of the initial interface: the view is placed into the window, where it and its subviews are visible to the user. Your view control-ler's `viewDidLoad` is also called at this time — another early opportunity for your code to run.

The app is now launched and running! It has an initial set of instances — at a mini-mum, the shared application instance, the window, the initial view controller, and the initial view controller's view and whatever interface objects it contains. Some of your code has run, and we are now off to the races: `UIApplicationMain` is still running (like Charlie on the M.T.A., `UIApplicationMain` never returns), and is just sitting there, watching for the user to do something, maintaining the *event loop*, which will respond to user actions as they occur.

App without a storyboard

In my description of the app launch process, I used several times the phrase "if there is a main storyboard." In the Xcode app templates, such as the Single View app template that we used to generate the Empty Window project, there *is* a main storyboard. It is possible, however, *not* to have a main storyboard. This way of structuring an app project is unusual nowadays, but it is quite viable, and was even fairly common years ago, before storyboards existed.

Without a storyboard, things like creating a window instance, giving it a root view controller, assigning it to the app delegate's window property, and calling makeKeyAnd-Visible on the window to show the interface, must be done by your code. To see what I mean, make a new iPhone project starting with the Single View app template; let's call it Truly Empty. Now follow these steps:

1. Edit the target. In the General pane, select "Main" in the Main Interface field and delete it (and press Tab to set this change).

2. In the Project navigator, delete *Main.storyboard* from the project.

3. Edit *AppDelegate.swift*; select and delete its entire code content.

4. To make a minimal working app, edit *AppDelegate.swift* in such a way as to recreate the AppDelegate class with just enough code to create and show the window, as shown in Example 6-1.

Example 6-1. An App Delegate class with no storyboard

```
import UIKit
@UIApplicationMain
class AppDelegate : UIResponder, UIApplicationDelegate {
    var window : UIWindow?
    func application(_ application: UIApplication,
        didFinishLaunchingWithOptions
        launchOptions: [UIApplicationLaunchOptionsKey : Any]?)
        -> Bool {
            self.window = self.window ?? UIWindow()
            self.window!.backgroundColor = .white
            self.window!.rootViewController = ViewController()
            self.window!.makeKeyAndVisible()
            return true
    }
}
```

The result is a minimal working app with an empty white window. You can prove to yourself that the app is working normally by editing *ViewController.swift* so that its viewDidLoad method changes the main view's background color:

```
override func viewDidLoad() {
    super.viewDidLoad()
    self.view.backgroundColor = .red
}
```

Run the app again; sure enough, the background is now red.

 You can omit steps 1 and 2, and Example 6-1 will still work. What you then have is an app that *has* a main storyboard, but *ignores* it at launch time: it creates its root view controller in code, overriding the automatic behavior of UIApplicationMain. This approach can be useful when you want the choice of root view controller to depend on the circumstances; a common case in point is an initial sign-in screen that shouldn't appear again once the user *has* signed in.

Frameworks and SDKs

A *framework* is a library of compiled code used by your code. Most of the frameworks you are likely to use when programming iOS will be Apple's built-in frameworks. These frameworks are already part of the system on the device where your app will run; they live in */System/Library/Frameworks* on the device, though you can't tell that on an iPhone or iPad because there's no way (normally) to inspect the file hierarchy directly.

Your compiled code also needs to be connected to those frameworks when the project is being built and run on your computer. To make this possible, the iOS device's *System/Library/Frameworks* is duplicated on your computer, inside Xcode itself. This duplicated subset of the device's system is called an *SDK* (for "software development kit"). Which SDK is used depends upon what destination you're building for.

Linking is the process of hooking up your compiled code with the frameworks that it needs, even though those frameworks are in one place at build time and in another place at runtime. Thus, for example:

When you build your code to run on a device
> A copy of any needed frameworks is used. This copy lives in *System/Library/ Frameworks* inside the iPhone SDK, which is located at *Xcode.app/Contents/ Developer/Platforms/iPhoneOS.platform/Developer/SDKs/iPhoneOS.sdk*.

When your code runs on a device
> The code, as it starts running, looks in the device's top-level */System/Library/ Frameworks* folder for the frameworks that it needs.

Used in this way, the frameworks are part of an ingenious mechanism whereby Apple's code is effectively incorporated dynamically into your app when the app runs. The frameworks are the locus of all the stuff that every app might need to do; they are Cocoa. That's a lot of stuff, and a lot of compiled code. Your app gets to share in the goodness and power of the frameworks because it is linked to them. Your code works as if the framework code were incorporated into it. Yet your app is relatively tiny; it's the frameworks that are huge.

Linking takes care of connecting your compiled code to any needed frameworks, but it isn't sufficient to allow your code to compile in the first place. The frameworks are full of classes (such as NSString) and methods (such as range(of:)) that your code will call. To satisfy the compiler, the frameworks publish their API in header files, which your code can import. Thus, for example, your code can speak of NSString and can call range(of:) because it imports the *NSString* header. Actually, what your code imports is the *UIKit* header, which in turn imports the *Foundation* header, which in turn imports the *NSString* header. And you can see this happening at the top of any of your own code's header files:

```
import UIKit
```

If you Command-click UIKit, you are taken to Swift's rendering of the *UIKit* header. There at the top is import Foundation. If you look at the *Foundation* header and scroll down, you'll see import Foundation.NSString. And if you look in the *NSString* header, you'll see the declaration of the range(of:) method.

Thus, using a framework is a two-part process:

Import the framework's header
> Your code needs this information in order to *compile* successfully. Your code imports a framework's header by using the import keyword, specifying either that framework or a framework that itself imports the desired framework. In Swift, you specify a framework by using its module name.

Link to the framework
> The compiled executable binary needs to be connected to the frameworks it will use while running, effectively incorporating the compiled code from those frameworks. As your code is built, it is linked to any needed frameworks, in accordance with the list of frameworks in the target's Link Binary With Libraries build phase.

Our project, however, does not do any explicit linking. If you look in the app target's Link Binary With Libraries build phase, it is empty. This is because Swift uses *modules*, and modules can perform *autolinking*. In Objective-C, modules and autolinking are optional features, and are governed by build settings. But in Swift, use of modules and autolinking is automatic.

Modules are cached information stored on your computer at *Library/Developer/ Xcode/DerivedData/ModuleCache*. Merely opening a Swift project causes any imported modules to be cached here. If you drill down into the *ModuleCache* folder, you'll see the modules for over a dozen frameworks and headers (*.pcm* files). Swift's use of modules simplifies the importing and linking process, and improves compilation times.

Modules are ingenious and convenient, but it is sometimes necessary to link to a framework manually. For example, let's say you want to use an MKMapView (Map Kit View) in your interface. You can configure this in a *.storyboard* or *.xib* file, but when you build and run your app, it crashes, complaining: "Could not instantiate class named MKMapView." The reason is that the nib, as it loads, finds that it contains an MKMapView but doesn't know what an MKMapView *is*. MKMapView is defined in the MapKit framework, but the nib doesn't know that.

Adding import MapKit at the top of your code doesn't solve the problem; you need to do that if your *code* wants to talk to the MKMapView, but it doesn't help the *nib* understand what an MKMapView is when it loads. The solution is to link to the MapKit framework manually:

1. Edit the target and look at the Build Phases pane.

2. Under Link Binary With Libraries, click the Plus button.

3. A list of available frameworks appears (along with dynamic libraries). Scroll down to *MapKit.framework*, select it, and click Add.

This solves the problem; your app now builds and runs.

You can also create your own framework as part of your project. A framework is a module, so this can be a useful way to structure your code, as I described in Chapter 5 when discussing Swift privacy. To make a new framework:

1. Edit the target and choose Editor → Add Target.

2. Select iOS; under Framework & Library, select Cocoa Touch Framework. Click Next.

3. Give your framework a name; let's call it Coolness. You can pick a language, but I'm not sure this makes any difference, as no code files will be created. The Project and Embed in Application pop-up menus should be correctly set by default. Click Finish.

A new Coolness framework target is created in your project. If you now add a *.swift* file to the Coolness target, and inside it define an object type *and declare it public*, then, back in one of your main app target's files, such as *AppDelegate.swift*, your code can import Coolness and will then be able to see that object type and its public members.

Renaming Parts of a Project

The name assigned to your project at creation time is used in many places throughout the project, leading beginners to worry that they can never rename a project without breaking something. But fear not!

First of all, you don't usually *need* to rename the project. Typically, what you want to change is the name of the *app* — the name that the user sees on the device, associated with this app's icon. The project name is *not* that name! Indeed, the project name is not a name that users will *ever* see. If all you want to do is change the name that appears visibly associated with the app on the device, change (or create) the "Bundle Display Name" in the *Info.plist*. In Xcode 8, you can do this easily by editing the Display Name text field in the General pane when you edit the target.

Still, you *can* rename a project, and it's easy to do: select the project listing at the top of the Project navigator, press Return to make its name editable, type the new name, and press Return again. Xcode presents a dialog proposing to change some other names to match, including the app target and the built app — and, by implication, various relevant build settings. You should feel free to accept.

Changing the project name (or target name) does not automatically change the scheme name to match. There is no particular need to do so, but you can change a scheme name freely; choose Product → Manage Schemes and click on the scheme name to make it editable.

Changing the project name (or target name) does not automatically change the main group name to match. There is no particular need to do so, but you can freely change the name of a group in the Project navigator, because these names are arbitrary; they have no effect on the build settings or the build process. However, the main group is special, because (as I've already said) it corresponds to a real folder on disk, the folder that sits beside your project file at the top level of the project folder. It's fine to change the group name, but beginners should not change the name of that folder *on disk*, as it is hard-coded into several build settings.

You can change the name of the project folder in the Finder at any time, and you can move the project folder in the Finder at will, because all build setting references to file and folder items in the project folder are relative.

CHAPTER 7

Nib Management

In Chapter 4, I talked about ways of obtaining an instance. You can directly instantiate an object type:

```
let v = UIView()
```

Or you can obtain a reference to an already existing instance:

```
let v = self.view.subviews[0]
```

But there is a third way: you can *load a nib*. A *nib* is a file, in a special format, filled with instructions for creating and configuring instances. To load a nib means, in effect, to tell that nib to follow those instructions: it *does* create and configure those instances.

My example of a UIView instance is apt, because a UIView is just the kind of instance a nib is likely to create. Nibs are edited in Xcode using a graphical interface, much like a drawing program. The idea is that you are designing some interface objects — mostly instances of UIView and UIView subclasses — that you want to use in your app when it runs. When your app does run, and when the moment comes where you actually need those interface objects (typically because you're about to display them in your visible interface), you load the nib, the nib-loading process creates and configures the instances, and you receive the instances and insert them into your app's actual interface.

You do not *have* to use nibs to create your interface objects. The loading of a nib does nothing that you could not have done directly, in code. You can instantiate a UIView or UIView subclass, you can configure it, you can construct a hierarchy of views, you can place that view hierarchy into your interface — manually, step by step, entirely in code. A nib is just a device for making that process simpler and more convenient. You design the nib beforehand, graphically; when the app runs, your code doesn't have to instantiate or configure any views. It has merely to load the nib and retrieve the

Are Nibs Necessary?

Since nibs are ultimately just sources of instances, you might wonder whether it is possible to do without them. Those same instances could be generated in code, so wouldn't it be possible to dispense with nibs altogether? The simple answer is: Yes, it would. It's quite possible to write a complex app that lacks a single *.storyboard* or *.xib* file (I've done it). The practical question, however, is one of balance. Most apps use nib files as a source of at least some interface objects; but there are some aspects of interface objects that can be customized only in code, and sometimes it's easier to generate those interface objects entirely in code at the outset. In real life your projects will probably involve some code-generated interface objects and some nib-generated interface objects (which may themselves be further modified or configured in code).

resulting instances and put them into your interface. And in fact, because you'll mostly be using view controllers (UIViewController), which are themselves designed with nibs in mind, you won't even have to do that! The view controller will load the nib and retrieve the resulting instances and put them into your interface for you, *automatically*.

Nibs are a simple and ingenious device for making the process of designing and con-figuring your app's interface simpler and more convenient than it would be if you had to do the same thing in code. But they are also probably the least understood aspect of iOS programming. Many beginners go on using nibs without knowing what they really are or how they really work. This is a huge mistake. It is crucial that you know what nibs are, how they work, and how to manipulate them in your code. Failure to understand nibs opens you up to all kinds of elementary, confusing mistakes that can be avoided or corrected merely by grasping a few basic facts. Nibs are *not magic*, nor are they hard to understand; so why not understand them? That's what this chapter is about.

 The name *nib*, or *nib file*, has nothing to do with fountain pens or bits of choco-late. The graphical nib-design aspect of Xcode, which I call the *nib editor*, used to be (up through Xcode 3.2.x) a separate application called Interface Builder. (The nib editor environment within Xcode is still often referred to as Interface Builder.) The files created by Interface Builder were given the *.nib* file extension, which was an acronym for "NeXTStep Interface Builder." Nowadays, the file you edit directly in the nib editor will be either a *.storyboard* file or a *.xib* file; when the app is built, they are compiled into nib files (see Chapter 6).

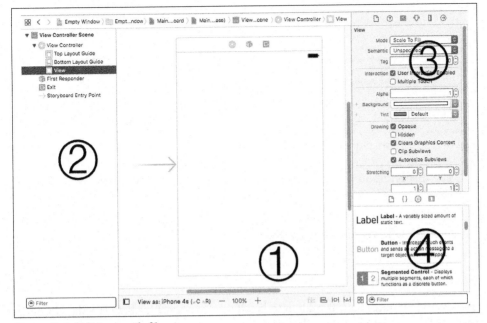

Figure 7-1. Editing a nib file

The Nib Editor Interface

Let's explore Xcode's nib editor interface. In Chapter 6, we created a simple iPhone project, Empty Window, directly from the Single View app template; it contains a storyboard file, so we'll use that. In Xcode, open the Empty Window project, locate *Main.storyboard* in the Project navigator, and click to edit it.

Figure 7-1 shows the project window after selecting *Main.storyboard*. (I've made some additional adjustments to make the screenshot fit on the page.) The interface may be considered in four pieces:

1. The bulk of the editor is devoted to the *canvas*, where you physically design your app's interface. The canvas portrays views in your app's interface and things that can contain views. A *view* is an interface object, which draws itself into a rectangular area. The phrase "things that can contain views" is my way of including view controllers, which are represented in the canvas even though they are not drawn in your app's interface; a view controller isn't a view, but it *has* a view (and controls it).

2. At the left of the editor is the *document outline*, listing the storyboard's contents hierarchically by name. It can be hidden by dragging its right edge or by clicking the button at the bottom left corner of the canvas.

Figure 7-2. A view controller selected in a storyboard

3. The inspectors in the Utilities pane let you edit details of the currently selected object.

4. The libraries in the Utilities pane, especially the Object library, are your source of interface objects to be added to the nib.

Document Outline

The document outline portrays hierarchically the relationships between the objects in the nib. This structure differs slightly depending on whether you're editing a *.storyboard* file or a *.xib* file.

In a storyboard file, the primary constituents are *scenes*. A scene is, roughly speaking, a single view controller, along with some ancillary material; every scene has a single view controller at its top level.

A view controller isn't an interface object, but it manages an interface object, namely its view (or *main view*). A view controller in a nib doesn't have to have its main view in the same nib, but it usually does, and in that case, in the nib editor, the view usually appears inside the view controller in the canvas. Thus, in Figure 7-1, the large rectangle in the canvas is a view controller's main view, and is actually inside a view controller.

The view controller itself can be readily seen and selected in the document outline. It is also represented as an icon in the *scene dock*, which appears above the view controller in the canvas when anything in this scene is selected (Figure 7-2). Each view controller in a storyboard file constitutes one scene. In the document outline, this scene is portrayed as a hierarchical collection of names. At the top level of the document outline are the scenes themselves. At the top level of each scene are (more or less) the same objects that appear in the view controller's scene dock: the view controller itself, along with two *proxy objects*, the First Responder token and the Exit token. These objects — the ones displayed as icons in the scene dock, and shown at the top level of the scene in the document outline — are the scene's *top-level objects*.

Objects listed in the document outline are of two kinds:

Nib objects

The view controller, along with its main view and any subviews that we care to place in that view, are real objects — potential objects that will be turned into actual instances when the nib is loaded by the running app. Such real objects to be instantiated from the nib are also called *nib objects*.

Proxy objects

The proxy objects (here, the First Responder and Exit tokens) do *not* represent instances that will come from the nib when it is loaded. Rather, they represent other objects, and are present to facilitate communication between nib objects and other objects (I'll give examples later in this chapter). You can't create or delete a proxy object; the nib editor shows them automatically.

(Also present in the document outline in Figure 7-2 is the Storyboard Entry Point. This isn't an object of any kind; it's just an indication that this view controller is the storyboard's initial view controller — in its Attributes inspector, Is Initial View Controller is checked — and corresponds to the right-pointing arrow seen at the left of this view controller in the canvas in Figure 7-1.)

Most nib objects listed in a storyboard's document outline will depend hierarchically upon a scene's view controller. For example, in Figure 7-2, the view controller has a main view; that view is listed as hierarchically dependent on the view controller. That makes sense, because this view belongs to this view controller. Moreover, any further interface objects that we drag into the main view in the canvas will be listed in the document outline as hierarchically dependent on the view. That makes sense, too. A view can contain other views (its *subviews*) and can be contained by another view (its *superview*). One view can contain many subviews, which might themselves contain subviews. But each view can have only one immediate superview. Thus there is a hierarchical tree of subviews contained by their superviews with a single object at the top. The document outline portrays that tree as an outline — hence the name.

In a *.xib* file, there are no scenes. What would be, in a *.storyboard* file, the top-level objects of a scene become, in a *.xib* file, the top-level objects of the nib itself. Nor is there any requirement that one of these top-level objects be a view controller; it can be, but more often the top-level interface object of a *.xib* file is a view. It might well be a view that is to serve as a view controller's main view, but that's not a requirement either. Figure 7-3 shows a *.xib* with a structure parallel to the single scene of Figure 7-2.

The document outline in Figure 7-3 lists three top-level objects. Two of them are proxy objects, termed Placeholders in the document outline: the File's Owner, and the First Responder. The third is a real object, a view; it will be instantiated when the nib is loaded as the app runs. The document outline in a *.xib* file can't be completely hidden; instead, it is collapsed into a set of icons representing the nib's top-level objects,

Figure 7-3. A .xib file containing a view

Figure 7-4. The dock in a .xib file

similar to a scene dock in a storyboard file, and often referred to simply as the *dock* (Figure 7-4).

At present, the document outline may seem unnecessary, because there is very little hierarchy; all objects in Figures 7-2 and 7-3 are readily accessible in the canvas. But when a storyboard contains many scenes, and when a view contains many levels of hierarchically arranged objects (along with their autolayout constraints), you're going to be very glad of the document outline, which lets you survey the contents of the nib in a nice hierarchical structure, and where you can locate and select the object you're after. You can also rearrange the hierarchy here; for example, if you've made an object a subview of the wrong view, you can reposition it within this outline by dragging its name.

If the names of nib objects in the document outline seem generic and uninformative, you can change them. The name is technically a *label*, and has no special meaning, so feel free to assign nib objects labels that are useful to you. Select a nib object's label in the document outline and press Return to make it editable, or select the object and edit the Label field in the Document section of the Identity inspector.

Figure 7-5. Dragging a button into a view

Canvas

The canvas provides a graphical representation of a view and its subviews, similar to what you're probably accustomed to in any drawing program. The canvas is scrollable and automatically accommodates however many graphical representations it contains; a storyboard canvas can also be zoomed (choose Editor → Canvas → Zoom, or use the contextual menu or the zoom buttons at the bottom of the canvas).

Our simple Empty Window project's *Main.storyboard* contains just one scene, so the only thing it represents in the canvas is the scene's view controller, with its main view inside and generally indistinguishable from it. It happens that this view controller will become our app's window's root view controller when the app runs; therefore its view will occupy the entire window, and will effectively be our app's initial interface (see Chapter 6). That gives us an excellent opportunity to experiment: any visible changes we make within this view should be visible when we subsequently build and run the app. To prove this, let's add a subview:

1. Start with the nib editor looking more or less like Figure 7-1.

2. Look at the Object library (Command-Option-Control-3). If it's in icon view (a grid of icons without text), click the button at the left of the filter bar to put it into list view. Click in the filter bar (or choose Edit → Filter → Filter in Library, Command-Option-L) and type "button" so that only button objects are shown in the list. The Button object is listed first.

3. Drag the Button object from the Object library into the view controller's main view in the canvas (Figure 7-5), and let go of the mouse.

A button is now present in the view in the canvas. The move we've just performed — dragging from the Object library into the canvas — is extremely characteristic; you'll do it often as you design your interface.

Much as in a drawing program, the nib editor provides features to aid you in designing your interface. Here are some things to try:

- Select the button: resizing handles appear. (If you accidentally select it twice and the resizing handles disappear, select the view and then the button again.)
- Using the resizing handles, resize the button to make it wider: dimension information appears.
- Drag the button near an edge of the view: a guideline appears, showing standard spacing. Similarly, drag the button near the center of the view: a guideline shows you when the button is centered.
- With the button selected, hold down the Option key and hover the mouse outside the button: arrows and numbers appear showing the distance between the button and the edges of the view. (If you accidentally clicked and dragged while you were holding Option, you'll now have two buttons. That's because Option-dragging an object duplicates it. Select the unwanted button and press Delete to remove it.)
- Control-Shift-click on the button: a menu appears, letting you select the button or whatever's behind it (in this case, the view, as well as the view controller because the view controller acts as a sort of top-level background to everything we're doing here).
- Double-click the button's title. The title becomes editable. Give it a new title, such as "Howdy!" Press Return to set the new title.

To prove that we really are designing our app's interface, we'll run the app:

1. Drag the button to a position near the *top left* corner of the canvas. (If you don't do this, the button could be off the screen when the app runs.)
2. Examine the Debug → Activate / Deactivate Breakpoints menu item. If it says Deactivate Breakpoints, choose it; we don't want to pause at any breakpoints you may have created while reading the previous chapter.
3. Make sure the destination in the Scheme pop-up menu is iPhone 6.
4. Choose Product → Run (or click the Run button in the toolbar).

After a heart-stopping pause, the iOS Simulator opens, and presto, our empty window is empty no longer (Figure 7-6); it contains a button! You can tap this button with the mouse, emulating what the user would do with a finger; the button highlights as you tap it.

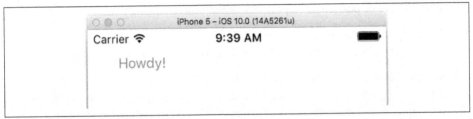

Figure 7-6. The Empty Window app's window is empty no longer

Inspectors and Libraries

Four inspectors appear in conjunction with the nib editor, and apply to whatever object is selected in the document outline, dock, or canvas:

Identity inspector (Command-Option-3)
The first section of this inspector, Custom Class, is the most important. Here you learn, and can change, the selected object's class. Some situations in which you'll need to change the class of an object in the nib appear later in this chapter.

Attributes inspector (Command-Option-4)
Settings here correspond to properties and methods that you might use to configure the object in code. For example, selecting our view and choosing from the Background pop-up menu in the Attributes inspector corresponds to setting the view's backgroundColor property in code. Similarly, selecting our button and typing in the Title field is like calling the button's setTitle(_:for:) method.

The Attributes inspector has sections corresponding to the selected object's class inheritance. For example, the UIButton Attributes inspector has three sections: in addition to a Button section, there's a Control section (because a UIButton is also a UIControl) and a View section (because a UIControl is also a UIView).

Size inspector (Command-Option-5)
The X, Y, Width, and Height fields determine the object's position and size within its superview, corresponding to its frame property in code; you can equally do this in the canvas by dragging and resizing, but numeric precision can be desirable.

If autolayout is turned on (the default for new *.storyboard* and *.xib* files), the rest of the Size inspector has to do with the selected object's autolayout constraints, plus the buttons at the lower right of the canvas help you manage alignment, positioning, and constraints.

Connections inspector (Command-Option-6)
I'll discuss and demonstrate use of the Connections inspector later in this chapter.

Two libraries are of particular importance when you're editing a nib:

Object library (Command-Option-Control-3)
   This library is your source for objects that you want to add to the nib.

Media library (Command-Option-Control-4)
   This library lists media in your project, such as images that you might want to drag into a UIImageView — or directly into your interface, in which case a UIImageView is created for you.

 I've now mentioned autolayout and constraints a couple of times, but I'm not going to explain here what they are. Nor am I going to discuss size classes and conditional constraints (trait variations). These are large topics having to do with views and view controllers, and are outside the scope of this book. I deal with these matters in full detail, including how to work with constraints and size classes in the nib editor, in *Programming iOS 10*.

Nib Loading

A nib file is a collection of potential instances — its nib objects. Those instances become real only if, while your app is running, the nib is *loaded*. At that moment, the nib objects contained in the nib are transformed into instances that are available to your app.

This architecture is a source of great efficiency. A nib usually contains interface; interface is relatively heavyweight stuff. A nib isn't loaded until it is needed; indeed, it might never be loaded. Thus this heavyweight stuff won't come into existence until and unless it is needed. In this way, memory usage is kept to a minimum, which is important because memory is at a premium in a mobile device. Also, loading a nib takes time, so loading fewer nibs at launch time — enough to generate just the app's initial interface — makes launching faster.

There's no such thing as "unloading" a nib. The job of the nib-loading process is to deliver some instances; when those instances are delivered, the nib's work, for that moment, is done. Henceforward it's up to the running app to decide what to do with the instances that just sprang to life. It must hang on to them for as long as it needs them, and will let them go out of existence when they are no longer needed.

Think of the nib file as a set of instructions for generating instances; whenever the nib is loaded, those instructions are followed. The same nib file can thus be *loaded multiple times*, generating a new set of instances each time. For example, a nib file might contain a piece of interface that you intend to use in several different places in your app. A nib file representing a single row of a table view might be loaded a dozen times in order to generate a dozen visible rows of that table view.

When Nibs Are Loaded

Here are some of the chief circumstances under which a nib file is commonly loaded while an app is running:

A view controller is instantiated from a storyboard

A storyboard is a collection of scenes. Each scene starts with a view controller. When that view controller is needed, it is instantiated from the storyboard. This means that a nib containing the view controller is loaded.

A view controller may be instantiated from a storyboard *automatically*. For example, as your app launches, if it has a main storyboard, the runtime looks for that storyboard's *initial view controller* (entry point) and instantiates it (see Chapter 6). Similarly, a storyboard typically contains several scenes connected by segues; when a segue is performed, the destination scene's view controller is instantiated.

It is also possible for your code to instantiate a view controller from a storyboard *manually*. To do so, you start with a UIStoryboard instance, and then:

- You can instantiate the storyboard's initial view controller by calling `instantiateInitialViewController`.

- You can instantiate any view controller whose scene is named within the storyboard by an identifier string by calling `instantiateViewController(withIdentifier:)`.

A view controller loads its main view from a nib

A view controller has a main view. But a view controller is a lightweight object (it's just some code), whereas its main view is a relatively heavyweight object. Therefore, a view controller, when it is instantiated, lacks its main view. It generates its main view later, when that view is needed because it is to be placed into the interface. A view controller can obtain its main view in several ways; one way is to load its main view from a nib.

If a view controller belongs to a scene in a storyboard, and if, as will usually be the case, it contains its view in that storyboard's canvas (as in our Empty Window example project), then there are *two* nibs involved: the nib containing the view controller, and the nib containing its main view. The nib containing the view controller was loaded in order to instantiate the view controller, as I just described; now, when that view controller instance needs its main view, the main view nib is loaded *automatically*, and the whole interface connected with that view controller springs to life.

Another fairly common configuration is that the view controller is instantiated in your code, *not* from a storyboard, by calling the UIViewController designated initializer `init(nibName:bundle:)`. The `nibName:` parameter tells this view controller instance the name of a nib — in this case, a nib generated from a *.xib* file in your project. When the view controller needs its main view, it *automatically* loads that nib and extracts its main view from it.

Your code explicitly loads a nib file
> If a nib file comes from a *.xib* file, your code can load it *manually*, by calling one of these methods:

`loadNibNamed(_:owner:options:)`
> A Bundle instance method. Usually, you'll direct it to `Bundle.main`.

`instantiate(withOwner:options:)`
> A UINib instance method. The nib in question was specified when UINib was instantiated and initialized with `init(nibName:bundle:)`.

Manual Nib Loading

In real life, most loading of nibs in your app will probably take place in one of the first two ways — a view controller nib is loaded automatically, or a view controller loads its main view nib automatically. But the third way, where you load a nib manually in code, is perfectly viable, and you might use it sometimes. And because you do it manually, it's the most educational way to understand the nib-loading process. So let's practice loading a nib manually.

First we'll create and configure a *.xib* file in our Empty Window project:

1. In the Empty Window project, choose File → New → File and specify iOS → User Interface → View. This will be a *.xib* file containing a UIView instance. Click Next.

2. In the Save dialog, accept the default name, View, for the new *.xib* file. Click Create.

3. We are now back in the Project navigator; our *View.xib* file has been created and selected, and we're looking at its contents in the editor. Those contents consist of a single UIView. It's too large, so select it and, in the Attributes inspector, change the Size pop-up menu, under Simulated Metrics, to Freeform. Handles appear around the view in the canvas; drag them to make the view smaller.

4. Populate the view with some arbitrary subviews, dragging them into it from the Object library. You can also configure the view itself; for example, in the Attributes inspector, change its background color (Figure 7-7).

Our goal now is to *load* this nib file, manually, in code, when the app runs. Edit *ViewController.swift* and, in the `viewDidLoad` method body, insert this line of code:

Figure 7-7. Designing a view in a .xib file

```
Bundle.main.loadNibNamed("View", owner: nil)
```

Build and run the app. Hey, what happened? Where's the designed view from *View.xib*? Did our nib fail to load?

No. Our nib did *not* fail to load. We loaded it! But we've omitted two further steps. Remember, there are *three* tasks you have to perform when you load a nib:

1. Load the nib.
2. Obtain the instances that it creates as it loads.
3. Do something with those instances.

We performed the *first* task — we loaded the nib — but we didn't obtain any instances from it. Thus, those instances were created *and then vanished in a puff of smoke!* In order to prevent that, we need to *capture* those instances somehow. The call to load-NibNamed(_:owner:options:) returns an array of the top-level nib objects instantiated from the loading of the nib. Those are the instances we need to capture! We have only one top-level nib object — the UIView — so it is sufficient to capture the first (and only) element of this array. Rewrite our code to look like this:

```
let arr = Bundle.main.loadNibNamed("View", owner: nil)!
let v = arr[0] as! UIView
```

We have now performed the *second* task: we've captured the instances that we created by loading the nib. The variable v now refers to a brand-new UIView instance, instantiated from the nib by loading it.

But *still* nothing seems to happen when we build and run the app, because we aren't *doing* anything with that UIView. That's the *third* task. Let's fix that by doing something clear and dramatic with the UIView: we'll put it into our interface! Rewrite our code once again:

Figure 7-8. A nib-loaded view appears in our interface

```
let arr = Bundle.main.loadNibNamed("View", owner: nil)!
let v = arr[0] as! UIView
self.view.addSubview(v)
```

Build and run the app. There's our view! This proves that our loading of the nib worked: we can *see*, in our running app's interface, the view that we designed in the nib (Figure 7-8).

Connections

A *connection* is something in a nib file. It unites two nib objects, running from one to the other. The connection has a direction: that's why I use the words "from" and "to" to describe it. I'll call the two objects the *source* and the *destination* of the connection.

There are two kinds of connection: outlet connections and action connections. The rest of this section describes them, explains how to create and configure them, and discusses the nature of the problems that they are intended to solve.

Outlets

When a nib loads and its instances come into existence, there's a problem: those instances are useless unless you can get a reference to them. In the preceding section, we solved that problem by capturing the array of top-level objects instantiated by the loading of the nib. But there's another way: use an outlet. This approach is more complicated — it requires some advance configuration, which can easily go wrong. But it is also more common, especially when nibs are loaded automatically.

An *outlet* is a connection that has a *name*, which is effectively just a string. When the nib loads, something unbelievably clever happens. The source object and the destina-

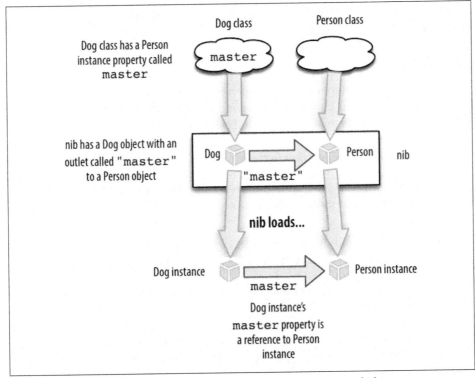

Figure 7-9. How an outlet provides a reference to a nib-instantiated object

tion object are no longer just potential objects in a nib; they are now real, full-fledged instances. The outlet's name is now immediately used to locate an *instance property* with that same name in the outlet's source object, and *the destination object is assigned to that property*. The source object now has a reference to the destination object!

For example, suppose there's a Dog object and a Person object in a nib, and suppose a Dog has a master instance property. Then if we make an outlet from the Dog object to the Person object in the nib, and if that outlet is named "master", then when the nib loads and the Dog instance and the Person instance are created, that Person instance will be assigned as the value of that Dog instance's master property (Figure 7-9).

The nib-loading mechanism can't magically *create* an instance property — that is, it doesn't cause the source object, once instantiated, to have an instance property of the correct name if it didn't have one before. The class of the source object has to have been defined with this instance property *already*. Thus, for an outlet to work, preparation must be performed in *two different places*: in the class of the source object, and in the nib. This is a bit tricky; Xcode does try to help you get it right, but it is still possible to mess it up. (I will discuss ways of messing it up, in detail, later in this chapter.)

The Nib Owner

To use an outlet to capture a reference to an instance created from a nib, we need an outlet that runs from an object *outside* the nib to an object *inside* the nib. This seems metaphysically impossible — but it isn't. The nib editor permits such an outlet to be created, using the *nib owner object*. Before I explain what the nib owner is, I'll tell you where to find the nib owner object in the nib editor:

- In a storyboard scene, the nib owner is the top-level view controller. It is the first object listed for that scene in the document outline, and the first object shown in the scene dock.

- In a *.xib* file, the nib owner is a proxy object. It is the first object shown in the document outline or dock, and is listed under Placeholders as the File's Owner.

So exactly what *is* the nib owner object in the nib editor? It represents an instance that *already* exists *outside* the nib at the time that the nib is loaded. When the nib is loaded, the nib-loading mechanism *doesn't* instantiate this object; it is *already* an instance. Instead, the nib-loading mechanism substitutes the real, already existing instance for the nib owner object, using it to fulfill any connections that involve the nib owner.

But wait! How does the nib-loading mechanism know *which* real, already existing instance to substitute for the nib owner object in the nib? It knows because it is told, in one of two ways, at nib-loading time:

- If your code loads the nib manually, either by calling `loadNib-Named(_:owner:options:)` or by calling `instantiate(withOwner:options:)`, you specify an owner object as the `owner:` argument.

- If a view controller instance loads a nib automatically in order to obtain its main view, the view controller instance specifies *itself* as the owner object.

For example, return to our Dog object and Person object. Suppose there is a Person nib object in our nib, but *no* Dog nib object. Instead, the *nib owner object* is a Dog. A Dog has a `master` instance property. We configure an outlet in the nib from the Dog nib owner object to the Person object — an outlet called `"master"`. We then load the nib *with an existing Dog instance as owner*. The nib-loading mechanism will match the Dog nib owner object with this already existing actual Dog instance, and will set the newly instantiated Person instance as that Dog instance's `master` (Figure 7-10).

Return now to Empty View, and let's reconfigure things to demonstrate this mechanism. We're already loading the View nib in code in *ViewController.swift*. This code is

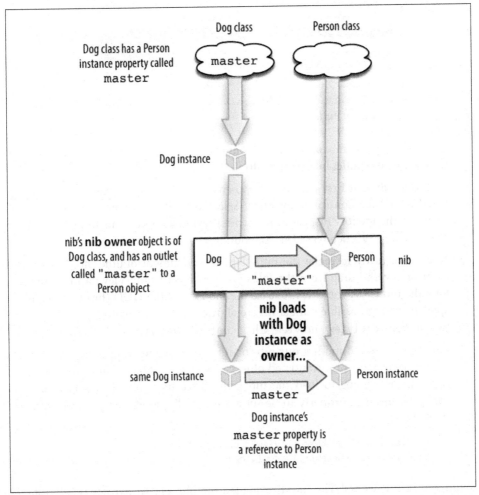

Dog class has a Person
instance property called
`master`

Dog class

master

Person class

Dog instance

nib's **nib owner** object is of
Dog class, and has an outlet
called `"master"` to a
Person object

Dog   Person   nib

`"master"`

**nib loads
with Dog
instance as
owner...**

same Dog instance   Person instance

`master`

Dog instance's
`master` property is
a reference to Person
instance

Figure 7-10. An outlet from the nib owner object

running inside a ViewController instance. So we'll use that instance as the nib owner.
This will be a little tedious to configure, but bear with me, because understanding
how to use this mechanism is crucial. Here we go:

1. First, we need an instance property in ViewController. At the start of the body of
   the ViewController class declaration, insert the property declaration, like this:

   ```
   class ViewController: UIViewController {
       @IBOutlet var coolview : UIView!
   ```

The `var` declaration you already understand; we're making an instance property
called `coolview`. It is declared as an Optional because it won't have a "real" value
when the ViewController instance is created; it's going to get that value through

Figure 7-11. Creating an outlet

the loading of the nib, later. The `@IBOutlet` attribute is a hint to Xcode to allow us to create the outlet in the nib editor.

2. Edit *View.xib*. Our first step must be to ensure that the nib owner object is designated as a ViewController instance. Select the File's Owner proxy object and switch to the Identity inspector. In the first text field, under Custom Class, set the Name value as `ViewController`. Tab out of the text field and save.

3. Now we're ready to make the outlet! In the document outline, hold down the Control key and drag from the File's Owner object to the View; a little line follows the mouse as you drag. Release the mouse. A little HUD (heads-up display) appears, listing possible outlets we are allowed to create (Figure 7-11). There are two of them: `coolview` and `view`. Click `coolview` (*not* `view`!).

4. Finally, we need to modify our nib-loading code. We no longer need to capture the top-level array of instantiated objects. That's the whole point of this exercise! Instead, we're going to load the nib *with ourself as owner*. This will cause our `coolview` instance property to be set automatically, so we can proceed to use it immediately:

```
Bundle.main.loadNibNamed("View", owner: self)
self.view.addSubview(self.coolview)
```

Build and run. It works! The first line loaded the nib *and set our `coolview` instance property* to the view instantiated from the nib. Thus, the second line can display `self.coolview` in the interface, because `self.coolview` now *is* that view.

Let's sum up what we just did. Our preparatory configuration was a little tricky, because it was performed in two places — in code, and in the nib:

- In code, there must be an instance property in the class whose instance will act as owner when the nib loads. (Not only did we create the property, but we also marked it as `@IBOutlet`.)

- In the nib editor, the class of the nib owner object must be set to the class whose instance will act as owner when the nib loads.

Figure 7-12. A view controller's view outlet connection

- In the nib editor, an outlet must be created, with the same name as the property, from the nib owner to some nib object. (This will be possible only if the other two configurations were correctly performed.)

If all those things are true, then, when the nib loads, *if* it is loaded with an owner of the correct class, that owner's instance property will be set to the outlet destination.

 When you configure an outlet to an object in the nib, that object's name as listed in the document outline ceases to be generic (e.g. "View") and takes on the name of the outlet (e.g. "coolview"). This name is still just a label — it has no effect on the operation of the outlet — and you can change it in the Identity inspector.

Automatically Configured Nibs

Now that we've created a nib owner outlet manually and loaded a nib manually, we can understand and appreciate what happens when a view controller gets its main view from a nib automatically. It all works exactly like what we just did! You can see this, for example, in our Empty Window project's *Main.storyboard*.

- We had to have an instance property in our nib owner class. Well, a UIView-Controller has a property — its `view` property! This is the property that needs to be set in order for the view controller to obtain its main view.

- In the nib editor, we had to make sure that the nib owner object's class was the class whose instance really will be the owner when the nib loads. Well, in *Main.storyboard*, in the single scene, the View Controller object *is* the nib owner, and if you select it and examine its class in the identity inspector, you'll see that it is of the correct class, namely ViewController (the class declared in the *ViewController.swift* file).

- In the nib editor, there needs to be an outlet with the same as the owner instance property, leading from the owner to the nib object. Well, in *Main.storyboard*, the ViewController object *is* the view nib owner, it *has* an outlet called `view`, and that outlet *is* connect to the main view. You can see this by selecting the view controller and examining its Connections inspector (Figure 7-12).

Thus, the storyboard has already been configured in a manner exactly parallel to how we configured *View.xib* in the preceding section. And the result is exactly the same. When the view controller needs its view, its loads the view nib with itself as owner, the nib-loading process sees the connected `view` outlet, the view at the end of that outlet is assigned to the view controller's `view` property, and voilà! The view controller has its main view.

Moreover, the view controller's main view is then placed into the interface. And *that* is why whatever we design in this view in the storyboard, such as putting into it a button whose title is "Howdy!", actually appears in the interface when the app runs.

Misconfigured Outlets

Setting up an outlet to work correctly involves several things being true at the same time. I guarantee that at some point in the future you will fail to get this right, and your outlet won't work properly. Don't be offended, and don't be afraid; be prepared! This happens to everyone. The important thing is to recognize the symptoms so that you know what's gone wrong. We're deliberately going to make things go wrong, so that we can explore the main ways that an outlet can be incorrectly configured:

Outlet name doesn't match a property name in the source class
Start with our working Empty Window example. Run the project to prove that all is well. Now, in *ViewController.swift*, change the property name to `badview`:

```
@IBOutlet var badview : UIView!
```

In order to get the code to compile, you'll also have to change the reference to this property in `viewDidLoad`:

```
self.view.addSubview(self.badview)
```

The code compiles just fine. But when you run it, the app crashes with this message in the console: "This class is not key value coding-compliant for the key `coolview`."

That message is just a technical way of saying that the name of the outlet in the nib (which is still `coolview`) doesn't match the name of a property of the nib's owner when the nib loads — because we changed the name of that property to `badview` and thus wrecked the configuration. In effect, we had everything set up correctly, but then we went behind the nib editor's back and removed the corresponding instance property from the outlet source's class. When the nib loads, the runtime can't match the outlet's name with any property in the outlet's source — the ViewController instance — and we crash.

There are other ways to bring about this same misconfiguration. For example, you could change things so that the nib owner is an instance of *the wrong class*:

```
Bundle.main.loadNibNamed("View", owner: NSObject())
```

We made the owner a generic NSObject instance. The effect is the same: the NSObject class has no property with the same name as the outlet, so the app crashes when the nib loads, complaining about the owner not being "key value coding-compliant." Another common way to make that same mistake is to make the nib owner class *in the nib* the wrong class.

No outlet in the nib

Fix the problem from the previous example by changing both references to the property name from `badview` back to `coolview` in *ViewController.swift*. Run the project to prove that all is well. Now we're going to mess things up at the other end! Edit *View.xib*. Select the File's Owner and switch to the Connections inspector, and disconnect the `coolview` outlet by clicking the X at the left end of the second cartouche. Run the project. We crash with this error message in the console: "Fatal error: unexpectedly found `nil` while unwrapping an Optional value."

We removed the outlet from the nib. So when the nib loaded, our ViewController instance property `coolview`, which is typed as an implicitly unwrapped Optional wrapping a UIView (`UIView!`), was *never set to anything*. Thus, it kept its initial value, which is `nil`. We then tried to *use* the implicitly unwrapped Optional by putting it into the interface:

```
self.view.addSubview(self.coolview)
```

Swift tries to obey by unwrapping the Optional for real, but you can't unwrap `nil`, so we crash.

No view outlet

I can't demonstrate this problem using a *.storyboard* file. What we'd like to do is *disconnect* the `view` outlet in *Main.storyboard*, but the storyboard editor guards against this. But if you *could* make this mistake, then trying to run the project would result in a crash at launch time, with a console message complaining that "the view outlet was not set."

A nib that is to serve as the source of a view controller's main view *must* have a connected `view` outlet from the view controller (the nib owner object) to the view. In a *.xib* file whose view is to function as a view controller's main view, you *can* make this mistake — usually by forgetting to connect the File's Owner `view` outlet to the view in the first place.

Deleting an Outlet

Deleting an outlet coherently — that is, without causing one of the problems described in the previous section — involves working in several places at once, just as creating an outlet does. I recommend proceeding in this order:

1. Disconnect the outlet in the nib.

2. Remove the outlet declaration from the code.

3. Attempt compilation and let the compiler catch any remaining issues for you.

Let's suppose, for example, that you decide to delete the `coolview` outlet from the Empty Window project. You would follow the same three-step procedure that I just outlined:

1. Disconnect the outlet in the nib. To do so, edit *View.xib*, select the source object (the File's Owner proxy object), and disconnect the `coolview` outlet in the Connections inspector by clicking the X.

2. Remove the outlet declaration from the code. To do so, edit *ViewController.swift* and delete or comment out the `@IBOutlet` declaration line.

3. Remove other references to the property. The easiest way is to attempt to build the project; the compiler issues an error on the line referring to `self.coolview` in *ViewController.swift*, because there is now no such property. Delete or comment out that line, and build again to prove that all is well.

More Ways to Create Outlets

Earlier, we created an outlet by first declaring an instance property in a class file, and then, in the nib editor, by control-dragging from the source (an instance of that class) to the destination in the document outline and choosing the desired outlet property from the HUD (heads-up display). Xcode provides many other ways to create outlets — too many to list here. I'll survey some of the most interesting.

We'll continue to use the Empty Window project and the *View.xib* file. Keep in mind that all of this works exactly the same way for a *.storyboard* file.

To prepare, delete the outlet in *View.xib* as I described in the previous section (if you haven't already done so). In *ViewController.swift*, create (or uncomment) the property declaration, and save:

```
@IBOutlet var coolview : UIView!
```

Now we're ready to experiment!

Drag from source Connections inspector
You can drag from a circle in the Connections inspector in the nib editor to connect the outlet. In *View.xib*, select the File's Owner and switch to the Connections inspector. The `coolview` outlet is listed here, but it isn't connected: the circle at its right is open. Drag from the circle next to `coolview` to the UIView object in the nib. You can drag to the view in the canvas or in the document outline. You don't

need to hold the Control key as you drag from the circle, and there's no HUD because you're dragging from a specific outlet, so Xcode knows which one you mean.

Drag from destination Connections inspector

Now let's make that same move the other way round. Delete the outlet in the nib. Select the View and look at the Connections inspector. We want an outlet that has this view as its destination: that's a "referencing outlet." Drag from the circle next to New Referencing Outlet to the File's Owner object. The HUD appears: click coolview to make the outlet connection.

Drag from source HUD

You can summon a HUD that effectively is the same as the Connections inspector. Let's start with that HUD. Again delete the outlet in the Connections inspector. Control-click the File's Owner. A HUD appears, looking a lot like the Connections inspector! Drag from the circle at the right of coolview to the UIView.

Drag from destination HUD

Again, let's make that same move the other way round. Delete the outlet in the Connections inspector. Either in the canvas or in the document outline, Control-click the view. There's the HUD showing its Connections inspector. Drag from the New Referencing Outlet circle to the File's Owner. A second HUD appears, listing possible outlets; click coolview.

Again, delete the outlet. Now we're going to create the outlet by dragging *between the code and the nib editor*. This will require that you work in two places at once: you're going to need an assistant pane. In the main editor pane, show *ViewController.swift*. In the assistant pane, show *View.xib*, in such a way that the view is visible.

Drag from property declaration to nib

Next to the property declaration in the code, in the gutter, is an empty circle. What do you think it's for? Drag from it *right across the barrier* to the View in the nib editor (Figure 7-13). The outlet connection is formed in the nib; you can see this by looking at the Connections inspector, and also because, back in the code, the circle in the gutter is now filled in. Hover over the filled circle, or click it, to learn what the outlet in the nib is connected to. You can click the little menu that appears when you click in the filled circle to navigate to the destination object.

Here's one more way — the most amazing of all. Keep the two-pane arrangement from the preceding example. Again, delete the outlet (you will probably need to use the Connections inspector or HUD in the nib editor pane to do this). Also delete the @IBOutlet line from the code! We're going to create the property declaration and connect the outlet, *all in a single move!*

Figure 7-13. Connecting an outlet by dragging from code to nib editor

Figure 7-14. Creating an outlet by dragging from nib editor to code

Drag from nib to code

Control-drag from the view in the nib editor across the pane barrier to just inside the body of the `class ViewController` declaration. A HUD offers to Insert Outlet or Outlet Collection (Figure 7-14). Release the mouse. A popover appears, where you can configure the declaration to be inserted into your code. Configure it as shown in Figure 7-15: you want an outlet, and this property should be named `coolview`. Click Connect. The property declaration is inserted into your code, and the outlet is connected in the nib, in a single move.

Figure 7-15. Configuring a property declaration

 Making an outlet by connecting directly between code and the nib editor is extremely cool and convenient, but don't be fooled: there's no such direct connection. There are always, if an outlet is to work properly, *two distinct and separate things* — an instance property in a class, and an outlet in the nib *with the same name* and *coming from an instance of that class*. It is the identity of the names and classes that allows the two to be matched at runtime when the nib loads. Xcode tries to help you get everything set up correctly, but it is *not* in fact magically connecting the code to the nib.

Outlet Collections

An *outlet collection* is an array instance property (in code) matched (in a nib) by multiple connections to objects of the same type.

For example, suppose a class contains this property declaration:

```
@IBOutlet var coolviews: [UIView]!
```

The outcome is that, in the nib editor, with an instance of this class selected, the Connections inspector lists `coolviews` — not under Outlets, but under Outlet Collections. This means that you can form *multiple* `coolviews` outlets, each one connected to a different UIView object in the nib. When the nib loads, those UIView instances become the elements of the array `coolviews`; the order in which the outlets are formed is the order of the elements in the array.

The advantage of this arrangement is that your code can refer to multiple interface objects instantiated from the nib by number (the index into the array) instead of your having to devise and manipulate a separate name for each one. This turns out to be particularly useful when forming outlets to such things as autolayout constraints and gesture recognizers.

Action Connections

An action connection, like an outlet connection, is a way of giving one object in a nib a reference to another. But it's not a property reference; it's a *message-sending* reference.

An *action* is a message emitted automatically by a Cocoa UIControl interface object (a *control*), and sent to another object, when the user does something to it, such as tapping the control. The various user behaviors that will cause a control to emit an action message are called *events*. To see a list of possible events, look at the UIControlEvents documentation. For example, in the case of a UIButton, the user tapping the button corresponds to the `UIControlEvents.touchUpInside` event.

For this architecture to work, the control object must know three things:

- What control event to respond to
- What message to send (method to call) when that control event occurs (the *action*)
- What object to send that message to (the *target*)

An action connection in a nib builds the knowledge of those three things into itself. It has the control object as its source; its destination is the target; and you tell the action connection, as you form it, what the control event and action message should be. To form the action connection, you need first to configure the class of the *destination* object so that it has a method suitable as an action message.

To experiment with action connections, we'll need a UIControl object in a nib, such as a button. You may already have such a button in the Empty Window project's *Main.storyboard* file. However, it's probable that, when the app runs, we've been covering the button with the view that we're loading from *View.xib*. So first clear out the ViewController class declaration body in *ViewController.swift*, so that there is no outlet property and no manual nib-loading code; this should be all that's left:

```
class ViewController: UIViewController {
}
```

Now let's arrange to use the view controller in our Empty Window project as a target for an action message emitted by the button's `.touchUpInside` event (meaning that the button was tapped). We'll need a method in the view controller that will be called by the button when the button is tapped. To make this method dramatic and obvious, we'll have the view controller put up an alert window. Insert this method into the *ViewController.swift* declaration body:

```
@IBAction func buttonPressed(_ sender: Any) {
    let alert = UIAlertController(
        title: "Howdy!", message: "You tapped me!", preferredStyle: .Alert)
    alert.addAction(
        UIAlertAction(title: "OK", style: .Cancel))
    self.present(alert, animated: true)
}
```

The `@IBAction` attribute is like `@IBOutlet`: it's a hint to Xcode itself, asking Xcode to make this method available in the nib editor. And indeed, if we look in the nib editor,

Figure 7-16. A HUD showing an action method

we find that it *is* now available: edit *Main.storyboard*, select the View Controller object and switch to the Connections inspector, and you'll find that `buttonPressed:` is now listed under Received Actions.

In *Main.storyboard*, in the single scene that it contains, the top-level View Controller's View should contain a button. (We created it earlier in this chapter: see Figure 7-5.) If it doesn't, add one, and position it in the upper left corner of the view. Our goal now is to connect that button's Touch Up Inside event, as an action, to the `button-Pressed(_:)` method in ViewController.

As with an outlet connection, there is a source and a destination. The source here is the button; the destination is View Controller, the ViewController instance acting as owner of the nib containing the button. There are many ways to form this outlet connection, all of them completely parallel to the formation of an action connection. The difference is that we must configure *both* ends of the connection. At the button (source) end, we must specify that the control event we want to use is Touch Up Inside; fortunately, this is the default for a UIButton, so we might be able to skip this step. At the view controller (destination) end, we must specify that the action method to be called is our `buttonPressed(_:)` method.

Let's form the action connection by simply Control-dragging from the button to the view controller in the nib editor:

1. Control-drag from the button (in the canvas or in the document outline) to the View Controller listing in the document outline (or to the view controller icon in the scene dock above the view in the canvas).

2. A HUD listing possible connections appears (Figure 7-16); it lists mostly segues, but it also lists Sent Events, and in particular it lists `buttonPressed:` (the Objective-C name of our `buttonPressed(_:)` method).

3. Click the `buttonPressed:` listing in the HUD.

The action connection has now been formed. This means that when the app runs, any time the button gets a Touch Up Inside event — meaning that it was tapped — it will call the `buttonPressed(_:)` method in the target, which is the view controller instance. We know what that method should do: it should put up an alert. Try it! Build and run the app, and when the app appears in the Simulator, tap the button. It works!

More Ways to Create Actions

Other ways in which you can form the action connection in the nib, having created the action method in *ViewController.swift*, include the following:

- Control-click the view controller. A HUD appears, similar to the Connections inspector. Drag from `buttonPressed:` (under Received Actions) to the button. Another HUD appears, listing possible control events. Click Touch Up Inside.

- Select the button and use the Connections inspector. Drag from the Touch Up Inside circle to the view controller. A HUD appears, listing the known action methods in the view controller; click `buttonPressed:`.

- Control-click the button. A HUD appears, similar to the Connections inspector. Proceed as in the previous case.

- Arrange to see *ViewController.swift* in one pane and the storyboard in the other. The `buttonPressed(_:)` declaration in *ViewController.swift* has a circle to its left, in the gutter. Drag from that circle across the pane barrier to the button in the nib.

As with an outlet connection, the most impressive way to make an action connection is to drag from the nib editor to your code, inserting the action method and forming the action connection in the nib *in a single move*. To try this, first delete the `buttonPressed(_:)` method in your code and delete the action connection in the nib. Arrange to see *ViewController.swift* in one pane and the storyboard in the other. Now:

1. Control-drag from the button in the nib editor to an empty area in the View-Controller class declaration's body. A HUD offering to create an outlet *or an action* appears in the code. Release the mouse.

2. The popover view appears. This is the tricky part. By default, the popover view is offering to create an outlet connection. That isn't what you want; you want an action connection! Change the Connection pop-up menu to Action. Now you can enter the name of the action method (`buttonPressed`) and configure the rest of the declaration (the defaults are probably good enough: see Figure 7-17).

Xcode forms the action connection in the nib, and inserts a stub method into your code:

Figure 7-17. Configuring an action method declaration

```
@IBAction func buttonPressed(_ sender: UIButton) {
}
```

The method is just a stub (Xcode can't read your mind and guess what you want the method to do), so in real life, at this point, you'd insert some functionality between those curly braces. As with an outlet connection, the filled circle next to the code in an action method tells you that Xcode believes that this connection is correctly configured, and you can click the filled circle to learn, and navigate to, the object at the source of the connection.

Misconfigured Actions

As with an outlet connection, configuring an action connection involves setting things up correctly at both ends (the nib and the code) so that they match. Thus, you can wreck an action connection's configuration and crash your app. The typical misconfiguration is that the name of the action method as embedded in the action connection in the nib no longer matches the name of the action method in the code.

To see this, change the name of the function in the code from `buttonPressed` to something else, like `buttonPushed`. Now run the app and tap the button. Your app crashes, displaying in the console the dreaded error message, "Unrecognized selector sent to instance." A selector is a message — the name of a method. The runtime tried to send a message to an object, but that object turned out to have no corresponding method (because we renamed it). If you look a little earlier in the error message, it even tells you the name of this method:

```
-[Empty_Window.ViewController buttonPressed:]
```

The runtime is telling you (using Objective-C notation) that it tried to call the `button-Pressed(_:)` method in your Empty Window module's ViewController class, but the ViewController class has no such method.

Connections Between Nibs — Not!

You cannot draw an outlet connection or an action connection between an object in one nib and an object in another nib. For example:

- You can't open nib editors on two different *.xib* files and Control-drag a connection from one to the other.

- In a *.storyboard* file, you cannot Control-drag a connection between an object in one scene and an object in another scene.

If you expect to be able to do this, you haven't understood what a nib is (or what a scene is, or what a connection is).

The reason is simple: objects in a nib together will become instances together, at the moment when the nib loads, so it makes sense to connect them in the nib, because we know what instances we'll be talking about when the nib loads. The two objects may both be instantiated from the nib, or one of them may be a proxy object (the nib owner), but they must both be represented *in the same nib*, so that the actual instances can be configured in relation to one another on a particular occasion when this nib loads.

If an outlet connection or an action connection were drawn from an object in one nib to an object in another nib, there would be no way to understand what actual future instances the connection is supposed to connect, because they are different nibs and will be loaded at different times (if ever). The problem of communicating between an instance generated from one nib and an instance generated from another nib is a special case of the more general problem of how to communicate between instances in a program, discussed in Chapter 13.

Additional Configuration of Nib-Based Instances

By the time a nib finishes loading, its instances are fully fledged; they have been initialized and configured with all the attributes dictated through the Attributes and Size inspectors, and their outlets have been used to set the values of the corresponding instance properties. Nevertheless, you might want to append your own code to the initialization process as an object is instantiated from a loading nib. This section describes some ways you can do that.

A common situation is that a view controller, functioning as the owner when a nib containing its main view loads (and therefore represented in the nib by the nib owner object), has an outlet to an interface object instantiated from the nib. In this architecture, the view controller can perform further configuration on that interface object, because it has a reference to it after the nib loads — the corresponding instance property. The earliest place where it can perform such configuration is its viewDidLoad method. At the time viewDidLoad is called, the view controller's view has loaded — that is, the view controller's view property has been set to its actual main view, instantiated from the nib — and all outlets have been connected; but the view is not yet in the visible interface.

Another possibility is that you'd like the nib object to configure itself, over and above whatever configuration has been performed in the nib. Often, this will be because you've got a custom subclass of a built-in interface object class — in fact, you might want to create a custom class, just so you have a place to put this self-configuring code. The problem you're trying to solve might be that the nib editor doesn't let you perform the configuration you're after, or that you have many objects that need to be configured in some identical, elaborate way, so that it makes more sense for them to configure themselves by virtue of sharing a common class than to configure each one individually in the nib editor.

One approach is to implement `awakeFromNib` in your custom class. The `awakeFromNib` message is sent to all nib-instantiated objects just after they are instantiated by the loading of the nib: the object has been initialized and configured and its connections are operational.

For example, let's make a button whose background color is always red, regardless of how it's configured in the nib. (This is a nutty example, but it's dramatically effective.) In the Empty Window project, we'll create a button subclass, RedButton:

1. In the Project navigator, choose File → New → File. Specify iOS → Source → Cocoa Touch Class. Click Next.

2. Call the new class RedButton. Make it a subclass of UIButton. Click Next.

3. Make sure you're saving into the project folder, with the Empty Window group, and make sure the Empty Window app target is checked. Click Create. Xcode creates *RedButton.swift*.

4. In *RedButton.swift*, inside the body of the RedButton class declaration, implement `awakeFromNib`:

```
override func awakeFromNib() {
    super.awakeFromNib()
    self.backgroundColor = .red
}
```

We now have a UIButton subclass that turns itself red when it's instantiated from a nib. But we have no instance of this subclass in any nib. Let's fix that. Edit the storyboard, select the button that's already in the main view, and use the Identity inspector to change this button's class to RedButton.

Now build and run the project. Sure enough, the button is red!

A further possibility is to take advantage of the User Defined Runtime Attributes in the nib object's Identity inspector. This can allow you to configure, in the nib editor, aspects of a nib object for which the nib editor itself provides no built-in interface. What you're actually doing here is sending the nib object, at nib-loading time, a `set-Value(_:forKeyPath:)` message; key paths are discussed in Chapter 10. Naturally,

Figure 7-18. Rounding a button's corners with a runtime attribute

the object needs to be prepared to respond to the given key path, or your app will crash when the nib loads.

For example, one of the disadvantages of the nib editor is that it provides no way to configure layer attributes. Let's say we'd like to use the nib editor to round the corners of our red button. In code, we would do that by setting the button's layer.corner-Radius property. The nib editor gives no access to this property. Instead, we can select the button in the nib editor and use the User Defined Runtime Attributes in the Identity inspector. We set the Key Path to layer.cornerRadius, the Type to Number, and the Value to whatever value we want — let's say 10 (Figure 7-18). Now build and run; sure enough, the button's corners are now rounded.

You can also configure a custom property of a nib object by making that property *inspectable*. To do so, add the @IBInspectable attribute to the property's declaration in your code. This causes the property to be listed in the nib object's Attributes inspector.

For example, let's make it possible to configure our button's border in the nib editor. At the start of the RedButton class declaration body, add this code:

```
@IBInspectable var borderWidth : CGFloat {
    get {
        return self.layer.borderWidth
    }
    set {
        self.layer.borderWidth = newValue
    }
}
```

That code declares a RedButton property, borderWidth, and makes it a façade in front of the layer's borderWidth property. It also causes the nib editor to display that property in the Attributes inspector for any button that is an instance of the RedButton class (Figure 7-19). The result is that when we give this property a value in the nib

Figure 7-19. An inspectable property in the nib editor

editor, that value is sent to the setter for this property at nib-loading time, and the button border appears with that width.

To intervene with a nib object's initialization even earlier, if the object is a UIView (or a UIView subclass), you can implement init(coder:). Note that, for a UIView, init(frame:) is *not called* during instantiation by the loading of a nib — init(coder:) is called instead. (Implementing init(frame:), and then wondering why your code isn't called when the view is instantiated from a nib, is a common beginner mistake.) A minimal implementation would look like this:

```
required init?(coder aDecoder: NSCoder) {
    super.init(coder:aDecoder)
    // your code here
}
```

CHAPTER 8

Documentation

Knowledge is of two kinds. We know a subject ourselves,
or we know where we can find information upon it.
—Samuel Johnson,
Boswell's Life of Johnson

No aspect of iOS programming is more important than a fluid and nimble relationship with the documentation. There is a huge number of built-in Cocoa classes, with many methods and properties and other details. Apple's documentation, whatever its flaws, is the definitive official word on how you can expect Cocoa to behave, and on the contractual rules incumbent upon you in working with this massive framework whose inner workings you cannot see directly.

Your primary access to the documentation is in Xcode, through the documentation window (Window → Documentation and API Reference, or Help → Documentation and API Reference, Command-Shift-0). So this chapter starts by talking about the documentation window and, in particular, its class documentation pages.

But there are other forms of documentation and assistance. Quick Help popovers and the Quick Help inspector provide documentation without leaving the code editor. You can examine the code headers, which provide a useful overview and often contain valuable comments; and you can jump quickly to any symbol declaration. Apple provides sample code, and there are lots of additional online resources. This chapter surveys all of that as well.

The Documentation Window

New in Xcode 8, the main documentation is included entirely within Xcode (in compressed form). The secondary documentation, however, needs to be downloaded manually from Apple; in the Components pane of the Preferences window, under

Documentation, click the download button for Guides and Sample Code. Until you do that, you'll be accessing guides and sample code over the Internet (and without a network connection, you won't be accessing them at all).

Within the documentation window, the primary way into the documentation is to do a search; for example, press Command-Shift-0 (or Command-L or Command-Shift-F if you're already in the documentation window) and type NSString. As you type, you're shown live search results pertinent to the language of your choice (Swift, Objective-C, or JavaScript), divided into API Reference, Tools Guides, and Sample Code. Besides choosing with the mouse, you can navigate these results with arrow keys, and press Return to select the desired hit. In this case, you probably want the top hit, which is the NSString class documentation page. Alternatively, you can choose Show All Results to see a page listing *all* results of the search, divided into the same three categories.

You can also perform a documentation window search starting from *within your code*. You'll very often want to do this: you're looking directly at a symbol (a class name, a method name, a property name, and so on) at its point of use in your code, and you want to know more about it. Hold Option and hover the mouse over a term in your code until a blue dotted underline appears; then (still holding Option) double-click the term. The documentation window opens, and you are taken to the full results page for a search on that term.

Alternatively, you can select text in your code (or anywhere else) and choose Help → Search Documentation for Selected Text (Command-Option-Control-/). Again, this is the equivalent of typing that text into the search field in the documentation window and asking to see the full results page.

The documentation window behaves basically as a glorified web browser. Multiple pages can appear simultaneously as tabs in the documentation window. To navigate to a new tab, hold Command as you navigate — for example, Command-click a link, or Command-click your choice in the pop-up search results window — or choose Open Link in New Tab from the contextual menu. You can navigate between tabs (Window → Show Next Tab), and each tab remembers its navigation history (Navigate → Go Back, or use the Back button in the window toolbar, which is also a pop-up menu).

A documentation page may be accompanied by a table of contents, displayed in a pane to the left of the documentation page; to see it if it isn't showing, choose Editor → Show Table of Contents, or click the Table of Contents icon in the window toolbar. As of this writing, class reference pages (such as NSString) do not have a table of contents, but guides do; a guide consists of multiple pages, and when you're viewing one, the Table of Contents pane lists all of them. To see an example, search for "Swift language" and click on The Swift Programming Language.

Figure 8-1. The start of the UIButton class documentation page

A full hierarchical table of contents for the whole documentation appears in the navigator area at the far left of the documentation window; to see it if it isn't showing, choose Editor → Show Navigator, or click the Navigator button in the window toolbar. Reference documents are displayed in one navigator (Editor → Show API Reference Navigator, or click the API Reference button); guides and sample code are displayed in another navigator (Editor → Show Guides and Sample Code Navigator, or click the Guides button).

When you encounter a documentation page to which you're likely to want to return, make it a bookmark: choose Add Bookmark from the contextual menu, or click the bookmark icon at the left of the page's title. To manage bookmarks, choose Editor → Show Bookmarks Navigator, or click the Bookmarks button. Click a bookmark in the Bookmarks navigator to jump to it in the documentation window. Bookmark management is simple but effective: you can rearrange bookmarks or delete a bookmark, and that's all.

To search for text *within* the current documentation page, use the Find menu commands. Find → Find (Command-F) summons a find bar, as in Safari.

Class Documentation Pages

In the vast majority of cases, your target documentation page will be the documentation for a class. It's important to be comfortable and conversant with the typical features and information provided by a class documentation page, so let's pause to notice them (Figure 8-1).

Breadcrumbs

At the top left of the page are breadcrumbs navigation links. These show you where you are, in more than one sense. UIButton is part of the UIKit framework; it is available to your code because you've imported UIKit. So now you know what to import in order to access this class. If you click the UIKit link, you're taken to an overview page listing *all* the major UIKit classes.

Bookmark icon

Click the bookmark icon at the left of the page's title to make a bookmark for rapid navigation to this page.

Language

Links let you choose between Swift and Objective-C as the language for display of class member names.

SDKs

This list tells you two important things:

- What sort of *hardware* you're programming for when you use this class. That's important because searches are not filtered by SDK. If you were to stumble accidentally into the NSViewController class documentation page, you might be confused about how this class fits into the rest of iOS programming, unless you notice that iOS is not listed among this class's SDKs.

- The lowest *version number* in which this class became available — also called the class's *availability*. The UIGraphicsImageRenderer page, for example, tells you that this class is available in iOS 10.0 and later. So you won't be able to use it in code intended to run on iOS 9.

On This Page

The class reference page is divided into sections, and these are links to them, in order:

Overview

If a page has an Overview section, read it! It explains what this class is for and how to use it. It may also contain valuable links to guides that provide related information.

Symbols

These are primarily the class's members — properties and methods — grouped by their purpose. Each member is accompanied by a short description; click the member itself to see further details. I'll talk more about that in a moment.

At the end of the Symbols section, there may be further subsections including Constants (such as enums used by this class's properties and methods) and Notifications (if this class emits any). For example, in the UIButton class documentation page, you'll find that, to create a UIButton instance in code, you can call the `init(type:)` initializer; its argument is a `UIButtonType`, listed in the Constants section.

Relationships
There are two chief kinds of relationship that a class can have, and you'll want to keep an eye on both of them:

Inherits from
This class's superclass. One of the biggest beginner mistakes is failing to consult the documentation up the superclass chain. A class inherits from its superclasses, so the functionality or information you're looking for may be in a superclass. You won't find `addTarget(_:action:for:)` among the UIButton class page symbols; it's in the UIControl class page. You won't find out that a UIButton has a `frame` property from the UIButton class page; that information is in the UIView class page (UIControl's superclass).

Conforms to
Protocols adopted by this class. Failing to consult the documentation for adopted protocols is a serious beginner mistake. For example, you won't find the `viewWillTransition(to:with:)` event among the UIView-Controller class page symbols: you have to look in the documentation for the UIContentContainer protocol, which UIViewController adopts.

See Also
A class documentation page may have a See Also section, linking to relevant guides.

When you click the name of a property or method in a class documentation page, you're taken to a separate page that describes it in detail. This page is laid out similarly to a class documentation page:

Breadcrumbs
The page has breadcrumbs leading back to the class documentation page.

Language
The page gives you a choice of languages.

SDKs
The page lists the SDKs in which this property or method is found, including its availability. Note that the availability for a property or method need not be the same as its class's availability, because a class can acquire (and lose) members over time. For example, the UIButton class is as old as iOS itself and is available starting in iOS 2.0, but the `init(type:)` initializer didn't appear until iOS 9.0.

(Before that, a button had to be created by a factory method `buttonWithType:`, which is still the Objective-C way and is displayed in the Objective-C version of the same page.)

On This Page

The sections of a method's page are particularly worth noting:

Overview

There is no separate Overview section, but there is always an initial summary of this method's purpose (the same summary that appears on the class documentation page).

Declaration

The formal declaration for this method, showing its parameters and return type.

Parameters

Separate explanations for each parameter.

Return Value

An explicit description of what this method returns.

Discussion

Often contains extremely important further details about how this method behaves. Always pay attention to this section!

See Also

Links to related methods and properties, as well as related guides. Very helpful for giving you a larger perspective on how this method fits into the overall behavior of this class.

Quick Help

Quick Help is a condensed rendering of the documentation on some single topic, usually a symbol name. It appears with regard to the current selection or insertion point automatically in the Quick Help inspector (Command-Option-2) if the inspector is showing. Thus, for example, if you're editing code and the insertion point or selection is within the term `viewDidLoad`, documentation for the `viewDidLoad` method appears in the Quick Help inspector if it is visible. Quick Help is also available in the Quick Help inspector for interface objects selected in the nib editor.

Quick Help documentation can also be displayed as a popover window, without the Quick Help inspector. Select a term and choose Help → Quick Help for Selected Item (Command-Control-Shift-?). Alternatively, hold down Option and hover the mouse over a term until the cursor becomes a question mark (and the term turns blue with a dashed underline); then Option-click the term.

When you're developing Swift code, Quick Help is of increased importance. If you click in the name of a Swift variable whose type is inferred, Quick Help shows the inferred type (see Figure 3-1). This can help you understand compile errors and other surprises.

The Quick Help documentation contains links. For example, click the Class Reference or Method Reference link to open the full documentation in the documentation window.

You can inject documentation for your own code into Quick Help. To do so, precede a declaration with a comment enclosed in /**...*/. Alternatively, use a sequence of single-line comments starting with ///. Within the comment, Markdown formatting can be used (see *http://daringfireball.net/projects/markdown/syntax*). The comment becomes the Description field for Quick Help; certain list items (paragraphs beginning with * or - followed by space) are treated in a special way:

- Paragraphs beginning with `Parameter` *paramname*: are incorporated into the Parameters field.

- A paragraph beginning with `Throws:` becomes the Throws field.

- A paragraph beginning with `Returns:` becomes the Returns field.

For example, here's a function declaration with a preceding comment:

```
/**
Many people would like to dog their cats. So it is *perfectly*
reasonable to supply a convenience method to do so:

* Because it's cool.
* Because it's there.

* Parameter cats: A string containing cats

* Returns: A string containing dogs
*/

func dogMyCats(_ cats:String) -> String {
    return "Dogs"
}
```

The double asterisk in the opening comment delimiter denotes that this is documentation, and the comment's location automatically associates it with the dogMyCats method whose definition follows. The word surrounded by asterisks is formatted as italics; the asterisked paragraphs become bulleted paragraphs; and the last two paragraphs become special fields. The outcome is that when dogMyCats is selected anywhere in my code, its documentation is displayed in Quick Help (Figure 8-2). The first paragraph of the description is also displayed as part of code completion (see Chapter 9).

```
Declaration  func dogMyCats(_ cats: String) -> String
Description  Many people would like to dog their cats. So it is
             perfectly reasonable to supply a convenience
             method to do so:

                  • Because it's cool.
                  • Because it's there.

Parameters   cats
                 A string containing cats
   Returns   A string containing dogs
```

Figure 8-2. Custom documentation injected into Quick Help

New in Xcode 8, you can generate a documentation comment automatically. Select within the declaration line and choose Editor → Structure → Add Documentation. The comment is inserted before the declaration. The description, and the parameters and returned value if this is a function declaration, are placeholders.

> There are additional special documentation fields. For more information about these, see the "Markup Functionality" page of Apple's *Markup Formatting Reference*.

Symbols

A *symbol* is a declared term, such as the name of a function, variable, or object type. If you can see the name of a symbol in your code in an editor in Xcode, you can jump quickly to the declaration of the symbol. Select text and choose Navigate → Jump to Definition (Command-Control-J). Alternatively, hold down Command and hover the mouse over a prospective term, until the cursor becomes a pointing finger (and the term becomes blue with a solid underline); Command-click the term to jump to the declaration for that symbol. When you do:

- If the symbol is declared in your code, you jump to that declaration in your code; this can be helpful not only for understanding your code but also for navigating it.

- If the symbol is declared in a framework, you jump to the declaration in the header file. If you started in a *.swift* file, the header file that you jump to is translated into Swift. (I'll talk more about header files in the next section.)

The precise meaning of the notion "jump" depends upon the modifier keys you use in addition to the Command key, and on your settings in the Navigation pane of Xcode's preferences. By default, Command-click jumps in the same editor, Command-Option-click jumps in an assistant pane, and Command-double-click jumps in a new window. Similarly, Command-Option-Control-J jumps in an assistant pane to the declaration of the selected term.

Another way to see a list of your project's symbols, and to navigate to a symbol declaration, is through the Symbol navigator (Chapter 6). If the second icon in the filter bar is highlighted, these are symbols declared in your project; if not, symbols from imported frameworks are listed as well.

To jump to the declaration of a symbol whose name you know, even if you don't see the name in the code before you, choose File → Open Quickly (Command-Shift-O). In the search field, type key letters from the name, which will be interpreted intelligently; for example, to search for `application(_:didFinishLaunchingWith-Options:)`, you might type `appdidf`. Possible matches are shown in a scrolling list below the search field; you can navigate this list with the mouse or by keyboard alone. Besides declarations from the framework headers, declarations in your own code are listed as well, so this, too, can be a rapid way of navigating your code.

Header Files

Often, a header file can be a useful form of documentation — possibly the *most* useful form of documentation. The header is necessarily accurate, up-to-date, and complete; the class documentation is not. A header consists chiefly of declarations, but it may also contain comments with helpful information; this, too, can tell you things that the class documentation might not. Also, a single header file can contain declarations for multiple classes and protocols. So it can be an excellent quick reference.

The simplest way to reach a header file is to jump to the declaration of a symbol there. For example, to reach *NSString.h* — the `Foundation.NSString` header file — Command-click on the term `NSString` wherever it may appear in your code. See the previous section for the various ways of jumping to a symbol declaration; since most symbols are declared in header files, these are ways of reaching header files.

When you jump to a header file from your code, if the code that you started from was a Swift file, the header file, if it is written in Objective-C, is spontaneously translated into Swift. That's good because it tells you what you can say in Swift. But it's bad if you were hoping to get a look at the actual Objective-C header! You can switch from a Swift translated (generated) header to the Objective-C original by choosing Navigate > Jump to Original Source (or choose Original Source from the Related Items menu at the left end of the jump bar).

You can learn a lot about the Swift language and the built-in library functions by examining the Swift header file. (There is also an excellent online presentation of the Swift header file at *http://swiftdoc.org.*) The special Swift header files for Core Graphics and Foundation are also likely to prove useful.

A useful trick is to write an import statement just so that you can Command-click it to reach a header. For example, if you import Swift at the top of a *.swift* file, the word Swift itself is a symbol that you can Command-click to jump to the Swift header.

Sample Code

Apple provides plenty of sample code projects, listed in the Guides and Sample Code navigator in the documentation window. You can view the code directly *in* the documentation window; sometimes this will be sufficient, but you can see only one file at a time, so it's difficult to get an overview. The alternative is to open the sample code project in Xcode; click the Open Project link at the top of a sample code page in the documentation window. If you're looking at the sample code in your browser at *http://developer.apple.com*, there's a Download Sample Code button. With the sample code project open as a project window, you can read the code, navigate it, edit it, and of course run the project.

As a form of documentation, sample code is both good and bad. It can be a superb source of working code that you can often copy and paste and use with very little alteration in your own projects. It is usually heavily commented, because the Apple folks are aware, as they write the code, that it is intended for instructional purposes. Sample code also illustrates concepts that users have difficulty extracting from the documentation. (Users who have not grasped UITouch handling, for instance, often find that the lightbulb goes on when they discover the MoveMe example.) But the logic of a project is often spread over multiple files, and nothing is more difficult to understand than someone else's code (except, perhaps, your own code). Moreover, what learners most need is not the *fait accompli* of a fully written project but the reasoning process that constructed the project, which no amount of commentary can provide.

My own assessment is that Apple's sample code is uneven. Some of it is a bit careless or even faulty, while some of it is astoundingly well-written. It is generally thoughtful and instructive, though, and is definitely a major component of the documentation; it deserves more appreciation and usage than it seems to get. But it is most useful, I think, after you've reached a certain level of competence and comfort.

Internet Resources

Programming has become a lot easier since the Internet came along and Google started indexing it. It's amazing what you can learn with a Google search. Your problem is very likely one that someone else has faced, solved, and written about on the Internet. Often you'll find sample code that you can paste into your project and adapt.

Apple's documentation resources are available at *http://developer.apple.com/library/*. These resources are updated before the changes are rolled into your doc sets for download. There are also some materials here that aren't part of the Xcode documentation on your computer. For example, you can download the videos for all WWDC 2016 sessions (as well as for some earlier years).

Apple also hosts some developer forums at *https://forums.developer.apple.com*. Some interesting discussions take place here, and they are patrolled by some very helpful Apple employees; but the interface remains extraordinarily clunky.

Other online resources have sprung up spontaneously as iOS programming has become more popular, and lots of iOS and Cocoa programmers blog about their experiences. One site that I'm particularly fond of is Stack Overflow (*http://www.stackoverflow.com*); it isn't devoted exclusively to iOS programming, of course, but lots of iOS programmers hang out there, questions are answered succinctly and correctly, and the interface lets you focus on the right answer quickly and easily.

CHAPTER 9

Life Cycle of a Project

This chapter surveys some of the main stages in the life cycle of an Xcode project, from inception to submission at the App Store. This survey will provide an opportunity to discuss some additional features of the Xcode development environment: configuring your build settings and your *Info.plist*; editing, debugging, and testing your code; running your app on a device; profiling; localization; and final preparations for the App Store.

Device Architecture and Conditional Code

As you create a project (File → New → Project), after you pick a project template, in the screen where you name your project, the Devices pop-up menu offers a choice of iPad, iPhone, or Universal. You can change this setting later, using the Devices pop-up menu in the General pane when you edit the app target. What you are ultimately determining here is your project's Targeted Device Family build setting:

1 *(iPhone)*
The app will run on an iPhone or iPod touch. It can also run on an iPad, but not as a native iPad app; it runs in a reduced enlargeable window, which I call the *iPhone Emulator* (Apple sometimes refers to this as "compatibility mode").

2 *(iPad)*
The app will run only on an iPad.

1,2 *(Universal)*
The app will run natively on both kinds of device.

Two additional project-level build settings determine what systems your device will run on:

Base SDK

The *latest* system your app can run on. As of this writing, in Xcode 8.0, you have just two choices, iOS 10.0 and Latest iOS (iOS 10.0). They sound the same, but the latter is better (and is the default for a new project). If you update Xcode to develop for a subsequent system, any existing projects that are already set to Latest iOS will automatically use that newer system's most recent SDK as their Base SDK, without you having to update their Base SDK setting manually.

iOS Deployment Target

The *earliest* system your app can run on: in Xcode 8, this can be any major iOS system as far back as iOS 8.0. To change the project's iOS Deployment Target setting easily, edit the project and switch to the Info tab, and choose from the iOS Deployment Target pop-up menu.

Backward Compatibility

Writing an app whose Deployment Target differs from its Base SDK — that is, an app that is *backward compatible* to an earlier system — is something of a challenge. There are two chief problems:

Changed behavior

With each new system, Apple permits itself to change the way some features work. The result is that certain features that exist on different systems may work differently depending what system it is. An entire area of functionality may be handled differently on different systems, requiring you to implement or call a whole different set of methods or use a completely different set of classes. It is even possible that the very same method may do two quite different things, depending on what system the app runs on.

Unsupported features

With each new system, Apple adds new features. Your app will crash if execution encounters features not supported by the system on which it is actually running.

Changed behavior is terribly troublesome, and I have little advice to give you. Often the issue is one of sheer breakage, or breakage and repair. For example, code using UIProgressView's `progressImage` property works in iOS 7.0, doesn't work at all from iOS 7.1 through iOS 8.4, and works in iOS 9 and iOS 10. You have no way of knowing this aside from trial and error, and working your way around it coherently is extremely tricky.

Unsupported features are a different story. If the compiler knows that a feature is unsupported by an earlier system, it will help prevent you from accidentally using that feature on that system. For example, here's how to start drawing a small image in iOS 10:

```
let r = UIGraphicsImageRenderer(size:CGSize(width:10,height:10))
```

The UIGraphicsImageRenderer class exists only in iOS 10.0 and later. If your deployment target is earlier than iOS 10.0, the compiler will stop you with an error: "UIGraphicsImageRenderer is only available on iOS 10.0 or newer." You cannot proceed until you guarantee to the compiler that this code will run only on iOS 10 or later. And Xcode's Fix-it feature will show you how to do that:

```
if #available(iOS 10.0, *) {
    let r = UIGraphicsImageRenderer(size:CGSize(width:10,height:10))
} else {
    // Fallback on earlier versions
}
```

The #available condition — an *availability check* — tests the current system against a set of requirements matching the actual availability of a feature as specified in its declaration. The UIGraphicsImageRenderer class declaration is preceded (in Swift) with this annotation:

```
@available(iOS 10.0, *)
```

For the detailed meaning of that annotation, consult the documentation. But you don't really need to understand it! Your #available condition should match that annotation, and Xcode's Fix-it will make sure that it does. You can use #available in an if condition or a guard condition.

You can annotate your own type and member declarations with an @available attribute, and your own code will then have to use an availability check. For example, if your method is declared @available(iOS 10.0, *), then you can't call that method, when the deployment target is earlier than iOS 10, without an availability check. Within such a method, you don't need any #available(iOS 10.0, *) availability checks, because you've already guaranteed that this method won't run on a system earlier than iOS 10.

To *test* your app on an earlier system, you'll need a device, real or simulated, *running* that earlier system. You can download an earlier Simulator SDK going back as far as iOS 8.1 through Xcode's Components preference pane (see Chapter 6), but to test on a system earlier than Xcode 8 will let you run, you'll need an older version of Xcode, or preferably an older device. This can be difficult to configure, and may not be worth the trouble.

Device Type

It can be useful, in the case of a universal app, to react to whether your code is running on an iPad, on the one hand, or an iPhone or iPod, on the other. The current UIDevice, or the traitCollection of any UIViewController or UIView in the hierarchy, will tell you the current device's type as its userInterfaceIdiom, which will be a UIUserInterfaceIdiom, either .phone or .pad.

You can load resources conditionally depending on the device type or screen resolution. In the case of images loaded from the top level of the app bundle, image files with the same name but different name suffixes can be used (such as @2x and @3x to indicate screen resolution, or ~iphone and ~ipad to indicate device type) so that the runtime will choose automatically the appropriate image variant for the current environment; but it is simpler wherever possible to use an asset catalog (see "Resources in an asset catalog" on page 323).

Similarly, certain *Info.plist* settings come with name suffixes, so you can adopt one setting on one device type and another setting on another. It is quite common, for example, for a universal app to adopt one set of possible orientations on iPhone and another set on iPad: typically, the iPhone version permits a limited set of orientations and the iPad version permits all orientations. You can configure this in the General pane when you edit the target:

1. Switch the Devices pop-up menu to iPhone and check the desired Device Orientation checkboxes for the iPhone.
2. Switch the Devices pop-up menu to iPad and check the desired Device Orientation checkboxes for the iPad.
3. Switch the Devices pop-up menu to Universal.

Even though you're now seeing just one set of orientations, both sets are remembered. What you've really done is to configure two groups of "Supported interface orientations" settings in the *Info.plist*, a general set (UISupportedInterface-Orientations) and an iPad-only set that overrides the general case when the app runs on an iPad (UISupportedInterfaceOrientations~ipad). Examine the *Info.plist* file to see that this is so.

In the same way, your app can load different nib files, and thus can display different interfaces, depending on the device type. For example, you can have two main storyboards, loading one of them at launch if this is an iPhone and the other if this is an iPad. Again, you can configure this in the General pane when you edit the target, and again, what you're really doing is telling the *Info.plist* setting "Main storyboard file base name" to appear twice, once for the general case (UIMainStoryboardFile) and once for iPad only (UIMainStoryboardFile~ipad). If your app loads a nib file by name, the naming of that nib file works like that of an image file: if there is an alternative nib file by the same name with ~ipad appended, it will load automatically if we are running on an iPad.

However, you are less likely than in the past to need to distinguish one device type from another. In iOS 7 and before, entire interface object classes (such as popovers) were available only on the iPad; in iOS 8 and later, there are no iPad-only classes, and the interface classes themselves adapt if your code is running on an iPhone. Similarly, in iOS 7 and before, a universal app might need a completely different interface, and hence a different set of nib files, depending on the device type; in iOS 8 and later, size classes allow a single nib file to be configured conditionally depending on the device type. And in general the physical distinction between an iPad and an iPhone is not so sharp as in the past: thanks to the intermediate iPhone 6 and (especially) the iPhone 6 Plus, it's more of a continuum.

Version Control

Sooner rather than later in the life of any real app, you should consider putting your project under version control. Version control is a way of taking periodic snapshots (technically called *commits*) of your project. Its purpose might be:

Security
> Version control can help you store your commits in a repository offsite, so that your code isn't lost in case of a local computer glitch or some equivalent "hit by a bus" scenario.

Collaboration
> Version control affords multiple developers ready, rational access to the same code.

Freedom from fear
> A project is a complicated thing; often, changes must be made experimentally, sometimes in many files, possibly over a period of many days, before a new feature can be tested. Version control means that I can easily retrace my steps (to some previous commit) if things go badly; this gives me confidence to start down some tentative programmatic road whose outcome may not be apparent until much later. Also, if I'm confused about what programmatic road I seem to be taking, I can ask a version control system to list the changes I've made recently. If an ancillary bug is introduced, I can use version control to pinpoint when it happened and help discover the cause.

Xcode provides various version control facilities, which are geared chiefly to git (*http://git-scm.com*) and Subversion (*http://subversion.apache.org*, also called svn). This doesn't mean you can't use any other version control system with your projects; it means only that you can't use any other version control system in an integrated fashion from inside Xcode. That's no disaster; there are many other ways to use version control, and even with git and Subversion, it is perfectly possible to ignore Xcode's integrated version control and rely on the Terminal command line, or use a specialized third-party GUI front end such as svnX for Subversion (*http://www.lacho seinteractive.net/en/products*) or SourceTree for git (*http://www.sourcetreeapp.com*).

If you prefer to manage your version control yourself, you can turn off Xcode's version control integration more or less completely. If you uncheck Enable Source Control in the Source Control preference pane, the only action you'll be able to take within Xcode is choose Check Out from the Source Control menu, to fetch code from a remote server. If you check Enable Source Control, three additional checkboxes let you select which automatic behaviors you want. Personally, I like to check Enable Source Control along with "Refresh local status automatically," so that Xcode displays a file's status in the Project navigator; I leave the other two checkboxes unchecked, because I'm a manual control kind of person.

When you create a new project, the Save dialog includes a checkbox that offers to place a git repository into your project folder from the outset. This can be purely local to your computer, or you can choose to associate it with a remote server. If you have no reason to decide otherwise, I suggest that you check that checkbox!

When you open an existing project, if that project is already managed with Subversion or git, Xcode detects this and is ready instantly to display version control information in its interface. If a remote repository is involved, Xcode automatically enters information for it in the Accounts preference pane, which is the unified interface for repository management. To use a remote server without having a working copy checked out from it, enter its information manually in the Accounts preference pane.

Source control actions are available in two places: the Source Control menu and the contextual menu in the Project navigator. To check out and open a project stored on a remote server, choose Source Control → Check Out. Other items in the Source Control menu are obvious, such as Commit, Push, Pull (or Update), Refresh Status, and Discard Changes. Note particularly the first item in the Source Control menu, which lists all open working copies by name and branch; its hierarchical menu items let you perform rudimentary branch management.

Files in the Project navigator are marked with their status. For example, if you're using git, you can distinguish modified files (M), new untracked files (?), and new files added to the index (A). (If you've unchecked "Refresh local status automatically," those markings may not appear until you choose Source Control → Refresh Status.)

When you choose Source Control → Commit, you're shown a comparison view of all changes in all changed files. Each change can be excluded from this commit (or reverted entirely), so it's possible to group related file hunks into meaningful commits. A similar comparison view is available for any commit by choosing Source Control → History. (But Xcode has nothing like the visual branch representation of git's own gitk tool.) Merge conflicts are also presented in a useful graphical comparison interface.

You can also see a comparison view for the file being currently edited, at any time, through the Version editor; choose View → Version Editor → Show Version Editor, or click the third Editor button in the project window toolbar. This handy feature is the main reason why I have Enable Source Control checked in the Source control

```
class LandscapeNavigationController :          5 class LandscapeNavigationController :
    UINavigationController {                         UINavigationController {
    override var                                6    override func
        supportedInterfaceOrientations :                supportedInterfaceOrientations() ->
        UIInterfaceOrientationMask {                    UIInterfaceOrientationMask {
        return .landscape                       7        return .landscape
    }                                           8    }
```

Figure 9-1. Version comparison

preference pane; I use it all the time to keep track of what I've done recently and to explore my project's commit history.

The Version editor actually has three modes: Comparison view, Blame view, and Log view (choose from View → Version Editor, or use the pop-up menu from the third Editor button in the toolbar). In Figure 9-1, I'm using Comparison view to see that in the more recent version of this file (on the left) I've changed my `supportedInterface-Orientations` implementation (because the Swift language changed). If I choose Editor → Copy Source Changes, the corresponding diff text (a patch file) is placed on the clipboard. If I switch to Blame view I can see my own commit message. The jump bar at the bottom of the Version editor permits me to view any commit's version of the current file in the editor.

Another way to learn how a line was changed is to select within that line (in the normal editor) and choose Editor → Show Blame For Line. A popover appears, describing the commit where this line changed to its current form; using buttons in that popover, you can switch to Blame view or Comparison view.

Editing and Navigating Your Code

Many aspects of Xcode's editing environment can be modified to suit your tastes. Your first step should be to pick a Source Editor font face and size you like in Xcode's Fonts & Colors preference pane. Nothing is so important as being able to read and write code comfortably! I like a largish size (13, 14 or even 16) and a pleasant monospaced font. New in Xcode 8, SF Mono is included and is the default; I think it's very nice. Other possibilities might be Menlo or Consolas, or the freeware Inconsolata (*http://levien.com/type/myfonts/*) or Source Code Pro (*https://github.com/adobe-fonts/source-code-pro*).

Xcode has some automatic formatting, autotyping, and text selection features. Their exact behavior depends upon your settings in the Editing and Indentation tabs of Xcode's Text Editing preference pane. I'm not going to describe these settings in detail, but I urge you to take advantage of them. Under Editing, I like to check just about everything, including Line Numbers; visible line numbers are useful when debugging. Under Indentation, I like to have just about everything checked too; I find the way Xcode lays out code to be excellent with these settings.

If you like Xcode's smart syntax-aware indenting, but you find that once in a while a line of code isn't indenting itself correctly, choose Editor → Structure → Re-Indent (Control-I), which autoindents the current line or selection.

With "Enable type-over completions" checked, Xcode helps balance delimiters. For example, suppose I intend to make a UIView by calling its initializer `init(frame:)`. I type as far as this:

```
let v = UIView(fr
```

Xcode automatically appends the closing right parenthesis, with the insertion point still positioned before it:

```
let v = UIView(fr)
// I have typed ^
```

That closing right parenthesis, however, is tentative; it's in gray. Now I finish typing the parameter; the right parenthesis is *still* gray:

```
let v = UIView(frame:r)
//        I have typed ^
```

I can now confirm the closing right parenthesis in any of several ways: I can actually type a right parenthesis, or I can type Tab or Right arrow. The tentative right parenthesis is replaced by a real right parenthesis, and the insertion point is now positioned after it, ready for me to continue typing. Xcode behaves similarly with double quotes, right curly braces, right square brackets, and so on.

Autocompletion

As you write code, you'll take advantage of Xcode's autocompletion feature. Cocoa type names and method names are astonishingly verbose, and whatever reduces your time and effort typing will be a relief. However, I personally do *not* check "Suggest completions while typing" under Editing; instead, I check "Use Escape key to show completion suggestions," and when I want autocompletion to happen, I ask for it manually, by pressing Esc.

For example, suppose I want my code to create an alert. I type as far as `UIAlert-Controller(` and press Esc. A menu pops up, listing the four initializers appropriate to a UIAlertController (Figure 9-2). You can navigate this menu, dismiss it, or accept the selection, using the mouse or the keyboard alone. I like to use the keyboard. So, if it were not already selected by default, I would navigate to `title:...` with the Down arrow key, and press Return to accept the selected choice.

When I choose from the autocompletion menu, the template for the method call is entered in my code (I've broken it into multiple lines here):

```
let alert = UIAlertController(|
    Ⓜ    UIAlertController ()
    Ⓜ    UIAlertController? (coder: NSCoder)
    Ⓜ    UIAlertController (nibName: String?, bundle: Bundle?)
    Ⓜ    UIAlertController (title: String?, message: String?, pr
```

Figure 9-2. The autocompletion menu

```
let alert = UIAlertController(
    title: <#String?#>,
    message: <#String?#>,
    preferredStyle: <#UIAlertControllerStyle#>)
```

The expressions in <#...#> are *placeholders*, showing the type of each parameter. They appear in Xcode as cartouche-like "text tokens" to prevent them from being edited accidentally. You can select the next placeholder with Tab or by choosing Navigate → Jump to Next Placeholder (Control-/). Thus I can select a placeholder and type over it, entering the actual argument I wish to pass, select the next placeholder and type that argument, and so forth. To convert a placeholder to a normal string without the delimiters, select it and press Return, or double-click it.

Autocompletion and its contextual intelligence works for object type names, method calls, and property names. It also works when you're entering a declaration for a function that's inherited or defined in an adopted protocol. You don't need to type even the initial func; just type the first few letters of the method's name. For example, in my app delegate class I might type:

```
applic
```

If I then press Esc, I see a list of methods such as application(_:didFinish-LaunchingWithOptions:); these are methods that might be sent to my app delegate (by virtue of its being the app delegate, as discussed in Chapter 11). When I choose one, the entire declaration is filled in for me, including the curly braces:

```
func application(_ application: UIApplication,
    didFinishLaunchingWithOptions
    launchOptions: [UIApplicationLaunchOptionsKey : Any]?) -> Bool {
        <#code#>
}
```

A placeholder for the code appears between the curly braces, and it is selected, ready for me to start entering the body of the function. If a function needs an override designation, Xcode's code completion provides it.

What you type in connection with autocompletion doesn't have to be the literal start of a symbol. As it does throughout the interface, Xcode will use intelligence in matching the components of the search term. If I know that the method I want to create is `application(_:didFinishLaunchingWithOptions:)`, I can get better search results by typing this:

```
appDidF
```

When I press Esc, `application(_:didFinishLaunchingWithOptions:)` is then *first* among the choices in the pop-up menu.

Snippets

Code autocompletion is supplemented by code snippets. A code snippet is a bit of text with an abbreviation. Code snippets are kept in the Code Snippet library (Command-Option-Control-2), but a code snippet's abbreviation is globally available to code completion, so you can use a snippet without showing the library: you type the abbreviation and the snippet's name is included among the possible completions.

For example, to enter a `class` declaration at the top level of a file, I would type `class` and press Esc, to get autocompletion, and choose Swift Subclass. The template for a class declaration appears in my code: the class name and superclass name are place-holders, the curly braces are provided, and the body of the declaration (between the curly braces) is another placeholder.

To learn a snippet's abbreviation, you must open its editing window — double-click the snippet in the Code Snippet library — and click Edit. If learning a snippet's abbre-viation is too much trouble, simply drag the snippet from the Code Snippet library into your text. The filter bar (Edit → Filter → Filter in Library, Command-Option-L) helps you reach a snippet by name quickly.

You can add your own snippets, which will be categorized as User snippets; the easiest way is to drag text into the Code Snippet library. Edit to suit your taste, providing a name, a description, and an abbreviation; the Completion Scopes pop-up menu lets you narrow the contexts in which the snippet will be available through code comple-tion. In the text of the snippet, use the <#...#> construct to form any desired place-holders.

For example, I've created an `outlet` snippet (Chapter 7) defined like this:

```
@IBOutlet var <#name#> : <#type#>!
```

And I've created an `action` snippet defined like this:

```
@IBAction func <#name#> (_ sender: Any) {
    <#code#>
}
```

My other snippets constitute a personal library of utility functions that I've devel-oped. For example, my `delay` snippet inserts my `DispatchQueue.main.asyncAfter` wrapper function (see "Delayed Performance" on page 516).

```
    let transform2 : CGAffineTransform = transform1.inverted
          ⊘ Function produces expected type 'CGAffineTransform'; did you mean to call it with '()'?



          ⊘ Function produces expected type 'CGAffineTransform'; did you mean to call it with '()'?
          Fix-it  Insert "()"

   12 : CGAffineTransform = transform1.inverted()
          ⊘ Function produces expected type 'CGAffineTransform'; did you mean to call it with '()'?
```

Figure 9-3. A compile error with a Fix-it suggestion

Fix-it and Live Syntax Checking

Xcode's Fix-it feature can make *and implement* positive suggestions on how to avert a problem. To summon it, click on an issue badge in the gutter. Such an issue badge will appear after compilation if there's a problem.

For instance, Figure 9-3, at the top, shows that I've accidentally forgotten the parentheses after a method call. This causes a compile error. But the stop-sign icon next to the error tells me that Fix-it has a suggestion. I click the stop-sign icon, and Figure 9-3, at the bottom, shows what happens: a Fix-it dialog pops up, telling me how it proposes to fix the problem — by inserting the parentheses. Moreover, Xcode is showing me what my code would look like if Fix-it *did* fix the problem in this way. If I press Return, or double-click the "Fix-it" suggestion in the dialog, Xcode *really* inserts the parentheses — and the error vanishes, because the problem is solved.

 If you're confident that Xcode will do the right thing, choose Editor → Fix All in Scope (Command-Option-Control-F), and Xcode will implement *all* nearby Fix-it suggestions without your even having to show the dialog.

Live syntax checking is like a form of continual compilation. Even if you don't compile or save, live syntax checking can detect the presence of a problem, and can suggest the solution with Fix-it. This feature can be toggled on or off using the "Show live issues" checkbox in the General preference pane.

Personally, I find live syntax checking intrusive. My code is almost never valid while I'm in the middle of typing, because the terms and parentheses are always half-finished; that's what it means to be typing! For example, merely typing the first letter of let will instantly cause the syntax checker to complain of an unresolved identifier; I hate that. So I've got "Show live issues" unchecked.

Navigation

Developing an Xcode project involves editing code in many files at once. Fortunately, Xcode provides numerous ways to navigate your code, many of which have been mentioned in previous chapters. Here are some of Xcode's chief forms of navigation:

The Project navigator

If you know something about the name of a file, you can find it quickly in the Project navigator (Command-1) by typing into the search field in the filter bar at the bottom of the navigator (Edit → Filter → Filter in Navigator, Command-Option-J). For example, type `story` to see just your *.storyboard* files. Moreover, after using the filter bar, you can press Tab and then the Up or Down arrow key to navigate the Project navigator; thus you can reach the desired file with the keyboard alone.

The Symbol navigator

If you highlight the first two icons in the filter bar (the first two are blue, the third is dark), the Symbol navigator lists your project's object types and their members. Click on a symbol to navigate to its declaration in the editor. As with the Project navigator, the filter bar's search field can help get you where you want to go.

The jump bar

Every path component of the code editor's jump bar is a menu:

The bottom level

At the bottom level (farthest right) in the jump bar is a list of your file's object and member declarations, in the order in which they appear (hold Command while choosing the menu to see them in alphabetical order); choose one to navigate to it. This menu can also be filtered; just start typing while any jump bar menu is open, to filter what the menu displays.

Higher levels

Higher-level path components are hierarchical menus; thus you can use any of them to work your way down the file hierarchy.

History

Each editor pane remembers the names of files you've edited in it. The Back and Forward triangles are both buttons and pop-up menus (or choose Navigate → Go Back and Navigate → Go Forward, Command-Control-Left and Command-Control-Right).

Related items

The leftmost button in the jump bar summons the Related Items menu, a hierarchical menu of files related to the current file, such as superclasses and adopted protocols. This list even includes functions that call or are called by the currently selected function.

 Your code can inject bold section titles into the jump bar's bottom-level menu using a comment whose first word is MARK:. To make a divider line in the menu, type a MARK: comment whose value is a hyphen. For example, try modifying *ViewController.swift* in our Empty Window project, and then look in the bottom-level jump bar menu:

```
// MARK: -
// MARK: view lifecycle
override func viewDidLoad() {
    super.viewDidLoad()
}
```

Similarly, comments starting with TODO: and FIXME: will appear in the bottom-level menu.

The Assistant pane
The Assistant pane lets you be in two places at once (see Chapter 6). Hold Option while navigating to open something in an Assistant pane instead of the primary editor pane. The Tracking menu in an Assistant pane's jump bar sets its automatic relationship to the main pane.

Tabs and windows
You can also be in two places at once by opening a tab or a separate window (again, see Chapter 6).

Jump to definition
Navigate → Jump to Definition (Command-Control-J) lets you jump to the declaration of the symbol already selected in your code.

Open quickly
File → Open Quickly (Command-Shift-O) opens a dialog where you can search for a symbol in your code and in the framework headers.

Breakpoints
The Breakpoint navigator lists all breakpoints in your code. Xcode lacks code bookmarks, but you can misuse a disabled breakpoint as a bookmark. Breakpoints are discussed later in this chapter.

Finding

Finding is a form of navigation. Xcode has both a global find (Find → Find in Project, Command-Shift-F), which is the same as using the Find navigator, and an editor-level find (Find → Find, Command-F); don't confuse them.

Figure 9-4. A call hierarchy in the Find navigator

Find options are all-important. For editor-level find, click the magnifying glass icon in the search field to get the Edit Find Options item. You can search for word middles or word starts, case sensitive or insensitive — you can even find using regular expressions. There's a lot of power lurking here!

The global find options appear above and below the search field, and include a scope, allowing you to specify in sophisticated ways which files will be searched: click the current scope to see the Search Scopes panel, where you can select a different scope or create a custom scope. Global find options above the search field include Text, Regular Expression, Definitions (where a symbol is defined), and References (where a symbol is used).

Don't neglect the Call Hierarchy global find option, which allows you to trace the nests of calls backward through your code. Click the second item in the search bar to summon the pop-up menu, and choose Call Hierarchy; alternatively, select a term in your code and choose Find → Find Call Hierarchy (Shift-Control-Command-H). The call hierarchy is displayed inverted in the Find navigator (Figure 9-4).

To replace text, click the word Find at the left end of the search bar to summon the pop-up menu, and choose Replace. You can replace all occurrences (Replace All), or select particular find results in the Find navigator and replace only those (Replace); you can also *delete* find results from the Find navigator, to protect them from being affected by Replace All. The Find navigator's Preview button summons a dialog that shows you the effect of each possible replacement, and lets you accept or reject particular replacements in advance of performing the replacement. For editor-level find, hold Option before clicking Replace All, to find-and-replace within only the current selection.

A sophisticated form of editor-level find is Editor → Edit All In Scope, which finds simultaneously all occurrences of the currently selected term within the same scope;

you can use this to change the name of a variable or function throughout its scope, or just to survey how the name is used.

Running in the Simulator

When you build and run with the Simulator as the destination, you run in the iOS Simulator application. The Simulator window represents a device. Depending on your app target's Base SDK, Deployment Target, and Targeted Device Family build settings, and on what SDKs you have installed, you may have choices about the device and system to be represented by the Simulator as you choose your destination before running (see Chapter 6).

The Simulator window can be displayed at various sizes: choose from Window → Scale. This is a matter of display merely, comparable to zooming the window. For example, you might run a double-resolution device in the Simulator at full size to see every pixel, or at half size to save space.

You can interact with the Simulator in some of the same basic ways as you would a device. Using the mouse, you can tap on the device's screen; hold Option to make the mouse represent two fingers moving symmetrically around their common center, and Option-Shift to represent two fingers moving in parallel. To click the Home button, choose Hardware → Home (Command-Shift-H). Items in the Hardware menu also let you perform hardware gestures such as rotating the device, shaking it, and locking its screen; you can also test your app by simulating certain rare events, such as a low-memory situation.

 Clicking the Home button to switch from the app you're running in Xcode to the home screen does *not* stop your app running, in Xcode or the Simulator. To quit your app in the Simulator, quit the Simulator, or switch to Xcode and choose Product → Stop.

The Debug menu in the Simulator is useful for detecting problems with animations and drawing. Toggle Slow Animations makes animations unfold in slow motion so that you can see in detail what's happening. The next four menu items (their names begin with Color) are similar to features available when running using Instruments, under the Core Animation instrument, revealing possible sources of inefficiency in screen drawing.

The Debug menu also lets you open the log in the Console application, and lets you set the simulated device's location (useful when testing a Core Location app).

Debugging

Debugging is the art of figuring out what's wrong with the behavior of your app as it runs. I divide this art into two main techniques: caveman debugging and pausing your running app.

Caveman Debugging

Caveman debugging consists of altering your code, usually temporarily, typically by adding code to dump informative messages into the console. The standard procedure is to read those messages in the project window's Debug pane as your app runs.

The Swift command for sending a message to the console is the print function. Using Swift's string interpolation and the CustomStringConvertible protocol (which requires a description property; see Chapter 4), you can pack a lot of useful information into a print call. Cocoa objects generally have a built-in description property implementation. For example:

```
print(self.view)
```

The output in the console reads something like this (I've formatted it for clarity here):

```
<UIView: 0x79121d40;
    frame = (0 0; 320 480);
    autoresize = RM+BM;
    layer = <CALayer: 0x79121eb0>>
```

We learn the object's class, its address in memory (useful for confirming whether two instances are in fact the same instance), and the values of some additional properties.

If you're importing Foundation — and in real-life iOS programming, you are — you also have access to the NSLog C function. It takes an NSString which operates as a format string, followed by the format arguments. A *format string* is a string containing symbols called *format specifiers*, for which values (the format arguments) will be substituted at runtime. All format specifiers begin with a percent sign (%), so the only way to enter a literal percent sign in a format string is as a double percent sign (%%). The character(s) following the percent sign specify the type of value that will be supplied at runtime. The most common format specifiers are %@ (an object reference), %d (an int), %ld (a long), and %f (a double). For example:

```
NSLog("the view: %@", self.view)
```

In that example, self.view is the first (and only) format argument, so its value will be substituted for the first (and only) format specifier, %@, when the format string is printed in the console:

```
2015-01-26 10:43:35.314 Empty Window[23702:809945]
  the view: <UIView: 0x7c233b90;
    frame = (0 0; 320 480);
    autoresize = RM+BM;
    layer = <CALayer: 0x7c233d00>>
```

I like NSLog's output because it provides the current time and date, along with the process name, process ID, and thread ID (useful for determining whether two logging statements are called on the same thread). Also, NSLog is thread-safe, whereas print is not. In addition, NSLog output appears in the device's console, whereas print output does not.

For the complete repertory of format specifiers available in a format string, see "String Format Specifiers" in Apple's *String Programming Guide*. The format specifiers are largely based on those of the C printf standard library function.

The main ways to go wrong with NSLog (or any format string) are to supply a different number of format arguments from the number of format specifiers in the string, or to supply an argument value different from the type declared by the corresponding format specifier. I often see beginners claim that logging shows a certain value to be nonsense, when in fact it is their NSLog call that is nonsense; for example, a format specifier was %d but the value of the corresponding argument was a float. Another common mistake is treating an NSNumber as if it were the type of number it contains; an NSNumber isn't any kind of number — it's an object (%@). Problems with signed vs. unsigned integers, or 32-bit vs. 64-bit numbers, can be tricky as well.

C structs are not objects, so they cannot provide a description. But Swift extends some of the most common C structs as Swift structs, and thus allows them to be printed with print. Thus, for example, this works:

```
print(self.view.frame) // (0.0,0.0,320.0,480.0)
```

However, you can't do the same thing with NSLog. For this reason, common Cocoa structs are usually accompanied by convenience functions that render them as strings. For example:

```
NSLog("%@", NSStringFromCGRect(self.view.frame))
// {{0, 0}, {320, 480}}
```

 Swift defines four special literals, particularly useful when logging because they describe their own position in the surrounding file: #file, #line, #column, and #function.

Another useful form of caveman debugging is deliberately aborting your app because something has gone seriously wrong. See the discussion of assert, precondition, and fatalError in Chapter 5. precondition and fatalError work even in a Release build. By default, assert never fails in a Release build, so it is safe to leave it in your code when your app is ready to ship; by that time, of course, you should be confident

Reducing the overhead of print

Even though `print` statements do not print into the device's console, they are executed even in a Release build and even on a device, and such execution may carry some overhead. In particular, the arguments are still evaluated. Here's a workaround for the common situation where your `print` call has only one argument. You can push evaluation of that argument back one level by overshadowing Swift's `print` function with your own custom `print` top-level function that uses `@autoclosure`, just as `assert` does (Chapter 5):

```
func print(_ item: @autoclosure () -> Any,
    separator: String = " ", terminator: String = "\n") {
        #if DEBUG
        Swift.print(item(), separator:separator, terminator: terminator)
        #endif
}
```

When you say `print(myExpensiveFunction())` now, that custom `print` function is called. This means that `myExpensiveFunction()` is wrapped in a closure and isn't evaluated. If you define -DDEBUG under the Other Swift Flags for the Debug configuration only, then when the app is built with the Release build configuration, `myExpensiveFunction()` will *never* be evaluated, because `item()` won't be called.

that the bad situation your `assert` was intended to detect has been debugged and will never actually occur.

Purists may scoff at caveman debugging, but I use it heavily: it's easy, informative, and lightweight. And sometimes it's the only way. Unlike the debugger, console logging works with any build configuration (Debug or Release) and wherever your app runs (in the Simulator or on a device). It works when pausing is impossible (because of threading issues, for example). It even works on someone else's device, such as a tester to whom you've distributed your app. It's a little tricky for a tester to get a look at the console so as to be able to report back to you, but it can be done: for example, the tester can connect the device to a computer and view its log in Xcode's Devices window.

The Xcode Debugger

When you're building and running in Xcode, you can pause in the debugger and use Xcode's debugging facilities. The important thing, if you want to use the debugger, is that the app should be built with the Debug build configuration (the default for a scheme's Run action). The debugger is not very helpful against an app built with the Release build configuration, not least because compiler optimizations can destroy the correspondence between steps in the compiled code and lines in your code.

Figure 9-5. A breakpoint

Figure 9-6. A disabled breakpoint

Breakpoints

There isn't a strong difference between running and debugging in Xcode; the main distinction is whether breakpoints are effective or ignored. The effectiveness of break-points can be toggled at two levels:

Globally (active vs. inactive)
Breakpoints as a whole are either *active or inactive*. If breakpoints are inactive, we won't pause at any breakpoints.

Individually (enabled vs. disabled)
A given breakpoint is either *enabled or disabled*. Even if breakpoints are active, we won't pause at this one if it is disabled. Disabling a breakpoint allows you to leave in place a breakpoint that you might need later without pausing at it every time it's encountered.

To create a breakpoint (Figure 9-5), select in the editor the line where you want to pause, and choose Debug → Breakpoints → Add Breakpoint at Current Line (Command-\). This keyboard shortcut toggles between adding and removing a breakpoint for the current line. The breakpoint is symbolized by an arrow in the gut-ter. Alternatively, a simple click in the gutter adds a breakpoint; to remove a break-point gesturally, drag it out of the gutter.

To disable a breakpoint at the current line, click on the breakpoint in the gutter to toggle its enabled status. Alternatively, Control-click on the breakpoint and choose Disable Breakpoint in the contextual menu. A dark breakpoint is enabled; a light breakpoint is disabled (Figure 9-6).

To toggle the active status of breakpoints as a whole, click the Breakpoints button in the bar at the top of the Debug pane, or choose Debug → Activate/Deactivate Break-points (Command-Y). The active status of breakpoints as a whole doesn't affect the enabled or disabled status of any breakpoints; if breakpoints are inactive, they are simply ignored *en masse*, and no pausing at breakpoints takes place. Breakpoint arrows are blue if breakpoints are active, gray if they are inactive.

Once you have some breakpoints in your code, you'll want to survey and manage them. That's what the Breakpoint navigator is for. Here you can navigate to a breakpoint, enable or disable a breakpoint by clicking on its arrow in the navigator, and delete a breakpoint.

You can also edit a breakpoint's behavior. Control-click on the breakpoint, in the gutter or in the Breakpoint navigator, and choose Edit Breakpoint; or Command-Option-click the breakpoint. This is a very powerful facility: you can have a breakpoint pause only under a certain condition or after it has been encountered a certain number of times, and you can have a breakpoint perform one or more actions when it is encountered, such as issuing a debugger command, logging, playing a sound, speaking text, or running a script.

A breakpoint can be configured to continue automatically after performing its action when it is encountered. This can be an excellent alternative to caveman debugging: instead of inserting a print or NSLog call, which must be compiled into your code and later removed when the app is released, you can set a breakpoint that logs and continues. By definition, such a breakpoint operates only when you're actively debugging the project; it won't dump any messages into the console when the app runs on a user's device, because breakpoints exist in Xcode, not on a user's device.

Certain special kinds of breakpoint can be created in the Breakpoint navigator — click the Plus button at the bottom of the navigator and choose from its pop-up menu — or by choosing from the Debug → Breakpoints hierarchical menu:

Exception breakpoint
> An exception breakpoint causes your app to pause at the time an exception is thrown or caught, without regard to whether the exception would crash your app later. I recommend that you create an exception breakpoint to pause on all exceptions when they are thrown, because this gives the best view of the call stack and variable values at the moment of the exception (rather than later when the crash actually occurs); you can see where you are in your code, and you can examine variable values, which may help you understand the cause of the problem. If you do create such an exception breakpoint, I also suggest that you use the contextual menu to say Move Breakpoint To → User, which makes this breakpoint global to all your projects.

> Sometimes Apple's code will throw an exception and catch it, deliberately. This isn't a crash, and nothing has gone wrong; but if you've created an exception breakpoint, your app will pause at it, which can be confusing.

Swift error breakpoint
> Similar to an exception breakpoint, but it pauses when your code says throw.

Symbolic breakpoint
> A symbolic breakpoint causes your app to pause when a certain method or function is called, regardless of what object called it. The method doesn't have to be

Figure 9-7. Paused at a breakpoint

your method! Thus, a symbolic breakpoint can help you understand Cocoa's behavior. A method may be specified in one of two ways:

Using Objective-C notation
The instance method or class method symbol (- or +) followed by square brackets containing the class name and the method name. For example:

```
-[UIApplication beginReceivingRemoteControlEvents]
```

By method name
The method name alone. The debugger will resolve this for you into all possible class–method pairs, as if you had entered them using the Objective-C notation that I just described. For example:

```
beginReceivingRemoteControlEvents
```

If you enter the method name (or class name) incorrectly, the symbolic breakpoint won't do anything. In general, you'll know if you got it right, because you'll see the resolved breakpoint listed hierarchically below yours.

Paused at a breakpoint

When the app runs with breakpoints active and an enabled breakpoint is encountered (and assuming its conditions are met, and so on), the app pauses. In the active project window, the editor shows the file containing the point of execution, which will usually be the file containing the breakpoint. The point of execution is shown as a green arrow; this is the line that is *about* to be executed (Figure 9-7). Depending on the settings for Running → Pauses in the Behaviors preference pane, the Debug navigator and the Debug pane may also appear.

Here are some things you might like to do while paused at a breakpoint:

See where you are
One common reason for setting a breakpoint is to make sure that the path of execution is passing through a certain line. Functions listed in the call stack in the Debug navigator with a User icon, with the text in black, are yours; click one to see where you are paused in that function. (Listings with the text in gray are functions and methods for which you have no source code, so there would be little point clicking one unless you know something about assembly language.) You can also view and navigate the call stack using the jump bar at the top of the Debug pane.

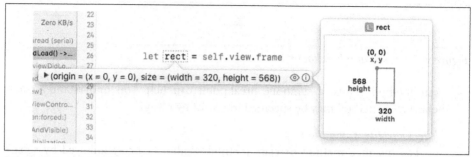

Figure 9-8. A data tip

Study variable values

In the Debug pane, variable values for the current scope (corresponding to what's selected in the call stack) are visible in the variables list. You can see additional object features, such as collection elements, properties, and even some private information, by opening triangles. (Local variable values are shown even if, at the point where you are paused, those variables have not yet been initialized; *such values are meaningless*, so ignore them.)

You can use the search field to filter variables by name or value. If a formatted summary isn't sufficiently helpful, you can send description (or, if this object adopts CustomDebugStringConvertible, debugDescription) to an object variable and view the output in the console: choose Print Description of [Variable] from the contextual menu, or select the variable and click the Info button below the variables list.

You can also view a variable's value graphically: select the variable and click the Quick Look button (an eye icon) below the variables list, or press Spacebar. For example, in the case of a CGRect, the graphical representation is a correctly proportioned rectangle. You can make instances of your own custom class viewable in the same way; declare the following method and return an instance of one of the permitted types (see Apple's *Quick Look for Custom Types in the Xcode Debugger*):

```
@objc func debugQuickLookObject() -> Any {
    // ... create and return your graphical object here ...
}
```

You can also inspect a variable's value in place in your code, by examining its data tip. To see a data tip, hover the mouse over the name of a variable in your code. The data tip is much like the display of this value in the variables list: there's a flippy triangle that you can open to see more information, plus an Info button that displays the value description here and in the console, and a Quick Look button for showing a value graphically (Figure 9-8).

Inspect your view hierarchy

You can study the view hierarchy while paused in the debugger. Click the Debug View Hierarchy button in the bar at the top of the Debug pane, or choose Debug → View Debugging → Capture View Hierarchy. Views are listed in an outline in the Debug navigator. The editor displays your views; this is a three-dimensional projection that you can rotate. The Object inspector and the Size inspector display information about the currently selected view.

Inspect your object graph

You can study your object graph (what objects you've created and how they are referring to one another) while paused in the debugger. I'll talk more about that later in this chapter.

Manage expressions

An expression is code to be added to the variables list and evaluated every time we pause. Choose Add Expression from the contextual menu in the variables list. The expression is evaluated within the current context in your code, so be careful of side effects.

Talk to the debugger

You can communicate directly with the debugger through the console. Xcode's debugger interface is a front end to the *real* debugger, LLDB (*http://lldb.llvm.org*); by talking directly to LLDB, you can do everything that you can do through the Xcode debugger interface, and more. Common commands are:

`fr v` *(short for* `frame variable`*)*
Alone, prints out all variables locally in scope, similar to the display in the variables list. Alternatively, can be followed by the name of a variable you want to examine.

`ty loo` *(short for* `type lookup`*)*
Followed by a type name, dumps a full declaration for the type, listing all its members (properties and methods).

`p` *(or* `expression`, `expr`, *or simply* `e`*)*
Evaluates, in the current context, any expression in the current language. Be careful of your expression's side effects!

`po` *(meaning "print object")*
Like `p`, but displays the value of the expression in accordance with its `description` or `debugDescription` (similar to Print Description).

Fiddle with breakpoints

You are free to create, destroy, edit, enable and disable, and otherwise manage breakpoints dynamically even while your app is running, which is useful because where you'd like to pause next might depend on what you learn while you're paused here. Indeed, this is one of the main advantages of breakpoints over caveman debugging. To change your caveman debugging, you have to stop the app, edit it, rebuild it, and start running the app all over again. But to fiddle with breakpoints, you don't have to be stopped; you don't even have to be paused! An operation that went wrong, if it doesn't crash your app, can probably be repeated in real time; so you can just add a breakpoint and try again. For example, if tapping a button produces the wrong results, you can add a breakpoint to the action handler and tap the button again; you pass through the same code, and this time you can work out what the trouble is.

Step or continue

To proceed with your paused app, you can either resume running until the next breakpoint is encountered (Debug → Continue) or take one step and pause again. Also, you can select in a line and choose Debug → Continue to Current Line (or Continue to Here from the contextual menu), which effectively sets a breakpoint at the chosen line, continues, and removes the breakpoint. The stepping commands (in the Debug menu) are:

Step Over

Pause at the next line.

Step Into

Pause in your function that the current line calls, if there is one; otherwise, pause at the next line.

Step Out

Pause when we return from the current function.

You can access these commands through convenient buttons in the bar at the top of the Debug pane. Even if the Debug pane is collapsed, the bar containing the buttons appears while running.

Start over, or abort

To kill the running app, click Stop in the toolbar (Product → Stop, Command-Period). Clicking the Home button in the Simulator (Hardware → Home) or on the device does *not* stop the running app in the multitasking world of iOS 4 and later. To kill the running app and relaunch it without rebuilding it, Control-click Run in the toolbar (Product → Perform Action → Run Without Building, Command-Control-R).

You can make changes to your code while the app is running or paused, but those changes are not magically communicated to the running app; there are programming milieus where that sort of thing is possible, but Xcode is not among them. You must stop the app and run in the normal way (which includes building) to see your changes in action.

Testing

A *test* is code that isn't part of your app target; its purpose is to make sure that your app works as expected. Tests can be of two kinds:

Unit tests

> A unit test exercises your app target *internally*, from the point of view of its *code*. For example, a unit test might call some method in your app target code, handing it various parameters and looking to see if the expected result is returned each time, not just under normal conditions but also when incorrect or extreme inputs are supplied.

Interface (UI) tests

> An interface test exercises your app *externally*, from the point of view of a *user*. Such a test guides your app through use case scenarios by effectively tapping buttons with a ghost finger, watching to make sure that the interface behaves as expected.

Tests should ideally be written and run constantly as you develop your app. It can even be useful to write unit tests *before* writing the real code, as a way of developing a working algorithm. Having initially ascertained that your code passes your tests, you continue to run those tests to detect whether a bug has been introduced during the course of development.

Tests are bundled in a separate target of your project (see Chapter 6). The application templates give you an opportunity to add a test target at the time you create your project: in the second dialog ("Choose options"), where you name your project, you can check Include Unit Tests or Include UI Tests, or both. Alternatively, you can easily create a new test target at any time: make a new target and specify iOS → Test → iOS Unit Testing Bundle or iOS UI Testing Bundle. Your tests do not run until you explicitly run them. Tests can be managed and run easily from the Test navigator (Command-5) as well as from within a test class file.

A test class is a subclass of XCTestCase (which is itself a subclass of XCTest). A test method is an instance method of a test class, returning no value and taking no parameters, whose name starts with test. The test target depends upon the app target, meaning that before a test class can be compiled and built, the app target must be compiled and built.

 To build your test target, so as to learn whether its code compiles successfully, choose Product → Build For → Testing.

A test method may call one or more test asserts; in Swift, these are global functions whose names begin with XCTAssert. For a list of these functions, see Apple's document *Testing With Xcode*, in the "Writing Test Classes and Methods" chapter, under

"Assertions Listed by Category." Unlike the corresponding Objective-C macros, the Swift test assert functions do *not* take format strings (the way NSLog does); each takes a single, simple message string. Test assert functions marked as being "for scalars" are not really for scalars in Swift, because in Swift there are no scalars (as opposed to objects): they apply to any types that adopt Equatable or Comparable.

A test class may also contain utility methods that are called by the test methods. In addition, you can override any of four special methods inherited from XCTestCase:

setUp *class method*
    Called once before *all* test methods in the class.

setUp *instance method*
    Called before *each* test method.

tearDown *instance method*
    Called after *each* test method.

tearDown *class method*
    Called once after *all* test methods in the class.

Running a test also runs the app. The test target's product is a bundle; a unit test bundle is loaded into the app as it launches, whereas an interface test bundle is loaded into a special test runner app generated for you by Xcode. Resources, such as test data, can be included in the bundle. You might use setUp to load such resources; you can get a reference to the bundle by way of the test class, as Bundle(for:type(of:self)).

Unit tests can see into the app target, because they are part of the same app; but, being a bundle, they also constitute a module. Therefore, the test target must import the app target as a module. To overcome privacy restrictions, the import statement should be preceded by the @testable attribute; this attribute temporarily changes internal (explicit or implicit) to public throughout the app target.

As an example of writing and running a unit test method, let's use our Empty Window project. Give the ViewController class a (nonsensical) instance method dogMyCats:

```
func dogMyCats(_ s:String) -> String {
    return ""
}
```

The method dogMyCats is supposed to receive any string and return the string "dogs". At the moment, though, it doesn't; it returns an empty string instead. That's a bug. Now we'll write a test method to ferret out this bug.

In the Empty Window project, choose File → New → Target and specify iOS → Test → iOS Unit Testing Bundle. Call the product *EmptyWindowTests*; observe that the target to be tested is the app target. Click Finish. In the Project navigator, a new group has been created, EmptyWindowTests, containing a single test file, *EmptyWindow-Tests.swift*. It contains a test class EmptyWindowTests, including stubs for two test methods, testExample and testPerformanceExample; comment out those two methods. We're going to replace them with a test method that calls dogMyCats and makes an assertion about the result:

1. At the top of *EmptyWindowTests.swift*, where we are importing XCTest, we must also import the app target:

   ```
   @testable import Empty_Window
   ```

2. Prepare an instance property in the declaration of the EmptyWindowTests class to store our ViewController instance:

   ```
   var viewController = ViewController()
   ```

3. Write the test method. Its name must start with test! Let's call it testDogMyCats. It has access to the ViewController instance as self.viewController:

   ```
   func testDogMyCats() {
       let input = "cats"
       let output = "dogs"
       XCTAssertEqual(output,
           self.viewController.dogMyCats(input),
           "Failed to produce \(output) from \(input)")
   }
   ```

We are now ready to run our test! There are many ways to do this. Switch to the Test navigator, and you'll see that it lists our test target, our test class, and our test method. Hover the mouse over any name, and a button appears to its right. By clicking the appropriate button, you can thus run all tests in every test class, all tests in the Emp-tyWindowTests class, or just the testDogMyCats test. But wait, there's more! Back in *EmptyWindowTests.swift*, there's also a diamond-shaped indicator in the gutter to the left of the class declaration and the test method name; when you hover the mouse over it, it changes to a Run button. You can click that button to run, respectively, all tests in this class or an individual test. Or, to run all tests, you can choose Product → Test. (After running a test, to run just that test again, choose Product → Perform Action → Test Again.)

So now let's run testDogMyCats. The app target is compiled and built; the test target is compiled and built. (If any of those steps fails, we can't test, and we'll be back on familiar ground with a compile error or a build error.) The app launches in the Simu-lator, and the test runs.

The test fails! (Well, we knew that was going to happen, didn't we?) The error is described in a banner next to the assert that failed in our code, as well as in the Issue navigator and the Report navigator. Moreover, red X marks appear everywhere — in the Test navigator next to testDogMyCats, in the Issue navigator, in the Report navigator, and in *EmptyWindowTests.swift* next to the class declaration and the first line of testDogMyCats.

Now let's fix our code. In *ViewController.swift*, modify dogMyCats to return "dogs" instead of an empty string. Now run the test again. It passes!

Recently run tests are listed in the Report navigator. When you select one, the editor displays two panes. The Tests pane lists in simple outline form what tests passed and failed, including the text of any assertion failure messages. The Logs pane goes into much more detail; by expanding transcripts, you can see the full console output from the test run, including any caveman debugging messages (print) that you may have sent from your test code.

When a test failure occurs, you might like to pause at the point where the assertion is about to fail. To do so, in the Breakpoint navigator, click the Plus button at the bottom and choose Add Test Failure Breakpoint. This is like an Exception breakpoint, pausing on the assert line in your test method just before it reports failure. You could then switch to the method being tested, for example, and debug it, examining its variables and so forth, to work out the reason for the impending failure.

There's a helpful feature allowing you to navigate between a method and a test that calls it: when the selection is within a method, the Related Items menu in the jump bar includes Test Callers. The same is true of the Tracking menu in an assistant pane.

In our example, we made a new ViewController instance in order to initialize EmptyWindowTests's self.viewController. But what if our test required us to get a reference to the *existing* ViewController instance? This is the same general problem of getting a reference to an instance that crops up so often in iOS programming (see "Instance References" on page 133, and Chapter 13). The test code runs inside a bundle that is effectively injected into your running app. This means that it can see app globals such as UIApplication.shared. From there, you can work your way to the desired reference:

```
if let viewController =
    (UIApplication.shared.delegate as? AppDelegate)?
        .window?.rootViewController as? ViewController {
            // ...
}
```

Organization of your test methods into test targets (suites) and test classes is largely a matter of convenience; it dictates the layout of the Test navigator and which tests will be run together, plus each test class has its own properties, its own setUp method, and so on. To make a new test target or a new test class, click the Plus button at the bottom of the Test navigator.

You can also edit a scheme's Test action to dictate what tests will be run when you choose Product → Test.

In addition to simple unit tests of the type I've just illustrated, there are two other forms of unit test:

Asynchronous testing

Allows a test method to be called back after a time-consuming operation. In your test method, you create an XCTestExpectation object by calling the factory method expectation(withDescription:); then you initiate an operation that takes a completion handler, and call waitForExpectations(with-Timeout:handler:). One of two things will happen:

The operation completes

The completion handler is called. In the completion handler, you perform any asserts having to do with the result of the operation, and then call fulfill on the XCTestExpectation object. This causes the timeout handler to be called.

The operation times out

The timeout handler is called. Thus, the timeout handler is called either way, allowing you to clean up as necessary.

Similarly, factory methods like expectation(for:evaluatedWith:handler:) allow you to wait without polling for a predicate to become true.

Performance testing

Allows you to test that the speed of an operation has not fallen off. In your test method, you call measure with a function argument in which you do something (possibly many times, so as to get a reasonable time measurement sample). If the block involves setup and teardown that you don't want included in the measurement, call measureMetrics(_:automaticallyStartMeasuring:for:) instead, and wrap the heart of the block with calls to startMeasuring and stop-Measuring.

The performance test runs your block several times, recording how long each run takes. The first time you run a performance test, it fails, but you establish a baseline measurement. On subsequent runs, it fails if the standard deviation of the runs is too far from the baseline, or if the average time has grown too much.

Now let's experiment with interface testing. I'm going to assume that you still have (from Chapter 7) a button in the Empty Window interface with an action method hooked to a ViewController method that summons an alert. We'll write a test that taps that button and makes sure that the alert is summoned. Add an iOS UI Testing Bundle to the project; call it *EmptyWindowUITests*.

Interface test code is based on *accessibility*, a feature that allows the screen interface to be described verbally and to be manipulated programmatically. It revolves around three classes: XCUIElement, XCUIApplication (an XCUIElement subclass), and XCUIElementQuery. To a large extent, you can avoid learning anything about these classes, because accessibility actions are *recordable*. This means that you can generate your code by performing the actual actions that constitute the test. Let's try it:

1. In the `testExample` stub method, create a new empty line and leave the insertion point within it.

2. Choose Editor → Start Recording UI Test. (Alternatively, there's a Record button at the bottom of the project window, in the debug bar.) The app launches in the Simulator.

3. Tap the button in the interface. When the alert appears, tap OK to dismiss it.

4. Return to Xcode and choose Editor → Stop Recording UI Test. Also choose Product → Stop to stop running in the Simulator.

The following code has been generated (assuming that your interface button's title is "Hello"):

```
let app = XCUIApplication()
app.buttons["Hello"].tap()
app.alerts["Howdy!"].collectionViews.buttons["OK"].tap()
```

The `app` object, obviously, is an XCUIApplication instance. Properties such as `buttons` and `alerts` return XCUIElementQuery objects. Subscripting such an object returns an XCUIElement, which can then be sent action methods such as `tap`.

Now run the test by clicking in the diamond in the gutter at the left of the `test-Example` declaration. The app launches in the Simulator, and a ghost finger performs the same actions we performed, tapping first the button in the interface and then, when the alert appears, the OK button that dismisses it. The test ends and the app stops running in the simulator. The test passes!

The important thing, however, is that if the interface stops looking and behaving as it does now, the test will *not* pass. For example, in *Main.storyboard*, select the button and, under Control in the Attributes inspector, uncheck Enabled. The button is still there, but it can't be tapped; we've broken the interface. Run the test. As desired, the test fails, and the Report navigator explains why: when we came to the Tap the "OK" Button step, we first had to perform Find the "OK" Button, and after two retries, we failed because there was no alert. Ingeniously, the report also incorporates screen shots so that we can inspect the state of the interface during the test. Hover the mouse over Tap the "OK" Button, and an Eye icon appears. Click it, and a screen shot shows the screen at that moment, displaying clearly the disabled interface button (and no alert).

Fix the bug by enabling the button once again. If you now choose Product → Test, all tests in all test suites are run, both the unit tests and the interface tests, and they all pass. Our app may be trivially simple, but it's definitely working!

During interface testing, your app is in effect being viewed from the outside, as a human being would view it. As I've already said, that depends upon accessibility. Standard interface objects are accessible, but other interface that you create might not be. Select an interface element in the nib editor to view its accessibility characteristics in the Identity inspector. Run the app in the Simulator and choose Xcode → Open Developer Tool → Accessibility Inspector to explore in real time the accessibility characteristics of whatever is under the cursor. For more about adding useful accessibility to your interface objects, see Apple's *Accessibility Programming Guide for iOS*.

Clean

From time to time, during repeated testing and debugging, and before making a different sort of build (switching from Debug to Release, or running on a device instead of the Simulator), it is a good idea to *clean* your target. This means that existing builds will be removed and caches will be cleared, so that all code will be considered to be in need of compilation and you can build your app from scratch.

Cleaning removes the cruft, quite literally. For example, suppose you have been including a certain resource in your app, and you decide it is no longer needed. You can remove it from the Copy Bundle Resources build phase (or from your project as a whole), but that doesn't remove it from your built app. This sort of leftover resource can cause all kinds of mysterious trouble. The wrong version of a nib may seem to appear in your interface; code that you've edited may seem to behave as it did before the edit. Cleaning removes the built app, and very often solves the problem.

I think of cleaning as having several levels or degrees:

Shallow clean
    Choose Product → Clean, which removes the built app and some of the intermediate information in the build folder.

Deeper clean
    Hold Option and choose Product → Clean Build Folder, which removes the entire build folder.

Insanely clean
    Quit Xcode. Open your user *Library/Developer/Xcode/DerivedData* folder and move all its contents to the trash. This is a complete clean for every project you've opened recently — plus the module cache. Removing the module cache can reset Swift itself, thus causing occasional mysterious compilation, code-completion, or syntax coloring issues to go away.

In addition to cleaning your project, you should also remove your app from the Simulator. This is for the same reason as cleaning the project: when the app is built and copied to the Simulator, existing resources inside the built app may not be removed (in order to save time), and this may cause the app to behave oddly. To clean out the current simulator while running the Simulator, choose iOS Simulator → Reset Content and Settings. To clean out *all* simulators, quit the Simulator and say, in the Terminal:

```
$ xcrun simctl erase all
```

Running on a Device

Sooner or later, you'll want to progress from running and testing and debugging in the Simulator to running and testing and debugging on a real device. The Simulator is nice, but it's only a simulation; there are many differences between the Simulator and a real device. The Simulator is really your computer, which is fast and has lots of memory, so problems with memory management and speed won't be exposed until you run on a device. User interaction with the Simulator is limited to what can be done with a mouse: you can click, you can drag, you can hold Option to simulate use of two fingers, but more elaborate gestures can be performed only on an actual device. And many iOS facilities, such as the accelerometer and access to the music library, are not present on the Simulator at all, so that testing an app that uses them is possible *only* on a device.

 Don't even think of developing an app without testing it on a device. You have no idea how your app *really* looks and behaves until you run it on a device. Submitting to the App Store an app that you have not run on a device is asking for trouble.

Obtaining a Developer Program Membership

Starting in Xcode 7, Apple provided the ability to configure your app to run on a device, for testing purposes, with no paid developer program membership. This ability, however, is limited, and I'm not going to document it here. Sooner or later, you're going to want a Developer Program membership, and you're going to accept that this is worth the annual fee. That's what this section is about.

Go to the Apple Developer Program web page (*https://developer.apple.com/programs/*) to initiate the enrollment process. When you're starting out, the Individual program is sufficient. The Organization program costs no more, but adds the ability to privilege additional team members in various roles. (You do *not* need the Organization program merely in order to distribute your built app to other users for testing.)

Your Developer Program membership involves two things:

An Apple ID

The user ID that identifies you at Apple's site (along with the corresponding password). You'll use your Developer Program Apple ID for all kinds of things. In addition to letting you prepare an app to run on a device, this same Apple ID lets you post on Apple's development forums, download Xcode beta versions, and so forth.

A team name

You, under the same Apple ID, can belong to more than one *team*. On each team, you will have one or more *roles* dictating your privileges. If you are the head (or sole member) of the team, you are the *team agent*, with roles Admin and Legal, meaning that you can do everything: you can develop apps, run them on your device, submit apps to the App Store, and receive the money for any paid apps that sell any copies there.

Having established your Developer Program Apple ID, you should enter it into the Accounts preference pane in Xcode. Click the Plus button at the bottom left and choose Add Apple ID. Provide the Apple ID and password. From now on, Xcode will identify you through the team name(s) associated with this Apple ID; you shouldn't need to tell Xcode this password again.

Signing an App

Running an app on a device is a remarkably complicated business. You will need to *sign* the app as you build it. An app that is not properly signed for a device will not run on that device (assuming you haven't jailbroken the device). Signing an app requires two things:

An identity

An identity represents Apple's permission for a given team to develop, on this computer, apps that can run on a device. It consists of two parts:

A private key

The private key is stored in the keychain on your computer. Thus, it identifies a computer where this team can *potentially* develop device-targeted apps.

A certificate

A certificate is a virtual permission slip from Apple. It contains the public key matching the private key (because you told Apple the public key when you asked for the certificate). With a copy of this certificate, any machine holding the private key can *actually* be used to develop device-targeted apps under the name of this team.

A provisioning profile
> A provisioning profile is a virtual permission slip from Apple, uniting four things:
>
> - An identity.
>
> - An app, identified by its bundle identifier.
>
> - A list of eligible devices, identified by their UDIDs (unique device identifiers).
>
> - A list of entitlements. An *entitlement* is a special privilege that not every app needs, such as the ability to talk to iCloud. You won't concern yourself with entitlements unless you write an app that needs one.
>
> Thus, a provisioning profile is sufficient for signing an app as you build it. It says that on *this* Mac it is permitted to build *this* app such that it will run on *these* devices.

There are two types of identity, and hence two types of certificate, and hence two types of provisioning profile: *development* and *distribution* (a distribution certificate is also called a *production* certificate). We are concerned here with the development identity, certificate, and profile; I'll talk about the distribution side later in this chapter.

Apple is the ultimate keeper of all information: your certificates, your provisioning profiles, what apps and what devices you've registered. Your communication with Apple, when you need to verify or obtain a copy of this information, will take place through one of two means:

The developer member center
> A set of web pages at *https://developer.apple.com/account/*. If you have a Developer Program membership, you can come here and click Certificates, IDs & Profiles (or go directly to *https://developer.apple.com/account/ios/certificate/*) to access all features and information to which you are entitled by your membership type and role. (This is the area of Apple's site formerly referred to as the Portal.)

Xcode
> Except for obtaining a distribution provisioning profile, just about everything you would need to do at the developer member center can be done through Xcode instead. When all goes well, using Xcode is a lot simpler! If there's a problem, you can head for the developer member center to iron it out.

Automatic Development Signing

New in Xcode 8, Apple provides two distinct ways of obtaining and managing development certificates and profiles — automatic signing, and manual signing. You distinguish between them on a per-app basis. For new projects, automatic signing is the

Figure 9-9. Xcode knows of no devices

Figure 9-10. Xcode offers to register a device

default. This is indicated by the fact that the "Automatically manage signing" check-box is checked in the Signing section of the General pane when you edit your project's app target (Figure 9-12).

Let's suppose that you have neither a development certificate in your computer's key-chain nor a development profile for any app. But you do have a Developer Program Apple ID, and you've entered it into Xcode's Accounts preference pane. Then, when you create a new project (File → New → Project) and specify a template (such as the iOS Single View app template), you'll see, on the next screen that appears, below where you type the new project's name, a pop-up menu listing all the teams with which your Apple ID is associated. If you belong to more than one team, specify the desired team here.

When you then create the project on disk and the project window opens, *everything happens automatically.* Your computer's keychain creates a private key for a development certificate. The public key is sent to Apple. The actual development certificate is created at the developer member center, and is downloaded and installed into your computer's keychain.

If you've never run on any device before, and if you haven't manually registered any devices at the developer member center, that's as far as Xcode can go for now. You'll see some alerts in the Signing section of the General pane when you edit the app target, as shown in Figure 9-9.

Now connect a device via USB to your computer. It will appear in the Scheme pop-up menu as unavailable. But choose it anyway. This causes the alert in Figure 9-9 to change: a Register Device button appears (Figure 9-10). Click it!

Figure 9-11. Xcode has registered a device for us

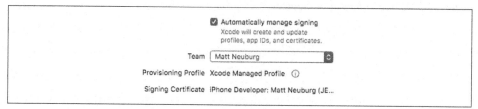

Figure 9-12. Xcode manages signing credentials automatically

New in Xcode 8, when Xcode resolves an automatic signing issue, it reports its actions in the Report navigator. Thus, having clicked the Register Device button, we can switch to the Report navigator to learn what just happened: Xcode has registered our device with Apple, as shown in Figure 9-11.

A development provisioning profile — a universal iOS Team Provisioning Profile, allowing you run any basic app on any device — is now created at the developer member center, and is downloaded and saved where Xcode can find it (in your ~/Library/MobileDevice/Provisioning Profiles folder). Figure 9-12 shows the resulting display in the Signing section of the General pane when you edit the app target.

You are now ready to run this project on this device, as I'll explain further in a moment.

The good news is that once you *already* have a development certificate, and once Xcode has *already* generated and downloaded a universal iOS Team Provisioning Profile, and once this device is *already* registered with Apple, none of that is necessary. When you create a new project, you supply your team name. Xcode thus knows everything it needs to know! The development certificate is valid for this computer, and the universal iOS Team Provisioning Profile is universal. Therefore, you should from now on be able to create a project and run it on your device *immediately*.

If you decide for any reason that you don't want a project's signing to be managed automatically by Xcode, simply uncheck the "Automatically manage signing" checkbox. This causes Xcode to take its hands off completely. Not only will it not automatically generate a development certificate or a development profile, but also it won't use any profile that it has created automatically; you will have to do *everything* manually and deliberately. (This, Apple hopes, should prevent the confusing situations we've seen in the past, where Xcode would try to assist automatically but would often mysteriously and silently fail, along with automatic generation of extra profiles and other unwanted behavior.)

Obtaining a Development Certificate Manually

Now let's go back a couple of steps and pretend that you don't want to manage signing automatically for this project, or that for some other reason you need to obtain a development certificate manually. How would you do it?

The full procedure, which is somewhat elaborate, is as follows. Instructions are also available at the developer member center as you initiate the process (go to the Certificates page and click the Plus button at the top right):

1. You launch Keychain Access and choose Keychain Access → Certificate Assistant → Request a Certificate from a Certificate Authority. Using your name and email address as identifiers, you generate and save to disk a 2048-bit RSA certificate request file. Your private key is stored in your keychain then and there; the certificate request containing your public key has been saved temporarily onto your computer. (For example, you might save it to the desktop.)

2. At the developer member center, you are presented with an interface allowing you to upload the saved certificate request file. You upload it, and the certificate is generated; click its listing at the developer member center to expose the Download button, and click Download.

3. Locate and double-click the file you just downloaded; Keychain Access automatically imports the certificate and stores it in your keychain, where Xcode is able to see it from now on.

You do not need to keep the certificate request file or the downloaded certificate file; your keychain now contains all the needed credentials. If this has worked, you can see the certificate in your keychain, read its details, and observe that it is valid and linked to your private key (Figure 9-13). Moreover, you should be able to confirm that Xcode now knows about this certificate: in the Accounts preference pane, click your Apple ID on the left and your team name on the right, and click View Details; a dialog opens where you should see an iOS Development signing identity listed at the top, with a Valid status.

If this is your very, very first time obtaining any certificate from the developer member center, you will need *another* certificate: the WWDR Intermediate Certificate. This is the certificate that certifies that certificates issued by WWDR (the Apple Worldwide Developer Relations Certification Authority) are to be trusted. (You can't make this stuff up.) Xcode should automatically install this in your keychain; if not, you can obtain a copy of it manually by clicking a link at the bottom of the page at the

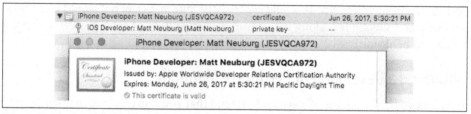

Figure 9-13. A valid development certificate

Figure 9-14. A universal development profile

developer member center where you begin the process of adding a certificate. (Manual installation of a new WWDR Intermediate Certificate actually became necessary last year when the old certificate expired and all developers had to scramble to acquire a new one.)

Obtaining a Development Provisioning Profile Manually

A provisioning profile, as I've already mentioned, unites an identity, a device, and an app bundle identifier. If things go well, in the simplest case, you'll be able to obtain a development provisioning profile automatically from within Xcode. You can confirm your possession of an applicable universal development provisioning profile by clicking the "i" button next to the words Xcode Managed Profile in the Signing section of the General pane when you edit the app target (Figure 9-12); a popover displays information about the provisioning profile, as shown in Figure 9-14.

The universal development profile allows you to run *any* app on the targeted device for testing purposes, provided that the app doesn't require special entitlements (such as using iCloud). If you turn on any entitlements for an app target (which you would do by making a change in the Capabilities pane when you edit the app target), and if you're using automatic signing, Xcode will communicate with the developer member center to attach those entitlements to your registered app; then it will create a new provisioning profile that includes those entitlements, download it, and use it for this project.

Now let's talk about what happens if you are *not* using automatic signing, and you want to obtain a development provisioning profile to run a certain app on your device. Most of the work happens at the developer member center:

1. First, the *device* must be registered at the developer member center. Look under Devices there to see if it is. If it isn't, click the Plus button and enter a name for this device along with its UDID. You can copy the device's UDID from its listing in Xcode's Devices window. Alternatively, you can submit a tab-delimited text file of UDIDs and names.

2. Next, the *app* must be registered at the developer member center. Look under Identifiers → App IDs there to see if it is. If it isn't, add it, as follows: Click Plus. Enter a name for this app. Don't worry about the nonsense letters and numbers that the developer member center adds as a prefix to your bundle identifier; use the Team ID. Enter the bundle identifier under Explicit App ID exactly as shown in Xcode, in the Bundle Identifier field under General when you edit the app target.

   (If your app uses special entitlements, this step is also where you'd associate those entitlements manually with the app.)

3. Under Provisioning Profiles, click Plus. Ask for an iOS App Development profile. On the next screen, choose the App ID. (You'll see an option to create a "wildcard" development profile; this is a universal development profile, but it's a *manually generated* universal development profile. Do *not* choose that! Create a development profile specifically targeted at this app.)

   On the next screen, check your development certificate. On the next screen, select the device(s) you want to run on. On the next screen, give this profile a name, and click Generate. Click the Download button.

4. On your computer, find the downloaded profile, and double-click it to open it in Xcode. You can then throw the downloaded profile away; Xcode has made a copy.

New in Xcode 8, when you elect to manage your app's signing manually, the General tab when you edit your app target sprouts Signing (Debug) and Signing (Release) sections describing and managing the situation with regard to your certificate and the profiles associated with this app (Figure 9-15). No automatic actions will be performed; Xcode will keep its hands off, and you will need do everything at the developer member center. If you have a profile for this app already, and if you switch on some entitlements in the Capabilities pane, you'll need to return to the member center, confirm that those entitlements are associated with your app, and create and download a new profile.

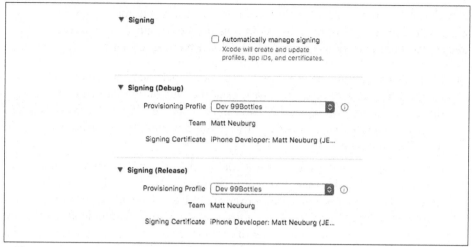

Figure 9-15. Manual code signing

 The Signing (Debug) and Signing (Release) sections that appear in the General tab are actually convenient ways of configuring the Provisioning Profile and Code Signing Identity build settings.

Running the App

Once you have a development profile applicable to an app and a device (or, in the case of the universal team profile, all apps and all registered devices), you can connect the device, choose it as the destination in the Scheme pop-up menu, and build and run the app. If you're asked for permission to access your keychain, grant it. If necessary, Xcode will install the associated provisioning profile onto the device.

The app is built, loaded onto your device, and runs there. As long as you launch the app from Xcode, everything is just as when running in the Simulator: you can run, or you can debug, and the running app is in communication with Xcode, so that you can stop at breakpoints, read messages in the console, profile your app with Instruments, and so on. The outward difference is that to interact physically with the app, you use the device (tethered physically to your computer), not the Simulator.

Running the app from Xcode on the device can also be used simply as a way of copying the current version of the app to the device. You can then stop the app (in Xcode), disconnect the device from your computer, and launch the app on the device and play with it for testing purposes.

Managing Certificates, Profiles, and Devices

Starting in Xcode 8, you're allowed to have more than one development certificate. Thus, management of development certificates may not be necessary. All you have to do, in order to run on a device on another computer, is do what you did on the first computer. If you're using automatic signing, a new certificate will be generated for you — one that doesn't conflict with the old certificate.

For distribution certificates, however, that's not the case. If you need to do a distribution build from more than one computer, you'll need to *export* your identities from the first computer and *import* them onto the second computer. To do so, go the Account preference pane on the first computer, where you have all the necessary credentials, and use the Gear menu at the bottom of the pane to choose Export Developer Accounts. Save the resulting file (called a *developer profile*), securing it with a password. Copy the exported file to the other computer. On the other computer, run Xcode and open the exported file, using the same password; like magic, the entire suite of teams and identities and certificates and provisioning profiles will then spring to life in that other copy of Xcode, including the entries in your keychain. You can then throw the developer profile away on both computers; it has done its job.

When you click the Accounts preference pane's View Details button, you see a dialog listing your certificates and provisioning profiles. This dialog provides yet another way to generate certificates. Provisioning profiles may be listed here as if they had not been downloaded, when in fact they have been; you can click Download All Profiles to get things back in sync, but with luck that won't be necessary.

When a device is attached to the computer, it appears in Xcode's Devices window (choose Window → Devices). Click a device's name to access information on the device. You can see (and copy) the device's UDID. You can see (and delete) apps that have been installed for development using Xcode. You can view the device's console log in real time. (The interface for this is a little obscure: click the tiny up-arrow at the bottom left of the main pane of the Devices window.) Using the Gear menu, you can see provisioning profiles that have been installed on the device. You can see log reports for crashes that took place on the device. And you can take screenshots that image your device's screen; you'll need to do this for your app when you submit it to the App Store.

 According to Apple, in macOS Sierra the Console app will display the console logs for any connected device; but I have not yet been able to confirm this for myself.

Profiling

Xcode provides tools for probing the internal behavior of your app graphically and numerically, and you should keep an eye on those tools. The gauges in the Debug navigator allow you to monitor key indicators, such as CPU and memory usage, any time you run your app. Memory debugging (new in Xcode 8) gives you a graphical view of your app's objects and their ownership chains, and can even reveal memory

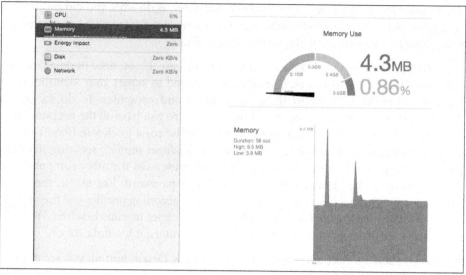

Figure 9-16. The Debug navigation gauges

leaks. And Instruments, a sophisticated and powerful utility application, collects profiling data that can help track down problems and provide the numeric information you need to improve your app's performance and responsiveness.

Gauges

The gauges in the Debug navigator are operating whenever you build and run your app. Click on a gauge to see further detail displayed in the editor. The gauges do not provide highly detailed information, but they are extremely lightweight and always active, so they provide an easy way to get a general sense of your running app's behavior at any time. In particular, if there's a problem, such as a prolonged period of unexpectedly high CPU usage or a relentless unchecked increase in memory usage, you can spot it in the gauges and then use Instruments to help track it down.

There are four basic gauges: CPU, Memory, Disk, and Network. Depending on the circumstances, you may see additional gauges. For example, an Energy Impact gauge appears when running on a device, and for certain devices, a GPU gauge may appear as well. If your app is iCloud-enabled, you'll also see an iCloud gauge.

In Figure 9-16, I've been heavily exercising my app for a few moments, repeatedly performing the most memory-intensive actions I expect the user to perform. These actions do cause some spikes in memory usage, but my app's memory usage then always settles back down and levels off, so I don't suspect any memory issues.

Figure 9-17. A memory graph

 Note that Figure 9-16 is the result of running *on a device*. Running in the Simulator gives completely different — and therefore misleading — results.

Memory Debugging

Memory debugging, new in Xcode 8, lets you pause your app and view a graphical display of your object hierarchy at that moment. This is valuable not only for detecting problems but simply for understanding your app's object structure.

To use memory debugging, run the app and click the Debug Memory Graph button in the debug bar (Figure 9-17). The app pauses, and you are shown a drawing of your app's objects, linked by their chains of ownership. The Debug navigator lists your objects hierarchically; click an object to see a different part of the graph. Double-click an object in the graph to refocus the graph on that object.

In Figure 9-17, we see that the UIWindow has as its root view controller a View-Controller, which has a board property which is a MyBoard, whose tiles property is an array of Tiles. Clicking the double-arrow button in the corner of the UIWindow object reveals more of the graph, showing how the UIWindow itself is retained.

At the cost of some additional overhead, you can enable the malloc stack before running your app: edit the scheme's Run action and check Diagnostic → Logging → Malloc Stack. When you've done that, selecting an object in the memory graph display provides a backtrace in the Memory inspector that tells you *how* each object came to be retained. Hover over a line of the backtrace and click the right-arrow button to jump to that line of your code.

Memory debugging also detects memory leaks. Such leaks will cause an error icon to appear, and are listed in the Runtime pane of the Issue navigator. For example, suppose we run the leaking Cat and Dog example from Chapter 5, where I have a Dog

Figure 9-18. The memory graph displays a leak

class instance and a Cat class instance with persisting references to one another and there are no other references to either instance, so they are both leaking. The leaking Cat and Dog are listed in the Issue navigator, and clicking one them displays a graph of the problem: the Cat and the Dog are retaining one another (Figure 9-18).

Instruments

You can use Instruments on the Simulator or the device. The device is where you'll do your ultimate testing, for maximum verisimilitude.

To get started with Instruments, set the desired destination in the Scheme pop-up menu in the project window toolbar, and choose Product → Profile. Your app builds using the Profile action for your scheme; by default, this uses the Release build configuration, which is probably what you want. If you're running on a device, you may see some validation warnings, but you can safely ignore them. Instruments launches; if your scheme's Instrument pop-up menu for the Profile action is set to Ask on Launch (the default), Instruments presents a dialog where you choose a trace template.

Alternatively, click Profile In Instruments in a Debug navigator gauge editor; this is convenient when the gauges have suggested a possible problem, and you want to reproduce that problem under the more detailed monitoring of Instruments. Instruments launches, selecting the appropriate trace template for you. A dialog offers two options: Restart stops your app and relaunches it with Instruments, whereas Transfer keeps your app running and hooks Instruments into it.

When the Instruments main window appears, it can be further customized to profile the kind of data that particularly interests you, and you can save the structure of the Instruments window as a custom template. You may have to click the Record button, or choose File → Record Trace, to get your app running. Now you should interact with your app like a user; Instruments will record its statistics.

Use of Instruments is an advanced topic, which is largely beyond the scope of this book. Indeed, an entire book could (and really should) be written about Instruments alone. For proper information, you should read Apple's documents, especially the *Instruments User Guide*. Also, many WWDC videos from current and prior years are about Instruments; look particularly for sessions with "Instruments" or "Perfor-

Figure 9-19. Instruments graphs memory usage over time

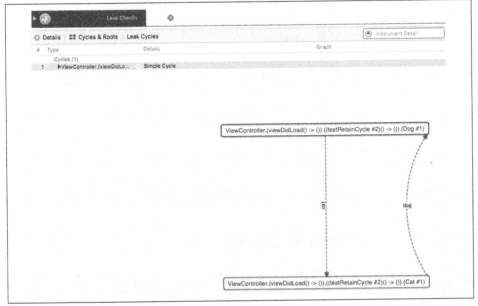

Figure 9-20. Instruments describes a retain cycle

mance" in their names. Here, I'll just demonstrate, without much explanation, the sort of thing Instruments can do.

Figure 9-19 shows me doing much the same thing in Instruments that I did with the Debug navigator gauges in Figure 9-16. I've set the destination to my device. I choose Product → Profile; when Instruments launches, I choose the Allocations trace template. With my app running under Instruments, I exercise it for a while and then pause Instruments, which meanwhile has charted my memory usage. Examining the chart, I find that there are spikes up to about 10MB, but the app in general settles down to a much lower level (less than 4MB). Those are very gentle and steady memory usage figures, so I'm happy.

Another field of Instruments expertise is the ability to detect memory leaks (similar to the memory graph leak detection I discussed earlier). In Figure 9-20, I've again run the retain cycle code from Chapter 5. I've profiled the app using the Leaks trace template. Instruments has detected the leak, and has diagrammed the issue.

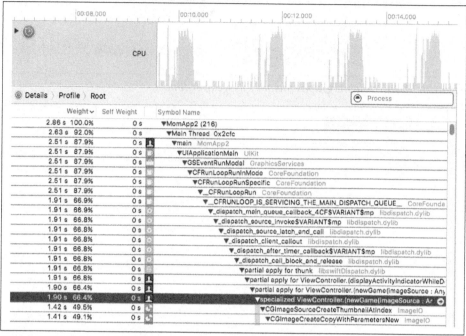

Figure 9-21. Drilling down into the time profile

In this final example, I'm curious as to whether I can shorten the time it takes my Diabelli's Theme app to load a photo image. I've set the destination to a device, because that's where speed matters and needs to be measured. I choose Product → Profile. Instruments launches, and I choose the Time Profiler trace template. When the app launches under Instruments on the device, I load new images repeatedly to exercise this part of my code.

In Figure 9-21, I've paused Instruments, and am looking at what it's telling me. Opening the triangles in the lower portion of the window, I can drill down to my own code, indicated by the user icon.

By double-clicking the listing of that line, I can see my own code, time-profiled (Figure 9-22). The profiler is drawing my attention to the call to CGImageSource-CreateThumbnailAtIndex; this is where we're spending most of our CPU time. That call is in the ImageIO framework; it isn't my code, so I can't make it run any faster. It may be, however, that I could load the image another way; for example, at the expense of some temporary memory usage, perhaps I could load the image at full size and scale it down by redrawing myself. If I'm concerned about speed here, I could spend a little time experimenting. The point is that now I know *what* the experiment should be. This is just the sort of focused, fact-based numerical analysis at which Instruments excels.

```
// load the CGImage at the desired size
let d = [
    kCGImageSourceShouldAllowFloat as String: true,
    kCGImageSourceCreateThumbnailWithTransform as String: true,
    kCGImageSourceCreateThumbnailFromImageAlways as String: true,
    kCGImageSourceThumbnailMaxPixelSize as String: max(Int(maxw), Int(maxh))
]
let imref = CGImageSourceCreateThumbnailAtIndex(src, 0, d)!                    71.6%

// turn it into a UIImage marked with the appropriate scale

let im = UIImage(cgImage: imref, scale: scaleToAskFor, orientation: .up)
```

Figure 9-22. My code, time-profiled

Localization

A device can be set by the user to prefer a certain language as its primary language. You might like the text in your app's interface to respond to this situation by appearing in that language. This is achieved by *localizing* the app for that language. You will probably want to implement localization relatively late in the lifetime of the app, after the app has achieved its final form, in preparation for distribution.

Localization operates through *localization folders* in your project folder and in the built app bundle. Let's say that a resource in one of these localization folders has a counterpart in the other localization folders. Then, when your app goes to load such a resource, it automatically loads the one appropriate to the user's preferred language.

Any type of resource can live in these localization folders; for example, you can have one version of an image to be loaded for one language, and another version of that image for another language. You will be most concerned, however, with *text* that is to appear in your interface. Such text must be maintained in specially formatted *.strings* files, with special names. For example:

- To localize your *Info.plist* file, use *InfoPlist.strings*.
- To localize your *Main.storyboard*, use *Main.strings*.
- To localize your code strings, use *Localizable.strings*.

You don't have to create or maintain these files manually. Instead, you can work with exported XML files in the standard *.xliff* format. Xcode will generate these files automatically, based on the structure and content of your project; it will also read them and will turn them automatically into the various localized *.strings* files.

To help you understand how the *.xliff* export and import process works, I'll start by explaining what you would have to do in order to create and maintain your *.strings* files manually. Then I'll describe how to do the same thing using *.xliff* files. I'll use our good old Empty Window project as the basis for the examples.

Localizing the Info.plist

I'll begin by localizing the string that appears in the Springboard under the app's icon — the visible title of the app. This string is the value of the "Bundle display name" key (CFBundleDisplayName) in our *Info.plist* file.

If our *Info.plist* file doesn't have a CFBundleDisplayName key, the first step is to make one. New in Xcode 8, you can easily do this by editing the target and entering a value in the Display Name text field in the General pane. Our Empty Window app already says "Empty Window" here, but it's in gray, indicating that this is merely an *automatic* display name; enter "Empty Window" explicitly (and press Tab), to make this an *actual* display name. You can look in the *Info.plist* afterward to confirm that the "Bundle display name" key now has a value of "Empty Window."

Now we're going to localize that string: we're going to make a different string appear in the Springboard when the device's language is French. How is the *Info.plist* file localized? It depends on another file, which by default is not created by the app template — *InfoPlist.strings*. So we need to create that file:

1. Choose File → New → File.
2. Select iOS → Resource → Strings File. Click Next.
3. Make sure this file is part of our app target, and name it *InfoPlist*. Get the name and capitalization exactly right! Click Create.
4. A file called *InfoPlist.strings* has appeared in the project navigator. Select it and, in the File inspector, click Localize.
5. A dialog appears offering us a choice of initial languages. The default is Base, which is fine. Click Localize.

We are now ready to add a language! Here's how to do it:

1. Edit the project. Under Info, the Localizations table lists our app's localizations. We are initially localized only for the development language (English in my case).
2. Click the Plus button under the Localizations table. From the pop-up menu that appears, choose French.
3. A dialog appears, listing files that are currently localized for English (because they came that way as part of the app template). We're dealing here with just *InfoPlist.strings*, so leave it checked but uncheck any other files that appear here. Click Finish.

We have now set up *InfoPlist.strings* to be localized for both English and French. In the Project navigator, the listing for *InfoPlist.strings* has acquired a flippy triangle. Open the triangle to reveal that our project now contains *two* copies of *Info-*

Plist.strings, one for Base (namely English) and one for French. Thus we can now edit either one individually.

Now let's edit our *InfoPlist.strings* files. A *.strings* file is a collection of key–value pairs in the following format:

```
/* Optional comments are C-style comments */
"key" = "value";
```

In the case of *InfoPlist.strings*, the key is the key name from *Info.plist* — the raw key name, not the English-like name. So the English *InfoPlist.strings* should look like this:

```
"CFBundleDisplayName" = "Empty Window";
```

The French *InfoPlist.strings* should look like this:

```
"CFBundleDisplayName" = "Fenêtre Vide";
```

That's all there is to it! Now let's try it out:

1. Build and run Empty Window in the Simulator.
2. In Xcode, stop the running project. In the Simulator, the home screen is revealed.
3. Examine the name of our app, as displayed in the Simulator home screen (the Springboard). It is Empty Window (perhaps truncated).
4. In the Simulator, launch the Settings app and change the language to French (General → Language & Region → iPhone Language → Français). Click Done. An action sheet asks to confirm that we want to Change to French. Do so.
5. After a pause, the language changes. Quit the Settings app and look at our app in the Springboard again. Its name is now displayed as Fenêtre Vide!

Is this fun or what? When you're done marveling at your own cosmopolitanism, change the Simulator's language back to English.

Localizing a Nib File

Now let's talk about how nib files are localized. Once upon a time, it was necessary to localize a copy of the entire nib. So, for example, if you wanted a French version of a nib file, you were constantly maintaining two separate nib files. If you created a button in one nib file, you had to create the same button in the other — except that in one, the title was in English, while in the other, the title was in French. And so on, for every interface object and every localization language. It doesn't sound like fun, does it?

Nowadays, happily, there's a better way. If a project uses base internationalization, then a correspondence can be created between a nib file in a *Base.lproj* folder and a *.strings* file in a localization folder. Thus the developer has just one copy of the nib file to maintain. If the app runs on a device that's localized for a language for which a *.strings* file exists, the strings in the *.strings* file are substituted for the strings in the nib file.

By default, our Empty Window project does use base internationalization, and its *Main.storyboard* file is in a *Base.lproj* folder. So we're ready to localize the storyboard file for French. You're going to need something in the storyboard file to localize:

1. Edit *Main.storyboard* and make sure that the initial main view contains a button whose title is "Hello". If there isn't one, add one. Make the button about 100 pixels wide, and save (that's important).

2. Still editing *Main.storyboard*, look at the File inspector. Under Localization, Base should be checked already. In addition, check French.

3. In the Project navigator, examine the listing for *Main.storyboard*. It now has a flippy triangle. Flip it open. Sure enough, there is now a base-localized *Main.storyboard* and a French-localized *Main.strings*.

4. Edit the French *Main.strings*. It has been created automatically, with keys corresponding to every interface item in *Main.storyboard* that has a title. You have to deduce, from comments and the key names, how this correspondence works. In our case, there's just one interface item in *Main.storyboard*, and anyway it's pretty easy to guess what interface item the key represents. It looks something like this:

   ```
   /* Class = "UIButton"; normalTitle = "Hello"; ObjectID = "PYn-zN-WlH"; */
   "PYn-zN-WlH.normalTitle" = "Hello";
   ```

5. In the second line, containing the key–value pair, change the value to "Bonjour". *Don't change the key!* It has been generated automatically, and correctly, so as to specify the correspondence between this value and the title of the button.

Run the project and view the interface. As we are now looking at our own app in action, there's a faster way to view it in any language for which it is localized: instead of switching the *device* language, you can change the *app* language. To do so, edit the scheme and, in the Run action's Options tab, change the Application Language pop-up menu to French (and close the scheme editor). Build and run again. Sure enough, the button's title appears as "Bonjour" when the app runs in French!

What happens if we now modify the nib? Suppose, for example, we add another button to the view in *Main.storyboard*. There's no automatic change to any *.strings* files corresponding to nibs; such files must instead be regenerated manually. (That's why, in real life, it's a good idea not to start localizing your nib files until your interface is pretty much finished.) But all is not lost:

1. Select *Main.storyboard* and choose File → Show in Finder.

2. Run Terminal. Type xcrun ibtool --export-strings-file output.strings followed by a space, and drag *Main.storyboard* from the Finder into the Terminal window. Press Return.

The result is that a new file called *output.strings* based on *Main.storyboard* is generated in your home directory (or whatever the current directory is). Merging this information with the existing localized *.strings* files based on *Main.storyboard* is up to you.

In that example, I made you widen the "Hello" button in advance, to make room for a longer localized title, "Bonjour". In real life, you'll probably use autolayout; this allows buttons and labels to grow and shrink automatically to accommodate different localized contents, while shifting other parts of the interface to compensate.

To test your interface under different localizations, you can also *preview* your localized nib files within Xcode, without running the app. Edit a *.storyboard* or *.xib* file and open an assistant pane, and switch the Tracking menu to Preview. A menu at the lower right lists localizations; choose from the menu to switch between them. A "double-length pseudolanguage" stress-tests your interface with really long localized replacement text.

Localizing Code Strings

What about localizing strings whose value is generated in code? In the Empty Window app, an example would be the alert summoned by tapping the button. It displays text — the title and message of the alert, and the title of the button that dismisses it:

```
@IBAction func buttonPressed(_ sender: Any) {
    let alert = UIAlertController(
        title: "Howdy!", message: "You tapped me!", preferredStyle: .Alert)
    alert.addAction(
        UIAlertAction(title: "OK", style: .Cancel))
    self.present(alert, animated: true)
}
```

How is that text to be localized? The approach is the same — a *.strings* file — but your code must be modified to use it explicitly. Your code calls the global NSLocalized-String function; the first parameter is a key into a *.strings* file, and the comment parameter provides an explanatory comment, such as the original text to be translated. NSLocalizedString takes several additional, optional parameters; if you omit them, the default is to use a file called *Localizable.strings*.

So, for example, we might modify our buttonPressed method to look like this:

```
@IBAction func buttonPressed(_ sender: Any) {
    let alert = UIAlertController(
        title: NSLocalizedString("ATitle", comment:"Howdy!"),
        message: NSLocalizedString("AMessage", comment:"You tapped me!"),
```

```
            preferredStyle: .Alert)
        alert.addAction(
            UIAlertAction(title: NSLocalizedString("Accept", comment:"OK"),
                style: .Cancel))
        self.present(alert, animated: true)
    }
```

Our code is now broken, of course, because there is no *Localizable.strings* file. Let's make one. The procedure is just as before:

1. Choose File → New → File.

2. Select iOS → Resource → Strings File. Click Next.

3. Make sure this file is part of our app target, and name it *Localizable*. Get the name and capitalization exactly right! Click Create.

4. A file called *Localizable.strings* has appeared in the project navigator. Select it and, in the File inspector, click Localize.

5. A dialog appears offering us a choice of initial languages. The default is Base, which is fine. Click Localize.

6. In the File inspector, check French.

The *Localizable.strings* file now exists in two localizations, Base (meaning English) and French. We must now provide these files with content. Just as we did with ibtool earlier, we can generate the initial content automatically using the genstrings tool. For example, on my machine I would now, in the Terminal, type xcrun genstrings followed by space. Then I drag *ViewController.swift* from the Finder into the Terminal window, and press Return. The result is a file *Localizable.strings* in the current directory, reading as follows:

```
/* OK */
"Accept" = "Accept";

/* You tapped me! */
"AMessage" = "AMessage";

/* Howdy! */
"ATitle" = "ATitle";
```

Now you copy and paste that content into the English and French versions of our project's *Localizable.strings* files, and go through those pairs, changing the value in each pair so that it reads correctly for the given localization. For example, in the English *Localizable.strings* file:

```
/* Howdy! */
"ATitle" = "Howdy!";
```

And in the French *Localizable.strings* file:

```
/* Howdy! */
"ATitle" = "Bonjour!";
```

And so forth.

Localizing With XML Files

Since Xcode 6, there's been another way do everything we just did. The surface mechanics of text localization can be made to revolve around the exporting and importing of *.xliff* files. This means that you typically won't actually have to press any Localize buttons or edit any *.strings* files! Instead, you edit the target and choose Editor → Export For Localization; when you save, a folder is created containing *.xliff* files for your various localizations. You then edit these files (or get a translation house to edit them for you) and import the edited files: edit the target and choose Editor → Import Localizations. Xcode reads the edited *.xliff* files and does the rest, automatically creating localizations and generating or modifying *.strings* files as needed.

To demonstrate, let's add another language — namely, Spanish — to our localizations:

1. Edit the target and choose Editor → Export For Localization.

2. We are offered a chance to export strings in our existing localizations as well as our base language. If we were planning to edit our French localization further, we would export it, but I'm not going to do that in this example. Instead, switch the Include pop-up menu to Development Language Only.

3. Specify a good place to save (such as the Desktop). You're creating a folder, so don't use the name of an existing folder in the same place. For example, if you're saving to the same folder that contains the project folder, you might call it *Empty Window Localizations*. Click Save.

4. In the Finder, open the folder you just created. It contains an *.xliff* file in your project's base language. For example, my file is called *en.xliff* because my development language is English.

Examine this *.xliff* file, and you will see that Xcode has done for us everything that we did manually. No *.strings* files need be present initially! Xcode does all the work:

- For every *Info.plist* file in your project, Xcode has created a corresponding `<file>` element. When imported, these elements will be turned into localized *Info-Plist.strings* files.

- For every *.storyboard* and *.xib* file, Xcode has run `ibtool` to extract the text, and has created a corresponding `<file>` element. When imported, these elements will be turned into eponymous localized *.strings* files.

- For every code file containing a call to NSLocalizedString, Xcode has run genstrings, and has created a corresponding <file> element. When imported, these elements will be turned into localized *Localizable.strings* files.

We now proceed to translate some or all of the strings in this file into some other language, save the edited *.xliff* file, and import it:

1. Open the *.xliff* file in a decent text editor (or an XML editor if you have one).

2. Just for the sake of this example, I'm going to localize only the "Hello" button in the storyboard. So delete (carefully, so as not to mess up the XML) all the <file>...</file> element groups except the one whose original attribute is "Empty Window/Base.lproj/Main.storyboard". And delete (carefully) all the <trans-unit>...</trans-unit> elements except the one whose <source> is "Hello".

3. To specify Spanish as the target language, add an attribute to the <file> element: target-language="es".

4. To provide an actual translation, add a <target> element after the <source> element, and give it some text, such as "Hola". Save. The file should now look something like this:

```
<?xml version="1.0" encoding="UTF-8" standalone="no"?>
<xliff xmlns="urn:oasis:names:tc:xliff:document:1.2"
  xmlns:xsi="http://www.w3.org/2001/XMLSchema-instance" version="1.2"
  xsi:schemaLocation="urn:oasis:names:tc:xliff:document:1.2
  http://docs.oasis-open.org/xliff/v1.2/os/xliff-core-1.2-strict.xsd">
  <file original="Empty Window/Base.lproj/Main.storyboard"
  source-language="en" target-language="es" datatype="plaintext">
    <header>
      <tool tool-id="com.apple.dt.xcode" tool-name="Xcode"
      tool-version="6.2" build-num="6C107a"/>
    </header>
    <body>
      <trans-unit id="PYn-zN-WlH.normalTitle">
        <source>Hello</source>
        <target>Hola</target>
        <note>Class = "UIButton"; normalTitle = "Hello";
          ObjectID = "PYn-zN-WlH";</note>
      </trans-unit>
    </body>
  </file>
</xliff>
```

5. Back in Xcode, edit the target and choose Editor → Import Localizations. In the Open dialog, select the edited *en.xliff* and click Open.

6. Xcode complains that we didn't translate everything there was to translate. Ignore that complaint and click Import.

Amazing things have now happened! With no visible prompting, Xcode has added Spanish to our localizations, and has created an additional *InfoPlist.strings* file, an additional *Main.strings* file, and an additional *Localizable.strings* file, all localized to Spanish. If you examine *Main.strings*, you'll see that it looks just as it would have looked if we had edited it manually:

```
/* Class = "UIButton"; normalTitle = "Hello"; ObjectID = "PYn-zN-WlH"; */
"PYn-zN-WlH.normalTitle" = "Hola";
```

Clearly, the round-trip to and from an *.xliff* file is an extremely convenient way to create and maintain your localizations. The *structure* of the localization within your project is exactly the same as I described earlier in this section, but the *.xliff* file externalizes that same information in a format that can be readily edited in a single file. The *.xliff* export process runs `ibtool` and `genstrings` for you, so your localized content is easy to maintain as you add interface and code.

Distribution

By *distribution* is meant providing to others who are not developers on your team your built app for running on their devices. There are two kinds of distribution:

Ad Hoc distribution
> You are providing a copy of your app to a limited set of known users so that they can try it on their specific devices and report bugs, make suggestions, and so forth.

App Store distribution
> You are providing the app to the App Store so that anyone can download it (possibly for a fee) and run it. An App Store distribution to the App Store is also the basis of another way of having known users test your app, namely through Test-Flight.

Making an Archive

To create a copy of your app for distribution, you need first to build an *archive* of your app. It is this archive that will subsequently be exported for Ad Hoc or App Store distribution. An archive is basically a preserved build. It has three main purposes:

Distribution
> An archive will serve as the basis for an Ad Hoc distribution or an App Store distribution.

Reproduction

Every time you build, conditions can vary, so the resulting app might behave slightly differently. But an archive preserves a specific built binary; every distribution from a particular archive is guaranteed to contain an identical binary, and thus will behave the same way. This fact is important for testing: if a bug report comes in based on an app distributed from a particular archive, you can Ad Hoc distribute that archive to yourself and run it, knowing that you are testing exactly the same app.

Symbolication

The archive includes a *.dSYM* file which allows Xcode to accept a crash log and report the crash's location in your code. This allows you to deal with crash reports from users.

Here's how to build an archive of your app:

1. Set the destination in the Scheme pop-up menu in the project window toolbar to Generic iOS Device. Until you do this, the Product → Archive menu item will be disabled. You do *not* have to have a device connected; you are not building to run on a *particular* device, but saving an archive that will run on *some* device.

2. If you like, edit the scheme to confirm that the Release build configuration will be used for the Archive action. This is the default, but it does no harm to double-check.

3. Choose Product → Archive. The app is compiled and built. The archive itself is stored in a date folder within your user *Library/Developer/Xcode/Archives* folder. Also, it is listed in Xcode's Organizer window (Window → Organizer) under Archives; this window may open spontaneously to show the archive you've just created. You can add a comment here; you can also change the archive's name (this won't affect the name of the app).

You've just signed your archive with a development profile; that's good, because it means you can run the archived build directly on your device. But it's also bad, because a development profile can't be used to make an Ad Hoc or App Store build of your app. You need a distribution profile! Not to worry; when you export the archive to form an Ad Hoc or App Store build, Xcode will *substitute* the appropriate distribution profile for the development profile that you used for archiving.

Obtaining a Distribution Certificate Manually

You can obtain a distribution certificate manually in one of two ways:

In Xcode's Accounts preference pane

In the Accounts preference pane, in the View Details dialog for your team, click the Create button to the right of iOS Distribution.

At the developer member center

You can obtain the distribution certificate manually, just as I described earlier for a development certificate.

Once you've done either of those things successfully, you'll see the distribution certificate in your keychain. It will look just like Figure 9-13, except that it will say "iPhone Distribution" instead of "iPhone Development."

Bear in mind that your account can have *only one* distribution certificate. Thus, it is not a trivial matter to perform a distribution from two different computers. You'll need to export a developer profile from one computer and import it on the other, as I explained earlier.

Obtaining a Distribution Profile Manually

If you're using automatic signing for this project, Xcode will probably be able to create an appropriate distribution profile for you automatically when you export your archive. In that case, you don't need to read this section!

 An automatically generated Ad Hoc distribution profile will be configured to run on all devices registered for your team at the developer member center.

However, if you're not using automatic signing, you're going to have to create your profiles manually, at the developer member center. Alternatively, if you *are* using automatic signing, but when you try to export your archive (as described in the next section) there's an error and the export fails, you'll have to *stop* using automatic signing and create your profiles manually instead.

Here's how to obtain a distribution profile manually:

1. If this is to be an Ad Hoc distribution profile, collect the UDIDs of all the devices where this build is to run, and make sure you've added each of them at the developer member center under Devices. (For an App Store distribution profile, omit this step.)

2. Make sure that the app is registered at the developer member center, as I described earlier in this chapter.

3. At the developer member center, under Provisioning Profiles, click the Plus button to ask for a new profile. In the Add iOS Provisioning Profile form, specify an Ad Hoc profile or an App Store profile. On the next screen, choose your app from the pop-up menu. On the next screen, choose your distribution certificate. On the next screen, for an Ad Hoc profile only, specify the devices you want this app to run on. On the next screen, give the profile a name.

Be careful about the profile's name, as you might need to be able to recognize it later from within Xcode! My own practice is to assign a name containing the term "AdHoc" or "AppStore" and the name of the app.

4. Click Generate to generate the profile. Click Download; find the downloaded profile on your computer, and double-click it to get Xcode to see it.

Ad Hoc Distribution

Apple's docs say that an Ad Hoc distribution build should include an icon that will appear in iTunes, but my experience is that this step, though it does work, is unnecessary. If you want to include this icon, it should be a PNG or JPEG file, 512×512 pixels in size, and its name should be *iTunesArtwork*, with *no file extension*. Make sure the icon is included in the build, being present in the Copy Bundle Resources build phase. (After adding this icon, you'll need to make a new archive of your app.)

Here are the steps for creating an Ad Hoc distribution file from an archive:

1. In the Organizer window, under Archives, select the archive and click the Export button at the upper right of the window. A dialog appears. Here, you are to specify a method; choose Save for Ad Hoc Deployment. Click Next.

2. You are now asked to select a Development Team. Select the correct team and click Choose.

3. At this point, you may see a dialog asking whether you want the exported app *thinned*, meaning that it will contain resources appropriate only to one type of device, simulating what the App Store will do when the user downloads the app to a device. You probably don't, though it might be interesting to learn the size of your thinned app.

4. The archive is prepared, and a summary window is displayed. The name of the provisioning profile is shown, so you can tell that the right thing is happening. Click Next.

5. The file is saved to the Desktop inside a uniquely named folder. It will have the suffix *.ipa* ("iPhone app").

6. Locate in the Finder the file you just saved. Provide this file to your users with instructions.

A user should copy the *.ipa* file to a safe location, such as the Desktop, and then launch iTunes and drag the *.ipa* file from the Finder onto the iTunes icon in the Dock (or double-click the *.ipa* file). Then the user should connect the device to the computer, make certain the app is present in the list of apps for this device *and that it will be installed on the next sync*, and finally sync the device to cause the app to be copied to it. (If this isn't the first version of your app that you've distributed to your Ad Hoc testers, the user might need to delete the current version from the device beforehand; otherwise, the new version might not be copied to the device when syncing.)

If you listed your own device as one of the devices for which this Ad Hoc distribution profile was to be enabled, you can obey these instructions yourself to make sure the Ad Hoc distribution is working as expected. First, remove from your device any previous copies of this app (such as development copies) and any profiles that might be associated with this app (you can do that through the Devices window in Xcode). Then copy the app onto your device by syncing with iTunes as just described. The app should run on your device, and you should see the Ad Hoc distribution profile on your device. Because you are not privileged over your other Ad Hoc testers, what works for you should work for them.

There is a registration limit of 100 devices per year per developer (not per app), which limits your number of Ad Hoc testers. Devices used for development are counted against this limit. You can work around this limit, and provide your betas more conveniently to testers, by using TestFlight beta testing instead.

TestFlight beta testing lifts the limit of 100 devices to a limit of 2000 testers, and is more convenient than Ad Hoc distribution because your users download and install prelease versions of your app directly from the App Store onto their devices through the TestFlight app (acquired by Apple in 2014 by buying Burstly). Configuration is performed at the iTunes Connect site; a prerelease version uploaded to iTunes Connect must be archived as if for App Store distribution (see the discussion of App Store submission later in this chapter). See the "TestFlight Beta Testing" chapter of Apple's *iTunes Connect Developer Guide*.

 Prerelease versions of your app intended for distribution to beta testers (as opposed to internal testers who have direct access to your iTunes Connect account) require review by Apple.

Final App Preparations

As the big day approaches when you're thinking of submitting your app to the App Store, don't let the prospect of huge fame and massive profits hasten you past the all-important final stages of app preparation. Apple has a lot of requirements, and failure to meet them can cause your app to be rejected. Take your time. Make a checklist and go through it carefully. See Apple's *App Distribution Guide* as well as the "Icon and Image Design" chapter of the *Human Interface Guidelines* for full details.

Icons in the App

The simplest way to provide your app with icons is to use the asset catalog. If you're not using an asset catalog for icons and you'd like to switch to using one, edit the target and, in the General pane, under App Icons and Launch Images, next to App Icons

Figure 9-23. Icon slots in the asset catalog

Source, click the Use Asset Catalog button. The Use Asset Catalog button then changes to a pop-up menu listing the asset catalog's name and the name of the image set within the catalog to be used for icons.

The image sizes needed are listed in the asset catalog itself. Select an image slot and look in the Attributes inspector. Confusingly, "2x" or "3x" means that the image should be double or triple the listed dimensions for an icon; thus, for example, an iPhone app icon listed as "60pt" or "60×60," but also with "3x," means that you should provide an image measuring 180×180. To determine which slots should be displayed, use the checkboxes in the Attributes inspector when you select an icon set or launch image set (Figure 9-23). To add an image, drag it from the Finder into the appropriate slot.

An icon file must be a PNG file, without alpha transparency. It should be a full square; the rounding of the corners will be added for you. Apple seems nowadays to prefer simple, cartoony images with a few bright colors and possibly a gentle gradient background.

When your app is built and the asset catalog is processed, the icons are written out to the top level of the app bundle and are given appropriate names (Figure 6-15); at the same time, an appropriate entry is written into the app's *Info.plist*, enabling the system to find and display the icon on a device. The details are complicated, but you won't have to worry about them — that is exactly why you're using the asset catalog!

App icon sizes have changed over the years. If your app is to be backward-compatible to earlier systems, you may need additional icons in additional sizes, corresponding to the expectations of those earlier systems. Conversely, new devices can come along, bringing with them new icon size requirements (this happened when the iPad Pro appeared on the scene). Again, this is exactly the sort of thing the asset catalog will help you with.

Optionally, you may elect to include smaller versions of your icon to appear when the user does a search on the device, as well as in the Settings app if you include a settings bundle. However, I never include those icons.

Other Icons

When you submit an app to the App Store, you will be asked to supply a 1024×1024 PNG or high-quality JPEG icon to be displayed at the App Store. Apple's guidelines say that it should not merely be a scaled-up version of your app's icon; but it must not differ perceptibly from your app's icon, either, or your app will be rejected (I know this from bitter experience).

The App Store icon does *not* need to be built into your app; indeed, it should not be, as it will merely swell the built app's size unnecessarily. On the other hand, you will probably want to keep it in your project (and in your project folder) so that you can find and maintain it easily. So I recommend that you import it into your project and copy it into your project folder, but do *not* add it to any target.

If you created an *iTunesArtwork* icon for Ad Hoc distribution, you may wish to delete it from the Copy Bundle Resources build phase now.

Launch Images

There is a delay between the moment when the user taps your app's icon to launch it and the moment when your app is up and running and displaying its initial window. To cover this delay and give the user a visible indication that something is happening, a launch image needs to be displayed during that interval.

The launch image needn't be detailed. It might be just a blank depiction of the main elements or regions of the interface that will be present when the app has finished launching. In this way, when the app *does* finish launching, the transition from the launch image to the real app will be a matter of those elements or regions being filled in.

In iOS 7 and before, the launch image was literally an image (a PNG file). It had to be included in your app bundle, and it had to obey certain naming conventions. As the variety of screen sizes and resolutions of iOS devices proliferated, so did the number of required launch images. The asset catalog, introduced in iOS 7, was helpful in this regard. But with the introduction of the iPhone 6 and iPhone 6 Plus, the entire situation threatened to become unmanageable.

For this reason, iOS 8 introduced a better solution. Instead of a set of launch images, you now provide a *launch nib file* — a single *.xib* or *.storyboard* file containing a single view to be displayed as a launch image. You construct this view using subviews and autolayout. Thus, the view is automatically reconfigured to match the screen size and orientation of the device on which the app is launching.

By default, a new app project comes with a *LaunchScreen.storyboard* file. This is where you design your launch image. The *Info.plist* points to this file as the value of its "Launch screen interface file base name" key (UILaunchStoryboardName). You can configure the *Info.plist*, if necessary, by editing the target and setting the Launch Screen File field (under App Icons and Launch Images).

You should take advantage of this feature — and not merely because it is convenient. The presence of a "Launch screen interface file base name" key in your *Info.plist* tells the system that your app runs natively on newer device types, such as the iPhone 6 and iPhone 6 Plus. Without it, your app will be displayed zoomed, as if the iPhone 6 were just a big iPhone 5S — in effect, you won't be getting all the pixels you're entitled to (and the display will be somewhat fuzzy).

Another reason for using a launch nib file is that it is localizable! As with any *.xib* or *.storyboard* file, strings displayed in a base-localized launch screen *.xib* or *.storyboard* file can be localized through individual *.strings* files.

As far as I can tell, custom fonts included in your app bundle cannot be displayed in a launch nib file. This is evidently because they have not yet been loaded at the time the launch screen needs to be displayed.

The bad news is that if your app is to be backward-compatible to earlier systems, you'll have to supply old-fashioned launch images *in addition to* the launch nib file. The requirements for launch images in iOS 7 and before are complicated — and are made more complicated by the fact that the rules have changed over the years, so that the more systems you want to be compatible with, the more requirements you'll have to satisfy. I have covered these requirements in earlier editions of this book, and I'm not going to repeat them here.

Apple provides an extremely helpful sample code project called Application Icons and Launch Images for iOS. It provides icons and launch images of all sizes and demonstrates the proper naming conventions.

Screenshots and Video Previews

When you submit your app to the App Store, you will be asked for one or more screenshots of your app in action to be displayed at the App Store. You should take these screenshots beforehand and be prepared to provide them during the app submission process. In the past, you had to provide at least one screenshot corresponding to the screen size of every device on which your app can run, in the corresponding resolution, but Apple says that you will now be allowed to have your largest-size screenshot reused for smaller sizes.

You can obtain screenshots either from the Simulator or from a device connected to the computer:

Simulator
Run the app in the Simulator, first setting the destination to get the desired device type. Choose File → Save Screen Shot.

Device
In Xcode, in the Devices window, locate your connected device under Devices and click Take Screenshot. Alternatively, choose Debug → View Debugging → Take Screenshot of [Device].

In both cases, the screenshot file is saved to wherever screenshots are normally saved on your computer (usually the Desktop).

You can also take a screenshot on a device by clicking the screen lock button and the Home button simultaneously. Now the screenshot is in the Camera Roll in the Photos app, and you can communicate it to your computer in any convenient way (such as by emailing it to yourself).

You can also submit to the App Store a video preview showing your app in action. It can be up to 30 seconds long, in H.264 or Apple ProRes format. Your computer can capture video of your device if it is running macOS 10.10 ("Yosemite") or later. Your device must be sufficiently modern to have a Lightning connector:

1. Connect the device to the computer and launch QuickTime Player. Choose File → New Movie Recording.

2. If necessary, set the Camera and Microphone to the device, using the pop-up menu from the down-pointing chevron button next to the Record button that appears when you hover the mouse over the QuickTime Player window.

3. Start recording, and exercise the app on the device. When you're finished, stop recording and save.

The resulting movie file can be edited in iMovie or Final Cut Pro to prepare it for submission to the App Store. For example, in iMovie:

1. After importing the movie file, choose File → New App Preview.

2. Edit! When you're done editing, choose File → Share → App Preview. This ensures the correct resolution and format.

For more details, see the "App Preview" section of the "First Steps" chapter of Apple's *iTunes Connect Developer Guide*.

Property List Settings

A number of settings in the *Info.plist* are crucial to the proper behavior of your app. You should peruse Apple's *Information Property List Key Reference* for full information. Most of the required keys are created as part of the template, and are given reasonable default values, but you should check them anyway. The following are particularly worthy of attention:

*Bundle display name (*CFBundleDisplayName*)*
> The name that appears under your app's icon on the device screen; this name needs to be short in order to avoid truncation. I talked earlier in this chapter about how to localize the display name. New in Xcode 8, you can enter this value directly in the General pane when you edit your app target.

*Supported interface orientations (*UISupportedInterfaceOrientations*)*
> This key designates the totality of orientations in which the app is ever permitted to appear. You can perform this setting with checkboxes in the General pane of the target editor. But you may also need to edit the *Info.plist* manually to rearrange the order of possible orientations, because on an iPhone the *first* orientation listed may be the one into which the app will actually launch.

*Required device capabilities (*UIRequiredDeviceCapabilities*)*
> You should set this key if the app requires capabilities that are not present on all devices. But don't use this key unless it makes no sense for your app to run *at all* on a device lacking the specified capabilities.

*Bundle version (*CFBundleVersion*)*
> Your app needs a version number. The best place to set it is the General pane of the target editor. Things are a little confusing here because there are two fields:

> *Version*
>> Corresponds in the *Info.plist* to "Bundle versions string, short" (CFBundle-ShortVersionString).

> *Build*
>> Corresponds in the *Info.plist* to "Bundle version" (CFBundleVersion).

> As far as I can determine, Apple will pay attention to the former if it is set, and otherwise will fall back on the latter. In general I play it safe and set both to the same value when submitting to the App Store. The value needs to be a version string, such as "1.0". The version string will be displayed at the App Store, distinguishing one release from another. Failure to increment the version string when submitting an update will cause the update to be rejected. It is legal, however, to increment the Build number without incrementing the Version number, and you will need to do so if you submit several successive builds of the same

prospective release (during the course of TestFlight testing, or because you found a bug and had to withdraw a submitted binary before it appeared on the App Store).

Submission to the App Store

When you're satisfied that your app works well, and you've installed or collected all the necessary resources, you're ready to submit your app to the App Store for distribution. To do so, you'll need to make preparations at the iTunes Connect web site. You can find a link to it on the iOS developer pages when you've logged in at Apple's site. You can go directly to *http://itunesconnect.apple.com*, but you'll still need to log in with your iOS Developer username and password.

 The first time you visit iTunes Connect, you should go to the Contracts section and complete submission of your contract. You can't offer any apps for sale until you do, and even free apps require completion of a contractual form.

I'm not going to recite all the steps you have to go through to tell iTunes Connect about your app, as these are described thoroughly in Apple's *iTunes Connect Developer Guide*, which is the final word on such matters. But here are some of the main pieces of information you will sooner or later have to supply:

Your app's name
This is the name that will appear at the App Store; it need not be identical to the short name that will appear under the app's icon on the device, dictated by the "Bundle display name" setting in your *Info.plist* file. Apple recommends that this be 25 characters or fewer, though it can be longer. You can get a rude shock when you submit your app's information to iTunes Connect and discover that the name you wanted is already taken. There is no reliable way to learn this in advance, and such a discovery can necessitate a certain amount of last-minute scrambling on your part. (Can you guess how I know that?)

Description
You must supply a description of fewer than 4,000 characters; Apple recommends fewer than 580 characters, and the first paragraph is the most important, because this may be all that users see at first when they visit the App Store. It must be pure text, without HTML and without character styling.

Keywords
This is a comma-separated list shorter than 100 characters. These keywords will be used, in addition to your app's name, to help users discover your app through the Search feature of the App Store.

Support

> This the URL of a web site where users can find more information about your app; it's good to have the site ready in advance.

Copyright

> Do not include a copyright symbol in this string; it will be added for you at the App Store.

SKU number

> This is arbitrary, so don't get nervous about it. It's just a unique identifier, unique within the world of your own apps. It's convenient if it has something to do with your app's name. It needn't be a number; it can actually be any string.

Price

> You don't get to make up a price. You have to choose from a list of pricing "tiers."

Availability Date

> There's an option to make the app available as soon as it is approved, and this will typically be your choice.

 As you submit information, click Save often! If the connection goes down and you haven't explicitly saved, all your work can be lost. (Can you guess how I know that?)

When you're ready to upload the app for which you've already submitted the information at iTunes Connect, you can perform the upload using Xcode. I'm assuming that you're able to archive and export your app, as I described already for Ad Hoc distribution; this time, you're going to export for App Store distribution. Select the archived build in the Organizer and click Upload to App Store. The upload will be performed, and the app will be validated at the far end.

Alternatively, you can use Application Loader. Export the archive as an *.ipa* file, as for an Ad Hoc distribution, but when selecting a method for export, choose Save for iOS App Store Deployment. Launch Application Loader by choosing Xcode → Open Developer Tool → Application Loader, and hand it the *.ipa* file.

After uploading the archive, you have one final step to perform. Wait for the binary to be processed at Apple's end. Then return to iTunes Connect, where you submitted your app information. You will now be able to select the binary, save, and submit the app for review.

You will subsequently receive emails from Apple informing you of your app's status as it passes through various stages: "Waiting For Review," "In Review," and finally, if all has gone well, "Ready For Sale" (even if it's a free app). Your app will then appear at the App Store.

PART III

Cocoa

The Cocoa Touch frameworks provide the general capabilities needed by any iOS application. Buttons can be tapped, text can be read, screens of interface can succeed one another, because Cocoa makes it so. To use the framework, you must learn to let the framework use you. You must put your code in the right place so that it will be called at the right time. You must fulfill certain obligations that Cocoa expects of you. You master Cocoa by being Cocoa's obedient servant. In this part of the book, that's what you'll learn to do.

- Chapter 10 describes how Cocoa is organized and structured through such Objective-C language features as subclassing, categories, and protocols. Then some important built-in Cocoa object types are introduced. The chapter concludes with a description of Cocoa key–value coding and a look at how the root NSObject class is organized.

- Chapter 11 presents Cocoa's event-driven model of activity, along with its major design patterns and event-related features — notifications, delegation, data sources, target–action, the responder chain, and key–value observing. The chapter concludes with some words of wisdom about managing the barrage of events Cocoa will be throwing at you, and how to escape that barrage momentarily with delayed performance.

- Chapter 12 is about Cocoa memory management. I'll explain how memory management of reference types works. Then some special memory management situations are described: autorelease pools, retain cycles, notifications and timers, nib loading, and CFTypeRefs. The chapter concludes with a discussion of Cocoa property memory management, and advice on how to debug memory management issues.

- Chapter 13 discusses the question of how your objects are going to see and communicate with one another within the confines of the Cocoa-based world. It concludes with some advice about adhering to the model–view–controller architecture.

Finally, don't forget to read Appendix A for more detail about how Objective-C and Swift interact and cooperate.

CHAPTER 10

Cocoa Classes

When you program iOS, you're programming Cocoa. So you need to be acquainted with Cocoa; you have to know, as it were, who you're talking to when you talk to Cocoa, and what sort of behavior Cocoa is likely to expect from you. Cocoa is a big framework, subdivided into many smaller frameworks, and it takes time and experience to become reasonably familiar with it. Nevertheless, Cocoa has certain chief conventions and primary components that can serve as guideposts from the outset.

The Cocoa API is written mostly in Objective-C, and Cocoa itself consists mostly of Objective-C classes, derived from the root class, NSObject. When programming iOS, you'll be using mostly the built-in Cocoa classes. Objective-C classes are comparable to and compatible with Swift classes, but the other two Swift object type flavors, structs and enums, are not matched by anything in Objective-C. Structs and enums declared originally in Swift cannot generally be handed across the bridge from Swift to Objective-C and Cocoa. Fortunately, some of the most important native Swift object types are also bridged to Cocoa classes. (See Appendix A for more details about the Objective-C language and how communications work between Swift and Objective-C.)

This chapter introduces Cocoa's class structure. It discusses how Cocoa is conceptually organized, in terms of its underlying Objective-C features, and then surveys some of the most commonly encountered Cocoa utility classes, concluding with a discussion of the Cocoa root class and its features, which are inherited by all Cocoa classes.

Subclassing

Cocoa effectively hands you a large repertory of objects that already know how to behave in certain desirable ways. A UIButton, for example, knows how to draw itself and how to respond when the user taps it; a UITextField knows how to display editable text, how to summon the keyboard, and how to accept keyboard input.

Often, the default behavior or appearance of an object supplied by Cocoa won't be quite what you're after, and you'll want to customize it. This does *not* necessarily mean that you need to subclass! Cocoa classes are heavily endowed with methods that you can call, and properties that you can set, precisely in order to customize an instance, and these will be your first resort. Always study the documentation for a Cocoa class to see whether instances can already be made to do what you want. For example, the class documentation for UIButton shows that you can set a button's title, title color, internal image, background image, and many other features and behaviors, without subclassing.

In addition, any built-in classes use *delegation* (Chapter 11) as the preferred way of letting you customize their behavior. For example, you wouldn't subclass UIApplication (the class of the singleton shared application instance) just in order to respond when the application has finished launching, because the delegate mechanism provides a way to do that — namely, the UIApplicationDelegate method `application(_:didFinishLaunchingWithOptions:)`. That's why the templates give us an AppDelegate class, which is *not* a UIApplication subclass, but which *does* adopt the UIApplicationDelegate protocol.

In fact (and you might be particularly surprised by this if you've used another object-oriented application framework), subclassing is one of the rarer ways in which your code will relate to Cocoa. Knowing when to subclass can be somewhat tricky, but the general rule is that you probably *shouldn't* subclass unless you're explicitly invited to do so. Most built-in Cocoa Touch classes will never need subclassing (and some, in their documentation, downright forbid it).

Nevertheless, sometimes setting properties and calling methods and using delegation won't suffice to customize an instance the way you want to. In such cases, a Cocoa class may provide methods that are called internally as an instance does its thing, allowing you to customize that class's behavior by subclassing and overriding (Chapter 4). You don't have the source code for any of Cocoa's built-in classes, but you can still subclass them, creating a new class that acts just like a built-in class except for the modifications you provide.

Certain Cocoa Touch classes are indeed subclassed routinely, constituting the exception that proves the rule. For example, a plain vanilla UIViewController, not subclassed, is very rare, and an iOS app without at least one UIViewController subclass would be practically impossible.

Another case in point is UIView. Cocoa Touch is full of built-in UIView subclasses that behave and draw themselves as needed (UIButton, UITextField, and so on), and you will rarely need to subclass any of them. On the other hand, you might create your *own* UIView subclass, whose job would be to draw itself in some completely new way. You don't actually draw a UIView; rather, when a UIView needs drawing, its draw(_:) method is called so that the view can draw itself. So the way to draw a UIView in some completely custom manner is to subclass UIView and implement draw(_:) in the subclass. As the documentation says, "Subclasses that ... draw their view's content should override this method and implement their drawing code there." The documentation is saying that you *need* to subclass UIView in order to draw content that is completely your own.

For example, suppose we want our window to contain a horizontal line. There is no horizontal line interface widget built into Cocoa, so we'll just have to roll our own — a UIView that draws itself as a horizontal line. Let's try it:

1. In our Empty Window example project, choose File → New → File and specify iOS → Source → Cocoa Touch Class, and in particular a subclass of UIView. Call the class MyHorizLine. Xcode creates *MyHorizLine.swift*. Make sure it's part of the app target.

2. In *MyHorizLine.swift*, replace the contents of the class declaration with this (without further explanation):

```
required init?(coder aDecoder: NSCoder) {
    super.init(coder:aDecoder)
    self.backgroundColor = .clear
}
override func draw(_ rect: CGRect) {
    let c = UIGraphicsGetCurrentContext()!
    c.move(to:CGPoint(x: 0, y: 0))
    c.addLine(to:CGPoint(x: self.bounds.size.width, y: 0))
    c.strokePath()
}
```

3. Edit the storyboard. Find UIView in the Object library (it is called simply "View"), and drag it into the View object in the canvas. You may resize it to be less tall.

4. With the UIView that you just dragged into the canvas still selected, use the Identity inspector to change its class to MyHorizLine.

Build and run the app in the Simulator. You'll see a horizontal line corresponding to the location of the top of the MyHorizLine instance in the nib. Our view has drawn itself as a horizontal line, because we subclassed it to do so.

In that example, we started with a bare UIView that had no drawing functionality of its own. That's why there was no need to call super; the default implementation of UIView's draw(_:) does nothing. But you might also be able to subclass a built-in UIView subclass to modify the way it already draws itself. For example, the UILabel documentation shows that two methods are present for exactly this purpose. Both `drawText(in:)` and `textRect(forBounds:limitedToNumberOfLines:)` explicitly tell us: "This method should only be overridden by subclasses that want to [modify how the label is drawn]." The implication is that these are methods that will be called for us, automatically, by Cocoa, as a label draws itself; thus, we can subclass UILabel and implement these methods in our subclass to modify how a particular type of label draws itself.

Here's an example from one of my own apps, in which I subclass UILabel to make a label that draws its own rectangular border and has its content inset somewhat from that border, by overriding `drawText(in:)`. As the documentation tells us: "In your overridden method, you can configure the current context further and then invoke super to do the actual drawing [of the text]." Let's try it:

1. In the Empty Window project, make a new class file, a UILabel subclass; call the class MyBoundedLabel.

2. In *MyBoundedLabel.swift*, insert this code into the body of the class declaration:

```
override func drawText(in rect: CGRect) {
    let context = UIGraphicsGetCurrentContext()!
    context.stroke(self.bounds.insetBy(dx: 1.0, dy: 1.0))
    super.drawText(in: rect.insetBy(dx: 5.0, dy: 5.0))
}
```

3. Edit the storyboard, add a UILabel to the interface, and change its class in the Identity inspector to MyBoundedLabel.

Build and run the app, and you'll see how the rectangle is drawn and the label's text is inset within it.

Categories and Extensions

A *category* is an Objective-C language feature that allows code to reach right into an existing class and inject additional methods. This is comparable to a Swift extension (see Chapter 4). Using a Swift extension, you can add class or instance methods to a Cocoa class; the Swift headers make heavy use of extensions, both as a way of organizing Swift's own object types and as a way of modifying Cocoa classes. In the same way, Cocoa uses categories to organize its own classes.

 Objective-C categories have names, and you may see references to these names in the headers, the documentation, and so forth. However, the names are effectively meaningless, so don't worry about them.

How Swift Uses Extensions

If you look in the main Swift header, you'll see that many native object type declarations consist of an initial declaration followed by a series of extensions. For example, after declaring the generic struct Array<Element>, the header proceeds to declare some half a dozen extensions on the Array struct. Some of these add protocol adoptions; most of them don't. All of them add declarations of properties or methods to Array; that's what extensions are for.

These extensions are not, of themselves, functionally significant; the header *could* have declared the Array struct with all of those properties and methods within the body of a single declaration. Instead, it breaks things up into multiple extensions. The extensions are simply a way of clumping related functionality together, organizing this object type's members so as to make them easier for human readers to understand.

In the Swift Core Graphics header, just about *everything* is an extension. Here Swift is adapting types defined elsewhere — adapting Swift numeric types for use with Core Graphics and the CGFloat numeric type, and adapting Cocoa structs such as CGPoint and CGRect as Swift object types.

How You Use Extensions

Swift permits you to write global functions, and there is nothing formally wrong with doing so. Nevertheless, for the sake of object-oriented encapsulation, you will often want to write a function as part of an existing object type. It will often be simplest and most sensible for you to inject such functions, as methods, into an existing object type with an extension. Subclassing merely to add a method or two is heavy-handed — and besides, it often wouldn't help you do what you need to do. (Also, extensions work on all three flavors of Swift object type, whereas you can't subclass a Swift enum or struct.)

For example, suppose you wanted to add a method to Cocoa's UIView class. You could subclass UIView and declare your method, but then it would be present only in your UIView subclass and in subclasses of that subclass: it would *not* be present in UIButton, UILabel, and all the other built-in UIView subclasses — because they are subclasses of UIView, not of *your* subclass, and you can't do anything to change that! An extension, on the other hand, solves the problem beautifully: you inject your method into UIView, and it is inherited by all built-in UIView subclasses as well.

You can use protocol extensions to inject functionality into classes in a selective but unified manner. Suppose I want UIButton and UIBarButtonItem — which is not a UIView, but does have button-like behavior — to share a certain method. I can declare a protocol with a method, implement that method in a protocol extension, and then use extensions to make UIButton and UIBarButtonItem adopt that protocol and thus acquire that method:

```
protocol ButtonLike {
    func behaveInButtonLikeWay()
}
extension ButtonLike {
    func behaveInButtonLikeWay() {
        // ...
    }
}
extension UIButton : ButtonLike {}
extension UIBarButtonItem : ButtonLike {}
```

Chapter 4 provides some examples of extensions I've written in my real iOS programming life (see "Extensions" on page 203). Also, as I explain there, I often use extensions in the same way as the Swift headers do, organizing my code for a single object type into multiple extensions simply for clarity.

How Cocoa Uses Categories

Cocoa uses categories as an organizational tool very much as Swift uses extensions. The declaration of a class will often be divided by functionality into multiple categories, and these will often appear in separate header files.

A good example is NSString. NSString is defined as part of the Foundation framework, and its basic methods are declared in *NSString.h*. Here we find that NSString itself, aside from its initializers, has just two members, length and character(at:), because these are regarded as the minimum functionality that a string needs in order to be a string.

Additional NSString methods — those that create a string, deal with a string's encoding, split a string, search in a string, and so on — are clumped into categories. These are shown in the Swift translation of the header as extensions. So, for example, after the declaration for the NSString class itself, we find this in the Swift translation of the header:

```
extension NSString {
    func substring(from: Int) -> String
    func substring(to: Int) -> String
    // ...
}
```

That, as it turns out, is actually Swift's translation of this Objective-C code:

```
@interface NSString (NSStringExtensionMethods)
- (NSString *)substringFromIndex:(NSUInteger)from;
- (NSString *)substringToIndex:(NSUInteger)to;
// ...
@end
```

That notation — the keyword @interface, followed by a class name, followed by another name in parentheses — is an Objective-C category.

Moreover, although the declarations for some of Cocoa's NSString categories appear in this same file, *NSString.h*, many of them appear elsewhere. For example:

- A string may serve as a file pathname, so we also find a category on NSString in *NSPathUtilities.h*, where methods and properties such as pathComponents are declared for splitting a pathname string into its constituents and the like.

- In *NSURL.h*, which is primarily devoted to declaring the NSURL class (and *its* categories), there's also another NSString category, declaring methods for dealing with percent-escaping in a URL string, such as addingPercentEncoding(with-AllowedCharacters:).

- Off in a completely different framework (UIKit), *NSStringDrawing.h* adds two further NSString categories, with methods like draw(at:withAttributes:) having to do with drawing a string in a graphics context.

This organization means that the NSString methods are not gathered in a single header file. In general, fortunately, this won't matter to you as a programmer, because an NSString is an NSString, no matter how it acquires its methods.

Protocols

Objective-C has protocols, and these are generally comparable to and compatible with Swift protocols (see Chapter 4). Since classes are the only Objective-C object type, all Objective-C protocols are seen by Swift as class protocols. Conversely, Swift protocols marked as @objc (which are implicitly class protocols) can be seen by Objective-C. Cocoa makes extensive use of protocols.

For example, let's talk about how Cocoa objects are copied. Some objects can be copied; some can't. This has nothing to do with an object's class heritage. Yet we would like a uniform method to which any object that *can* be copied will respond. So Cocoa defines a protocol named NSCopying, which declares just one required method, copyWithZone:. Here's how the NSCopying protocol is declared in Objective-C (in *NSObject.h*):

```
@protocol NSCopying
- (id)copyWithZone:(nullable NSZone *)zone;
@end
```

That's translated into Swift as follows:

```
protocol NSCopying {
    func copy(with zone: NSZone? = nil) -> Any
}
```

The NSCopying protocol declaration in *NSObject.h*, however, is not a statement that NSObject conforms to NSCopying. Indeed, NSObject does *not* conform to NSCopying! This doesn't compile:

```
let obj = NSObject().copy(with:nil) // compile error
```

But this does compile, because NSString *does* conform to NSCopying:

```
let s = ("hello" as NSString).copy(with: nil)
```

Here's another example. A typical Cocoa pattern is that Cocoa wants to say: "An instance of any class will do here, provided it implements the following methods." That, obviously, is a protocol. For example, consider how a protocol is used in connection with a table view (UITableView). A table view gets its data from a data source. For this purpose, UITableView declares a `dataSource` property, like this:

```
@property (nonatomic, weak, nullable) id <UITableViewDataSource> dataSource;
```

That's translated into Swift as follows:

```
weak var dataSource: UITableViewDataSource?
```

UITableViewDataSource is a protocol. The table view is saying: "I don't care what class my data source belongs to, but whatever it is, it should conform to the UITableViewDataSource protocol." Such conformance constitutes a promise that the data source will implement at least the required instance methods `tableView(_:numberOf-RowsInSection:)` and `tableView(_:cellForRowAt:)`, which the table view will call when it needs to know what data to display. When you use a UITableView, and you want to provide it with a data source object, the class of that object *will* adopt UITableViewDataSource and *will* implement its required methods; otherwise, your code won't compile:

```
let obj = NSObject()
let tv = UITableView()
tv.dataSource = obj // compile error
```

Far and away the most pervasive use of protocols in Cocoa is in connection with the delegation pattern. I'll discuss this pattern in detail in Chapter 11, but you can readily see an example in our handy Empty Window project: the AppDelegate class provided by the project template is declared like this:

```
class AppDelegate: UIResponder, UIApplicationDelegate { // ...
```

AppDelegate's chief purpose on earth is to serve as the shared application's delegate. The shared application object is a UIApplication, and UIApplication's `delegate` property is declared like this:

```
unowned(unsafe) var delegate: UIApplicationDelegate?
```

(I'll explain the `unsafe` modifier in Chapter 12.) The `UIApplicationDelegate` type is a protocol. This is how the shared UIApplication object knows that its delegate might be capable of receiving messages such as `application(_:didFinishLaunchingWith-Options:)`. So the AppDelegate class officially announces its role by explicitly adopting the UIApplicationDelegate protocol.

 Some clever beginners may try to inject a method into a class that adopts a delegate protocol by extending the protocol and implementing the delegate method in the protocol extension. That isn't going to work, because Objective-C can't see protocol extensions (see Appendix A). You can call such a method from Swift, but Cocoa is never going to call it, because it doesn't know that the method implementation exists.

A Cocoa protocol has its own documentation page. When the UIApplication class documentation tells you that the `delegate` property is typed as a UIApplicationDelegate, it's implicitly telling you that if you want to know what messages a UIApplication's delegate might receive, you need to look in the UIApplicationDelegate protocol documentation. You won't find `application(_:didFinishLaunchingWith-Options:)` mentioned anywhere on the UIApplication class documentation page! It's documented in the UIApplicationDelegate protocol documentation page.

This separation of information can be particularly confusing when a class adopts a protocol. When a class's documentation mentions that the class conforms to a protocol, don't forget to examine that protocol's documentation! The latter might contain important information about how the class behaves. To learn what messages can be sent to an object, you need to look upward through the superclass inheritance chain; you also need to look at any protocols that this object's class (or superclass) conforms to. For example, as I already mentioned in Chapter 8, you won't find out that UIView-Controller gets a `viewWillTransition(to:with:)` event by looking at the UIView-Controller class documentation page: you have to look in the documentation for the UIContentContainer protocol, which UIViewController adopts.

Informal Protocols

You may occasionally see, online or in the documentation, a reference to an *informal protocol*. An informal protocol isn't really a protocol at all; it's just a way of providing the compiler with a knowledge of a method name so that it will allow a message to be sent without complaining.

There are two complementary ways to implement an informal protocol. One is to define a category on NSObject; this makes any object eligible to receive the messages listed in the category. The other is to define a protocol to which no class formally conforms; instead, messages listed in the protocol are sent only to objects typed as id (AnyObject), thus suppressing any possible objections from the compiler (see "Suppressing type checking" on page 213).

These techniques were widespread in Cocoa before Objective-C protocols could declare methods as optional; now they are largely unnecessary, and are also mildly dangerous. Nowadays, very few informal protocols remain — but they do exist. For example, NSKeyValueCoding (discussed later in this chapter) is an informal protocol; you may see the term NSKeyValueCoding in the documentation and elsewhere, but there isn't actually any such type: it's a category on NSObject.

Optional Methods

Objective-C protocols, and Swift protocols marked as @objc, can have optional members (see "Optional Protocol Members" on page 185). The question thus arises: How, in practice, is an optional method feasible? We know that if a message is sent to an object and the object can't handle that message, an exception is raised and your app will likely crash. But a method declaration is a contract suggesting that the object *can* handle that message. If we subvert that contract by declaring a method that might or might not be implemented, aren't we inviting crashes?

The answer is that Objective-C is both dynamic and introspective. Objective-C can ask an object whether it can really deal with a message without actually sending it that message. The key method here is NSObject's `responds(to:)` method, which takes a selector parameter (see Chapter 2) and returns a Bool. Thus it is possible to send a message to an object only if it would be safe to do so.

Demonstrating `responds(to:)` in Swift is generally a little tricky, because it's hard to get Swift to throw away its strict type checking long enough to let us send an object a message to which it might not respond. In this artificial example, I start by defining, at top level, a class that derives from NSObject, because otherwise we can't send `responds(to:)` to it, along with an @objc protocol to declare the message that I want to send conditionally (an informal protocol!):

```
class MyClass : NSObject {
}
@objc protocol Dummy {
    func woohoo()
}
```

Now I can say this:

```
let mc = MyClass()
if mc.responds(to: #selector(Dummy.woohoo)) {
    (mc as AnyObject).woohoo()
}
```

Note the cast of mc to AnyObject. This causes Swift to abandon its strict type checking (see "Suppressing type checking" on page 213); we can now send this object any message that Swift knows about, provided it is susceptible to Objective-C introspection — that's why I marked my protocol declaration as @objc to start with. As you know,

Swift provides a shorthand for sending a message conditionally — append a question mark to the name of the message:

```
let mc = MyClass()
(mc as AnyObject).woohoo?()
```

Behind the scenes, those two approaches are exactly the same; the latter is syntactic sugar for the former. In response to the question mark, Swift is calling responds(to:) for us, and will refrain from sending woohoo to this object if it *doesn't* respond to this selector.

That explains also how optional protocol members work. It is no coincidence that Swift treats optional protocol members like AnyObject members. Here's the example I gave in Chapter 4:

```
@objc protocol Flier {
    @objc optional var song : String {get}
    @objc optional func sing()
}
```

When you call sing?() on an object typed as a Flier, responds(to:) is called behind the scenes to determine whether this call is safe. That is also why optional protocol members work only on @objc protocols and classes derived from NSObject: Swift is relying here on a purely Objective-C feature.

You wouldn't want to send a message optionally, or call responds(to:) explicitly, before sending just any old message, because it isn't generally necessary except with optional methods, and it slows things down a little. But Cocoa does in fact call responds(to:) on your objects as a matter of course. To see that this is true, implement responds(to:) on AppDelegate in our Empty Window project and instrument it with logging:

```
override func responds(to aSelector: Selector) -> Bool {
    print(aSelector)
    return super.responds(to:aSelector)
}
```

The output on my machine, as the Empty Window app launches, includes the following (I'm omitting private methods and multiple calls to the same method):

```
application:handleOpenURL:
application:openURL:sourceApplication:annotation:
application:openURL:options:
applicationDidReceiveMemoryWarning:
applicationWillTerminate:
applicationSignificantTimeChange:
application:willChangeStatusBarOrientation:duration:
application:didChangeStatusBarOrientation:
application:willChangeStatusBarFrame:
application:didChangeStatusBarFrame:
application:deviceAccelerated:
```

```
application:deviceChangedOrientation:
applicationDidBecomeActive:
applicationWillResignActive:
applicationDidEnterBackground:
applicationWillEnterForeground:
application:didResumeWithOptions:
application:handleWatchKitExtensionRequest:reply:
application:shouldSaveApplicationState:
application:supportedInterfaceOrientationsForWindow:
application:performFetchWithCompletionHandler:
application:didReceiveRemoteNotification:fetchCompletionHandler:
application:willFinishLaunchingWithOptions:
application(_:didFinishLaunchingWithOptions:)
```

That's Cocoa, checking to see which of the optional UIApplicationDelegate protocol methods (including a couple of undocumented methods) are actually implemented by our AppDelegate instance — which, because it is the UIApplication object's delegate and formally conforms to the UIApplicationDelegate protocol, has explicitly agreed that it *might* be willing to respond to any of those messages. The entire delegate pattern (Chapter 11) depends upon this technique. Observe the policy followed here by Cocoa: it checks all the optional protocol methods once, when it first meets the object in question, and presumably stores the results; thus, the app is slowed a tiny bit by this one-time initial bombardment of responds(to:) calls, but now Cocoa knows all the answers and won't have to perform any of these same checks on the same object later.

 In Swift 3, when implementing a method of a Cocoa protocol, you should always do so in a class declaration or extension that *explicitly declares adoption* of that protocol. Otherwise, the compiler not be able to resolve the correspondence between your Swift method declaration and Cocoa's Objective-C method declaration; even worse, the compiler might not complain, but Cocoa might not be able to see your method implementation (and won't call it as expected). I regard this as a bug in the language (due to renamification; see Appendix A).

Some Foundation Classes

The Foundation classes of Cocoa provide basic data types and utilities that will form the basis of your communication with Cocoa. Obviously I can't list all of them, let alone describe them fully, but I can survey those that you'll probably want to be aware of before writing even the simplest iOS program. For more information, start with Apple's list of the Foundation classes in the Foundation framework documentation page.

In many situations, you can use Foundation classes implicitly, while working with Swift classes. That's because of Swift's ability to *bridge* between its own classes and those of Foundation. For example, String is bridged to NSString (Chapter 3), and

Array is bridged to NSArray (Chapter 4). Thus, a String and an NSString can be cast to one another, and an Array (of the right sort) and an NSArray can be cast to one another; a String can be passed where an NSString is expected, and an Array (of the right sort) can be passed where an NSArray is expected. Moreover, when you use String or Array in the presence of Foundation, some NSString and NSArray properties and methods spring to life.

New in Swift 3, the Swift "overlay" puts a native Swift interface in front of many other Foundation types. The Swift interface is distinguished by dropping the "NS" prefix that marks Foundation class names; for example, Objective-C NSData is accessed through Swift Data, and Objective-C NSDate is accessed through Swift Date — though you can still use NSData and NSDate directly if you really want to. Again, the Swift and Objective-C types are bridged to one another, so casting and passing works as you would expect. The Swift types provide many conveniences that the Objective-C types do not; for example, they may declare adoption of appropriate Swift protocols such as Equatable and Comparable, and, in some cases, they may be value types (structs) where the Objective-C types are reference types (classes).

 There are two kinds of bridging to be distinguished here. String and Array are native Swift types, with an independent existence. Date and Data, on the other hand, aren't native Swift types; they are façades for NSDate and NSData, meaning that you cannot use them *at all* except in the presence of Cocoa's Foundation framework.

Useful Structs and Constants

NSRange is a C struct (see Appendix A) of importance in dealing with some of the classes I'm about to discuss. Its components are integers, location and length. For example, an NSRange whose location is 1 starts at the second element of something (because element counting is always zero-based), and if its length is 2 it designates this element and the next.

Cocoa supplies various convenience functions for dealing with an NSRange. Swift helps out by bridging NSRange as a Swift struct, and you can convert between an NSRange and a Swift Range whose endpoints are Ints: Swift gives NSRange an initializer that takes a Swift Range, along with a toRange method.

New in Swift 3, you may encounter some difficulty initializing an NSRange from a Range — because what you think is a Range isn't one. For example, this code won't compile:

```
let r = 1...3
let rang = NSRange(r) // compile error
```

The reason is that 1...3 is actually something called a CountableClosedRange. Luckily, you can coerce a CountableClosedRange to a Range, and from there you can coerce to an NSRange:

```
let rang = NSRange(Range(r))
```

Another new Swift 3 issue is that you can't print an NSRange; you get an opaque struct in the console. The workaround is to pass the NSRange through Cocoa's NSStringFromRange function:

```
print(NSStringFromRange(rang))
```

NSNotFound is a constant integer indicating that some requested element was not found. The true numeric value of NSNotFound is of no concern to you; always compare against NSNotFound itself, to learn whether a result is meaningful. For example, if you ask for the index of a certain object in an NSArray and the object isn't present, the result is NSNotFound:

```
let arr = ["hey"] as NSArray
let ix = arr.index(of:"ho")
if ix == NSNotFound {
    print("it wasn't found")
}
```

Why does Cocoa resort to an integer value with a special meaning in this way? Because it has to. The result could not be 0 to indicate the absence of the object, because 0 would indicate the first element of the array. Nor could it be -1, because an NSArray index value is always positive. Nor could it be nil, because Objective-C can't return nil when an integer is expected (and even if it could, it would be seen as another way of saying 0). Contrast Swift, whose Array index(of:) method returns an Int wrapped in an Optional, allowing it to return nil to indicate that the target object wasn't found.

If a search returns a range and the thing sought is not present, the location component of the resulting NSRange will be NSNotFound. As I mentioned in Chapter 3, Swift will sometimes do some clever automatic bridging for you, thus saving you the trouble of comparing with NSNotFound. The canonical example is NSString's range(of:) method. As defined in Cocoa, it returns an NSRange; the corresponding Swift String method returns a Swift Range (of String.Index) wrapped in an Optional, returning nil if the NSRange's location is NSNotFound:

```
let s = "hello"
let r = s.range(of:"ha") // nil; an Optional wrapping a Swift Range
```

That's great if what you wanted is a Swift Range, suitable for further slicing a Swift String; but if you wanted an NSRange, suitable for handing back to Cocoa, you'll need to cast your original Swift String to an NSString to start with — thus causing the result to remain in the Cocoa world:

```
let s = "hello" as NSString
let r = s.range(of:"ha") // an NSRange
if r.location == NSNotFound {
    print("it wasn't found")
}
```

NSString and Friends

NSString is the Cocoa object version of a string. NSString and Swift String are bridged to one another, and you will often move between them without thinking, passing a Swift String to Cocoa where an NSString is expected, calling Cocoa NSString methods on a Swift String, and so forth. For example:

```
let s = "hello"
let s2 = s.capitalized
```

In that code, s is a Swift String and s2 is a Swift String, but the capitalized property actually belongs to Cocoa. In the course of that code, a Swift String has been bridged to NSString and passed to Cocoa, which has processed it to get the capitalized string; the capitalized string is an NSString, but it has been bridged back to a Swift String. In all likelihood, you are not conscious of the bridging; capitalized feels like a native String property, but it isn't — as you can readily prove by trying to use it in an environment where Foundation is not imported (you can't do it).

In some cases, Swift may fail to cross the bridge implicitly for you, and you will need to cross the bridge yourself by casting explicitly. For example, if s is a Swift string, you can't call appendingPathExtension on it directly:

```
let s = "MyFile"
let s2 = s.appendingPathExtension("txt") // compile error
```

You have to cast explicitly to NSString:

```
let s2 = (s as NSString).appendingPathExtension("txt")
```

Also, trouble can arise where you need to provide an index on a string. For example:

```
let s = "hello"
let s2 = s.substring(to:4) // compile error
```

The problem here is that the bridging is in your way. Swift has no objection to your calling the substring(to:) method on a Swift String, but then the index value must be a String.Index, which is rather tricky to construct (see Chapter 3):

```
let s2 = s.substring(to:s.index(s.startIndex, offsetBy:4))
```

If you don't want to talk that way, you must cast the String to an NSString beforehand; now you are in Cocoa's world, where string indexes are integers:

```
let s2 = (s as NSString).substring(to:4)
```

As I explained in Chapter 3, however, those two calls are not equivalent: they can give different answers! The reason is that String and NSString have fundamentally different notions of what constitutes an element of a string (see "The String–NSString Element Mismatch" on page 95). A String must resolve its elements into characters, which means that it must walk the string, coalescing any combining codepoints; an NSString behaves as if it were an array of UTF-16 codepoints. On the Swift side, each increment in a String.Index corresponds to a true character, but access by index or range requires walking the string; on the Cocoa side, access by index or range is extremely fast, but might not correspond to character boundaries. (See the "Characters and Grapheme Clusters" chapter of Apple's *String Programming Guide*.)

Another important difference between a Swift String and a Cocoa NSString is that an NSString is immutable. This means that, with NSString, you can do things such as obtain a new string based on the first — as capitalized and substring(to:) do — but you can't change the string *in place*. To do that, you need another class, a subclass of NSString, NSMutableString. NSMutableString has many useful methods, and you'll probably want to take advantage of them; but Swift String isn't bridged to NSMutableString, so you can't get from String to NSMutableString merely by casting. To obtain an NSMutableString, you'll have to make one. The simplest way is with NSMutableString's initializer init(string:), which expects an NSString — meaning that you can pass a Swift String. Coming back the other way, you can cast all the way from NSMutableString to a Swift String in one move:

```
let s = "hello"
let ms = NSMutableString(string:s)
ms.deleteCharacters(in:NSRange(location: ms.length-1, length:1))
let s2 = (ms as String) + "ion" // now s2 is a Swift String
```

As I said in Chapter 3, native Swift String methods are thin on the ground. All the real string-processing power lives over on the Cocoa side of the bridge. So you're going to be crossing that bridge a lot! And this will not be only for the power of the NSString and NSMutableString classes. Many other useful classes are associated with them.

For example, suppose you want to search a string for some substring. All the best ways come from Cocoa:

- An NSString can be searched using various range methods, with numerous options such as ignoring diacriticals, ignoring case, starting at the end, and insisting that the substring occupy the start or end of the searched string.

- Perhaps you don't know exactly what you're looking for: you need to describe it structurally. A Scanner (Objective-C NSScanner) lets you walk through a string looking for pieces that fit certain criteria; for example, with Scanner (and CharacterSet, Objective-C NSCharacterSet) you can skip past everything in a string that precedes a number and then extract the number.

- By specifying the option .regularExpressionSearch, you can search using a regular expression. Regular expressions are also supported as a separate class, NSRegularExpression, which in turn uses NSTextCheckingResult to describe match results.

- More sophisticated automated textual analysis is supported by some additional classes, such as NSDataDetector, an NSRegularExpression subclass that efficiently finds certain types of string expression such as a URL or a phone number, and NSLinguisticTagger, which actually attempts to analyze text into its grammatical parts of speech.

In this example, our goal is to replace all occurrences of the word "hell" with the word "heaven." We don't want to replace mere occurrences of the *substring* "hell" — for example, "hello" should be left intact. Thus our search needs some intelligence as to what constitutes a word boundary. That sounds like a job for a regular expression. Swift doesn't have regular expressions, so everything has to be done by Cocoa:

```
let s = NSMutableString(string:"hello world, go to hell")
let r = try! NSRegularExpression(
    pattern: "\\bhell\\b",
    options: .caseInsensitive)
r.replaceMatches(
    in: s, range: NSRange(location:0, length:s.length),
    withTemplate: "heaven")
// s is "hello world, go to heaven"
```

NSString also has convenience utilities for working with a file path string, and is often used in conjunction with URL (Objective-C NSURL), which is another Foundation type worth looking into, along with its companion types, URLComponents (Objective-C NSURLComponents) and URLQueryItem (Objective-C NSURLQueryItem). In addition, NSString — like some other classes discussed in this section — provides methods for writing out to a file's contents or reading in a file's contents; the file can be specified either as a string file path or as a URL.

An NSString carries no font and size information. Interface objects that display strings (such as UILabel) have a font property that is a UIFont; but this determines the *single* font and size in which the string will display. If you want styled text — where different runs of text have different style attributes (size, font, color, and so forth) — you need to use NSAttributedString, along with its supporting classes NSMutableAttributedString, NSParagraphStyle, and NSMutableParagraphStyle. These allow you to style text and paragraphs easily in sophisticated ways. The built-in interface objects that display text can display an attributed string.

String drawing in a graphics context can be performed with methods provided through the NSStringDrawing category on NSString and on NSAttributedString.

NSDate and Friends

A Date (Objective-C NSDate) is a date and time, represented internally as a number of seconds since some reference date. Calling Date's initializer init() — i.e., saying Date() — gives you a date object for the current date and time. Many date operations will also involve the use of DateComponents (Objective-C NSDateComponents), and conversions between Date and DateComponents require use of a Calendar (Objective-C NSCalendar). Here's an example of constructing a date based on its calendrical values:

```
let greg = Calendar(identifier:.gregorian)
let comp = DateComponents(calendar: greg,
    year: 2016, month: 8, day: 10, hour: 15)
let d = comp.date // Optional wrapping Date
```

Similarly, DateComponents provides the correct way to do date arithmetic. Here's how to add one month to a given date:

```
let d = Date() // or whatever
let comp = DateComponents(month:1)
let greg = Calendar(identifier:.gregorian)
let d2 = greg.date(byAdding: comp, to:d) // Optional wrapping Date
```

Because a Date is essentially a wrapper for a TimeInterval (a Double), Swift can overload the arithmetic operators so that you can do arithmetic directly on a Date:

```
let d = Date()
let d2 = d + 4 // i.e. 4 seconds later
```

New in iOS 10, you can express the range between two dates as a DateInterval (Objective-C NSDateInterval). DateIntervals can be compared, intersected, and checked for containment:

```
let greg = Calendar(identifier:.gregorian)
let d1 = DateComponents(calendar: greg,
    year: 2016, month: 1, day: 1, hour: 0).date!
let d2 = DateComponents(calendar: greg,
    year: 2016, month: 8, day: 10, hour: 15).date!
let di = DateInterval(start: d1, end: d2)
if di.contains(Date()) { // are we currently between those two dates?
```

You will also likely be concerned with dates represented as strings. If you don't take explicit charge of a date's string representation, it is represented by a string whose format may surprise you. For example, if you simply print a Date, you are shown the date in the GMT timezone, which can be confusing if that isn't where you live. A simple solution is to call description(with:), whose parameter is a Locale (Objective-C NSLocale) comprising the user's current time zone, language, region format, and calendar settings:

```
print(d)
// 2016-08-10 22:00:00 +0000
print(d.description(with:Locale.current))
// Wednesday, August 10, 2016 at 3:00:00 PM Pacific Daylight Time
```

For exact creation and parsing of date strings, use DateFormatter (Objective-C NSDateFormatter), which takes a format string similar to NSLog (and NSString's init(format:)). In this example, we call the class method dateFormat(from-Template:options:locale:) with the current locale, thus surrendering completely to the user's preferences. The template: is a string listing the date components to be used, but their order, punctuation, and language are left up to the locale:

```
let df = DateFormatter()
let format = DateFormatter.dateFormat(
    fromTemplate:"dMMMMyyyyhmmaz", options:0,
    locale:Locale.currentLocale())
df.dateFormat = format
let s = df.string(from:Date())
```

The result is the date shown in the user's time zone and language, using the correct linguistic conventions. It involves a combination of region format and language, which are two separate settings. Thus:

- On my device, the result might be "July 16, 2016, 7:44 AM PDT."
- If I change my device's *region* to France, it might be "16 July 2016 7:44 AM GMT-7."
- If I also change my device's *language* to French, it might be "16 juillet 2016 7:44 AM UTC–7."

NSNumber

An NSNumber is an object that wraps a numeric value. The wrapped value can be any standard Objective-C numeric type (including BOOL, the Objective-C equivalent of Swift Bool). In Swift, everything is an object — a number is a Struct instance — so it comes as a surprise to Swift users that NSNumber is needed. But an ordinary number in Objective-C is not an object (it is a scalar; see Chapter 1), so it cannot be used where an object is expected. Thus, NSNumber solves an important problem, converting a number into an object and back again.

Swift does its best to shield you from having to deal directly with NSNumber. It bridges Swift numeric types to Objective-C in two different ways:

As a scalar
    If Objective-C expects an ordinary number, a Swift number is bridged to an ordinary number (a scalar). For example:

```
UIView.animate(withDuration: 1,
    animations: whatToAnimate, completion: whatToDoLater)
```

Objective-C `animateWithDuration:animations:completion:` takes a C double as its first parameter. The Swift numeric object that you supply as the first argument to `animate(withDuration:animations:completion:)` becomes a C double.

As an NSNumber

If Objective-C expects an object, a Swift basic numeric type is bridged to an NSNumber. A basic numeric type is Int, UIInt, Float, or Double — and also Bool, because NSNumber can wrap an Objective-C BOOL. For example:

```
UserDefaults.standard.set(1, forKey:"Score")
```

Objective-C `setObject:forKey:` takes an Objective-C object as its first parameter. The Swift numeric object that you supply as the first argument to `set(_:forKey:)` becomes an NSNumber.

Naturally, if you need to cross the bridge explicitly, you can. You can cast a Swift number (of a basic numeric type) to an NSNumber:

```
let n = 1 as NSNumber
```

If you need an NSNumber to wrap a numeric type that isn't automatically bridged, call its `init(value:)` initializer:

```
let i : UInt8 = 1
// let n = i as NSNumber // compile error, not bridged
let n = NSNumber(value:i)
```

Coming back from Objective-C to Swift, a value will typically arrive as an Any object and you will have to cast down. NSNumber comes with properties for accessing the wrapped value by its numeric type. Recall this example from Chapter 5, involving an NSNumber extracted as a value from a Notification's `userInfo` dictionary:

```
if let prog = (n.userInfo?["progress"] as? NSNumber)?.doubleValue {
    self.progress = prog
}
```

An NSNumber can also be cast down to a basic Swift numeric type. Therefore, so can an Any object wrapping an NSNumber. Thus, the same example can be rewritten like this, without explicitly mentioning NSNumber:

```
if let prog = n.userInfo?["progress"] as? Double {
    self.progress = prog
}
```

In the second version, Swift is actually doing behind the scenes exactly what we did in the first version — treating an Any object as an NSNumber and getting its `doubleValue` property to extract the wrapped number.

An NSNumber object is just a wrapper and no more. It can't be used directly for numeric calculations; it isn't a number. It *wraps* a number. One way or another, if you want a number, you have to extract it from the NSNumber.

An NSNumber subclass, NSDecimalNumber, on the other hand, *can* be used in calculations, thanks to a bunch of arithmetic methods:

```
let dec1 = NSDecimalNumber(value: 4.0)
let dec2 = NSDecimalNumber(value: 5.0)
let sum = dec1.adding(dec2) // 9.0
```

NSDecimalNumber is useful particularly for rounding, because there's a handy way to specify the desired rounding behavior.

Underlying NSDecimalNumber is the Decimal struct (Objective-C NSDecimal); it is an NSDecimalNumber's `decimalValue`. In Objective-C, NSDecimal comes with C functions that are faster than NSDecimalNumber methods. In Swift 3, things are even better, because the arithmetic operators are overloaded to allow you to do Decimal arithmetic; thus, you are likely to prefer working with Decimal over NSDecimalNumber:

```
let dec1 = Decimal(4.0)
let dec2 = Decimal(5.0)
let sum = dec1 + dec2
```

NSValue

NSValue is NSNumber's superclass. It is used for wrapping nonnumeric C values, such as C structs, where an object is expected. The problem being solved here is parallel to the problem solved by NSNumber: a Swift struct is an object, but a C struct is not, so a struct cannot be used in Objective-C where an object is expected.

Convenience methods provided through the NSValueUIGeometryExtensions category on NSValue allow easy wrapping and unwrapping of CGPoint, CGSize, CGRect, CGAffineTransform, UIEdgeInsets, and UIOffset; additional categories allow easy wrapping and unwrapping of NSRange, CATransform3D, CMTime, CMTimeMapping, CMTimeRange, MKCoordinate, and MKCoordinateSpan. You are unlikely to need to store any other kind of C value in an NSValue, but if you do need to, you can.

Swift will *not* magically bridge any of these C struct types to or from an NSValue. You must manage them explicitly, exactly as you would do if your code were written in Objective-C. In this example from my own code, we use Core Animation to animate the movement of a button in the interface from one position to another; the button's starting and ending positions are each expressed as a CGPoint, but an animation's `fromValue` and `toValue` must be objects. A CGPoint is not an Objective-C object, so we must wrap the CGPoint values in NSValue objects:

```
let ba = CABasicAnimation(keyPath:"position")
ba.duration = 10
ba.fromValue = NSValue(cgPoint:self.oldButtonCenter)
ba.toValue = NSValue(cgPoint:goal)
self.button.layer.add(ba, forKey:nil)
```

Similarly, you can make an array of CGPoint in Swift, because CGPoint becomes a Swift object type (a Swift struct), and a Swift Array can have elements of any type; but such an array isn't meaningful to Objective-C, because an Objective-C NSArray must have objects as its elements, and a CGPoint, in Objective-C, is not an object. Thus, if you want Objective-C to do anything with those CGPoints, you must wrap them in NSValue objects. This is another animation example, where I set the values array (an NSArray) of a keyframe animation by turning an array of CGPoints into an array of NSValues:

```
anim.values = [oldP,p1,p2,newP].map {NSValue(cgPoint:$0)}
```

NSData

Data (Objective-C NSData) is a general sequence of bytes; basically, it's just a buffer, a chunk of memory. In Objective-C, NSData is immutable; the mutable version is its subclass NSMutableData. In Swift, however, where Data is a bridged value type imposed in front of NSData, a Data object is mutable if it was declared with var, just like any other value type. Moreover, because a Data object represents a byte sequence, Swift makes it a Collection (and therefore a Sequence), causing Swift features such as enumeration with for...in, subscripting, and append(_:) to spring to life. Thus, although you can work with NSData and NSMutableData if you want to (by casting to cross the bridge), you are much more likely to prefer Data.

In practice, Data tends to arise in two main ways:

- When downloading from the Internet. For example, URLSession (Objective-C NSURLSession) supplies whatever it retrieves from the Internet as Data. Transforming it from there into (let's say) a string, specifying the correct encoding, would then be up to you.

- When storing an object as a file or in user preferences (UserDefaults). For example, you can't store a UIColor value directly into user preferences. So if the user has made a color choice and you need to save it, you transform the UIColor into a Data object (using NSKeyedArchiver) and save that:

```
let ud = UserDefaults.standard
let c = UIColor.blue
let cdata = NSKeyedArchiver.archivedData(withRootObject:c)
ud.set(cdata, forKey: "myColor")
```

NSMeasurement and Friends

New in iOS 10, the Measurement type (Objective-C NSMeasurement) embodies the notion of a measurement by some unit (Unit, Objective-C NSUnit). A unit may be along some dimension that may be expressible in different units convertible to one another; by reducing values in different units of the same dimension to a base unit, a Measurement permits you to perform arithmetic operations and conversions.

The dimensions, which are all subclasses of the (abstract) Dimension class (Objective-C NSDimension, an NSUnit subclass), have names like UnitAngle and UnitLength (Objective-C NSUnitAngle, NSUnitLength), and have class properties vending an instance corresponding to a particular unit type; for example, UnitAngle has class properties degrees and radians and others, and UnitLength has class properties miles and kilometers and others.

To illustrate, I'll add 5 miles to 6 kilometers:

```
let m1 = Measurement(value:5, unit: UnitLength.miles)
let m2 = Measurement(value:6, unit: UnitLength.kilometers)
let total = m1 + m2
```

The answer, total, is 14046.7 meters under the hood, because meters are the base unit of length. But it can be converted to any length unit:

```
let totalFeet = total.converted(to: .feet).value // 46084.9737532808
```

If your goal is to output a measurement as a user-facing string, use a Measurement-Formatter (Objective-C NSMeasurementFormatter). Its behavior is locale-dependent by default, expressing the value and the units as the user would expect:

```
let mf = MeasurementFormatter()
let s = mf.string(from:total) // "8.728 mi"
```

My code says nothing about miles, but the MeasurementFormatter outputs "8.728 mi" because my device is set to United States and English. If my device is set to France and French, the very same code outputs "14,047 km" — using the French decimal point notation and the French preferred unit of distance measurement.

Equality and Comparison

In Swift, the equality and comparison operators can be overridden for an object type that adopts Equatable and Comparable ("Operators" on page 274). But Objective-C operators can't do that; they are applicable only to scalars. Objective-C therefore performs comparison of object instances in a special way, and it can be useful to know about this when working with Cocoa types.

To permit determination of whether two objects are "equal" — whatever that may mean for this object type — an Objective-C class must implement isEqual: — Swift isEqual(_:) — which is inherited from NSObject. Swift will help out by treating NSObject as Equatable and by permitting the use of the == operator, implicitly converting it to an isEqual(_:) call. Thus, if a class derived from NSObject implements isEqual(_:), ordinary Swift comparison will work. For example:

```
let n1 = NSNumber(value:1)
let n2 = NSNumber(value:2)
let n3 = NSNumber(value:3)
let ok = n2 == 2 // true ❶
let ok2 = n2 == NSNumber(value:2) // true ❷
let ix = [n1,n2,n3].index(of:2) // Optional wrapping 1 ❸
```

That code seems to do three impossible things before breakfast:

❶ We directly compare an Int to an NSNumber, and we get the right answer, as if we were comparing the Int to the integer wrapped by that NSNumber.

❷ We directly compare two NSNumber objects to one another, and we get the right answer, as if we were comparing the integers that they wrap.

❸ We treat an array of NSNumber objects as an array of Equatables and call the index(of:) method, and we successfully determine which NSNumber object is "equal" to an actual number.

There are two parts to this apparent magic:

- The numbers are being wrapped in NSNumber objects for us.
- The == operator (also used behind the scenes by the index(of:) method) is being converted to an isEqual(_:) call. NSNumber implements isEqual(_:) to compare two NSNumber objects by comparing the numeric values that they wrap; therefore the equality comparisons all work correctly.

If an NSObject subclass *doesn't* implement isEqual(_:), it inherits NSObject's implementation, which compares the two objects for identity (like Swift's === operator). For example, these two Dog objects can be compared with the == operator, even though Dog does not adopt Equatable, because they derive from NSObject — but Dog doesn't implement isEqual(_:), so == defaults to NSObject's identity comparison:

```
class Dog : NSObject {
    var name : String
    init(_ name:String) {self.name = name}
}
let d1 = Dog("Fido")
let d2 = Dog("Fido")
let ok = d1 == d2 // false
```

Similarly, in Objective-C it is up to individual classes to supply ordered comparison methods. The standard method is compare: — Swift compare(_:) — which returns one of three cases of ComparisonResult (Objective-C NSComparisonResult):

.orderedAscending
>   The receiver is less than the argument.

.orderedSame
>   The receiver is equal to the argument.

.orderedDescending
>   The receiver is greater than the argument.

Swift comparison operators (< and so forth) do *not* magically call compare(_:) for you. You can't compare two NSNumber values directly:

```
let n1 = NSNumber(value:1)
let n2 = NSNumber(value:2)
let ok = n1 < n2 // compile error
```

You will typically fall back on calling compare(_:) yourself:

```
let n1 = NSNumber(value:1)
let n2 = NSNumber(value:2)
let ok = n1.compare(n2) == .orderedAscending // true
```

On the other hand, where Swift overlays its own type in front of a Foundation type, that type *can* adopt Equatable and Comparable, and now comparison operators *do* work. For example, you can't compare two NSDate values with <, but you *can* compare two Date values:

```
let d1 = // ... some Date ...
let d2 = // ... some Date ...
let ok = d1 < d2 // fine!
```

NSArray and NSMutableArray

NSArray is Objective-C's array object type. It is fundamentally similar to Swift Array, and they are bridged to one another; but NSArray elements must be objects (classes and class instances), and they don't have to be of a single type. For a full discussion of how to bridge back and forth between Swift Array and Objective-C NSArray, implicitly and by casting, see "Swift Array and Objective-C NSArray" on page 228.

An NSArray's length is its count, and an element can be obtained by index number using object(at:). The index of the first element, as with a Swift Array, is zero, so the index of the last element is count minus one.

Instead of calling object(at:), you can use subscripting with an NSArray. This is not because NSArray is bridged to Swift Array, but because NSArray implements an

Objective-C method, `objectAtIndexedSubscript:`, which is the Objective-C equivalent of a Swift `subscript` getter. In fact, when you examine the NSArray header file translated into Swift, this method is shown as a `subscript` declaration!

You can seek an object within an array with `index(of:)` or `indexOfObject-Identical(to:)`; the former's idea of equality is to call `isEqual(_:)`, whereas the latter uses object identity (like Swift's `===`). As I mentioned earlier, if the object is not found in the array, the result is `NSNotFound`.

Unlike a Swift Array, and like an Objective-C NSString, an NSArray is immutable. This doesn't mean you can't mutate any of the objects it contains; it means that once the NSArray is formed you can't remove an object from it, insert an object into it, or replace an object at a given index. To do those things while staying in the Objective-C world, you can derive a new array consisting of the original array plus or minus some objects, or use NSArray's subclass, NSMutableArray. Swift Array is not bridged to NSMutableArray; if you want an NSMutableArray, you must create it. The simplest way is with the NSMutableArray initializers, `init()` or `init(array:)`.

Once you have an NSMutableArray, you can call methods such as NSMutableArray's `add(_:)` and `replaceObject(at:with:)`. You can also assign into an NSMutable-Array using subscripting. Again, this is because NSMutableArray implements a special Objective-C method, `setObject:atIndexedSubscript:`; Swift recognizes this as equivalent to a `subscript` setter.

Coming back the other way, you can cast from NSMutableArray down to a Swift array:

```
let marr = NSMutableArray()
marr.add(1) // an NSNumber
marr.add(2) // an NSNumber
let arr = marr as NSArray as! [Int]
```

Cocoa provides ways to search or filter an array by passing a function. You can also derive a sorted version of an array, supplying the sorting rules in various ways, or if it's a mutable array, you can sort it directly. You might prefer to perform those kinds of operation in the Swift Array world, but it can be useful to know how to do them the Cocoa way. For example:

```
let pep = ["Manny", "Moe", "Jack"] as NSArray
let ems = pep.objects(
    at: pep.indexesOfObjects(options:[]) {
        (obj, idx, stop) -> Bool in
        return (obj as! NSString).range(
            of: "m", options:.caseInsensitive
        ).location == 0
    }
) // ["Manny", "Moe"]
```

NSDictionary and NSMutableDictionary

NSDictionary is Objective-C's dictionary object type. It is fundamentally similar to Swift Dictionary, and they are bridged to one another. But NSDictionary keys and values must be objects (classes and class instances), and they don't have to be of a single type; the keys must conform to NSCopying and be hashable. See "Swift Dictionary and Objective-C NSDictionary" on page 233 for a full discussion of how to bridge back and forth between Swift Dictionary and Objective-C NSDictionary, including casting.

An NSDictionary is immutable; its mutable subclass is NSMutableDictionary. Swift Dictionary is not bridged to NSMutableDictionary; you can most easily make an NSMutableDictionary with an initializer, init() or init(dictionary:).

The keys of an NSDictionary are distinct (using isEqual(_:) for comparison). If you add a key–value pair to an NSMutableDictionary, then if that key is not already present, the pair is simply added, but if the key is already present, then the corresponding value is replaced. This is parallel to the behavior of Swift Dictionary.

The fundamental use of an NSDictionary is to request an entry's value by key (using object(forKey:)); if no such key exists, the result is nil. In Objective-C, nil is not an object, and thus cannot be a value in an NSDictionary; the meaning of this response is thus unambiguous. Swift handles this by treating the result of object(forKey:) as an Any? — that is, an Optional wrapping an Any.

Subscripting is possible on an NSDictionary or an NSMutableDictionary for similar reasons to why subscripting is possible on an NSArray or an NSMutableArray. NSDictionary implements objectForKeyedSubscript:, and Swift understands this as equivalent to a subscript getter. In addition, NSMutableDictionary implements setObject:forKeyedSubscript:, and Swift understands this as equivalent to a subscript setter.

You can get from an NSDictionary a list of keys (allKeys), a list of values (allValues), or a list of keys sorted by value. You can also walk through the key–value pairs, and you can even filter an NSDictionary by a test against its values.

NSSet and Friends

An NSSet is an unordered collection of distinct objects. "Distinct" means that no two objects in a set can return true when they are compared using isEqual(_:). Learning whether an object is present in a set is much more efficient than seeking it in an array, and you can ask whether one set is a subset of, or intersects, another set. You can walk through (enumerate) a set with the for...in construct, though the order is of course undefined. You can filter a set, as you can an NSArray. Indeed, much of what you can do with a set is parallel to what you can do with an array, except that of course you can't do anything with a set that involves the notion of ordering.

To escape even that restriction, you can use an *ordered set*. An ordered set (NSOrderedSet) is *very* like an array, and the methods for working with it are very similar to the methods for working with an array — you can even fetch an element by subscripting (because it implements `objectAtIndexedSubscript:`). But an ordered set's elements must be distinct. An ordered set provides many of the advantages of sets: for example, as with an NSSet, learning whether an object is present in an ordered set is much more efficient than for an array, and you can readily take the union, intersection, or difference with another set. Since the distinctness restriction will often prove no restriction at all (because the elements were going to be distinct anyway), it is worthwhile to use NSOrderedSet instead of NSArray wherever possible.

 Handing an array over to an ordered set *uniques* the array, meaning that order is maintained but only the first occurrence of an equal object is moved to the set.

An NSSet is immutable. You can derive one NSSet from another by adding or removing elements, or you can use its subclass, NSMutableSet. Similarly, NSOrderedSet has its mutable counterpart, NSMutableOrderedSet (which you can insert into by subscripting, because it implements `setObject:atIndexedSubscript:`). There is no penalty for adding to a set an object that the set already contains; nothing is added (and so the distinctness rule is enforced), but there's no error.

NSCountedSet, a subclass of NSMutableSet, is a mutable unordered collection of objects that are *not* necessarily distinct (this concept is often referred to as a *bag*). It is implemented as a set plus a count of how many times each element has been added.

Swift Set is bridged to NSSet. But NSSet elements must be objects (classes and class instances), and they don't have to be of a single type. For details, see "Swift Set and Objective-C NSSet" on page 240. NSMutableSet, NSCountedSet, NSOrderedSet, and NSMutableOrderedSet are easily formed from a set or an array using an initializer. Coming back the other way, you can cast an NSMutableSet or NSCountedSet up to NSSet and down to a Swift Set (similar to an NSMutableArray). NSOrderedSet comes with "façade" properties that present it as an array or a set. Because of their special behaviors, however, you are much more likely to leave an NSCountedSet or NSOrderedSet in its Objective-C form for as long you're working with it.

NSIndexSet

IndexSet (Objective-C NSIndexSet) represents a collection of unique whole numbers; its purpose is to express element numbers of an ordered collection, such as an array. Thus, for instance, to retrieve multiple elements simultaneously from an array, you specify the desired indexes as an IndexSet. It is also used with other things that are array-like; for example, you pass an IndexSet to a UITableView to indicate what sections to insert or delete.

NSIndexSet is immutable; it has a mutable subclass, NSMutableIndexSet. As with other Swift types imposed in front of Foundation types, however, IndexSet gets to do all sorts of convenient Swift magic. IndexSet is a value type, so it is mutable if the declaration uses var. Comparison and arithmetic operators work directly with IndexSet values. Even more important, an IndexSet acts like a Set: it adopts the SetAlgebra protocol, and methods like contains(_:) and intersection(_:) spring to life. Thus you probably won't need NSMutableIndexSet at all.

To take a specific example, let's say you want to speak of the elements at indexes 1, 2, 3, 4, 8, 9, and 10 of an array. IndexSet expresses this notion in some compact implementation that can be readily queried. The actual implementation is opaque, but you can imagine that this IndexSet might consist of two Ranges, 1...4 and 8...10, and IndexSet's methods actually invite you to think of it as a Set of Ranges:

```
let arr = ["zero", "one", "two", "three", "four", "five",
    "six", "seven", "eight", "nine", "ten"]
var ixs = IndexSet()
ixs.insert(integersIn: Range(1...4))
ixs.insert(integersIn: Range(8...10))
let arr2 = (arr as NSArray).objects(at:ixs)
// ["one", "two", "three", "four", "eight", "nine", "ten"]
```

To walk through (enumerate) the index values specified by an IndexSet, you can use for...in; alternatively, you can walk through an IndexSet's indexes or ranges by calling various enumerate... methods that let you pass a function returning a Bool.

NSNull

The NSNull class does nothing but supply a pointer to a singleton object, NSNull(). This singleton object is used to stand for nil in situations where an actual Objective-C object is required and nil is not permitted. For example, you can't use nil as the value of an element of an Objective-C collection (such as NSArray, NSSet, or NSDictionary), so you'd use NSNull() instead.

You can test an object for equality against NSNull() using the ordinary equality operator (==), because it falls back on NSObject's isEqual(_:), which is identity comparison. This is a singleton instance, and therefore identity comparison works.

Immutable and Mutable

Beginners sometimes have difficulty with the Cocoa Foundation notion of class pairs where the superclass is immutable and the subclass is mutable. This notion is reminiscent of the Swift distinction between a constant (let) and a true variable (var), and has similar consequences. For example, the fact that NSArray is "immutable" means much the same thing as the fact that a Swift Array is referred to with let: you can't append or insert into this array, or replace or delete an element of this array; but if its elements are reference types — and of course, for an NSArray, they *are* reference types — you can mutate an element in place.

The reason why Cocoa needs these immutable/mutable pairs is to prevent unauthorized mutation. These are ordinary classes, so an NSArray object, say, is an ordinary class instance — a reference type. If a class has an NSArray property, and if this array were mutable, the array could be mutated by some other object, behind this class's back. To prevent that from happening, a class will work internally and temporarily with a mutable instance but then store and vend to other classes an immutable instance, thus protecting the value from being changed accidentally or behind its own back. (Swift doesn't face the same issue, because its fundamental built-in object types such as String, Array, and Dictionary are structs, and therefore are value types, which cannot be mutated in place; they can be changed only by being replaced, and that is something that can be guarded against or detected through a setter observer.)

The documentation may not make it completely obvious that the mutable classes obey and, if appropriate, override the methods of their immutable superclasses. For example, dozens of NSMutableArray methods are not listed on NSMutableArray's class documentation page, because they are inherited from NSArray. And when such methods are inherited by the mutable subclass, they may be overridden to fit the mutable subclass. For example, NSArray's init(array:) generates an immutable array, but NSMutableArray's init(array:) — which isn't even listed on the NSMutableArray documentation page, because it is inherited from NSArray — generates a mutable array.

That fact also answers the question of how to make an immutable array mutable, and *vice versa*. If init(array:), sent to the NSArray class, yields a new immutable array containing the same objects in the same order as the original array, then the same initializer, init(array:), sent to the NSMutableArray class, yields a *mutable* array containing the same objects in the same order as the original. Thus this single method can transform an array between immutable and mutable in either direction. You can also use copy (produces an immutable copy) and mutableCopy (produces a mutable copy), both inherited from NSObject; but these are not as convenient because they yield an Any which must then be cast.

These immutable/mutable class pairs are all implemented as *class clusters*, which means that Cocoa uses a secret class, different from the documented class you work with. You may discover this by peeking under the hood; for example, saying `NSStringFromClass(type(of:s))`, where s is an NSString, might yield a mysterious value "__NSCFString". You should not spend any time wondering about this secret class. It is subject to change without notice and is none of your business; you should never have looked at it in the first place.

Property Lists

A *property list* is a string (XML) representation of data. The Foundation classes NSString, NSData, NSArray, and NSDictionary are the only classes that can be converted into a property list. Moreover, an NSArray or NSDictionary can be converted into a property list only if the only classes it collects are these classes, along with NSDate and NSNumber. (This is why, as I mentioned earlier, you must convert a UIColor into a Data object in order to store it in user defaults; the user defaults *is* a property list.)

The primary use of a property list is to store data as a file. It is a way of *serializing* a value — saving it to disk in a form from which it can be reconstructed. NSArray and NSDictionary provide convenience methods `write(toFile:atomically:)` and `write(to:atomically:)` that generate property list files given a string pathname or file URL, respectively; conversely, they also provide initializers that create an NSArray object or an NSDictionary object based on the property list contents of a given file. For this very reason, you are likely to start with one of these classes when you want to create a property list. (The NSString and NSData `write` methods just write the data out as a file directly, not as a property list.)

Here, for example, I'll create an array of strings and write it out to disk as a property list file:

```
let arr = ["Manny", "Moe", "Jack"]
let fm = FileManager()
let temp = fm.temporaryDirectory
if let f = try? temp.appendingPathComponent("pep.plist") {
    (arr as NSArray).write(to: f, atomically: true)
}
/*
<?xml version="1.0" encoding="UTF-8"?>
<!DOCTYPE plist PUBLIC "-//Apple//DTD PLIST 1.0//EN"
    "http://www.apple.com/DTDs/PropertyList-1.0.dtd">
<plist version="1.0">
<array>
    <string>Manny</string>
    <string>Moe</string>
```

```
      <string>Jack</string>
    </array>
    </plist>
    */
```

When you reconstruct an NSArray or NSDictionary object from a property list file in this way, the collections, string objects, and data objects in the collection are all immutable. If you want them to be mutable, or if you want to convert an instance of one of the other property list classes to a property list, you'll use the PropertyListSerialization class (Objective-C NSPropertyListSerialization; see the *Property List Programming Guide*).

Accessors, Properties, and Key–Value Coding

An Objective-C instance variable is structurally similar to a Swift instance property: it's a variable that accompanies each instance of a class, with a lifetime and value associated with that particular instance. An Objective-C instance variable, however, is usually private, in the sense that instances of other classes can't see it (and Swift can't see it). If an instance variable is to be made public, an Objective-C class will typically implement *accessor methods*: a getter method and (if this instance variable is to be publicly writable) a setter method. This is such a common thing to do that there are naming conventions:

The getter method

A getter should have the same name as the instance variable (without an initial underscore if the instance variable has one). Thus, if the instance variable is named myVar (or _myVar), the getter method should be named myVar.

The setter method

A setter method's name should start with set, followed by a capitalized version of the instance variable's name (without an initial underscore if the instance variable has one). The setter should take one parameter — the new value to be assigned to the instance variable. Thus, if the instance variable is named myVar (or _myVar), the setter should be named setMyVar:.

This pattern — a getter method, possibly accompanied by an appropriately named setter method — is so common that there's a shorthand: an Objective-C class can declare a *property*, using the keyword @property and a name. Here, for example, is a line from the UIView class declaration:

```
    @property(nonatomic) CGRect frame;
```

(Ignore the material in parentheses.) Within Objective-C, this declaration constitutes a promise that there is a getter accessor method frame returning a CGRect, along with a setter accessor method setFrame: that takes a CGRect parameter.

When Objective-C formally declares a @property in this way, *Swift sees it as a Swift property*. Thus, UIView's frame property declaration is translated directly into a Swift declaration of an instance property frame of type CGRect:

```
var frame: CGRect
```

An Objective-C property name, however, is mere syntactic sugar. When you set a UIView's frame property, you are actually calling its setFrame: setter method, and when you get a UIView's frame property, you are actually calling its frame getter method. In Objective-C, use of the property is optional; Objective-C code can, and often does, call the setFrame: and frame methods *directly*. But you can't do that in Swift! If an Objective-C class has a formal @property declaration, *the accessor methods are hidden from Swift*.

An Objective-C property declaration can include the word readonly in the parentheses. This indicates that there is a getter but no setter. So, for example (ignore the other material in the parentheses):

```
@property(nonatomic,readonly,strong) CALayer *layer;
```

Swift will reflect this restriction with {get} after the declaration, as if this were a computed read-only property; the compiler will not permit you to assign to such a property:

```
var layer: CALayer { get }
```

An Objective-C property and its accompanying accessor methods have a life of their own, independent of any underlying instance variable. Although accessor methods may literally be ways of accessing an invisible instance variable, they don't have to be. When you set a UIView's frame property and the setFrame: accessor method is called, you have no way of knowing what that method is really doing: it might be setting an instance variable called frame or _frame, but who knows? In this sense, accessors and properties are a façade, hiding the underlying implementation. This is similar to how, within Swift, you can set a variable without knowing or caring whether it is a stored variable or a computed variable.

Swift Accessors

Just as Objective-C properties are actually a shorthand for accessor methods, so Objective-C treats Swift properties as a shorthand for accessor methods — even though no such methods are formally present. If you, in Swift, declare that a class has a property prop, Objective-C can call a prop method to get its value or a setProp: method to set its value, *even though you have not implemented such methods*. Those calls are routed to your property through *implicit* accessor methods.

In Swift, you should *not* write *explicit* accessor methods for a property; the compiler will stop you if you attempt to do so. If you need to implement an accessor method explicitly and formally, use a computed property. Here, for example, I'll add to my UIViewController subclass a computed `color` property with a getter and a setter:

```
class ViewController: UIViewController {
    var color : UIColor {
        get {
            print("someone called the getter")
            return .red
        }
        set {
            print("someone called the setter")
        }
    }
}
```

Objective-C code can now call explicitly the implicit `setColor:` and `color` accessor methods — and when it does, the computed property's setter and getter methods are in fact called:

```
ViewController* vc = [ViewController new];
[vc setColor:[UIColor redColor]]; // "someone called the setter"
UIColor* c = [vc color]; // "someone called the getter"
```

This proves that, in Objective-C's mind, you *have* provided `setColor:` and `color` accessor methods. You can even change the Objective-C names of these accessor methods! To do so, add an `@objc(...)` attribute with the Objective-C name in parentheses. You can add it to a computed property's setter and getter methods, or you can add it to a property itself:

```
@objc(hue) var color : UIColor?
```

Objective-C code can now call `hue` and `setHue:` accessor methods directly.

If, in speaking to Objective-C, you need to pass a selector for an accessor method, precede the contents of the `#selector` expression with `getter:` or `setter:`. For example, `#selector(setter:color)` is `"setHue:"` if we have modified our `color` property's Objective-C name with `@objc(hue)` (or `"setColor:"` if we have not).

If all you want to do is add functionality to the setter, use a setter observer. For example, to add functionality to the Objective-C `setFrame:` method in your UIView subclass, you can override the `frame` property and write a `didSet` observer:

```
class MyView: UIView {
    override var frame : CGRect {
        didSet {
            print("the frame setter was called: \(super.frame)")
        }
    }
}
```

Key–Value Coding

Cocoa can dynamically call an accessor method (or access an Objective-C instance variable) based on a string name specified at runtime, through a mechanism called *key–value coding* (KVC). The string name is the *key*; what is passed or returned is the *value*. The basis for key–value coding is the NSKeyValueCoding protocol, an informal protocol; it is actually a category injected into NSObject. A Swift class, to be susceptible to key–value coding, must therefore be derived from NSObject.

The fundamental key–value coding methods are value(forKey:) and set-Value(_:forKey:). When one of these methods is called on an object, the object is introspected. In simplified terms, first the appropriate accessor method is sought; if it doesn't exist, the instance variable is accessed directly. Another useful pair of methods is dictionaryWithValues(forKeys:) and setValuesForKeys(_:), which allow you to get and set multiple key–value pairs by way of a dictionary with a single command.

The value in key–value coding must be an Objective-C object, and is typed in Swift as Any. When calling value(forKey:), you'll receive an Optional wrapping an Any; you'll want to cast this down safely to its expected type.

A class is *key–value coding compliant* (or *KVC compliant*) on a given key if it provides the accessor methods, or possesses the instance variable, required for access through that key. An attempt to access a key for which a class is *not* key–value coding compliant will cause an exception at runtime. It is useful to be familiar with the message you'll get when such a crash occurs, so let's cause it deliberately:

```
let obj = NSObject()
obj.setValue("hello", forKey:"keyName") // crash
```

The console says: "This class is not key value coding-compliant for the key keyName." The last word in that error message, despite the lack of quotes, is the key string that caused the trouble.

What would it take for that method call *not* to crash? The class of the object to which it is sent would need to have a setKeyName: setter method (or a keyName or _keyName instance variable). In Swift, as I demonstrated in the previous section, an instance property implies the existence of accessor methods. Thus, we can use key–value coding on an instance of any NSObject subclass that has a declared property, provided the key string is the string name of that property. Let's try it! Here is such a class:

```
class Dog : NSObject {
    var name : String = ""
}
```

And here's our test:

```
let d = Dog()
d.setValue("Fido", forKey:"name") // no crash!
print(d.name) // "Fido" - it worked!
```

Uses of Key–Value Coding

Key–value coding allows you, in effect, to decide at runtime, based on a string, what accessor to call. In the simplest case, you're using a string to access a dynamically specified property. That's useful in Objective-C code; but such unfettered introspective dynamism is contrary to the spirit of Swift, and in translating my own Objective-C code into Swift I have found myself accomplishing the same effect in other ways.

Here's an example. In a flashcard app, I have a class Term, representing a Latin word. It declares many properties. Each card displays one term, with its various properties shown in different text fields. If the user taps any of three text fields, I want the interface to change from the term that's currently showing to the next term whose value is different for the particular property that this text field represents. Thus this code is the same for all three text fields; the only difference is *which property* to consider as we hunt for the next term to be displayed. In Objective-C, by far the simplest way to express this parallelism is through key–value coding:

```
NSInteger tag = g.view.tag; // the tag tells us which text field was tapped
NSString* key = nil;
switch (tag) {
    case 1: key = @"lesson"; break;
    case 2: key = @"lessonSection"; break;
    case 3: key = @"lessonSectionPartFirstWord"; break;
}
// get current value of corresponding instance variable
NSString* curValue = [[self currentCardController].term valueForKey: key];
```

In Swift, however, it's easy to implement the same dynamism using an array of anonymous functions:

```
let tag = g.view!.tag - 1
let arr : [(Term) -> String] = [
    {$0.lesson}, {$0.lessonSection}, {$0.lessonSectionPartFirstWord}
]
let f = arr[tag]
let curValue = f(self.currentCardController().term)
```

Nevertheless, key–value coding remains valuable in programming iOS, especially because a number of built-in Cocoa classes permit you to use it in special ways. For example:

- If you send value(forKey:) to an NSArray, it sends value(forKey:) to each of its elements and returns a new array consisting of the results, an elegant shorthand. NSSet behaves similarly.

- NSDictionary implements value(forKey:) as an alternative to object(forKey:) (useful particularly if you have an NSArray of dictionaries). Similarly, NSMutableDictionary treats setValue(_:forKey:) as a synonym for set(_:for-

Key:), except that the first parameter can be `nil`, in which case `remove-Object(forKey:)` is called.

- NSSortDescriptor sorts an NSArray by sending `value(forKey:)` to each of its elements. This makes it easy to sort an array of dictionaries on the value of a particular dictionary key, or an array of objects on the value of a particular property.

- NSManagedObject, used in conjunction with Core Data, is guaranteed to be key–value coding compliant for attributes you've configured in the entity model. Thus, it's common to access those attributes with `value(forKey:)` and `set-Value(_:forKey:)`.

- CALayer and CAAnimation permit you to use key–value coding to define and retrieve the values for *arbitrary* keys, as if they were a kind of dictionary; they are, in effect, key–value coding compliant for *every key*. This is extremely helpful for attaching identifying and configuration information to an instance of one of these classes. That, in fact, is my own most common way of using key–value coding in Swift.

KVC and Outlets

Key–value coding lies at the heart of how outlet connections work (Chapter 7). The name of the outlet in the nib is a string. It is key–value coding that turns the string into a hunt for a matching property at nib-loading time.

Suppose, for example, that you have a class Dog with an `@IBOutlet` property `master`, and you've drawn a `"master"` outlet from that class's representative in the nib to a Person nib object. When the nib loads, the outlet name `"master"` is translated though key–value coding to the accessor method name `setMaster:`, and your Dog instance's `setMaster:` implicit accessor method is called with the Person instance as its parameter — thus setting the value of your Dog instance's `master` property to the Person instance (Figure 7-9).

If something goes wrong with the match between the outlet name in the nib and the name of the property in the class, then at runtime, when the nib loads, Cocoa's attempt to use key–value coding to set a value in your object based on the name of the outlet will fail, and will generate an exception, complaining that the class is *not key–value coding compliant* for the key (the outlet name) — that is, your app will crash at nib-loading time. A likely way for this to happen is that you formed the outlet correctly but then later changed the name of (or deleted) the property in the class (see "Misconfigured Outlets" on page 352).

Key Paths

A *key path* allows you to chain keys in a single expression. If an object is key–value coding compliant for a certain key, and if the value of that key is itself an object that is key–value coding compliant for another key, you can chain those keys by calling value(forKeyPath:) and setValue(_:forKeyPath:). A key path string looks like a succession of key names joined using dot-notation. For example, valueForKeyPath("key1.key2") effectively calls value(forKey:) on the message receiver, with "key1" as the key, and then takes the object returned from that call and calls value(forKey:) on that object, with "key2" as the key.

To illustrate this shorthand, imagine that our object myObject has an instance property theData which is an array of dictionaries such that each dictionary has a name key and a description key:

```
var theData = [
    [
        "description" : "The one with glasses.",
        "name" : "Manny"
    ],
    [
        "description" : "Looks a little like Governor Dewey.",
        "name" : "Moe"
    ],
    [
        "description" : "The one without a mustache.",
        "name" : "Jack"
    ]
]
```

We can use key–value coding with a key path to drill down into that array of dictionaries:

```
let arr = myObject.value(forKeyPath:"theData.name") as! [String]
```

The result is an array consisting of the strings "Manny", "Moe", and "Jack". If you don't see why, review what I said earlier about how NSArray and NSDictionary implement value(forKey:).

Typing a key path as a literal string risks typing the string incorrectly, with possibly disastrous results. In that example, the Swift compiler knows that myObject has a property theData that's an array of dictionaries, but it does not know that every dictionary has a "name" key. Thus, you are compelled to pass a string as your key path, and hope that the string is correct. If, however, a key path corresponds to known properties, you can get the compiler to check it for you. To do so, use #keyPath syntax, new in Swift 3 (similar to #selector syntax).

For example, suppose the class Dog (derived from NSObject) has a String name property, and the class DogOwner (derived from NSObject) has a dogs property that is an Array of Dog. Then you can say this:

```
let owner = // ... a DogOwner ...
let names = owner.value(forKeyPath:#keyPath(DogOwner.dogs.name)) as! [String]
```

No law requires that the path should consist of multiple nodes. Thus, you can also use #keyPath notation with a simple key. For example:

```
let dog = // ... a Dog ...
let dogName = dog.value(forKey:#keyPath(Dog.name)) as! String
```

That may seem like a silly example, because we could simply have fetched dog.name. But sometimes you *have* to supply a key or a key path, and #keyPath syntax can then save you from the risk of typing the key string incorrectly. I'll show an example in Chapter 11.

 Recall also the discussion of user-defined runtime attributes, in Chapter 7. This feature uses key–value coding! The string you're entering in the first column when you define a runtime attribute in an object's Identity inspector in a nib is a key path.

Array Accessors

Key–value coding is a powerful technology with many additional ramifications. (See Apple's *Key-Value Coding Programming Guide* for full information.) I'll illustrate just one of them. Key–value coding allows an object to synthesize a key whose value appears to be an array (or a set), even if it isn't. You implement specially named accessor methods; key–value coding sees them when you try to use the corresponding key.

To illustrate, I'll add these methods to the class of our object myObject:

```
func countOfPepBoys() -> Int {
    return self.theData.count
}
func objectInPepBoysAtIndex(_ ix:Int) -> Any {
    return self.theData[ix]
}
```

By implementing countOf... and objectIn...AtIndex, I'm telling the key–value coding system to act as if the given key — "pepBoys", in this case — exists and is an array. An attempt to fetch the value of the key "pepBoys" by way of key–value coding will succeed, and will return an object that can be treated as an NSArray, though in fact it is a proxy object (an NSKeyValueArray). Thus we can now say things like this:

```
let arr = myObject.value(forKey:"pepBoys")!
let arr2 = myObject.value(forKeyPath:"pepBoys.name")!
```

In that code, `arr` is the array proxy, and `arr2` is the same array of the names of the three Pep Boys as before. The example seems pointless: the underlying implementation is *already* an array, so how does saying `"pepBoys"` here differ from saying `"theData"`, as we did before? It doesn't. But it could! Imagine that there is no simple actual array — that the result of `countOfPepBoys` and `objectInPepBoysAtIndex(_:)` is obtained through some completely different sort of operation. In effect, we have created a key that acts as an NSArray façade; we could have anything at all hiding behind it.

The Secret Life of NSObject

Because every Objective-C class inherits from NSObject, it's worth taking some time to explore NSObject. NSObject is constructed in a rather elaborate way:

- It defines some native class methods and instance methods having mostly to do with the basics of instantiation and of method sending and resolution.

- It adopts the NSObject protocol. This protocol declares instance methods having mostly to do with memory management, the relationship between an instance and its class, and introspection. Because all the NSObject protocol methods are required, the NSObject class implements them all. In Swift, the NSObject protocol is called NSObjectProtocol, to avoid name clash.

- It implements convenience methods related to the NSCopying, NSMutableCopying, and NSCoding protocols, without formally adopting those protocols. NSObject intentionally doesn't adopt these protocols because this would cause all other classes to adopt them, which would be wrong. But thanks to this architecture, if a class *does* adopt one of these protocols, you can call the corresponding convenience method. For example, NSObject implements the `copy` instance method, so you can call `copy` on any instance, but you'll crash unless the instance's class also adopts the NSCopying protocol and implements `copy(with:)`.

- A large number of methods are injected into NSObject by more than two dozen categories on NSObject, scattered among various header files. For example, `awakeFromNib` (see Chapter 7) comes from the UINibLoadingAdditions category on NSObject, declared in *UINibLoading.h*.

- A class object is an object. Therefore all Objective-C classes, which are objects of type Class, inherit from NSObject. Therefore, *any instance method of NSObject can be called on a class object as a class method!* For example, `responds(to:)` is defined as an instance method by the NSObject protocol, but it can (therefore) be treated also as a class method and sent to a class object.

Taken as a whole, the NSObject methods may be considered under the following rough classification:

Creation, destruction, and memory management

Methods for creating an instance, such as alloc and copy, along with methods for learning when something is happening in the lifetime of an object, such as initialize and dealloc, plus methods that manage memory.

Class relationships

Methods for learning an object's class and inheritance, such as superclass, isKind(of:), and isMember(of:).

Object introspection and comparison

Methods for asking what would happen if an object were sent a certain message, such as responds(to:), for representing an object as a string (description), and for comparing objects (isEqual(_:)).

Message response

Methods for meddling with what does happen when an object is sent a certain message, such as doesNotRecognizeSelector(_:). If you're curious, see the *Objective-C Runtime Programming Guide*.

Message sending

Methods for sending a message dynamically. For example, perform(_:) takes a selector as parameter, and sending it to an object tells that object to perform that selector. This might seem identical to just sending that message to that object, but what if you don't know what message to send until runtime? Moreover, variants on perform allow you to send a message on a specified thread, or send a message after a certain amount of time has passed (perform(_:with:afterDelay:) and similar).

CHAPTER 11

Cocoa Events

All of your app's executable code lies in its functions. The impetus for a function being called must come from somewhere. One of your functions may call another, but who will call the first function in the first place? How, ultimately, will *any* of your code *ever* run?

After your app has launched, as I said in Chapter 6, "UIApplicationMain is just sitting there, watching for the user to do something, maintaining the *event loop*, which will respond to user actions as they occur." The event loop is the key. The runtime is watching and waiting for certain things to happen, such as the user making a gesture on the screen, or some specific stage arriving in the lifetime of your app. When such things do happen, Cocoa calls your code.

But Cocoa can call your code only if your code is there to be called. Your code is like a panel of buttons, waiting for Cocoa to press one. If something happens that Cocoa feels your code needs to know about and respond to, it presses the right button — if the right button is there.

The art of Cocoa programming lies in knowing what Cocoa wants to do. You organize your code, right from the start, with Cocoa's behavior in mind. Cocoa makes certain promises about how and when it will dispatch messages to your code. These are Cocoa's *events*. You know what these events are, and you arrange for your code to be ready when Cocoa delivers them.

The specific events that you can receive are listed in the documentation. The overall architecture of how and when events are dispatched and the ways in which your code arranges to receive them is the subject of this chapter.

Reasons for Events

Broadly speaking, the reasons you might receive an event may be divided informally into four categories. These categories are not official; I made them up. Often it isn't completely clear which of these categories an event fits into; an event may well appear to fit two categories. But they are still generally useful for visualizing how and why Cocoa interacts with your code:

User events

The user does something interactive, and an event is triggered directly. Obvious examples are events that you get when the user taps or swipes the screen, or types a key on the keyboard.

Lifetime events

These are events notifying you of the arrival of a stage in the life of the app, such as the fact that the app is starting up or is about to go into the background, or of a component of the app, such as the fact that a UIViewController's view has just loaded or is about to be removed from the screen.

Functional events

Cocoa is about to do something, and turns to you in case you want to supply additional functionality. I would put into this category UIView's draw(_:) (your chance to have a view draw itself) and UILabel's drawText(in:) (your chance to modify the look of a label), with which we experimented in Chapter 10.

Query events

Cocoa turns to you to ask a question; its behavior will depend upon your answer. For example, the way data appears in a table (a UITableView) is that whenever Cocoa needs a cell for a row of the table, it turns to you and asks for the cell.

Subclassing

A built-in Cocoa class may define methods that Cocoa itself will call and that you are invited (or required) to override in a subclass, so that your custom behavior, and not (merely) the default behavior, will take place.

An example I gave in Chapter 10 was UIView's draw(_:). This is what I call a functional event. By overriding draw(_:) in a UIView subclass, you dictate the full procedure by which a view draws itself. You don't know exactly when this method will be called, and you don't care; when it is, you draw, and this guarantees that the view will always appear the way you want it to. (You *never* call draw(_:) yourself; if some underlying condition has changed and you want the view to be redrawn, you call setNeedsDisplay and let Cocoa call draw(_:) in response.)

Built-in UIView subclasses may have other functional event methods you'll want to customize through subclassing. Typically this will be in order to change the way the view is drawn, without taking command of the entire drawing procedure yourself. In Chapter 10 I gave an example involving UILabel and its `drawText(in:)`. A similar case is UISlider, which lets you customize the position and size of the slider's "thumb" by overriding `thumbRect(forBounds:trackRect:value:)`.

UIViewController is a class meant for subclassing. Of the methods listed in the UIViewController class documentation, just about all are methods you might have reason to override. If you create a UIViewController subclass in Xcode, you'll see that the template already includes a couple of method overrides to get you started. For example, `viewDidLoad` is called to let you know that your view controller has obtained its main view (its `view`), so that you can perform initializations; it's an obvious example of a lifetime event. And UIViewController has many other lifetime events that you can and will override in order to get fine control over what happens when. For example, `viewWillAppear` means that your view controller's view is about to be placed into the interface; `viewDidAppear` means that your view controller's view *has* been placed into the interface; `viewDidLayoutSubviews` means that your view has been positioned within its superview; and so on.

A UIViewController method like `supportedInterfaceOrientations` is what I call a query event. Your job is to return a bitmask ("Option sets" on page 238) telling Cocoa what orientations your view can appear in at this moment — whenever that may be. You trust Cocoa to call this method at the appropriate moments, so that if the user rotates the device, your app's interface will or won't be rotated to compensate, depending on what value you return.

 In iOS 10, `supportedInterfaceOrientations` is expressed as a property that you'll override (as a computed variable). But it's still a query event, and your override's getter is still effectively a method that Cocoa will call.

When looking for events that you can receive through subclassing, be sure to look upward though the inheritance hierarchy. For example, if you're wondering how to be notified when your custom UILabel subclass is embedded into another view, you won't find the answer in the UILabel class documentation; a UILabel receives the appropriate event by virtue of being a UIView. In the UIView class documentation, you'll learn that you can override `didMoveToSuperview` to be informed when this happens. By the same token, look upward through adopted protocols as well. If you're wondering how to be notified when your view controller's view is about to undergo app rotation, you won't find out by looking in the UIViewController class documentation; a UIViewController receives the appropriate event by virtue of adopting the UIContentContainer protocol. In the UIContentContainer protocol documentation, you'll learn that you can override `viewWillTransition(to:with:)`.

Nevertheless, as I said in Chapter 10, subclassing and overriding is far from being the most important or common way of arranging to receive events. Aside from UIView-Controller, it is hard to think of *any* built-in Cocoa class that you will *regularly* subclass for this purpose. The majority of your communication from Cocoa will be through other means.

Notifications

Cocoa provides your app with a single NotificationCenter instance (Objective-C NSNotificationCenter), informally called the *notification center*. This instance, available as `NotificationCenter.default`, is the basis of a mechanism for sending messages called *notifications*. A notification is a Notification instance (Objective-C NSNotification). The idea is that any object can be registered with the notification center to receive certain notifications. Another object can hand the notification center a notification to send out (this is called *posting* the notification). The notification center will then send that notification to all objects that are registered to receive it.

Cocoa itself posts notifications through the notification center, and your code can register to receive them. Thus, notifications are a way of receiving events from Cocoa. You'll find a separate Notifications section in the documentation for a class that provides them.

You may also want to post notifications yourself, as a way of communicating with your own code. The notification mechanism is often described as a dispatching or broadcasting mechanism, and with good reason. It lets an object send a message without knowing or caring what object or how many objects receive it. This relieves your app's architecture from the formal responsibility of somehow hooking up instances just so a message can pass from one to the other (which can sometimes be quite tricky or onerous, as discussed in Chapter 13). When objects are conceptually "distant" from one another, notifications can be a fairly lightweight way of permitting one to message the other.

A Notification instance has three pieces of information associated with it, which can be retrieved through properties:

name
> A string which identifies the notification's meaning.

object
> An instance associated with the notification; typically, the instance that posted it.

userInfo
> Not every notification has a userInfo; it is a dictionary, and can contain additional information associated with the notification. What information this dictionary will contain, and under what keys, depends on the particular notification;

you have to consult the documentation. For example, the documentation tells us that UIApplication's `UIApplicationDidChangeStatusBarOrientation` notification includes a `userInfo` dictionary with a key `UIApplicationStatusBar-OrientationUserInfoKey` whose value is the status bar's previous orientation. When you post a notification yourself, you can put anything you like into the `userInfo` for the notification's recipient(s) to retrieve.

 New in Swift 3, a Notification's `name` string is typed as a `Notification.Name`, a struct adopting RawRepresentable with a String `rawValue`. Built-in Cocoa notification names are vended as static `Notification.Name` properties of this struct. In this way, notification name constants are all namespaced inside `Notification.Name`, and can be referred to using dot-notation. I'll show examples in a moment.

Receiving a Notification

To register to receive a notification, you send one of two messages to the notification center. One is `addObserver(_:selector:name:object:)`. The parameters are as follows:

`observer`:
    The instance to which the notification is to be sent. This will typically be `self`; it would be quite unusual for one instance to register a different instance as the receiver of a notification.

`selector`:
    The message to be sent to the observer instance when the notification occurs. The designated method should return no result and should take one parameter, which will be the Notification instance. The selector must specify correctly a method that is exposed to Objective-C; Swift's `#selector` syntax will help you with that (see Chapter 2).

`name`:
    The `name` of the notification you'd like to receive. If this parameter is `nil`, you're asking to receive *all* notifications associated with the object designated in the `object:` parameter.

`object`:
    The `object` of the notification you're interested in, which will usually be the object that posted it. If this is `nil`, you're asking to receive *all* notifications with the name designated in the `name:` parameter. (If both the `name:` and `object:` parameters are `nil`, you're asking to receive all notifications!)

For example, in one of my apps I want to change the interface whenever the device's built-in music player starts playing a different song. The API for the music player belongs to the MPMusicPlayerController class; this class provides a notification to tell me when the music player changes what song is being played, listed under Notifications in the MPMusicPlayerController class documentation as `MPMusicPlayer-ControllerNowPlayingItemDidChange`.

It turns out, looking at the documentation, that this notification won't be posted at all unless I first call MPMusicPlayerController's `beginGeneratingPlayback-Notifications` instance method. This architecture is not uncommon; Cocoa saves itself some time and effort by not sending out certain notifications unless they are switched on, as it were. So my first job is to get an instance of MPMusicPlayer-Controller and call this method:

```
let mp = MPMusicPlayerController.systemMusicPlayer()
mp.beginGeneratingPlaybackNotifications()
```

Now I register myself to receive the desired playback notification:

```
NotificationCenter.default.addObserver(self,
    selector: #selector(nowPlayingItemChanged),
    name: .MPMusicPlayerControllerNowPlayingItemDidChange,
    object: nil)
```

(As I mentioned earlier, I can refer to the notification name using dot-notation. There is no need for me to specify explicitly that this is a `Notification.Name`, as Swift already knows that.)

As a result, whenever an `MPMusicPlayerControllerNowPlayingItemDidChange` notification is posted, my `nowPlayingItemChanged` method will be called:

```
func nowPlayingItemChanged (_ n:Notification) {
    self.updateNowPlayingItem()
    // ... and so on ...
}
```

Heavy use of `addObserver(_:selector:name:object:)` means that your code ends up peppered with methods that exist solely in order to be called by the notification center. There is nothing about these methods that tells you what they are for — you will probably want to use explicit comments in order to remind yourself — and the methods are separate from the registration call, all of which makes your code rather confusing.

This problem is solved by using the *other* way of registering to receive a notification — by calling `addObserver(forName:object:queue:using:)`. It returns a value, whose purpose I'll explain in a moment. The queue: will usually be nil; a non-nil queue: is for background threading. The name: and object: parameters are just like those of `addObserver(_:selector:name:object:)`. Instead of an observer and a selector, however, you provide a Swift function consisting of the actual code to be executed when the notification arrives. This function should take one parameter — the Notification itself. If you use an anonymous function, your response to the notification becomes part of the registration:

```
let ob = NotificationCenter.default.addObserver(
    forName: .MPMusicPlayerControllerNowPlayingItemDidChange,
    object: nil, queue: nil) {
        _ in
        self.updateNowPlayingItem()
        // ... and so on ...
}
```

 Use of addObserver(forName:...) can impose some additional memory management complications that I'll talk about in Chapter 12.

Unregistering

It is up to you, for every object that you register as a recipient of notifications, to unregister that object before it goes out of existence. If you fail to do this, and if the object does go out of existence, and if a notification for which that object is registered is posted, the notification center will attempt to send the appropriate message to that object, which is now missing in action. The result will be a crash at best, and chaos at worst.

To unregister an object as a recipient of notifications, call the notification center's removeObserver(_:) method. Alternatively, you can unregister an object for just a specific set of notifications with removeObserver(_:name:object:). The object passed as the first argument is the object that is no longer to receive notifications. What object that is depends on how you registered in the first place:

You called addObserver(_:selector:name:object:)
You *supplied* an observer originally; that is the observer you must now unregister. This will typically be self.

You called addObserver(forName:object:queue:using:)
The call *returned* an observer token object typed as an NSObjectProtocol (its real class and nature are no concern of yours); that is the observer you must now unregister.

The trick is finding the right moment to unregister. The fallback solution is the registered instance's deinit method, this being the last lifetime event an instance is sent before it goes out of existence.

If you're calling addObserver(forName:object:queue:using:) multiple times from the same class, you're going to end up receiving from the notification center multiple observer tokens, which you need to preserve so that you can unregister all of them later. If your plan is to unregister everything at once, one way to handle this situation is through an instance property that is a mutable collection. My favored approach is a Set property:

```
var observers = Set<NSObject>()
```

Each time I register for a notification by calling addObserver(for-Name:object:queue:using:), I capture the result and add it to the set:

```
let ob = NotificationCenter.default.addObserver(
    forName: .MPMusicPlayerControllerNowPlayingItemDidChange,
    object: nil, queue: nil) {
        _ in
        self.updateNowPlayingItem()
        // ... and so on ...
    }
self.observers.insert(ob as! NSObject)
```

When it's time to unregister, I enumerate the set and empty it:

```
for ob in self.observers {
    NotificationCenter.default.removeObserver(ob)
}
self.observers.removeAll()
```

 NotificationCenter cannot be introspected: you cannot ask the NotificationCenter what objects are registered with it as notification recipients. This is a major gap in Cocoa's functionality, and can make it difficult to track down bugs if you make a mistake such as unregistering an observer prematurely (as usual, I know this from bitter experience).

Posting a Notification

Although you'll mostly be interested in receiving notifications from Cocoa, you can, as I mentioned earlier, take advantage of the notification mechanism as a way of communicating between your own objects. One reason for doing this might be that two objects are conceptually distant or independent from one another. You should probably avoid using notifications too freely, or as an excuse for not bothering to devise proper lines of communication between objects; but they are certainly appropriate in some circumstances. (I'll raise this point again in Chapter 13.)

To use notifications in this way, your objects must play both roles in the communication chain. One of your objects (or more than one) will register to receive a notification, identified by name or object or both, as I've already described. Another of your objects will post a notification, identified in the same way. The notification center will then pass the message along from the poster to the registered recipient(s).

To post a notification, send to the notification center the message post(name:object:userInfo:). You are defining the name: yourself, so you'll have to turn a string into a Notification.Name. There are two ways to do this:

By coercion
> For example, you can pass Notification.Name("myNotificationName") as the name: argument. This is an easy approach, but it's error-prone: you'll need to perform the same coercion in order to register to receive this notification, and now you're using this string literal twice, an invitation to make a typing mistake and have things mysteriously go wrong.

By extending Notification.Name
> You define a namespaced constant, and you use that constant both when posting the notification and when registering for it. This approach localizes the coercion in a single place; it's a little more work than the first approach, but it's the correct approach, and you should use it.

For example, one of my apps is a simple card game. The game needs to know when a card is tapped. But a card knows nothing about the game; when it is tapped, it simply emits a virtual shriek by posting a notification. I've defined my notification name by extending Notification.Name:

```
extension Notification.Name {
    static let cardTapped = Notification.Name("cardTapped")
}
```

When a card is tapped, I respond like this:

```
NotificationCenter.default.post(name: .cardTapped, object: self)
```

The game object has registered for the .cardTapped notification, so it hears about this and retrieves the notification's object; now it knows what card was tapped and can proceed correctly.

Timer

A Timer (Objective-C NSTimer) is not, strictly speaking, a notification; but it behaves very similarly. It is an object that gives off a signal (*fires*) after the lapse of a certain time interval. The signal is a message to one of your instances. Thus you can arrange to be notified when a certain time has elapsed. The timing is not perfectly accurate, but it's pretty good.

Timer management is not exactly tricky, but it is a little unusual. A timer that is actively watching the clock is said to be *scheduled*. A timer may fire once, or it may be a *repeating* timer. To make a timer go out of existence, it must be *invalidated*. A timer that is set to fire once is invalidated automatically after it fires; a repeating timer repeats until *you* invalidate it by sending it the invalidate message. An invalidated timer should be regarded as off-limits: you cannot revive it or use it for anything further, and you should probably not send any messages to it.

For example, one of my apps is a game with a score; I want to penalize the user, by diminishing the score, for every ten seconds that elapses after each move without the user making a further move. So each time the user makes a move, I create and schedule a repeating timer whose time interval is ten seconds (and I also invalidate any existing timer); in the method that the timer calls, I diminish the score.

The straightforward way to create a timer is with one of two scheduledTimer class methods. These methods both create the timer and schedule it, so that the timer begins watching the clock immediately:

scheduledTimer(timeInterval:target:selector:userInfo:repeats:)
> The target and selector determine what message will be sent to what object when the timer fires; the method in question should take one parameter, which will be a reference to the timer. The userInfo is just like the userInfo of a notification.

scheduledTimer(withTimeInterval:repeats:block:)
> New in iOS 10, you can provide a function to be called when the timer fires; the function should take one parameter, which will be a reference to the timer.

A Timer has a tolerance property, which is a time interval signifying how long after the timer *would* fire you're willing to grant before it really *does* fire. The documentation suggests that you can improve device battery life and app responsiveness by supplying a value of at least 10 percent of the timeInterval.

 Timers have some memory management implications that I'll discuss in Chapter 12.

Delegation

Delegation is an object-oriented design pattern, a relationship between two objects, in which a primary object's behavior is customized or assisted by a secondary object. The secondary object is the primary object's *delegate*. No subclassing is involved, and indeed the primary object is agnostic about the delegate's class.

As implemented by Cocoa, here's how delegation works. A built-in Cocoa class has an instance property, usually called delegate (it will certainly have delegate in its name). For some instance of that Cocoa class, you set the value of this property to an instance of one of *your* classes. At certain moments in its activity, the Cocoa class promises to turn to its delegate for instructions by sending it a certain message: if the Cocoa instance finds that its delegate is not nil, and that its delegate is prepared to receive that message, the Cocoa instance sends the message to the delegate.

Recall the discussion of protocols from Chapter 10. Delegation is one of Cocoa's main uses of protocols. In the old days, delegate methods were listed in the Cocoa class's documentation, and their names were made known to the compiler through an informal protocol (a category on NSObject). Now, though, a class's delegate methods are usually listed in a genuine protocol with its own documentation. There are over 70 Cocoa delegate protocols, showing how heavily Cocoa relies on delegation. Most delegate methods are optional, but in a few cases you'll discover some that are required.

Cocoa Delegation

To customize a Cocoa instance's behavior through delegation, you start with one of your classes, which adopts the relevant delegate protocol. When the app runs, you set the Cocoa instance's `delegate` property (or whatever its name is) to an instance of your class. You might do this in code; alternatively, you might do it in a nib, by connecting an instance's `delegate` outlet (or whatever it's called) to an appropriate instance that is to serve as delegate. Your delegate class will probably do other things besides serving as this instance's delegate. Indeed, one of the nice things about delegation is that it leaves you free to slot delegate code into your class architecture however you like; the delegate type is a protocol, so the actual delegate can be an instance of *any* class.

In this simple example, I want to ensure that my app's root view controller, a UINavigationController, doesn't permit the app to rotate — the app should appear only in portrait orientation when this view controller is in charge. But UINavigationController isn't my class; it belongs to Cocoa. My own class is a *different* view controller, a UIViewController subclass, which acts as the UINavigationController's child. How can the child tell the parent how to rotate? Well, UINavigationController has a `delegate` property, typed as UINavigationControllerDelegate (a protocol). It promises to send this delegate the `navigationControllerSupportedInterface-Orientations(_:)` message when it needs to know how to rotate. So my view controller, in response to a very early lifetime event, sets itself as the UINavigationController's delegate. It also implements the `navigationControllerSupported-InterfaceOrientations(_:)` method. Presto, the problem is solved:

```
class ViewController : UIViewController, UINavigationControllerDelegate {
    override func viewDidLoad() {
        super.viewDidLoad()
        self.navigationController?.delegate = self
    }
    func navigationControllerSupportedInterfaceOrientations(
        _ nav: UINavigationController) -> UIInterfaceOrientationMask {
            return .portrait
    }
}
```

An app's shared application instance, `UIApplication.shared`, has a delegate that serves such an important role in the life of the app that the Xcode app templates automatically supply one — a class called AppDelegate. I described in Chapter 6 how an app gets started by calling `UIApplicationMain`, which instantiates the AppDelegate class and makes that instance the delegate of the shared application instance (which it has also created). As I pointed out in Chapter 10, AppDelegate formally adopts the UIApplicationDelegate protocol, signifying that it is ready to serve in this role; `responds(to:)` is then sent to the app delegate to see what UIApplicationDelegate protocol methods it implements. Thereafter, the application delegate instance is sent messages letting it know of major events in the lifetime of the app. That is why the UIApplicationDelegate protocol method `application(_:didFinishLaunchingWith-Options:)` is so important; it is one of the earliest opportunities for *your* code to run.

 The UIApplication delegate methods are also provided as notifications. This lets an instance other than the app delegate hear conveniently about application lifetime events, by registering for them. A few other classes provide duplicate events similarly; for example, UITableView's `tableView(_:didSelectRowAt:)` delegate method is matched by a notification `UITableViewSelectionDidChange`.

By convention, many Cocoa delegate method names contain the modal verbs `should`, `will`, or `did`. A `will` message is sent to the delegate just before something happens; a `did` message is sent to the delegate just after something happens. A `should` method is special: it returns a Bool, and you are expected to respond with `true` to permit something or `false` to prevent it. The documentation tells you what the default response is; you don't have to implement a `should` method if the default response is always acceptable.

In many cases, a property will control some overall behavior, while a delegate method lets you modify that behavior based on circumstances at runtime. For example, whether the user can tap the status bar to make a scroll view scroll quickly to the top is governed by the scroll view's `scrollsToTop` property; but even if this property's value is `true`, you can prevent this behavior for a *particular* tap by returning `false` from the scroll view delegate's `scrollViewShouldScrollToTop(_:)`.

When you're searching the documentation for how you can be notified of a certain event, be sure to consult the corresponding delegate protocol, if there is one. You'd like to know when the user taps in a UITextField to start editing it? You won't find anything relevant in the UITextField class documentation; what you're after is `text-FieldDidBeginEditing(_:)` in the UITextFieldDelegate protocol. And so on.

Implementing Delegation

The Cocoa pattern of a delegate whose responsibilities are described by a protocol is one that you will want to imitate in your own code. Setting up this pattern takes some

---

practice, and can be a little time-consuming, but it is often the correct approach, because it appropriately assigns knowledge and responsibility to the various objects involved.

Consider an actual case. In one of my apps I present a view controller whose view contains three sliders that the user can move to choose a color. Appropriately, this view controller is a UIViewController subclass called ColorPickerController. When the user taps Done or Cancel, the view should be dismissed; but first, the code that presented this view needs to hear about what color the user chose. So I need to send a message from the ColorPickerController instance *back to the instance that presented it*.

Here is the declaration for the message that I want the ColorPickerController to send before it goes out of existence:

```
func colorPicker (_ picker:ColorPickerController,
    didSetColorNamed theName:String?,
    to theColor:UIColor?)
```

The question is: where and how should this method be declared?

Now, it happens that in my app I know the class of the instance that will in fact present the ColorPickerController: it is a SettingsController. So I could simply declare this method in SettingsController. But this, if it is all I do, means that the Color-PickerController, in order to send this message to the SettingsController, must *know* that the instance that presented it *is* a SettingsController. But surely it is merely a *contingent* fact that the instance being sent this message is a SettingsController; it should be open to *any* class to present and dismiss a ColorPickerController, and thus to be eligible to receive this message.

Therefore we want ColorPickerController *itself* to declare the method that *it itself is going to call*; and we want it to send the message blindly to some receiver, without regard to the class of that receiver. That's what a protocol is for! The solution, then, is for ColorPickerController to define a protocol, with this method as part of that protocol, and for the class that presents a ColorPickerController to conform to that protocol. ColorPickerController also has an appropriately typed `delegate` property; this provides the channel of communication, and tells the compiler that sending this message is legal:

```
protocol ColorPickerDelegate : class {
    // color == nil on cancel
    func colorPicker (_ picker:ColorPickerController,
        didSetColorNamed theName:String?,
        to theColor:UIColor?)
}
```

```
class ColorPickerController : UIViewController {
    weak var delegate: ColorPickerDelegate?
    // ...
}
```

(On the meaning of and reasons for the weak attribute, see Chapter 5.) When my SettingsController instance creates and configures a ColorPickerController instance, it also sets itself as that ColorPickerController's delegate — which it can do, because it adopts the protocol:

```
extension SettingsController : ColorPickerDelegate {
    func showColorPicker() {
        let colorName = // ...
        let c = // ...
        let cpc = ColorPickerController(colorName:colorName, color:c)
        cpc.delegate = self
        self.present(cpc, animated: true)
    }
    func colorPicker (_ picker:ColorPickerController,
        didSetColorNamed theName:String?,
        to theColor:UIColor?) {
            // ...
    }
}
```

Now, when the user picks a color, the ColorPickerController *knows* to whom it should send colorPicker:didSetColorNamed:to: — namely, its delegate! And the compiler allows this, because the delegate has adopted the ColorPickerDelegate protocol:

```
@IBAction func dismissColorPicker(_ sender : Any?) { // user tapped Done
    let c : UIColor? = self.color
    self.delegate?.colorPicker(self, didSetColorNamed: self.colorName, to: c)
}
```

Data Sources

A *data source* is like a delegate, except that its methods supply the data for another object to display. The chief Cocoa classes with data sources are UITableView, UICollectionView, UIPickerView, and UIPageViewController. In each case, the data source must formally adopt a data source protocol with required methods.

It comes as a surprise to some beginners that a data source is necessary at all. Why isn't a table's data just part of the table? Or why isn't there at least some fixed data structure that contains the data? The reason is that such an architecture would violate generality. Use of a data source separates the object that displays the data from the object that manages the data, and leaves the latter free to store and obtain that data however it likes (see on model–view–controller in Chapter 13). The only requirement is that the data source must be able to supply information quickly, because it will be asked for it in real time when the data needs displaying.

Another surprise is that the data source is different from the delegate. But this again is only for generality; it's an option, not a requirement. There is no reason why the data source and the delegate should not be the same object, and most of the time they probably will be. Indeed, in most cases, data source methods and delegate methods will work closely together; you won't even be conscious of the distinction.

In this example from one of my apps, I implement a UIPickerView that allows the user to configure a game by saying how many stages it should consist of ("1 Stage," "2 Stages", and so on). The first two methods are UIPickerView data source methods; the third method is a UIPickerView delegate method. It takes all three methods to supply the picker view's content:

```
extension NewGameController: UIPickerViewDataSource, UIPickerViewDelegate {
    func numberOfComponents(in pickerView: UIPickerView) -> Int {
        return 1
    }
    func pickerView(_ pickerView: UIPickerView,
        numberOfRowsInComponent component: Int) -> Int {
            return 9
    }
    func pickerView(_ pickerView: UIPickerView,
        titleForRow row: Int, forComponent component: Int) -> String? {
            return "\(row+1) Stage" + ( row > 0 ? "s" : "")
    }
}
```

Actions

An *action* is a message emitted by an instance of a UIControl subclass (a *control*) reporting a significant user event taking place in that control. The UIControl subclasses are all simple interface objects that the user can interact with directly, such as a button (UIButton) or a segmented control (UISegmentedControl).

The significant user events (*control events*) are listed under UIControlEvents in the Constants section of the UIControl class documentation. Different controls implement different control events: for example, a segmented control's Value Changed event signifies that the user has tapped to select a different segment, but a button's Touch Up Inside event signifies that the user has tapped the button. Of itself, a control event has no external effect; the control responds visually (for example, a tapped button looks tapped), but it doesn't automatically share the information that the event has taken place. If you want to know when a control event takes place, so that you can respond to it in your code, *you* must arrange for that control event to trigger an *action message*.

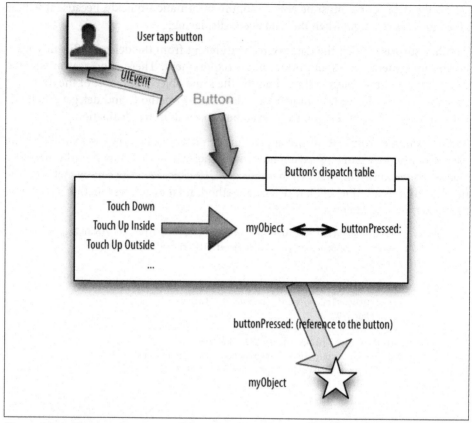

Figure 11-1. The target–action architecture

Here's how it works. A control maintains an internal dispatch table: for each control event, there can be any number of target–action pairs, in each of which the *action* is a message selector (the name of a method) and the *target* is the object to which that message is to be sent. When a control event occurs, the control consults its dispatch table, finds all the target–action pairs associated with that control event, and sends each action message to the corresponding target (Figure 11-1).

There are two ways to manipulate a control's action dispatch table:

Action connection

You can configure an action connection in a nib. I described in Chapter 7 how to do this, but I didn't completely explain the underlying mechanism. Now all is revealed: an action connection formed in the nib editor is a visual way of configuring a control's action dispatch table.

Code

You can use code to operate directly on the control's action dispatch table. The key method here is the UIControl instance method addTarget(_:action:for:), where the target: is an object, the action: is a selector, and the for: parameter is a UIControlEvents bitmask ("Option sets" on page 238). Unlike a notification center, a control also has methods for introspecting the dispatch table.

Recall the example of a control and its action from Chapter 7. We have a button-Pressed(_:) method:

```
@IBAction func buttonPressed(_ sender: Any) {
    let alert = UIAlertController(
        title: "Howdy!", message: "You tapped me!", preferredStyle: .Alert)
    alert.addAction(
        UIAlertAction(title: "OK", style: .Cancel))
    self.present(alert, animated: true)
}
```

This sort of method is an *action handler*. Its purpose is to be called when the user taps a certain button in the interface. In Chapter 7, we arranged for that to happen by setting up an action connection in the nib: we connected the button's Touch Up Inside event to the ViewController buttonPressed(_:) method. In reality, we were forming a target–action pair and adding that target–action pair to the button's dispatch table for the Touch Up Inside control event.

Instead of making that arrangement in the nib, we could have done the same thing in code. Suppose we had *never* drawn that action connection. And suppose that, instead, we have an outlet connection from the view controller to the button, called button. Then the view controller, after the nib loads, can configure the button's dispatch table like this:

```
self.button.addTarget(self,
    action: #selector(buttonPressed),
    for: .touchUpInside)
```

 A control event can have multiple target–action pairs. You might configure it this way intentionally, but it is also possible to do so accidentally. Unintentionally giving a control event a target–action pair without removing its *existing* target–action pair is an easy mistake to make, and can cause some very mysterious behavior. For example, if we had formed an action connection in the nib *and* configured the dispatch table in code, a tap on the button would cause button-Pressed(_:) to be called *twice*.

The signature for the action selector can be in any of three forms:

- The fullest form takes two parameters:
  - The control.
  - The UIEvent that generated the control event.
- A shorter form, the one most commonly used, omits the second parameter. `buttonPressed(_:)` is an example; it takes one parameter. When `button-Pressed(_:)` is called through an action message emanating from the button, its parameter will be a reference to the button.
- There is a still shorter form that omits both parameters.

What is the UIEvent, and what is it for? Well, a *touch event* is generated whenever the user does something with a finger (sets it down on the screen, moves it, raises it from the screen). UIEvents are the lowest-level objects charged with communication of touch events to your app. A UIEvent is basically a timestamp (a Double) along with a collection (Set) of touch events (UITouch). The action mechanism deliberately shields you from the complexities of touch events, but by electing to receive the UIEvent, you can still deal with those complexities if you want to.

 Curiously, none of the action selector parameters provide any way to learn *which* control event triggered the current action selector call! Thus, for example, to distinguish a Touch Up Inside control event from a Touch Up Outside control event, their corresponding target–action pairs must specify two different action handlers; if you dispatch them to the same action handler, that handler cannot discover which control event occurred.

The Responder Chain

A *responder* is an object that knows how to receive UIEvents directly (see the previous section). It knows this because it is an instance of UIResponder or a UIResponder subclass. If you examine the Cocoa class hierarchy, you'll find that just about any class that has anything to do with display on the screen is a responder. A UIView is a responder. A UIWindow is a responder. A UIViewController is a responder. Even a UIApplication is a responder. Even the app delegate is a responder!

A UIResponder has four low-level methods for receiving touch-related UIEvents:

- `touchesBegan(_:with:)`
- `touchesMoved(_:with:)`
- `touchesEnded(_:with:)`
- `touchesCancelled(_:with:)`

These methods — the *touch methods* — are called to notify a responder of a touch event. No matter how your code ultimately hears about a user-related touch event — indeed, even if your code *never* hears about a touch event (because Cocoa reacted in some automatic way to the touch, without your code's intervention) — the touch was initially communicated to a responder through one of the touch methods.

The mechanism for this communication starts by deciding which responder the user touched. The UIView methods `hitTest(_:with:)` and `point(inside:with:)` are called until the correct view (the *hit-test view*) is located. Then UIApplication's `send-Event(_:)` method is called, which calls UIWindow's `sendEvent(_:)`, which calls the correct touch method of the hit-test view (a responder).

The responders in your app participate in a *responder chain*, which essentially links them up through the view hierarchy. A UIView can sit inside another UIView, its *superview*, and so on until we reach the app's UIWindow (a UIView that has no superview). The responder chain, from bottom to top, looks like this:

1. The UIView that we start with (here, the hit-test view).
2. If this UIView is a UIViewController's `view`, that UIViewController.
3. The UIView's superview.
4. Go back to step 2 and repeat! Keep repeating until we reach...
5. The UIWindow.
6. The UIApplication.
7. The UIApplication's delegate.

The next responder up the responder chain is a responder's *next responder*, which is obtained from a responder through its `next` property (which returns an Optional wrapping a UIResponder). Thus the responder chain can be walked upward from any responder to the top of the chain.

Deferring Responsibility

The responder chain can be used to let a responder defer responsibility for handling a touch event. If a responder receives a touch event and can't handle it, the event can be passed up the responder chain to look for a responder that *can* handle it. This can happen in two main ways:

- The responder doesn't implement the relevant touch method.
- The responder implements the relevant touch method to call `super`.

For example, a plain vanilla UIView has no native implementation of the touch methods. Thus, by default, even if a UIView is the hit-test view, the touch event effectively falls through the UIView and travels up the responder chain, looking for someone to respond to it. In certain situations, it might make sense for you to defer responsibility for this touch to the main background view, or even to the UIViewController that controls it.

Here's an example from one of my apps. The app is a game that's a simple jigsaw puzzle: a rectangular photo is divided into smaller pieces, and the pieces are shuffled. The user's job is to tap two pieces in succession to swap them. The background view is a UIView subclass called Board; the puzzle pieces are generic UIView objects, and are subviews of the Board. Knowledge of how a piece should respond when tapped resides in the Board, which knows the overall layout of the pieces; thus, I don't need a puzzle piece to contain any tap detection logic. Therefore I take advantage of the responder chain to defer responsibility: the puzzle pieces don't implement any touch methods, and a tap on a puzzle piece falls through to the Board, which *does* perform touch detection and handles the tap, and tells the tapped piece what to do. The user, of course, knows nothing about that: outwardly, you touch a piece and the piece responds.

Nil-Targeted Actions

A *nil-targeted action* is a target–action pair in which the target is nil. There is no designated target object, so the following rule is used: starting with the hit-test view (the view with which the user is interacting), Cocoa walks up the responder chain, one responder at a time, looking for an object that can respond to the action message:

- If a responder is found that handles this message, that method is called on that responder, and that's the end.
- If we get all the way to the top of the responder chain without finding a responder to handle this message, the message goes unhandled (with no penalty) — in other words, nothing happens.

Suppose, for example, that we were to configure a button in code, like this:

```
self.button.addTarget(nil,
    action: #selector(buttonPressed),
    for: .touchUpInside)
```

That's a nil-targeted action. So what happens when the user taps the button? First, Cocoa looks in the UIButton itself to see whether it responds to buttonPressed. If not, it looks in the UIView that is its superview. And so on, up the responder chain. If self is the view controller that owns the view that contains the button, and if the class of this view controller does in fact implement buttonPressed, tapping the button will cause the view controller's buttonPressed to be called!

It's obvious how to construct a nil-targeted action in code: you set up a target–action pair where the target is nil, as in the preceding example. But how do you construct a nil-targeted action in a nib? The answer is: you form a connection to the First Responder proxy object (in the dock). This is what the First Responder proxy object is for! The First Responder isn't a real object with a known class, so before you can connect an action to it, you have to define the action message within the First Responder proxy object, like this:

1. Select the First Responder proxy in the nib, and switch to the Attributes inspector.

2. You'll see a table (probably empty) of user-defined nil-targeted First Responder actions. Click the Plus button and give the new action a name; it must take a single parameter (so that its name will end with a colon).

3. Now you can Control-drag from a control, such as a UIButton, to the First Responder proxy to specify a nil-targeted action with the name you specified.

Key–Value Observing

Key–value observing, or *KVO*, is a notification mechanism that doesn't use the NotificationCenter. It allows one object to be registered *directly with a second object* so as to be notified when a value in the second object changes. Moreover, the second object — the observed object — doesn't actually have to *do* anything; it needn't even be conscious of the fact that this registration has taken place. When the value in the observed object changes, the registered object — the observer — is automatically notified. (Perhaps a better architectural analogy would be with the target–action mechanism; this is a target–action mechanism that works between *any* two objects.)

When you use KVO, the observer will be *your* object; you will write the code that will respond when the observer is notified of the change for which it has registered. But the observed object, the one with which you register to hear about changes, needn't be your object at all; in fact, it often will not be. Many Cocoa objects promise to behave in a KVO compliant way, and you are invited and expected to use KVO on them. Typically, KVO is used in place of delegation or notifications.

The process of using KVO may be broken down into three stages:

Registration
> To hear about a change in a value belonging to the observed object, we must be registered with the observed object. This typically involves calling the observed object's addObserver(_:forKeyPath:options:context:) method. (All objects derived from NSObject have this method, because it is injected into NSObject by

the NSKeyValueObserving informal protocol, which is actually a set of categories on NSObject and other classes.)

Change

The change takes place in the value belonging to the observed object, and it must take place in a special way — a KVO compliant way. Typically, this means using a key–value coding compliant accessor to make the change. Setting a property passes through a key–value coding compliant accessor.

Notification

The observer is automatically notified that the value in the observed object has changed: its `observeValue(forKeyPath:of:change:context:)` method, which we have implemented for exactly this purpose, is called by the runtime.

It is also necessary, sooner or later, to unregister with the observed object when we no longer want to receive this notification, by sending it `removeObserver(_:forKey-Path:context:)`. This is for the same reason that we must unregister for NotificationCenter notifications: if we don't, the app can crash if the notification is sent to an observer that has gone out of existence. You must explicitly unregister the observer for every key path for which it is registered; you can't use `nil` as the second argument to mean "all key paths." The last possible moment to unregister is the observer's `deinit`; obviously, this requires that the observer have a reference to the observed object.

But there's more. All observers must be unregistered from an observed object before *the observed object* goes out of existence! If an object goes out of existence with observers still registered with it, your app will crash, with a helpful message in the console: "An instance was deallocated while key value observers were still registered with it."

Here's an example from my actual code. An AVPlayerViewController is a view controller whose view displays video content. When the view first appears, there can be a nasty flash, because the view is black until the video content is ready, which may take a little time. The solution is to make the view initially invisible, until the video content *is* ready. Thus, we want to be notified when the video content is ready. AVPlayerViewController has an `isReadyForDisplay` property — so we want to be notified when that property becomes `true`. But AVPlayerViewController has no delegate, and provides no notifications. The solution is to use KVO: we register ourself with the AVPlayerViewController to hear about changes in its `isReadyForDisplay` property. Here's the part of my code that configures and shows an AVPlayerViewController's view:

```
let readyForDisplay = #keyPath(AVPlayerViewController.readyForDisplay)
func setUpChild() {
    // ...
    let av = AVPlayerViewController()
    av.player = player
    av.view.frame = CGRect(x:10, y:10, width:300, height:200)
    av.view.isHidden = true // looks nicer if we don't show until ready
    av.addObserver(self,
        forKeyPath: readyForDisplay,
        options: .new, context: nil) ❶
    // ...
}
override func observeValue(forKeyPath keyPath: String?,
    of object: Any?, change: [NSKeyValueChangeKey : Any]?,
    context: UnsafeMutableRawPointer?) { ❷
        guard keyPath == readyForDisplay else {return}
        guard let vc = object as? AVPlayerViewController else {return}
        guard let ok = change?[.newKey] as? Bool else {return}
        guard ok else {return} ❸
        vc.removeObserver(self, forKeyPath:keyPath!)
        DispatchQueue.main.async {
            vc.view.isHidden = false
        }
}
```

❶ The AVPlayerViewController's view starts out invisible (isHidden is true). We register to hear about any change in its isReadyForDisplay property. The options: argument is a bitmask (NSKeyValueObservingOptions). One of the things it lets us do is ask for the new value of the changed property to be sent to us in the change: dictionary.

❷ The AVPlayerViewController's isReadyForDisplay property changes, and we hear about it because our observeValue is called. We make sure this is the right notification; as I suggested in Chapter 5, a sequence of guard statements reads nicely here. Note that the observed object (the AVPlayerViewController) arrives as the object parameter; this not only helps us identify the notification, but also allows us to communicate with that object.

❸ The last guard statement confirms that isReadyForDisplay actually changed from false to true. This is the moment we've been waiting for! We unregister — we only need to hear about this change once — and proceed to make the view visible (isHidden is false). There are no guarantees about the thread on which observeValue will be called, so we step out to the main thread before doing anything that would affect the interface.

You're probably wondering about the context: parameter in addObserver and observeValue. On the whole, I recommend against using this parameter, but I'll tell

you about it anyway. It is said to represent "arbitrary data" that is handed into add-
Observer and retrieved in observeValue. You have to be careful with its value, however, because it is typed as an UnsafeMutableRawPointer. This means that its memory
is not managed while the runtime has hold of it; *you* must manage its memory by
keeping a persistent reference to the value elsewhere. The usual approach is to use a
global variable (a variable declared at the top level of a file); to prevent it from being
too global, you can declare it private, like this:

```
private var con = "ObserveValue"
```

When you call addObserver, you pass the address of this variable, &con, as the
context: argument. When you are notified in observeValue, you can use the
context: parameter as an identifier by comparing it to &con:

```
override func observeValue(forKeyPath keyPath: String?,
    of object: Any?, change: [NSKeyValueChangeKey : Any]?,
    context: UnsafeMutableRawPointer?) {
        guard context == &con else { return } // wrong notification
        // ...
}
```

In that code, the *value* stored in the global variable is irrelevant; we are using its
address as an identifier. If you want to *use* the value stored in the global variable,
rebind the UnsafeMutableRawPointer to an UnsafeMutablePointer specified as the
underlying type. Now you can access the underlying value as the UnsafeMutablePointer's pointee property. In our example, con is a String:

```
let c = context?.bindMemory(to: String.self, capacity: 1)
if let s = c?.pointee { // ...
```

Key–value observing is a deep mechanism; consult Apple's *Key-Value Observing
Guide* for full information. (For example, it is possible to observe a mutable NSArray,
but the mechanism is more elaborate than I have described here.) KVO also has some
unfortunate shortcomings. For one thing, all notifications arrive by calling the same
bottleneck method; that's a pity. And keeping track of who's observing whom, and
making sure both observer and observed have appropriate lifetimes and that unregis-
tration takes place in a timely fashion, can be tricky. But in general, KVO is useful for
keeping values coordinated in different objects; and, as I've already said, certain parts
of Cocoa will expect you to use it.

 Both the observed and the observer in KVO must derive from NSObject. Moreover, if the property to be observed is declared in Swift, it *must* be marked
dynamic — otherwise, KVO won't work. (The reason is that KVO works by swiz-
zling the accessor methods; Cocoa needs to be able to reach right in and change
your object's code, and it can't do that unless the property is dynamic.)

Swamped by Events

Your code runs only because Cocoa sends an event and you had previously set up a method ready to receive it. Cocoa has the potential to send *lots* of events, telling you what the user has done, informing you of each stage in the lifetime of your app and its objects, asking for your input on how to proceed. To receive the events that you need to hear about, your code is peppered with methods that are *entry points* — methods that you have written with just the right name and in just the right class so that they can be called by Cocoa through events. In fact, it is easy to imagine that in many cases your code for a class will consist almost entirely of entry points.

Arranging all those entry points is one of your primary challenges as an iOS programmer. You know what you want to do, but you don't get to "just do it." You have to divide up your app's functionality and allocate it in accordance with when and how Cocoa is going to call into your code. Before you've written a single line of your own code, the skeleton structure of a class is likely to have been largely mapped out for you by the need to be prepared to receive the events that Cocoa is going to want to send you.

Suppose, for example, that your iPhone app presents an interface consisting of a table view. (This is in fact an extremely probable scenario.) You're likely to have a corresponding UITableViewController subclass; UITableViewController is a built-in UIViewController subclass, and an instance of your UITableViewController subclass will own and control the table view, plus you'll probably use this same class as the table view's data source and delegate. In this single class, then, you're likely to want to implement *at a minimum* the following methods:

init(coder:) *or* init(nibName:bundle:)
  UIViewController lifetime method, where you perform instance initializations.

viewDidLoad
  UIViewController lifetime method, where you perform view-related initializations.

viewDidAppear
  UIViewController lifetime method, where you set up states that need to apply only while your view is onscreen. For example, if you're going to register for a notification or set up a timer, this is a likely place to do it.

viewDidDisappear
  UIViewController lifetime method, where you reverse what you did in viewDid-Appear. For example, this would be a likely place to unregister for a notification or invalidate a repeating timer that you set up in viewDidAppear.

`supportedInterfaceOrientations`
> UIViewController query method, where you specify what device orientations are allowed for this view controller's main view.

`numberOfSections(in:)`

`tableView(_:numberOfRowsInSection:)`

`tableView(_:cellForRowAt:)`
> UITableView data source query methods, where you specify the contents of the table.

`tableView(_:didSelectRowAt:)`
> UITableView delegate user action method, where you respond when the user taps a row of the table.

`deinit`
> Swift class instance lifetime method, where you perform end-of-life cleanup.

Suppose, further, that you did in fact use `viewDidAppear` to register for a notification and to set up a timer, and the notification and the timer each has a selector; you must therefore also implement the methods specified by those selectors.

We already have, then, about a dozen methods whose presence is effectively a matter of boilerplate. These are not *your* methods; *you* are never going to call them. They are *Cocoa's* methods, which you have placed here so that each can be called at the appropriate moment in the life story of your app.

The logic of a program laid out in this fashion is by no means easy to understand! I'm not criticizing Cocoa here — indeed, it's hard to imagine how else an application framework could work — but, purely as an objective matter of fact, the result is that a Cocoa program, even your own program, even *while you're developing it,* is hard to read, because it consists of numerous disconnected entry points, each with its own meaning, each called at its own set moment which is not in any way obvious from looking at the program. To understand what our hypothetical class does, you have to know *already* such things as when `viewDidAppear` is called and how it is typically used; otherwise, you don't even know where to look to find the program's logic and behavior, let alone how to interpret what you see when you do look there. And this difficulty is greatly compounded when you try to read someone else's code (this is one reason why, as I mentioned in Chapter 8, sample code is not all that helpful to a beginner).

Looking at the code of an iOS program — even your own code — your eyes can easily glaze over at the sight of all these methods called automatically by Cocoa under various circumstances. To be sure, experience will teach you about such things as the overridden UIViewController methods and the table view delegate and data source methods. On the other hand, no amount of experience will tell you that a certain method is called as a button's action or through a notification. Comments really help, and I strongly advise you, as you develop any iOS app, to comment every method, quite heavily if need be, saying what that method does and under what circumstances you expect it to be called — especially if it is an entry point, where it is Cocoa itself that will do the calling.

Adding to your challenges is that fact that you can't really know *precisely when* an entry point will be called. The documentation may give you a general sense, but in most cases there are no guarantees about when events will arrive and in what order. What you think is going to happen, and even what the documentation leads you to believe is going to happen, might not be quite what really does happen. Your own code can trigger unintended events. The documentation might not make it clear just when a notification will be sent. There could even be a bug in Cocoa such that events are called in a way that seems to contradict the documentation. And you have no access to the Cocoa source code, so you can't work out the underlying details. Therefore I also recommend that as you develop your app, you instrument your code heavily with caveman debugging (print and NSLog; see Chapter 9). As you test your code, keep an eye on the console output and check whether the messages make sense. You may be surprised at what you discover.

Perhaps the most common kind of mistake in writing a Cocoa app is not that there's a bug in your code itself, but that you've put the code *in the wrong place*. Your code isn't running, or it's running at the wrong time, or the pieces are running in the wrong order. I see questions about this sort of thing all the time on the various online user forums (these are all actual examples that appeared over the course of just two days):

- *There's a delay between the time when my view appears and when my button takes on its correct title.*

  That's because you put the code that sets the button's title in viewDidAppear. That's *too late*; your code needs to run earlier, perhaps in viewWillAppear.

- *My subviews are positioned in code and they're turning out all wrong.*

  That's because you put the code that positions your subviews in viewDidLoad. That's *too early*; your code needs to run later, when your view's dimensions have been determined.

- *My view is rotating even though my view controller's supportedInterface-Orientations says not to.*

  That's because you implemented supportedInterfaceOrientations in the *wrong class*; it needs to be implemented in the UINavigationController that contains your view controller (or by using the delegate's navigationController-SupportedInterfaceOrientations, as I described earlier in this chapter).

- *I set up an action connection for Value Changed on a text field, but my code isn't being called when the user edits.*

That's because you connected the *wrong control event*; a text field emits Editing Changed, not Value Changed.

Delayed Performance

Your code is executed in response to some event; but your code in turn may trigger a new event or chain of events. Sometimes this causes bad things to happen: there might be a crash, or Cocoa might appear not to have done what you said to do. To solve this problem, sometimes you just need to step outside Cocoa's own chain of events for a moment and wait for everything to settle down before proceeding.

The technique for doing this is called *delayed performance*. You tell Cocoa to do something, not right this moment, but in a little while, when things have settled down. Perhaps you need only a very short delay, possibly even as short as zero seconds, just to let Cocoa finish doing something, such as laying out the interface. Technically, you're allowing the current run loop to finish, completing and unwinding the entire current method call stack, before proceeding further with your own code.

When you program iOS, you're likely to be using delayed performance a lot more than you might expect. With experience, you'll develop a kind of sixth sense for when delayed performance might be the solution to your difficulties.

The main way to get delayed performance in iOS programming is by calling DispatchQueue's `after(when:execute:)` method. It takes a function stating what should happen after the specified time has passed. Here's a utility function that encapsulates the call:

```
func delay(_ delay:Double, closure:@escaping ()->()) {
    let when = DispatchTime.now() + delay
    DispatchQueue.main.asyncAfter(deadline: when, execute: closure)
}
```

That utility function is so important that I routinely paste it at the top level of the AppDelegate class file in every app I write. It's going to come in handy, I know! To use it, I call `delay` with a delay time (usually a very small number of seconds such as `0.1`) and an anonymous function saying what to do after the delay. Note that what you propose to do in this anonymous function will be done later on; you're deliberately breaking out of your own code's line-by-line sequence of execution. So a delayed performance call will be the last call in its own surrounding function, and cannot return any value.

In this actual example from one of my own apps, the user has tapped a row of a table, and my code responds by creating and showing a new view controller:

```
override func tableView(_ tableView: UITableView,
    didSelectRowAt indexPath: IndexPath) {
        let t = TracksViewController(
            mediaItemCollection: self.albums[indexPath.row])
        self.navigationController?.pushViewController(t, animated: true)
}
```

Unfortunately, the innocent-looking call to my TracksViewController initializer `init(mediaItemCollection:)` can take a moment to complete, so the app comes to a stop with the table row highlighted — very briefly, but just long enough to startle the user. To cover this delay with a sense of activity, I've rigged my UITableViewCell subclass to show a spinning activity indicator when it's selected:

```
override func setSelected(_ selected: Bool, animated: Bool) {
    if selected {
        self.activityIndicator.startAnimating()
    } else {
        self.activityIndicator.stopAnimating()
    }
    super.setSelected(selected, animated: animated)
}
```

But there's a problem: the spinning activity indicator never appears and never spins. The reason is that the events are stumbling over one another here. UITableViewCell's `setSelected(_:animated:)` isn't called until the UITableView delegate method `tableView(_:didSelectRowAt:)` has finished. But the delay we're trying to paper over is *during* `tableView(_:didSelectRowAt:)`; the whole problem is that it *doesn't* finish fast enough.

Delayed performance to the rescue! I'll rewrite `tableView(_:didSelectRowAt:)` so that it finishes immediately — thus triggering `setSelected(_:animated:)` immediately and causing the activity indicator to appear and spin — and I'll use delayed performance to call `init(mediaItemCollection:)` later on, when the interface has ironed itself out:

```
override func tableView(_ tableView: UITableView,
    didSelectRowAt indexPath: IndexPath) {
        delay(0.1) {
            let t = TracksViewController(
                mediaItemCollection: self.albums[indexPath.row])
            self.navigationController?.pushViewController(t, animated: true)
        }
}
```

CHAPTER 12

Memory Management

Class instances, both in Swift and in Objective-C, are reference types (see "Value Types and Reference Types" on page 146). Behind the scenes, Swift and Objective-C memory management for reference types works essentially the same way. Such memory management, as I pointed out in Chapter 5, can be a tricky business.

Fortunately, Swift uses ARC (automatic reference counting), so that you don't have to manage the memory for every reference type object explicitly and individually, as was once necessary in Objective-C. Thanks to ARC, you are far less likely to make a memory management mistake, and more of your time is liberated to concentrate on what your app actually does instead of dealing with memory management concerns.

But even with ARC it is still possible to make a memory management mistake, or to be caught unawares by Cocoa's memory management behavior. A memory management mistake can lead to runaway excessive memory usage, crashes, or mysterious misbehavior of your app, and even in Swift it is possible to make such a mistake. Cocoa memory management can be surprising in individual cases, and you need to understand, and prepare for, what Cocoa is going to do.

Principles of Cocoa Memory Management

The reason why reference type memory must be managed at all is that references to reference type objects are merely pointers. The real object pointed to occupies a hunk of memory that must be explicitly set aside when the object is brought into existence and that must be explicitly freed up when the object goes out of existence. The memory is set aside when the object is instantiated, but how is this memory to be freed up, and when should it happen?

At the very least, an object should certainly go out of existence when no other objects exist that have a pointer to it. An object without a pointer to it is useless; it is occupying memory, but no other object has, or can ever get, a reference to it. This is a *memory leak*. Many computer languages solve this problem through a policy called *garbage collection*. Simply put, the language prevents memory leaks by periodically sweeping through a central list of all objects and destroying those to which no pointer exists. But garbage collection would be an expensive strategy on an iOS device, where memory is strictly limited and the processor is relatively slow (and may have only a single core). Thus, memory in iOS must be managed more or less manually, on an individual basis; each object needs to go out of existence exactly when it is no longer needed.

The hard part in that sentence is the word "exactly." An object must go out of existence neither too late nor too soon. Multiple objects can have a pointer (a reference) to the very same object. If both the object Manny and the object Moe have a pointer to the object Jack, and if Manny somehow tells Jack to go out of existence now, poor old Moe is left with a pointer to nothing (or worse, to garbage). A pointer whose object has been destroyed behind the pointer's back is a *dangling pointer*. If Moe subsequently uses that dangling pointer to send a message to the object that it thinks is there, the app will crash. On the other hand, if both Manny and Moe go out of existence, and if no other object has a pointer to Jack, Jack must go out of existence too, or he will leak.

To prevent both dangling pointers and memory leakage, there is a policy of manual memory management based on a number, maintained by every reference type object, called its *retain count*. The rule is that other objects can increment or decrement an object's retain count — and that's all they are allowed to do. As long as an object's retain count is positive, the object will persist. No object has the direct power to tell another object to be destroyed; rather, as soon as an object's retain count is decremented to zero, it is destroyed automatically.

By this policy, every object that needs Jack to persist should increment Jack's retain count, and should decrement it once again when it no longer needs Jack to persist. As long as all objects are well-behaved in accordance with this policy, the problem of manual memory management is effectively solved:

- There cannot be any dangling pointers, because any object that has a pointer to Jack has incremented Jack's retain count, thus ensuring that Jack persists.
- There cannot be any memory leaks, because any object that no longer needs Jack decrements Jack's retain count, thus ensuring that eventually Jack will go out of existence — namely, when the retain count reaches zero, indicating that no object needs Jack any longer.

Rules of Cocoa Memory Management

An object is well-behaved with respect to memory management as long as it adheres to certain very simple, well-defined rules in conformity with the basic concepts of memory management. The underlying ethic is that each object that has a reference to a reference type object is responsible solely for its own memory management of that object, in accordance with these rules. If all objects that ever get a reference to this reference type object behave correctly with respect to these rules, the object's memory will be managed correctly and it will go out of existence exactly when it is no longer needed.

Consider three objects: Manny, Moe, and Jack. Poor old Jack is going to be the victim here: we're going to manage his memory, and if Jack's memory is managed correctly, Jack will go out of existence correctly. Manny and Moe are going to participate in managing Jack's memory. How will they do that? Everything will be fine as long as Manny and Moe follow these rules:

- If Manny or Moe *explicitly instantiates* Jack — by directly calling an initializer — then the initializer *increments* Jack's retain count.

- If Manny or Moe *makes a copy* of Jack — by calling copy or mutableCopy or any other method with copy in its name — then the copy method *increments* the retain count of this new, duplicate Jack.

- If Manny or Moe *acquires* a reference to Jack (not through explicit instantiation or copying), and needs Jack to *persist* — long enough to work with Jack in code, or long enough to be the value of an instance property — then he himself *increments* Jack's retain count. (This is called *retaining* Jack.)

- If and only if Manny or Moe, himself, has done any of those things — that is, if Manny or Moe has ever directly or indirectly caused Jack's retain count to be incremented — then when he himself no longer needs his reference to Jack, before letting go of that reference, he *decrements* Jack's retain count to balance exactly all previous increments that he himself has performed. (This is called *releasing* Jack.) Having released Jack, Manny or Moe should then assume that Jack no longer exists, because if this causes Jack's retain count to drop to zero, Jack *will* no longer exist. This is the *golden rule of memory management* — the rule that makes memory management work coherently and correctly.

A general way of understanding the golden rule of memory management is to think in terms of *ownership*. If Manny has created, copied, or retained Jack — that is, if Manny has ever incremented Jack's retain count — Manny has asserted ownership of Jack. Both Manny and Moe can own Jack at once, but each is responsible only for managing his own ownership of Jack correctly. It is the responsibility of an owner of Jack eventually to decrement Jack's retain count — to release Jack, thus resigning ownership of Jack. The owner thus says: "Jack may or may not persist after this, but as for me, I'm done with Jack, and Jack can go out of existence as far as I'm concerned." At the same time, a nonowner of Jack must *never* release Jack. As long as all objects behave this way with respect to Jack, Jack will not leak nor will any pointer to Jack be left dangling.

What ARC Is and What It Does

Once upon a time, retaining and releasing an object was a matter of you, the programmer, literally sending `retain` and `release` messages to it. NSObject still implements `retain` and `release`, but under ARC (and in Swift) you can't call them. That's because ARC is calling them for you! That's ARC's job — to do for you what you would have had to do if memory management were still up to the programmer.

ARC is implemented as part of the compiler. The compiler is literally modifying your code by inserting `retain` and `release` calls behind the scenes. Thus, for example, when you receive a reference type object by calling some method, ARC immediately retains it so that it will persist for as long as this same code continues to run; then ARC releases it when the code comes to an end. Similarly, when you create or copy a reference type object, ARC knows that its retain count has been incremented, and releases it when the code comes to an end.

ARC is very conservative, but also very accurate. In effect, ARC retains at every juncture that might have the slightest implications for memory management: it retains when an object is received as an argument, it retains when an object is assigned to a variable, and so forth. It may even insert temporary variables, behind the scenes, to enable it to refer sufficiently early to an object so that it can retain it. But of course it eventually also releases to match.

How Cocoa Objects Manage Memory

Built-in Cocoa objects will take ownership of objects that you hand to them, by retaining them, if it makes sense for them to do so, and will of course then balance that retain with a release later. Indeed, this is so generally true that if a Cocoa object is *not* going to retain an object you hand it, there will be a note to that effect in the documentation.

A collection, such as an NSArray or an NSDictionary, is a particularly obvious case in point (see Chapter 10 for a discussion of the common collection classes). An object can hardly be an element of a collection if that object can go out of existence at any time; so when you add an element to a collection, the collection asserts ownership of the object by retaining it. Thereafter, the collection acts as a well-behaved owner. If this is a mutable collection, then if an element is removed from it, the collection

---

releases that element. If the collection object goes out of existence, it releases all its elements.

Prior to ARC, removing an object from a mutable collection constituted a potential trap. Consider the following Objective-C code:

```
id obj = myMutableArray[0]; // an NSMutableArray
[myMutableArray removeObjectAtIndex: 0]; // bad idea in non-ARC code!
// ... could crash here by referring to obj ...
```

As I just said, when you remove an object from a mutable collection, the collection releases it. So, without ARC, the second line of that code involves an implicit release of the object that used to be element 0 of myMutableArray. If this reduces the object's retain count to zero, it will be destroyed. The pointer obj will then be a dangling pointer, and a crash may be in our future when we try to use it as if it were a real object. With ARC, however, that sort of danger doesn't exist. Assigning a reference type object to a variable retains it! But we *did* assign this object to a variable, obj, *before* we removed it from the collection. Thus that code is perfectly safe, and so is its Swift equivalent:

```
let obj = myMutableArray[0]
myMutableArray.removeObject(at:0)
// ... safe to refer to obj ...
```

The first line retains the object. The second line releases the object, but that release balances the retain that was placed on the object when the object was placed in the collection originally. Thus the object's retain count is still more than zero, and it continues to exist for the duration of this code.

Autorelease Pool

When a method creates an instance and returns that instance, some memory management hanky-panky has to take place. For example, consider this simple code:

```
func makeImage() -> UIImage? {
    if let im = UIImage(named:"myImage") {
        return im
    }
    return nil
}
```

Think about the retain count of im, the UIImage we are returning. This retain count has been incremented by our call to the UIImage initializer UIImage(named:). According to the golden rule of memory management, as we pass im out of our own control by returning it, we should decrement the retain count of im, to balance the increment and surrender ownership. But when can we possibly do that? If we do it *before* the line return im, the retain count of im will be zero and it will vanish in a

puff of smoke; we will be returning a dangling pointer. But we can't do it *after* the line
`return im`, because when that line is executed, our code comes to an end.

Clearly, we need a way to vend this object without decrementing its retain count *now*
— so that it stays in existence long enough for the caller to receive and work with it
— while ensuring that at some future time we *will* decrement its retain count, so as to
balance our `init(named:)` call and fulfill our own management of this object's memory. The solution is something midway between releasing the object and not releasing
it — ARC *autoreleases* it.

Here's how autoreleasing works. Your code runs in the presence of something called
an *autorelease pool*. When ARC autoreleases an object, that object is placed in the
autorelease pool, and a number is incremented saying how many times this object has
been placed in this autorelease pool. From time to time, when nothing else is going
on, the autorelease pool is automatically *drained*. This means that the autorelease
pool releases each of its objects, the same number of times as that object was placed in
this autorelease pool, and empties itself of all objects. If that causes an object's retain
count to be zero, so be it; the object is destroyed in the usual way. So autoreleasing an
object is just like releasing it, but with a proviso, "later, not right this second."

In general, autoreleasing and the autorelease pool are merely an implementation
detail. You can't see them; they are just part of how ARC works. So why am I telling
you about them? It's because sometimes, on very rare occasions, you might want to
drain the autorelease pool yourself. Consider the following code (it's slightly artificial,
but that's because demonstrating the need to drain the autorelease pool isn't easy):

```
func test() {
    let path = Bundle.main.path(forResource:"001", ofType: "png")!
    for j in 0 ..< 50 {
        for i in 0 ..< 100 {
            let im = UIImage(contentsOfFile: path)
        }
    }
}
```

That method does something that looks utterly innocuous; it loads an image. But it
loads it repeatedly in a loop. As the loop runs, memory climbs constantly
(Figure 12-1); by the time our method comes to an end, our app's memory usage has
reached almost 34MB. This is not because the images aren't being released each time
through the loop; it's because a lot of *intermediate* objects — things you've never even
heard of, such as NSPathStore2 objects — are secondarily generated by our call to
`init(contentsOfFile:)` *and are autoreleased*, and are all sitting there, piling up in
the autorelease pool by the tens of thousands, waiting for the pool to be drained.
When our code finally comes to an end, the autorelease pool *is* drained, and our
memory usage drops precipitately back down to almost nothing.

Figure 12-1. Memory usage grows during a loop

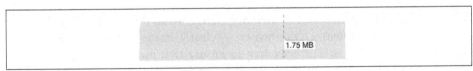

Figure 12-2. Memory usage holds steady with an autorelease pool

Granted, 34MB isn't exactly a massive amount of memory. But you may imagine that a more elaborate inner loop might generate more and larger autoreleased objects, and that our memory usage could potentially rise quite significantly. Thus, it would be nice to have a way to drain the autorelease pool *manually* now and then during the course of a loop with many iterations. Swift provides such a way — the global `autoreleasepool` function, which takes a single argument that you'll supply as a trailing anonymous function. Before the anonymous function is called, a special temporary autorelease pool is created, and is used for all autoreleased objects thereafter. After the anonymous function exits, the temporary autorelease pool is drained and goes out of existence. Here's the same method with an `autoreleasepool` call wrapping the inner loop:

```
func test() {
    let path = Bundle.main.path(forResource:"001", ofType: "png")!
    for j in 0 ..< 50 {
        autoreleasepool {
            for i in 0 ..< 100 {
                let im = UIImage(contentsOfFile: path)
            }
        }
    }
}
```

The difference in memory usage is dramatic: memory holds roughly steady at less than 2MB (Figure 12-2). Setting up and draining the temporary autorelease pool probably involves some overhead, so if possible you may want to divide your loop into an outer and an inner loop, as shown in the example, so that the autorelease pool is not set up and torn down on every iteration.

Memory Management of Instance Properties

Before ARC, managing memory for instance properties (Objective-C instance variables, Chapter 10) was one of the trickiest parts of Cocoa programming. The correct behavior is to retain a reference type object when you assign it to a property, and then release it when either of these things happens:

- You assign a different value to the same property.
- The instance whose instance property this is goes out of existence.

In order to obey the golden rule of memory management, the object taking charge of this memory management — the owner — clearly needs to be the object whose instance property this is. The only way to ensure that memory management of a property is handled correctly, therefore, is to implement it *in the setter method* for that property. The setter must release whatever object is currently the value of the property, and must retain whatever object is being assigned to that property. The exact details can be quite tricky (what if they are the same object?), and before ARC it was easy for programmers to get them wrong. And that, of course, is not the *only* memory management needed; to prevent a leak when the owner goes out of existence, the owner's `dealloc` method (the Objective-C equivalent of `deinit`) had to be implemented to release every object being retained as the value of a property.

Fortunately, ARC understands all that, and the memory of instance properties, like the memory of all variables, is managed correctly for you.

This fact also gives us a clue as to how to release an object on demand. This is a valuable thing to be able to do, because an object may be using a lot of memory. You don't want to put too great a strain on the device's memory, so you want to release the object as soon as you're done with it. Also, when your app goes into the background and is suspended, the Watchdog process will terminate it in the background if it is found to be using too much memory; so you might want to release this object when you are notified that the app is about to be backgrounded. (I talked about that problem in Chapter 3.)

You can't call `release` explicitly, so you need another way to do it, some way that is consonant with the design and behavior of ARC. The solution is to assign something else — something small — to this property. That causes the object that was previously the value of this property to be released. A commonly used approach is to type this property as an Optional — possibly, to simplify matters, an implicitly unwrapped Optional. This means that `nil` can be assigned to it, purely as a way of replacing the object that is the instance property's current value and releasing it.

Retain Cycles and Weak References

As I explained in Chapter 5, you can get yourself into a retain cycle where two objects have references to one another — for example, each is the value of the other's instance property. If such a situation is allowed to persist until no other objects have a reference to either of these objects, then neither can go out of existence, because each has a retain count greater than zero and neither will "go first" and release the other. Since these two objects, *ex hypothesi*, can no longer be referred to by any object except one another, this situation can now never be remedied — these objects are leaking.

The solution is to step in and modify how the memory is managed for one of these references. By default, a reference is a *persisting* reference (what ARC calls a *strong* or *retain* reference): assigning to it retains the assigned value. In Swift, you can declare a reference type variable as weak or as unowned to change the way its memory is managed:

weak

> A weak reference takes advantage of a powerful ARC feature. When a reference is weak, ARC does *not* retain the object assigned to it. This seems dangerous, because it means that the object might go out of existence behind our backs, leaving us with a dangling pointer and leading to a potential crash later on. But ARC is very clever about this. It keeps track of all weak references and all objects assigned to them. When such an object's retain count drops to zero and the object is about to be destroyed, ARC sneaks in and assigns nil to the reference — that's why a weak reference in Swift must be an Optional declared with var, so that ARC can do that. Thus, provided you handle the Optional coherently, nothing bad can happen.

unowned

> An unowned reference is a different kettle of fish. When you mark a reference as unowned, you're telling ARC to take its hands off completely: it does no memory management at all when something is assigned to this reference. This really *is* dangerous — if the object referred to goes out of existence, you really *can* be left with a dangling pointer and you really *can* crash. That is why you must never use unowned unless you know that the object referred to will *not* go out of existence: unowned is safe, provided the object referred to will outlive the object that refers to it. That is why an unowned object should be some single object, assigned only once, without which the referrer cannot exist at all.

In real life, a weak reference is most commonly used to connect an object to its delegate (Chapter 11). A delegate is an independent entity; there is usually no reason why an object needs to claim ownership of its delegate, and indeed an object is usually its delegate's servant, not its owner. Ownership, if there is any, often runs the other way; Object A might create *and retain* Object B, and make itself Object B's delegate. That's potentially a retain cycle. Therefore, most delegates should be declared as weak references:

```
class ColorPickerController : UIViewController {
    weak var delegate: ColorPickerDelegate?
    // ...
}
```

```
libobjc.A.dylib'objc_retain:
    0x110706d00 <+0>:   xorl    %eax, %eax
    0x110706d02 <+2>:   testq   %rdi, %rdi
    0x110706d05 <+5>:   je      0x110706d0c              ; <+12>
    0x110706d07 <+7>:   jns     0x110706d0d              ; <+13>
    0x110706d09 <+9>:   movq    %rdi, %rax
    0x110706d0c <+12>:  retq
    0x110706d0d <+13>:  movq    (%rdi), %rax
->  0x110706d10 <+16>:  testb   $0x2, 0x20(%rax)    Thread 1: EXC_BAD_ACCESS (code=1, address=0x24)
    0x110706d14 <+20>:  jne     0x110706d25              ; <+37>
```

Figure 12-3. A crash from messaging a dangling pointer

Unfortunately, properties of built-in Cocoa classes that keep weak references are sometimes *non-ARC* weak references (because they are old and backward-compatible, whereas ARC is new). Such properties are declared using the keyword assign. For example, AVSpeechSynthesizer's delegate property is declared like this:

```
@property(nonatomic, assign, nullable)
    id<AVSpeechSynthesizerDelegate> delegate;
```

In Swift, that declaration is translated like this:

```
unowned(unsafe) var delegate: AVSpeechSynthesizerDelegate?
```

The Swift term unowned and the Objective-C term assign are synonyms; they tell you that there's no ARC memory management here. The unsafe designation is a further warning inserted by Swift; unlike your own code, where you won't use unowned unless it is safe, Cocoa's unowned is potentially dangerous and you need to exercise caution.

Even though *your* code is using ARC, the fact that Cocoa's code is *not* using ARC means that memory management mistakes can still occur. A reference such as an AVSpeechSynthesizer's delegate can end up as a dangling pointer, pointing at garbage, if the object to which that reference was pointing has gone out of existence. If anyone (you or Cocoa) tries to send a message by way of such a reference, the app will then crash — and, since this typically happens long after the point where the real mistake occurred, figuring out the cause of the crash can be quite difficult. The typical sign of such a crash is that EXC_BAD_ACCESS is reported in connection with memory management activity (Figure 12-3). (This is the sort of situation in which you might need to turn on zombies in order to debug, as I'll describe later in this chapter.)

Defending against this kind of situation is up to you. If you assign some object to a non-ARC unsafe reference, such as an AVSpeechSynthesizer's delegate, and if that object is about to go out of existence at a time when this reference still exists, *you* have a duty to assign nil (or some other object) to that reference, thus rendering it harmless.

Unusual Memory Management Situations

If you are using NotificationCenter to register for notifications (Chapter 11), and if you registered with the notification center by calling add-Observer(_:selector:name:object:), you handed the notification center a reference to some object (usually self) as the first argument; the notification center's reference to this object is a non-ARC unsafe reference, and there is a danger that after this object goes out of existence the notification center will try to send a notification to whatever is referred to, which will be garbage. That is why you must unregister before that can happen. This is similar to the situation with delegates that I was talking about a moment ago.

If you registered with the notification center by calling addObserver(for-Name:object:queue:using:), memory management can be even more tricky, because:

- The observer token object returned from the call to addObserver(for-Name:object:queue:using:) is retained by the notification center until you unregister it.
- The observer token may also be retaining you (self) through the function that you provided as the last parameter, if that function refers to self — because functions are closures. If so, then until you unregister the observer token from the notification center, the notification center is retaining you. This means that you will leak until you unregister. But you cannot unregister from the notification center in deinit, because deinit isn't going to be called so long as you are registered.
- In addition, if you also retain the observer token, then if the observer token is retaining you, you have a retain cycle on your hands.

Thus, use of addObserver(forName:object:queue:using:) can put you into the same situation that I described in "Weak and Unowned References in Anonymous Functions" on page 287. And the solution is the same: mark self as weak or (preferably) unowned in the anonymous function that you pass in as the last argument.

Consider, for example, this (artificial) code, in which we, a view controller, register for a notification and assign the observer token to an instance property:

```
var observer : Any!
override func viewWillAppear(_ animated: Bool) {
    super.viewWillAppear(animated)
    self.observer = NotificationCenter.default.addObserver(
        forName: .woohoo, object:nil, queue:nil) {
```

```
        _ in
        print(self.description)
    }
}
```

Our intention is eventually to unregister the observer; that's why we're keeping a reference to it. It's natural to do this in viewDidDisappear:

```
override func viewDidDisappear(_ animated: Bool) {
    super.viewDidDisappear(animated)
    NotificationCenter.default.removeObserver(self.observer)
}
```

This works in the sense that the observer is unregistered; but the view controller itself is leaking. We can see this by logging on deinit:

```
deinit {
    print("deinit")
}
```

In a situation where this view controller should be destroyed — for example, it was a presented view controller, and now it is being dismissed — deinit is never called. We have a retain cycle! The simplest solution is to mark self as unowned as it enters the anonymous function; this is safe because self will not outlive the anonymous function:

```
self.observer = NotificationCenter.default.addObserver(
    forName: .woohoo, object:nil, queue:nil) {
        [unowned self] _ in
        print(self.description)
    }
```

Another unusual case is Timer (Chapter 10). The Timer class documentation says that "run loops maintain strong references to their timers"; it then says of scheduled-Timer(timeInterval:target:selector:userInfo:repeats:) that "The timer maintains a strong reference to target until it (the timer) is invalidated." This should set off alarm bells in your head: "Danger, Will Robinson, danger!" The documentation is warning you that as long as a repeating timer has not been invalidated, the target is being retained by the run loop; the only way to stop this is to send the invalidate message to the timer. (With a non-repeating timer, the problem arises less starkly, because the timer invalidates itself immediately after firing.)

When you called scheduledTimer, you probably supplied self as the target: argument. This means that you (self) are being retained, and cannot go out of existence until you invalidate the timer. So when will you that? You can't do it in your deinit implementation, because as long as the timer is repeating and has not been sent the invalidate message, deinit won't be called. You therefore need to find another appropriate moment for sending invalidate to the timer. There's no good way out of this situation; you simply have to find such a moment, and that's that. For example,

you could balance creation and invalidation of the timer by doing them in viewWill-
Appear and viewDidDisappear:

```
var timer : Timer!
override func viewWillAppear(_ animated: Bool) {
    super.viewWillAppear(animated)
    self.timer = Timer.scheduledTimer(timeInterval: 1, target: self,
        selector: #selector(fired), userInfo: nil, repeats: true)
    self.timer.tolerance = 0.1
}
func fired(_ t:Timer) {
    print("timer fired")
}
override func viewDidDisappear(_ animated: Bool) {
    super.viewDidDisappear(animated)
    self.timer.invalidate()
}
```

New in iOS 10, you can call scheduledTimer(withTimeInterval:repeats:block:)
instead. Here you must take the normal precautions that apply to any retained function. If the timer is a repeating timer, you are retaining it so that you can invalidate it
later; but the timer is retaining the function you hand to it as the block: argument. If
that involves a reference to self, it will retain self, causing a retain cycle. But you
already know how to break such a retain cycle: use an anonymous function, and mark
self as weak or unowned ("Weak and Unowned References in Anonymous Functions"
on page 287). Having done that, you *can* invalidate the timer in deinit. Thus, the following does *not* leak; deinit is called, the timer is invalidated, and everything goes
out of existence in good order:

```
var timer : Timer!
override func viewWillAppear(_ animated: Bool) {
    super.viewWillAppear(animated)
    self.timer = Timer.scheduledTimer(withTimeInterval: 1, repeats: true) {
        [unowned self] // *
        t in
        self.fired(t)
    }
    self.timer.tolerance = 0.1
}
func fired(_ t:Timer) {
    print("timer fired")
}
deinit {
    self.timer.invalidate()
}
```

Other Cocoa objects with unusual memory management behavior will usually be
called out clearly in the documentation. For example, the UIWebView documentation
warns: "Before releasing an instance of UIWebView for which you have set a delegate,

you must first set its `delegate` property to `nil`." And a CAAnimation object *retains its delegate*; this is exceptional and can cause trouble if you're not conscious of it.

There are also situations where the documentation fails to warn of any special memory management considerations, but you can wind up with a retain cycle anyway. Discovering the problem can be tricky. Areas of Cocoa that have given me trouble include UIKit Dynamics (a UIDynamicBehavior's `action` handler) and WebKit (a WKWebKit's WKScriptMessageHandler).

Three Foundation collection classes — NSPointerArray, NSHashTable, and NSMapTable — are similar respectively to NSMutableArray, NSMutableSet, and NSMutableDictionary, except that (among other things) their memory management policy is up to you. A HashTable created with the class method `weakObjects`, for example, maintains ARC-weak references to its elements, meaning that they are replaced by `nil` if the retain count of the object to which they were pointing has dropped to zero. You may find uses for these classes as a way of avoiding retain cycles.

Nib Loading and Memory Management

When a nib loads, it instantiates its nib objects (Chapter 7). What happens to these instantiated objects? A view retains its subviews, but what about the top-level objects, which are not subviews of any view? The answer is, in effect, that they do not have elevated retain counts; if someone doesn't immediately retain them, they'll simply vanish in a puff of smoke.

If you don't want that to happen — and if you did, why would you be loading this nib in the first place? — you need to capture a reference to the top-level objects instantiated from the nib. There are two mechanisms for doing this.

The first approach is to capture the result of the nib-loading code. When a nib is loaded by calling Bundle's `loadNibNamed(_:owner:options:)` or UINib's `instantiate(withOwner:options:)`, an array is returned consisting of the top-level objects instantiated by the nib-loading mechanism. So it's sufficient to retain this array, or the objects in it. We did that in Chapter 7 when we loaded a nib and assigned the result to a variable, like this:

```
let arr = Bundle.main.loadNibNamed("View", owner: nil)!
let v = arr[0] as! UIView
self.view.addSubview(v)
```

The other possibility is to configure the nib owner with outlets that will retain the nib's top-level objects when they are instantiated. We did that in Chapter 7 when we set up an outlet like this:

```
class ViewController: UIViewController {
    @IBOutlet var coolview : UIView!
```

We then loaded the nib with this view controller as owner:

```
Bundle.main.loadNibNamed("View", owner: self)
self.view.addSubview(self.coolview)
```

The first line instantiates the top-level view from the nib, and the nib-loading mechanism assigns it to `self.coolview`. Since `self.coolview` is a strong reference, it retains the view. Thus, the view is still there when we insert it into the interface in the second line.

It is common, however, for `@IBOutlet` properties that you declare to be marked weak. This is not obligatory, and it probably does no harm to omit the weak designation. The reason such outlets work properly even when they *are* designated weak is that you use this designation only when this is an outlet to an object that you know will be retained by someone else — for example, it's already a subview of your view controller's main view. A view controller retains its main view, and a view is retained by its superview, so the nib-loading process will cause this view to be retained, and there is no need for your `@IBOutlet` property to retain it as well.

Memory Management of CFTypeRefs

A CFTypeRef is a pure C analog to an Objective-C object. In Objective-C, CFTypeRef types are distinguished by the suffix `Ref` at the end of their name. In Swift, however, this `Ref` suffix is dropped. For example, a CGContextRef is a CFTypeRef, and is known in Swift as a CGContext.

A CFTypeRef is a pointer to an opaque C struct (see Appendix A), where "opaque" means that the struct has no directly accessible components. This struct acts as a pseudo-object; a CFTypeRef is analogous to an object type. In Objective-C, the fact that this thing is not an object is particularly obvious, because the code that operates upon a CFTypeRef is not object-oriented. A CFTypeRef has no properties or methods, and you do not send any messages to it; you work with CFTypeRefs entirely through global C functions. In Swift 3, however, those global C functions are hand-tweaked to *look* like methods; for example, the `CGContextDrawLinearGradient` C function is called, in Swift, by sending the `drawLinearGradient` message to a CGContext pseudo-object, just as if a CGContext were an object and `drawLinear-Gradient` were an instance method.

For example, here's some Swift code for drawing a gradient; `con` is a CGContext, `sp` is a CGColorSpace, and `grad` is a CGGradient (all of them being CFTypeRefs):

```
let con = UIGraphicsGetCurrentContext()!
let locs : [CGFloat] = [ 0.0, 0.5, 1.0 ]
let colors : [CGFloat] = [
    0.8, 0.4, // starting color, transparent light gray
    0.1, 0.5, // intermediate color, darker less transparent gray
```

```
            0.8, 0.4, // ending color, transparent light gray
    ]
    let sp = CGColorSpaceCreateDeviceGray()
    let grad = CGGradient(colorSpace: sp,
        colorComponents: colors, locations: locs, count: 3)!
    con.drawLinearGradient(grad,
        start: CGPoint(x:89,y:0), end: CGPoint(x:111,y:0), options:[])
```

Despite being only a pseudo-object, a CFTypeRef is a reference type, and its memory must be managed in just the same way as that of a real object. Therefore, a CFTypeRef pseudo-object has a retain count! And this retain count works exactly as for a true object, in accordance with the golden rule of memory management. A CFTypeRef must be retained when it comes within the sphere of influence of an owner who wants it to persist, and it must be released when that owner no longer needs it.

In Objective-C, the golden rule, as applied to CFTypeRefs, is that if you obtained a CFTypeRef object through a function whose name contains the word `Create` or `Copy`, its retain count has been incremented. In addition, if you are worried about the object persisting, you'll retain it explicitly by calling the `CFRetain` function to increment its retain count. To balance your `Create`, `Copy`, or `CFRetain` call, you must eventually release the object. By default, you'll do that by calling the `CFRelease` function; some CFTypeRefs, however, have their own dedicated object release functions — for example, for CGPath, there's a dedicated `CGPathRelease` function. There's no ARC management of CFTypeRefs in Objective-C, so you have to do all of this yourself, explicitly.

In Swift, however, you will *never* need to call `CFRetain`, or any form of `CFRelease`; indeed, you cannot. Swift will do it for you, behind the scenes, automatically.

Think of CFTypeRefs as living in two worlds: the CFTypeRef world of pure C, and the memory-managed object-oriented world of Swift. When you obtain a CFTypeRef pseudo-object, it *crosses the bridge* from the CFTypeRef world into the Swift world. From that moment on, until you are done with it, it needs memory management. Swift is aware of this, and for the most part, Swift itself will use the golden rule and will apply correct memory management. Thus, for example, the code I showed earlier for drawing a gradient is in fact memory-management complete. In Objective-C, we would have to release `sp` and `grad`, because they arrived into our world through `Create` calls; if we failed to do this, they would leak. In Swift, however, there is no need, because Swift will do it for us. (See Appendix A for more about how objects move between the CFTypeRef world and the memory-managed object world.)

Working with CFTypeRefs in Swift is thus much easier than in Objective-C. In Swift, you can treat CFTypeRef pseudo-objects as actual objects! For example, you can assign a CFTypeRef to a property in Swift, or pass it as an argument to a Swift function, and its memory will be managed correctly; in Objective-C, those are tricky things to do.

It is possible, however, that you may receive a CFTypeRef through some API that lacks memory management information. Such a value will come forcibly to your attention, because it will arrive into Swift, not as a CFTypeRef, but as an Unmanaged generic wrapping the actual CFTypeRef. This is a form of warning that Swift does not know how to proceed with the memory management of this pseudo-object. You will in fact be *unable* to proceed until you unwrap the CFTypeRef by calling the Unmanaged object's `takeRetainedValue` or `takeUnretainedValue` method. You will call whichever method tells Swift how to manage the memory for this object correctly. For a CFTypeRef with an incremented retain count (usually acquired through a function with `Create` or `Copy` in its name), call `takeRetainedValue`; otherwise, call `takeUnretainedValue`.

Property Memory Management Policies

In Objective-C, a `@property` declaration (see Chapter 10) includes a statement of the memory management policy that is followed by the corresponding setter accessor method. It is useful to be aware of this and to know how such policy statements are translated into Swift.

For example, earlier I said that a UIViewController retains its `view` (its main view). How do I know this? Because the `@property` declaration tells me so:

```
@property(null_resettable, nonatomic, strong) UIView *view;
```

The term `strong` means that the setter retains the incoming UIView object. The Swift translation of this declaration doesn't add any attribute to the variable:

```
var view: UIView!
```

The default in Swift is that a variable referring to a reference object type *is* a strong reference — a persisting reference. This means that it retains the object. Thus, you can safely conclude from this declaration that UIViewController retains its `view`.

The possible memory management policies for a Cocoa property are:

`strong`, `retain` *(no Swift equivalent)*
    The default. The two terms are pure synonyms of one another; `retain` is the term inherited from pre-ARC days. Assignment to this property retains the incoming value and releases the existing value.

`copy` *(no Swift equivalent, or @NSCopying)*
    The same as `strong` or `retain`, except that the setter copies the incoming value by sending `copy` to it; the incoming value must be an object of a type that adopts NSCopying, to ensure that this is possible. The copy, which has an increased retain count already, becomes the new value.

weak *(Swift* weak*)*

An ARC-weak reference. The incoming object value is not retained, but if it goes out of existence behind our back, ARC will magically substitute nil as the value of this property, which must be typed as an Optional declared with var.

assign *(Swift* unowned(unsafe)*)*

No memory management. This policy is inherited from pre-ARC days, and is inherently unsafe (hence the additional unsafe warning in the Swift translation of the name): if the object referred to goes out of existence, this reference will become a dangling pointer and can cause a crash if you subsequently try to use it.

You'd probably like to hear more about the copy policy, as I haven't mentioned it until now. This policy is used by Cocoa particularly when an immutable class has a mutable subclass (such as NSString and NSMutableString, or NSArray and NSMutable-Array; see Chapter 10). The idea is to deal with the danger of the setter's caller passing in an object of the mutable subclass. A moment's thought will reveal that this is possible, because, in accordance with the substitution principle of polymorphism (Chapter 4), wherever an instance of a class is expected, an instance of its subclass can be passed. But it would be bad if this were to happen, because now the caller might keep a reference to the incoming value and, since it is in fact mutable, could later mutate it behind our back. To prevent this, the setter calls copy on the incoming object; this creates a new instance, separate from the object provided — and belonging to the immutable class.

In Swift, this problem is unlikely to arise with strings and arrays, because on the Swift side these are value types (structs) and are effectively copied when assigned, passed as an argument, or received as a return value. Thus, Cocoa's NSString and NSArray property declarations, when translated into Swift as String and Array property declarations, don't show any special marking corresponding to Objective-C copy. But Cocoa types that are *not* bridged to Swift value types *do* show a marking: @NSCopying. For example, the declaration of the attributedText property of a UILabel appears like this in Swift:

```
@NSCopying var attributedText: NSAttributedString?
```

NSAttributedString has a mutable subclass, NSMutableAttributedString. You've probably configured this attributed string as an NSMutableAttributedString, and now you're assigning it as the UILabel's attributedText. UILabel doesn't want you keeping a reference to this mutable string and mutating it in place, since that would change the value of the property without passing through the setter. Thus, it copies the incoming value to ensure that what it has is a separate immutable NSAttributedString.

You can do exactly the same thing in your own code, and you will want to do so. Merely providing the @NSCopying designation on a property is sufficient; Swift will enforce the copy policy and will take care of the actual copying for you when code assigns to this property:

```
class StringDrawer {
    @NSCopying var attributedString : NSAttributedString!
    // ...
}
```

If, as is sometimes the case, your own class wants the internal ability to mutate the value of this property while preventing a mutable value from arriving from outside, put a private computed property façade in front of it that transforms it to the corresponding mutable type:

```
class StringDrawer {
    @NSCopying var attributedString : NSAttributedString!
    private var mutableAttributedString : NSMutableAttributedString! {
        get {
            if self.attributedString == nil {return nil}
            return NSMutableAttributedString(
                attributedString:self.attributedString)
        }
        set {
            self.attributedString = newValue
        }
    }
    // ...
}
```

@NSCopying can be used *only* for instance properties of classes, not of structs or enums — and only in the presence of Foundation, because that is where the NSCopying protocol is defined, which the type of a variable marked as @NSCopying must adopt.

Debugging Memory Management Mistakes

Though far less likely to occur under ARC (and Swift), memory management mistakes still *can* occur, especially because a programmer is prone to suppose (wrongly) that they can't. Experience suggests that you should use every tool at your disposal to ferret out possible mistakes. Here are some of those tools (and see Chapter 9):

- The memory gauge in the Debug navigator charts memory usage whenever your app runs, allowing you to observe possible memory leakage or other unwarranted heavy memory use. Note that memory management in the Simulator is not necessarily indicative of reality! Always observe the memory gauge with the app running on a device before making a judgment.

- Instruments (Product → Profile) has excellent tools for noticing leaks and tracking memory management of individual objects.

- Good old caveman debugging can help confirm that your objects are behaving as you want them to. Implement `deinit` with a `print` call. If it isn't called, your object is not going out of existence. This technique can reveal problems that even Instruments will not directly expose.

- Memory graphing (new in Xcode 8, see "Memory Debugging" on page 421) will draw you a picture of the ownership relations between your objects; in conjunction with Malloc Stack, it will trace that ownership through the actual retain calls.

- Dangling pointers are particularly difficult to track down, but they can often be located by "turning on zombies." This is easy in Instruments with the Zombies template. Alternatively, edit the Run action in your scheme, switch to the Diagnostics tab, and check Enable Zombie Objects. The result is that an object that goes out of existence is replaced by a "zombie" that will report to the console if a message is sent to it ("message sent to deallocated instance"). Be sure to turn zombies back off when you've finished tracking down your dangling pointers. Don't use zombies with the Leaks instrument: zombies *are* leaks.

- The Address Sanitizer (also in the scheme's Run action's Diagnostics tab) lets you debug even more subtle forms of memory misuse. Here, for example, we're doing a Very Bad Thing, writing directly into memory that doesn't belong to us:

  ```
  let b = UnsafeMutablePointer<CGFloat>.allocate(capacity:3)
  b.initializeFrom([0.1, 0.2, 0.3])
  b[4] = 0.4
  ```

  Even worse, that code probably won't crash; it corrupts memory silently. But if we run our app under Address Sanitizer, it detects the problem and reports a heap buffer overflow.

Even these tools may not help you with every possible memory management issue. For example, some objects, such as a UIView containing a large image, are themselves small (and thus may not cause the memory gauge or Instruments to register large memory use) but require a large backing store nevertheless; maintaining references to too many such objects can cause your app to be summarily killed by the system. This sort of issue is not easy to track down.

CHAPTER 13

Communication Between Objects

As soon as an app grows to more than a few objects, puzzling questions can arise about how to send a message or communicate data between one object and another. The problem is essentially one of architecture. It may require some planning to construct your code so that all the pieces fit together and information can be shared as needed at the right moment. This chapter presents some organizational considerations that will help you arrange for one object to be able to communicate with another.

The problem of communication often comes down to one object being able to *see* another: the object Manny needs to be able to find the object Jack repeatedly and reliably over the long term so as to be able to send Jack messages.

One obvious solution is an instance property of Manny whose value *is* Jack. This is appropriate particularly when Manny and Jack share certain responsibilities or supplement one another's functionality. The application object and its delegate, a table view and its data source, a view controller and the view that it controls — these are cases where the former must have an instance property pointing at the latter.

This does not necessarily imply that Manny needs to assert ownership of Jack as a matter of memory management policy (see Chapter 12) — but it might. An object does not typically retain its delegate or its data source; similarly, an object that implements the target–action pattern, such as a UIControl, does not retain its target. By using a weak reference and typing the property as an Optional, and then treating the Optional coherently and safely, Manny can avoid owning Jack while coping with the possibility that his supposed reference to Jack will turn out to be nil. On the other hand, a view controller is useless without a view to control; once it has a view, it will retain it, releasing it only when it itself goes out of existence.

Objects can perform two-way communication without both of them holding references to one another. It may be sufficient for *one* of them to have a reference to the other — because the former, as part of a message to the latter, can include a reference to himself. For example, Manny might send a message to Jack where one of the parameters is a reference to Manny; this might merely constitute a form of identification, or an invitation to Jack to send a message back to Manny if Jack needs further information while doing whatever this method does. Manny thus makes himself, as it were, momentarily visible to Jack; Jack should not wantonly retain Manny (especially since there's an obvious risk of a retain cycle). Again, this is a common pattern. The parameter of the delegate message `textFieldShouldBeginEditing(_:)` is a reference to the UITextField that sent the message. The first parameter of a target–action message is a reference to the control that sent the message.

But how is Manny to obtain a reference to Jack in the first place? That's a very big question. Much of the art of iOS programming, and of object-oriented programming generally, lies in one object *getting a reference* to some other object (see "Instance References" on page 133). Every case is different and must be solved separately, but certain general patterns emerge, and this chapter will outline some of them.

There are also ways for Manny to send a message that Jack *receives* without having to send it directly *to* Jack — possibly without even knowing or caring who Jack is. Notifications and key–value observing are examples, and I'll mention them in this chapter as well.

Finally, the chapter ends with a section on the larger question of what kinds of objects *need* to see one another, within the general scope of a typical iOS program.

Visibility by Instantiation

Every instance comes from somewhere and at someone's behest: some object sent a message commanding this instance to come into existence in the first place. The commanding object therefore has a reference to the instance at that moment. When Manny creates Jack, Manny has a reference to Jack.

That simple fact can serve as the starting point for establishing future communication. If Manny creates Jack and knows that he (Manny) will need a reference to Jack in the future, Manny can keep the reference that he obtained by creating Jack in the first place. Or, it may be that what Manny knows is that Jack will need a reference to Manny in the future; Manny can supply that reference immediately after creating Jack, and Jack will then keep it.

Delegation is a case in point. Manny may create Jack and immediately make himself Jack's delegate, as in my example code in Chapter 11:

```
let cpc = ColorPickerController(colorName:colorName, color:c)
cpc.delegate = self
```

Indeed, if this crucial, you might endow Jack with an initializer so that Manny can create Jack and hand Jack a reference to himself *at the same time*, to help prevent any slip-ups. Compare the approach taken by UIBarButtonItem, where three different initializers, such as init(title:style:target:action:), require as a parameter the target to which future messages will be sent by the UIBarButtonItem.

When Manny creates Jack, it might not be a reference to Manny himself that Jack needs, but to something that Manny knows or has. You will presumably endow Jack with a method so that Manny can hand that information across; again, it might be reasonable to make that method Jack's initializer, if Jack simply cannot live without the information.

Recall this example from Chapter 11. It comes from a table view controller. The user has tapped a row of the table. We create a secondary table view controller, a Tracks-ViewController instance, handing it the data it will need, and display the secondary table view. I have deliberately devised TracksViewController to have a designated initializer init(mediaItemCollection:), making it virtually obligatory for a Tracks-ViewController to have access, from the moment it comes into existence, to the data it needs:

```
override func tableView(_ tableView: UITableView,
    didSelectRowAt indexPath: IndexPath) {
        delay(0.1) {
            let t = TracksViewController(
                mediaItemCollection: self.albums[indexPath.row])
            self.navigationController?.pushViewController(t, animated: true)
        }
}
```

In that example, self does not keep a reference to the new TracksViewController instance, nor does the TracksViewController acquire a reference to self. But self does create the TracksViewController instance, and so, for one brief shining moment, it has a reference to it. Therefore self takes advantage of that moment to hand the TracksViewController instance the information it needs. There will be no better moment to do this. Knowing the moment, and taking care not to miss it, is part of the art of data communication.

Nib-loading is also a case in point. The loading of a nib is a way of instantiating objects from the nib. Proper preparation is essential in order to ensure that there's a reference for those objects, so that they don't simply vanish in a puff of smoke ("Nib Loading and Memory Management" on page 532). The moment of the nib loading is the moment when the nib's owner or the code that loads the nib is in contact with those objects; it takes advantage of that moment to secure those references.

Beginners are often puzzled by how two objects are to get a reference to one another if they will be instantiated from *different* nibs — either different *.xib* files or different scenes in a storyboard. It is frustrating that you can't draw a connection between an object in nib A and an object in nib B; it's particularly frustrating when you can see both objects sitting right there in the same storyboard. But, as I explained earlier ("Connections Between Nibs — Not!" on page 361), such a connection would be meaningless, which is why it's impossible. These are different nibs, and they will load at different times. However, some object (Manny) is going to be the owner when nib A loads, and some object (Jack) is going to be the owner when nib B loads. Perhaps they (Manny and Jack) can then see each other, in which case, given all the necessary outlets, the problem is solved. Or perhaps some third object (Moe) can see both of them and will introduce them to one another, providing a communication path for them.

For example, when a segue in a storyboard is triggered, the segue's destination view controller is instantiated, and the segue has a reference to it. At the same time, the segue's source view controller already exists, and the segue has a reference to it as well. So the segue sends the source view controller the prepare(for:sender:) message, containing a reference to itself (the segue) as the first parameter. Think of the segue as Moe; it is bringing Manny (the source view controller) and Jack (the destination view controller) together. This is the source view controller's chance (Manny's moment) to obtain a reference to the newly instantiated destination view controller (a reference to Jack), by asking the segue for it — and now the source view controller can make itself the destination view controller's delegate, hand it any needed information, and so forth.

Visibility by Relationship

Objects may acquire the ability to see one another automatically by virtue of their position in a containing structure. Before worrying about how to supply one object with a reference to another, consider whether there may *already* be a chain of references leading from one to the other.

For example, a subview can see its superview, through its superview property. A superview can see all its subviews, through its subviews property, and can pick out a specific subview through that subview's tag property, by calling the viewWithTag(_:) method. A subview in a window can see its window, through its window property. Thus, by working your way up or down the view hierarchy by means of these properties, it may be possible to obtain the desired reference.

Similarly, a responder (Chapter 11) can see the next object up the responder chain, through the next property — which also means, because of the structure of the responder chain, that a view controller's main view can see the view controller. In this code from one of my apps, I work my way up from a view some way down the view hierarchy to obtain a reference to the view controller that's in charge of this whole scene (and there are similar examples in Chapter 5):

```
var r : UIResponder! = sender
repeat { r = r.next } while !(r is UIViewController)
```

Similarly, view controllers are themselves part of a hierarchy and therefore can see one another. If a view controller is currently presenting a view through a second view controller, the latter is the former's `presentedViewController`, and the former is the latter's `presentingViewController`. If a view controller is the child of a UINavigationController, the latter is its `navigationController`. A UINavigation-Controller's visible view is controlled by its `visibleViewController`. And from any of these, you can reach the view controller's view through its `view` property, and so forth.

All of these relationships are public. So if you can get a reference to just one object within any of these structures or a similar structure, you can effectively navigate the whole structure through a chain of references and lay your hands on any other object within the structure.

Global Visibility

Some objects are globally visible — that is, they are visible to all other objects. Object types themselves are an important example. As I pointed out in Chapter 4, it is perfectly reasonable to use a Swift struct with static members as a way of providing globally available namespaced constants ("Struct As Namespace" on page 145).

Classes sometimes have class methods or properties that vend singleton instances. Some of these singletons, in turn, have properties pointing to other objects, making those other objects likewise globally visible. For example, any object can see the singleton UIApplication instance as `UIApplication.shared`. So any object can also see the app's primary window, because that is the singleton UIApplication instance's `keyWindow` property, and any object can see the app delegate, because that is its `delegate` property. And the chain continues: any object can see the app's root view controller, because that is the primary window's `rootViewController` — and from there, as I said in the previous section, we can navigate the view controller hierarchy and the view hierarchy.

You, too, can make your own objects globally visible by attaching them to a globally visible object. For example, a public property of the app delegate, which you are free to create, is globally visible by virtue of the app delegate being globally visible (by virtue of the shared application being globally visible).

Another globally visible object is the shared defaults object obtained as `UserDefaults.standard`. This object is the gateway to storage and retrieval of user defaults, which is similar to a dictionary (a collection of values named by keys). The user defaults are automatically saved when your application quits and are automatically available when your application is launched again later, so they are one of the ways in which your app maintains information between launches. But, being globally visible, they are also a conduit for communicating values within your app.

For example, in one of my apps there's a preference setting I call `hazyStripy`. This determines whether a certain visible interface object (a card in a game) is drawn with a hazy fill or a stripy fill. This is a setting that the user can change, so there is a preferences interface allowing the user to make this change. When the user displays this preferences interface, I examine the `hazyStripy` setting in the user defaults to configure the interface to reflect it in a segmented control (called `self.hazyStripy`):

```
func setHazyStripy () {
    let hs = UserDefaults.standard
        .object(forKey:Default.hazyStripy) as! Int
    self.hazyStripy.selectedSegmentIndex = hs
}
```

Conversely, if the user interacts with the preferences interface, tapping the `hazyStripy` segmented control to change its setting, I respond by changing the actual `hazyStripy` setting in the user defaults:

```
@IBAction func hazyStripyChange(_ sender: Any) {
    let hs = self.hazyStripy.selectedSegmentIndex
    UserDefaults.standard.set(hs, forKey: Default.hazyStripy)
}
```

But here's the really interesting part. The preferences interface is not the only object that uses the `hazyStripy` setting in the user defaults; the drawing code that actually draws the hazy-or-stripy-filled card also uses it, so as to know how the card should draw itself! When the user leaves the preferences interface and the card game reappears, the cards are redrawn — consulting the `hazyStripy` setting in UserDefaults in order to do so:

```
override func draw(_ rect: CGRect) {
    let hazy : Bool = UserDefaults.standard
        .integer(forKey:Default.hazyStripy) == HazyStripy.hazy.rawValue
    CardPainter.shared.drawCard(self.card, hazy:hazy)
}
```

Thus there is no need for the card object and the view controller object that manages the preferences interface to be able to see one another, because they can both see this common object, the `hazyStripy` user default. UserDefaults becomes, in itself, a global conduit for communicating information from one part of my app to another.

Notifications and Key–Value Observing

Notifications (Chapter 11) can be a way to communicate between objects that are conceptually distant from one another without bothering to provide *any* way for one to see the other. All they really need to have in common is a knowledge of the name of the notification. Every object can see the notification center — it is a globally visible object — so every object can arrange to post or receive a notification.

Using a notification in this way may seem lazy, an evasion of your responsibility to architect your objects sensibly. But sometimes one object doesn't need to know, and indeed shouldn't know, what object (or objects) it is sending a message to.

Recall the example I gave in Chapter 11. In a simple card game app, the game needs to know when a card is tapped. A card, when it is tapped, knowing nothing about the game, simply emits a virtual shriek by posting a notification; the game object has registered for this notification and takes over from there:

```
NotificationCenter.default.post(name: .cardTapped, object: self)
```

Here's another example, taking advantage of the fact that notifications are a broadcast mechanism. In one of my apps, the app delegate may detect a need to tear down the interface and build it back up again from scratch. If this is to happen without causing memory leaks (and all sorts of other havoc), every view controller that is currently running a repeating Timer needs to invalidate that timer (Chapter 12). Rather than my having to work out what view controllers those might be, and endowing every view controller with a method that can be called, I simply have the app delegate shout "Everybody stop timers!", by posting a notification. *All* my view controllers that run timers have registered for this notification, and they know what to do when they receive it.

By the same token, Cocoa itself provides notification versions of many delegate and action messages. For example, the app delegate has a method for being told when the app goes into the background, but other objects might need to know this too; those objects can register for the corresponding notification.

Similarly, key–value observing can be used to keep two conceptually distant objects synchronized with one another: a property of one object changes, and the other object hears about the change. As I said in (Chapter 11), entire parts of Cocoa routinely expect you to use this when you want to be notified of a change in an object property. You can configure the same sort of thing with your own objects.

Model–View–Controller

In Apple's documentation and elsewhere, you'll find references to the term *model–view–controller*, or *MVC*. This refers to an architectural goal of maintaining a distinction between three functional aspects of a program where the user can view and edit information — meaning, in effect, a program with a graphical user interface. The notion goes back to the days of Smalltalk, and much has been written about it since then, but informally, here's what the terms mean:

Model

The data and its management, often referred to as the program's "business logic" — the hard-core stuff that the program is really all about.

View

What the user sees and interacts with.

Controller

The mediation between the model and the view.

Consider, for example, a game where the current score is displayed to the user:

A label displays the score (View)

A UILabel that shows the user the current score for the game in progress is *view*; it is effectively nothing but a pixel-maker, and its business is to know how to draw itself. The knowledge of *what* it should draw — the score, and the fact that this *is* a score — lies elsewhere.

A rookie programmer might try to use the score displayed by the UILabel as the actual score: to increment the score, read the UILabel's string, turn that string into a number, increment the number, turn the number back into a string, and present that string in place of the previous string. That is a gross violation of the MVC philosophy! The view presented to the user should *reflect* the score; it should not *store* the score.

The score is maintained (Model)

The score is data being maintained internally; it is *model*. It could be as simple as an instance property along with a public `increment` method or as complicated as a Score object with a raft of methods.

The score is numeric, whereas a UILabel displays a string; this alone is enough to show that the view and the model are naturally different.

The score is updated (Controller)

Telling the score when to change, and causing the updated score to be reflected in the user interface, is the work of the *controller*. This will be particularly clear if we imagine that the model's numeric score needs to be transformed in some way for presentation to the user.

For example, suppose the UILabel that presents the score reads: "The score is 20." The model is presumably storing and providing the number 20, so what's the source of the phrase "The score is..."? Whoever is causing this phrase to precede the score in the presentation of the score to the user is a controller.

Even this simplistic example (Figure 13-1) illustrates very well the advantages of MVC. By separating powers in this way, we allow the aspects of the program to evolve with a great degree of independence. Do you want a different font and size in the pre-

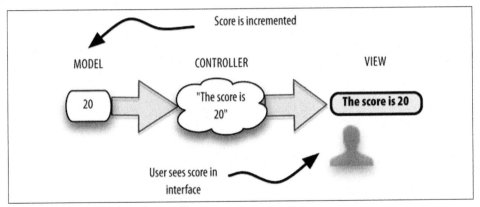

Figure 13-1. Model–view–controller

sentation of the score? Change the view; the model and controller need know nothing about it, but will just go on working exactly as they did before. Do you want to change the phrase that precedes the score? Change the controller; the model and view are unchanged.

Adherence to MVC is particularly appropriate in a Cocoa app, because Cocoa itself adheres to it. The very names of Cocoa classes reveal the MVC philosophy that underlies them. A UIView is a view. A UIViewController is a controller; its purpose is to embody the logic that tells the view what to display. In Chapter 11 we saw that a UIPickerView does not hold the data it displays; it gets that data from a data source. So the UIPickerView is a view; the data maintained by the data source is model (and the data source itself is probably a controller).

A further distinction, found in Apple's documentation, is this: true model material and true view material should be quite reusable, in the sense that they can be transferred wholesale into some other app; controller material is generally not reusable, because it is concerned with how *this* app mediates between the model and the view.

MVC helps to provide answers about what objects need to be able to see what other objects in your app. A controller object will usually need to see a model object and a view object. A model object, or a group of model objects, usually won't need to see outside itself. A view object typically doesn't need to see outside itself *specifically*, but structural devices such as delegation, data source, and target–action allow a view object to communicate agnostically with a controller.

C, Objective-C, and Swift

You are an iOS programmer, and you've chosen to adopt Apple's new language, Swift. And this means that you'll never have to concern yourself with Apple's *old* language, Objective-C, right? Wrong.

Objective-C is not dead. Far from it. *You* may be using Swift, but Cocoa is not. Programming iOS involves communicating with Cocoa and its supplementary frameworks. The APIs for those frameworks are written in Objective-C — or in its underlying base language, C. Messages that you send to Cocoa using Swift are being translated for you into Objective-C. Objects that you send and receive back and forth across the Swift/Objective-C bridge are Objective-C objects. Some objects that you send from Swift to Objective-C are even being translated for you into other object types, or into nonobject types.

You need to understand what Objective-C expects from you when you are sending messages across the language bridge. You need to know what Objective-C is going to *do* with those messages. You need to know what is coming *from* Objective-C, and how it will be represented in Swift. Your app may include some Objective-C code as well as Swift code, so you need to know how the parts of your own app will communicate with each other.

This appendix summarizes certain linguistic features of C and Objective-C, and describes how Swift interfaces with those features. I do not explain here how to write Objective-C! For example, I'll talk about Objective-C methods and method declarations, because you need to know how to call an Objective-C method from Swift; but I'm not going to explain how to call an Objective-C method *in Objective-C*. Earlier editions of this book teach C and Objective-C systematically and in detail, and I recommend consulting one for information about those languages.

The C Language

Objective-C is a superset of C; to put it another way, C provides the linguistic under-pinnings of Objective-C. Everything that is true of C is true also of Objective-C. It is possible, and often necessary, to write long stretches of Objective-C code that are, in effect, pure C. Some of the Cocoa APIs are written in C. Therefore, in order to know about Objective-C, it is necessary to know about C.

C statements, including declarations, must end in a semicolon. Variables must be declared before use. A variable declaration consists of a data type name followed by the variable name, optionally followed by assignment of an initial value:

```
int i;
double d = 3.14159;
```

The C `typedef` statement starts with an existing type name and defines a new syno-nym for it:

```
typedef double NSTimeInterval;
```

C Data Types

C is not an object-oriented language; its data types are not objects (they are *scalars*). The basic built-in C data types are all numeric: char (one byte), int (four bytes), float and double (floating-point numbers), and varieties such as short (short integer), long (long integer), unsigned short, and so on. Objective-C adds NSInteger, NSUInteger (unsigned), and CGFloat. The C bool type is actually a numeric, with zero represent-ing false; Objective-C adds BOOL, which is also a numeric. The C native text type (string) is actually a null-terminated array of char.

Swift explicitly supplies numeric types that interface directly with C numeric types, even though Swift's types are objects and C's types are not. Swift type aliases provide names that correspond to the C type names: a Swift CBool is a C bool, a Swift CChar is a C char (a Swift Int8), a Swift CInt is a C int (a Swift Int32), a Swift CFloat is a C float (a Swift Float), and so on. Swift Int interchanges with NSInteger; Swift UInt interchanges with NSUInteger. Swift Bool interchanges with Swift ObjCBool, which represents Objective-C BOOL. CGFloat is adopted as a Swift type name.

A major difference between C and Swift is that C (and therefore Objective-C) implic-itly coerces when values of different numeric types are assigned, passed, or compared to one another; Swift doesn't, so you must coerce explicitly to make types match exactly.

The native C string type, a null-terminated array of char, is typed in Swift either as an array of Int8 or, for reasons that will be clear later, as UnsafePointer<Int8> (recall that CChar *is* Int8). A C string can't be formed as a literal in Swift, but you can pass a Swift String where a C string is expected. If you need to create a C string variable, the

NSString utf8String property or NSString cString(using:) method can be used to form a C string. Alternatively, you can use the String utf8CString property or the withCString method; in this example, I cycle through the "characters" of the C string until I reach the null terminator (I'll explain the pointee property a bit later):

```
"hello".withCString {
    var cs = $0
    while cs.pointee != 0 {
        print(cs.pointee)
        cs += 1 // or: cs = cs.successor()
    }
}
```

In the other direction, a UTF-8 C string (including ASCII) can be rendered into a Swift String by way of a Swift String initializer such as init(cString:).

C Enums

A C enum is numeric; values are some form of integer, and can be implicit (starting from 0) or explicit. Enums arrive in various forms into Swift, depending on exactly how they are declared. Let's start with the simplest (and oldest) form:

```
enum State {
    kDead,
    kAlive
};
typedef enum State State;
```

(The typedef in the last line merely allows C programs to use the term State as the name of this type instead of the more verbose enum State.) The C enumerand names kDead and kAlive are not "cases" of anything; they are not namespaced. They are constants, and as they are not explicitly initialized, they represent 0 and 1 respectively. An enum declaration can specify the integer type further; this one doesn't, so the values are typed in Swift as UInt32.

This old-fashioned sort of C enum arrives as a Swift struct adopting the RawRepresentable protocol. This struct is used automatically as a medium of interchange wherever a State enum arrives from or is expected by C. Thus, if a C function setState takes a State enum parameter, you can call it with one of the State enumerand names:

```
setState(kDead)
```

I'm sure you noticed that I didn't say .kDead. As in C, enumerand names are not namespaced in Swift; there's no such thing as State.kDead. In this way, Swift has done its best to import these names helpfully and usefully, trying to represent State as a type even though, in C, it really isn't one. If you are curious about what integer is represented by the name kDead, you have to take its rawValue. You can also create an arbitrary State value by calling its init(rawValue:) initializer — there is no compiler or runtime check to see whether this value is one of the defined constants. But you aren't expected to do either of those things.

Starting back in Xcode 4.4, a new C enum notation was introduced, using the NS_ENUM macro:

```
typedef NS_ENUM(NSInteger, UIStatusBarAnimation) {
    UIStatusBarAnimationNone,
    UIStatusBarAnimationFade,
    UIStatusBarAnimationSlide,
};
```

That notation explicitly specifies the integer type and associates a type name with this enum as a whole. Swift imports an enum declared this way *as a Swift enum* with the name and raw value type intact. This is a true Swift enum, so the enumerand names become namespaced case names. Moreover, Swift automatically subtracts the common prefix from the case names:

```
enum UIStatusBarAnimation : Int {
    case none
    case fade
    case slide
}
```

Going the other way, a Swift enum with an Int raw value type can be exposed to Objective-C using the @objc attribute. Thus, for example:

```
@objc enum Star : Int {
    case blue
    case white
    case yellow
    case red
}
```

Objective-C sees that as an enum with type NSInteger and enumerand names Star-Blue, StarWhite, and so on.

There is another variant of C enum notation, using the NS_OPTIONS macro, suitable for bitmasks:

```
typedef NS_OPTIONS(NSUInteger, UIViewAutoresizing) {
    UIViewAutoresizingNone              = 0,
    UIViewAutoresizingFlexibleLeftMargin   = 1 << 0,
    UIViewAutoresizingFlexibleWidth     = 1 << 1,
    UIViewAutoresizingFlexibleRightMargin  = 1 << 2,
    UIViewAutoresizingFlexibleTopMargin    = 1 << 3,
    UIViewAutoresizingFlexibleHeight    = 1 << 4,
    UIViewAutoresizingFlexibleBottomMargin = 1 << 5
};
```

An enum declared this way arrives into Swift as a struct adopting the OptionSet protocol. The OptionSet protocol adopts the RawRepresentable protocol, so this is a struct with a `rawValue` instance property holding the underlying integer. The C enum case names are represented by static properties, each of whose values *is an instance of this struct*; the names of these static properties are imported with the common prefix subtracted:

```
struct UIViewAutoresizing : OptionSet {
    init(rawValue: UInt)
    static var flexibleLeftMargin: UIViewAutoresizing { get }
    static var flexibleWidth: UIViewAutoresizing { get }
    static var flexibleRightMargin: UIViewAutoresizing { get }
    static var flexibleTopMargin: UIViewAutoresizing { get }
    static var flexibleHeight: UIViewAutoresizing { get }
    static var flexibleBottomMargin: UIViewAutoresizing { get }
}
```

Thus, for example, when you say `UIViewAutoresizing.flexibleLeftMargin`, it *looks* as if you are initializing a case of a Swift enum, but in fact this is an instance of the UIViewAutoresizing *struct*, whose `rawValue` property has been set to the value declared by the original C enum — which, for `.flexibleLeftMargin`, is `1<<0`. Because a static property of this struct *is* an instance of the same struct, you can, as with an enum, omit the struct name when supplying a static property name where the struct is expected:

```
self.view.autoresizingMask = .flexibleWidth
```

Moreover, because this is an OptionSet struct, set-like operations can be applied — thus permitting you to manipulate the bitmask by working with instances as if this were a Set:

```
self.view.autoresizingMask = [.flexibleWidth, .flexibleHeight]
```

 In Objective-C, where an `NS_OPTIONS` enum is expected, you pass 0 to indicate that no options are provided. In Swift, where a corresponding struct is expected, you pass `[]` (an empty set) or omit the `options:` parameter entirely. Some `NS_OPTIONS` enums have an explicit option that *means* 0; Swift 3 sometimes won't bother to import its name, because passing `[]` means the same thing. For example, to set a UIViewAutoresizing value to `UIViewAutoresizingNone` in Swift 3, set it to `[]` (not `.none`).

Unfortunately, you may occasionally encounter a bitmask enum whose Cocoa API hasn't been marked `NS_OPTIONS`, and thus isn't imported into Swift as an OptionSet. Here's an example:

```
typedef enum NSGlyphProperty : NSInteger {
    NSGlyphPropertyNull = (1 << 0),
    NSGlyphPropertyControlCharacter = (1 << 1),
    NSGlyphPropertyElastic = (1 << 2),
    NSGlyphPropertyNonBaseCharacter = (1 << 3)
} NSGlyphProperty;
```

That's obviously a bitmask, but in Swift it's a simple enum. To work with it as a bit-mask, you'll have to take its raw value and use the arithmetic bitwise-or and bitwise-and operators, just as in Objective-C:

```
let property = self.lm.propertyForGlyph(at:lastCharRange)
let mask1 = property.rawValue
let mask2 = NSGlyphProperty.controlCharacter.rawValue
return mask1 & mask2 != 0 // can't say .contains here
```

Also, some common lists of alternatives are not implemented as enums in the first place. This is not problematic, but it is inconvenient. For example, the names of the AVFoundation audio session categories are just global NSString constants:

```
NSString *const AVAudioSessionCategoryAmbient;
NSString *const AVAudioSessionCategorySoloAmbient;
NSString *const AVAudioSessionCategoryPlayback;
// ... and so on ...
```

Even though this is a list of alternatives with an obvious common prefix, Swift doesn't magically transform it into an AVAudioSessionCategory enum or struct with abbreviated names. When you want to specify the Playback category, you have to use the whole name, AVAudioSessionCategoryPlayback.

C Structs

A C struct is a compound type whose elements can be accessed by name using dot-notation after a reference to the struct. For example:

```
struct CGPoint {
    CGFloat x;
    CGFloat y;
};
typedef struct CGPoint CGPoint;
```

After that declaration, it becomes possible to talk like this in C:

```
CGPoint p;
p.x = 100;
p.y = 200;
```

A C struct arrives wholesale into Swift as a Swift struct, which is thereupon endowed with Swift struct features. Thus, for example, CGPoint in Swift has x and y CGFloat instance properties, as you would expect; but it also magically acquires the implicit memberwise initializer! In addition, a zeroing initializer with no parameters is injected; thus, saying CGPoint() makes a CGPoint whose x and y are both 0. Extensions can supply additional features, and the Swift CoreGraphics header adds a few to CGPoint:

```
extension CGPoint {
    static var zero: CGPoint { get }
    init(x: Int, y: Int)
    init(x: Double, y: Double)
}
```

As you can see, a Swift CGPoint has additional initializers accepting Int or Double arguments, along with another way of making a zero CGPoint, `CGPoint.zero`. CGSize is treated similarly. CGRect is particularly well endowed with added methods and properties in Swift, allow you to do things in a Swiftier way. (I'll talk more about this in a bit.)

The fact that a Swift struct is an object, while a C struct is not, does not pose any problems of communication. You can assign or pass a Swift CGPoint, for example, where a C CGPoint is expected, because CGPoint came from C in the first place. The fact that Swift has endowed CGPoint with object methods and properties doesn't matter; C doesn't see them. All that C cares about are the x and y elements of this CGPoint, which are communicated from Swift to C without difficulty.

C Pointers

A C pointer is an integer designating the location in memory (the *address*) where the real data resides. Allocating and disposing of that memory is a separate matter. The declaration for a pointer to a data type is written with an asterisk after the data type name; a space can appear on either or both sides of the asterisk. These are equivalent declarations of a pointer-to-int:

```
int *intPtr1;
int* intPtr2;
int * intPtr3;
```

The type name itself is `int*` (or, with a space, `int *`). Objective-C, for reasons that I'll explain later, uses C pointers heavily, so you're going to be seeing that asterisk a lot if you look at any Objective-C.

A C pointer arrives into Swift as an UnsafePointer or, if writable, an UnsafeMutablePointer; this is a generic, and is specified to the actual type of data pointed to. (A pointer is "unsafe" because Swift isn't managing the memory for, and can't even guarantee the integrity of, what is pointed to.)

For example, here's an Objective-C UIColor method declaration; I haven't discussed this syntax yet, but just concentrate on the types in parentheses:

```
- (BOOL) getRed: (CGFloat *) red
    green: (CGFloat *) green
    blue: (CGFloat *) blue
    alpha: (CGFloat *) alpha;
```

CGFloat is a basic numeric type. The type `CGFloat *`, despite the space, states that these parameters are all `CGFloat*` — that is, pointer-to-CGFloat.

The Swift 3 translation of that declaration looks like this:

```
func getRed(_ red: UnsafeMutablePointer<CGFloat>,
    green: UnsafeMutablePointer<CGFloat>,
    blue: UnsafeMutablePointer<CGFloat>,
    alpha: UnsafeMutablePointer<CGFloat>) -> Bool
```

UnsafeMutablePointer in this context is used like a Swift `inout` parameter: you declare and initialize a `var` of the appropriate type beforehand, and then pass its address as argument by way of the & prefix operator. When you pass the address of a reference in this way, you are in fact creating and passing a pointer:

```
var r : CGFloat = 0
var g : CGFloat = 0
var b : CGFloat = 0
var a : CGFloat = 0
c.getRed(&r, green: &g, blue: &b, alpha: &a)
```

In C, to access the memory pointed to by a pointer, you use an asterisk before the pointer's name: `*intPtr` is "the thing pointed to by the pointer `intPtr`." In Swift, you use the pointer's `pointee` property.

In this example, we receive a `stop` parameter typed originally as a `BOOL*`, a pointer-to-BOOL; in Swift, it's an `UnsafeMutablePointer<ObjCBool>`. To set the BOOL at the far end of this pointer, we set the pointer's `pointee`:

```
// mas is an NSMutableAttributedString, r is an NSRange
mas.enumerateAttribute("HERE", in:r) {
    value, r, stop in
    if let value = value as? Int, value == 1  {
        // ...
        stop.pointee = true
    }
}
```

The most general type of C pointer is pointer-to-void (`void*`), also known as the *generic pointer*. The term `void` here means that no type is specified; it is legal in C to use a generic pointer wherever a specific type of pointer is expected, and *vice versa*. In effect, pointer-to-void casts away type checking as to what's at the far end of the pointer. This will appear in Swift as a "raw" pointer, either UnsafeRawPointer or UnsafeMutableRawPointer. In general, when you encounter pointers of this type, if you need to access the underlying data, you'll start by rebinding its memory to an unsafe pointer generic specified to the underlying type:

```
// context is an UnsafeMutableRawPointer
let c = context.bindMemory(to: String.self, capacity: 1)
// now c is an UnsafeMutablePointer<String>
```

C Arrays

A C array contains a fixed number of elements of a certain data type. Under the hood, it is a contiguous block of memory sized to accommodate this number of elements of this data type. For this reason, the name of an array in C is the name of a pointer — to the first element of the array. For example, if arr has been declared as an array of int, the term arr can be used wherever a value of type int* (a pointer-to-int) is expected. The C language will indicate an array type either by appending square brackets to a reference or as a pointer.

(That explains why C strings are often typed in Swift as an unsafe pointer to Int8 or CChar: a C string is an array of char, so it's a pointer to char.)

For example, the C function CGContextStrokeLineSegments is declared like this:

```
void CGContextStrokeLineSegments(CGContextRef c,
    const CGPoint points[],
    size_t count
);
```

The second parameter is a C array of CGPoints; that's what the square brackets tell you. A C array carries no information about how many elements it contains, so to pass this C array to this function, you must also *tell* the function how many elements the array contains; that's what the third parameter is for. A C array of CGPoint is a pointer to a CGPoint, so this function's declaration is translated into Swift 3 like this:

```
func __strokeLineSegments(
    between points: UnsafePointer<CGPoint>?,
    count: Int)
```

Now, you're not expected to call this function; the CGContext Swift overlay provides a pure Swift version, strokeLineSegments, which takes a Swift array of CGPoint (with no need to provide a count). But let's say you wanted to call __strokeLine-Segments instead. How would you do it?

To call __strokeLineSegments and pass it a C array of CGPoints, it would appear that you need to *make* a C array of CGPoints. A C array is not, by any stretch of the imagination, a Swift array; so how on earth will you do this? Surprise! You don't have to. Even though a Swift array is not a C array, you can pass a pointer to a Swift array here. In fact, you don't even need to pass a pointer; you can pass a reference to a Swift array *itself*. And since this is not a mutable pointer, you can declare the array with let; indeed, you can even pass a Swift array literal! No matter which approach you choose, Swift will convert to a C array for you as the argument crosses the bridge from Swift to C:

```
let c = UIGraphicsGetCurrentContext()!
let arr = [CGPoint(x:0,y:0),
    CGPoint(x:50,y:50),
    CGPoint(x:50,y:50),
    CGPoint(x:0,y:100),
]
c.__strokeLineSegments(between: arr, count: arr.count)
```

However, you *can* form a C array if you really want to. To do so, you must first set aside the block of memory yourself: declare an UnsafeMutablePointer of the desired type, calling the class method allocate(capacity:) with the desired number of elements. You can then write the element values directly into memory. You could do this by manipulating the pointee, but you can also use subscripting, which might be a lot more convenient. Finally, since the UnsafeMutablePointer *is* a pointer, you pass *it*, not a pointer to it, as argument:

```
let c = UIGraphicsGetCurrentContext()!
let arr = UnsafeMutablePointer<CGPoint>.allocate(capacity:4)
arr[0] = CGPoint(x:0,y:0)
arr[1] = CGPoint(x:50,y:50)
arr[2] = CGPoint(x:50,y:50)
arr[3] = CGPoint(x:0,y:100)
c.__strokeLineSegments(between: arr, count: 4)
```

If you're going to do that, however, you really need to take upon yourself the full details of memory management. Having allocated this pointer's memory and assigned values into it, you should remove the values and deallocate the memory:

```
let arr = UnsafeMutablePointer<CGPoint>.allocate(capacity:4)
defer {
    arr.deinitialize()
    arr.deallocate(capacity:4)
}
```

The same convenient subscripting is available when you *receive* a C array. For example:

```
let comp = col.cgColor.__unsafeComponents // col is a UIColor
```

comp is typed as an UnsafePointer to CGFloat. This is really a C array of CGFloat — and so you can access its elements by subscripting:

```
if let comp = col.cgColor.__unsafeComponents,
    let sp = col.cgColor.colorSpace,
    sp.model == .rgb {
        let red = comp[0]
        let green = comp[1]
        let blue = comp[2]
        let alpha = comp[3]
        // ...
}
```

C Functions

A C function declaration starts with the return type (which might be void, meaning no returned value), followed by the function name, followed by a parameter list, in parentheses, of comma-separated pairs consisting of the type followed by the parameter name. The parameter names are purely internal. C functions are global, and Swift can call them directly.

For example, here's the C declaration for an Audio Services function:

```
extern OSStatus
AudioServicesCreateSystemSoundID(
    CFURLRef inFileURL,
    SystemSoundID* outSystemSoundID)
```

Ignoring the term extern, which I'm not going to explain, an OSStatus is basically an Int32. A CFURLRef is a CFTypeRef ("Memory Management of CFTypeRefs" on page 533), called CFURL in Swift. A SystemSoundID is a UInt32, and the * makes this a C pointer, as we already know. The whole thing thus translates directly into Swift:

```
func AudioServicesCreateSystemSoundID(
    _ inFileURL: CFURL,
    _ outSystemSoundID: UnsafeMutablePointer<SystemSoundID>) -> OSStatus
```

CFURL is (for reasons that I'll explain later) interchangeable with NSURL and Swift URL; so here we are, calling this C function in Swift:

```
let sndurl = Bundle.main.url(forResource: "test", withExtension: "aif")!
var snd : SystemSoundID = 0
AudioServicesCreateSystemSoundID(sndurl as CFURL, &snd)
```

In iOS programming, the vast majority of commonly used C global functions operate on a struct; they have the name of that struct as the first element of their name, and have that struct itself as their first parameter. In Swift 3, such functions are often overshadowed by instance method representations; the struct name is stripped from the name of the function, and the function is applied as a method to an instance of that struct.

For example, in Objective-C, the way to construct a CGRect from scratch is with the CGRectMake function, and the way to divide a CGRect is with the CGRectDivide function:

```
CGRect rect = CGRectMake(10,10,100,100);
CGRect arrow;
CGRect body;
CGRectDivide(rect, &arrow, &body, ARHEIGHT, CGRectMinYEdge);
```

In Swift, CGRectMake is overshadowed by the CGRect struct initializer init(x:y:width:height:), and CGRectDivide is overshadowed by the CGRect divided method:

```
let myRect = CGRect(x: 10, y: 10, width: 100, height: 100)
let (arrowRect, bodyRect) =
    myRect.divided(atDistance: Arrow.ARHEIGHT, from: .minYEdge)
```

In C, a function has a type based on its signature, and the name of a function is a reference to the function, and so it is possible to pass a function — sometimes referred to as a *pointer-to-function* — by using the function's name where a function of that type is expected. In a declaration, a pointer-to-function may be symbolized by an asterisk in parentheses.

For example, here's the declaration for a C function from the Audio Toolbox framework:

```
extern OSStatus
AudioServicesAddSystemSoundCompletion(SystemSoundID inSystemSoundID,
    CFRunLoopRef __nullable inRunLoop,
    CFStringRef __nullable inRunLoopMode,
    AudioServicesSystemSoundCompletionProc inCompletionRoutine,
    void * __nullable inClientData)
```

(I'll explain the term __nullable later.) What's an AudioServicesSystemSoundCompletionProc? It's this:

```
typedef void (*AudioServicesSystemSoundCompletionProc)(
    SystemSoundID ssID,
    void* __nullable clientData);
```

A SystemSoundID is a UInt32, so that tells you, in the rather tortured syntax that C uses for these things, that an AudioServicesSystemSoundCompletionProc is a pointer to a function taking two parameters (typed UInt32 and pointer-to-void) and returning no result.

Amazingly, you can pass a Swift function where a C pointer-to-function is expected! As always when passing a function, you can define the function separately and pass its name, or you can form the function inline as an anonymous function. If you're going to define the function separately, it must be a *function* — meaning that it cannot be a method. A function defined at the top level of a file is fine; so is a function defined locally within a function.

So here's my AudioServicesSystemSoundCompletionProc, declared at the top level of a file:

```
func soundFinished(_ snd:UInt32, _ c:UnsafeMutableRawPointer?) -> Void {
    AudioServicesRemoveSystemSoundCompletion(snd)
    AudioServicesDisposeSystemSoundID(snd)
}
```

And here's my code for playing a sound file as a system sound, including a call to AudioServicesAddSystemSoundCompletion:

```
let sndurl = Bundle.main.url(forResource: "test", withExtension: "aif")!
var snd : SystemSoundID = 0
AudioServicesCreateSystemSoundID(sndurl as CFURL, &snd)
AudioServicesAddSystemSoundCompletion(snd, nil, nil, soundFinished, nil)
AudioServicesPlaySystemSound(snd)
```

Objective-C

Objective-C is built on the back of C. It adds some syntax and features, but it continues to use C syntax and data types, and remains C under the hood.

Unlike Swift, Objective-C has no namespaces. For this reason, different frameworks distinguish their contents by starting their names with different prefixes. The "CG" in "CGFloat" stands for Core Graphics, because it is declared in the Core Graphics framework. The "NS" in "NSString" stands for NeXTStep, a historical name for the framework that later became Cocoa. And so on.

Objective-C Objects and C Pointers

All the data types and syntax of C are part of Objective-C. But Objective-C is also object-oriented, so it needs a way of adding objects to C. It does this by taking advantage of C pointers. C pointers accommodate having anything at all at the far end of the pointer; management of whatever is pointed to is a separate matter, and that's just what Objective-C takes care of. Thus, Objective-C object types are expressed using C pointer syntax.

For example, here's the Objective-C declaration for the addSubview: method:

```
- (void)addSubview:(UIView *)view;
```

I haven't discussed Objective-C method declaration syntax yet, but focus on the type declaration for the view parameter, in parentheses: it is UIView*. This appears to mean "a pointer to a UIView." It does mean that — and it doesn't. *All* Objective-C object references are pointers. Thus, the fact that this is a pointer is merely a way of saying it's an object. What's at the far end of the pointer is a UIView instance.

The Swift translation of this method declaration doesn't appear to involve any pointers:

```
func addSubview(_ view: UIView)
```

In general, in Swift, you will simply pass a reference to a class instance where Objective-C expects a class instance; the fact that an asterisk is used in the Objective-C declaration to express the fact that this is an object won't matter. What you pass as argument when calling addSubview(_:) from Swift is a UIView instance. There is, of course, a sense in which you *are* passing a pointer when you pass a class instance — because classes are reference types! Thus, a class instance is actually seen the same way by both Swift and Objective-C. The difference is that Swift doesn't use pointer *notation.*

Objective-C's id type is a general pointer to an object — the object equivalent of C pointer-to-void. Any object type can be assigned or cast to or from an id. Because id is itself a pointer, a reference declared as id doesn't use an asterisk; it is rare (though not impossible) to encounter an id*.

Objective-C Objects and Swift Objects

Objective-C objects are classes and instances of classes. They arrive into Swift more or less intact. You won't have any trouble subclassing Objective-C classes or working with instances of Objective-C classes.

The same is true in reverse. If Objective-C expects an object, it expects a class, and Swift can provide it. In the most general case, where Objective-C expects an id, you can pass a class instance, and Objective-C will be able to deal with it. But the only kind of object that Objective-C can *fully* deal with is an instance of an NSObject sub-class. Instances of other classes can't be introspected by Objective-C, and everything else has to be bridged or boxed in order to survive the journey into Objective-C's world, as I'll explain in the next section.

Swift can see just about all aspects of an Objective-C class type (for how Swift sees Objective-C properties and accessors, see Chapter 10). But much of Swift, while not problematic for Objective-C, is simply invisible to it. Objective-C can't see any of the following:

- Swift enums, except for an @objc enum with an Int raw value
- Swift structs, except for structs that come ultimately from C (or that are bridged, as I'll describe in the next section)
- Swift classes not derived from NSObject
- Swift protocols not marked @objc
- Protocol extensions
- Generics
- Tuples
- Nested types

What, precisely, do I mean by "can't see" a type? I mean that it can't cope with it as a type, and therefore whatever uses it as a type becomes invisible. For example, suppose we have a class MyClass not derived from NSObject. It is perfectly fine to hand Objective-C an instance of this type where an id is expected. But if your UIView-Controller subclass has a property typed as a MyClass, Objective-C is unaware of it. If your UIViewController subclass has a method that receives or returns a value typed as a MyClass, Objective-C is unaware of it.

Nevertheless, you are perfectly free to use such properties and methods, even in a subclass or extension of an Objective-C class type such as UIViewController; they won't give Objective-C any difficulty, because as far as Objective-C is concerned, they won't be present at all.

The @objc attribute exposes to Objective-C something that it normally would not be able to see, provided it is legal for Objective-C to see it; for example, you can use it to expose to Objective-C an individual method of a class not derived from NSObject. And it has another purpose: when you mark something with @objc, you can add parentheses containing the name by which you want Objective-C to see this thing. You are free to do this even for a class or a class member that Objective-C can see already, as in this example:

```
@objc(ViewController) class ViewController : UIViewController { // ...
```

That code demonstrates something that is in fact useful to do. By default, Objective-C sees your class's name as being namespaced (prefixed) by the module name (typically, the project name). Thus, this ViewController class might be seen by Objective-C as MyCoolApp.ViewController. This can wreck the association between the class name and something else. For example, when you're translating an existing Objective-C project into Swift, you may want to use @objc(...) syntax to prevent a nib object or an NSCoding archive from losing track of its associated class.

Bridged Types and Boxed Types

Swift will convert certain native nonclass types to their Objective-C class equivalents for you. The following native Swift structs are bridged to Objective-C class types:

- String to NSString
- Int, UInt, Double, Float, and Bool to NSNumber
- Array to NSArray
- Dictionary to NSDictionary
- Set to NSSet

New in Swift 3, Cocoa Foundation classes are overlaid by Swift types, whose names are the same but without the "NS" prefix. Often, extra functionality is injected to make the type behave in a more Swift-like way; and, where appropriate, the Swift type may be a struct, thus allowing you to take advantage of Swift value type semantics. For example, NSMutableData becomes largely otiose, because Data, the overlay for Objective-C NSData, is a struct with mutating methods and can thus be declared with let or var. And Date, the overlay for Objective-C NSDate, adopts Equatable and

Comparable, so that (for example) an NSDate method like `earlierDate:` can be replaced by the > operator.

The Swift overlay types are all bridged to their Foundation counterparts, and Swift will prefer the Swift types wherever possible. For example, a Cocoa method that takes or returns an NSDate in Objective-C will take or return a Date in Swift. If necessary, you can access the Objective-C Foundation type by casting.

Also new in Swift 3, any type of object can be handed to Objective-C, even if Objective-C wouldn't see it as an object and the type isn't bridged to an Objective-C class type. Objective-C can't *do* anything with such an object; but the compiler won't complain and the app won't crash. For example, this code is legal:

```
let lay = CALayer()
lay.setValue(CGPoint(x:100,y:100), forKey: "point")
lay.setValue([CGPoint(x:100,y:100)], forKey: "pointArray")
```

Where Objective-C expects an object, we provide a CGPoint and then an array of CGPoint. But a CGPoint is not an Objective-C object — it's a struct — and an Objective-C array must contain only objects (not structs). How can this be?

The answer, in a nutshell, is that when a Swift object is handed to Objective-C by way of an Any value, if that object can't be bridged and Objective-C can't see it as an object, Swift *boxes* it into something that Objective-C *can* see as an object. How Swift does this is irrelevant; it's an implementation detail, and none of your business. It happens that in this case, the two objects are a `_SwiftValue` and a `_SwiftDeferred-NSArray`, but those names are secret and subject to change, and knowing them is useless. What's important is that they are Objective-C objects, wrapping the values we provided. In this way, Objective-C is able to store these objects for us, in their boxes, and hand them back to us intact upon request. Like Pandora, Objective-C will cope perfectly well as long as it doesn't look in the box!

Objective-C Methods

In Objective-C, method parameters can (and nearly always do) have external names, and the name of a method as a whole is not distinct from the external names of the parameters. The parameter names are *part* of the method name, with a colon appearing where each parameter would need to go. For example, here's a typical Objective-C method declaration from Cocoa's NSString class:

```
- (NSString *)stringByReplacingOccurrencesOfString:(NSString *)target
                            withString:(NSString *)replacement
```

The Objective-C name of that method is `stringByReplacingOccurrencesOfString:withString:`. The name contains two colons, so the method takes two parameters, which the declaration tells us are NSString parameters.

The declaration for an Objective-C method has three parts:

- Either + or -, meaning that the method is a class method or an instance method, respectively.

- The data type of the return value, in parentheses. It might be void, meaning no returned value.

- The name of the method, split after each colon so as to make room for the parameters. Following each colon is the data type of the parameter, in parentheses, followed by a placeholder (internal) name for the parameter.

When Swift calls an Objective-C method, there's an obvious mismatch between the rules and conventions of the two languages. A Swift method is a function; it has parentheses, and if its parameters have external names (labels), they appear inside the parentheses. The function name that precedes the parentheses is clearly distinct from the parameter labels inside the parentheses. But an Objective-C method name involves no parentheses. So where should the Swift parentheses go?

Before Swift 3, the general solution to this mismatch was a simple algorithm. Everything before the first colon in Objective-C precedes the parentheses in Swift, and the first Swift parameter will therefore have no external name:

```
func stringByReplacingOccurrencesOfString(
    _ target:String, withString replacement:String) // Swift 2.2 and before
```

Swift 3, however, goes further: it takes this opportunity to render the Objective-C method's Swift name more Swift-like, by a rather involved process called *renamification*, which is performed by a component called the *Clang importer*, mediating between the two languages.

The renamification rules are rather elaborate, but you don't need to know the details; you can get a sense of how they behave from the way they transform the stringBy-ReplacingOccurrencesOfString:withString: method into a Swift function:

- Swift prunes redundant initial type names. We're starting with a string, and it's obvious from the return type that a string is returned, so there's no point saying string at the start. We are thus left with byReplacingOccurrencesOf-String:withString:.

- Swift prunes initial by. That's a common Cocoa locution, but Swift finds it merely verbose. Now we're down to replacingOccurrencesOfString:withString:.

- Swift prunes redundant final type names. It's obvious that the parameters are strings, so there's no point saying string at the end of the parameter names. That leaves replacingOccurrencesOf:with:.

- Finally, Swift decides where to split the first parameter name into the Swift method name (before the parentheses) and the external first parameter name (inside the parentheses). Here, Swift sees that what's left of the first parameter name ends with a preposition, of, so it splits before that preposition.

Here's the resulting Swift 3 renamification of this method:

```
func replacingOccurrences(
    of target:String, with replacement:String) // Swift 3
```

And here's an actual example of calling it:

```
let s = "hello"
let s2 = s.replacingOccurrences(of: "ell", with:"ipp")
// s2 is now "hippo"
```

How does Objective-C see methods declared in Swift? The simplest case is that the first parameter should have no externalized name. For example, here's a Swift method intended as the action method of a button in the interface:

```
@IBAction func doButton(_ sender: Any?) {
    // ...
}
```

That method is seen by Objective-C as doButton:. That is the canonical form for an action method with one parameter, and for that reason I like to declare my action methods along those lines.

If a Swift method's first parameter does have an externalized name, then, as seen by Objective-C, that externalized name is appended to what precedes the parentheses — in general, by inserting a preposition with. For example, here's a Swift method:

```
func makeHash(ingredients stuff:[String]) {
    // ...
}
```

That method is seen by Objective-C as makeHashWithIngredients:. But if the externalized name of the first parameter is a preposition, then it is appended *directly* to what precedes the parentheses. For example:

```
func makeHash(of stuff:[String]) {
    // ...
}
```

That method is seen by Objective-C as makeHashOf:.

What about internal parameter names? When you *call* an Objective-C method from Swift, Objective-C's internal names for the parameters don't matter; you don't use them, and you don't need to know or care what they are. When you *override* an Objective-C method in Swift, on the other hand, code completion will suggest internal names corresponding to the Objective-C internal names, but you are free to change them. For example, here's the Objective-C declaration of the UIViewController prepareForSegue:sender: instance method:

```
- (void)prepareForSegue:(UIStoryboardSegue *)segue sender:(nullable id)sender;
```

When you override that method in your UIViewController subclass, the suggested template, in accordance with the renamification rules, looks like this:

```
override func prepare(for segue: UIStoryboardSegue, sender: Any?) {
    // ...
}
```

But, as I just said, you are free to change the internal names; they are local variable names for your use inside the function body, and Objective-C doesn't care about them. This is a valid (but weird) override of prepareForSegue:sender: in Swift:

```
override func prepare(for war: UIStoryboardSegue, sender bow: Any?) {
    // ...
}
```

Unlike Swift, Objective-C does not permit overloading of methods. Two View-Controller instance methods called myMethod: returning no result, one taking a CGFloat parameter and one taking an NSString parameter, would be illegal in Objective-C. Therefore, two such Swift methods, though legal as far as Swift is concerned, would be illegal if they were both visible to Objective-C. You can use the @nonobjc attribute to *hide* from Objective-C something that it would normally be able to see. Thus, marking all but one of the overloaded methods @nonobjc solves the problem.

Objective-C has its own version of a variadic parameter. For example, the NSArray instance method arrayWithObjects: is declared like this:

```
+ (id)arrayWithObjects:(id)firstObj, ... ;
```

Unlike Swift, such methods in Objective-C must somehow be told explicitly how many arguments are being supplied. Many such methods, including arrayWith-Objects:, use a nil terminator; that is, the caller supplies nil after the last argument, and the callee knows when it has reached the last argument because it encounters nil. A call to arrayWithObjects: in Objective-C would look something like this:

```
NSArray* pep = [NSArray arrayWithObjects: manny, moe, jack, nil];
```

Objective-C cannot call (or see) a Swift method that takes a variadic parameter. Swift, however, *can* call an Objective-C method that takes a variadic parameter, provided that it is marked NS_REQUIRES_NIL_TERMINATION. arrayWithObjects: is marked in this way, so you can say NSArray(objects:1, 2, 3) and Swift will supply the missing nil terminator.

Objective-C Initializers and Factories

Objective-C initializer methods are instance methods; actual instantiation is performed using the NSObject class method alloc, for which Swift has no equivalent (and doesn't need one), and the initializer message is sent to the instance that results. For example, this is how you create a UIColor instance by supplying red, green, blue, and alpha values in Objective-C:

```
UIColor* col = [[UIColor alloc] initWithRed:0.5 green:0.6 blue:0.7 alpha:1];
```

The name of that initializer, in Objective-C, is initWithRed:green:blue:alpha:. It's declared like this:

```
- (UIColor *)initWithRed:(CGFloat)red green:(CGFloat)green
    blue:(CGFloat)blue alpha:(CGFloat)alpha;
```

In short, an initializer method, to all outward appearances, is just an instance method like any other in Objective-C.

Swift, nevertheless, is able to detect that an Objective-C initializer *is* an initializer, because the name is special — it starts with init! Therefore, Swift is able to translate an Objective-C initializer into a Swift initializer. The word init is stripped from the start of the method name, and the preposition with, if it appears, is stripped as well. What's left is the external name of the first parameter. Thus, Swift translates Objective-C initWithRed:green:blue:alpha: into the Swift initializer init(red:green:blue:alpha:), which is declared like this:

```
init(red: CGFloat, green: CGFloat, blue: CGFloat, alpha: CGFloat)
```

And you'd call it like this:

```
let col = UIColor(red: 0.5, green: 0.6, blue: 0.7, alpha: 1.0)
```

The same principle operates in reverse: for example, a Swift initializer init(value:) is visible to and callable by Objective-C under the name initWithValue:.

There is a second way to create an instance in Objective-C. Very commonly, a class will supply a *class* method that is a *factory* for an instance. For example, the UIColor class has a class method colorWithRed:green:blue:alpha:, declared as follows:

```
+ (UIColor*) colorWithRed: (CGFloat) red green: (CGFloat) green
                 blue: (CGFloat) blue alpha: (CGFloat) alpha;
```

Swift detects a factory method of this kind by some pattern-matching rules — a class method that returns an instance of the class, and whose name begins with the name of the class, stripped of its prefix — and translates it *as an initializer*, stripping the class name (and the with) from the start of the first parameter name. If the resulting initializer exists already, as it does in this example, then Swift treats the factory method as superfluous and suppresses it completely! Thus, the Objective-C class method colorWithRed:green:blue:alpha: isn't callable from Swift, because it would be identical to the init(red:green:blue:alpha:) that already exists.

Selectors

An Objective-C method will sometimes expect as parameter the name of a method to be called later. Such a name is called a *selector*. For example, the Objective-C UIControl `addTarget:action:forControlEvents:` method can be called as a way of telling a button in the interface, "From now on, whenever you are tapped, send this message to this object." The message, the `action:` parameter, is a selector.

You may imagine that, if this were a Swift method, you'd be passing a function here. A selector, however, is not the same as a function. It's just a name. Objective-C, unlike Swift, is so dynamic that it is able, at runtime, to construct and send an arbitrary message to an arbitrary object based on the name alone. But even though it is just a name, a selector is not exactly a string, either. It is, in fact, a separate object type, designated in Objective-C declarations as SEL and in Swift declarations as Selector.

Before Swift 2.2, the only way to form a selector in Swift was to use a literal string. In most cases, you could use a bare literal string:

```
b.addTarget(self, action: "doNewGame:",
    forControlEvents: .TouchUpInside) // before Swift 2.2
```

The trouble with this syntax is that it is error-prone. Forming a literal selector string by hand is an invitation to form the string incorrectly, resulting in a selector that at best will fail to work, and at worst will cause your app to crash. As I explained in Chapter 2, this problem is solved starting in Swift 2.2 by the introduction of `#selector` syntax. In Swift 3, that example would be written like this:

```
b.addTarget(self, action: #selector(doNewGame), for: .touchUpInside)
```

The `#selector` syntax means that you will probably never need to form a selector from a literal string. Nevertheless, you can do so if you want to. The rules for forming the string from the method name are completely mechanical:

1. The string starts with everything that precedes the left parenthesis in the method name.

2. If the method takes *no parameters*, stop. That's the end of the string.

3. If the method's first parameter has an external parameter name, append With and a capitalized version of that name, unless it is a preposition, in which case append a capitalized version of it directly.

4. Add a colon.

5. If the method takes exactly *one parameter*, stop. That's the end of the string.

6. If the method takes more than one parameter, add the external names of all remaining parameters, with a colon after each external parameter name.

Observe that this means that if the method takes any parameters, its Objective-C name string *will end with a colon*. Capitalization counts, and the name should contain no spaces or other punctuation except for the colons.

To illustrate, here are some Swift method declarations, with their Objective-C name strings given in a comment:

```
func sayHello() -> String // "sayHello"

func say(_ s:String) // "say:"

func say(string s:String) // "sayWithString:"

func say(of s:String) // "sayOf:"

func say(_ s:String, times n:Int) // "say:times:"
```

 Objective-C cannot use a selector to call a method that it can't see! An attempt to do so will cause a crash at runtime. Use of the #selector syntax will allow the compiler to stop you from making this mistake.

CFTypeRefs

A CFTypeRef is a pointer to an opaque struct that acts as a pseudo-object. CFTypeRef functions are global C functions. Swift can call C functions, as I've already said; and before Swift 3, CFTypeRef code would appear almost as if Swift were C. For example:

```
// before Swift 3:
let con = UIGraphicsGetCurrentContext()!
let sp = CGColorSpaceCreateDeviceGray()
// ... colors and locs are arrays of CGFloat ...
let grad = CGGradientCreateWithColorComponents (sp, colors, locs, 3) ❶
CGContextDrawLinearGradient (
    con, grad, CGPointMake(89,0), CGPointMake(111,0), []) ❷
```

In Swift 3, as part of renamification, many commonly used CFTypeRef functions (such as those in the Core Graphics framework) are recast as if the CFTypeRef objects were class instances, with the functions themselves recast as instance methods, parallel to what I described for CGRect structs earlier. The last two lines of the preceding code are a case in point:

❶ In Objective C, a CFTypeRef is created with some sort of Create function. In Swift 3, the CFTypeRef is treated as an object type name, and the syntax looks more like an initializer, complete with external parameter names.

❷ In Objective C, a CFTypeRef function operating on a CFTypeRef pseudo-object takes that object *as its first parameter*. In Swift 3, the pseudo-object is treated as a real object, and the function becomes a method call sent to it, again with external parameter names.

Thus, those lines are recast in Swift 3 like this:

```swift
let con = UIGraphicsGetCurrentContext()!
let sp = CGColorSpaceCreateDeviceGray()
// ... colors and locs are arrays of CGFloat ...
let grad = CGGradient(colorSpace: sp,
    colorComponents: colors, locations: locs, count: 3)
con.drawLinearGradient(grad,
    start: CGPoint(x:89,y:0), end: CGPoint(x:111,y:0), options:[])
```

For CFTypeRef pseudo-objects and their memory management, see Chapter 12. A CFTypeRef is a pointer, so it is interchangeable with C pointer-to-void. And because it is a pointer to a pseudo-object, it is interchangeable with Objective-C id.

Many CFTypeRefs are *toll-free bridged* to corresponding Objective-C object types. For example, CFString and NSString, CFNumber and NSNumber, CFArray and NSArray, CFDictionary and NSDictionary are all toll-free bridged (and there are many others). Such pairs are interchangeable by casting. Again, this is much easier in Swift than in Objective-C. In Objective-C, ARC memory management doesn't apply to CFType-Refs. Therefore you must perform a *bridging cast*, to tell Objective-C how to manage this object's memory as it crosses between the memory-managed world of Objective-C objects and the unmanaged world of C and CFTypeRefs. But in Swift, CFTypeRefs *are* memory-managed, and so there is no need for a bridging cast; you can just cast, plain and simple.

For example, in this code from one of my apps, I'm using the ImageIO framework. This framework has a C API (which has not been renamified) and uses CFTypeRefs. `CGImageSourceCopyPropertiesAtIndex` returns a CFDictionary whose keys are CFStrings. The easiest way to obtain a value from a dictionary is by subscripting, but you can't do that with a CFDictionary, because it isn't an object — so I cast it to an NSDictionary. The key `kCGImagePropertyPixelWidth` is a CFString, but when I try to use it directly in a subscript, Swift allows me to do so:

```swift
let result = CGImageSourceCopyPropertiesAtIndex(src, 0, nil)! as NSDictionary
let width = result[kCGImagePropertyPixelWidth] as! CGFloat
```

Similarly, in this code, I form an NSDictionary d using CFString keys — and then I pass it to the `CGImageSourceCreateThumbnailAtIndex` function where a CFDictionary is expected:

```swift
let d : NSDictionary = [
    kCGImageSourceShouldAllowFloat : true,
    kCGImageSourceCreateThumbnailWithTransform : true,
    kCGImageSourceCreateThumbnailFromImageAlways : true,
    kCGImageSourceThumbnailMaxPixelSize : w
]
let imref = CGImageSourceCreateThumbnailAtIndex(src, 0, d)!
```

Blocks

A *block* is a C language feature introduced by Apple starting in iOS 4. It is very like a C function, but it is not a C function; it behaves as a closure and can be passed around as a reference type. A block, in fact, is parallel to and compatible with a Swift function, and indeed the two are interchangeable: you can pass a Swift function where a block is expected, and when a block is handed to you by Cocoa it appears as a function.

In C and Objective-C, a block declaration is signified by the caret character (^), which appears where a function name (or an asterisk in parentheses) would appear in a C function declaration. For example, the NSArray instance method `sortedArrayUsing-Comparator:` takes an NSComparator parameter, which is defined through a `typedef` like this:

```
typedef NSComparisonResult (^NSComparator)(id obj1, id obj2);
```

To read that declaration, it helps to start in the middle and work your way outward; it says: "NSComparator is the type of a block taking two `id` parameters and returning an NSComparisonResult." In Swift, therefore, that `typedef` is translated as `(Any, Any) -> ComparisonResult`. It is then trivial to supply a function of the required type as argument when you call `sortedArray(comparator:)` in Swift.

In many cases, there won't be a `typedef`, and the type of the block will appear directly in a method declaration. Here's the Objective-C declaration for a UIView class method that takes two block parameters:

```
+ (void)animateWithDuration:(NSTimeInterval)duration
    animations:(void (^)(void))animations
    completion:(void (^ __nullable)(BOOL finished))completion;
```

In that declaration, `animations:` is a block taking no parameters (void) and returning no value, and `completion:` is a block taking one parameter, a BOOL, and returning no value. Here's the Swift translation:

```
class func animate(withDuration duration: TimeInterval,
    animations: () -> Swift.Void,
    completion: ((Bool) -> Swift.Void)? = nil)
```

Those are examples of methods that you would *call*, passing a function as argument where a block parameter is expected. Here's an example of a method that you would *implement*, where a function is passed *to you*. This is the Objective-C declaration:

```
- (void)webView:(WKWebView *)webView
    decidePolicyForNavigationAction:(WKNavigationAction *)navigationAction
    decisionHandler:(void (^)(WKNavigationActionPolicy))decisionHandler;
```

You implement this method, and it is called when the user taps a link in a web view, so that you can decide how to respond. The third parameter is a block that takes one parameter — a WKNavigationActionPolicy, which is an enum — and returns no value. The block is passed to you as a Swift function, and you respond by *calling* the function to report your decision:

```
func webView(_ webView: WKWebView,
    decidePolicyFor navigationAction: WKNavigationAction,
    decisionHandler: @escaping (WKNavigationActionPolicy) -> Swift.Void) {
        // ...
        decisionHandler(.allow)
    }
```

A C function is not a block, but you can also use a Swift function where a C function is expected, as I demonstrated earlier. Going in the other direction, to declare a type as a C pointer-to-function, mark the type as @convention(c). For example, here are two Swift method declarations:

```
func blockTaker(_ f:()->()) {}
func functionTaker(_ f:@convention(c)() -> ()) {}
```

Objective-C sees the first as taking an Objective-C block, and the second as taking a C pointer-to-function.

API Markup

As soon as Swift was first introduced to the programming public in June of 2014, it was evident that Swift's strict, specific typing was a poor match for Objective-C's dynamic, loose typing. The chief problems were:

Too many implicitly unwrapped Optionals
In Objective-C, any object instance reference can be nil. But in Swift, only an Optional can be nil.

The default solution was to use implicitly unwrapped Optionals as the medium of object interchange between Objective-C and Swift. But this was a blunt instrument, especially because most objects arriving from Objective-C were never *in fact* going to be nil.

Too many collections of AnyObject
In Objective-C, a collection type such as NSArray can contain elements of multiple object types, and the collection itself is agnostic as to what types of elements it may contain. But a Swift collection type can contain elements of just one type, and is itself typed according that element type.

The default solution was for every collection to arrive from Objective-C typed in the most general way, using AnyObject; it then had to be cast down explicitly on the Swift side. It was particularly galling to ask for a view's subviews, for example, and get back an [AnyObject] which had to be cast down to a [UIView] — when nothing could be more obvious than that a view's subviews would in fact all be UIView objects.

These problems have subsequently been solved by modifying the Objective-C language to permit *markup* of declarations in such a way as to communicate to Swift a more specific knowledge of what to expect.

An Objective-C object type can be marked as nonnull or nullable, to specify, respectively, that it will never be nil or that it might be nil. In the same way, C pointer types can be marked __nonnull or __nullable. Using these markers obviates all need for implicitly unwrapped Optionals as a medium of interchange; every type can be either a normal type or a normal Optional. Thus, implicitly unwrapped Optionals are a rare sight in the Cocoa APIs nowadays.

If you're writing an Objective-C header file and you don't mark up any of it as to nullability, you'll return to the bad old days: Swift will see your types as implicitly unwrapped Optionals. For example, here's an Objective-C method declaration:

```
- (NSString*) badMethod: (NSString*) s;
```

In the absence of markup, Swift sees that as follows:

```
func badMethod(_ s: String!) -> String!
```

As soon as your header file contains any markup, the Objective-C compiler will complain until it is completely marked up. To help you with this, you can mark an entire stretch of your header file with a default nonnull setting; you will then need to mark up only the exceptional nullable types:

```
NS_ASSUME_NONNULL_BEGIN
- (NSString*) badMethod: (NSString*) s;
- (nullable NSString*) goodMethod: (NSString*) s;
NS_ASSUME_NONNULL_END
```

Swift sees that with no implicitly unwrapped Optionals:

```
func badMethod(_ s: String) -> String
func goodMethod(_ s: String) -> String?
```

To mark an Objective-C collection type as containing a certain type of element, the element type can appear in angle brackets (<>) after the name of the collection type but before the asterisk. This is an Objective-C method that returns an array of strings:

```
- (NSArray<NSString*>*) pepBoys;
```

Swift sees the return type of that method as [String], and there will be no need to cast it down.

In the declaration of an actual Objective-C collection type, a placeholder name stands for the type in angle brackets. For example, the declaration for NSArray starts like this:

```
@interface NSArray<ObjectType>
- (NSArray<ObjectType> *)arrayByAddingObject:(ObjectType)anObject;
// ...
```

The first line says that we're going to use ObjectType as the placeholder name for the element type. The second line says that the `arrayByAddingObject:` method takes an object of the element type and returns an array of the element type. If a particular array is declared as `NSArray<NSString*>*`, the ObjectType placeholder would be resolved to `NSString*`. (You can see why Apple refers to this as a "lightweight generic.")

In Swift 3, classes marked up as lightweight generics are imported into Swift as actual generics even if they are not bridged collection types. For example, suppose I declare my own Objective-C class, parallel to NSArray:

```
@interface Thing<ObjectType> : NSObject
- (void) giveMeAThing:(nonnull ObjectType)anObject;
@end
```

The Thing class arrives into Swift declared as a generic `class Thing<ObjectType : AnyObject> : NSObject`, and has to be instantiated by resolving the generic somehow. Often, it will be resolved explicitly:

```
let t = Thing<NSString>()
t.giveMeAThing("howdy") // an Int would be illegal here
```

The details are quite involved; for full information, see proposal SE-0057 at *https:// github.com/apple/swift-evolution*.

Bilingual Targets

It is legal for a target to be a *bilingual target* — one that contains both Swift files and Objective-C files. A bilingual target can be useful for various reasons. You might want to take advantage of Objective-C language features. You might want to incorporate third-party code written in Objective-C. You might want to incorporate your own *existing* code written in Objective-C. Your app itself may have been written in Objective-C originally, and now you want to migrate part of it (or all of it, in stages) into Swift.

The key question is how, within a single target, Swift and Objective-C hear about one another's code in the first place. Recall that Objective-C, unlike Swift, has a visibility problem already: Objective-C files cannot automatically see one another. Instead, each Objective-C file that needs to see another Objective-C file must be instructed explicitly to see that file, usually with an `#import` directive at the top of the first file. In order to prevent unwanted exposure of private information, an Objective-C class declaration is conventionally spread over *two* files: a header file (*.h*) containing the `@interface` section, and a code file (*.m*) containing the `@implementation` section.

Also conventionally, only *.h* files are ever imported. Thus, if declarations of class members, constants, and so forth are to be public, they are placed in a *.h* file.

Visibility of Swift and Objective-C to one another depends upon this convention: it works through *.h* files. There are two directions of visibility, and they operate separately through two special *.h* files:

How Swift sees Objective-C

When you add a Swift file to an Objective-C target, or an Objective-C file to a Swift target, Xcode offers to create a *bridging header*. This is a *.h* file *in the project*. Its default name is derived from the target name — for example, *MyCoolApp-Bridging-Header.h* — but the name is arbitrary and can be changed, provided you change the target's Objective-C Bridging Header build setting to match. (Similarly, if you decline the bridging header and you decide later that you want one, create a *.h* file manually and point to it in the target's Objective-C Bridging Header build setting.)

An Objective-C *.h* file will then be visible to Swift provided you `#import` it in this bridging header.

How Objective-C sees Swift

If you have a bridging header, then when you build your target, the appropriate top-level declarations of *all* your Swift files are *automatically* translated into Objective-C and are used to construct a *hidden* bridging header inside the *Intermediates* build folder for this target, deep inside your *DerivedData* folder. The easiest way to see this is with the following Terminal command:

```
$ find ~/Library/Developer/Xcode/DerivedData -name "*Swift.h"
```

This will reveal the name of the hidden bridging header. For example, for a target called MyCoolApp, the hidden bridging header is called *MyCoolApp-Swift.h*. The name may involve some transformation; for example, a space in the target name is translated into an underscore. Alternatively, examine (or change) the target's Objective-C Generated Interface Header Name build setting.

Your Objective-C files will be able to see your Swift declarations, provided you `#import` this hidden bridging header into each Objective-C file that needs to see it.

For simplicity, I will refer to these two bridging headers as the *visible* and *invisible* bridging headers, respectively.

For example, let's say that I've added to my Swift target, called MyCoolApp, a Thing class written in Objective-C. It is distributed over two files, *Thing.h* and *Thing.m*. Then:

- For Swift code to see the Thing class, I need to #import "Thing.h" in the *visible* bridging header (*MyCoolApp-Bridging-Header.h*).

- For Thing class code to see my Swift declarations, I need to import the *invisible* bridging header (#import "MyCoolApp-Swift.h") at the top of *Thing.m*.

> Once you've imported the invisible bridging header into an Objective-C file, you can Command-click its name to open it. This shows you your app's entire Swift API as seen as by Objective-C!

On that basis, here's the procedure I use for turning my own Objective-C apps into Swift apps:

1. Pick a *.m* file to be translated into Swift. Objective-C cannot subclass a Swift class, so if you have defined both a class and its subclass in Objective-C, start with the subclass. Leave the app delegate class for last.

2. Remove that *.m* file from the target. To do so, select the *.m* file and use the File inspector.

3. In every Objective-C file that #imports the corresponding *.h* file, remove that #import statement and import in its place the invisible bridging header (if you aren't importing it in this file already).

4. If you were importing the corresponding *.h* file in the visible bridging header, remove the #import statement.

5. Create the *.swift* file for this class. Make sure it is added to the target.

6. In the *.swift* file, declare the class and provide stub declarations for all members that were being made public in the *.h* file. If this class needs to adopt Cocoa protocols, adopt them; you may have to provide stub declarations of required protocol methods as well. If this file needs to refer to any other classes that your target still declares in Objective-C, import their *.h* files in the visible bridging header.

7. The project should now compile! It doesn't work, of course, because you have not written any real code in the *.swift* file. But who cares about that? Time for a beer!

8. Now fill out the code in the *.swift* file. My technique is to translate more or less line-by-line from the original Objective-C code, even though the outcome is not particularly idiomatic or Swifty.

9. When the code for this *.m* file is completely translated into Swift, build and run and test. If the runtime complains (probably accompanied by crashing) that it can't find this class, find all references to it in the nib editor and reenter the class's name in the Identity inspector (and press Tab to set the change). Save and try again.

10. On to the next *.m* file! Repeat all of the above steps.

11. When all of the other files have been translated, translate the app delegate class. At this point, if there are no Objective-C files left in the target, you can delete the *main.m* file (replacing it with a `@UIApplicationMain` attribute in the app delegate class declaration) and the *.pch* (precompiled header) file.

Your app should now run, and is now written in pure Swift (or is, at least, as pure as you intend to make it). Now go back and think about the code, making it more Swifty and idiomatic. You may well find that things that were clumsy or tricky in Objective-C can be made much neater and clearer in Swift.

Note also that you can do a *partial* conversion of an Objective-C class by extending it in Swift. This can be useful as a stage along the path to total conversion, or you might quite reasonably write only one or two methods of an Objective-C class in Swift, just because Swift makes it so much easier to say or understand certain kinds of thing. However, Swift cannot see the Objective-C class's members unless they are made public, so methods and properties that you were previously keeping private in the Objective-C class's *.m* file may have to be declared in its *.h* file.

Index

A

aborting, 271
access control, 277
accessibility, 408
accessors, 478
Accounts preferences, 384, 411, 419
actions, 357, 503
    connections, 357
    connections, creating, 359
    handler, 505
    misconfiguring, 361
    nil-targeted, 508
    selector signatures, 505
    target, 504
Ad Hoc distribution, 433, 436
address, 38, 555
address operator, 38, 556
Address Sanitizer, 538
adopt a protocol, 180
Allocations instrument, 423
ampersand, 38, 556
anonymous functions, 46
    abbreviated syntax, 48
    capture list, 288
    define-and-call, 52
    parameter list and return type, 47
    retain cycles, 287
    throws, 264
    trailing, 50
Any, 211
AnyClass, 215
AnyHashable, 233
AnyObject, 212-214
    object identity, 214
    suppressing type checking, 213
API, xii
app bundle, 317
app delegate, 500
app delegate instance, 326
app launch process, 326
app name, 332, 442, 443
app name, localizing, 426
App Store, 443
App Store distribution, 433
app target, 309
app version number, 442
app without main storyboard, 328
app, registering, 417
append, 92, 223
Apple ID, 411
ARC, 519
    (see also memory management)
architecture, 26
archive, 433
arguments, 29
arithmetic operators, 87
Array, 216
arrays, 216-230
    C arrays, 557
    casting, 217
    concatenating, 223
    declaration, 216
    enumerating, 225
    equality, 218
    flattening, 224
    indexing, 219
    initializers, 217
    literal, 216

mutating, 220
nested, 220
Optional, 218
properties and methods, 221
searching, 222
sorting, 224
subscripting, 219
testing element type, 218
transforming, 225
uniquing, 236, 474
ArraySlice, 219
arrow operator, 28
as, 170, 183, 249
assert, 271
asset catalog, 323, 438
asset catalog, compiled, 318
asset catalog, nonimage resources, 324
assignment, 7
assignment, compound, 89
assignment, conditional, 253
assignment, multiple, 101
assistant pane, 305, 391
associated type, 192
associated type chains, 197
associated value, 138, 250, 256, 257
Attributes inspector, 303, 341
autoclosure, 272
autocompletion, 386
autolayout, 342
autolinking, 330
automatic signing, 413
automatic variables, 71
autorelease, 524
autorelease pool, 524
availability, 370
available, 381
awakeFromNib, 363

B

backward compatibility, 380
bag, 474
balancing delimiters, 386
base class, 151
Base SDK build setting, 380
Behaviors preferences, 298, 306
beta testing, 437
bilingual target, 575
binary executable, 311
binary numbers, 84

binding, conditional, 243, 255, 272
bindMemory, 512
bitmask, 238
bitwise operators, 88, 238
    (see also option sets)
blame, 385
blocks (flow control), 242
blocks, C, 46, 572
body of a function, 28
bookmarking a documentation page, 369
bookmarking a line of code, 391
Bool, 82
BOOL, 465
Boolean operators, 83
boxing, 564
branching, 241-254
branching, shortcircuiting, 260
break, 260
Breakpoint navigator, 302
breakpoints, 397
bridged types, 563, 564
    (see also boxing)
    Any and id, 211
    AnyObject and id, 212
    Array and NSArray, 228, 471
    casting, 173
    CFTypeRefs, 571
    Dictionary and NSDictionary, 233
    Error and NSError, 267
    Foundation, 459, 564
    number and NSNumber, 465
    Set and NSSet, 474
    String and NSString, 94, 461
bridging header, 576
build, 296
build configurations, 313
build phases, 310
build settings, 312
bundle display name, 332, 426
bundle identifier, 294
bundle, app, 317
bundle, test, 404

C

C, 550-560
    (see also Objective-C)
    arrays, 557
    blocks, 572
    data types, 550

enums, 551
functions, 559
numeric types, 86
pointer-to-function, 560, 573
pointer-to-void, 556
pointers, 555
strings, 551
structs, 467, 554
Calendar, 464
call stack, 301, 399
calling a function, 8, 29
canvas, 335, 339
capabilities, 416
capitalization, 8
capture list, 288
captured variable references, 53
captured variable references, preserving, 59
captured variable references, setting, 58
case (of enum), 135
case (of switch statement), 245
casting, 169-174
casting safely, 171, 249
categories, 450
caveman debugging, 394
certificate, 411
certificate, exporting, 419
CFTypeRefs, 570
CFTypeRefs, memory management, 533
chains, associated type, 197
chains, Optional, 109
Character, 95
character sequence, 95
characters vs. codepoints, 95
characters, escaped, 91
class clusters, 477
class documentation page, 369
class members, 16
class methods, 129
class methods of NSObject, 486
class methods vs. static methods, 165
class of object in nib, changing, 341
class properties, 70, 127
class properties vs. static properties, 166
class protocols, 186
classes, 146-166
    (see also object types)
    class methods, 165
    class properties, 166
    deinitializers, 164

documentation, 369
generic, subclassing, 197
hierarchy, 152
inheritance, 153
initializers, 156
initializers, inheritance, 159
instances, multiple references, 149
instances, mutating, 40, 148
methods, overriding, 154
methods, overriding, preventing, 156, 280
Objective-C name, 563
omitting type name, 136
polymorphism, 166
properties, overriding, 164
reference types, 146
references to, 215
static methods, 165
static properties, 166
subclass and superclass, 152
subclassing, preventing, 156, 280
subscripts, overriding, 156
umbrella type, 212, 215
cleaning, 409
closures, 53-61
    (see also anonymous functions)
    captured variable references, 53
    captured variable references, preserving, 59
    captured variable references, setting, 58
    escaping, 60
    returned from function, 56
Cocoa, 447-547
    actions, 503
    categories, 450
    data sources, 502
    delegation, 498
    events, 489
    Foundation classes, 458
    key–value coding, 481
    key–value observing, 509
    memory management, 519
    notifications, 492
    protocols, 453
    responder chain, 506
    subclassing, 448, 490
code completion, 386
code signing (see signing an app)
Code Snippet library, 304, 388
code, location, 8, 489
codepoints, Unicode, 93

codepoints, Unicode, vs. characters, 95
coercion, numeric, 85, 550
coercion, Range and NSRange, 100, 459
coercion, String and Int, 92
collections, Foundation, 475-476
collections, memory management, 522, 532
collections, Swift, 216-240
colon
    adopting protocol, 180
    argument label, 33
    enum raw value type, 137
    generic type constraint, 194
    key–value, 231
    label, 260
    parameter name, 28
    superclass, 153
    ternary operator, 253
    variable type, 72
comma
    arguments, 29
    array literal, 216
    condition list, 244
    dictionary literal, 231
    generic constraints, 201
    generic placeholders, 193
    parameters, 28
    protocol, 180, 182
    switch case, 251
    tuples, 100
    variadics, 36
comments, 4
comments, self-documenting, 373
communication between objects, 539
Comparable, 195
compare, 471
comparison of Objective-C objects, 471
comparison operators, 90
ComparisonResult, 471
compatibility, backward, 380
compile error, 4
compile single file, 296
Compile Sources build phase, 310
compiler, 4
completion, code, 386
completion, type-over, 386
Components preferences, 316, 368
composition of protocols, 184
compound assignment operators, 89
computed variable initializer, 74

computed variables, 75
concatenating arrays, 223
concatenating strings, 91
condition list, 244
conditional assignment, 253
conditional binding, 243, 255, 272
conditional constraints, 342
conditional evaluation, 253
conditional initialization, 73
conditions, 82, 241
configurations, 313
conform to a protocol, 180
connections, 346
    action, 357
    between nibs, 361, 542
    creating, 349, 354, 359
    deleting, 353
    outlet, 347, 483
Connections inspector, 303, 351, 354
console, 301, 394
constants, 7, 71, 145, 147
constraints in nib files, 341
constraints, type, 194
constraints, type, extensions, 209
constraints, type, multiple, 200
contains, 96, 99, 222
continue, 260
control events, 358, 503
control flow (see flow control)
convenience initializers, 157
convention(c), 573
Copy Bundle Resources build phase, 311
copying instances, 149
count, 93, 221, 235
covariant, 169, 197
crash
    class not key–value coding compliant, 352,
        481, 483
    could not cast value, 171
    could not instantiate class, 331
    deallocated object, 528
    loaded nib but view outlet was not set, 353
    unexpectedly found nil, 108, 353
    unrecognized selector, 66, 361
creating an action connection, 359
creating an enum, 135
creating an instance, 15, 119
creating an outlet, 354

curly braces, 4, 28, 47, 75, 79, 91, 117, 119, 131, 164, 184, 203, 242
currying, 61
CustomReflectable, 282
CustomStringConvertible, 182

D

dance, weak–strong, 288
dangling pointers, 520
Data, 468
data sources, 502
data tips, 400
Date, 464
DateComponents, 464
DateFormatter, 465
DateInterval, 464
dates, 464
Debug menu (Simulator), 393
Debug navigator, 300, 399, 420
Debug pane, 301, 399
debugger, Xcode, 396
debugging, 394-402
debugging memory management, 421, 537
debugPrint, 282
Decimal, 467
decimal point, 84
declaration of arrays, 216
declaration of dictionaries, 231
declaration of enums, 135
declaration of extensions, 203
declaration of functions, 27
declaration of generics, 192
declaration of object types, 117
declaration of operators, 274
declaration of protocols, 184
declaration of sets, 236
declaration of variables, 71
declaration, jumping to, 374
defer statement, 269
deferred initialization, 113
define-and-call, 52
deinit, 164
deinit not called, 283, 529
delayed performance, 516
delegate, 498
delegate, memory management, 527
delegating initializers, 124
delegation, 498
deleting an outlet, 353

delimiters, balancing, 386
Deployment Target build setting, 380
description, 182
Design Patterns, 26
designated initializers, 157, 159
destinations, 315
developer member center, 412
development provisioning profile, 416
device types, running on different, 381
device, registering, 413, 417
device, running on, 410
Devices window, 419
dictionaries, 231-235
    casting, 232
    declaration, 231
    enumerating, 232
    keys, 233
    literals, 231
    mutating, 231
    properties, 232
    subscripting, 231
    testing type, 232
    values, 233
Dictionary, 231
didSet, 78
dispatch table, 504
dispatch, dynamic, 169
dispatch_once, 80
display name, 332, 426
distributing your app, 433
distribution provisioning profile, 435
do construct, 268
do...catch, 262
dock, 336
document outline, 336
documentation, 367-377
    class, 369
    comments, 373
    delegate, 500
    downloading, 368
    immutable vs. mutable classes, 476
    protocols, 455
    searching, 368
    table of contents, 368
documentation window, 367
doom, pyramid of, 244
dot-notation, 5, 14
    function references, 65
    key paths, 484

Optionals, 109
tuples, 102
Double, 84
downcasting (see casting)
drawing a view, 449
drawing text, 463
dropFirst, 97, 224
dropLast, 97, 224
dynamic, 512
dynamic dispatch, 169

E

early exit, 259
edit all in scope, 392
editing a storyboard, 335
editing a xib file, 337
editing the project, 309
editing the target, 309
editing your code, 385
editor, 304
elementsEqual, 222
Empty Window example project, 294, 339, 449
encapsulation, 23
endIndex, 97, 222
ensure code is executed, 269
entitlements, 412, 416
entry point, code, 325, 513
entry point, storyboard, 337
enumerate, 257
enumerated, 101, 225
enums, 135-143
    (see also object types)
    associated value, 138, 250, 256, 257
    C enums, 551
    declaration, 135
    equality, 136
    indirect, 151
    initializers, 139
    initializing, 135
    methods, 141
    omitting type name, 135
    properties, 140
    raw value, 137
    subscripts, 142
equal sign, 7
equality of Objective-C objects, 469
equality of Swift objects, 276
equality operators, 90
Equatable, 276

Error, 261
ErrorPointer, 266
errors, 261-268
    catching, 262
    Objective-C, 266
    throwing, 262
errors, compiler, 4
    ambiguous, 34
    method with Objective-C selector conflicts,
        35
    only available on iOS 10.0 or newer, 381
    protocol can only be used as a generic con-
        straint, 195
    required initializer must be provided, 188
    return from initializer without initializing,
        121
    value of optional type not unwrapped, 105
escaped characters, 91
escaping, 60
evaluation, conditional, 253
event-based programming, 513
events, 358, 489
exception breakpoint, 398
exclamation mark, 105, 106, 112, 170, 186
exit, early, 259
explicit specialization, 196
explicit variable type, 72
exporting certificates, 419
extensions, 203-210, 451
    (see also categories)
    declaring, 203
    generics, 209
    generics, type constraints, 209
    object types, 204, 205
    protocols, 206, 452
    restrictions on, 203
    structs, 205
external parameter names, 32
    initializers, 119
    methods, 564
    subscripts, 131

F

factory for functions, 57
factory for instances, 176
factory methods, Objective-C, 568
failable initializers, 125, 160
fallthrough, 252, 260
false, 82

Fast, Whole Module Optimization, 169, 314
fatal error (see crash)
fatalError, 271
File inspector, 303
File Template library, 304
file templates, 324
file, Swift, structure, 9
fileprivate, 278
File's Owner, 348
filter, 97, 225
final, 156
Find navigator, 299, 392
finding, 391
    (see also searching)
first, 96, 221
First Responder proxy object, 509
Fix-it, 389
flag, 82
flatMap, 226
flavors (of object type), 6
Float, 86
flow control, 241-273
folders in an Xcode project, 322
font, 463
for case, 257
for loop, 256
for...in, 256
forced unwrap operator, 105
forEach, 225
format string, 394
Foundation framework, 14, 458
frameworks, 14, 329
    creating, 331
    embedded, 331
    importing, 330
    linking, 329
    Swift, 319
function in function, 41
functional events, 490
functions, 8, 27-67
    anonymous, 46
    anonymous, retain cycles, 287
    anonymous, throws, 264
    body, 28
    C blocks, 572
    C functions, 559
    calling, 8, 29
    closures, 53
    curried, 61
    declaration, 8, 27
    default parameter values, 35
    define-and-call, 52
    external parameter names, 32
    generic, 193
    global, 9, 14
    global, class method instead, 204
    global, instance method instead, 208
    ignored parameters, 36
    internal parameter names, 29
    local, 41
    mathematical, 89
    modifiable parameters, 37
    overloading, 34
    recursion, 43
    reference, 62
    reference types, 151
    result, 27
    result, ignoring, 30
    rethrows, 268
    return value, 28
    returned from function, 56
    signature, 32
    throws, 264
    throws, calling, 265
    trailing, 50
    type, 43
    values, 43
    variadic parameters, 36

G

garbage collection, 282, 520
gauges, 301, 419
generate, 256
generated interface, 304
generic pointer, 556
generics, 190-203
    associated type chains, 197
    classes, subclassing, 197
    declaration, 192
    extensions, 209
    functions, 193
    object types, 193
    protocols, 192
    protocols, constraining associated type, 201
    resolving, 191
    resolving explicitly, 196
    specializing, 191
    specializing explicitly, 196

type constraints, 194
type constraints, extensions, 209
type constraints, multiple, 200
type, telling compiler, 195
where clauses, 200
where clauses, extensions, 209
getter, 75, 478
git, 383
global constants, 145
global functions, 9, 14
global functions, class method instead, 204
global functions, instance method instead, 208
global variables, 9, 70
global variables, initialization, 80
globally visible instances, 543
golden rule of memory management, 521
groups, 298, 308
guard case, 273
guard let, 272
guard statement, 245, 272

H

handler, action, 505
handlers, 46
Hashable, 231
hasPrefix, 92
hasSuffix, 92
header files, 375
    bridging, 576
    Core Graphics, 451
    jumping to, 375
    Objective-C, 576
    Swift, 15, 376
heads-up display, 350
hexadecimal number, 84
hierarchy of classes, 152
hierarchy of views, 337
HUD, 350

I

IBAction, 359
IBInspectable, 364
IBOutlet, 350
IBOutlet, weak, 533
icons, 318, 438
id, 211, 212
identity, 411
Identity inspector, 303, 341
identity operator, 214

if case, 251
if construct, 242
if let, 243
image files, 323
immutable Objective-C classes, 476
iMovie, 441
implicitly unwrapped Optional, 106
import statement, 9, 330
index, 96, 97, 222
index, enumerate with, 101, 225, 257
indexing a string, 97, 100
indexing an array, 219
IndexSet, 474
indices, 222
indirect, 151
inferred variable type, 72
inferred variable type, learning, 87
Info.plist, 318, 320, 442
    (see also property list settings)
informal protocols, 455
inheritance, 153
inheritance of initializers, 159
init, 119
init with self, 124
init with super, 159
init with type reference, 176
init(coder:), 188
initialization, 6, 71
initialization of enums, 135
initialization of nib-based instances, 363
initialization of Optionals, 108
initialization of properties, 121, 126
initialization, conditional, 73
initialization, deferred, 113
initialization, lazy, 80
initializers, 119
    class, 156
    convenience, 157
    delegating, 124
    designated, 157
    enum, 139
    failable, 125, 160
    implicit, class, 157
    implicit, enum, 135
    implicit, struct, 144
    inheritance, 159
    Objective-C, 568
    overriding, 160
    required, 163, 177, 187

required by Cocoa, 188
struct, 144
inout, 38
insert, 98, 223
instance methods, 16, 128
instance properties, 16, 70, 127
instance variables, Objective-C, 478
instances, 15-20, 133
    copying, 149
    creation, 15, 119, 133
    getting a reference, 133, 539
    globally visible, 543
    initial, 326
    lifetime, 133
    literals instead, 189
    multiple references, 149
    mutating, 40, 148
    nib-based, 342
    nib-based, memory management, 532
    relationships between, 542
    type, 167
    type, learning, 174
    type, telling compiler, 169
    type, testing, 171
instantiation, 15, 119, 133
instantiation, nib-based, 333
Instruments, 420, 537
Int, 84
Interface Builder, 334
interface tests, 403
internal, 278
internal identity principle, 166
internal parameter names, 29
internationalization (see localization)
Internet as documentation, 376
interpolation, string, 91, 93
interval operators, 98
introspection, 281, 456, 481
invisible bridging header, 576
iOS Deployment Target build setting, 380
is, 171, 183
isEmpty, 92, 221, 235
isEqual, 470
Issue navigator, 300
issues, live, 389
iteration, 242
Iterator.Element, 200
iTunes Connect, 443

J

joined, 92, 224
jump bar, 304, 390
    Debug pane, 399
    injecting comments, 391
    Related Items menu, 304
    Tracking menu, 305
jumping, 259-273
jumping to declaration, 374
jumping to header files, 375

K

Key Bindings preferences, 297
key paths, 484, 484
keyboard shortcuts in Xcode, 297
Keychain Access, 415
keys (dictionary), 231
key–value coding, 481-486
key–value coding compliant, 481
key–value observing, 509
key–value pairs, 231
KVC, 481
KVO, 509

L

labels in flow control, 260
labels in function calls, 32
    (see also external parameter names)
labels in nib editor, 338
labels in nib editor, changed by outlet, 351
labels in tuples, 102
last, 96, 221
launch images, 439
launch nib, 440
launch process of an app, 326
layer, configuring in the nib, 364
lazy initialization, 80
Leaks instrument, 423
leaks, memory, 282, 420, 422, 520, 527
let, 7, 71, 147
lifetime, 7, 12, 133
    (see also scope)
lifetime events, 490
LIFO, 23
lightweight generics, 230, 574
line, 3
Link Binary With Libraries build phase, 311
linking, 329

literals where instance expected, 189
literals, array, 216
literals, dictionary, 231
literals, logging, 395
literals, numeric, 84
literals, string, 90
live issues, 389
LLDB, 401
loading a nib, 333, 342
local variables, 71
Locale, 464
localization, 425-433
logging, 394
logging C structs, 395
logical operators, 83
looping, 242, 254
looping, shortcircuiting, 260
lowercased, 92

M

main function, 325
main storyboard, 321, 327, 382
main storyboard, app without, 328
main view loaded from nib, 343
main view of view controller, 336
main.swift file, 9, 325
maintenance of state, 23
map, 226
Markdown, 373
math functions, 89
max, 223
Measurement, 469
MeasurementFormatter, 469
Media library, 304, 342
member center, 412
members, 13
memberwise initializer, 144
memory graph, 421
memory leaks, 282, 420, 422, 520, 527
memory management, 282-290, 519-538
    anonymous functions, 287
    ARC, 522
    autorelease pool, 524
    CFTypeRefs, 533
    collections, 522, 532
    dangling pointers, 520
    debugging, 537
    delegates, 527
    golden rule, 521

graph, 421
leaks, 282, 422, 520
mutable Objective-C classes, 536
nib-loaded objects, 532
nilifying unsafe references, 528
notifications, 529
ownership, 522
properties, 526
properties, Objective-C, 535
protocol references, 290
retain cycles, 282, 527
retains, unusual, 532
timers, 530
Unmanaged, 535
unowned references, 286, 527
unsafe references, 528
weak references, 284, 527
messages, 5
    sending optionally, 186, 456
    to Optionals, 109
    to self, 19
metatype, 176, 177
methods, 13, 128
    (see also functions)
    class, 129
    enums, 141
    external parameter names, 564
    inheritance, 153
    instance, 16, 128
    instance, secret life, 131
    mutating, 142, 145, 147
    Objective-C, 564, 564
    omitting type name, 136
    optional, 185, 456
    overriding, 154
    overriding and polymorphism, 167
    overriding, preventing, 156, 280
    selectors, 66
    static, 129
    static vs. class, 165
    structs, 145
min, 223
Mirror, 281
model–view–controller, 545
modules, 9, 14, 330
modules, importing, 330
modules, privacy, 280
mutable Objective-C classes, 476
mutable Objective-C classes, NSCopying, 536

mutating an instance, 40, 148
mutating methods, 142, 145, 147
MVC, 545

N

name of app, 442, 443
name of app, localizing, 426
names of accessors, 478
names of accessors, changing, 480
namespaces, 13, 132, 145, 204
namespaces, Objective-C, 561
naming image files, 323
navigating your code, 390
Navigation preferences, 303
Navigator pane, 297
nested arrays, 220
nested scopes, 268
nested types, 13, 117, 132
Never, 271
NeXTStep, 334
nib editor, 334
nib files, 321, 333-365
nib files, launch, 440
nib files, loading, 342
nib files, localizing, 427
nib objects, 337
nib owner, 348
nib-based instantiation, 333, 532
nibs, connections between, 361, 542
nil, 107
nil in Objective-C collections, 475
nil signaling failure, 114
nil signaling no data, 113
nil, unwrapping, 108
nil-coalescing operator, 254
nil-targeted actions, 508
nilifying unsafe references, 528
nonnull, 574
nonobjc, 567
Notification, 492
Notification.Name, 493
    forming from string, 497
NotificationCenter, 492
notifications, 492
    matching delegate methods, 500
    posting, 496
    registering, 493
    retain cycles, 529
    unregistering, 495, 529

when appropriate, 496, 545
NSArray, 228, 471
NSArray proxy (key–value coding), 485
NSAttributedString, 463
NSCoding, 188, 563
NSCopying, 453, 536
NSCountedSet, 474
NSDataAsset, 324
NSDecimalNumber, 467
NSDictionary, 233, 473
NSError, 262
NSErrorPointer, 266
NSFastEnumeration, 256
NSHashTable, 532
NSKeyedArchiver, 468
NSLinguisticTagger, 463
NSLog, 394
NSMapTable, 532
NSMutableArray, 229, 472
NSMutableDictionary, 235, 473
NSMutableOrderedSet, 474
NSMutableSet, 474
NSMutableString, 462
NSNotFound, 115, 460
NSNull, 254, 475
NSNumber, 465
NSObject, 152, 486-487
NSObject, equality, 470
NSObjectProtocol, 486
NSOrderedSet, 474
NSPointerArray, 532
NSRange, 100, 459
NSRegularExpression, 463
NSSet, 473
NSString, 94, 461
NSValue, 467
nullable, 574
numeric literals, 84
numeric types, C, 86
numeric types, Swift, 84
numericCast, 87

O

objc, 67, 185, 213, 290, 480, 552, 563
Object library, 304, 339
object types, 117-166
    declaration, 117
    definition over multiple files, 205, 452
    extensions, 204

flavors, 6
generic, 193
generic, extensions, 209
initializers, 119
methods, 128
nested, 132
Objective-C, 562
passing or assigning, 175
polymorphism, 175
printing, 175
properties, 125
reference vs. value, 146
references to, 174
references to, Objective-C, 561
scope, 117
subscripts, 130
umbrella type, 211
Objective-C, 549-575
  (see also bridged types)
  accessors, 77, 478
  categories, 450
  collections, 475-476
  comparison, 471
  equality, 469
  factory methods, 568
  header files, 576
  id, 211, 212, 562
  immutable vs. mutable classes, 476
  initializers, 568
  instance variables, 478
  lightweight generics, 230, 574
  methods, 564
  namespaces, 561
  object references, 561
  object types, 562
  Optionals and, 112
  properties, 478
  protocols, 453
  protocols, adopting in Swift, 458
  setter, 79
  subscripts, 472-474
  Swift features invisible to, 562
  Swift, in one target with, 575
  Swift, translating app into, 577
objects, 5
  (see also object types)
  communication between, 539
  graphing, 421
  identity of two, 214

octal numbers, 84
on-demand resources, 324
open, 278
operator syntax, 5, 274
operators, 274-277
  arithmetic, 87
  bitwise, 88, 238
    (see also option sets)
  Boolean, 83
  comparison, 90
  compound assignment, 89
  creating, 276
  declaration, 274
  equality, 90
  identity, 214
  interval, 98
  nil-coalescing, 254
  overriding, 275
  ternary, 253
  unwrap, 105, 109
Optimization Level build setting, 314
optimizing, 420
option sets, 238, 553
option sets, empty, 239
Optional chains, 109
optional message sending, 186, 456
optional methods, 185, 456
optional properties, 185
optional unwrap operator, 109
Optionals, 103-115
  casting, 172
  chain, 109
  comparison, 112
  creating, 103
  declaration, 104
  deferred initialization, 113
  double-wrapped, 185, 221
  empty, 107
  enum, 139
  enum, generic, 190
  equality, 112
  implicitly unwrapped, 106
  initialization, 108
  messages to, 109
  nil, 107
  Objective-C and, 112
  properties, 123
  type, 103
  type, testing, 172

unwrapping, 105
unwrapping safely, 109, 243, 248, 254, 255, 272
wrapping, 104
wrapping array elements, 218
OptionSet, 238, 553
organization identifier, 294
Organizer window, 434
orientation of interface, 442
outlet collections, 357
outlet connections, 347, 483
outlets, 347
    creating, 354
    deleting, 353
    misconfiguring, 352
overflow, 88
overlay, Swift, 459, 564
overloading, 34
overriding, 154
overriding and polymorphism, 167
overriding, initializers, 160
overriding, preventing, 156, 280
owner (memory management), 522
owner (nib), 348

P

parameter list, 28
parameter list in anonymous function, 47
parameter list, omitting, 50
parameters, 27
    default values, 35
    external names, 32
    external names, initializers, 119
    external names, methods, 564
    external names, subscripts, 131
    functions as, 43
    ignoring, 36
    internal names, 29
    modifiable, 37
    variadic, 36
parentheses
    calling a function, 29
    coercion, 85
    declaring a function, 28
    instantiating an object type, 15, 119
    order of operations, 83, 89
    signifying Void, 32, 103
    tuples, 100
patterns, switch statement, 247

persistence (see lifetime)
persisting references, 284
placeholders, generic, 190
    (see also generics)
placeholders, nib editor (see proxy objects)
playgrounds, xiii
pointee, 39, 556
pointer-to-void, 556
pointers, 39, 149
pointers, C, 555
pointers, dangling, 520
pointers, generic, 556
polymorphism, 166
pool, autorelease, 524
popFirst, 224
popLast, 224
Portal, 412
posting a notification, 492
precondition, 272
prefix, 97, 221
previews, video, 441
print, 3, 36, 93, 394
    (see also logging)
privacy, 20, 277
private, 278
product name, 294
profile (see provisioning profile)
profiling, 420
project, 293
project file, 307
project folder, 306, 332
Project navigator, 298, 390
project templates, 294
project window, 296
project, renaming, 332
properties, 13, 69, 125
    (see also variables)
    accessors, 479
    class, 70, 127
    classes, overriding, 164
    computed initialization, 75
    deferred initialization, 113
    dynamic, 512
    enums, 140
    initialization, 121, 126
    initialization, classes, 156
    inspectable, 364
    instance, 16, 70, 127
    lazy initialization, 81

memory management, 526
Objective-C, 478
Objective-C, memory management, 535
omitting type name, 136
Optional, 123
optional, 185
overriding, 164
private, 22
releasing, 526
static, 70, 127
static vs. class, 166
static, initialization, 80
static, struct, 145
structs, 145
property list settings, 320, 442
dependent on device type, 382
property lists, 477
protocols, 179-190, 453
adopter, 192
adopting, 180
associated type, 192
associated type, chaining, 197
associated type, constraining, 201
casting, 183
class, 186
composition, 184
conforming to, 180
declaration, 184
delegate, 501
documentation, 455
extensions, 206, 452
extensions, constraining associated type, 210
extensions, invisible to Objective-C, 455
generic, 192
generic, constraining associated type, 201
implicitly required initializers, 187
informal, 455
literal convertible, 189
memory management, 290
Objective-C, 453
optional members, 185, 456
testing type, 183
provisioning profile, 412
provisioning profile, development, 416
provisioning profile, distribution, 435
provisioning profile, exporting, 419
provisioning profile, universal, 416
proxy objects, 337, 348

public, 278
pyramid of doom, 244

Q

query events, 490
question mark, 104, 112, 171, 186, 248, 253, 254
Quick Help, 303, 372
Quick Look a variable, 400

R

Range, 98
range, indexing with, 100, 219
range, string, 94
raw value, 137
RawRepresentable, 208
read-only variables, 76
recursion, 43
recursive initializers, 124
recursive references, 150
reduce, 227
Refactoring, 26
reference types, 146
reference types, memory management, 282
reference, getting, 133, 539
reference, persisting, 284
reference, recursive, 150
reference, strong, 284
reference, unowned, 286, 527
reference, unsafe, 528
reference, weak, 284, 527
references to class types, 215
references to functions, 62
references to object types, 174
references to object types, Objective-C, 561
references to same object, 149, 214
registering a device, 413, 417
registering an app, 417
registering for a notification, 493
regular expressions, 463
Related Items menu, 304
releasing a property, 526
remove, 98, 223
removeFirst, 223
removeLast, 223
removeSubrange, 100
removeValue, 232
renamification, xv, 565
renaming a project or target, 332
REPL, xiii

replaceSubrange, 100
replacing, 392
Report navigator, 302, 406
required initializers, 163, 177, 187
resolution, screen, 323, 381
resolving a generic, 191, 196
resources, 321
resources in an asset catalog, 323
resources in the app bundle, 322
resources, dependent on device type, 382
resources, on-demand, 324
responder, 506
responder chain, 507
responds, 456
result of a function, 27
result of a function, ignoring, 30
retain count, 520
retain cycles, 282, 527
    anonymous functions, 287
    notifications, 529
    timers, 530
retains, unusual, 532
rethrows, 268
return function from function, 56
return statement, 28
return value of anonymous function, 47
return value of function, 28
return, omitting, 50
reversed, 99, 224
root class, 151
root view controller, 327
run, 296
running on a device, 410

S

sample code, Apple's, 376
scalars, 6, 465, 550
Scanner, 462
scene, 336
scene dock, 336
Scheme pop-up menu, 315
schemes, 314
scientific notation, 84
scope, 11
scope, exiting early, 259
scope, nested, 268
scope, object types, 117
scope, variable, 69
screen resolution, 323, 381

screencasts, 441
screenshots, 440
SDKs, 316, 329
SDKs, earlier, 381
searching arrays, 222
searching for symbols, 374, 375
searching the documentation, 368
searching your code, 391
Selector, 569
selectors, 66, 569
self, 19
    in escaping functions, 61
    in initializers, 123, 158
    in instance methods, 20, 118
    in property initialization, 126
    in static/class methods, 118
    polymorphism, 168
    polymorphism in class methods, 177
    with type name, 176
Self, 178, 192, 199
semicolon, 3
Sequence, 256
sequence, 258
sequence, array initializer, 217
sequence, character, 95
sequence, enumerating multiple, 259
sequence, enumerating with index, 101, 257
sequence, generating, 256
sequence, range indexing, 99
sequence, transforming, 258
serialization, 477
Set, 235
sets, 235-240, 474
    declaration, 236
    equality, 236
    initializers, 236
    literals, 236
    mutating, 236
    operations, 237
    option sets, 238, 553
    sampling, 236
    transformations, 236
setter, 75, 478
setter observers, 78
setter, private, 279
shared application instance, 326
shortcircuiting, 260
should, delegate method names with, 500
side effects, 30

signature of a function, 32
signing an app, 411
   automatic, 413
   manual, 417
Simulator, 393
Single View app template, 294
singleton, 80
size classes, 342
Size inspector, 303, 341
slice, 219
snippets, 388
sort, 224
sorted, 224
sorting arrays, 224
Source Control preferences and menu, 383
specializing a generic, 191, 196
splatting, 36
split, 97, 225
square brackets, 130, 216, 231
stack, 23
startIndex, 97, 222
starts, 222
state, maintenance, 23
statement, 3
static members, 16
static methods, 129
static methods vs. class methods, 165
static properties, 70, 127
static properties vs. class properties, 166
static properties, initialization, 80
static properties, struct, 145
stepping, 402
stored variables, 75
storyboard files, 321
   (see also main storyboard)
   compiled, 318
   dependent on device type, 382
   editing, 335
   entry point, 337
   launch, 440
stride, 258
String, 90
String.Index, 97
strings, 90-100
   C strings, 551
   characters, 95
   coercion, 92
   comparison, 92
   concatenating, 91

equality, 92
format, 394
indexing, 97, 100
initializers, 92
interpolation, 91, 93
length, 93, 95
literals, 90
localizing, 429
modifying, 97, 100
notification names, 497
range, 94
searching, 94
substrings, 94-100, 462
Unicode, 93
strong references, 284
structs, 143-146
   (see also object types)
   C structs, 467, 554
   C structs, logging, 395
   initializers, 144
   initializers, extensions, 205
   methods, 145
   omitting type name, 136
   properties, 145
   static properties, 145
   subscripts, 145
styled text, 463
subclass, 151
subclassing in Cocoa, 448, 490
subclassing UIApplication, 448
subclassing UILabel, 450
subclassing UIView, 449, 490
subclassing UIViewController, 448, 491
subclassing, preventing, 156, 280
subscripting, 97, 100, 219, 231
subscripting, Objective-C, 472-474
subscripts, 130
   classes, 156
   enums, 142
   overriding, 156
   structs, 145
substitution principle, 166
Subversion, 383
subview, 337
suffix, 97, 221
super, 155
super in initializers, 159
superclass, 151
superview, 337

supported interface orientations, 442
svn, 383
swapping variables, 101
Swift, xi, 3-290
Swift and Objective-C in one target, 575
Swift header, 15
Swift overlay (Foundation), 459, 564
switch statement, 245
Symbol navigator, 299, 390
symbolic breakpoint, 398
symbols, searching for, 374, 375
syntax checking, 389

T

tabs in Xcode, 306
target, 309
target, action, 504
target, bilingual, 575
target, framework, 331
target, test, 403
Targeted Device Family build setting, 379
team, 411
templates, file, 324
templates, project, 294
ternary operator, 253
test bundle, 404
Test Failure breakpoint, 406
Test navigator, 300
test target, 403
testable, 404
TestFlight, 437
tests, 403
text, drawing, 463
text, styled, 463
thinning an app, 436
throw, 262
throws, 264
Time Profiler instrument, 424
Timer, 497
timers, 497
timers and retain cycles, 530
times, 464
top-level, 14
    (see also global)
top-level objects (nib), 336
tracking, 305
Tracking menu, 305
trailing function, 50
true, 82

try, 265
tuples, 100
Type, 175
type alias, 46, 103
type checking, suppressing, 213
type constraints, 194
type constraints, multiple, 200
type eraser, 233
type name, omitting, 135
type of function, 43
type of instance vs. type of variable, 167
type of instance, testing, 171
type of Optional, 103
type of variable, 7, 72
type placeholders, 190
    (see also generics)
type references, 174
type(of:), 174
type-over completions, 386
typecasting (see casting)
types, 117
    (see also object types)

U

UDID, 412
UI tests, 403
UIApplication, 326, 448
UIApplicationMain, 326
UIBackgroundTaskIdentifier, 73
UIControl, 358, 503
UILabel, 450
UIPickerView, 503
UIResponder, 506
UIView, 449, 490
    (see also views)
UIViewController, 448, 491
    (see also view controller)
umbrella types, 212
underflow, 88
underscore
    argument label, 33
    assignment to, 30, 101
    mop-up switch case, 247
    parameter name, 36, 63
    parameter name, anonymous function, 49
Unicode, 91
UnicodeScalar, 93
unique an array, 236, 474
Unit, 469

unit tests, 403
universal app, 379
universal development provisioning profile,
    416
Unmanaged, 535
unowned references, 286, 527
unregistering for a notification, 495, 529
unsafe references, 528
UnsafeMutablePointer, 39, 555
UnsafeMutableRawPointer, 512, 556
UnsafePointer, 555
until, 255
unwrapping an Optional, 105
updateValue, 232
uppercased, 92
URL, 463
User Defined Runtime Attributes, 363
user events, 490
UserDefaults, 145, 543
UTF-8, UTF-16, UTF-32, 93
Utilities pane, 303

V

value types, 146
values (dictionary), 231
var, 7, 71, 147
variables, 6, 69-82
    coercion, 85
    computed, 75
    declaration, 6, 71
    façade, 78
    functions as value of, 43
    global, 9, 70
    global, initialization, 80
    initialization, 6
    initialization of Optional, 108
    lazy, 80
    lifetime, 7, 69
    local, 71
    read-only, 76
    scope, 69
    setter observers, 78
    stored, 75

    swapping, 101
    type, 7, 72
    type vs. instance type, 167
variables list, 301, 400
variadic parameters, 36
version control, 383
version string, 442
video previews, 441
view controller, 336, 343
view controller, initial, 327, 337, 343
view debugging, 401
views, 335
views, drawing, 449
visibility (see scope)
visibility, instance, 539
visible bridging header, 576
Void, 31, 103
void, 556

W

warnings, compiler, 4
weak references, 284, 527
weak–strong dance, 288
where, 200, 209, 248, 257
while case, 256
while let, 255
while loop, 254
Whole Module Optimization, 169, 314
willSet, 78
windows, secondary, in Xcode, 306
WWDR Intermediate Certificate, 415

X

Xcode, 293-444
    (see also nib editor)
xib files, 321
xib files, editing, 337
xliff files, 431

Z

zip, 259
zombies, 538

About the Author

Matt Neuburg started programming computers in 1968, when he was 14 years old, as a member of a literally underground high school club, which met once a week to do timesharing on a bank of PDP-10s by way of primitive teletype machines. He also occasionally used Princeton University's IBM-360/67, but gave it up in frustration when one day he dropped his punch cards. He majored in Greek at Swarthmore College, and received his PhD from Cornell University in 1981, writing his doctoral dissertation (about Aeschylus) on a mainframe. He proceeded to teach Classical languages, literature, and culture at many well-known institutions of higher learning, most of which now disavow knowledge of his existence, and to publish numerous scholarly articles unlikely to interest anyone. Meanwhile he obtained an Apple IIc and became hopelessly hooked on computers again, migrating to a Macintosh in 1990. He wrote some educational and utility freeware, became an early regular contributor to the online journal *TidBITS*, and in 1995 left academe to edit *MacTech* magazine. In August 1996 he became a freelancer, which means he has been looking for work ever since. He is the author of *Frontier: The Definitive Guide*, *REALbasic: The Definitive Guide*, and *AppleScript: The Definitive Guide*, as well as *Programming iOS 10* (all for O'Reilly Media), and *Take Control of Using Mountain Lion* (TidBITS Publishing).

Colophon

The animal on the cover of *iOS 10 Programming Fundamentals with Swift* is a harp seal (*Pagophilus groenlandicus*), a Latin name that translates to "ice-lover from Greenland." These animals are native to the northern Atlantic and Arctic Oceans, and spend most of their time in the water, only going onto ice packs to give birth and molt. As earless ("true") seals, their streamlined bodies and energy-efficient swimming style make them well-equipped for aquatic life. While eared seal species like sea lions are powerful swimmers, they are considered semiaquatic because they mate and rest on land.

The harp seal has silvery-gray fur, with a large black marking on its back that resembles a harp or wishbone. They grow to be 5–6 feet long, and weigh 300–400 pounds as adults. Due to their cold habitat, they have a thick coat of blubber for insulation. A harp seal's diet is very varied, including several species of fish and crustaceans. They can remain underwater for an average of 16 minutes to hunt for food, and are able to dive several hundred feet.

Harp seal pups are born without any protective fat, but are kept warm by their white coat, which absorbs heat from the sun. After nursing for 12 days, the seal pups are abandoned, having tripled their weight due to their mother's high-fat milk. In the subsequent weeks until they are able to swim off the ice, the pups are very vulnerable to predators and will lose nearly half of their weight. Those that survive reach maturity after 4–8 years (depending on their gender), and have an average lifespan of 35 years.

Harp seals are hunted commercially off the coasts of Canada, Norway, Russia, and Greenland for their meat, oil, and fur. Though some of these governments have regulations and enforce hunting quotas, it is believed that the number of animals killed every year is underreported. Public outcry and efforts by conservationists have resulted in a decline in market demand for seal pelts and other products, however.

The cover image is from Wood's *Animate Creation*. The cover fonts are URW Typewriter and Guardian Sans. The text font is Adobe Minion Pro; the heading font is Adobe Myriad Condensed; and the code font is Dalton Maag's Ubuntu Mono.

Get even more for your money.

Join the O'Reilly Community, and register the O'Reilly books you own. It's free, and you'll get:

- $4.99 ebook upgrade offer
- 40% upgrade offer on O'Reilly print books
- Membership discounts on books and events
- Free lifetime updates to ebooks and videos
- Multiple ebook formats, DRM FREE
- Participation in the O'Reilly community
- Newsletters
- Account management
- 100% Satisfaction Guarantee

Signing up is easy:

1. Go to: oreilly.com/go/register
2. Create an O'Reilly login.
3. Provide your address.
4. Register your books.

Note: English-language books only

To order books online:
oreilly.com/store

For questions about products or an order:
orders@oreilly.com

To sign up to get topic-specific email announcements and/or news about upcoming books, conferences, special offers, and new technologies:
elists@oreilly.com

For technical questions about book content:
booktech@oreilly.com

To submit new book proposals to our editors:
proposals@oreilly.com

O'Reilly books are available in multiple DRM-free ebook formats. For more information:
oreilly.com/ebooks

O'REILLY®

CPSIA information can be obtained
at www.ICGtesting.com
Printed in the USA
LVOW02s1135230117
521852LV00020BA/724/P

santa clara
county
library district

Renewals: (800) 471-0991

www.sccl.org

iOS 10 Programming Fundamentals with Swift

Move into iOS development by getting a firm grasp of its fundamentals, including the Xcode IDE, the Cocoa Touch framework, and Swift 3—the latest version of Apple's acclaimed programming language. With this thoroughly updated guide, you'll learn Swift's object-oriented concepts, understand how to use Apple's development tools, and discover how Cocoa provides the underlying functionality iOS apps need to have.

"Neuburg is my favorite programming book writer, period."

—John Gru
Daring Fir

- Explore Swift's object-oriented concepts: variables and functions, scopes and namespaces, object types and instances

- Become familiar with built-in Swift types such as numbers, strings, ranges, tuples, Optionals, arrays, dictionaries, and sets

- Learn how to declare, instantiate, and customize Swift object types: enums, structs, and classes

- Discover powerful Swift features such as protocols and generics

- Catch up on Swift 3 innovations: revised APIs, new Foundation bridged types, and more

- Tour the lifecycle of an Xcode project from inception to App Store—including Xcode's new automatic code signing and debugging features

- Construct app interfaces with the nib editor, Interface Builder

- Understand Cocoa's event-driven model and its major design patterns and features

- Find out how Swift communicates with Cocoa's C and Objective-C APIs

Matt Neuburg has a PhD in Clas and has taught at many colleges and universities. He has served a editor of *MacTech* magazine and as contributing editor for *TidBIT* He has written many OS X and i(applications. Previous books inc several editions of *iOS Programm Fundamentals*, as well as *REALbc The Definitive Guide* and *AppleSc The Definitive Guide* (all O'Reilly)

Once you master the fundamentals, you'll be ready to tackle the details of iOS app development with author Matt Neuburg's companion guide, *Programming iOS 10*.

Programming iOS 10
978-1-491-97016-4

Twitter: @oreillymedia
eilly